VEDIC ECONOMY

RAMA PROSAD BANERJEE

PUBLISHERS & DISTRIBUTORS (P) LTD

7/22, Ansari Road, Darya Ganj, New Delhi
Tel.: +91-11-4077 5252, 2327 3880
E-mail: orders@atlanticbooks.com
Web: www.atlanticbooks.com

Published by Atlantic Publishers & Distributors (P) Ltd 2023

Disclaimer

- The author and the publisher have taken every effort to the maximum of their skill, expertise and knowledge to provide correct material in the book. Even then if some mistakes persist in the content of the book, the publisher does not take responsibility for the same. The publisher shall have no liability to any person or entity with respect to any loss or damage caused, or alleged to have been caused directly or indirectly, by the information contained in this book.
- The author has fully tried to follow the copyright law. However, if any work is found to be similar, it is unintentional and the same should not be used as defamatory or to file legal suit against the author.
- If the readers find any mistakes, we shall be grateful to them for pointing out those to us so that these can be corrected in the next edition.
- All disputes are subject to the jurisdiction of Delhi courts only.

Printed & bound in India by Atlantic Print Services

Offered to the Lotus Feet of
Lord Krishna
&
Dedicated to the spirit of the Vedic Sages,
Kautilya and Yudhisthira

Preface

Economic Emergence for All

The recent experience of the world of having absorbed the physical and mental pains due to the impacts of the deadly Corona virus, understood in the name of COVID-19, has a very widespread effect on a long term scale. The disruption has caused massive blockage and restrictions in the economic flow and movement of value from one end to the other, creating short-term and long-term impacts on the life and activities of humans on earth. As has been nicely put across by the World Bank in its World Development Report, 2022 which says: "The mobility restrictions, lockdowns, and other public health measures necessary to address the pandemic rapidly produced the largest global economic crisis in more than a century. This was compounded by a drop in demand as the pandemic affected consumer behavior. Economic activity contracted in 2020 in about 90 percent of countries, exceeding the number of countries seeing such declines during two world wars, the Great Depression of the 1930s, the emerging economy debt crises of the 1980s, and the 2007–09 global financial crisis. In 2020, the first year of the COVID-19 pandemic, the global economy shrank by approximately 3 percent, and global poverty increased for the first time in a generation."

Glaring Red Eyes of Context

The world is confronted with the impacts of two-year long pandemic on one hand and the chaotic relations among countries resulting out of the conflicts and invasions in western part of the world, on the other. The fallout has been certain categories of direct and indirect impacts on human living and national existence. The trauma of the war between Russia and Ukraine has actually shattered the fuel economy of the world to such an extent that most part of Europe has been experiencing volatility in stock market, turbulence in consumer price movement and sustained uncertainties in the wholesale price indices covering goods and services of all kinds. The impact can be categorized in three different ways:

(1) Living standard and living index of human being has a direct impact and got affected by the price indices both Wholesale Price Index(WPI) and Consumer Price Index(CPI) curbing the scope and flexibility of the human consumption at an individual and collective level.

(2) The required flow of finances for the developmental and transformational technologies have become costlier than before making the nations unable to invest in renewing existing infrastructure, creating new physical infrastructure, developing new mega manufacturing and distribution hubs, exploring new areas of resources through mega investment and investing in the new thoughts arising out of knowledge transactions and interactions at individual or collective level.

(3) A gloomy mind has been allowed to prevail across, enjoying a perceptive share of influence larger than its own actual size. As a whole, the world has stopped or reduced the pace of its wheels of growth benefitting human emergence for future.

The Bright Sun Ahead

Even though things have trooped as mentioned above to be justified with those words, there are new areas and avenues of growth identified in different parts of world. The concentration of riches and wealth that the world has experienced post-World War II period until early 2019, may be described in the following terms:

(A) The Asian region has actually got in hand a clear opportunity to derive direct and indirect benefit out of these chaotic and conflicting positions of the world.

(B) The Indian policy of keeping itself neutral to the events occurring across, has actually given strong dividend in terms of directly creating impact on productivity, investments, consumption, flow of finances, dispersion of infrastructure, investments and elevations in technology and as a whole creating better futures for human being.

(C) Seven Tigers of Asian region, including Japan, Singapore, Taiwan, Indonesia, Malaysia, have actually identified ways and means to get benefitted out of the chaos and conflicts occurring in the West.

(D) The resultant effect of shifting the locus of technology from the exclusive possession of the West to creative dimensions of the East.

(E) The future of investment-worthy knowledge products has shifted its locus already to the East, in general, and India and China, in particular. With the strong support from the fiscal authorities of India, having derived the benefit of accumulated surplus from GST, the financial sector along with certain others have emerged out of the traumatic impact of the lame technologies of pre-nineties, creating a new horizon for the mega and mini manufacturing activities for electronics, consumer durables of other varieties, general consumer products, general value-added products and several new dimension products.

(F) Indian industry has shown the power and resilience to withstand the trauma of the pandemic. Now the time has reached to see its emergence, in realistic terms, as a whole.

Economic doctrines, policies and modules have so far served nations and societies in fragmented or skewed manner benefitting certain segments of human population through a process of zero-sum game as an underlying principle of relocating wealth and riches from one corner of the globe to the other. Trade and commerce, though have seen the change in identity with a shift of locus in the origin and manufacture of new dimension products and services, economic and social justice are yet to reach the kitchens and floors of people residing throughout the world. It is true that the collective efforts of the last seven decades have changed the face of many have-nots and 'bottom of pyramid livers', the perennial problems of poverty, inequality, ill-health, lack of providence of services for good life and light of knowledge remains widespread as fundamental issues of global economy. Apart from this the consumption economy has proved a skewed tendency, in terms of over consumption in certain areas and sectors and deprivation, dissatisfaction in certain other areas of the world. The peace and poise of mind gets strongly shattered with the imbalance between the expectations and achievements.

Vedic Economy corrects imbalances through certain basic values at the individual level and at the collective. It urges upon understanding the issues and problems of others by each on one hand and combining the social and human potentials in such a way that growth and fulfillment take place in the context of peace and poise.

The world deserves the best spirit of economic management for its own practice and implementation at different corners of the globe. The sooner it is done, the better it is for human society. Vedic Economy does not exclude a single individual from its domain, rather, it offers to include every person to unleash her/his dormant potentials to transform the same into economically and socially applicable values.

I recommend all nations on earth to adapt, practice and implement the spirit of Vedic Economy within their own framework and experience better individual and collective life of human beings on earth and create a better new world.

Prof. (Dr.) R. P. Banerjee
30 January, 2023

Contents

1

Poverty, the Menace of Human Civilization

Poverty is an age-old menace for the human civilization. It has many facets starting from economic poverty, poverty of wealth, poverty of skill, poverty of resources and poverty of mind. Poverty of human civilization is a combination of all or some of the factors mentioned above. Any attempt to remove or reduce spell of poverty has to go along with the concurrent attempt to remove or reduce it in the respective segments.

The other way of understanding poverty is the lack of wellbeing and happiness in human beings. Society represents the collective standards of happiness and wellbeing whereas individuals sometimes deviate from the concept and requirement of collectiveness of well-being and happiness. The standards which the society sets for itself and promotes as a required standard of living a good life is essentially the standard or bench mark to identify the span of poverty and scope of poverty. The ideas, ideals and dreams which the society cherishes for itself pre-determine the scale with which it sets the standards and target for it. The moments, the ideas, ideals and dreams undergo specific change as they transform the standard for society.

The progress of civilization has brought in changes in the expectations of a good life and thereby changes in the standards and contents of the ingredients and components of a good life.

Basically, an agrarian mode of civilization had a mere expectation of simple living and good thinking for the living of a good life. A person having got a square meal for the day, minimum clothing for a human look, a reasonable shade over the head used to be considered as a standard of a good life. With the change and progress of civilization, particularly at the advent of industrialization, the requirements and ingredients of a good life started changing with the addition of gadgets to the agrarian sector. For example, the standard of living at the agrarian level of satisfaction was mostly natural and things tested based on the living experience of the seniors and the forerunners. There were hardly any measuring instruments to measure the worth of content and the spread of content. But the industrial mind wanted to become scientific in its own nature and measures the calories, vitamin and mineral or the other contents of food and accordingly create a basket of food to be treated as a balanced content of food for a good life. However, this view of balance content keeps changing over a period of time, sometimes even over a short period. The level of satisfaction in an industrial society goes beyond a minimum position to survive and grow, rather it has spearheaded the concept of multiplied wants and demands to be considered as the basis of living a good life that hardly gets limited to the want and demand fulfilled.

Poverty is a fact of deprivation and a sense of deprivation as well. However, we have to measure the standard for identification of poverty; the fact of deprivation has to be taken care of. On the other hand, a source of deprivation is the feeling of deprivation and its persistence in people with abundance of economic resources. The global standard purchasing power of 1 dollar a day and the next level of standard as purchasing power for 2 dollars a day considered only the minimum requirement of a good life. It takes care of the minimum fund required. The minimum health and hygiene required for a marginal living in some cases, and good living in other cases, define poverty. Poverty of mind persists at each level of attainment. A sense of deprivation and an urge to come up to a particular standard, according to the mental framework, is perceptive poverty. Though recovered from the first level, most advanced economies are suffering from a form of perceptive poverty at each level of their collective and individual living.

Whereas, we need to address the issues of the economic poverty in general, there is an urgent need to identify and take care of the issues of perceptive poverty as well. But, global society has taken into account the issues of the economic poverty for a large section of population and thereby tries to solve the issues of perceptive poverty in the process of its accomplishment.

Perceived Objective of Work

Whereas technology drives the means of production, so far it has failed to drive down a significant change in the mode of human involvement in the productive system. One of the very old companies, which is present in almost all countries in the world and has survived and threats, resilience of global market situation, withstood World War-I, World War-II, onslaughts and many more cross-currents in the global scenario for a long period of close to two centuries, remains still on the top of the world trying to be present in the minds of consumers across the globe with the intrinsic value offered through the brand, product and services everywhere, still maintains its name, from its very inception is 'Procter & Gamble'. The journey of nearly two hundred years could have been a journey succumbing to the pressures and threats from the gallops in technology, productive system, human behaviour, spread of knowledge in a new era and the rapid changing pattern in consumerism on one hand and the changing faces of global relations, cultures and political identities and occasional devastations by nature, on the other.

This is not just a single example for durability, sustainability, continued reengineering, adaptability, inclusiveness and growth through providing intrinsic value and connecting with relevant people throughout the world, there are so many other examples as well spread in most of the continents of the world. Truthful, Honest, Cooperative, Sincere, Simple, Integrity in Character, Positive Intent, Positive Values, Universality in Approach, Supportive to Global Minds, Positive Spirit, Urge to Transform, Strong Commitment to Work and Organization are the fundamental aspects of the character of an ideal person who can drive the organizations to the levels of success and achievements.

Let Goodness Prevail

Technology has gifted us with instant communication, cosmic travel, non-human, robotic activities, reengineered organism on one hand and creating a human intellect in a non-human context, on the other. However, in all the situations technology has failed to transform the intrinsic attributes of human being in any way. The bad and corrupt remain bad and corrupt. Moreover, with the power of technology in hand the bad and corrupt finds better penetration in the global context to create an edge for them and perpetuate more aggressively to defeat the goodness of the world society. However, technological change has favoured the most productive firm in each industry and helped reallocation of the resources towards growth across the potential markets. In the beginning of 20th century, most firms in the world used to harp on the domestic boundaries more than the overseas markets. It was in the beginning of 21st century in general, and the recent period in particular, the firms have chosen wider boundaries taking advantage of trade agreements, fiscal permissibility, cross border trade, contractual trade and free trade agreements, globally.

Emergence of Super Star Firms

The emergence of electronic commerce and the Business-to-Business functioning on a wider scale on one hand and business to consumers on the other have actually provided a better solution to ease the barriers to trade, barriers to distribution, barriers to reach out, barriers to demographic identities and other restrictive elements in the business process. The world has gone in favour of two extremes, on one hand the world has paved the ways to create Superstar Firms and on the other, technology has eased out the access of knowledge to the business process as a whole and scale the business without significant component of 'resource-mass'. The economic doctrines which were usually followed during the eighteenth, nineteenth and early and middle period of 20th century have all taken a back seat with the capital market indicators coming up in a big way to determine the industrial prospect of nations and enterprises. The World Bank in its survey on the world development, published in World Development Report 2019 has identified the role of superstar firms in a big manner, which reads as follows:

> "Large firms dominate the global economy: 10 percent of the world's companies are estimated to generate 80 percent of all profits. Superstar firms shape a country's exports. One study of 32 developing countries found that, on average, the five largest exporters in a country account for a third of its exports, nearly half of export growth, and a third of growth due to export diversification."
>
> (World Bank, *World Development Report 2019*, p. 37)

The large firms have a beneficial effect on two aspects:

- Large firms can accelerate domestic economic growth through enhanced capacity of pulling resources, replacing the fatigued and old technology by the new, upgrading the skill unfolding potential of manpower and creating a new business process.

- The large firms are accelerators in economic chain, wherein instead of limiting its thrust on the direct productivity or the direct business system it creates a multiplier platform for a large number of new generation activities and entrepreneurship.

The World Bank study has supported the view and importance of large firms from a third point of view which highlights the emergence of latest technology. Digitalization, automation, robotization, creation of machine intelligence and machine-neurons have actually changed the focus of the world business from mere brick and mortar to a knowledge centric, continuously innovative and competitive, throughout emergent a business design. The job market thereby has focused on two broad categories with respect to the quality and nature of job as follows:

1. Brand seeking jobs
2. Jobs on creative platforms

Whereas jobs are the focus of every economy, creation of the same depends on the factors of consumption, distribution, production, innovations, quality of manpower and resources. Hindu Economy assumes that resources are of three types:

1. Knowledge Resources
2. Value Resources
3. Spiritual Resources

A self-contented economy that is free from factors of greed, aggressive ego, utter selfishness, cooperative in nature, takes care of all, oriented to the spirit of sacrifice and goodness.

The Emergence of Super Consumption

While the brand seeking jobs are supported by the existing brands who are present in any domain and who can operate from any geographical location, the other one is available to a person of any description to adapt and move for a job design nurtured and created through the active intervention of potential knowledge.

Physical presence in the context of job is gradually getting replaced by the virtual presence of relevant people backed by certain types of physical identities brought through the combination of material, financial and human resources. As the markets move forward to a higher number and degree of different faces of startups, the competition in the market rises higher and higher. The startups require supporting ambience and congenial market parameters. However, a higher degree of competition thrown open by new range of startups redefined the market realities, in most of the cases, in favour of consumption. In the process, the market experiences a phenomenon of redistributive resources and creation of new range of value for the society and the nation. As the World Bank has observed, the process of facilitation offered by technology has to be garnered by a search for continuous receptivity in the society by way of creation of a new horizon and connecting it with different shades of consumers through new pathways. According to the World Bank:

> "Technological progress leads to the direct creation of jobs in the technology sector. People are increasingly using smartphones, tablets, and other portable electronic devices to work, organize their finances, secure and heat their homes, and have fun. Workers create the online interfaces that drive this growth. With consumer interests changing fast, there are more opportunities for people to pursue careers in mobile app development and virtual reality design."
>
> (The *World Development Report 2019*, p. 20.)

At one point of time, population was argued as a negative factor towards economic growth and world was not ready in proper sense of the term to accommodate everybody in the process of growth, which used to occur in certain sectors and some parts of the globe and also some sections of the population within the national boundaries.

However, during the middle of previous century it came to the understanding of the thinkers and practitioners that the human being can be considered as a resource and proper utilization and management of the said resource could lead to an expansion of the global economic standard and distributive development of the economics of the world. This, however, has been further fine-tuned in different ways and different aspects and levels of technology. This has been provided with converting the human power into a more resourceful element in the chain of business in the world. Culturally the pattern of Economy Management has a broad divide between:

- Dominant Rational
- Dominant Intuitive

The dominant rational has always banked on the externalities like tools, technologies, in hard and soft form with applications through systems, structures, procedures and formal agenda, whereas the dominant intuitive have backed on the creative, perceptive, intuitive and sixth sense of doing things.

Economic leadership transcends with a combination of these two. With the emergence of two major global economies in the Asian continent, namely China and India, the need to look at Economic leadership from a different perspective has become urgent. The Western model emphasizes more on the first category and has pushed global business from a people-friendly to a profit-friendly process. The new reality of the world demands new breed of leadership based on tradition and millennia through the tested wisdom of China and India. The wisdom centric attitude to life, as ancient India had lived on during its Vedic period, has a strong relevance for the future shape of economy in the world. This process will not only tend to develop leadership with a balance between the two varieties but also shall attempt to inculcate the ancient wisdom in the developmental process for real survival and growth of economy in a holistic manner in future.

The Poor, The Rich, The Global Man

In 2010, the total global wealth has reached around US $200 trillion. In 2020, this was around US $300 trillion. The dollar millionaires have crossed the size of the Australian continent by number. The Gini coefficient is far away from the mark of global equality, zero. The dollar millionaires are far away from getting the happiness they were otherwise expected to have drawn from the wealth that they have amassed. The economic pyramid still persists. The pyramid of wealth has a wide base and sharp apex signifying the higher degree of concentration in the hands of a few leaving the vast majority between the spaces of frying pan to fire. The richest one percent of global adults control close to 45 percent of global assets. The wealthiest 10 percent have close to 85 percent of that. However, the bottom 50 percent of the global adult population has only 2 percent of the global wealth to their command. The current estimate of nearly 5 billion global adults show the per percent average wealth to their command have also risen significantly. The major magazines, listing, richest persons on earth do now consider those having US$1 billion as the minimum size of the par.

Yet, profuse cries are in the air. Sumantra from India, Nasir from Bangladesh, Haris from East Europe, Hof from the Nordic, Elzen from South America, Wilson from Africa and many other from across the globe have their cries unheard but echoed through the winds of change swiping through the barriers of cultures and countries.

Sumantra lives alone in a shanty shelter to park the bicycles for the traders, customers and others visiting the market in Salt Lake, Kolkata. He takes pleasure in a wonderful bed to go to sleep in the night on a rotten and torn mat picked up from the garbage. Some of the cloths are made of some banners of some political parties and thrown away jute bags rejected by the shoppers for being cut in 100 places by the rats. Sumantra has a breakfast. The tea stall gives him half a cup of tea in an earthen small jar which is already used by a customer and thrown in the bins. Sumantra gives a smile with this morning's hot half full cup of tea. For the biscuits he has to fight with the dog and pick up one or two broken, thrown away by some 'Good-hearted' householders visiting the tea stall after completing the stretch of morning walks. Sumantra is allowed to take the shelter as he provides an essential service of watching the bicycles from the back side of the store. He guards it against the stealing away of bicycles parts by those interested. The lunch, at times available, most of other times not. Sumantra has a source of water, after everybody gets their jars and containers filled in from the public place of water supply by the side of the market, he gets a few drops to fill in the same empty earthen jar to quench his thirst for water. He fortunately gets bits and pieces of food residuals for his consumption thrown away by the 'Good-hearted' householders and others. Sumantra's dinner is, however, secured. The owner of the bicycle parking place is gracious to offer him two pieces of thin hand-made bread and some pickles or other items to get a part of his stomach filled in for his dinner. Sumantra goes to his bed with immense pleasure and reviews his life.

He was there in a village remote from the place from where he is right now. He had his parents. Sumantra, now aged around 45, looks back at those days when he was 4 to 5. His mother, Laxmi Devi, was so kind to him. Sumantra, the fifth child of the parents was so profusely cared for. They had a small piece of land with a yield of one crop a year. The yield was not insufficient for them to fill in their belly for a period of 4 months a year. Sumantra's father, Narayan, a hard-working person was so stout, confident and responsible that he did hardly trouble the children to garner the earnings for the family. Narayan used to work in the field of others as an agricultural labourer. He could work beyond the normal hours of time and earn higher than others in his category. Narayan never cared for his personal health. He was always keen to see that he himself manages and fulfils the needs of the family. However, Laxmi Devi was not idle, she used to work in the household as a housemaid and whatever little amount she could earn would always add a value to the stream of income for the family. Laxmi Devi wanted her children to grow as good citizens and a good person and at the same time established themselves economically to live a good life. She wanted to get her children educated. All the children were sent to a free school slightly away from their cottage at the other end of the village. The school opens and closes every day but for the teachers. Students who are most eager to learn used to come and go back home empty every day. Classrooms, mostly broken and wretched. Library mentioned on the door of it as the books of the Library remain at the same positions throughout. The door lock has caught deep rust because of not being touched for a long period of time. Only one attendant of the school, who lives in the school premises with the family, opens the outside gate for willing students to come in and go back forthwith. Biju Sardar, the gate keeper advises the students to come to the school on the last day of the calendar month and first day of the calendar month only to have the benefit of meeting the teacher in the classroom for a while. Laxmi Devi's children had a moment of meeting the teachers, occasionally on the first working day of the calendar month, when they visit their school to complete formalities for their salaries. Laxmi Devi was truly illiterate. She had developed the conviction that her children would grow with intellect and rank with others enjoying the benefits of the world by virtue of the power of their intellect. Laxmi Devi had a dream that each child would grow in intellect and have a footage in the world like others. She knew the new rule of the world, "If you want to have a position in the world, you need to be strong in either intellect or capital, or both". In the absence of both of these, you have a grand position in the dark path and horizons of the world where you will have hardly a stretch of good life lead by many other. In the race of life, you need to understand what makes you grow up and up on the ladder to finally get a footing on the horizontals of the average economic plate. Laxmi Devi and Narayan together with their children were just maintaining a life of happiness with a standard of living far below that of a global standard. Sumantra recounts the occasions when the mother had offered exclusive love and affection to him. Hardly once or twice a week Sumantra had a chance to get the mother free from her works and duties. They had a single room cottage and a cot inside that. The cottage shed was covered by long leaves of Palm and Coconut trees fitted on a framework made on bamboos and tied with knots given by ropes made of coconut fibers. It gave a cool and pleasant living during the hot summer, relatively warm one living during the winter. The walls of the cottage made of special type of mud made the inside of the room counter active to the external temperature. Narayan could not do the repair for the house for last five years because of the paucity of the funds required for it. The disaster came on a day there was a massive cyclone. The roof cover got blown up. Flying in the air getting smashed and dropped at a place untraceable. The village turned into shanties. Trees, homes all structures have broken to the lakes. And a massive shower thereafter. Shower continued for the third day inviting a massive flood. The barrage authority nearby had no other options but to open the locks of the gates and allow the rush of water towards the areas populated by human beings. Sumantra among others were carried away by the waves of flood. He got his senses back in the district hospital under the care of 'semi-doctors'. The eyes could not trace any known person. Sumantra, now lost in the woods of the world, cried. He got a shelter near the hospital at the mercy of a person running a small tea stall. He grew over there and learned so many things in life. He learned how to make tea, how to get the breads toasted and offer it on a plate with butter and sugar added to, how to clean the stall, how to speak to people and how to collect money. Till then Sumantra was on his knees contribute effectively to the stall owner and help him earn. In the process earned his own living in the form of kinds. The stall owner gave him the food and shelter for living still the time he was contributing labour. As he grew further, Sumantra faced severe problems with his knees and the joints of hips. People had advised him to visit the hospital for the remedy. With permission from the stall owner, he visited the hospital 4/5 times and got a chance to reach the doctor only once. The hospital belonged to the Government and offered free treatments for poor patients. Sumantra belongs to that category as per definition of the term. However, Sumantra was not wearing the right kind of dress to be chosen by the doctor's crew nor was he having any connection with the person collecting Rs.10 for a quick visit with the doctor. Finally, when he could reach the doctor's table on the last day, the doctor was on his feet to go out and gave a prescription to him for some medicine for his problems. The hospital store did not have the medicines prescribed for Sumantra. The only option remained was to buy those from the open market. Sumantra tried hard to get some support from the stall owner for the medicine, but failed. He talked to many a tea drinkers about the issue. Finally, got a person working with a medicine shop assuring him to get a few samples collected from the medical representative for him. Sumantra got some medicine through the same person. He had consumed them. Till that time Sumantra was walking, doing his work even though lot of pains. After the medicine course was over, Sumantra found his knees were unable to bear the load of his body and getting folded. Sumantra cannot stand up now. He walks sitting. Can he continue work sitting? 'No, get lost!' the stall owner proclaimed. 'I can't bear with you further. Find your own way.' Sumantra had an acquaintance with a helper of a bus of a long-distance operator. The bus goes to Kolkata and finally parks in Salt Lake. Sumantra came to the final destination Salt Lake with the helper of the bus riding a long distance by the help of the bus. Sumantra is now disconnected from his own past, his own heritage, his own relations, his own connections. The nearest market is his next phase of life's destination where he is now residing. His earning is two pieces of handmade bread in the dinner through his contribution of work to the bicycle shed owner. He works while sitting, can't get up straight. Some people consider him a mad person as he is always in scabies. However, there are others casting compassionate eyes on this silent man Sumantra. He does never utter a single word to anybody but lips in himself.

Is Sumantra a real poor? What kind of poverty he is residing in? If you go by standards of defining poverty Sumantra is nowhere close to the lowest level of poverty line. The purchase power of US $1 a day is far above the upper limits of Sumantra's estimation. Look at the components of human developments index:

- The basic requirements for the purchasing power of US$1 a day.
- Basic education for a proper understanding of world and life.
- Facilities for basic health for survival at a minimal.

- Fundamentals of living condition.
- The facilities for sewerage and sanitation.
- Thriving on the issues of sustainability through keeping parity with the requirements of the Green Earth.
- Minimum calorie requirement for survival and proper growth of body and mind.
- Hazard free boundaries of life.

Let us look into the case of Sumantra to examine the points mentioned above.

1. **The basic requirements for the purchasing power of US $1 a day:** Sumantra has reached an age of 45 years. According to the estimation of population scientist the maturity and fulfillment of life should begin within the age bracket of 25–45. If someone has been able to create something for his/her own life has to have a seeding within that period of life. However, there are good number of exceptions in the world who have gone beyond or started before for an exceptional fulfillment and contributions for the world. In the Indian context, Mohandas Karamchand Gandhi, generally called Gandhiji, identified as the Father of Indian Nation started his stigma after he crossed fifty years of his formative life in different parts of the world. For Mahatma Gandhi, the span between years 50–80 was the most active and effective. Another Indian, Swami Vivekananda had made a mark in the global and national context at a very young age, starting in his teens. His earlier name was Narendra Nath Datta. Swami Vivekananda was a disciple of Sri Ramakrishna, considered as God embodied on earth. Vivekananda had carried a message from his master Ramakrishna to spread across the world for salvation of humanity. He was voice with a form; considered a voice without a form by many contemporary thinkers of the world. He finished his journey of life at thirty-nine only, but creating a huge impact on the entire landmarks of India, among all segments of the population and many corners of the world. Swami Vivekananda's mission was to spread the idea of divinity in human being and arousing the downtrodden of the country and the world. His idea was to uplift the economically deprived people from their conditions of economic deprivation to a situation

of significant economic identity. The special situation of India was properly taken care of by Vivekananda. The social divide across caste, religion and other identities were in prime focus for him. He wanted to bring on par all downtrodden people and make them join the mainstream of social and economic life of the nation. Vivekananda's heart used to bleed at the cry of human beings in any part of the world. He was the messenger of salvation for humanity from deprived crying and downtrodden condition to a condition of a new understanding of life and a proper positioning of life in the emerging context of the world. Swami Vivekananda could finish his global duties in the span of around 20 years from the age of 20 up to close to 40. On the other hand, the case of Gandhi ji was slightly different. He had two parallel initiatives for his movement. The first time in the history of the world having arisen a large mass movement, Mahatma Gandhi had again focussed on rejuvenating the lives and aspirations of the weaker sections of the society. He used to call them by the term 'Harijan', Men of the God. Those who are backward in social class and backward in economic activities have received deprivation of any kind for long are otherwise unacceptable by the upper state of the society were termed as 'Harijan', the Men of God. Gandhi ji used to work on behalf of them at social and political fronts to liberate them from the clutches of the neglect of life. It was indeed his unique contribution that a movement for political freedom led to a massive participation of people in general which thereby garnered a collective strength to throw out impositions on the system.

Happiness

Neither in the case of Swami Vivekananda, nor in the case of Mahatma Gandhi a quantified definition of poverty was mentioned. Poverty is an index of mind relating to the expectations of the same person. Let us look at the case of a person residing near the temple of Lord Viswanath (Lord of World) at Varanasi, India. The person is a shoe mender. He is a beautiful shoe mender. Very perfect in his work. Knows the art of mending shoes properly and can mend any kind of shoe at the quickest interval of time given to him. The person sits at his designated place by the side of the road which runs towards the main gate of the temple. He sits in the morning hours for a brief period and again in the afternoon hours for short period. The man charges very nominal and reasonable rate and does not speak to anybody except for a brief word for communicating the requirements related to the works. He is thoroughly engrossed in his work, but always seems fresh with a smile on his face. Then once, very surprisingly, the man does not come in the afternoon many of the days. Sometimes he is there, but sometimes he is not. A sage, a regular visitor to the temple, had observed this shoe mender doing his work in the morning but disappearing from his work many a times in the afternoon hours. The shoe mender was really very popular. Most people requiring the mending of their shoes would come to him for the best remedy of their problems. Even then this man was not continuing his work beyond certain limits most of the days. Why? The sage was curious to know. What makes him remain away from such a high demanding work? How come that this man refrains from charging higher when others are freely charging much higher. This shoe mender's demand was the highest because of the quality of his work, the sincerity in the service and the exact payment, very reasonable and nominal that he was charging. The sage could not restrain himself and asked the shoe mender these questions. 'Why don't you continue this work everyday afternoon hours when the demand is so high? Why don't you charge higher? Do you have any other thing to do during that time? Where do you stay?' The man had only one answer with a smile saying, 'I am happy'. He doesn't want to indulge in these kinds of discussion beyond this. The sage thought he will watch what the person does after work. The sage wanted to follow this man down to his destination. Few days he followed him and found the same thing happening. The shoe mender had counted the coins earned. Bagged them and journeyed back walking by the side of the road down to his destination near the river Ganges. He was staying in a small space of less than 40 sq. ft. and 200 cu. ft. It was by the side of the footpath beneath the extended ground floor balcony of a house with a flat stone as the door cover. The man had to creep into get inside. He had a small idol of Lord Sri Ramachandra. Reaching the small space of his residence, he kept the idol open before him, put the stone piece as the barrier serving as the entrance door and started his work there. The stone piece was not adequate to cover the length and breadth of the opening to enter that small space. Therefore, sound from inside came out, and if someone peeped in, they could even see the interior from the footpath. The sage was following the man as he wanted to understand his next action. To his surprise the sage found the shoe mender chanting the holy name of Lord Rama with an idol of Lord Rama having kept in front. As the chanting continued for long, the man got into a deep ecstasy with tears rolling down both the eyes and was fully absorbed in the bliss of realization. The name of this shoe mender was not known, but the sage found the shoe mender far superior to many sages who are otherwise known. The sage had understood the style of living of this man. He worked for his daily need but didn't work beyond that. He worked till the time he was in a position to acquire the money needed for daily survival. The shoe mender considered the time available with his life as God's time. He took away that much of time from the God's time which is essentially required for his survival only. He doesn't work beyond that limit and considers the fulfillment of life lying in the realization of divine. He believes that this life is blessed with the faculty to realize the divine. Therefore, it is an imperative upon humans to thrive on the process identified for the realization of divine. He does so. The shoe mender is blessed with happiness. How much does he earn a day? Probably, his earning a day accumulated for close to a week would come closer to purchasing power of US $1 a day. The shoe mender is extremely poor. The shoe mender is extremely happy on the other hand. He considers his life as a life blessed with God's boon. He can visit the Lord Viswanath every day, he can chant before Lord Rama every day and on top of it he can contribute his service towards the devotees of Lord Viswanath through mending the shoes of devotees requiring that. The shoe mender is happier that most of the happy people on earth.

Sumantra is not that much happy. Sumantra is not unhappy either. He has lost his physical abilities. His eyesight is very poor, can't see far. His entire body carries patches of infections oppressed by the realities of the world; Sumantra is living a self-content graceful life. "Sumantra, do you want some money?"

"Only tea, half a cup in a small size earthen jar." Sumantra does not have any expectation from the world nor does he want to revolt against the world. He feels the world as it appears to him. He can see the morning sun rising in the east. Sumantra prostrates before the sun offering him the highest regard. Is it that he has seen his life having been extended by one fresh day? Will he be able to carry the smile he exchanges with the rising sun, down the hours and minutes of the day? Probably yes at times. Probably not. Sumantra does not differentiate between the eating pot for him and that of a street dog. He still survives as many street dogs do. Sumantra has developed a unique friendship with these street dogs. The nights belong to the street dogs. The day to Sumantra. He watches the parked bicycles throughout the day from the corner he sits in. His friends, the street dogs carry the mantle of watching throughout the night allowing Sumantra to take a rest in the small place designated for him at the back corner with a small shed above. When it rains lightly Sumantra is safe. However, when it rains profusely, Sumantra has to take a shelter at the back of the boundary wall of the market having a better shed on top yet getting drenched in rains. During winters Sumantra has plastic bags to cover with and get protection from the chills of deep winter. Sumantra is not unhappy nor is he very happy. He is thankful to the world for having provided to him the basic sustenance as he considers whatever he has in his possession as the best that could be for a man like him.

"I do not have any money. I do not want any money. What do I do with this winter jacket? My friend Bitu, the black colour street dog needs it more. If you are giving me, I will give it to him." No begging at all. Sumantra does not beg to anyone. He doesn't beg for money. He doesn't beg for anything else required of a life. He maintains his life and thinks that as a good life.

How do we define this life? A poor man's life? An unfortunate life? Life of a person who needs caring and nurturing by the world? An underprivileged life? A backward life? The conditions which reign in the realm of these types of people would need experiencing it to understand the fallout. Let Sumantras survive the way they are maintaining their lives of earth till the time a new messenger brings in the holy message of divinity for everybody. Till the time the wealth of the world finds its way to flow across and flood every deserving place or person.

The earth does not have the providence for close to a trillion billionaires in the next fifty years' time. However, the earth has got immense potential to create happy lives everywhere—at every corner of it, long and short.

Let all the economic evils be chased away by the essential humanistic happiness of life. Let all the yields of society be swayed by the waves of divinity, considering everyone is the embodiment of the divine. Consider everyone having a proper share of the cake of global wealth, to the benefit and satisfaction of those souls.

Let all Sumantras stand up, have their health hazards parked away, get a glowing face and be in a position to tell 'Oh the world! What a nice place to live in. What a nice place to grow across. What a nice place to experience. What a nice place to share the unconsumed bread with the next.'

2. **Basic education for a proper understanding of world and life:** The millennium goal as spelt out by the global organizations, the World Bank, the UNESCO and other regional institutions went forward to make people educated across the globe. Target 2C of the World Bank had mentioned the promise to ensure that by 2015 children everywhere, boys and girls alike will be able to complete a full course of primary schooling. The goal of educating every child at least through primary school was announced in 1990 by 'Jomitien Conference' on 'Education for all'. The progress has not been significant and very satisfactory for all. Till 2000 Europe and Central Asia, Latin America and Caribbean, East Asia and Pacific had shown three

distinct trends on the same. There has been a sharp increase in enrolment rate in Sub-Saharan Africa despite a steep rise in the population growth. As of 2010, an estimate of 100 million children worldwide have lost the chances of getting into schools for a proper education and nearly 150 million children have lost the chance to complete their first length of the primary education. About half of this total number have faced the perils of economic disadvantage as the first barrier to get themselves enrolled for the introductory education. East Asia and Pacific on one hand and other parts of Asia on the other have experienced scattered disadvantages for the children of their homes.

There have been various ways to define literacy. Experience of life teaches a person the most. A person having never visited a formal intuition of learning can have a wise assimilation of knowledge of life. We call it wisdom. Let us try to understand the formal definition of literacy as advocated by global institutions first.

Literacy comes closer to a general measure of the outcome of educational initiative. The first spell of outcome for any educational initiative should process through various steps of literacy, starting from the basic language, understanding and being adept in communication, basic sciences, culture and art, realms of commerce and transactions, understanding the nature and its various footfalls, understanding the biomass and the inert objects scattered around. The laws of nature discovered at various phases of our evaluation and the laws of the world as imposed by human institutions do contribute to the assimilation of knowledge in the process of education. The views about education differ widely from one civilization to the other.

'Gnothi Sheaton' (know thyself) was uttered by the great philosopher Socrates long back in the western hemisphere of the world. A few millennia years before that 'AtmanoViddhi' (know your true self) was uttered by the Vedic sages of India in general and the phase 'Yajna Valka', in particular. Discovering the world within person has been advocated in the Indian civilization, as the true intend of education. Swami Vivekananda's view about education stands as, "education is the manifestation of perfection residing already within". The idea is, a human person, by virtue of his/her having inherited the intrinsic quality, does carry the same throughout. It is the art and science of unfoldment that makes the person liberate those in intrinsic qualities, hither to dormant and lying beneath the material scales of life. The view further says, a process of self-identification and introspection would facilitate getting hold of the inner dimension of the person and liberate the person from the unfortunate impositions of the externalities of the world.

The concept further argues that this life is blessed with the presence and touch of divine and, therefore, all best qualities coveted for a life do reside within. A consistent and persistent endeavour can truly make it exhibit before the functional ingredients of the life. Your thoughts, your actions, your perceptions, your beliefs, your imagination, your ideas and your ideals have the chance to raise its head out of the impositions of the material desire and want. A normal human self would always be driven by material instincts and desires. More you try to put the fire of desire down by fulfilling it, more it becomes vigorous. One particular level of desire having been quenched by the provision of it would encourage the multiplication of the same in a different form with a different attire. The view suggests that this life is like a chariot which is being driven by the intellect of a human person, whereas the divine embodied residing silently in the back. Till the time you give unto Him, the driving force of life, imagination and thoughts and actions are left in the hands of the worldly intellect and knowledge. The sages of Upanishad in India had identified the connection in a nice manner as follows:

"AtmanoRathinamViddhi, ShariramRatham Eva Tu

Buddhi Tu SarathiViddhi, ManahPragraham Eva Cha"

(Know that this body is like a chariot, the supreme self-resides within in the form of Atman. The life being lived at the instance of human intellect whereas the mind acts as a connecting cord between the human driving force and the divine seated within.)

Through persistent endeavours the unfoldment of inner self is absolutely possible. The person then acquires knowledge which is universally applicable both for material conduct of life and its spiritual quest. Let us take an example from recent past in India. A few highlighting lines about a person who was considered a God-man by a great European thinker Romain Rolland. His name is Sri Ramakrishna, the spiritual master of Swami Vivekananda whose name has appeared before.

Ramakrishna did not have any formal education from any formal educational institutions. He had no chance to learn language, mathematics, basic sciences, rationality and reasoning, philosophies, scriptures, literature and any other significant piece of knowledge of the world. The person did not have any tutor to tuition him the elements of knowledge required him living a modern life. Yet Romain Rolland finds in him the 'highest wisdom' a human person can collect on earth. A man having never studied the scriptures and literatures could spell out the highest intrinsic truth of the Nature and the universe by being absolutely one with it. In the process of his being absorbed in the universal consciousness, he used to unfold the untold truth of human existence. God was real to him. As real as an individual identifying the next person sitting in the sequence. The divine light which had emanated out of him was full of empowerment and strength for those believing in him, among many others Swami Vivekanandawas the most prominent of this category. The burning fire of belief that Vivekananda had carried throughout, made him accepted in the world as a prophet of new era. His address at the Parliament of the world religions at Chicago, USA held in 1893 had conveyed an electrifying spiritual spirit among the sensitive minds of the western world, the best thinkers of the world, the best scientists, technologists, best personalities of art, culture and literature with great eagerness. To take a few names Madam Kalve from Europe, Leo Tolstoy from Russia, Romain Rolland from Europe and a large number of dignitaries from United States and other parts of the world started considering this man as the prophet for a new civilization. Vivekananda used to consider a noble and value-based character as the first intent of education. Literacy and knowledge would follow. If a person understands intrinsic divine qualities, understanding the cries of the deprived souls becomes omnipresent in him or her. Global institutions have taken a different route.

The objective of education has gone to the sedimentary granules of understanding a life on earth. The person is expected to acquire and garner information available across. Application of knowledge becomes more important than knowledge itself. The Socratic view of 'pure knowledge' has been replaced by the concept of 'effective knowledge' as advocated by Xenophane, Descarte and other Western philosophical thinkers. This school of thought has influenced the minds of global institutions more than the other schools.

Education has a great impact on economic transformations. Proper education for all individuals in the world would create an ideal place for all humans in this globe, creating a homogeneous and happy environment for all to live happy.

We would classify the objective of education as follows.

1. Education driving towards the height of wisdom.
2. Education driving down the lanes of life. This may be called a practical school.

Whereas the wisdom school includes the driving motive of Socrates, the Indian sages, universal God-Man Ramakrishna, and the prophet of modern era Vivekananda and the like, the practical school considers formal education as its goal. Assimilation of information of various qualities and imperatives becomes the ultimate objective of this school. The idea is, a person acquires intellect and knowledge such that it can earn a benefit in exchange. The intellect has to be accumulated in such a fashion that it gets a proper market value at an appropriate point of time. The knowledge and intellect acquired as such is considered as sellable commodity in the world. One develops knowledge and intellect with a view to get the monetized equivalents of it. The idea goes further, wherein knowledge is equated to wealth. If the knowledge has the power to create new ideas, tools, technologies and process, the knowledge is rated higher than the other inputs of knowledge which is otherwise unable to do the same. A tradable commodity in the market place, the knowledge of a person should dress up in a fashion rated higher by the takers in the market. The knowledge should find effective and matching avenues to carry the essential elements down to the place appropriate for its final application. A scientific discovery or an invention which fails to fetch a market value is a waste in the eye of the world. Any item of thought and idea has to get its own client to have its footing on earth. If the idea or the elements of knowledge fails to get a client it does not have any value, material or otherwise. The knowledge should blend itself with the elements of application contributing to the enhancement of value for life. If the knowledge is replaced by an idea or an ideal that fails to garner a cliental, it finds a place in the garbage of human society. The global institutions have developed this pattern of educational framework throughout. This may be branded as a process of 'exteriorization'. Value of life is estimated through the value of the things in possession of life. Ideas and ideals contributing to the spread of noble thoughts and noble practices of living do not have a significant place to pace up. The global institutions have chosen the process of exteriorization as it has the following attributes:

1. It is measurable.
2. It is quantifiable.
3. It can be separated out of the clout of the many.
4. It has got individual identity separate from others.
5. It is a disconnect with the time past and time present.
6. It has a chance and prospect to grow big individually and become unique and distinct in its features and outlays. The United Nations education and scientific and cultural organizations advocate this through the institute of statistics and other fora. It addresses the issue of literacy to read and write with understanding a short, simple sentence about everyday life. Pushing the objective of life down to the level of day to day mundane, elements and parameters.
7. It identifies the philosophy of life as 'appearance first, quality next'.

Whereas the wisdom school is unfit for the apparent practicality of life, the practical school fits in. The wisdom school has identified the goals of life on a very long term, whereas the practical school wants to have it in the short run. Let us look at a comparison of the two:

Sl. No.	Description	Wisdom School	Practical School
1.	Measurable	It tries to understand a person through the broadness and vastness of his/her mind. It wants to see that this life is for 'me' and for 'many others'.	It considers that achievements are always measurable, in terms of external possession and personal achievements. The person's intrinsic content proves secondary to the external possessions, achievement and recognition.

2.	Quantifiable	The view says the human being is an embodiment of the infinite divine soul. Hence, he/she is essentially infinite in quality and potent. Quantifying the person reduces him/her to a minute granule of his/her ultimate potentials.	Quantification is judged as the ultimate credential of the person. A dollar millionaire is rated low with respect to a dollar billionaire. Right at this moment the world enjoys of vast number of dollar millionaire is more than the number of people residing in the Australian continent. Quantification is a feature of rating the countries on their development. Gross domestic product (GDP) and the rate of change in it is being considered as one of the ultimate parameters to judge the position of a country. Even the state of happiness is being measure in quantified terms to understand how happy people in the country or region are.
3.	Separable	A human life is inseparable from the universal existence. This life is essentially the focus of consciousness and not a bundle of material component comprising it.. The consciousness makes and drives this life, has a connect with the universal consciousness. If separated out the life loses the ultimate chance to grow noble and great.	The life has to be lived to extract the best enjoyment out of the world. An interesting observation can be mentioned here. Millionaire parents of children meeting other parents in public schools in the United States are seen bewildered at the sight of billionaire parent over there. The comparisons are sometimes visible, sometimes dormant. People do compare on their possessions and achievements because of their focus on the externalities of their life alone.

4.	Individuality	The wisdom suggests that an individual is an integral component of the whole.. Not only that, the whole represents through the individual and essentially makes the individual the embodied face of the whole. The supreme consciousness not only travels through, but remains in synthesis always.	Individuality makes the person different from others with the continued satisfaction of his/her human ego. Each individual considers his/her entity as distinctly different from other and expects a unique achievement and recognition valued by the rest.

Living for Better Life

The history of human emergence has depicted concerns for personal fulfillment and kinds of developments suited to the will and wish of the person or the group of people surrounding the person. Throughout the history of human existence, living a better life has become one of the central themes in the making of an honourable and respectable context of the human person. The objective of life plays a very important role in this entire journey of human civilization. At some point of time, this journey has been the journey of human endeavours, throughout different phases and periods of human emergence. At different phases of human history, we come across a mix of qualities and attributes, which have created diverse impacts on the progress of human journey at different corners of the world in diversified ways. It has been found in many cases of known periods of history that winners have become those who had the might and wit to dominate or defeat others with a view to snatch or take away the riches and potent lying with others. Those victorious are usually people having cultivated certain kinds of attributes and emotions which otherwise might have been considered as demonic or they are entities having negative impacts on the surrounding and the environment. The driving force of human history has been the heroes with potential power of destruction and domination. In most cases, they have either created their authority through destruction, domination or maintained it in a way that feeds the restructuring or changes in the human context.

Athah Arthashatakam (Eight Ways to Depict Economic Ills)

The journey of human being in an organized manner has occurred during the historical period and certain observations about this journey from a realistic point of view shows the unpleasant situations created in the modern era, particularly during the current period, which could be depicted in the following terms as:

1. Unhappiness in living a life in general and specific situation of unhappiness for taking the agenda of life forward.
2. Sense of deprivation and realistic assessment proving facts of deprivation causing problems and troubles in life at individual level and having the impact of such at the community or collective level.
3. Getting defeated in life on a relative measurement and scale and withdrawing from the stream of competitiveness and the central focus of life.
4. Poverty as measured and understood in material terms—the have-nots in life and society.
5. Poverty of mind having the sense and perception of not being able to come up to the standard of life as desired for herself or himself.
6. A relative position of the person's existence with respect to others in the society and the surrounding giving rise to the sense of deprivation of different kinds.
7. Perceptive loss of faith and hope on herself/himself because of intrinsic factors or externalities featuring across.
8. The stressed, the obsessed, the victim of calamities of nature or of situations leading to either loss of possession or developed inability to have the possession required for good life.

In its study of the global economy after the spell of COVID-19 pandemic which had almost crippled the global activities to lowest of the low or negative level, the World Bank group has come up with an understanding through their worldwide finding that it has been a period of crisis, though the countries have been affected in a different scale, the patterns of recovery and emergence are more or less either common or homogeneous at almost all places in the world. The observation by World Bank comes with a conclusion that inequality between and among countries have actually increased during the last few years, with a higher level of impac of that during the last three years of COVID-19 pandemic. The World Bank's observation runs as follows:

"Within countries, the crisis disproportionately affected disadvantaged groups. In 2020, in 70 percent of countries, the incidence of temporary unemployment was higher for workers who had completed only primary education. Income losses were similarly larger among youth, women, the self-employed, and casual workers with lower levels of education. Women, in particular, were affected by income and employment losses because they were more likely to be employed in sectors most affected by lockdown and social distancing measures of childcare centres and schools. According to a high-frequency phone-survey data collected by the World Bank, in the initial phase of the pandemic, up to July 2020, 42 percent of women lost their jobs, compared with 31 percent of men, further underscoring the unequal impact of the crisis by gender."

[World Bank, *World Bank Report 2022: Finance for an Equitable Recovery*, p. 5]

According to the observation, with respect to global financial system as depicted in the World Bank Study as mentioned above, the impacts of the COVID problem, through unusual, has certain ground level similarities with the impacts of such calamities that occurred periodically throughout the history of human progress. The economic power though lies in the brains and muscles of an individual, at the collective level this delves in the possibility or not of having entities with a gradually increased size, in terms of participation by people in more and larger numbers. It is, thus, more important to find that impacts of the problems remain grounded in the intent of the individual, apart from the power of muscle and brain. However, distress at an individual level touches down the pathways of living at a cluster and collective level. The impact of COVID-19 pandemic has been directly identified as an impact on the global economic cycle including production, distribution and consumption. However, the most important of this has been considered as a basic problem in the global financial system. The World Bank has observed this problem as to be in the proportion of a distress in the financial system having impact on investment, recovery, redistribution and growth on the cycle of financial emergence and movement throughout. The observation of the World

Bank group which has come through their study of the period of the COVID-19 until the early period of 2022 as:

"The pandemic and the associated policy responses have significantly affected the financial position of households, firms, and governments. The payment and enforcement moratoria described earlier (chapter 1) have supported borrowers by allowing a temporary halt in their bank repayment obligations. In applying these moratoria, banks have been able to help mitigate the economic fallout from COVID-19 (coronavirus).

It is not yet clear which borrowers will be permanently affected by the pandemic and how debtors will adjust to the structural changes in the economy. It is evident, however, that many borrowers are facing financial difficulties that go beyond liquidity stress. This situation is an unprecedented challenge for banks and bank supervisors because the magnitude of the ongoing shock, the uncertainty of the impact, risk extremely difficult."

[*World Bank Report 2022*, p. 80.]

Crisis in the field of economic activities looms because of the parameters including factors as depicted in *Artha shastakam*. Let us have an understanding from the ancient literature of India, the *Mahabharata*. The largest epic in the world is not only a wonder in terms of its literary content and expanse but also the factual description of society and the world ruled by different kings and kingdoms in one of the most important human habitat, Bharat Varsha. Bharat Varsha includes a much larger and wider boundary than the largest territorial dimension of India as depicted by scholars of geographical, political, historical, sociological and relevant other streams of observations and thoughts. It was very vast and wide, connected inhabitants or people of different shapes and varieties through belief and orientation of life. The most fundamental belief that was very widely depicted in the minds and hearts of people, living at the extreme North to the extreme South, the extreme West to the extreme East, had nurtured people to the level of culminating growth with a common belief and orientation to life. This common belief and orientation to life had a sequential under pinning where the facts of life were construed through different phases having different types of aspiration as expectations to get filled in from. In the described facts of the *Mahabharata* there was a war called the war of Kurukshetra. This war became inevitable because of the fact that the evil-doer king had lost the power of fairness in judgement and deprived good people of their legitimate possessions in life. The immediate causative factor to the war was however the gross insult or an ugly behaviour with a respectable lady, demeaning her in the public, putting her into extreme distress without any salvage or support from anyone. The war was waged against the ruling king Dhritarashtra represented through his son Duryodhana on one side and five Pandavas on the other. The main strength of the king called Kaurav Raja (the Kaurav Emperor) was a very senior and a great warrior named Bhishma. Bhishma was a man of wisdom having very wide knowledge and experience of how to develop, manage and maintain a fair socio-economic standard and position for people in the country and the world. The principal warrior on the side of Pandavas was the Arjuna. He was not only the top most warriors but also the dearest devotee of Lord Krishna, the god incarnate on earth. After the war, Bhishma was on the verge of death and made to lie and rest on a bed of arrows created by Arjuna. Packed with all his senses and eager to share the wisdom of life, Bhishma had a detailed long conversation or a one-to-one with the would-be king of the entire Bharat Varsha after they win in the war. Yudhisthira, the next king had eagerly approached to Bhishma for sharing his mind on the acquired and experienced wisdom in life with respect to Raja dharma or attributes of a righteous king. Bhishma had said:

"Rishi Namaapihi Rajendra Satyameva Param Dhanam
Tatharagyam Param Satyaha Anyathahna Viswashahkaranam"

[Vedavyas, *The Mahabharatam*, trans. Haridas Siddhanta Bagis Bhattacharya, Viswabani Prakashani, and Shantiparva, 1992, vol. 32, verse no.18, p. 505.]

That means the king shall depend on and maintain truth in all respects of holding and running the State. Bhishma is urging Yudhisthira upon holding the statehood with certain basic attributes as mentioned in the next verse.

"Gunovan Shilovan Danto Mridu Dharmaha Jitaha Indriaha
Sudarsha Sthulalakshah Cha Na Vrashyaet Sadashreya"

[*The Mahabharatam*, vol. 32, verse no. 19, p. 505.]

That means the king shall possess and nurture the attributes like positive qualities in life, good character with a mind full of calm and peace, having cool and gentle nature, positive behaviour, fair in dealing, open to give up things for others, eager to help and support others and ready to work for taking forward the wealth and content and always in favour of the collective good.

Bhishma goes on telling,

"Pratyekshena Anumanena Tatha Oupaman Sadrishanopi
Parikshante Maharaja Sve Pare Cha Eva Nityashah"

[*The Mahabharatam*, vol. 32, verse no. 41, p. 510.]

That means the king reconsiders appropriate things and information as fair only when any kind of assumption, kind of example or expert saying in favour of something or against it by one or many people, are properly directly and if possible physically observed and examined by herself/himself or independent entity.

"YathadeshangYathakalangYathabuddhimYathabalam
AnushishyetPraja Raja Dharma Artharthe Tat Rite Rataha"

[*The Mahabharatam*, vol. 33, verse no. 2, p. 841.]

That means the king shall examine in right perspective the positions, timings with the physical and potential resources and might and shall attempt to provide goodness and maintain wellbeing for everyone on a constant basis.

Bhishma continues providing active advice to Yudhisthira and he says:

"Sarva Samyam Anayasham Satyah Vakyah Cha Bharata
Nirvedah Cha Vidhitsaha ChaYasha Sat Sa Sukhi Narahah"

[*The Mahabharatam*, vol. 34, verse no. 2, p. 1650.]

That means the position of equality in varied conditions and thoughts and attainment can be attained through practice and endeavours. A man who can go beyond the greed for personal attainment and satisfaction, maintains the truth of the world, attains total fulfilment even encircled with things not recommendable.

"AtmanaAnarthaYuktena Pape NibishateManaha
SadharmaKolushangKirtahaKryeche Loke Bidhiote"

[*The Mahabharatam*, vol. 34, verse no. 2, p. 1692.]

Meaning, self-driven unethical and unfair work captures the mind of a person into sinful stream of activities. This compels the person to destroy continuously the probable prospects of the person lying within.

Bhishma continues:

"Durachara Durbichestaha Duspragyaha Priyosahasa
Asanta Sthitih Bikhata Santaha Achara Chara Lakshnam"

[*The Mahabharatam*, vol. 34, verse no. 2, p. 1791.]

That means people with ill habits, devil intention, wrong tendencies and negative character with strength to pursue and win are detrimental to the economic concerns of a nation. On the other hand, people with good character and tendency, good intent and behaviour are considered honest and good for nation and the economy.

With respect to the approaches to cleanliness and social life Bhishma tells Yudhisthira as:

"PurishamYadiba Mutrang Ye Na Kurbanti Manaba
Rajamarge Gabang Madhye Dhanyamodhye Cha Te Subha"

[*The Mahabharatam*, vol. 34, verse no. 3, p. 1791.]

Which means people who litter on or by the side of civil pathways or at the place of domestic habitat or places of getting and making food are people to be considered as evil for economic emergence of a nation or a society.

On a fundamental principle of life Bhishma advises Yudhisthira on setting the basic philosophy of outlook of life for the purpose attaining economic emergence. He continues saying:

"Mahi Mahi Jah PabanahaAntariksha
Jalaha Ekaha Sa Cha Eba Jalang Dibam Cha
Dibaha Ekaha Cha Api Yataha Prasutaha
Astat Uchhatam Me Bhagabana Puranam"

[*The Mahabharatam*, vol. 34, verse no. 6, p. 1889.]

That means, Bhishma continues telling Yudhisthira an advisory directive for a better life saying, every individual should have the thought about the contributions made by the broader entities for the sustainability and development of his/her life to create a selfless view about the world, society and its economy. He mentions, this earth, the plants and trees, air, the sky, water, lives inside water, the heavenly contributions and heavenly qualities supporting our life on earth enhances the mental frame of the person and induces the person to a better thought on a better perspective. This man is a positive force for the economic development of an individual.

the Government of China making their net surplus non-relocatable from the Chinese territory. This has already strained the relation between the equity investors, fund providers and industrial enterprises in China. Many of these equity investors carry the fund portfolio participated by Japanese, European and American Bankers. And they are on the look-out for an alternative destination for their investment fund, with equal or enhanced growth potential. Many of them have chosen India to relocate their investment destinations. The result of the spell of investment is economic prosperity for the people of the nation.

B. India's Economy

The first physical symptom was the Sensex and Nifty dropped down little bit. However, both Sensex and Nifty have bounced back. With the rationalization of corporate taxation, better repatriation norms, cases of cross-industry penetration, rationalisation of labour laws, better bankruptcy norms and wider flexibility in mergers, acquisitions and take over norms, India has really positioned itself as the investment focal point in the world. Media looks at the matter from a short view angle and they identify that India has Sensex of 36000–40000 and has a crash point. Forecasts about the Sensex is that it shall go well beyond 50000. Media has also mentioned that certain sectors, such as the automobile sector, in Indian economy have reached the irrecoverable position.

Sensex during 2019 beginning till today has been hovering around the 60,000–65,000 from January 21 2019. Let us look back 10 years ago. The Sensex was below 10000.

January2014: Sensex was still hovering around 10000 to little bit more than 10000.

June 2014: Sensex suddenly grew up to 15000.

2023 mid-January sensex is around 60,000.

From that time onward Indian economy not only has grown steady but fabulous.

September 2019: India's position was still on the top of the World on major parameters. If we look at the changes at the capital market indicators, the resilience has been very strong, which reveals certain intrinsic possible factors created in the economy.

Intrinsic Factors

These possible intrinsic factors are:

1. Major spread of the medium and small sector in the economy.
2. Growth of new factories and start-ups.
3. Tenured investment implemented at the bottom level of economy both in agricultural industry and business.
4. GDP and GDP percentage was considered as a major economic determinant by the economic thinkers in the early part of the last century.

After World War II the world has seen three different phases of oil crash (a) 1969, (b) 1978–79, (c) 1998–2000.

Now each of these has actually transformed global technology in industry, business and distribution.

The first transformation occurred immediately after the World War-II on the process technology. Manufacturing had undergone massive changes from manual driven to process driven across the globe, which was first adopted in the automobile industry, shipping, aircraft making, electronics, consumer durables and home appliances. Some impact of this was in medicine and medical technology. Cancer detection, PET scan, MRI are some of the technologies that emerged during this period globally. So there was a massive transformation from manual to process. And in the economic parlance the meaning of this is a change from labour-intense economy to a technology-intense economy. The moment there is a labour to technology transformation, the indicators which had been considered as GDP centric fail to catch hold of the reality. At the moment there is a transformation in the process technology, we do not have a factory run by 20 thousand people, but a better factory can be run by 2 thousand people. For example, TATA traditionally have been manufacturing steel. In one of the plants, for a particular level of each metric ton output, the number of labour force which was needed previously, and which is now being utilized was reduced to almost one twentieth by the managers with a better quality, speedy production, more output, better finishing. The advent of computers and the massive spread of computers in

1980s and 1990s and subsequent period, led to the next phase of transformation, the knowledge economy.

The world had opted for knowledge economy, computer driven processes everywhere with an emphasis on manufacturing on large scale initially, then the entire 1990s, whereas 2020s onwards it is shifting the manufacturing from Mega to Mini. Given this background, immediately after World War-II mega industrialization was the process in the entire world.

At India too the first three 5-year plans had a consistent emphasis on large scale industries. But it underwent changes thereafter. India could not catch hold of global trade. 1980s, 1990s and remaining period the global trade was more of from MEGA to MIDI, the emergence of SME. During this period the world has witnessed changes in the academic portfolio also. The industry was supported by thoughts from academics.

Emergence of Behavioural School of Managing Societies

If we look at the thoughts for running the world, human psychology leading to consumer taste preference had dominated the scenario during the 1890s and the subsequent period and therefore we have got a behavioural school of thought for managing enterprises wherein organisational behaviour plays a major role. Consumer behaviour plays a major role in consumer dynamics. We have behavioural finance to identify the global finance and finally the behavioural school of economics to see how psychology impacts on the economic process. If we look at the value created in the market of an enterprise, it has got two different aspects, one is the physical-material, and the other one is perceptive-psychological, which are added together for the total value. The physical-material is determined through the fundamental analysis of the company or the market whereas the perceptive-psychological keep on changing rapidly in the market. Capital markets globally thrive on a portfolio and a mix of both. A segment of the price comes from the physical-material value whereas other segment perceptive-psychological is normally ignored by people who don't penetrate deep into the subject.

Whereas a company does not change its profile overnight normally, the perception about the company's position in the market keeps on changing. That is what we call volatility factors of the market. Product markets show a steady pattern for a while, but the share markets do not. However, if you take a look at the steady return from the share market, we get the pattern. This is what we understand from the global financial market as of now. Whereas China has gone much ahead of India in terms of its manufacturing base, for the total physical-material value created in the economy, total global trade, accumulation and creation of wealth and exhibiting the indicators in accordance, however, India has proven edge over many other economies. Also in terms of the growth in participation by the consumers, depth and breadth of consumer involvement in the market and thereby enhancing the potential value of the market significantly. That is the reason why Indian capital market has gone beyond many leading economies in growth parameters during the last five years. Major economies like USA, China, Japan, France, Germany and England have tried to focus on India's emergence of capital market during the last 5 years to find more prospects for their own economies. USA and most of the other leading economies have Indian market of consumption as the most attractive place on earth now. If we take the PPP in the global economy, India has already attained a close to US $10 trillion on 30 June 2019. However, the way IMF and the World Bank calculates and the media reports India's economic size is less than US $3 Trillion as of now. India is close to reaching out the target of US $5 Trillion within the next few years and poised to go beyond.

This will have a tremendous amount of impact during the next two decades. The target that India has fixed of US $5 Trillion within the period of two to three will not only be over fulfilled but also there are chances of making it double in a period shorter than a decade. Two important reasons to be kept in mind are:

1. The West European model of SME development (particularly Sweden, Denmark, Norway and Scandinavia), and
2. Participation of educated youth in the process of industry in larger numbers in the years to come.

The Walled General Theory and After

John Maynard Keynes made a remarkable contribution to the thoughts of national and global economies of the world by introducing the General Theory of Economics, largely accepted due to its wide range. It transformed, in various forms, economies with significant influences in economic thoughts during the world war periods and post-World War-II period as well. The General Theory however, had a wide focus on creation of wealth and distribution of the same in the interest of global humanity. Since the emergence of new modes of business post technological revolution of several generations, currently in its 5th generation, the economic thoughts have travelled to the grassroots, shifting the focus basically from the general to the specific. Whereas, the general approach of economic theory values the intermediaries as secondary form of capital, the new technologies have connected the primary capital to tertiary capital through direct distribution of manufactures and proceeds from the origins to its consumption end. The world has chosen a medium-less or intermediary-less connectivity for economic distribution assuming that to be a better way out for creation and proper distribution of wealth across the globe. During the last 50 years, the world has driven itself towards massive globalization creating connectivity among people and organizations, providing direct access of the benefits of connectivity to the individuals. However, during the same period, the emergence of similar phenomena of sticking to the local prerogatives and individual aspirations have shown prominence in the world.

The World Bank has observed very recently in its World Development Report 2020 that creating a value chain on a global scale has become important in transforming the economic conditions of people in the societies of the world. The focus of Global Value Chain (GVC) has been on the new technologies per se and impact of new technology in the life and activities of the people in the world. This talks about the impacts of new technology in creating new manufacturing, process and systems, distribution on a global scale for a local person, creation of wealth of through different modes and allowing access to the wealth to everyone wherever it has potential to get parked in and progress to fulfill the agenda of societies and economies. The issues of poverty, illiteracy, ill-health require to think in a manner that would connect and involve individuals in a way hitherto untouched upon by human society for offering solution to economic problems of Nations. An Asian initiative towards creating a homogenous Asia focused on a combination of the scope and potential of technology, impact of resources natural and created, role of organizations and Nations and overall, the role of an individual. Song of Asia as it reads below reveals an integrated approach among all towards creating an agenda that would finally resolve the economic, social and cultural problems of the world.

Song of Asia

A
Asia..............Asia..............Asia
Chariot of Asian Sun enters the horizon
Infusing the path of earth with illuminations
Divine wisdom spreads
In the minds and hearts
Realizing the Blissful Supreme Brahman within.
Asia.............Asia.............Asia

B
For the building of new one Asia
Let's put our strength of brain and minds
Together we combine our strength
of innovation creative potential and dreams
Into the reality of making Finest products and services
Asia.............Asia.............Asia

C
We grow together endlessly
We grow continuously
We win the world.
Asia emerges on top of the globe
Integrated Asia holds hands
of the people of the world
Asia now all set to create
Asia.............Asia.............Asia

D
New Global Man
To make
World free from poverty-illiteracy-ill health
A new world of happiness
World of harmony
Asia.............Asia.............Asia

E
"Sarve Bhavantu Sukhinah
Sarve Santu Niramayah"
Let all be happy and well
Asia calls.........Rise Unite.
Asia..............Asia..............Asia

Homogeneity in an economy requires total involvement of the individuals in a wholesome manner. An example of Indian Economy 2019 until beginning of 2020 is a remarkable pathway of some ground thoughts of economy. The points to consider are:

1. The capital market indicator surging very strongly up from nearly a BSE Sensex point of close to 70000 mark few months ago and hovering around 55000 to 60000 in the first week of July 2022. On the other hand, forecasts on the overall economic growth looms around 7.5% to 8% during the current period. Beginning January 2023, sensex stood around 60,000–61,000.
2. The hue and cry raised by some people, the media and some political forces about Indian economy saying that it is collapsing is on one hand. On the other, the government thrust to make from less than $3 trillion to $5 trillion size of economy poses very high hope for the economy and focusing on certain areas which may not appear to be directly leading to provide economic benefits.
3. The large impact of the unofficial economy in the nation, wherein the value created over a long period of time through unofficial means, without contributing to economic agenda and estimation, thereby failing to impact on the GDP Growth Index for the nation, has created this kind of doubtful situation.
4. A strong liquidity in the capital market, having created an impact on the Sensitivity Indices of the market is basically receiving contribution from both ends of the economy (the White Economy and the parallel Black Economy).
5. The evils of parallel black economy reduced or eroded would immediately push up the economic indicators of nations. It holds true for an economy like India.

Sir Maynard Keynes has observed and mentioned the global economic positions in general terms while formulating the General Theory. A highlight of which is as follows:

"The Classical economics presupposes that the factors of production desire and receive as the reward of their efforts nothing but a predetermined share of the aggregate output of all kinds which they can produce, both the demand and the supply of each factor depending upon the expected amount of their reward in terms of output in general. It is not necessary that the factors should receive their shares of the output in kind in the first instance; the position is substantially the same if they are paid in money, provided they all of them accept the money merely as a temporary convenience, with a view to spending the whole of it forthwith on purchasing such part of current output as they choose. Nor is it necessary that current output should comprise the whole of wealth; the position is still substantially the same if the factors of production swap their wage in respect of current output for other forms of wealth, provided that those with whom they swap intend to employ the whole sum forthwith to purchase some part of current output. It may even be the case that the supply function of a factor, in terms of what it can produce in terms of something which it cannot produce. The essential point is that by whatever roundabout methods every factor of production ultimately accepts as its reward a predetermined share of the expected current output either in kind or in terms of something which has an exchange value equal to that of the predetermined share."

Several thousand years ago the Indian Sage Kautilya had formulated his *Arthashastra* called 'Kautilya's *Arthashastra*'. This was basically based on the thoughts, beliefs and philosophies visualized and realized by Indian sages during the entire Vedic period in India. Kautilya's principles of economy was the first in the history of human civilization where the economic thoughts had embraced all aspects of human life considering a human being as an integral one. Kautilya believed in the following:

1. Individual human being is the unit of all economic activities.
2. Individual has to combine with other individuals to create a collective and form institutions to engineer collective activities. The belief in the formation of this collectivity lies on the Vedic principle of collective mind which reads as,

   "Samgachhadhawam Sambadadhwam Samvo Manamsi Janotam. Deva Bhage Yatha Purbe Sam Janana Upasata."

   [Combine your minds together with all others as because all minds are gifted by the Divine. Pure minds so united will create a collectivism as it is there in the Divine world.]

   Therefore, individual minds with purity connecting with other individual minds with purity desist from anything

He also mentions,

"Prajaha Srishta Manasha Karmana Cha
Davoi Eka Ataha Sat Pathaha LokoYushta
Dristam Karmam Saswatam Cha Antabat
Cha Manaha Tyaga Karanam Na Anyataste"

[*The Mahabharatam*, vol. 34, verse no. 15, p. 1892.]

That means the creator has made this creation of individual human being with a mind full of potentials for the work of the world and herself/himself and therefore person should apply her/his mind and mental energy for doing good work for herself/himself and for other people around with full of mental and physical energy as available and to develop and cultivate the concept of giving and not fall a pray to the concept of grabbing in the context of the economic position of the society. There is no other alternative for true economic growth.

Indian Economy: Current and Prospects

A. There are two aspects of Indian economy

(i) Revealed campaign about it; and

(ii) Realistic position about it.

Let's have a brief look at these two aspects.

(i) Revealed Campaign: I call it Media Myopia—the journalistic view of Indian Economy that create ripples, reverberating upon the points that it is all sinking. It is reported that economy is sinking to the doom and this has been the case since a couple of months back.

(ii) However, if we take a realistic look at the economy of India vis-a-vis the world, we find new prospects emerging.

Result of which are as follows:

(a) Changing locus of investments from one region to the other within Asian continent.

(b) Reinforcement of investments into the new set of technology built up in traditional industries.

1. Investors like, Blackstone, BlackRock, Abubakar and some midsize investors from the US, Europe and Japan who are investing into equity participation in Chinese manufacturing have been facing problems with the recent repatriation rules empowered by

evil to occur and thereby the question of parallel black economy will not arise at all.

3. Kautilya had considered individual belief, way of life, individual's practiced culture, social norms, social structure, condition of health, level of knowledge earned though education or practice very important in giving a shape to the economy.
4. Kautilya wanted that the leaders of economic zones, called the 'Raja' or King has to be a person fully spiritually oriented. He has mentioned that the 'Raja' should be Brahma Gyani, a person having realized the wisdom of Supreme Lord. The meaning of this is when a person attains a state of Brahma Gyan, he/she is above all discriminations, he is very simple, he dedicates his life to the cause of others, he serves the world first before thinking of serving himself and he has concern for everyone in the Nation or the World.

This is the basic tenet of Hindu Economy—to create a person free from greed, anger, gluttony, envy, zealously, etc. The person should be a giver, not a grabber, acquisition should be for the minimum maintenance and fairness of living only, acquisition not for piling up wealth and depriving others. Never to deceit, cheat, betray, disregard, abandon anybody in the world. On the other hand, trying to contain embrace, establish cooperate, offer care and support, considering that the supreme self is present in every individual. Therefore, every individual is important.

Kautilya came forward with the doctrine, that king should have primacy of the interest of the citizens. A leader should have the primacy of the wellbeing of people. "Thou first, me next" is the fundamental view of Hindu Economy. This "me" is a realized and liberated self who considers everyone of earth as equal. This view of life should be the guiding and governing view for the economies and societies of the world. Hindu economy stands for that and advocates the same for the entire world, with a view to make the world free from poverty, illiteracy, ill health and all kinds of discriminations that have prevailed over during the several millennia of human civilization. Economic evils can only be resolved fully by appropriate application of the Hindu economy. Kautilya's *Arthashastra* provides a highlighting dimension of the Hindu economy. This particular work is based on the principles garnered by Kautilya, drawn from the thoughts and realizations of Vedic sages. This economic principle can offer solutions to the economic problems of any kind that prevail in the modern world at different parts of the world. Let this be applied in the context of the nations and the world.

उत्थान बद्कम् (Utthana Shatakam)

Six Principles of Economic Emergence

(i) Creating a Synthesis - समन्ययम (Samannyam)

(ii) Developing Equi-rhythm - सं छन्दम् (Sam Chhandam)

(iii) Collective Emergence - समाधृतम् (Samadhritam)

(iv) Distributive Justice in Demand and Consumption - समानी आकूति: (Samani Aakutih):

(v) Emergence through Knowledge - प्रज्ञानार्थम् (Pranjanartham)

(vi) Collective Unfoldment अपावृणु वयम (ApavrinuVayam)

The Vedic economy offers fundamental solutions to the economic ills and evils of human society. It considers the individual human being as the most important element in the framework of societies and context of activities. Having given emphasis on individual human being, the Vedic sages developed various aspects of initiatives and coordination, having direct impact on the human living as a whole and human economic positions and conditions, in particular. The basic belief is that every human person has got sufficient potential for rising and growing based on the individual's capacity of self-development and mental orientation to the work and the world. Starting from the earliest Vedic period until the end of it and the emergent lives in the Harappan and Mohenjo-Daro times were actually principle centric and principle driven. The post-*Mahabharata* war empire of Yudhisthira had embraced and followed the principles for life and society as proposed by the sages during the Vedic period at different points of time. The common understanding among the sages about managing, running and participating in a human society is that it is full of individual and collective potent. Utthana Shatakam or the Collective Emergence, in sequence, explains these eternal principles in six different ways in order to develop a comprehensive and durable model for everyone in the society. Kautilya had coined it in the principle of Prajanam

Sukham Cha Hitam as the priority in and objective of managing and running a society towards best and most optimum happiness of everyone in the collective. The active principles as followed by Yudhisthira in Mahabharatian period and that by Kautilya by historical period attempts to create a society full of happiness and individual minds oriented to a superior truth identified as the cosmic truth in the theory and concept of Supreme Brahman. In a sequence, both Yudhisthira and Kautilya have actually adhered to and followed all the elements of Utthana Shatakam, as mentioned above as Samannyam, Sam Chhandam, Samadhritam, Samani Akutihih, Pranjanartham, Apavrinu Vayam. The core approach in economic management as elaborated and spelled out in specific terms in the following chapters have been periphery first, center next.

"पराबृत्यम् प्रथमम्

केन्द्रातिग अभिज्ञानम्"

(Parabrityam Prathamam / Kendratiga Abhigyanam)

Attempt the periphery first and then take care of the centre. In simple terms the economic management would look into the most marginal and highest deserving first and then attempt to undertake the central focus of emergence in future in different ways subsequently. This principle was very successfully followed in India during and subsequent to the period of Kautilya. During this period, the social, collective and personal lives of individuals were not only highly honourable but graceful, according to most parameters applied now in understanding the economic wellbeing of an individual and a collective of masses.

Bibliography

Vedavyas. *The Mahabharatam*. Translated by Haridas Siddhanta Bagis Bhattacharya. Viswabani Prakashani, and Shantiparva, 1992.

World Bank. *World Development Report 2019: The Changing Nature of Work*, 2019.

World Bank. *World Development Report 2022: Finance for an Equitable Recovery*, 2022.

2
Outline of Vedic Economic Philosophy

The law of influence on the economic system stands just outside the admitted periphery of Economics. Barring few modern economists, it would possibly take a few centuries to grasp the theory. Few among the Nobel Laureates of the last four decades have thought that the radical law for solving the problem of economic systems lies just outside the index of economics.

It was Kautilya who first thought elaborately of a total economic theory and also made arrangements for its application. Kautilya's economics is a completely applicable theory of determining the solution and prevention of problems relating to state, society, family and individual life. Kautilya has got an inheritance of a state with just and noble principles offering happiness and wellbeing to all.

After the war of Kurukshetra was over in the *Mahabharata*, Yudhishthira had set up a state which was based on certain eternal values, such as:

1. THOU FIRST, ME NEXT.
2. LET'S SHARE THE RICHES AND DEFICITS.
3. LET'S RHYTHM THE SPIRIT OF WE.
4. PRACTISE THE SPIRIT OF COLLECTIVE EMERGENCE.
5. MAINTAIN AND ESTABLISH EQUALITY, FRATERNITY, UNITY, SHARED RESPONSIBILITY.
6. CULTIVATE TRUTH BASED THOUGHTS AND ACTIONS.
7. ASPIRE FOR REALISATION OF THE ETERNAL TRUTH (BRAHMA GYAN) IN LIFE.

Kautilya's *Arthashastra* (Economics) has presented in detail the clue for the solutions to the impediments for setting up of a theocratic state that wants to and works for the eternal principles for ultimate happiness and wellbeing of people. The principles put across by Kautilya were mostly tested in real life and society by Yudhisthira, the Righteous King. Kautilya had included those practices proven over ages for its effectiveness in developing and establishing a society free from poverty, illiteracy, inequality and ill-health both in the short run and long period.

Kautilya's *Arthashastra* is a theory of total development and extension of the principles of economics. Among these, the main are:

- Individual person: Creating fundamental connections between the natural and secondary capital and human person.
- Society-centric composition: Lives of the people in all parts of the society would be natural, beautiful and happy. For this, is required opening up of the paths of all possibilities and exposition of character; and to rear this line of activities correctly.
- Appropriate arrangement: For development, comfort and safety through enterprises of the state.
- World enterprises: To establish right dignity and pleasure within extended identity of an individual and the collective in totality and to initiate appropriate endeavour to ensure fulfillment.
- All works are to be so accomplished in the right perspective of time, as these may extend beyond time.
- A comprehensive outlook and methods of application: Kautilya set up a background for composition of economics. His proposal is a special directive of the principles of economics. At the very beginning Kautilya has informed that this economics has been composed for the right of this world and to observe them properly.

Kautilya puts it as:

> Prithibya Labhe palanecayabat anta *Arthashastra*
> nipurbacaryah o prasthapitani prayasantani
> samhrtyaek amidam *Arthashastra* amkstam.
>
> (*Arthashastra*, 1/1/1).

In this book *Vedic Economics,* a completely comprehensive form of all the thoughts and theories promulgated so far by the preceptors of previous ages, regarding acquiring and observing the rights of the world has been presented along with the addition of new thoughts. Thoughts span from the Vedic era through the periods of the *Mahabharata* and down until the modern and current era. The thoughts have passed through the tests of applications of nearly thirty thousand years from the early Vedic era until a thousand years ago.

Most of the big publication of Kautilya's *Arthashastra* in other languages have presented the same partially and in accordance with their own wish. Some have shown it to be a treatise on politics and diplomacy. Some again have presented the *Arthashastra* in such a manner as it deals more with protection of the state, diplomacy, etc. than the thoughts and theories of economics and as such it is better not to call it economics but a treatise on detective-diplomacy and politics.

But, Kautilya's *Arthashastra* is the first complete document of economic system in the history of the world. It is such a system where starting from man's activities of life, urge of work, thoughts and character/ feelings right up to the theory of complete manifestation—all are there. *Arthashastra* has not stopped after stating a theory only. It includes all the wings of the act of living and the influence thereof.

Kautilya has made the individual man the pivot. Starting from the taste, habits, objects and target of an individual, his character is especially important for the economic arrangement of a country. Where an individual makes his personal interest, habits and his wants and gains the sole concern, no thought and work for the totality can crystallize there, unless there is a totally consented mind. Good or bad of the totality on feelings for the totality cannot be specially arranged. Unless the power of oneness is manifested in a national periphery or in an economic environment, its economic freedom remains a remote aspiration. That is why Kautilya has felt that building up of the character of the totality and thought the phases of building up of character of individuals is of utmost importance. Economic growth will be effected thought building up of the character of the totality. Plato had thought that it is possible to build up a free economic environment through a speciality entrusted situation.

Man, individually, is worth a mention for such an enterprise. Mental formation and character of an individual man, his outlook of the life's path—all are worth a mention. Society gets developed centring on the observance of rules of life of an individual. Blooming of the individual gradually leaves a compacted impression upon civilization and national and international environment. When a flow of lifestyle grows by an individual's concepts, activities and endeavours of the society move along with the same flow. As taste and character appear rather great for an individual, so also in a society's life, the taste and character of individuals cast influence to pave a path for the society. Unit of society is an individual man. The influence has got twofold action—in one way society is influenced by an individual, while in the other way society's influence falls on an individual. Wherever may be the field of action of the individual, the society comes to terms with it. Society is a common field where different types of influences of different people flow in to represent the background in varied forms, alterations or changes being the rule.

Kautilya's *Arthashastra* is a coupling and well-arranged economic theory between an individual and the society. This economic theory is full of accounts that teach one to control one's temptation, infatuation, greed and petty interest and to think for others. This is even more applicable to a person who has to develop himself into a leader or a king. The chief characteristic of his would be 'You first, I next'. That is, he who would be a king would have to think more of others and be involved in others' problems. He would have to move along others' path; extend opportunity to others. The king will not be confined by his own personal interests, but he would think of the interests of the totality and bring in the totality to prior consideration. The prime duty of the king would be to accord not his own but others' welfare, as welfare of the subjects would be that of the king's. If woe is inflicted on the lives of the subjects, it would affect the king also. First the king would share the sorrows of the subjects. Second, he would try his best to remove that. According to Kautilya, a king will be such as:

"Prajasukhe'sukham rajanam prajanam
tu hite hitam prajanam
Natma priyam sukham rajam; prajanam
tu hitam priyam."

[The king will be happy with the happiness of his subjects, subjects' welfare would be his/The king will not be contented with his own happiness; welfare of the subjects would be dear to him]

But how can such character be built up? Kautilya wanted the one who likes to be a king to have knowledge of the Vedas. The knowledge of Vedas is actually the knowledge of the Absolute soul. This is essential for one to be considered as a leader. If knowledge of the Absolute self is acquired, in the mind of the person would arise attraction for all good things on the earth. Truth, wisdom and reverence have converged in the knowledge of the Absolute self so this knowledge of the Absolute self ends in union—where truth, wisdom and reverence have merged, but any one of these would have to be glorified in his character. So a sense of similarity of mind or an equilibration gets firmly established. Just as 'Yatah bai imani bhutani jayante…'(Whatever has born on earth till date and whatever is expected to come hereinafter all represent the Divine). Whatever life has been born so far; whatever has manifested so far —all are some forms of the Absolute Self. He himself has assumed life-form in different manifestations. He exists in different forms. So high and low, rich and poor are his special appearances. He has been many. He is male and female—all. He who knows the Absolute Self he was developed the sense that the Absolute Self is the absolute. Now how this Absolute Self is to be welcomed, how should he be served? Narayana (Lord) stays in all the creatures, so in the life Narayana spends within crores of people, extended far and wide, he stays in the form of the One and a general Truth. The same substance exists in all. The King has responsibility to blossom the real and infuse total unity in all. That is why a king should be eager to cause happiness to everybody in this world. And the arrangement for this happiness will be from the realization of life emerged for a combined outlook of all.

The realization of the life of an individual builds up the social background anew. And because the society is a totality of individuals, moving with the society, in any way whatsoever, demands a modulation of outlook. Kautilya has stressed on a society-centred lifestyle. The endeavour of economic solution keeping the society at the centre is much more moralistic. If society is bold, it gains the ability to look after all the people of the society. The ability that develops comes out mainly from the influence of the people in the society. If this economic development and solution of economic problem be thought of in the light of social outlook and in view of requirements of the society, then it would be totalistic. Blooming of life is development of an individual on one side, it is necessary to solved everything required for the living of an individual; but on the other side to create a totalistic environment, background and situation for arranging the endeavour. The background which is to be built up for this personal arrangement of an individual is totalistic. Development takes place on the basis of this totalistic background. If a suitable background may be set up **for the manifestation of whatever is these with for individual** the totalistic economic development will be sounder.

General acquaintance with a multitude reveals its economic characteristic. When the cheerful people move about, then when they engage themselves in endeavours, when different enterprises are launched out of zeal, it is then that the background of development is setup Economic development becomes possible through support and participation of all. Activities of a few big concerns or a few regions may be developed but in total it does not signify economic development. Big industries and enterprises have direct and indirect consequence. Directly, it can create a tried destiny in me; indirectly by this coordinate an associate industry may be build up. Extension and spread of economic ability may be possible through uniting enterprises of many people and moving forward along with it. United enterprises of many may show the right direction of economic freedom to a country and through this economic ability gets extended. Again, the economic environment gets nourished by newer economic possibilities. This constitutes a union between totalistic enterprises of individuals and society. Economic environment thus gets resounded and development of an individual also comes in the purview of individual winning. The economic environment thus facilitates economic development. This link between society and individual ultimately nourishes both. Society builds up its own path. It is quite natural that the path of society would be different. Society hare spontaneous accepts an individual where undertaking given by the society accept the lively observances of an individual for his proper exposition.

In order to build up this connecting link and concord between an individual and society, the state system and the world system should have been properly exposed. Wealth of a society is generally limited. It is impossible for the society to set up and offer an economic system with this limited ability. But the whirlpool of the state system, the big endeavour, and the works of it is able to cast special influence.

Kautilya's *Arthashastra* has laid special stress on society and individual. In the background that is set up as a consequence of joint ventures of an individual and society, state or multistate enterprises are possible. At the root of state enterprises is the collection of tax by states. A state allows an enterprise to flourish only after collection tax. Both in case of income and over income, a tax is fixed by the state. The state has to invest money collected by it in the form of taxes for running the state and for effecting economic progress. The ability of the investment is determined by how much it expends for running the state. In order to ascertain the ability to invest, a state considers what would be the size of his enterprise. That is, through that enterprise the periphery of the life of the state would be extended besides being benevolent in all the contexts stated by Kautilya. One of the main themes as identified different Vedic sages and a basic belief of Kautilya is:

"Sukha grahana bijneyam tattva a artha pada niscitam
Kautilyena kartam sastram bimuktam
grantha bistaram." (1/1/19)

The theory that has been propounded here has been in a simple manner free from the influence of many a literature and a certain and definite method of affording happiness in life has been expected by Kautilya's experience.

Arthashastra has laid importance on providing happiness through balanced arrangement of settlements, on proper use of cultivable and uncultivable lands. This mode of using lands will have to be set up in such a manner that agriculture and industry move on through a balanced design, instead of conflict.

"Tasmat Svadhanma bhlitanam raja
No byabhi carayer
Svadharma samdadhano hi pretya
Caiha ca nandati. By a basthitam aryam aryad krtabar
Nasrama sthitih
Trayalniraksitau lokah prasida iti
No sidatih." (1/3/16-17)

[So, a king kin of people should not behave otherwise, sticking to his own principle and pleasing all he would be pleased in himself. He should establish the position and respect for all should keep the traders in respective dignified position and thus by adoring the three class he becomes benevolent to others and himself does never become exhausted.]

In case of running the state, the rules should establish people in respective places in accordance with their qualifications and thus by creating opportunities in their own spheres of work, suitable situation should be created for their advancement. In a spirited royal system, as the stage of development is fixed according to the qualification and working order so also the economic development will rise to be the best in that stage. Judgement of the wealth at the primary, secondary and ternary stage of economics has been included in the culture of modern age. In the publication *Small Is Beautiful,* E. F. Schumacher has considered three types of primary wealth. Basic primary wealth exists in nature in the form of component of creation. For example, whatever is in direct contact with earth as minerals under the ground or as plants above and whatever exists in the form of living wealth as men, animals, birds etc. all one shall basic primary wealth identity of primary basic wealth act the entry point is its possibility. All should be considered as the basic and primary wealth. Any possibility of arrangements leading to the blossoming is to be considered as the derivative of the primary wealth, therefore secondary in nature. In these there will be no arrangement for flowering of the primary wealth i.e., if the primary wealth does not find suitable law of probating, it would be difficult for it to be real wealth. When developed wealth becomes a burden if suitable probability law is not, undeveloped human wealth is a burden, uncultivated land is a burden and so on. Agriculture, livestock, farming, trade, artistry—in all of these lies dormant the law of blossoming.

Kautilya has recommended suitable endeavour for economic development. And to undertake such endeavour men of suitable character would be necessary. Those whose character fits up this economic development should be entrusted with the responsibility of this economic development. For this Kautilya wanted special knowledge, special arrangement for transmission of knowledge. On transmission of Vedic knowledge in man new order of character would be developed. It is such a character as can open up a life full of possibilities with special care.

> "Tat vidya binaya hetuh indriya jayah
> kama krodh abbhamana manaharsa tyagat karyah"
>
> (1/6/8/1)

Knowledge is accessible with character bent with modesty. This character bent with modesty can be built up through becoming free of the influence of six sense organs, lust, anger, greed, etc. which are vices of character. Kauitlya has wanted domination of state and to bring about prosperity through nourishment of economy to those who are engaged specially in development of economic environment of state. To action fourfold gains and salvation of society, Kautilya has prescribed running of economic system by such good charactered men. In the Vedic tradition, economic concern has been given high priority for human living.

"Artha ebo pradhana iti Kautilyah.
Artha mulyam hi dharma kamah abi iti" (1/7/6-7)

Money is the main thing. Development of a state is to be judged in the standard of money. For this Kautilya has wanted a king of pure character just like a hermit, who is engaged in realizing truth and resorted to truth. It is not enough just for a state leader to be such charactered, rather if it is possible for all types of men, in all spheres, engaged in the position of directions of the king, to rise to be like a hermit, then that would be a just background for the ultimate development of a state.

"Tasmat arilsad barga tyage yagena
Indriya jayam kurbitam
Brddha samyogena prajman carena
Caksuh, ulthanena jogo ksema sadhanam
Karya anusasena suadharma slhapanam
Binayam vidya upadesena
Loka apriga tvam artha sainyo gena hitena
Brttim" (1/7/1)

Purification of the character of one who would rise to be the controller of state and world, and who would run the economy of it, is primary. The main enemies of the directors are the six inherent vices. These enemies lust, anger, greed, infatuation, vanity and vices spoil the character and, as a result of that different influences and edition of degeneration grow in the economic system. The opportunity that may append as the consequence of association with the serve organs at the centre of an endeavour may inspire wisdom for the performance at all stage of the endeavour. A life controlled or possessed by the six inherent vices builds up an uneven society. To build up an even society, characters of all concerned are built up by placement at the night position through purification of character and earnest desire for the spiritual path. A character who worked with modesty can earn wisdom through proper purification process. After acquiring wisdom, he can move forward through economic consequences and altruistic consequence.

Kautilya has cited various example from the past to make us realize that direction of kings who are possessed with inherent vies is ruinous. On the other side, kings resorting to righteousness and truth may always rise to be helpful to and associated with their kingdom. A king truly is to be like a hermit. A self-denying, truthful, content, faithful with absolute self, altruistic and suitably wise man is fit for being a king. A king will always be benevolent to his subjects. Thinking for others in the only and chief speciality of his.

> "Sahaya asadhyam rajatvam cakram
> Ekam na bartate
> Kurbita cacibamsa tasmat tesam
> Co srnuan matam." (1/7/9)

For successful ruling of the state a king requires his support group. The members of the supporting group for running the state should be having righteous character like the king himself and should be true associates in running the state quite selflessly. Right there this is the way of running the economic system ably and evenly whereas when the associates who have been otherwise, i.e., in whom greed, infatuation, anger, etc. are appended are kept away from the royal sphere. The way in which the way of economic progress is exposed would be most filling for the particular group of people. That is the way Kautilya's *Arthashastra* has begun with the stage of training. The act of training is generally the training for purification of character, training for conquering the sense organs and the training for acquiring wisdom. Acquiring wisdom means Vedic wisdom. Knowledge of the Rig, Sam, Yajur Vedas being ultimately mixed with principal knowledge of the Athrava Veda infuses real wisdom. For a person in whom the Vedic wisdom has been infused it is possible to bring about a balanced arrangement for an economic system through selfless service with state. Man builds up his life and world with the right of a free life being free of the dreadful influences of poverty, sorrow, fear, etc.

He who likes to be the controller of a state or region should have a complete vision and integral character. The qualities he should be in possession of are:

Honesty, devotion, enthusiasm, and he should be self-denying, fearless, able to work, compassionate, efficient, wise, faithful, of good character and a believer in God.

Leadership from such a person can rightly solve the problems. Solution of economic problems is possible when knowledge is to be acquired on the basis of what have been gathered as experiences by the individual or in totality and is applied on the basis of the storing of this knowledge. That is why a king is to begin the stage of acquiring direct knowledge about human habits. Often clue for the accurate solution of these may be had only if one gets acquitted with their nature and can dive deep into the problems. Kautilya's complete outlook has been revealed in the plans of the *Arthashastra*. The *Arthashastra* has been divided into fifteen chapters. The chapters are as follows:

Vinay Adhikari kami (Directorate of modesty): In this chapter acquisition of knowledge and details of endeavours on the basis of application of the knowledge has been described. He who would be in charge of economic regions shall have to be studying the Vedas, conquering sense organs is necessary and, above all, one is to fixup one duties and should always be engaged in observing the duties. Manager propaganda: In the stage Kautilya opines that the king would acquire proper knowledge about the real problem of the human habitations. The problems which burden and exhaust the habitation are to be properly considered and the solutions are to be planned right from him and the application thereof is to be assured.

Besides there are:

> "dharmasthiyam, kantakasodhanam, yogobrttam,
> mandalayogin, sadagunyam, byasanadhikarakam,
> abhi a syatkarma, samsramikm, samghabrttam,
> abaliyasam, durga lambaupayah, a
> upanisardakamand tantra yukkh,"

Kautilya's *Arthashastra* is not a document of the past. It is meant for the future world. Almost all of the noble laurels in economics during past half country have acquired that knowledge and presented it before men the outline of pure world considering the past of some region of the world. Of all the subjects thus considered, the main one is related with economic assessment. Assessing the economic status with statistics Kautilya has composed the proposal on the basis of that new statistic. All the economic theories considered and applied so far are in comparison with Kautilya's *Arthashastra* single eyed or myopic economic thoughts.

It is only Kautilya who has presented a complete theory of economic development. The basis of Kautilya's *Arthashastra* is individual for the blooming of an individual when both his inner and outer situation are active. Inner situation has to be prepared. For this Kautilya has demanded a spiritual basis. All the subjects of the inner sense of an individual have to be prepared through Vedic knowledge. Background of a noble character in an individual has to be setup by acquiring Vedic knowledge and with that the situation for development is set up. This is possible within every man. The inner environment is built up for position of the possibility. When the inner environment is built up, the individual concerned likes to develop whatever possibility there is in him, when the spiritual wisdom is established the mind grows in dimension within that man. The formation of the mind gets changed. A solemn resolve comes to mind. When the lamp of will glows, wind sets in the soil of the will, summon for work rises along the path of the will; when the will-force become strong in an individual all the external opposition just free away for strong flow of will to be built up. Kautilya likes everyone to struggle. There is something among all of the things on the stage of this world or among all the lines of linking which casts no influence on economic development of man. Everything in life has an economic measure, the flow of thinking and everything among the observance of life cast an influence on the economic system. Each factor in the selection of food and practice of life has an economic stand point, Practice, wheel of culture, spiritual glow, endeavour for work, determination for action all these form pillars of economics.

When an Individual gets established, his family become settled. Man can earn his livelihood by his education or proficiency of work. Stages appear in terms of high education, a very expert personality when men get established in their different stages. On one hand when a person gets something, finds happiness. On the other hand for not getting something grief stores in the person. Both, the propensity of getting and the pain for not getting may end in greed, hatred, vanity, provocation and the like. Through exposition of these at different stage of life may turn the environment of an individual life just extremely distressing.

A healthy and beautiful mind in man can render every part of his work beautiful. If inspiration rises in men, variety comes in his work and activities take speed. Such marks are also visible in state struggles. Such a wonderful situation had arisen in case of the national movement of India. During this period extraordinary inspiration gathered momentum in all spheres of activities of society like literature, art, science, technology. In this period world-class works were accomplished in science so also was in the field of literature. Stags out and decrepit ties of society had begun to be severed then to a great extent. Swami Vivekananda had set out a call for the uprise of the lioness and the people of the lowest level of the society. Stir created in society in this period resulted in alteration of positions. Situation of the society had also changed. Social communication and exchange among different states of the society was initialised and, as a consequence, a phase of complete awareness had just started. Initiation of such phase do not take the same form always. Sometimes understanding and harmony hidden inside conflict gets exposed. Sometimes new kind of harmony comes out through gradual gyration of conflict and agreement. Thus, the stage of evolution in a society does create a newer stage in society.

In this startling stage of the society an eagerness grows in everybody to act sometimes. And as a result, a newer life of economic activity sets in. The outline of this economic progress gets built through different types of small, medium and big enterprises. The economic environment of the world has grown up on one side through big industries and on the other through various small and medium enterprises. Small and medium enterprises can make the foundation of economic system sound. Large extension of limited wealth and property can bring greater progress in the society. The national system of India is centred in the society. The lamp of the state glows by the combination of societies.

What Kautilya aspired is to construct; other economists are mainly interested in analysis and criticism. Kautilya has presented a complete structure which goes on blooming through thinking, feeling and intending. All the aspects of the possibilities in all thus depended continue to bloom. As in inspiration so also in development all the avenues of development open up at the touch of inspiration. The divine existence uncalled in a man owing to Vedic wisdom and or due to character gets exposed. Through the extension and depth of Vedic wisdom a permanent glow in the character of man becomes apparent.

With respect to wealth, all land, immovable property, financial property, and human resource build up the background of economic development. In judging about wealth in them becomes evident that every wealth item has the possibility of special use and application. Every item can be used for welfare of state, social and individual. As the state used its wealth after considering the total treasure so also in the life of an individual there would be new call in his life. This call to an individual is to welcome all he has and to flourish. For someone, this flourishing is in agreement with some long enterprise. For others, it means to advance slowly step by step.

The fundamental significance of Hindu economic theory is to restrain enjoyment. Virtue-wealth, lust-salvation these four items form life structure in the flow of life. But the basis of life is the fetching of virtue and the purity is in final salvation. Kautilya wants every enterprising man to have spiritual experience. The mode of his dealings of a man who enters the field of work through divine feeling and realization and has l purity of character is quite different. He may, at some moments, think of the status of his personal interest but in course of time he would drop his own interest and engage himself at the interest of the society and of many people. Renunciation is acceptance. If there be firmness in this believe a balanced economic system is pleasant and the fascinating world system have would have a balanced position for everyone wherever.

3

Integrated Mind is The Background of Economic Development

Lion's share of necessity is built at the background of desire. From necessity grows demand and the supply is arranged in accordance with demand and behind that come production, distribution, circulation and other economic endeavours. The background of mind can bring endeavour, inspiration of work and again all types of men e.g., drowsy, over from work indifferent, diligent, lazy and with the under led power; of them, those with integrated minds can built up the society. In human civilization the poor, distressed, desired and weak people always move backwards. In the history of civilization these distressed and helpless people get engaged in the whirlpool of darkness and these people have been waiting aloud in impressed grief all along. A time comes when all abilities and possibilities fully sink and they get to the bottom. Hopes of life moves to a whirlpool of hopeless future. These can be traced out from the factors of nativity and culture, may be had in the bonding of a state and territory of the society. These must be sought out. They are obsolete in economic views and all fields of different orders in notions and systems of the same, still in pretext of these many bombastic theories have been framed. To set up a correct order of economic system, communication with the mental ideas of a group of people is needed. It was Kautilya who first forwarded this theory that in being an enthusiastic expert of the integrated mind lies the theory of elimination of poverty. But this view of Kautilya was accorded after hundreds of thousands of years. World Bank in its World Development Report of 2015 had brought a suggestion of integrated vasospastic mind for the elimination of poverty and economic development.

"Individuals are not calculating automation, rather, people are malleable and emotional actors whose decision making is influenced by contextual cues, local social network and social norms and signed mental models. All of these play a role in determining what individuals perceive as desirable, possible or even linkable for their lives...."

World Bank, *World Development Report 2015*: Mind, Society and Behaviour, p. 3

Man is responsible for considering machine made, spontaneous accounts- but he must not be confined within the same. The mental environment of man determines his work. The socio-economic situation grows in the background of the influence of external situation and environment the relations determined by social and human feelings and conceptions. And the true economic solution may be possible only on the basis of these.

World Bank has put a proposal before the countries for eliminating poverty and discommendation in economic system of the world with some portion of the proposal put forth in Kautilya's *Arthashastra*. Kautilya's proposal is more balanced and collective. All of the professional works, wings feelings, thoughts and procedure of life and made familiar in the form of economic identity in Kautilya's *Arthashastra* and the true solution is possible only when we are initiated into the solution through amalgamating all side like use and giving an collective look at the life. Fundamental background of the demand of the market is formed by the backgrounds of desire. As demand grows up all the matters of supply are framed being consistent with that of effective supply. There should be arrangement of production and fitting process of distribution. All arrangements in the long run have ways of dividing and distribution. If demand is cancelled, there remains no use of supply. If there is no need of supply, there would be no need for production. Economic order may grow up depending on what is called modern thoughts and ideas of economic progress.

"From the hundreds of empirical papers on human decision making that from the basis of the report, three principles stand out as providing the direction for new approaches to understanding behaviour and designing and implementing development policy. First people make most judgements and most choices automatically not deliberatively. We call this thinking automatically, second how people act and think often depends on what others around these do and think. We call this thinking society. Third individuals in a given society share a common perspective on making sense of the world around them and understanding themselves. We call this thinking with mental models."

(*World Development Report 2015*, p 3.)

In case of taking decision, what count much is one man's nature, specialties of his character and how he is to be taken at the background of the society. Wave of linking naturally moves into the mental compartment from the flow of life upon a matter of one's depending.

It depends on how one looks upon a matter and how one's demands are developed. That is the influence of the inference one determines on the flow of collective thoughts or the thought of the market. A common demand or the background of the demand is formed from the collective thoughts of a society.

The sphere of influence of mind gets united with the society and forms a stream of social feelings. This stress of social feelings forms a norm of the market. A combined form of all that comes to life with a beckon holds cancelled in the power of the market. The determining factor and inspiration of the movement of the market as a whole are formed under such special circumstance.

The power of the market suppresses all other powers for a long-time, the power of society, culture, tradition and the like get defeated by the power of the market. But the market changes its form with the background of change of technology. The basis of new technology brings demands for new articles or new kind of service. So, in order to solve economic problems, knowledge of mental movements, passion, character, manners, culture and ideas of life of an individual, a society and a group of people is essential.

"Na jatu kamah kamanam upobhogena samyati
Habisha krishna bbaratm eva bhuyaha eva abhibardhate."
(*Mahabharata* 1/37/12)

[Lust is not satisfied through enjoyment of desired object rather just as fire increases with ghee, lust also just increases through enjoyment of desired things]

Cessation of desire and longing does not be an enjoyment, it is rather a basis of renunciation. Renunciation does not curtail life. Renunciation may make other things reduced but the mind gets enhanced. A big mind has a big dimension—the power to feel is also big, A big mind may take noble influence, a little bit of it begets satisfaction. Waves of boundless desire can no longer set up a stallion in this mind. A mind strikes with pain of non-fulfilment, creates alms here of not getting the desired object.

"Psychological and anthropological research also suggests that poverty generates a mental model through which the poor see themselves and their opportunities. In particular, it can dull the capacity to imagine a better life. Evidence also shows that interventions and designs that alter this mental model so that people can recognize their own potential more easily or that at least spare important development outcomes such as school achievement labour market participation and the take up of anti-poverty programs."

[*World Development Report 2015*, p. 14]

As poverty comes to overcast the mental background so also it creates a seaman of poverty-stricken mind. Determination to build up improved mind gets damaged in such a situation of mind. Continuous change in the mental background of the combination in the mental state in the state of social life sets up a fresh newer quest for possibility. Let all the endeavours for exposition of possibility in spreading education, fulfilment of labour, power and elimination of poverty be glaring.

The Vedic Economic Mind

The first step for eradication of poverty has come through different modes of economic line of linking and processes. Endeavour of work and cooperation takes life to the path of progress and victory. Endeavour of work does not remain confined to the world and proposals. To perform works defined by Kautilya, development of true acquaintance with the inner significance of work.

"Karmakarasye karma sambandhan asana bijhh "(*Arthashastra* 3/13/26)

Details of the action of the workers are to be enquired of during the period of work and from the factors of the relevant happening.

If the control over work and the endeavour is correct, work may take a speed, with the speed of work remains associated the mentality of the worker. If the work is with king of the worker, it becomes worker and that work becomes the idea of economic progress. While doing the work the enterprising and sympathetic worker augment the quality of the work to turn the same into an the offering of worship for economic progress.

"Yat prtuibyah bhiyabani hiranyam
Pasabah striyah
Ekasya api na paryaptam tasmat
Trsnam parityjet." [*Mahabharata* 1/37/13]

[All of the food stores, money and wealth, animal resources, human (male and female) appears to take all together and cannot put the society longing for enjoyment of an individual. So, it is good to spur the longing for enjoyment]

A mind that likes to enjoy knows how to enjoy. At a certain stage of enjoyment, such a moving state is active as there are only constantly increasing enjoyment. Endeavours for economic programs accomplishes enterprising sympathetic and enthusiastic works. Longing for enjoyment is an enterprise that creates corruption. The static path gets deviated to build up crooked path. A creative individual may become a worker and at the same time an enjoyer. When the control over the mind gets lessened the longing for enjoyment increases.

"Mental model and social beliefs and practices often become deeply rooted in individuals. We tend to internalize aspects of society taking them for granted as in evitable social facts. People central models shape their understanding what is right, what is natural and what is possible in life. Social relations and structures in turn are the basis socially constructed. Common-sense which represents the evidence, ideologies and aspirations that individuals take for granted and use to make decisions and which in some cases increase social differences. (*World Development Report 2015*, p. 12.)

The flow of mental thought root deep in the individuals so that this can bind the life tightly at the social background. The direction of the path for the movement of the society is tied up in accordance with the mental framework of the people. Economic framework is set up at the instance of how the society moves on or how it likes to move. When mental background in framed at the social background of the people to lend a form, write life to build up a common land of consciousness, at the instance of values of land, the inferences keep the society well nourished, it takes the entire group forward, winning the hazards and resistances in life.

The complete social influence always calls upon the society towards a bigger background. To make this a complete influence, moving an effective state enterprise takes to hail economic freedom. The state policy of economy is built up at the background of the social confidence formed at the influence of the complete cogitation. In a democratic system mental state and outlook for directing lives of majority of people from the basis of state system. In is thus that life become more nourished and moves to the path of completeness.

"Yah duh tyaja durmatih abhih yah
Na jiryati tiryatab
Yah asau pranantiko rogaah tam
Trsham tyajatah sukham." (*Mahabharata* 1.37.14)

[A person who happens to be extended with vile thoughts cannot easily shun desire, desire does not wane ever with decaying of body. The thirst which is like a fatal desire must be shunned and this happiness achieved.]

An individual often gets passionate with desires and to serve his own self is instigated to be involved in activities of mean linking. Venture by hook or by crook goes on for the achievement of whatever is required for the satisfaction of his own desire when people of the lower stratum become strong by virtue of the state power, their macho behaviours gets spontaneously influenced by those at the upper starta, previous identity becomes rather secondary.

"The produce of industry is what it adds to the subject or materials upon which it is employed. In proportion as the value this produce is great or small, so will like this be the profits of the employer. But the annual value of every society is always precisely equal to the exchangeable value of the whole annual produce of its industry, or rather is precisely the same thing with that exchangeable value. By preferring the support of domestic to that foreign industry, be intends only his own security; and by directing that industry is such manner as its produce may be of the greatest value, he intendeds only his own gain, and he is in this, as many other cases led by an invisible hand to promote an end which was no part of his intention. By pursuing his own interest, he frequently promotes that of the society more effectively than when he really intends to promote it."

Adam Smith, *The Wealth of Nations* (New York: Bantem Dell, 2003), p. 572.

Economic growth goes on increasing continuously through communication in the part of production. Annual income is estimated form this complete cost of production—alternatively annual income may be estimated with exchangeable produce. Movement of the produce inside the country and abroad depends on the market price of that produce. Balance of market gets fixed by the direction of an invisible cooperative hand. The final position it stays in depends of its past history. Market grows these in the form of a medium of satisfying personal interest of innumerable people. Adam Smith's outlook converges to the present identity of a society.

The principle of 'realization of personal interest' is to jump with it in the field of world-activity to get all other interests accumulated in the mind privately and publicly vanished. Sense of satisfaction and pleasure comes not from welcoming the desire but in its abandonment. When the market assumes this form, the very basic of economic structure changes.

A lesson from the *Mahabharata* is worthy of deep attention. Yayati, the king being stricken with sex-urge in his mind got youth from his son, enjoyed the same for thousand years and in the long run being tired of the same returned the youth to his son and expressed his experience in the following lines.

"Purnam sahasram barsam asakta chetasah
Tatha api anudinam trsna mimatsva avhijayate".

(*Mahabharata* 1/37/15)

[Desires in life inclined to the fulfilment had been for thousand years, but still must and desire constantly had been arising in my mind]

Placing the bricks of desire one by one in a structure, a free mind can be affecting a noble ascent. Through having release from the trouble of poverty of individuals' captivity from desire may be removed. an attentive being and enthusiastic enterprise in every family towards a venture for the new work is the main wealth of info. A worker sympathetic but free from desire is the carrier of modern economy.

"The first requirement of the concept of poverty is of a criterion as to who should be the focus of our concern. The specification of certain consumption norms or a poverty line, may be part of the enjoyment in life; the poor one those people whose consumption standard's fall short of the norms or whose income lie below the poverty line.

If society feels some responsibility for providing of wellbeing beyond more mere existence, for example, good physical health, then it will add to its list of necessities the resources required to prevent or cure sickness. At any given time, a policy definition reflects a balancing of community capabilities and desires...."

Amartya Kumar Sen and Jean Drèze, *The Amartya Sen and Jean Drèze Omnibus: Comprising Poverty and Famines, Hunger and Public Action, India: Economic Development and Social Opportunity* (New Delhi: Oxford University Press, 1998), p. 9–5.

Poverty level is estimated on the basis of the fitting expenditure limit of human enjoyment. The level below is of poverty. If the pervasion of the arrangements for men to be well reaches all, then as men will come forward to solve economic poverty so also pleasure would bloom in society. In the findings of Amartya Sen and Dreze, poverty in India gets expressed in the background of line.

The role of the state is to be considered here with importance. All the powers that are to be considered deeply tell upon the strength of the market in a combined form. Thus, the nature of the market undergoes changes. If the governance of the state goes on controlling the administration, movement, rules and principles and giving and taking, then a balance is set up in that market in respect of buyers and sellers and ultimately the market aligns into a steady state. The state is accountable to its people for components required for satisfaction at the time of preliminary and urgent necessity and to hail those in a justified way may be assured. State is responsible for meeting the requirement and to facilitate the processes of a balanced life.

"Rajno hi bratam utthanam Yannah
Karyah anusasanam
Daksina brttih samyam tu diksha
Tasya abhisevanam." (Kautilya 1/19/33)

Through observance of vow a king becomes special and great; the basis of the order of the state is renunciation. And the object of processing money for the state treasury is to set up an equilibrated order. The king will see all in the same way.

The responsibility of the state is to endeavour for this equilibrated order. Through having impartial view for all, the king will set up a consistent arrangement in the whole state. For this the king would be conversant with the true position of everyone and in accordance with that the arrangement of the economic status of the state would be set up. The king would endeavour for economic development of all.

"There are three main fronts on which progress must be made if we are to deepen our understanding of way poverty occurs, and significantly improve the effectiveness of poverty reduction policies. First, poverty research needs to focus on poverty, dynamics over the life cause and across generations ... Second, there is need to move efforts to measure poverty dynamics beyond more income and consumption to more multi-dimensional concept and measures, of poverty—This is increasingly common in static analysis but is pure in work on poverty dynamics. This might involve assets or more ambitiously, using concepts of human development on wellbeing. Third, a thorough understanding of poverty reduction requires cross-disciplinary research, Using strengths of different disciplines and methods, and quantitative and qualitative approaches to poverty analysis."

[Tony Addison, ed., *Poverty Dynamics: Interdisciplinary Perspectives* (New York: Oxford University Press, 2009), p. 3.]

For eradication of poverty these fundamental factors are to be stressed upon—how does poverty change spot, in the path of life situation and measure change, the sequence of lives and as a consequence there is constantly change in demand of enjoyment in the market and its measure is essential. Secondly, before enjoyment varied identities of man gets exposed in this stage and discovering the true nature in of it is essential. Thirdly, it is essential to know the real nature of poverty or to take all necessary steps to solve that. Material right, priced wealth or real blooming of human resource—through true pervasion of these and through society culture, sequence, tradition, technical knowledge and the like, the principle of possibility of economic arrangement gets evident.

In recent times thoughts have come forward go to realise that depiction of economic philosophy is not possible merely by solving economic problems. For the development of economic system of the state, influence of natural mental movement of individual and collectively, their complete or private behaviour and all the wings of life are essential. Kautilya's *Arthashastra* is the very first economic theory that has looked upon the human civilization in an integrated form and called upon for balanced development and setting up of economic equality.

"Tasmat tat utthito raja kuryat anusasanam
Arthasya mulam vtthanam anarthasya biparyayah"
(Kautilya 1/19/35)

A king, always active, would run the administration of his kingdom knowing that endeavour for work lies at the root of all economic upraise. Through enthusiasm for work he would make the economic system free of any disaster.

Endeavour of work comes with the advent of a great power in society and state. If the dormant power in man gets exposed, this very power becomes proper for society and state to move on. This exposition of the dormant power in man makes the foundation of the economy of the state sounder, Kautilya's economic wisdom has always insisted on always being earnest in the exposition of this power dormant in man and this would make the economic progress the highest.

"At least since the time of Adam Smith, competition has played a central role in economics. It is because of competition that individuals and firms pursuing their own self-interest are led, as of by invisible hand, to do what is common good... Markets work partly because of competition and partly because of advantages that result from decentralization. Competition is important because it provides incentives. ...There is no strategic corporate policy to outwit rivals. To be sure, profits are maximized if firms minimize their costs of production. But to get customers as many as the firm could possibly want all the firms made to do is charge ever so slightly less than 'the market price'."

Joseph E. Stiglitz, *Whither Socialism?* (Massachusetts: MIT Press Cambridge, 1994), p. 109–10.

Kautilya wanted to set up such an arrangement as would enable the benefit of economic measures to reach all concerned. Kautilya is the very first creator and propounded of theory who opined that the set-up and structure of economy are conjoined with everything in life. State system, culture, social system, religious life, work culture of men, integrated native all together are essential for shaping economic policy. Longing and getting of men are estimated on the basis of a complete feeling about life. Ways of life and out work of life for differ from person to person. The possibility of solution of economic problem are all embedded in the background of the combined power of the society.

"Krtva ca kalusa buddhirupachabhin caturbidha
Naga tu antam nibarten a sthita satubatah ghrtau."

[The mind which has been blemished with different types of glooms, the respective judgement gets also blemished. If this mind be inspired in a steady form like a glowing flame, befitting characters are built up for a state.

Kautilya has liked an open system for administration of state. A complete economic system may grow up through a democratic system of reaching a consensus after considering the important opinions of all. This is the richest wealth in the field of building up a balanced and equilibrated environment of life at the state or social level.

If we look beyond the 20th century and adopt a very long-term view the idea of a stable capital–labour split must somehow deal with the fact that the nature of capital itself has changed radically (from land and other real estate in the 18th century to industrial financial capital in the 21st century). There is also the idea, wide spread among economists, that modern economic growth depends largely on the rise of human capital.

"The truth is that economics should never have sought to divorce itself from the other social science and can advance only in consumption with them. The social sciences collectively know too little to waste time on foolish disciplinary squabbles. If we are to progress in our understanding of the historical dynamics of the wealth distribution and to structure of social classes, we must obviously take a pragmatic approach and prevail ourselves of the methods of historians, sociologists and political scientists as well as economists."

[Thomas Piketty, *Capital in the Twenty-First Century* (Harvard University Press, 2013) 2013, p. 33.]

If future invitation is hailed, it will be observed that as during last three centuries the diversion between invested wealth and labour has changed form, so also it would happen in future also.

A true economic system does never remain limited within a common boundary of economy when reasoning all the changes of history that has risen up to the prevent stage in conjunction with all the aspects of social science, we attempt to see it would be evident that a complete economic system is to be built up conjointly will all the wings of state life.

Kautilya was the first to propound an integrated form to economics. The basic outlook expressed in Kautilya's *Arthashastra* is the land of faith of an individual. By way of enlivening the land of faith of an individual that can be cragged quite indifferently into the very depth of the problem. The way to cross a problem lies in entering dep into the problem. When the inquisitiveness gets mingled up with the inquisitiveness of an individual the way to cross over the problem may be found out by a state. So in accordance with the ancient sequence of feastings Kautilya desired for the gestation of inner spiritual power in man and the exposition of his spiritual consciousness.

Now the problem is: are poverty and dissatisfaction the same measure? All dissatisfactions are not criteria for poverty. Different measures of dissatisfactions get revealed in different ways in the background of time. If disappointment, alarm, anxiety, dirtiness of mind gets conjoined with dissatisfaction, then it is to be understood that poverty must be a reason there of.

The group of dual people bent down thus unveils the acuteness of poverty. With development of economic condition, a change comes through in the complete form of man. Only change cannot remove dimness.

If all the people are to be possessers of fair lives, then the spiritual path is only the right one for him. That is why Kautilya wanted:

"Tasmat ari barga tyage yogena
Indria jayam krubitam"

[Kautilya 1/7/1]

[I can query the six vices the king will be free from the control the sense organs]

Those who would be in the administration must cross the limit of sex-passion-anger-greed-infatuation-verity-envy, etc. Then and then only would he be engaged properly in extending welfare and happiness to all. Otherwise, wealth of a society or of a state would not be bloomed and he will be rather confined to a limited number of spots.

From this emerges inequality in society and disaster in the economic status of a state. Kautilya has prescribed procurement of Vedic knowledge of keeping the mental background free of demands.

This procurement of Vedic Knowledge does not mean going through the tests, it aims at setting the Vedic Wisdom in. The central idea of Vedic Wisdom is acquiring knowledge of God, the absolute Self.

For this, a way of the paths like that of reverence, practice of yoga or any other spiritual practice is essential. A religious devotee as would contract his desire for enjoyment so also, he would form the pillars of the Hindu economic policy. There lies the key to bringing total change in the civilization. Through this a newer society free, liberal and biotical to all will be set up.

Bibliography

Addison, Tony, ed. *Poverty Dynamics: Interdisciplinary Perspectives*. New York: Oxford University Press, 2009.

Piketty, Thomas. *Capital in the Twenty-First Century*. Harvard University Press, 2013.

Sen, Amartya Kumar, and Jean Drèze. *The Amartya Sen and Jean Drèze Omnibus: Comprising Poverty and Famines, Hunger and Public Action, India: Economic Development and Social Opportunity*. New Delhi: Oxford University Press, 1998.

Smith, Adam. *The Wealth of Nations*. New York: Bantem Dell, 2003.

Stiglitz, Joseph E. *Whither Socialism?* Massachusetts: MIT Press Cambridge, 1994.

World Bank. *World Development Report 2015: Mind, Society, and Behavior*, 2015.

4

Economic System of States: Vedic Ways

Introduction

Some fundamental aspects of economic system of states have been stressed upon in Kautilya's *Arthashastra*. In the state circle, question of leadership has become much prominent. In *Arthashastra* the subject has been dealt with very carefully. The aspect of leadership has been viewed in two-fold manner; traditional or sequential leadership and built up or elected leadership. The question has not been considered only once and then left out, it has been assessed continuously. *Arthashastra* has laid stress on the components of continuous assessment.

As this consideration is useful to a king, so also it is for others. Training, imparting knowledge, personal discussion and observance and study would continue right before coming to leadership. If a prince happens to have a chance to be a king, minister or councillor, he also will have to pass through these stages. This is applicable in case of ministers, monocrats or officers. How much knowledge and training is to be imparted, on whom, would depend on the time allowed to him at present or the duties awaiting him in future. Thus, the nature of trailing suitable for an individual as officer is to be judged and training is to be arranged accordingly.

Basics of Economic Thought

At the root of financial solvency is the cooperation of people. If some route is to searched for economic progress of a country, then first of all an able leadership will have to be looked for and also the factors which the needs of the country depend on and the flow of movement of the economic system of its own. Of these, three factors are worthy of mention.

1. Collective strength of population
2. Strength of money
3. Strength of materials

Kautilya's *Arthashastra* has laid greatest stress on the strength of people. Strength of people does not only mean the number of the population and the ability grown upon the basis of that. It means a collective endeavour of beginning right from the local people extending to the people of all levels. If assessed correctly the dignity of the strength of the people should be an extension of people's cooperation. That is the state of affairs built up by the concerted efforts of many persons is manifested in the strength of the people.

The strength of money is financial ability. Strength of money becomes more useful when strength of people falls short. Money begets money. That is, money is to be produced starting with money. Enterprises become valuable if alterable strength of capital is available as investment, when there is investment the flower of possibilities blossom there. In some cases, investment is able to create the environment and infrastructure for appropriate enterprise. This ability is the ability of application of investment.

Strength of materials is a principal support of economic progress and development. Economic development needs money and needs cooperation too. If supply of materials remains proper, equally needful strength of people and strength of wealth also become valid. Strength of material augments the usefulness of strength of wealth and people. As strength of material on one side facilitates the path of people and use of wealth of a country so also it facilitates the path of creation of strength of material and its supply. The strength of population, money and material depends on the merits and demerits of economic outlook. In considering leadership, Kautilya has stressed on the personal merits and demerits. He has contemplated an ascetic king as a sage king. Here the personal qualities of and character of king has been looked into. It cannot be accurately said that for being an ascetic-king or a sage-king it is not necessary for being so in that family, in that time age or in that very sequence.

For being a sage-king, there should be observation and exercise. Study and cultivation of spiritual burning is essential. For spiritual study, the Vedas have been selected. Studying Rig, Sam and Yajur

Veda and initials of the same in life is necessary for state leadership. Kautilya has asserted that as getting rid of the six inherent vices is essential for a king. It is not so much for common people. The leadership must be free of the six inherent vices and should have to work for great multitude of people in selflessness and devoid of self-orientation. As a result, this leadership would get established in the hearts of the people. All will follow the leadership and would this accord cooperation.

State leadership would be abiding by duties and obligation of Kshatriyas culture of valour and strength is primary for that. He will think for the protection of the state, at the same time to assure the same continuously, he will take up necessary steps and ways. This has generally been taken to be the duty of a king. Kautilya has proceeded further and has cast light on the sanctification of character and spiritual realization. According to Kautilya, without sanctification of character one cannot get rid of the vices like sex-passion, anger, greed, infatuation, verity, etc. These are antagonistic for men to be great or for growth. The vices are not only injurious to individuals, Kautilya has very rightly placed in his *Arthashastra* the proposals for the removal of vices and egotism for officials of all stages. Destruction of vices and egotism in case of a common man brings good result to him only. On the other hand, if it happens in the case of an official, as someone entrusted with responsibilities from the state, the result spreads faraway. The effects of sex-passion, anger, etc. in a man of the stature of a leader result in the people of large kingdom getting ruined with the sin of the king. If the character of the king is blemished that blemish gets transfused into the subjects. That is why Kautilya asserts what are required are discipline, regularity, strength of character, Vedic learning and obedience to spirituality. Discipline is key to Vedic learning and obedience to spirituality. It is harmful on the part of leadership to be selfish and occupied with egotism. If the leader becomes selfish, he will invest the power on the state to meet his own interest. Strength of materials would be invested by such a leader in his own interest.

If a king moves in the path of spirituality assets. Like qualities and sage like properties get manifested by him. One part of one who is at the helm of the monetary affairs should never be selfish and obsessed by sex-passion, anger etc. Such a person shall have to be of good character and be a possessor of spirituality. He would be captured and drenched in the nectar-like downpour of traditional sequence. He would bear what is true and what is great.

A sage-king would be an ideal economic and political leader of the state environment. Kautilya has offered the basic responsibility of creating a background for economic that should be present in the leadership. But for an ideal leadership economic discipline does not appear within the people. Without having an inspiration from the leadership, the cooperation needful for economic development of people also does not grow. That is why Kautilya has approached Vedic learning and Vedic culture for developing economic situation.

Strength of Population in the Field of Spirituality

A single stick may be broken easily, but if ten sticks are bundled to break this becomes rather very hard. People's enterprise is to be tied up with the rope of cooperation. A number of economic theories have explained cooperation in a number of ways. Some have explained in terms of cooperation, some again through union of classes. In such cases necessity or interest has played the promotion role. When a worker's marks are read from the standpoint of class interest and become incorporated, in that case what actually acts at the root in his non-cooperation of the negative mind. Whatever action is negative, mind initials are negative.

So, the fundamental change that the incorporation of workers on the basis of interests of the workers can be brought about in the economic system is by the control of the representative of worker on the factors of production. The aim of this process of control is that the benefit of the economic system reaches all. It does not happen in the extreme case in line of a tried route. Just as the service of the interest of an individual only serves him, so also the service of interest of a growth tends to serve only the members of that family. So, if region of workers be active then sinful action prevails. The leadership coming out hand in hand with the workers gets entangled in sex-passion-anger, greed-infatuation and extort the people exorbitantly. The sin pledging emancipation from which revolution is set in. Such leadership creates a deeper ditch of that very sin.

Spiritual wealth is thus necessary for economic leadership. Just as spiritual practice is necessary for cleaning monk observing a vow, still more essential is observing spiritual life for a king for a leadership in social and economic affairs. Not with the help of popular demoniac power, but the leadership should have to be possessor of beneficial divine power. It is quite befitting for giving leadership to one who is devoid of sex-passion, anger, greed and infatuation. He becomes the inspiration for development. His power to give a call is his strength of character. His personality glowing with wisdom would build up an environment of economic awaking.

A sage-king would remember two opportunities with contradictory inclination. Firstly, there is an inspiration of inner awakening and secondly moving along the part of inner awakening he would build up the propensity of a clean external awakening. As the lotus of inner awakening would be blossoming gradually single petalled, bi-petalled and multi-petal lotus would be bloomed, so would the force of.inspiration of external awakening be condensed.

As inner awakening opens up the closed door of consciousness in an individual, so would the external weakening bring about development of less consciousness. Exposition of the consciousness of the individual who has been installed by the leadership would be ensuring that other. Consciences become transformed. The strength of consciousness of enterprising and spiritual-minded leadership becomes the gate for freedom of mass-consciousness. At the light naming touch of divine consciousness wake up the dormant consciousness of many people. Invocation of consciousness will be exposed. Under such circumstances he forgets his intimate and own self. Man, then becomes eager to serve others, urging others to forget self-interest, self-inclination and a network for complete identity and multipurpose flow of work is to be setup.

What can be accomplished through leadership of awakening consciousness has been tested in different countries. At the moment of awakening millions of people leap up at the call of self-sacrificing leadership dedicated to the masses, they leap up practically without caning for anything whatsoever. The sacrifice their own interest, own ability and even own lives. We have seen in connection with the freedom movement of different countries that large number of people have rushed out to sacrifice lives. Present situation of the self-feastings for future and pull from the back and nothing of the like could prevent them, because an indomitable call rang in their ears. These great-hearted men rushed out at the lofty attraction, have scarified their lives for their mother countries.

This is possible due to the spread of mass-consciousness. The mantra of consciousness rings in the container of leadership and with this mantra the mass-intention becomes sanctified through ascetic practice with this mantra. It is just like exciting the suppressed fire inside. The strength of leadership become able to open up the flow of consciousness within itself, the effect of its glow falls on the mental stands of the masses.

As there is a mind inside an individual self, there is a conscious force in totality. The collective mind and collective consciousness is sensitive. As the conscious plea of an individual is influenced by the touch of some other country, so also is collective consciousness. Eagerness, enthusiasm, enterprise all become fruitful in the reforms and strength of character lying in the fundamental dark.

It can be said with certainty that mental reforms would get controlled at all. Mental exercise of an individual can take place even without any reformation. Reforms sometime remains suppressed just like the undercurrent flow of the Phalgoo River. It is true that the reform suppressed within cannot be confined for long it begins to be exposed. As a result, the personal propensity of an individual finds an opening for exposition. The best transformation of this gets accomplished in the way of reformation of the nation.

A nation that is individualistic has to be developed along that very way. If an individualistic nation is to develop it will have to understand deeply the path of blossoming of an individual. The nation will move forward along the path of the blossoming of individuals. The exposition of every individual would constitute the exposition of the nation. Every individual on the basis of his own being and becoming would build up the structure of national improvement. Individual awakening is the main word. So an individualistic state would encourage awakening of the self.

The path of progress of a moralistic nation is quite different. Here the collective mind and the collective consciousness are to be incited. The nation is to move forward resorting collectively. Any call, any appeal all are to be aimed at collectively. Here personal appeal will yield no result. The mantra for awakening of a moralistic nation would enterprise. Since there is reform of the collectivity call is to be aired on the basis of collectivity.

In case of a nation when a particular criterion works best where a special appeal acts through tradition and consequences, then that very characteristic would be the best means for bringing mass-exposition there.

In case of India, for earning the strength of people the exercise of inner world is recommended. Kautilya was right in his principle. In the Indian perspective he has put forward the proposal of spiritual learning and spiritual exercise for state leadership. Subdual of inherent vices is the initial preparation for spiritual exercise. The social background considered for subdual inherent vices is just something external. Its basic sensitivity is rather extreme. The phase of awakening starts in the mind of an individual. Inspiration of good and truth, inspiration of beauty and pleasure gets surged in the mind. The seed of realization is to be sowed in the mind. In the mind occurs the germination of realization and granules flourish with stem branches and flowers. It is in the mind where the old narrowness leaning towards the back gets shattered and something big and great emerges.

Awakening takes place in the heart. In his mind the chariot of awakening is called by the individual himself, the companionship and inspiration that the individual gain through this call sets the phase of formation in the individual. Here from gradually occurs the invocation of light. With this invocation the individual recedes gradually from darkness. Darkness gets destroyed at the touch of light. As a result, all the guilt and faults of character of an individual gets dissipated. The subdual of the inherent vice gets transformed then. There remains no need to look back towards these vices.

In him who has taken the God in himself, welcomed God in his life no blemish can get accumulated. The wide and open flow of godliness fills out all the spots and blemishes of mind. The mind becomes free of blemishes. It is a clear and open mind. In this clear and open mind, the root of sex-passion, anger, infatuation, etc. cannot move far.

The vices, so far accumulated, disappear altogether. Only noble and great leadership free of blemishes can feel rightly the measure of the strength of the people's hand. If for enjoyment and egotism creep in the leadership, then it spreads more widely in the public. If on the other hand, the propensity of greed and enjoyment gets disbarred from the leadership, people's strength becomes more eager for cooperation. The situation required for cooperation also comes to the leadership as a source of inspiration. Self-damaging leadership paleness noble. And this very nobility begets in him the magnetic power of call. In one who has welcomed in one's own life, own exercise, the true and beautiful mind, a clear desire, the propensity of renunciation and nobility become silent features of his character. The wheels of the chariot set forth by him for economic progress acquiring greater and greater velocity with time. The strength of the people gets associated with it.

Strength of Money and Material in Spiritual Field

Strength of population begets strength of money. If the temple of Kalighat present of money is offered at the feet of the idol of kali, the mother, the very high quanta of such little presents in total makes a huge amount of money. Similarly, in the Devasthanam (abode of the god) organization of Tirupati, a huge amount of endowment has grown up. Tiny savings in the course of time grows up into huge treasure. Strength of money spreads in two ways. One is increasing money through investing the source of money. It is possible with whom and where there is ample plentiness of money. Kautilya's *Arthashastra* has not praised this type of money. *Arthashastra* has sought for strength of money with the strength of population. Through this proposal as the aphoriser, Kautilya hinted at a far-reaching affair. If money is procured through heating up of money, then the process would be what is called capitalism in modern terminology. On the other hand, if it grows through support and cooperation of the masses, it would be called mass money.

Merits and demerits of capitalism are tested. It has shattered the other economic system of modern society. Under the process of capitalism Marxist and socialist system have been utterly twisted and broken. New learnings and wisdom, new ways of life and new flow of thought have served as the carriers of capitalist system. This has brought expensive transformation into clean dreamland of paradise. America is an example. The whole young community of the world now dreams of going to America. Almost everybody is up and ready to go there. It is as if it is a dreamland on this earth. American dollar is as if a God's currency. All together have extended their grip on this treasure and are running with some blind hope. Such saturations are present in Eastern Europe, Australia and some African countries, in all ends of Asia and even in China and India. The strength of money which has built up places and building in America has at its root the brandishing of money. Money gets created by the force of money. This is the main principle of capitalism. Money here comes first; money comes second, and money is the last word. The perspective of mass-money is of course different.

As the empire of prosperity of capitalism is being built up, so also an empire of sorrow is there, prosperity has grown up, it has been more expensive and along with it has increased starvation, poverty, torture disparity and extreme sadness. When a group of people is busy in spending time in Honolulu they are busy in their own construction and experiencing of satisfaction came across with children who are starvation-stricken and sickly. The same situation occurs in the forest area called Sundarbans shatters the heart of mother earth. Where would voice the wonders of hundreds and thousands of people who are being paired in the muddy field of affiliate go? The hope of vanity of revolution has been demolished. The words and endeavour of class strength has been futile. Drag for the interests of individuals and society has extinguished the flame of revolution. Perspective of newer feeling is required. High tide of newer thoughts crashing the dam of orthodoxy is required.

It is the time for standing up. It is now the time to be glowing with power and valour. It is the time for awakening. Swami Pranabananda has called this age to be one of the great awakening. It is not the time to be mortified being drenched in hidden terms under the covering of the inherent vices. Fie is to be cried upon that past which has boiled in bringing a flow of truth and has been a trial. Fie is also to be cried upon that present, which does not cover essence of its own self, which is absorbed to build up that flawless true of drop of and grain of which would be inscribed by the intrinsic name or the note of Brahman (the absolute Self) and which would be quite implicated in the feeling of that Brahman. It is not for leadership only. This call is for all, for the public. It is for all, for me, for you.

One is not to approach anybody for mass money. If the nation wakes up, mass-money in naturally provided with. Only cooperation is needed, what is needed more is a positive outlook. I can, we can, my country can—such forceful and positive feeling is required. At the stage of ability there a would be a free advent of the hints for what I can, what we can and why my country can. Pointed direction of awakening also comes automatically. People of the country only know how to rouse the country and again the people of the country can also push the country on the verge of destruction.

When it is settled what we can, the provision for the second thoughts also comes in. Along with the material factors is settled. Strength of people and money in its connections begets the strength of material. Strength of people, money and material all are connected in a row. Just the flow of three streams. One is conjoined with the other. Material is dependent on procuring and also on creative ability. Inspiration for material comes in man's mind, in man's desire. At the time of awakening the inspiration for material becomes as if multiplied many times.

During national movement of India came a high tide of natural enterprise for work. The integral vow that came in minds of the nation in post-war Japan dragged that nation upwards. Japan has acquired a lofty position of monetary strength. Enthusiasm for creation of materials has arrived in China, India, Japan, Korea, Taiwan, Singapore, Malaysia and elsewhere. The expedition of materials is in the expedition of the carriers of newer technology. Technology also has adjusted itself to the attraction of the market. Material strength has been formed from materials saturated with newer and newer measures.

Conclusion

The excellence of Kautilya lies in the sensitivity of his thought and depth of arguments. His strength lies hidden in the topics introduced by him in creating a perspective of state economics. At the very initiation of the *Arthashastra* Kautilya has brought the context of shaping proper men for economic system and has raised the case of proper arrangement for those men to become interested in spiritually. Men made powerful with Vedic learning and Vedic wisdom are proper for Kautilya's economic system. Economic development and explosion of solvency would also take place in this system.

5

Wisdom is Compulsory for Economic Liberation

Spiritual realization is the path of wisdom: Without a basis of spiritual knowledge, proper outlook and pull for society and civilization do not develop. Selfishness becomes stronger in an individual devoid of knowledge. The deeper the touch of wisdom, the deeper moves the sharpness of outlook. As an outlook saturated with wisdom becomes free from personal assets and liabilities, so also it becomes full of kindness. With wisdom, kindness develops spontaneously. That is at the touch of wisdom meanness gets lost, nobility develops.

Wisdom is one and undivided. Wisdom means wisdom in Absolute self. Infiltration of feelings for this means wisdom. Feelings for the Absolute gets the exposition of wisdom along with. As feelings proceed, so proceeds wisdom. Wherever there is a bit of touch of wisdom right, there is the beginning of the expedition in the path of wisdom. It is the capping of the tree of wisdom that develops into the tree of wisdom. Germinated wisdom widens outlook. Widening of heart rises for electorate knowledge. All blemishes of an individual burn up in the flame of wisdom, services of egotism vanish. With the advent of knowledge, the thought of personal interest or feelings of personal good or bad become insignificant. Kautilya has liked that on being emanated a system devoid of anger and sex-passion, economic arrangements would be set properly.

> "Avidyavinayah purusabyasanhertuh
> Avinauti hi byasanadosat no pasyati"

(*Arthashastra* 8/3/1)

[Blemish of character does not become visible due to local conceal of wisdom not because a man devoid of wisdom stays as afflicted with faults.]

In an economic system exposition of knowledge of individuals is necessary. With exposition of knowledge, the ability for running an economic system blooms up in an individual. Thereby the economic system gains momentum. On gaining momentum proportionality comes back to the economic system.

"Raja rajyam iti prakrti samksepah."
(*Arthashastra* 8/2/1)

"Rajyah abhyantarau bah youba
Kopah iti" (*Arthashastra* 8/2/2)

"A bhayat abhiyantarah kopau
Bahya kopal papiyan
Antaram ati kopat ca antah kopat"
(*Arthashastra* 8/2/3)

[Lion's share of king's responsibility is bestowed on the correction of the nature of the public. This mention of nature of the public is essential, or the administration and sovereignty of the state with end, angered by enmity. Evil people and evil power will try to harm the state from inside and outside respectively. These evil people and powers are like venomous snakes, bite naturally, for and without any purpose.

Basis of Wisdom is Essential for Economic Development

Purification of character is essential for administrating a state and moving the economic system. Different personalities act within the people. Generally lower possibility and lower taste predominate and due to predominance of low taste, people become accustomed with beastly propensity. Initial acquaintance with the beastly propensity in men is with selfishness inside oneself. Selfishness in the first exposition of bad taste. Initiating with selfishness what is tell of working for others one cannot even think for others in the least. So, the cooperation that is needed for working for others and many is practically ruled out. The matter of cooperation is of utmost importance is running a state. Development of the state is not possible without cooperation of the people. This cooperation of people may be manifested in two ways.

One as is the nature so is the cooperation, two, cooperation is sought for after transformation of the nature.

A common and general characteristic in people is the downward propensity. These consist of setting one's own affairs in due order, thinking of only one's own good and bad, rise and such and working accordingly. If in such attempts, the context of others happens to appear it shall have to be pushed back. That is, one moves forward undauntedly to meet one's own interest and if in doing so the affairs of others are interrupted, others are harmed, one remains unperturbed. Such an individual looks at the world in the light of his own interest. On the other hand, transformation brings widening of vision. Man no longer remains contained in the boundary of his own petty interests. Crossing the boundary of this interest, a new ability to back practically all the others begin to develop in him. A few eastern and western beliefs are worthy of mention here.

Gandhi and Kant

The belief inherent in Mahatma Gandhi's home rule movement was recognition of people in the light of his own realization to build up people accordingly. According to Mahatma, home rule will come only if people get themselves rightly prepared. Transformation of the inner propensity of the people is essential for building up an ideal society and state. If there is no transformation of propensity, the people would just stand hindrance against formation of an ideal society.

According to Gandhi ji, the roots of all the human problems are two things. And these are desire and greed. People filled with desire and greed become out and out connected with their own interests. That vision becomes normal and they are unable to work with a greater perspective. This remains true for all activities, thoughts and vows as a fundamental objective and that is how the self-interest, the products for self-satisfaction, may be fulfilled. If all the objects are reviewed only from the angle of personal viewpoint, the bigger subjects would be left unattained. All is yellow to a jaundiced eye. A narrow boundary of man imparts narrowness to the view. Narrow view makes all men of the world look to be worshippers of narrow views. To one who is engaged in fulfilment one's narrow interest only, faith becomes evident that all in this world are running after their own interests. His feelings get so much more placed that he tries to present explanations of even self-sacrifice and self-demeaning with forms of different colour. So, such a man cannot be associated with any noble job with an open mind. Even if he is engaged in the flow of work, he would seek in it, at every moment, the blooming of his own interest.

Coming out of the enclosure of mere personal interest, some are there in whom has arisen some particular group-interest. That is to be a judge in the light of group interest and not personal interest. He struggles for the group, thinks also thus. It is just the class concord of the working class and on this basis theory of struggle is propounded. It is also termed struggle of the proletariat. In both cases struggle is known after the group concerned and the individual involved in such activity crosses his own personal interest and moves forward for the greater interest. For this, there may be a possibility of blossoming of a vibration of noble feelings within the individual existence. But in most cases, in such possibilities, bindings of selfish action may be exposed. That is a selfish feeling actually rooms all the feelings if one type of selfishness gets inspired it directly helps other types of selfishness to be manifested. That is, reforms of selfishness get reaped. And along with such reforms more personal interest often emerges in time.

The basis of the ideal of utopian rule of Rama contrived by Gandhi ji is the locator of stoicism. This wealth of stoicism with sense of an individual. According to Gandhi ji, 'the wealth of spices' means awakening of an individual. From stoicism comes salvation. According to Gandhi with the advent of stoicism, longing and desire vanished from an individual. He then does not beg anybody. Practically, he loses all the things to be begged for. Awakening of this stoicism makes self-dependence flourish in an individual. The inner home-rule of one's own sets in. This inner home rule makes an individual deserving for the greater home rule. The best way to set up a real home rule for the country is to help most of the people of the country stand on their own integrity. When the larger fraction of society or state would be engaged in ouster practice for home-rule in the very personal existence it is them that there would really be the situation for an integral home-rule. Integral home-rule is the feeling of a completeness both within and outside. Inner home-rule maintains the endeavour for outer home-rule. Without an inspiration of inner home-rule outer movement for home-rule becomes rather hollow and such as the word for word's sake.

According to Gandhi ji, for inner home-rule to be effective impetus for indifference is to be awakened. And this indifference would be generated in the way of self-restraint. Stoicism would come out of indifference and when as a result of salvation and stoicism all influence of greed and infatuation comes to an end, such a person will then not impart any injury to others because for doing so consideration driven by one's own selfish motive has to be active. The flow of home-rule comes only when stoicism is woken up in an individual. It becomes free from the sheath of longing and desire of his inner self and engages himself in the attempt of freedom for others and setting home-rule for the whole world. Economic freedom is a part of this home-rule.

On the contrary, Immanuel Kant thought otherwise. Kant's theory is rather a big pillar of Western inquisitiveness of life. Kant has classified human nature in two groups to bring into discussion. These are universality and individual characteristic, when the sense of universality within man wakes up, the range of his vision gets expanded towards completeness. Contrarily, cultivation of personal characteristics makes man restricted. The more one becomes attentive towards personal characteristics, the more will generate in him a nation of differentiation. Difference would grow among men. The conflicting aspects in men, the factors of disproportionation and the principle of non-cooperation will be exposed. According to Kant, but for cultivation of personal characteristic awakening in man cannot happen. Through cultivation of personal character man inaugurates his power of enterprise. That is, by changing transfusion of enterprise, man becomes desirous for work and becomes real to make his identity long-lasting in the world.

Kant has stated four principles of personal characteristics. These are the power of expression of individuals, power of feelings of individual collection of personal experiences of individual and general flow of thoughts. Personal characteristics are formed by a combination of exposition, feelings, experience, and thoughts within a man. Man will have to stand on the basis of his personal characteristic. But only looking at everything from the perspective of personal characteristic will not do it. If there is no awakening of universality, he would be turned into an entity befitting a lower animal. Kant has stated three means for awakening of universality. These are: universal knowledge of nature; universal ability of study and universal treasure of utterances. Universal knowledge of nature is the first step of universality. This universal feeling is required for transformation of individuality to collectively. Universal feelings widen the individual. Once this universal feeling wakes up a liberal feeling in an individual, then such a feeling gets transfused in an individual as all are to be looked at equally, that dealing with others is reasonable which would seem to be reasonable to one's own self. Inaugurating the power and co-operative spirit an individual rises to be an associated power at the background of greater necessity of the society and the world. According to Kant, a man gets engaged in looking out for society and the world only when there is a wide expansion of universality in him. For widening of universality, the transfusion of universal attitude is of utmost importance. On awakening of the universal attitude, the sense of freedom within oneself is never wiped out. Universality is to be roused on the very basis of this sense of freedom. At the background of freedom, universality truth turns a man into worker, enterpriser, creative, cooperative and worshipper of completeness in the world affair.

For this, Kant has spoken of freedom and universality at a time as the basis of freedom of one and all. Gandhiji has longed for personal home-rule of an individual life. Kant liked the universality in an individual. Home rule means freedom from the personal bondage within an individual. If home rule does arrive in the personal life of an individual, then he carries the very message of this to the background of the world and thence rises the atmosphere of cooperation. One learns how to offer cooperation to others and gets engaged in cooperative activities.

The mission between personal exposition and universality as contemplated by Kant has the message of cooperation dormant in it. According to Kant, cooperation is transformed on applied form of the inner inspiration within an individual. When an individual realizes that not the sense of ownership, but man at large, society at large is the circle of his acquaintance, then would come the power endeavour for cooperation, an individual would extend his cooperative hand. This would be the basis of his economic development. For economic awakening, such a strong background in essential.

A sensation would grow there for a large number of men within the mind of an individual. Not only for personal status, personal sorrows, sufferings, pains but a congenial situation for thinking for others would be created for man. The limit of the personal interest would then no longer be able to influence an individual, rather thoughts or feelings of greater interest would emerge; only thoughts for somethings great would prevail.

At the very basis of the thoughts of both Gandhi and Kant, there is an impetus for moving to the great. In the proposals of both is manifested a statement of cooperation in a wide background. The same gets manifested in a wide situation crossing the sheath of the identity of an individual and builds up above all an environment of cooperation for complete awakening. The problem met within both is the basic identity of man. The more this basic identity would be evident, the more would grow an extreme consciousness in men. It is this extreme consciousness of an individual which enlivens the dormant beneficial wealth within him. In this connection Kautilya has directly raised the context of the godliness in man.

Kautilya and Kant

Kautilya has given primary importance to the awakening of godliness in an individual whose role is in the administration of a state and controlling the same. Paying primary importance to administration and control of state means when Vedic learning gets transfused in both state and people, the divine qualities dormant in man begin to be awakened. That is, the man proceeds to realize and recognize the basic identity of his, the feeling that he himself is part of the undivided universal entity be too evident within him; inheritance of the divine is infused in him and so he is adorned with the divine qualities, the divine qualities are wealth of his life. And the effect of the divine qualities is such the man naturally becomes of expanded mind and heart. Temperament for narrowness, selfishness, Conflict, envy and hatred are shredded off noble qualities get blossomed. Altruism then seems to be more essential than selfish attitude. Kautilya has remarked:

"Vidya vinayah hetuh indriya vijayah"

(*Arthashastra*, 1/6/1)

"Artha eka pradhanah iti Kautilya...
Arthamhlau hi dharmakama itih"

(*Arthashastra*, 1/7/6-7)

(One must conquer the sense organs with vedic knowledge. Money is the main thing because it is necessary even for acquiring religious feelings.)

"Sahya sadhyam rajatvam cakram
Ekam na bartate" (*Arthashastra* 1/7/1)

(To run the wheel for running a state is not in the range of one's capability, for this cooperation and assistance of many are required.)

"Rajh hi bratam utthanam yajram
Karyah anusasanam,
Daksina brtti samyamtu diksatasya

Abhisecanam." (*Arthashastra*, 1/19/33)

"Praja sukham rajnam prajanam
Hite hitam
Na atumapriyam hitam rajnam prajanam
Tu priyan hitam" (*Arthashastra*, 1/19/34)

(The king will observe his vow, will offer himself to spiritual practice and observance, will maintain spiritual practice for his people. A king will be completely devoted to his people. He will consider the pleasure of his people to be his own. The benefit of the people is benefit of the king. To achieve something coveted of his own or enjoyment of pleasure is not at all adorable, for the king will find pleasure in the accomplishment of length and enjoyment of pleasure for his people.)

According to Kautilya the king enlightened in spiritual practice would be processor of spiritual realization and feelings and would inspire his subject for having spiritual realization. The king would rise to be of a divine character. His vow of life would be to accomplish benefit and pleasure for his people.

Kautilya wanted to induce a fundamental character in man and to see him engaged is an environment of work, flow of activities. That is, the intimate propensity in a man will not only be of importance but of cooperation as well. The basis of Kautilya's economic philosophy is cooperation. The more the cooperative spirit spreads among men the more would be developed the background for economic development. It is cooperation that bring about development and also creates proper situation for development.

As Kautilya has wanted cooperation. So also he has demanded greatness of character. When there is a glow of fundamental identity in a man, specialty of a great character appears then, and only then. The deeper would be the glow of the fundamental identity, the more extended would be the wakeful consciousness and watchful conscience, the sphere of his influence would be all pervading. The more a man would learn to cross his personal narrowness, the more would be his pervasiveness in the world. This pervasiveness in the world is a change in the inner attitude of man. The external nature of the world remains the same, but it gets expressed through outlook, behaviour, cooperation and activities. This wave of change carries man to a newer position. When there is an expansion of outlook, man becomes fit for realizing pains, sorrows and problems of others. He learns how to think for others. Not only that, he considers others affairs with due importance. Thus, is created a proper situation for cooperation.

There is a possibility of greatness in the philosophy of Gandhi and Kant. But for becoming a factor of cooperation in the economic system man would have to proceed on the basis of the spirituality, gained by experience. Kautilya has rightly realized that cooperation is the main factor in an economic system. But for cooperation, the economic system would be a rather transitory and frail structure. Collection of inspiration and power of cooperation would be created from the wealth of personal conscience of man. On the very basis of cooperation, an individual comes out to be a unit of economic foundation of state. Stationing of such persons brings in the flow of cooperation in a state. This is the very first and foremost step of economic awakening. When the force of cooperation becomes strong an individual begins to recognize anew a state's own wealth. Economic power wakes up.

6
Economics for National Leadership

National Leadership

The identity of a nation or a state comes from the quality of leadership it possesses. For the rule of Ram is required the leadership a Ram. In the same way, the waking of a state and its economic stability demands proper leadership. A state is not always known by the identity of the leadership only. If the blooming of leadership does not occur in proper measure the development of a state also remains incomplete. If leadership blooms properly the process of development of state becomes hastened, Kautilya's *Arthashastra* has presented a philosophy of highly idealized philosophy of leadership.

Without leadership the question of upliftment remains unsolved, as leadership becomes deeper and more active, the stronger becomes the flow of the development of a state. The more relaxed the leadership becomes, the more flaccid becomes the flow of state development. Leaving the question of leadership unconsidered, it is not at all possible to introduce a system of economic development of a state. As leadership is essential for running a state, so also is it equally essential for its economic development.

One of the knowledgeable points of the theories of economic development is to fix a leadership compatible with the flow of development. Some of the economic theories have liked leadership of democratic system. Some again liked the leadership of individual dominance. Some again demanded individual leadership with a coordinating group. Besides there is the option of selecting leadership by a class and to bring the economic system of a state under the control of a particular class. The control of the economic system may not be controlled by the state leadership. For shaping the system, the application of the principle useful for the leadership, drawing up of the principle with suitable modification of it, is essential.

Influence and utility of leadership are many, great for development of a state. No theory can flourish without proper leadership. The question remains that of identity of theory. The future of the state and its economic system depends on the nature of the leadership. Leadership may be of many types. It cannot be said that under the same system leadership will also be of a similar nature. Just as leadership depends on theory and principle, it also depends on the current situation of the surroundings and the state. The question of principle is far reacting, but the question of situation is transitory. According to far-reacting ideas, the internal situation is looked upon in the light of instance coming from a distance. The work system of leadership depends on immediate situation and situation coming from a distance. How far a creative leadership is effective in consensus with another depends on the effectiveness of that leadership?

Different Types of State Leadership

Mentionable factors of exploration of the nature of state leadership are methods of taking decision by leadership, methods of making the decision effective, judgement of the field of application and the trend of measuring problem and possibility and the worthiness of leadership.

Methods of Taking Decision by Leadership

The methods of taking decision by leadership depends on the consequence of the system directed by the leadership.

The following four figures shed light on this subject.

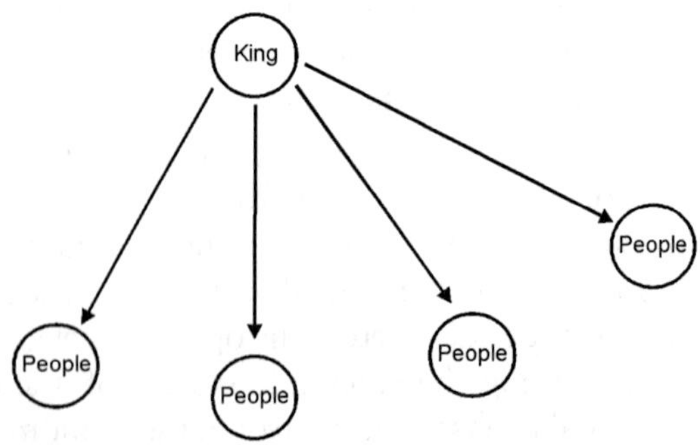

Figure 1: Authoritative Leadership

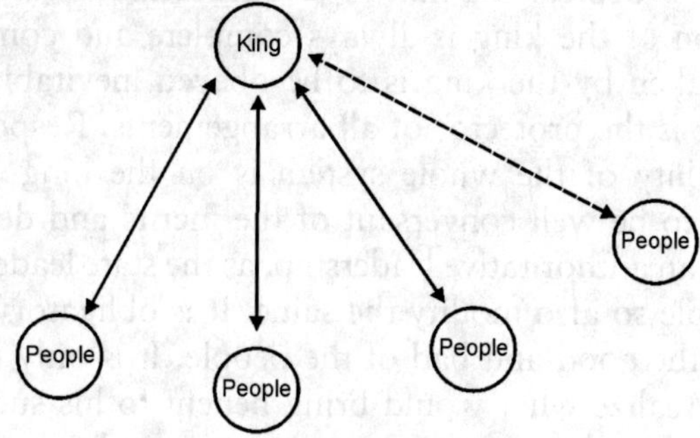

Figure 2: Democratic Leadership

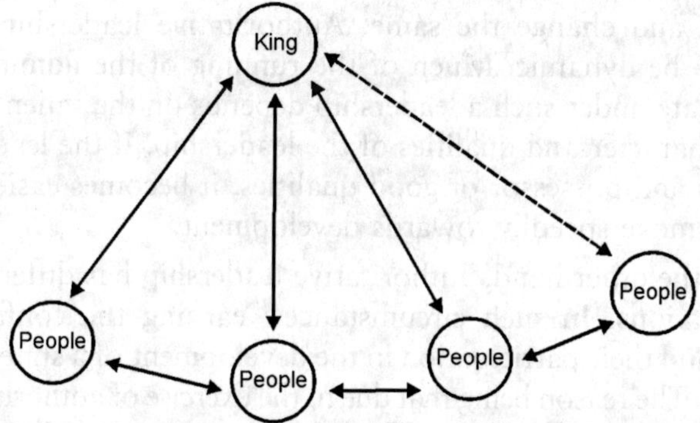

Figure 3: Council of Equals

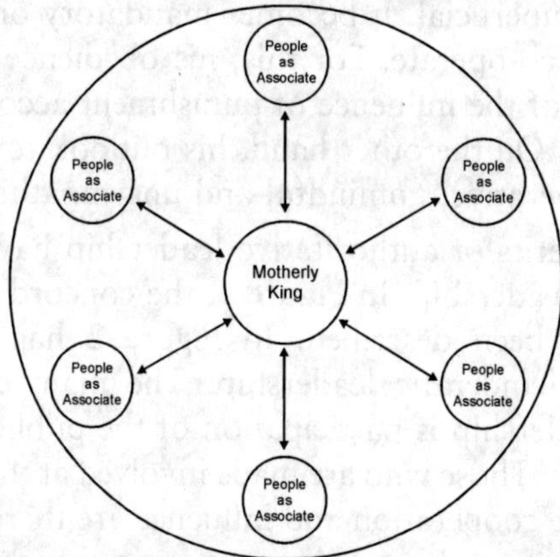

Figure 4: Mother Leadership Framework

Figure 1 depicts the nature of authoritative leadership. Here the opinion of the king is always complete and compulsive. The decision taken by the king is to be obeyed inevitably by all. The king alone is the protector of all arrangements. Responsibility and accountability of the whole system is on the king. So, the king himself is to be well conversant of the merits and demerits of the system. In an authoritative leadership, as the state leader implements the principle so also modify the same. It is obligatory for the king to realize the good and bad of the people. It is only the king who is able to realize what would bring benefit to his subjects. People are assumed to be ignorant and so may not know accurately of their good and bad, the leadership is to realize the same. So, it is necessary for him to frame land laws and equally implement these laws. It is much easier for an authoritative king to take instant decision and change the same. Authoritative leadership may be taken to be dynamic. Much of the running of the administration of the state under such a leadership depends on the salient features of the character and qualities of the leadership. If the leadership is a genius and possessor of good qualities, it becomes easier for the state to move speedily towards development.

On the other hand, authoritative leadership has different types of limitations. In such circumstances, earning the confidence of people and their participation in the development of a state is hardly possible. The reason being that due to the exercise of authoritativeness participation of people in taking decision is also hardly expected. Who is not incorporated in taking a decision can really lend hearty cooperation in implementation of the same. Cooperation for such a person is just superficial. It becomes mandatory or compelling for that person to co-operate. For this, his obedience is to be gained by application of the influence of punishment according to rule or administration. On the other hand, his outlook towards authority turns non-cooperative, unmindful and unsympathetic.

These demerits of authoritative leadership have been nullified in democratic leadership. In Figure 1, the concord of authoritative leadership has been described. In Figure 2 has been described the status of democratic leadership. The main characteristic of democratic leadership is participation of the public at the stage of taking decisions. Those who are made involved at the stage of taking decision, whose cooperation and influence are there in the decision would quite easily and naturally support in the implementation of the decision. Democratic leadership promises to move on through decisions with all, in all cases. The greatest merit of this is that having cooperation of all becomes easy.

Just as it is easy for democratic leadership to win cooperation, so also arise many problems in the path of cooperation. In taking a decision with many people, many problems are also raised. Every man offers pains of cooperation with his cooperation. This often causes inconvenience in taking decision. Taking decisions may not even be possible in some cases. Due to the propensity of making the decision in an assembly of many people, the decision also changes qualitatively.

Despite many demerits, the democratic system stays ahead in the measure of judgement. Development becomes easier in the democratic system of leadership. It has become a special advantage of democracy that criticism of the state system comes out. People associated with such criticism actually reveal the points of regression and staying behind of the state. As a result, the attention of the state leadership is sure to be drawn to those points.

It is often rather difficult for democratic leadership to take any epoch-making step or to take instant decisions. Much time is wasted or much time is lost in doing some work by persuading all or taking opinions. Because of this, it is often difficult for a democratic state to take any bold step. Besides on the part of a democratic leadership, the independent exposition of a state leader often remains suppressed under the influence of so many people.

These demerits of democratic leadership can be avoided in combined leadership. Combined leadership actually is formed of cooperation and consistency of all people. Here as cooperation becomes the leadership and the people is built up so also mutual agreement among common people has also for revealed. What is the predominance of all at the time of taking decision and implementation thereof. In case of taking and implementing decision as cooperation attributes merit to the decision, so also it reveals association of all with respective specialties in the implementation of a decision. As a result, state can explore its paths of multipurpose development. Multiple flows of exposition lend mobility and enterprise to the state.

Problems arise in a combination leadership with respect to mutual understanding and mutual exchange of thoughts. As an individual user all the wealth of his genius is used towards giving cooperation to a state, so also with the reform and judgement of taste grown side by side with the genius, he moves forward to the collectively. The judgement and application of personal taste lends to an individual a perspective novel and unthought of. Satisfaction of the personal interest becomes the primarily an important thing to an individual. As a consequence, the subject of leadership becomes dependent on the characteristic features of an individual.

At the background of the society a good man, an honest man, a man of liberal and progressed character becomes more active. Such men will not spend lives only on the basis of justice and principle. Others will be associated with their struggle in life. But for this is required the blooming of personal character at the primary stage. Only men of noble character and those depending on honest and justified principle are capable of building up a combined leadership. The combination of ordinary people is likely to point downwards. Being bonded to lower taste and propensity, such persons actually will have little basis for appeal of combination. Rather they might sully the same. Besides the real purpose of combination gets blurred if the persons in the sphere of the attempt of combination just give priority to the fulfilment of their personal longings. As a result, the combined leadership will crumble down with the state system also at stake.

Keeping in mind the flaws of combined leadership, it becomes evident that another leadership is needed that would be even more forceful than combined leadership to be able to hasten cooperation. Within a given set of features nations should come out with adequate assurances. Only the motherly leadership can accomplish this difficult job. It is motherly leadership which can create such an enjoined situation. Motherly leadership is at the same time democratic and combined plus something more. In it there are essential features of authoritativeness and the good aspects of combined and democratic leadership.

The aspects motherly leadership are specially engaged with are economic success, honesty, devotion, working with attachment and full measure of cooperation. As a consequence, an individual gradually slows down the influence of his egoism. Due to the reduction of the limit of personal interest, cooperation does cast its real influence. That is cooperation become nearly successful. This is because both sides of motherly leadership are dominant—the instant and the distant. Just as the instant arrangement is for a small range of time, so also motherly leadership pays alteration to arrangements for long duration.

At the background of motherly leadership, modulation of the character of an individual and laying the ethical foundation in state systems thus becomes essential. On the part of motherly leadership, the subdual of one's inherent vices and modulation of character are essential. The power of subdual of inherent vices brings about purification of mind. Purification of the mind makes spiritual practice easier. Spiritual wisdom blooms up easily before a purified mind. Such a person is an easy wanderer in the background of the world. Social truth and the complete state of affairs are caught in the domain of individual feelings.

Motherly leadership has a mind as caring, charitable and sympathetic as a mother. For such leadership, working for long duration and permanent results becomes easier. Kautilya in his *Arthashastra* has mentioned many such qualities of motherly leadership. *Arthashastra* has presented a step for landing into motherly leadership. Kautilya's *Arthashastra* has presented a unique proposal in the discussion on leadership. He has brought all the good qualities in the purview of leadership. As a result, just through analysis of the character of a leader, the stand and measure of ideal would be revealed. A leader himself would be the indicative of ideal.

Context Of Leadership In *Arthashastra*

Kautilya has brought the context of high descent of leadership. In this context Kautilya's assertion is that family affairs and traditional identity of a king is important. This traditional identity is essential for expression of the fundamental character of a leader. As the traditional identity reveals the basis outlook of leadership, so also does it point out specially towards the pervasion of the same. In describing the essential qualities of the leader of state, Kautilya says:

Mahakult nau daibabuddhi sattvasampannau
Barddhadarsau dharmical
Satyagabisambadakah krtajhah
Sthulalakhksmau
Mohotsahah adtrghasutruah sakyasamantakh
Hrdbuddhirksudraparisaktau birayakamah
Ityabhisasika gunah
[*Arthashastra* 1/2/3]

[The leader of state should come from a big family or lineage. He would be honest in intelligence, he would be a wise man of pure instinct, he would receive advice from the old, he would be religious. Such a king would be truthful and righteous, He would be gratitude embodied and would move on to reach the goal of fulfilling his earthly longing. Such a king would be expert in looks and would select proper companions and groups. The king would cross all meanness by chastisement of his mind and would be modesty embodied—these are the primary qualities for leaders]

Kautilya has not given prominence to the family identity of leadership, nor has he disregarded the same. The leadership would be honest intelligence-wise, of very superior instinct and truthful. That is, he would be such an observer as exposition of the good quality of life would be naturally evident. This leadership would be careful about others. He would speak the truth and as a result in the periphery of the leadership i.e., in the kingdom of the king there would be excessiveness of virtuous practice and intense devotion to truth. In order to create an environment of gratitude, the chief would have to develop gratefulness. An environment of gratefulness extends the field of natural exchange and understanding.

Good qualities are expected of a king, at the same time e endeavour for work and enterprise are expected. In case of enterprise, a king is to be up and doing with full of energy. If an enterprising person is energetic, the path of accomplishment of his work becomes rather easy. Through the earnestness of the king, development of the state is hastened. For the development of the kingdom are required a king of the high degree of qualities and noble character so also his enterprise and ability to work.

Without enterprise and ability, it is not possible for a king to be up and working for his state. As a result of this, the state values the ability to work and several able person are available to meet the needs of the state. The point of force and valour of ability is worth men thinking. A valorous king may develop arrogance and temperament. But if the valorous king possesses virtuous feelings, he can never turn arrogant. A king with virtuous feeling gradually by virtue of his characteristic fairness and behaviour may become valorous and would prolong or extend the enterprise for state. The virtuous emotion would make the king modest. He would not ignore the seniors, rather would consult with them in all matters. Advice of the seniors is very valuable. The essence of experience gathered by the seniors becomes much more useful to the administration. The advice received from the seniors may help the king know what should be the nature of the ministers. In other words, he can thus select portfolio and ministers. This selection is very important—Become the king, work with all ministers and councilors, push the work further. The more a king is up and doing in this manner, the greater would be his ability and suitability.

The qualities mentioned by Kautilya in respect of a king are applicable to all types of leaders. It can also be applied to the administration of any organisation. It is applicable to all organisations—business organisation, charity organisation, and religious organisations.

Leadership should be based on justice and virtue. At the same time, the leader should be active and up and doing. For the leadership devoted to religion and respectful to seniors, moving towards development of the state is possible. The qualities developed and extended thus are equally applicable for instant progress of the same. Matters of periodic necessity for a state are poverty, lack of education, lack of wealth, lack of understanding among the public, etc. and the matter of extended duration or the extended programme taken for the development of the state. In this extended programme, there remain sole enterprises which have instant needs or needs for small duration rather limited.

There have all along been a conflict between feelings and activities for short and long durations. There are many such examples that would witness the hindrance in a programme of short duration caused by one of long duration. To take an example, the work of short duration should fit into the same for long duration in the interest of continued development. An enterprise of long duration needs investment of a large amount of money. Many a times, because of such big investment common people of the state often land in great difficulty. If a large investment has already been made for a programme of long duration, necessary funds to be invested for the problems of hunger, poverty, health education and the like would naturally fallshort.

Under such circumstances the inner feelings of a leader become much relevant. If the leader is large heartened and righteous, his attention will surely go to the weaker section of society. Shaping of a project of long duration will not be possible excluding hunger, poverty, back to education and lack of health. Just for this, ordinary arrangement of relations is necessary. Ordinary arrangement of relation between projects of short and long duration becomes a must. This arrangement becomes possible if the leadership within its heart, in the deepest core of mind is a loving and affection-aligned. This entity always weeps for the weak people. It is not possible for him to take up any project depriving the weak people. So along with projects of long duration one becomes initiated into projects of short duration also. Due to the very possession of the qualities of leadership proposed by Kautilya, he would be able to accomplish this difficult job. Leadership describe by Kautilya in this sense just resembles motherly leadership. Just as motherly leadership calls for large heartedness with enterprise so also is the leadership described by Kautilya—the state leader in that sense is an ideal state leader.

Effectiveness of a State Leader

Kautilya has paid attention to the effectiveness of a state leader. He wanted that the effectiveness qualities of a state leader would be such as it becomes possible for him to pay attention to all sides. Kautilya has said that a state should be curious to know all things. He should also be a good listener. An important responsibility of a state leader is his power to listen. He should have to listen painlessly to the problems, wants and complaints of the people. If the thoughts and feelings at the root of the enterprises owned by the state are correct and universal, the context of wants and complaints become baseless. The thoughts and enterprises of a state primarily depend on the principle share of thinking and movement of thoughts of the leadership. If the leadership assures a motherly presence, his principle, sphere of thinking and movement of thoughts become far-reaching and bring everyone in the country good results.

On the other side, in spite of there being, in general, ample attention and much endeavor, some lapses of different grades are also possible. So all aspects of the activities of leadership cannot yield good results. There are always some aspects which in a different field and at different times create problems. As there are fundamental problems of common measure of people so also are some attributed and contemplated problems. If people can raise their problems and the state authority realises the same attentively, surely some way for their solution can be found out.

Kautilya has said that the responsibility of the state leader is not to listen for listening's sake. A state-leader should be a proper listener and he should acquire the power of retaining the subjects heard by himself. That is, retaining in his mind the subjects heard like those of want and complaint, description of same contexts, advice and supports and finding them out in suitable hours and translating them into action with earnest ness.

But a state-leader is not only to be listener and one who retains, according to Kautilya, he is to be able to understand. He is to understand the subjects in the very language in which people narrate them. The meaning of understanding in the same language is to have the correct version of a statement. Kautilya has said that a state leader should be earnest. To know the feelings and words of the people. In these to be ascertained, the statements of the people are to be followed closely. Kautilya has said that one should not be restless at the very first hearing. People should be listened to understand after listening to what is to be taken and what is to be left out. What is worth taking is to be translated into action and what is not, what is to be discarded. Kautilya has warned the leader in the truth that through such consideration of taking and leaving a state leader would be able to recognize the truth. The truth is to be accepted and the untruth is to be discarded.

Accordingly to Kautilya, a king or state leader should have truth as his goal. He will recognize the truth chose the same and make it the basis of all works. Standing on the truth the king will be eager to perform all his duty. Kautilya has said that a king should have some qualities for this. These are courage, ability to protest, earnestness and multipurpose expertise to work.

According to Kautilya, the basis of the courage, earnestness and agility to be earned by a state leader is truth. Standing on the basis of truth, he would reveal the token of his courage. The courage spoken of here is, according to Kautilya, to be mixed with truth only to prevent any injustice from getting entry.

But for the basis of truth, the ability to protest also becomes futile. Political parties and leadership of modern times have had a practice of erecting protest on the path of spreading truth, siding with the untruth. A state leader should have to practice truth for this. This practice of truth will get into him an ability to be protesting in the true sense.

A state leader should be earnest. If there is no speed in the work, it becomes difficult on the part of a leader to retain his leadership. To get that speed in work the state leader should have a compassionate mind. Only if a state leader has compassion for the people, can he be up and completing and fulfilling his work. For this again is required multipurpose expertise. A state leader has to concentrate on many factors and earn multipurpose expertise. For this what is needed is indomitable endeavour. It is possible only in motherly leadership. The ideal of a leader fixed in Kautilya's *Arthashastra* is rightly reassembling the motherly one. Both are benevolent and able. This is a proper ideal for future states.

7

Spirituality Oriented State Can Only Constitute A Society Free from Exploitation

Kautilya's Proposal

Spiritually-oriented state is a jewel among all the states. Only a spiritually-oriented state can develop the basis of equality and collective understanding for justice to all and build up a social system free from exploitation.

State-system built up on the basis of religion brings about the blooming of possibility among all. For economic development of a state Kautilya has recommended the waking up of spiritual power in all. As a consequence of this there would be a complete change in the state system. The administration of a state shall have to be of pure spiritual character like that of a renunciate person. Due to the development of spiritual power these administraters would spend lives based on spirituality. At the same time, they would build up a social system on the basis of which there would be the theory of procuring and using universal wealth. As a result, there would be equal rights for the destitute, the pauper, for those who have to depend on social wealth for everything. So, a society free from exploitation and poverty would grow up.

Expedition Against Inherent Personal Ego

Kautilya wanted self-restraint of sensual appetites for all in society. In case of expedition against the inherent vices, Kautilya has inspired everybody.

"Vidya binaya hetuh indriya jayah
kamah krodhah lobhah mohah madah matsaryah
Etya gat karyah" (*Arthashastra* 1/6/1)

[A modest and wise person shuns sex-passion, anger, greed, pride, attachment, restlessness and becomes content.]

"Vidyabinitau rajah hi prajanam binaya ratah
Ananyam prthibim bhunkte sarba bhuthite ratah."
(*Arthashastra*1/5/17)

[A king rich in spiritual knowledge would become modest and righteous and would also make his people modest and righteous. This unrivalled king would build up a state free of troubles and would conduct benevolent activities]

"Karnah twak aksih jihbah ghranau indriyanam
Sabdas sparsah rupah rasah gandhah
Esa bai pratipattih indriya jayah
Sastranusthanam ba."
(*Arthashastra* 1/6/2)

Sound, touch, grace, flavour, smell should be allowed in influence the sense-organs ear, skin, eye, tongue, nose. By being content through practice of scriptures, one can be worthy.)

Kautilya wanted to build up a religious environment. He liked it to be everywhere. Just as a religious environment is required for an individual so also it is required in totality for a state. Inherent senses make man subhuman. Man, then behaves like a beast. So, adventure against inherent senses is actually that better against beastliness. But for abolition of sexual passion and other vices mind is not purified, and without a pure mind divine feelings do not set in.

Some modern psychologists have begun to assert that sexual passion, anger, etc. are necessary. According to them, sex-passion is the binding force of the society, i.e., through the network of desire and passion mutual relation gets a permanent form. Psychologists have understood that as a human, a person becomes a consumer and buyer of different objects and services. That is, in persons confined to the network of passion and desire, different types of cravings get initiated. Man is encircled by desires one by one, until it becomes an explosion of desires.

Initiation of passion and desire causes an explosion of demands in the market, e.g. the essential commodities for one's livelihood like food clothing and resort come as initial demand. This is essential for life. In every part of this list gradual changes occur. Newer demands start through changes in the quality of food, clothing and shelter. For these changes to occur in the form of demands, ability is needed and what is more, acute support of mind helps bring support of ability. As ability creates favourable conditions of mind, so also inspiration of mind may get fitting ability. Fitting ability inspires the mind and makes a man enterprising. As a result, a man filled with the strength of mind now gets exposed to newer search. Since the inner ego comes from passion, desirability of mind gets involved in the satisfaction of those passions and desires.

Passion begets inequality: attempts for satisfaction of passion and desire of an individual influences the sphere of trade and commerce. The effect of increase of desire falls on commerce as objects for satisfaction of desire are to be procured from the market with a price. Thus, desire creates market, causes expansion in markets. Through explosion of desire not only are newer demands created but basic changes also may come in demands. Desire is like a bird; it springs from one branch to another in a tree. The desire of a fluctuating mind may remain still for periodic satisfaction, but soon it comes back with a newer desire.

Commerce entangled in the network of desire moves on at the liberation of desire. An example will make the point clear. There is not much profit in the market of rice and other essential items. Though in such cases, the rate of profit is small, but there is a balance as the extent is vast. That is, such trade is dependent on quality. But there is not much interest in such trade. Interest is where the profit is enormous. Consumers impelled by desire sometimes manage to forget their ability and limit of purchase.

Such events are now used by the market to move forward. Diversity of demands can be offered by companies, as also mental awareness may be created by them. Diversity of demands expended by diversity of demands of individuals is the producer of new commodities or new service and it also helps give new shape to old commodities and service. Demands mingled with desire are not connected with basic needs. This measure of trade is something otherwise. There is not much scope of profit in trading of goods of daily use, but the goods mingled with desire bear ample scope of profit.

For this reason, extensive competition goes on among different organization for creating the market for commodities emerged from desire and to take possession of that. This type of competition often presents a naked picture of the market. The naked picture of the market takes through the presentation and distribution of commodities by the companies and expression of basic trend of the market. Commodities and services emerging from desire set up a value-added economic system which is apt for collecting extra pride. The world of longing and desire sets up a separateness in the economic system. These have been set up in modern and post-modern periods in the economic system. The economic system of these modern and postmodern periods has given permanent shape to exploitation and inequality. Both capitalist and communist systems have given soundness to inequality and exploitation. Both the capitalist and communist systems are in the same position with respect to longing and desire. Both have basis on the inherent vices within men. Both the systems have given their own solutions to the individuals chased by the inherent vices. The capitalist system thinks about individuals, the communist system is engaged in solving problems of groups. Both of them are imparting and creating, in their own ways, inequality and exploitation. Not only that, but they have also engaged themselves to give exploitation a permanent shape. The path of winning over this exploitation is in a theocratic state. It is a theocratic state that can reduce exploitation and build up a society free from exploitation.

Anger Begets Destruction

Kautilya has inspired struggle against inherent vices. He asserts, these vices are to be conquered, sense organs should be controlled. Longings and desire must not captivate men, they are to be got rid of. Kautilya has urged men to be rid of anger. Anger is a great enemy to men. Under the influence of anger, much gets deviated from normality; anger disrupts normality.

Anger mesmerizes an individual and keeps him engaged in worldly possessions. Anger makes one forget the past. An individual then becomes quite ignorant of the current context and as a result he loses his understanding. In this world, the state of an individual devoid of understanding in just as good as death. That is, as a consequence of anger an individual gradually gets away from his own identity and possibility. Such persons cannot cast normal sympathetic looks at others. Anger just shuts all the doors, possibilities for the man and makes him blind.

So, men under the influence of anger cannot get united. Anger rather separates them. Such a person is quite unable to be an associate of the other. For him it is not possible to build up a united system. An angry person becomes unable to move hand in hand with others. That is why it is not possible for him to be an associate in a basis economic system. Anger renders one into an individual unit; not only that, sometimes the result becomes to the contrary. Anger makes one always stand in the role of a critic since such a person is confined in the whirl of anger, he often makes criticism his sole profession. Others and all the efforts of the others in his view become food for criticism.

Cooperation cannot be established in economics by the persons susceptible to rage. These people always place themselves contrary to the cooperation in the economic system. But in the economic system cooperation reigns supreme. But for cooperation, economic insurgence cannot be possible. There are many ways of economic insurgence. The easiest and the most successful one of these is the participation of everyone; in an economic system, the greater the number of people associated the more vigorous it would be.

Anger stands as a great impediment to participation in an economic system. For both India and China participation is very much essential for economic growth. Due to the communist rule China has been able to make participation mandatory. She has suppressed temper and agitation strictly. Desire of the state has to be abided compulsorily by all, millions of protesters had been punished and criticized by military tanks at Tiananmen square. The scepter of the state got pierced in the chest and hands of the people quite forcibly. As a result, a very fearful situation prevails. China has assured association of the people in the economic system through creation of such fearful environment. Of course, this path of forcing to take part cannot be a stable one, collapse of the same is quite inevitable.

The situation so long reared in India has at its root a democratic system and democratic temperaments. India is a kind of source of the democratic nations and feeling. The ground here is, as it were, the exponent of democracy. Classical scriptures and philosophy of India has given the liberty to all for maintaining and expressing personal opinions so also given scope of applying the same. Due to foreign occupancy for a long period of time, different types of propensities have grown in Indian people. People following India's old tradition, flow of feelings and culture, have in many ways been associated or timed to be endeavour charioting the economic development within the country. But the followers of Moghul and Pathan reigns in the middle age seldom did so. As in the struggle for freedom of India and so also in economic development, such people did not get involved to a considerable extent.

Followers of foreign invaders of the middle age have not only been indifferent in being cooperative in the economic development of the country but they have rather been opposing the same. They had shared cooperation augmented the business of bulk money and underworld. Rage and protest reign supreme in them. Being raged they did not accept the age-old classical nation of India. Whenever the hour of economic awakening has been furnished by the people respectful towards tradition of course, what does cooperation for the stage of waking means needs to be clarified.

Cooperation means to conjoin or to join. To conjoin or join with the work of the stage of the endeavour and activity of an organization or a man or that of the endeavour and activity for the state. State wants the effect of activities of all to come under the national perspective. Activities going on in fields, stages, factories, offices, courts, hospitals, schools, temples, at windows, on roads, vehicles bring consequences to state. Gross Domestic Production (GDP) is calculated on the basis of summation of these.

Non-Cooperation Weakens the Economic System

Results of black-market, movement of black money or black propensity do not add to the GDP. These reduce GDP. Factors registered in the national economic system, which give indications whose effects, to some extent at least, come to national treasury. combine to form GDP. The effect of the black market, movement of black money and black propensity affect GDP in an opposite way. These do not increase GDP. Yet in accordance with basic responsibility of the state, the people in spite of being associated with the black market, flow of black money and black propensity are partners or sharers of the basic resources of the state. Consequently, net national product falls much below the expected value.

India has endured this condition for a long time. Forbearance is there in the Indian tradition; we have endured through ages. There had been oppression, there had been torture at the very tinseling of bells at the corners of rooms, in the foyers of the temple. They would do much to create pressure through torture for proselytism. In spite of that we have tolerated it. Toleration, toleration, toleration—India has risen through toleration. India is again rising. This time cooperation is at a high tide. The law of cooperation has come from the trends of modern economy, what is needed for enlivening the ever-increasing demand of the market is participation. Partners of black market and sharers of the system now find little opportunities. Not in the interest of upliftment of the state, but for future protection of their own, they inspire to being sharers of black monetary arrangement and they are inspired to gradually shift from the stream of black monetary arrangements and rush to the main road of economy. Once the stage of development begins the flow tide is quite natural. But it takes time. Sometimes flow tide comes in favour of the market and sometimes in the enlivenment of the economic states. If the flow tide of enlivenment of the economic states has cooperation at the root, then it brings a permanent economic rise.

Continence and Economic Order

Kautilya has urged everyone to be continent. Continence is essential on the part of a leader of the market and equally for the people also. What is the nature of a continent person? What is the form of his demands? How does he find his place in the economic system? These questions are very pertinent. A continent person possess individuality as a feature of his character. Every being a man he seems to be possessing mere improved specialties. So, temperament movement and gamut of living are quite different. He is not a servant of longing and desire. His demands are just or those required for normal act of living. He has a craving for food, clothing and residence. Demands for a beautiful and more improved life is not unlikely. But there is no earnest and eager effort of consumption function of the same.

A continent man is an elevated man, a godly man. He does not look after self-interest and his own happiness. Such a person does not cause others harm, he does not even think of harming others. He always extends cooperation. Increase in humbleness of such persons in society gradually changes the other structure and inner arrangement of a society. Society takes a new shape. In that new form some factors become prominent, e.g., unification, cooperation and equality.

The form of unification becomes strong and visible among the people. If there is a look of unification, some feelings surpassing that of desire and gain come to occupy a place. Not a feeling of desire and gain but a propensity of searching out qualifications and disqualifications in man. Unification cares the background of confidence between one another. Cooperation grows up on the basis of unification.

The reference to cooperation has been mentioned earlier. Cooperation is a strong pillar of modern economic system. Revolution in the economic system comes through cooperation. Working hand in hand, the union of many hands form a great venture. Cooperation gives this measure. As a result of cooperation, the worth of the enterprises goes up. These points need elaboration through example.

Let us understand the point through a discussion about two companies. Let the first be 'Sunrise Limited' and these second is 'Sunset Limited'. Both of these deal in computer software. Both have a demand in national and international markets. Both have earned a reputation in this line.

Sunrise Limited believes that an organization earns reputation depending upon inner wealth. Inner wealth consists of these big divisions. Monetary resources and natural resources are most property utilized when human wealth becomes cooperative. That is, the more energetic enterprising and co-operative is the human resource, the more propensity to utilize the monetary and critical resources and will be gradually available therefrom.

Sunrise Limited therefore attributes high value to human resources. The company look at a decision that the matters right from its proprietorship to its administration and day to day activities- all would be vested with the employees of the organization. That is, from the framing of policies to all of the matters of the workers will be important. Everywhere they would decide what is to be done and what not. They will discern the course to be taken by the company. In other words, the workers would be the true steersmen of the company. Bestowal of all powers on the workers has over, termed by them, all power to the executives.

Bestowal of power on the workers. This means the workers will struggle with best and till the last for their company. Not to speak of the congeal situation, in the adverse situation also the workers of the company would bring favourable outcome for their company. That is why Sunrise Limited has flourished so much. This is evident everywhere in the market, viz stock markets, product and service market and so on.

On the contrary Sunset Limited thinks otherwise. It believes that efficiency is the only measure of progress. And efficient people are always to be kept under control. The highest work or return can be extracted from the efficient people kept under control. A man is to be known in the light of efficiency and that is the mode of treatment with them.

As Sunset Limited judges everything in terms of the measure of efficiency, it becomes difficult for it to be apprised of the possibilities. Possibility hides behind efficiency. An efficient man of today is the full-grown form of a man of possibilities in the past. An efficient man of today carries along with him a continuous way of possibility. So also, a man of possibilities at present is the efficient and expert man of the future. Sunset Limited has no patience at all. So, it finds no time to look back upon the possibilities. That is why Sunset Limited can only deal with the present resources only, it is not possible for it to go beyond.

The environment created by Sunrise Limited is one of co-operation. As a result, all of the possibilities of Sunrise Limited would get materialized and the company would progress day by day very rapidly. If the situation of self-discretion comes in the purview of Sunset Limited, a non-co-operative mindset would grow within the efficient people. A non-cooperation environment can destroy both the companies. Cooperation makes them sound. For Sunrise Limited, achievement of cooperation is rather spontaneous.

The example furnished in the case of companies may be applied in the case of states also. The economic development of a state depends on cooperation. The more dependable and forceful is the cooperation, the more sound would be the foundation of the economy of the state.

A man with cooperative spirit is godly. A beasty man is a slave to his inherent vices. Urging by the inherent vices they would be engaged totally in beastly activities. He will not find satisfaction anywhere. Money has been procured, still there is a constant chase after money. Such a beastly man for satisfaction of sensual pleasure and fulfilment of passion and desire, to satisfy his longings would venture even through killing others. If such a man becomes enterprising, he would utilize all the profits of his enterprise for others. He would deprive and exploit the workers and employees to the most of his capacity to increase his own wealth. Here nothing else is worthy to him, what is only important is satisfaction of his own passion and longings. So, any enterprise of his whatsoever would remain as an instance of deprivation of man. But there would be no exploitation and inequality in a theocratic state.

The main principle of discrimination lies in this passion and longing. Explosion of passion causes great expansion of discrimination. Poison of passion serves as the bricks of discrimination. Chasing passion induces deprivation to others. In godly and continent persons passion has no entry. When the influence passion and longing get dispersed a feeling of unification for all does appear. So, the path centered at passion is to be avoided in the capitalist system.

The dictatorship of the proletariat in a communist system also has the same consequence. The interest of the labour class converges at the urge of the combined passion and desires of the labourers. This also follows the same route. Just as a capitalist system creates discrimination and exploitation in case of the individuals, so also a communist system creates class-discrimination and class-exploitation. A labourer in power is in all senses a wealthy capitalist. The difference is that his authority in many cases is much more than that of a wealthy capitalist. So, a communist system inflicts greater discrimination and exploitation.

If godly persons are able to institute a theocratic state, they can extend true cooperation in support of them. Thus, it becomes easier for them to build up a newer society and economic system. Such a new social system can bring in development of all in an open atmosphere just like the company already cited as an example. Thus, invite cooperation of all in the economic system. This rule will be the beginning of the end of exploitation and discrimination.,

8
Vedic Spirit and Capital Market

Role of Capital Market in a State

There was no capital market at the time of Kautilya, but he has presented such a philosophy as would be a guide of economic liberty to the present world as it had been in ancient time. Profound is the role of capital market in the modern state system. In case of rich countries, capital market has constantly been observing increased responsibility. All the rich countries have been developed in the working of capital market. Capital market has as if been a part of modern economic system. The more a country has been associated with the world system, the more it has increased the appreciation of the capital market. The influence of the capital market is felt everywhere. Even in countries which have differences in opinion with the rich countries of the west, the role of capital market has gradually been growing important. The pillars capital market stands on are rather unstable. Modern arrangement has not yet been able to get enough dependability. Kautilya's *Arthashastra* has some such laws in it which can turn modern capital market into a more firm and dependable system.

Familiarity of *Arthashastra*

Chandragupta Maurya knew the dignity of *Arthashastra*. The Maurya empire is not the only deed of Kautilya. As the economic system of our country is dependent on ancient tradition and sequence, Kautilya's economics has created an age defying economic sequence, mainly based on the Indian pattern. Kautilya's economic system has also attracted the attention of the world. The *Arthashastra* has been presented in English through the elaborate translation of R. P. Kangle. Consequently, familiarity of the *Arthashastra* among the intelligentsia of the world has increased. Of course, there are much defects in the translation of Kangle. Going through this translation, Kautilya often seems to be inconclusive and sometimes puts off people. Sometimes it would appear that Kautilya is eager to keep up the interest of the king.

All sympathy is as if bestowed on the king in the *Arthashastra* and as if there is no hint of any possibility of mass liberation.

Again, there are plenty of positive things in the translation of Kangle, who was a professor of Sanskrit at the University of Bombay. Bombay University published this between 1960 and 1964. There had been a necessity of complete and flowing translation of the *Arthashastra* in English. Kangle has met the requirement successively. What Kangle has done as an outsider has left no scope of doubt in his devotion and expertness. There are many such fields and parts of the *Arthashastra* that are naturally beyond the grasp of the linguists.

A sincere translation of this book is possible if there is mastery over language, along with knowledge and experience in economics. If true knowledge of Indian traditions and sequence gets added, then only an able and a true translation becomes possible. If this problem is kept in mind, then only one world realizes why true evaluation and application of the *Arthashastra* have not yet been made, why there is moreover many types of a parity in different spheres with the *Arthashastra*. It was Dr. Shyamashastri of Mysore who first translated the *Arthashastra* in 1915. It has at the root a feeling of the sequence of India. So, a basis dissimilarity has been evident between this first translation and that of Kangle. The present deliberation is not depending on this translation though all translation has been addressed with proper weightage here.

Kautilya composed the *Arthashastra* at the time of Chandragupta Maurya. He was also called by Visnugupta. Chandragupta had set up the vast Maurya empire overthrowing the Nanda empire. In the 4th century BCE Dhanananda's state was spread in North India and was very powerful. Alexander could not touch the Nanda empire. Some also say that Alexander had to return due to revolt in his army. Factually, great fear infiltrated in the army of Alexander at the news of the enormous power of the Nanda empire and revolt burst out and Alexander had to go back. Chandragupta not only conquered the Nanda empire, but he set up a big Indian empire which extended even beyond Afganistan. Behind this success of Chandragupta was the intelligence and philosophy of Kautilya alias Chanakya.

After two futile attempts to overflow the Nanda empire, Chandragupta was one day moving in hiding round a settlement. Meanwhile he had been popular. People wanted him but were blaming his wrong procedure for his failure. Standing near a house he heard a common mother scolding her son for his stupidity by saying, 'you are a fool just like Chandragupta. Actually, the boy liked hot food. Since food was heaped at the center of the dish, he tried to eat food from there. But as the food was too hot there, he got his palm scorched, making it difficult for him to eat food again. That is why his mother was scolding him and said that he should have started not from the centre, but from the circumference.

Chandragupta then came to senses. He realized why Chanakya has repeatedly advised him to get hold of the smaller peripheral kingdoms and then to strike with a combined face. Then and then only Nanda emperor could be defeated, and his empire seized. This procedure brought them success. Kautilya's *Arthashastra* is a big political philosophy that made the Maurya empire of Chandragupta vast and powerful. Alexander returned to his country in 393 BCE and died. After few years, Selucas, like Alexander, set out on invasion and, like Alexander, he arrived at the border of India. This time the Greek regiment was utterly routed by Chandragupta and forced to flee. Selucas was compelled to enter into a peace agreement with Chandragupta and give back to Chandragupta Alexander and the adjacent places conquered by his army. In such a vast Indian empire Chandragupta had set up such an economic system good effects of which were enjoyed by the common people most.

Kautilya's Economic Philosophy for Managing State

"Prajasukha Sukham rajnah prajanam ca hite hitam.
Natmapriyam ca hitam rajnah prajanam Tu priyajam hitam"

(*Arthashastra* 1/19/34)

[Contentment of the people is the contentment of the king; benefit of the people is king's own benefit. King's object is not to do good for himself; to do good to the people should be the true object of the king.]

Some of the western scholars have called Kautilya's to be anti-people. From the principle depicted above regarding the outlook of a king, one can understand the characterization of a king.

Kautilya had laid stress on a king to be fully pro-people but possessor of full authority and devotion.

Division of secretariats is a big step of Kautilya in administration of a state. Among the division of secretariats designed by him include:

(a) Department of earning and development of mineral resources

(b) Department of increasing agricultural products and price of commodities.

(c) Department involving different duties and various objects being increasingly brought under justice.

(d) Department for public convenience duty being service to people.

(e) Department for developing balance among different classes of society.

(f) Labour department for workers of different fields.

(g) Department for defense of the state; it would be internal and state defense.

(h) Department for future planning

(i) Department for collection of information for ascertaining the weal and woe of the people.

(j) Department for farming and applying laws.

Cabinet of minister was there to keep vigilance on the working of the secretariats for administration of the state and to guide the working of the departments properly. Its main object was to keep the department properly active and effective through proper control. Works of every department were controlled by one or more principles of the *Arthashastra*. For example, the principle of the labour- department for ascertaining price of labour is:

"Rtvik, acaryah, mantra, purohitah Senapatih
Yubarajah, rajamata, rajamahisi
Astscatvarimsat sahasrah (panah)"

(*Arthashastra* 5/3/3)

[Family priests, teachers, ministers, priests, princes, king's mother, queen all of them would get forty-eight thousand para as salary.]

Such classification of salary was also for other classes. For example, for directors, regional army commanders, officers in charge of provincial authorities to be enterprising in works twenty-four thousand coins was fixed up as salary. In this way, in *Arthashastra* salary structure has been designed for all. State would estimate from all sides salaries and income of workers of all stages. Thus, the minister remuneration for labour would be such as it is sufficient for the worker concerned. Salary would be judged on the basis of ability and type of work of a worker.

"Etene bhutanam bhutanam ca
Vidyakarmabhyam
Bhaktabetanabisesam ca kuryat"

(*Arthashastra* 5/3/33)

[Thus, salary would be judged for regular and periodical workers on the basis of the nature of the work and the efficiency of workers.]

We come across these principles in the modern global economic system. Fixing up of salaries of workers in accordance with nature of work and capability of workers is an important direction propounded by Kautilya. If salary is not given or payment is not made in accordance with judgment of work, state has the right to punish the man or organization concerned. Where state is the enterpriser, enough punishment is prescribed for the violating supervisors entrusted with the direction of job. Besides if workers have developed reasonable dues in non-government organizations, this organizer will be amenable to punishment. State here is not only maker of the rule but also the enforcer.

"Karmakarasya Karmasambandham asana vidguh"

(*Arthashastra* 3/10/26)

[He would judge the work of a lobourer who would be able to observe the work from close proximity]

"Yathasambhasitam betanam labhet
Karmakatanurupam sambhasitam betanan."

(*Arthashastra* 3/13/27)

[Worker would get requisite salary in accordance with time and nature of work and contract.]

"Karsakah sasyanam gopalakah sarpisam vaidehakah
Panyatmana byabahrtanam
Dasabhagamsabhasitam betanau ladhte
Sambhasitabetanastu yatha sambhasitam"

(*Arthashastra* 3/13/28-29)

[Farmers, cowherds, businessman would get crop or butter if there is no contract at the initiation. If there be a contract, then they will get salary in accordance with the contract]

As there are arrangements for observation and control of the labour of workers, so also there are arrangements to see that they are not deceived. Where there is a contract with labour joining the works, all payments are to be made in accordance with that contract. In case of no contract made, one tenth of the produce would be the due for the worker.

Kautilya's Principle and Modern Share Market

The evaluation of the market has been so designed as to note the balance between the interest of the buyers and sellers.

> "Sulkedhyaksah sulkasalam dhvajam ca
> Pranmukham udanmnkham ba
> Mahadvarabhyase nibesayet."
>
> (*Arthashastra* 2/21/1)

[Director of tax-department would place a state-flag in front of the main gate at the East-northern point of the director for procuring taxes.]

From the state treasury of the tax-directorate all sorts of taxes are regulated. Coming at the front of the flag, all sellers would announce the price of their merchandise.

> "Dhvajamule upasthitasyapraman amardham
> Daidehakah
> Panyasyakratuh
> 'Etat pramanena arthena panya midem kah kreta iti
> Trirudghositam arthebhyah dadyay
> Kretrsamgharse mulyabrdhih sasulkahkasam gacchet"
>
> (*Arthashastra* 2/21/7-9)

[Businessman standing near that flag would be shout aloud thrice, the quantity merchandise they have brought and the principle expected. Buyers would be attracted by this announcement. The enthusiastic buyer would have to pay the price after completion all formalities. If due to clash of interests among the buyers attracted by the announcement, higher price is finalized, the excess amount will be deposited with the government treasury.]

The above principle makes it clear that the sentience of price has been given just twofold importance. The interest of the buyer has been placed by the side of that of the market. The mode of announcement of price in modern terminology is called auction sale. This auction sale was applicable to the capital market and a number of markets of commodities applied this process to ascertain the price of commodities like tea, coffee, rubber, etc. Before the introduction of computer, the process of fixing up of price in the share market was to cry aloud that with me are lying so and so saleable shares of so and so company and price per share is so and so.

After computerization, there is no need to cry aloud in the share market; now quotation of quantity and price of share are conveyed to the buyers through computer. The external feature of the process is the same but there is difference in the extreme end. There are different organization for full control of the modern share-markets. Securities and Exchange Commission of America and Securities Exchange Board of India (SEBI) are engaged in such works. Their duty is to look after the interest of the buyers and sellers and side by side of the state. Main interest of such organization is directed to the stability of the market.

At the very beginning of the principle of buying and selling Kautilya has insisted on declaring price before the flag. It is just like an oath. It is like the custom of allowing to give declaration after taking an oath. The oath was to be repeated thrice. As a result, it becomes imperative on the person to be more caring about selling. Excess money collected in the process would go to tax fund, i.e., the state-treasury. For this, even the smaller companies get a chance to occupy a reasonable position in the market.

Most of the scandals that are heard of in capital markets in different countries have their problem initiating from the shortage of liability. Usually that is quite natural following the path of Kautilya and that is very essential for capital market. With the declaration of price, the stock is also to be announced; if by transfer of share some one runs into debt, it would not be possible for him to come back through natural procedure of the market.

In our country, a great part of the total market has had a stain of scandal. In the measure of Kautilya, all buyers and sellers should be mutually liable to each other. Besides there is the problem of maintaining the interest of common buyers. In other words, in order to bring a boom, the capital market's greater stress is to be laid on bringing many people within share market, than on insisting on purchase of huge amount of share by only few buyers and to stop disparity in during and selling of shares.

If the capital market runs in Kautilya's line it must spread all over the world. In India capital market is gradually becoming strong and attractive in the field of movement and investment of money. The problem lies in the protection of buyers and controlling the price. Price control through Government order in an old system. Kautilya did not support this. If anyone in the market fails to read the market properly the very existence of the market becomes at stake. Kautilya's *Arthashastra* has set up a basis of firm opinion on this subject. From Kautilya's philosophy this subject has seriously hinted at the setting up of an ideal capital market.

9

Faith and World Economic System

Faith may be of an individual or even of the people in totality. The centre of gravity of confidence is the heart of the individual as the 'group' mind of the totality. Individual proceeds on the path of life resting on the wings of faith. It casts its influence on the livelihood of an individual, on the outlook towards society and nation, on the measure of the act of living, work, pursuit of science, art, literature, economy and economic system. Many scientific and technological achievements have been accomplished on the basis of confidence. The pursuit of scientific researches of Albert Einstein and Acharya Jagadish Chandra Bose are examples. In the scientific research of Acharya Jagadish Chandra Bose, faith had cast deep influence. Belief in God and feeling of dignity of the tradition of the country were so deep in the Acharya that true confidence appeared in prominence in his scientific lectures and theories. In the beginning of 1901, he was getting prepared for a lecture to be delivered before the scientists in a meeting of the Royal Society of London, the goddess of the mother country appeared before him and vanished. This sight filled up Jagadish Chandra, the scientist with great enthusiasm, the glow of that inspiration filled up the content of his lecture.

"He had been occupied till the very last moment presenting the instruments for the experiment. And he had had the strongest of experiences on the afternoon before the day. Acharya Jagadish Chandra Bose had his confidence concentrated on the altar of his country and the mother country. Such a feeling was always wakeful in his mind as he was entrusted with the responsibility of representing his country. He advanced in his pursuit of science with this confidence. Sara Bull, an American known otherwise as 'Mrs.

Ole Bull' after her Norwegian violinist husband, was Nivedita's friend, who like Nivedita became Bose's friend admirer and protector. Bose came to address her as 'mother' and she called him 'son' to the extent that she was able to persuade Bose to apply for a patent for his galena receiver. The patent application for a director of electrical disturbances was filled on 30 September 1901—(Bose was then still in England) by Jagadish Chandra Bose, of Calcutta, India, Assignor of one half to Sara Chapman Bull of 755,840 on 29 March 1904".

(*Prof. Jagadish Chandra Bose and Indian Response to Western Science* by Subrata Dasgupta, Oxford University Press, 1999, p. 92.)

Faith of a Scientist

Acharya Jagadish Chandra Bose had deep self-confidence, love for his country and severance to the tradition of the country. The theory presented by him before the intelligentsia of the world had at its root the theory of non-dualism

Sarvam khalvidam Brahma

All is Brahma. Whatever is being seen, whatever is unseen, whatever has been born and whatever is inanimate, all is Brahma. for this Jagadish Chandra got prepared to define life force in a new and novel way. In the Paris lecture of 1901, he said there is no break of continuity between the living and the non-living. One could draw a line demarcating the purely physical phenomenon for the physiological, the phenomenon dead matter for the peculiar to the living.

(Ibid p. 189)

Acharya Jagadish Chandra Bose was deeply impressed and inspired by the sayings of the Vedanta of Swamiji. When they met each other in Paris. Swamiji has remarked about him.

Heroic Bengali and Indian who had stepped forth from among the whole galaxy of genius to proclaim the motherland name and reputation amidst all those from Germany, France, England and Italy, who had charmed a western audience by the force of his genius and had infused new life into the half dead body of the motherland. (ibid p. 110.)

Acharya Bose met the great scientist Patrick Geddes who had been impressed by Swami Vivekananda. Geddes was impressed by Vivekananda and quite familiar with sister Nivedita gave much publicity for the Acharya before the society of the scientists; later he also wrote a biography of the Acharya.

Spread of Faith

Scientific work dependent on faith made his pervasion durable. Faith also brings in the creation of science a new significance and perspective. Creation of science and technology always emerges as a basic inspiration. The inspiration may be theoretical, social, ethical, economic or just symbolic. Enlightened through inspiration, a scientist marches on in the path of his as cretinism. Scientists enlightened through inspiration engage themselves with enthusiasm in new discoveries and creations in the world. Discovery and creation bring forth the offering to be paid to enthusiasm.

A scientist merges along the path of this world through his discovery and creation. Merely mundane affairs do not impress a scientist. A scientist is ready to sacrifice all his wealth of life for that necessity which has behind it an important incrusting as are made by mankind. Society and civilization would have satisfaction and by which newer installments would be there. A new faith has been firm in sciences, technology and trade and commerce, law of acquisition and possession, what is acquired and accepted call for attachment multiplied many times. So, in trade and commerce this process of acquisition and possession becomes evident through continuously appearing new inventions, new articles, new materials, new science and new technology. Insisting on confidence in this novelty brings in inspiration for newer creations in science technology and trade and commerce. This has been evident in recent research.

"An object is worth more to you if you already own it. Research found that some Cornell students who would choose a chocolate bar over a coffee mug start to prefer the mug once they have been given one. This endowment effect has been spotted will all sorts of things, from basketball tickets to shares and petrol vouchers. The question that has puzzled economists is just why a supposedly clever species like, how sapiens, should fall a prey to something so irrational.

Now scientists may have provided an answer. The endowment effect has been seen in brain imaging studies in people and in ellipse, which suggest it is an evolutionary adoption. Trade was risky when there were no contracts, Law or Language. The bird in the hand was worth even more when bushes were dangerous. ("The Future of Energy." *The Economist*, 21 June 2008, p. 18) in favour of this has been found in the history of science. Science has marched towards newer and newer discoveries in search of nature, source and application of energy. Energy liberated from coal, steam, oil solar energy and other types of natural energy; combustion energy, atomic energy and other types of energy obtained from animals—exposition of all there and discovery of the process of their application have a feeling of necessity and faith the necessity is mundane and real. The faith is also mundane, but it is sensitive. Faith brings the firmness which helps discovery of science, and the phase of new creation may move on. Endeavour of world-science is moving in different routes owing to high price of fuel and to get rid of the world-wide problem of fuel. Biofuel is something very important in this respect. Besides biofuel, fuel-oil has also caught the attention for fuels scientists. Scientists are moving towards different enterprises in small and big fields. In future cars on the road will be energized only by re-charging the fuel by all.

"Nothing ages faster than future. A few years ago, these was general agreement that if the internal combustion even was replaced by something clean. That something would be the fuel cell. A fuel can have a way of reacting to hydrogen and oxygen together in a controlled way and extracting electricity from the processors. It was to be the possessors of what was known as the hydrogen economy, in which that gas would replace fossil smells and power almost everything.

(*The Economist*, ibid, p. 60/17.)

Faith in Civilization

Fuel is very intimately connected with the growing of human civilization. With the demand for fuel, our mode of use has moved on from stage to stage. Processes and attempts of science and technology have reached the age of plug-in hybrid. A Japanese company has tried to introduce Toshiko Nuclear Battery. Such a battery will be able to supply up to 10 megawatts of electricity for about 15 to 30 years. It will be possible to use the same at will and at suitable hour. After expiry it will be sent back to the company. The company will never let it go to waste. In the history of science thoughts of future and enterprise in accordance with the same is quite natural.

"As Samuel Golden Wisely observed, "you should never make predictions, especially about the future is concerned. People almost always either overshoot or undershoot. Holidays on the moon by the 2000 as in the 1969? not exactly. A quick look out of the atmosphere is the limit of that vision for the moment. On the other hand, a seemingly boring way of linking computer files full of data, on sub atomic physics can turn into a world wide web of information in half a decade."

(*The Economist*, ibid, p. 60/21.)

The longing hidden behind the invasion of science has not been fulfilled no doubt, but it is true that much of the same has been turned as real. The longing of the future will also turn into reality. Gradually Man's victory march has moving towards constant fulfillment.

Economic world lying with thought of science. The economic system of the world is moving on with a faith that money is the basic wealth, money is success. Now through day-to day worry, incitement and fatigue a great uncertainty has occupied minds of and hours of the people. Through study of the markets for investment, especially the share market, it has been realized that increase in the provision of wealth has taken place under the secret cover in a restless atmosphere.

"Welcome to the age of anxiety over the past year bean betrayal and confusion have railed investor confidence, leaving stomachs query and unsettled. Every day, it seems some giant bank or wall street Titan discovers a few billion dollars more in troubled assets it did not realize it owned and has to write down. Whether it's been the immolation of Bear Steam, the descent of home prices, of the credit fruit—weren't even going to talk about sky rocketing price for food and energy the news has been wrenching.

With all that turmoil perhaps, it's surprising, then that the major stock indexes haven't sustained more calamitous dentine."

(*Fortune*, 23 June 2008)

As much and as how dependence has been achieved, so much has been the advancement.

Kautilya has liked the introduction of an economic system right with the firm faith in the path of movement. Movement for the introduction of an economic system should be with firm faith in God then and only then would the marching on in the fields of both science technology and trade commerce reach fulfillment.

10
Kautilya and State-System of Economy

Philosophical Basis of the Vedic Economy

Kautilya's *Arthashastra* is based on the very ancient wisdom and mentality of India. In his *Arthashastra* as Kautilya has discussed vividly on economic system and economic philosophy, so also he has made electorate discussion on state and political directives. Factually the very first reading of the *Arthashastra* would depict that Kautilya has presented his philosophy keeping the temporary requirement of state politics in mind. But after going deep into it its permanent relevance would be realized.

It not only has depicted the time befitting directives of times prior to Kautilya, but it is a complete economic and political philosophy. Foreign scholars of course opine differently. They have mentioned Rousseau and Habbo's in comparison to say that Kautilya's *Arthashastra* has failed to present to state its history or a complete political philosophy. R. P. Kangle had published the translation the *Arthashastra* in the decade of sixty in the last century. This translation has been the source book in discussion on Kautilya's *Arthashastra*. But if read with attention some discrepancy would be noticed in the translated *Arthashastra*. He has displaced many words for its true sense and has attribute a temporary meaning to them. Again, in many cases he has ignored the common meaning to attribute a new one. A small example will make the thing clear. He has translated 'Yoga-kshema' as security and well-being. There is no doubt about the derivation of the word 'Yoga'. 'Yoga-Kshema' has together been used to depict some mundane and spiritual need. In the same sense Yoga has been projected as the connect to the superior spiritual source. But Kangle calls Yoga to be security and kshema well-being. In the same way the role and say of the *Arthashastra* have been belittled by deviation of the actual meaning.

At the very beginning of the *Arthashastra* Kautilya has paid obeisance to Sukra (the mentor of the demons) and Brhaspati (the mentor of the gods) as:

"Prithibyahtable palane ca yabanta
Arthashastra ni
Samihrtyaukmidam *Arthashastram* Krtam" (1/1)

(This new *Arthashastra* has been composed by compiling together the political philosophy and scientific knowledge so far discovered by the earlier mentor to acquire and rear a kingdom)

This declaration of Kautilya clarifies that the *Arthashastra* is based right on the ancient sequence. 'Parthiban tabhe' through translation of this phrase and analysis thereof Kautilya has especially hinted at the fact that the *Arthashastra* is written for a king aspiring to occupy a kingdom and willing to set up an empire.

As instructions in it are aimed at such a king aspiring to set up an empire, this must be anti-people, As we would enter into the discussion, it would be clear to us that such explanations offered by some scholars are to be avoided carefully. The *Arthashastra* is based on just opposite philosophy. The *Arthashastra* in eager to bring discipline in the administration of a kingdom by a king only because sharing of justice and principle in such administration only causes the people to prosper. The *Arthashastra* has brought the whole thing under the purview of the state in the interest of proper control and right administration. The basis object of control and administration is the welfare of the masses.

Let us first look at the list of the topics discussed in the *Arthashastra*.

"Tasyayam prakarana adhikarana
Samuddesah" (1/1/2)

(Here the division of the scripture is being classified)

"Vidyasamuddesah brdhasamyagol
Indriyajayah,
Amatyaotpatti, mantripurohitot pattih" (1/1/3)

(Practice of different section of knowledge and science, organization for the welfare of the aged, liberation for the influence of the desires emerging from the sense-organs, appointment and setting of the administrators of the state, appointment and directions for practicing virtues of the minister and the priests.)

The significance of the first part of the third verse is given above. The basic outlook of the *Arthashastra* of Kautilya is very clear here. Some basic principles have been emphasized on proper training of all ministers and officers for the state and council for administration and management of the state.

These principles are:

(i) Attainment of complete worthiness through study and cultivation of knowledge and science.

(ii) To accept in administration of the state the essence of experience through combination of all of those who are aged and experienced in the society.

The most valuable aspect of the administration of a state is being too free from the influence of desires those who are associated with administration. They will be impartial and able administrators, if and only they become free from desires.

Economic System Free from the Influence of Desires

The philosophy on which Kautilya has placed his economic principle is indicative of the extreme aspiration of the man. The economic conviction stands upon the object which has been indicated by the Vedas and Upanishads. Those who will be helmsmen of society, on whom the directive force of economy will be vested should be self-denying and free from longing and desires. Economic policy and state administration also is considered here as asceticism. The chief helmsmen in the administration of state should be self-denying and devoid of self-interest. They should be free from the luxury of longing.

So, at the very beginning of his description of the economic system, Kautilya has argued strongly in favour of being above longing and desire. He first tried to build up character. Really the building up of character is not only applicable to those who have taken the heirs but also to the public. Actually, advice is provided here for the public to rise above the influence of longing and desire. Kautilya's *Arthashastra* is here the real founder of modern economic processes.

The real key to a modern market dependent economy lies in the demand. And the root of creation of the demand is the peremptory to menace of longing and desires. The more pervasive will be the longing and desires the more a man will be restless with desire, the more will be submerged in the lust of longing and the more will increase the demand of the market.

There would be an explosion of demand. That is demand would go on increasing. On the other hand, if man becomes contented easily, demand will fall. New types of commodities and services are results of the explosion of demands. As the consequence on one side goes to the buyers and consumers so also the markets of the producers and distributers get increased. The more the market of the commodities would expand the more would grow the demand for supply of monetary wealth. That is the supply of money is also to be increased. As a result, inflation results in the market of money.

Explosion of demands not only creates an explosion in the markets of commodities, services or money but it also helps explosion of wealth gradually in different direction. That is inflation of demand collectively moves to the inflation of wealth. But this does not cause solution of basic problems of man.

There are bites of longing and inflammatory poison of desires at the root of the explosion demanded. As a result, social wealth sets out in the quest of satisfaction. All persons do not get the touch of this satisfaction. There remains the problem of poverty and discrimination.

Thoughts on poverty and discrimination flew in different channels. Persons adhering to different opinions have put forth different contradictory theories on poverty and discrimination. But all the opinions so long cultivated converge to one point and that is the basis of an economic system would grow through satisfaction of longing and desires. Longing and desires only change forms, take different shapes. Man moves on gradually from one type of desire to another. It is just like searching for fruits from one branch to another. Satisfaction of one longing is just the staircase for certain of other types of longings. Prosperity comes to the society by this process, it has come no doubt, but thereby discrimination increases, poverty lingers on. So long as man will be considered as a worm of desire, an economic system cannot yield full result.

An economic system free from the slavery of longings causes dense pervasion of commodities and services. Value added product is the main thing corroborated by an economic system influenced by longing and desires. Improved economy grows on the basis of value-added products. Among the ways meant for developing improved standard of livelihood the main thing is to accept those things which have the very basis of high standard. Due to attribution of higher values, greater incentive is caused in production, distribution and transport of commodities. Competition grows among different companies in production and this competition is to reach the buyers in greater measure.

The merit of competition is two folds.

1. Increase in the extent of activity of the company by choice results in increase of wealth and pervasion thereof.
2. A collection of consumable goods comprising a large number of products and services for the buyers.

As a result, as facilities of companies increase so buyers also get advantages. In comparison to the smallest number of products and services buyers would get before, they now have at their disposal a much greater number of products and services for consumption. Man is so satisfied.

Competition brings much more satisfaction to him. This results in uplifting of the standard of the act of living. The advancement of the company also in effected. The more the companies grow in the extent, any place and promotion, the greater is the effect on the economic order. As a result of competition, usage of commodities increases and at the same time development of economic order continues as a subsequence. The connection of this economic order with expansion of the market is quite direct. Due to this direct connection the market gets involved in bringing about a transformation of the economic order. Expansion of desire acts as the main driving force behind the expansion of the market and consequential economic progress. As a result, on one side there is an explosion of prosperity in one section of the society and at the same time in hunger prevails in the other section of the society. Along with the explosion of slavery there are poverty, lack of education and disparity.

Basis of renouncement: Solution of this problem is quite unattainable on the basis of greed and desire. Discontentment of non-fulfillment continues to be accumulated more and more in the people who are guardedly greedy and desire. Due to this discontentment of non-fulfillment such belief grows in them as desire are there are to be fulfilled by them by hook by crook. Then immorality gains ground in society. Not to speak of velvet from immoral activities man jumps by nature into immoral ones. For this reason, we find gradual increase in injustice, heinous acts, highway robbery, making others embarrassed annoyed and destitute becomes quite natural. As if deciding on the basis of injustice is quite natural. To manage one's own affairs by deceiving others becomes quite natural. As a result of this persons specially these who hold power cast influence on the wealth of the society exploit the society, social power gets weakened and a person on grout becomes more powerful. Consequently, there is a disbalance in the equilibrium of society. When equilibrium gets disturbed, society becomes weak. A person or society then stands on the predominance of money. All the powers of the state now go under the control of money. Money then becomes the supreme power. Achievements, quality of consumption, victory in lives all that are thought of and done are assured by the monetary power.

But in spite of that, a happy ending has not been achieved. Cultivation of economic affairs done so long has comprised some subjects e.g.

1. Political background
2. Social judgement and background
3. Applied economics
4. Unexpected incidents

But do not judge the type of people for whom this economic system is contemplated. What is absent from these is man. The role of man is of utmost importance in an economic system. An individual takes part in an economic system with all his propriety. Kautilya has remarked:

> "Manusam nayanapanayau, devayanayau.
> Devamanusam hi karma lokam yapayati."
>
> (*Arthashastra* 6/2/6-7)

[Man goes through good and bad works in a new endeavour and in the activities of godly man the benevolent side of work becomes evident.]

Man fixes up his path based on his character and his own circle. But when a man transforms into a godly man, he casts his influence not only on himself but on others of this earth and hastens the change. Now the question is: Who is this godly man. From where does godliness come?

A man who is a slave to desire and longings is merely entangled in human instincts, may even be in beastliness. A godly man is self-denying. He gives up all his desires for earthly pressures, longing for property and becomes inclined to a transparent and natural life. The step for becoming a godly man is to turn the direction of life. The market becomes inflated through fulfilling the desires of a life smeared with longings but on the other side, disparity becomes heaped up, poverty becomes augmented. If a wind of renunciation blows in this life, if the aim of this life becomes attainment of divinity, if it only attributes value to the path of renunciation, then the change brought about within brings extensive external changes.

Spiritual practice is needed for economic development. That is why Kautilya has recommended an attempt for continence for everyone including king, ministers and officers. Those who are slaves to the superguns are slaves to desire and longing. Thus, they are eager not for society nor for men but to satisfy their own desires. The renunciation and offering that are essential for coming out piercing the actuation can come through sole dedication to God, through austerity and through fixing up one's aim towards the path of godliness,

That is why Kautilya has laid so much importance on continence. A continent leader or worker would bring change in society, organization or company. They would help to design the whole economic system of the rest. Because at this point no government enterprise would be required to control the market. Market would become spontaneously influenced by free and dedicated person. So, market would not act on the wealth in quite a murky way. In the conflicts between monetary power and people's power in the market, the latter would get the victory.

This victory of people's power is of utmost importance in the perspective of the big chakras of charity and extensive distribution. Now such a system would be built up which would end in distribution of wealth. The economic system we would reach along the following the theory of Kautilya may be termed as state principle of economy on the basis of spirituality. This in the present world is a device for curing all diseases.

11

Vedic Economic Philosophy: Basis of Spritual Economy

The object of composing the *Arthashastra* of Kautilya was to find out the means of setting up and controlling a state on the basis of wisdom. The *Arthashastra* is a scripture well-written in a very simple and easy language. For ascertainment of this scripture the author has written down in all six thousand verses distributed in fifteen parts, one hundred and fifty chapters and one hundred eighty sections. In the first chapter of the first part there is a description of the scripture. In the second and third chapters there is the theory or philosophy of the *Arthashastra*. In every part of the *Arthashastra*, there are ingredients of its philosophy. In that sense the *Arthashastra* is a complete philosophical scripture.

Kautilya's *Arthashastra* is based on the Vedas and Vedic wisdom. Its philosophical basis rests on the Vedas, history, puranas and Indian succession. It rests on the Indian succession it as deals with the subjects relating to kingdom and king, so also it has deals with subjects relating who people. The *Arthashastra* believes that dealing with subjects relating to people's needs is very essential. It has laid special stress on this. That is why as the *Arthashastra* may be taken as a field of spiritual economics so also it can be announced as a field of mass economics.

Spiritual Economics: Kautilya's Proposal

All those who will be connected to economics and economic system need spiritual education. Only being educated in spiritual education will not do, they must acquire spiritual knowledge; they would have to be spiritual persons.

According to the *Arthashastra* three types of knowledge are required for judging the statement on learning.

"Samah Rig Yajuh devah trayah trayz"

(*Arthashastra*, 1/3/1)

"Atharvavedah Itihasa vedau ca vedah."

(*Arthashastra*, 1/3/2)

[Sama, Rig and Yajurveda —these three economic form the tri of knowledge. Attain expertise in these words of wisdom to cultivate also the Atharvaveda and history.]

People of different acquaintances, profession and trade have different takes on life. He who will be the controller of a state needs to acquire knowledge of the Vedas and histories and he should try to apply that knowledge. The spiritual quest introduced and the basis of the knowledge set up by the Vedas should be applied in controlling a state. Target and object of the Vedas are indispensable for a state. A state would bear at its bosom the glow of Vedic knowledge. For a man engaged in controlling a state the job would be easy and natural if it is on the basis of wisdom.

So, Kautilya wanted cultivation and practice of varied subjects. He liked to introduce in society cultivation of education, the portion of Vedic literature depicting mode of worship (kalpa), grammar, etymology (nirukta), prosody, etc. for men engaged in different professions and some on professions which are natural to them and there are others which are procured by them. Consideration of naturalness is essential because if one gets engaged in some work according to one's own characteristic, specialty and taste, the work has a greater chance of being successful. Factors which befit one's own characteristic and taste are those which are spontaneously acceptable through usual norms and get bloomed up speedily. It is not a matter of time or hour; it is a question of one's deservingness. As for example, it is rather easy for a distinguished farmer to be engaged in cultivation judging properly the trends of the nature. He can understand what the trend of the nature and he would be would act accordingly.

A distinguished farmer knows the symptoms of the land, trend of the nature and seed and the conjunction of consequences. He can accomplish the job of cultivation at times of both hardship and favour. In the same way the mystic word for gaining profit in a business flow in the blood of a person whose family tradition has been business. He knows quite well the good and bad, rise and fall and beginning and end of business.

It is quite natural for such a person to be successful in business. Just in the same way it becomes quite natural to set up newer forums and newer stages in the path of knowledge for one who has kept oneself engaged in cultivation of knowledge. So, it is rather pleasant and relieving to move along the path of sequence. That is why Kautilya has fixed up learning, teaching, act of worshiping on behalf of one's own self as well as on behalf of others, charity, acceptance, etc., for the framing. For the Kautilyas (people of the second caste) were fixed daily teaching, act of worshiping on behalf one's own self, charity and protection of those who practice scriptures and accepting offering. For the Vaishyas (traders, the third caste) duties fixed were daily reading, worshiping, charity, farming, livestock farming and trade. To the shudras duties assigned were service, crafts and handiwork. Duties assigned to the householders were, depending on the judgement of their position, were observance of one's own religion, judgement of material world attempt for satisfaction of needs, service for the dependents, observance of religious rites and protection of all. A celibate (Brahmachari) would be engaged in daily reading and sacrificial activities. Those who would leave for forest after the period of domestic life(vanaprastha) would observe celibacy, cultivate scriptures and spend lives conforming to scriptural prescripts. Mendicants are sannyasi would be devoid of all cravings and would be content and forsake all contacts, would live with earnest desire of reaching God. He will be merciful to all, will possess kindness, forgiveness, devotion to truth and non-violence, would be engaged in a godly life free of rage, of malice and create an environment of truth and justice.

Kautilya has spoken of arrangements of profession and quality in the society. The main object of this arrangement is the extension of effectiveness and proficiency in society. The effectiveness and efficiency of an endeavour glorifies the same and at the same time makes the basis of the economy of the country sounder. Kautilya has remarked:

"Tasmat swadharmam bhutanam ca raja
Byabhicarayet
Swadharmam Samdadhatri hi pretya
Ca iha ca nandati" (*Arthashastra* 1/3/6)

[The king and the people will stay in their respective position and would never shun their own position in spite of strong oppositions]

Positions of persons attached to different professions and status may easily be determined if their characters assessed in terms of their professions. A person engaged in a profession that calls for honest, diligent, developed, self-denying person should be a possessor of honest, diligent, devoted and self-denying personality. Persons belonging professions sheltered in power, ability and valour must be powerful, able and valorous.

If looked at the subject on behalf of the state and society, it will be ascertaining how much important the principle is:

There are few steps of observing one's own positions:

- Assessment of character.
- Definite conception regarding aims and objects.
- Judgement of consequences.

Role and effectiveness of that activity on greater population and state system. Action according to one's own position on the part of the state and people is required for shaping the economic system. In an economic system, we judge the points of production and productivity with utmost importance, these points are backbones of economic system. Whatever may be the stage of technology an economic excellence in production and productivity, among the arrangements essential for getting long term results of an economic system productivity occurs at the topmost position. Rearrangement of technology becomes essential for keeping up and increasing productivity. Investment would be required for implementing change in technology.

Newer investments will be required in newer and newer technologies. The quality and quantity of investment will depend on technology. Among the factors, other than technological fix-up, that requires investment, special mention may be made of the condition of the market, eagerness and ability of buyers, supply of essential components and arrangement for movement of money and commodities.

Among the factors Kautilya has emphasized on, for judging the respective positions, the main are continence, observance of religion and building of character. Kautilya has advised that judgment of character is very much essential where there is monetary power of the state to be organized. Arrangement and extension of monetary power depends on those people who are bearers of and nearer to the economic system. If the bearers of economic systems are not of restrained character, wastage of monetary wealth becomes inevitable.

Enterprise is Essential

In the economic policy of Kautilya there is a concrete attempt to make every individual an ideal. Kautilya wants both the king and the people to work as per their own nature and position. Among the activities of theirs in accordance with their own nature, the matter of satisfying personal interests become rather secondary. Those who attempt to serve their own purpose according to Kautilya are inexperts and unacceptable.

To give a permanent basis to an economic system Kautilya has advised a suitable right of succession of the authority. Qualities that are essential for a king should all be bestowed on his successors. Kautilya is very careful about this right of succession. He has stressed on training of the persons engaged in state and economic systems. There are all types of subjects in the proposal for training. For example, there is provision of training in mechanism and skill training in temperament and moral behaviour.

The most important direction for a state and economic policy is to provide contentment to the people. Kautilya *Arthashastra* insists on attempts for providing contentment to the people.

> "Tasmat nityah utthitah raja kuryat arthanu sastram
> Arthasya mulam uttranam arthasya biparyayah."
>
> (*Arthashastra* 1/19/35)

[The king will always be on the alert for meaningful attempt to work and edition of the principles for the benefit of the people. Trouble and disaster may befall if the basic source of money is neglected.]

On the part of a king to promote wellbeing of the people belongs to his normal program activities. A king always keeps his eye on effectual matters in promoting the wellbeing of the people. King's aim would be to be eager at the same time to promote the wellbeing of the people and state. For these, it would be required to provide means to speed-up the economic arrangements. King's responsibility would be promoting such arrangements of production, distribution of assimilation of different products as to make the persons concerned to come forward in totality to society— the desired object of the state. Kautilya knows well that but for the cooperation of all types and all classes of people, economic development and expansion would not be possible.

Cooperation and Active Participation

The foundation of on the basis of cooperation and active participation but for endeavour comes along a ruinous consequence.

"Anutthanc dhrubau na sah praptasya
Anagatasya ca
Prapyate phalam utthana alabhate ca arthapadam."
(*Arthashastra* 1/19/36)

[At the conclusion of endeavour a havoc is inevitable, what has been secured and what are waiting to be secured are all destroyed. Endeavour brings the desired result. Money and power get stabilized.]

Kautilya has attributed great value to endeavour. Cooperation stands at the basis of endeavour. Long-term and far-expanded attainment stands behind an endeavour that has grown on the basis of cooperation. Both wealth and possibility get destroyed due to the dearth of endeavour. On the other hand, the result of endeavour is far expanding. Endeavour fetches money, as well as relations, reputation and power.

Just an individual endeavour causes the path of monetary rise and reputation, so does monetary rise and power collectivity come out of the economic system built on the basis of cooperation of many people.

That is why Kautilya has advised the king to be active and always remain active. A king is to be active and is to remain always active, not for the sake of his own self but for the whole state and state system for the people.

The endeavour spoken of by Kautilya is applicable for both mundane and spiritual fields. In the mundane field, the chief initiator will be the state leadership. The responsibility of the state leadership would be to endeavour and make others also endeavour. On endeavouring the basis of the development of the state would be sounder.

Just as an individual is solely responsible for his own enterprise, so also the responsibility of a state enterprise is vested on the steersman of the state. There are two aspects of the state enterprise: one individual; two collective. An individual is to take the initiative on his own for his advancement, so also, he is to take active part in state enterprises. For one's own progress the endeavour should be to his liking and taste. On the other hand, a state enterprise may not always be so though extending cooperation to same. The two enterprises are naturally quite different. Of course, the main source of inspiration for both these types of enterprises is the desire for growth of the individual in his mind.

When steersman state creates sonorous by his weight and desires of the result of the action. The result is from both the sides. Just as for an individual so also for a state the result would be such as the enterprises would receive best actions for required activity and thereby benefit the most.

Judgement of Work

There are many aspects of the work of the steersman of a state. These include for example economic awakening of the state, being companion of weal and woe of the people, to assure security and stability of the state. The steersman of a state would observe his own duties and obligation like a warrior (Kautilya) and at the same time would cooperate with the persons engaged in observing other activities for running the state. A king will observe his own duties and also see that there be no impediment in his state for observing duties of others also.

For this the steersman of a state should have:

Instant endeavour and technical capability arising out of judgement and endeavour and judicious application for reaching results to possible subjects.

Agnayagaragatah karyapasyet etat
Pasuinam
Purohitah acarya sakhah pratyuttha
Abhibadya ca (*Arthashastra* 1/19/31)

[The king will pay special attention to the fact that there be no obstruction in observing vedic rites. The king will give proper respect to the priests, mentors and the respected and revered person of the society and will always be conversant of them.]

Tapasvinam tu karyani traividyauh
Saha karayet
Mayayogavidyam caiba na savayam
Kopakaranat. (*Arthashastra* 1/19/32)

(The king will be zealous in providing comfort to the hermits, the persons engaged in the study of the three Vedas but he himself would not care fot others, announce by crossing the limit of his knowledge and right for this the king would seek advice and help from suitable persons.)

Kautilya has laid stress on religious dealings, spiritual reverence and observance of one's own rights and duties. The king is to move cautiously so that in spite of being zealous to perform his own duties, he may not commit something dangerous or destructive. Kautilya has kept vigilance on him so that too much influence does not occur, in case of his observance of realized and depiction of duties. Responsibilities for this have been laid down not only for the steersmen of states but also for common people. In the *Arthashastra* composed by him. Kautilya has sought means for a total development of economy.

Economy of Spiritual Thought

Spiritual thoughts bring a fundamental change in a man. That change comes from within. Advancing on the path of austerity when the phase of incitation gets initiated, he finds the petals being unfolded just as the petals of a lotus opening. The obstructed flow of possibility within him gets exposed. An individual now gradually crosses his own limit to extend himself. Attempt to cross his own limit after knowing and realizing the same moves the individual forward in the path of being impersonal.

The egotistic limit of an individual gets smashed by the incitation of spirituality. Egotism moves away and the spring of godliness gets exposed in him. This individual then no longer remains eager and engrossed with individual and selfish thoughts. He then becomes synonymous with totality. The structure of his mind gets extended from one to many. So, his thoughts blow up for many, for multitude and for people at large.

In an attempt to prepare the philosophy of economics, Kautilya has firstly laid stress on learning and practice of the Rig, Sam and Yajur Vedas. According to him, that knowledge of the Vedas and through acquiring Vedic wisdom a king or a steersman of the state would be relived of egotism. He would go beyond his own self under the influence of divine feelings, would break down the small boundary of his own self and would try to bring happiness and cause development to all. As a result, the king would conquer his common human instincts and would gradually arrive at the level of greatness. This waking of a king is required not only for a state =or its people but also for the incitation of civilization.

Cooperation comes from an individual in the state affairs when demands of right and freedom of an individual get satisfied. If extreme needs and hunger of mind are satisfied, cooperation from him gets multiplied. The state eagerly waits for this cooperation. Just as a family prospers on the basis of cooperation of all its members, in case of a state its economy would advance by the help of mutual co-operators of the citizens. Spiritual knowledge and spiritual feeling facilitate the path of cooperation. In economics participation and cooperation do bring possibility. Intellect, genius and possibilities for an individual bloom up through cooperation. If things like 'I have a role to play in such an enterprise' or 'I have got some basis duties', them in him rises the will to add something, to do something extra. An individual then rises to be a fundamental particle of totality. This is the seed of the inspiration of totality. The totality which would move with such individuals, endeavour for work, and would naturally grow in them.

Not as an individual, but as a fundamental component of totality would now get a perspective of waking. In this perspective of weakening desire to do something to build something up would rise up in him. Above all, an attraction for being offered to many would arise. As a consequence, the economic system would prosper extensively. Many endeavours, many creations of many people get shaped up into a moving economic system, powerful, combined and offered for the benefit of multitude. This is the basis of spiritual economics.

12
The Royal Office

Kautilya's Reflection

What is meant by the royal office? In his *Arthashastra*, Kautilya has vivid description on what would be the attitude of persons placed at the helm of a state. Is royal office only an office placed at the disposal of a king? What should be the basic principle for founding a state and security of the same? Kautilya has given his correct opinion on matters such as how a state should develop its wealth, how should it use this wealth and so on. The opinions narrated in the *Arthashastra* are not confined merely into an essay of opinion; it has also been applied rightly.

Austerity remains behind the rise of a state. The state which has moved forward depending on such austerity has had it blooming. Austerity of a state does not only mean to determine and absence the boundary, but it also rather has a greater implication. If everyone is not in some way or other benefitted by the austerity of a state is to be considered a failure. Universal questions that have always been discussed and where the significance of a state lies—Why would all be bonded to a state? What is the limit of the evolution of a state? Where would a state serve king, subjects or something else?

Kautilya expressed solution to all these in the part of a state by expounding his knowledge. In Kausalya's proposal there are some things which are engaged in a universal need of a state and again there are somethings which finds clue for daily works.

According to a European doctrine subjects worthy of consideration among those which are relevant to requirement of a state are:

1. Sovereignty of state
2. Society of state
3. Matters related to requirements and the rise of the people.

4. Orderly placement of relations with other states.
5. Role of a state with respect to requirements of the mankind.

But Kautilya has placed these topics in a different order.

He has reviewed the problem from a different corner and judged it quite differently.

According to Kautilya, the important topic of development of a state are:

1. Character and leadership ability of a king
2. Advancement of moral character of the people and relevant matters.
3. Movement of the state along the traditional path of the state in accordance with teaching of the state.
4. To assure security and sovereignty of the state
5. Assuring the position of one's own state with respect of other states and developing cooperation.

There is a basic difference between the austere services of European states and the Indian ones. Europe has laid stress on the points of security, sovereignty and the like. This has resulted in an attempt by the state for expansion. A state wants to cross its own boundary to build a new one. With the extension of the boundary of the state come the other aspects of adaptation, viz. eagerness for occupation of foreign states and exploitation of them. That is why in some cases European powers in an attempt to invade and seize foreign states have turned into competitors among themselves. The character of a state that becomes evident at the phase of seizing and exploiting foreign states is just an act of brandishing might and ability. The direct consequence of this is aspiration for power and ability. The practice of power has made European countries invaders of different parts of the world. They have occupied many parts of this world, extended their mode of administration there, established their civilization at their will. That is why we find that at different phases of this a vast portion of Asia and Africa has been quite demolished under European rules.

As this practice of power and ability has augmented the defense system of the state also it has brought discipline in internal administration also. The power and ability of the people have been stressed upon in the internal administration of the state. As a result, the state has had people full of power and ability. Not just by the infrastructure and will of the state, a state becomes developed by the power and ability of every individual.

Europe has been able to make a state weapon for earning the capability of its people. As a result, on one hand, the state has been invading other countries, on the other the state is more stable than others, The state has been inspiring or supporting people in their effort for practice of stability. State has made an individual stand on his ability.

The target of aspiration of a state in India is quite different. At the basis of the practice of states in India there are balanced arrangements, balanced outlook and balanced promotion. So, the basis of the austere practice of states in India is the character of the state. An Indian state does not invade others. India's desire is not to trample on others to occupy and enjoy. So, India has developed as a state depending on its own ability, in the type of its own position. In India character and outlook of the controllers of the state have been shaped. In running a state there is definitely an influence of moral feeling; state, here, has been seen as a background for holding moral and spiritual feelings. State would continuously ensure the same through its varied endeavours and activities. The State would be eager to see that moral wakening of the people is possible and that spiritual longing can be transformed in their lives.

Kautilya has fixed up his endeavour for austere activity of state right at this point. Kautilya has recommended a king who is synonymous with the existence of the state, A king would develop himself such as he would be able to ensure the importance of the people in all his activities. This was the desire of Kautilya. That is why he has been earnest by engaged in purifying the character of the king and drawing ideal characters at every step. According to Kautilya, a king is not only to be set in the role of leadership to the people. The main significance of a king is in his service to the people. A king is to be a servant of the people; service to the people has been designed for him. Such as a king would use the administration of the state as an instrument for service.

Kautilya's Philosophy of State

In Kautilya's arrangement, the state is not the carrier for satisfying enjoyment of the people, it is also for attempting to discover and fulfill newer requirements of the people and at the same time it is also for uplifting their life. That is why Kautilya has said that the spiritual development of the king and the people should occur simultaneously. Along with spiritual development of the king, there should be spiritual development of the people also. The basic question of Kautilya is why should a state be there? What purpose would be served by the state? Would its role be complete if it is not helpful in the awakening of the individuals? Kautilya opines—No it would not be. The state would have to be the partner of the day-to-day life of the people, companion of warp and wool craving and satisfaction of daily life. At the same time the state would rise to be a field of adaptation of a complete life for an individual.

Kautilya, therefore, has made the state its jewel for the head, penal system, principle of government, rule of adaption, path of development of a state. All these rather smoothen the spiritual blooming of the state and its people. As such, just as immediate and periodical factors are important in duties of a state, so also future and distant future have gained prominence. The blooming of an individual is blending of insensate and spiritual blooming. Both these are required simultaneously. Insensate blooming would serve immediate purpose, while spiritual blooming would flourish the mental world of an individual. So, Kautilya has looked upon the state as a carrier of advancement and stability for the inner and other lives of the people.

For a king, Kautilya put forth the proposal of building up and purification of character. Side by side Kautilya has been advising the king to look after proper arrangement for administration of a state. That is, the king would be r welcoming all and at the same time everyone would come in the circle of his government. Side by side with the security of a state, Kautilya has judged with proper value the stability of the reign of the king.

Many scholars have misconceived the attempt of Kautilya to give stability to the king and called it an aggressive attitude. This is an unjust complaint. Kautilya particularly wanted stability for the king. Not only that, but he has also sought that a king would have recourse to diplomatic means of different sorts to have stability of his reign. For example, the king will always be on his guard against revolts or conspiracies. If he gets any scent of conspiracy, he would nip the same in the bud. If the neighboring state is aggressive in nature the king would keep a watchful sight on it, so that the neighboring state may not get an opportunity to strike against him. The king would have to be particularly careful, and he would have to be ever ready. The king would have to acquire the ability not only to defend against abuse but also to crush down any blow or attack that may befall.

Kautilya has this timed to give bonding of state a stable form. Many have complained that Kautilya in his proposal has laid excessive stress on secret service for a king to ascertain quelling of enemies and set up defense against the same. Kautilya has laid much importance to secret service. The complaint in one sense is true. In Kautilya's terminology, a king should have many eyes to see, many ears to hear. So, the way in which he has advised for collecting secret news may often be compared with the three-stage secret collection of news by KGB in Soviet Union. In the Soviet Union there was a three-stage detective arrangement for keeping a watch on a probable rebel. The significance of Kautilya's principle of detective service is quite different. He liked to provide enough time to a king for administration of his state. If the king finds enough time, he would be able to build up a system fit for the development of the state in accordance with his own opinion and feelings. As a consequence of this the development of the state would be complete. The king also would get a chance for rectification of his faults. Kautilya therefore has urged for the state leadership to be always alert. According to him, as there are enemies of the state outside so also, they are within. If there is unification between the external enemy with the internal, it becomes rather dangerous for a state. So, the king should always be on his guard against such unification. Collecting all news is not only in the interest of the king but in the interest of the whole state. In order to keep a state free from any probable danger, the king must keep the arrangement of collecting secret news rather than fighting.

One more thing that Kautilya especially wanted for the welfare of the state is religious and spiritual practice by the king and his people. Kautilya has designated Vedic knowledge and practice as the primary duty. This means blossoming of the spiritual sense of an individual through Vedic knowledge and practice. This will cause an awakening of spiritual power in an individual and ensure liberty of the inner self of an individual does happen. Kautilya has placed the austere services of the state for attaining liberation of both the state and the people.

Function of a State

> "Avidyah atinayah purusa byasan hetuh
> Abinitau hi byasanah dosan na pasyati"
>
> (*Arthashastra* 8/3/1–2)

[Destructive mentality comes from lack of knowledge and modesty. Immodest man does not find fault with man going against the state]

> "Kaupajah tribangah kamajah catur-bargah
> Tayuh kopau gartan
> Sasbatra hi kopah carati.
> Prayasah ca kopabasa rajanah Prakrtikupah arhatah srayante,
> kamabasah ksaya nimittam arih byadhibhiriti"
> (*Arthashastra* 8/3/4–7)

[Rage transfuses three types of vices, lust four types of vices. Of this more serious in rage, because it has unrestricted movement. By the influence of rage, a king can invite natural fury. Yielding to lust causes erosion of power and by this a king is fiend by simultaneous attack of enemy and disease.

> "Asatam pragrah kamah aaupah ca
> A babrah satam.
> Byasabam dosabahu lyat atyantam
> ubhayam matam
> Tasmat kopam ca kamam ca byasanah
> Arambham atmatam
> Parityajena mulaharam brdhasebi
> Jitendriyah" (*Arthashastra* 8/3/65–66)

[A lustful man gives indulgence to the dishonest and a wrathful person reproaches honest person. Both possess many vices and so both are to be avoided. He who has been self-conscious, shuns rage and lust and uproots the vices and places the aged person on respectful position and became continent.]

In case of administration of a state, Kautilya has laid greatest importance on the human resource. As a consequence of this development of state also. A state can be directed towards supporting the desire of the people, on being carried away by the movement of the bell weather of guiding the people in the desired path. Kautilya has called for avoiding filthy character and filthy feelings in the state. Of the two, the leader of rage and lust is very injurious. They bring in filthy of different types and measures. According to Kautilya, rage and lust brings illness in an individual, destroys the ability to judge between good and evil. If there is no real wisdom, an arrogant attitude comes in. Such an attitude is especially harmful. An individual must remain very cautious so that any arrogant attitude might not cast harmful effect for the state and its people. Such family aspect as might lead a state to purification must be avoided very carefully.

Biological urge and rage get the influenced person devoid of any competence to do good things. He just augments the destructive power of the state. An individual blind in rage completely losses his sense. In him rises an infatuating effect which gets a special infatuation even on his power and influence. Effectually his attitude becomes obstinate and one-sided. As a consequence, the sense of judgement gets lost. The ability to sense which is honest and which dishonest disappears. The judgement as to which deeds would weaken up the power congenial to the state, which would develop good advent in men disappears completely. At that moment, he relies on the subject of his rage and nothing else. Consequently, all the endeavours under the spell of rage become rather oppositely effective. The individual concerned bring about his own downfall and at the same time open the path of the calamity for his state too.

Loss of power is the inevitable result of sexual urge. A lustful person is quite unfit for administration. If a lustful person is entrusted with administration of a state, many social diseases appear within the state. The state gradually becomes weak consequently both the sovereignty and security get impeded. A lustful person also becomes powerless and so becomes quite unable to defend against foreign invasion and attack of diseases. The state gets deviated from its ideal and desire and gets turned to a path of bad taste and bad measures. Lust and rage lead an individual to a path of utter destruction.

"Bak parusyam artha dusanam dandaparu
Syam iti" (*Arthashastra*, 8/3/23)

"Iti kopajah arih tribargah" (*Arthashastra*, 8/36/37)

"Kamajah tu mrgayah dutah striyam Panam
Iti caturbar gah" (*Arthashastra* 8/3/38)

"Saprtyadeyam jyutam nisprat yadeyam Stribyasanam.
Adarsanah karyanirbedah kalati Patanat anarthah
Dharmatopah ca tantradaurbalyam
Panah anubandhah caiti"
(*Arthashastra*, 8/3/53–54)

[Speech and sound pollution, wealth pollution and physical pollution these three types of pollution are generated from rage. From rage these three enemies are formed. Vices come out of sexual urge is of four types hunting, gambling, attachment to woman and addiction to wine. Detachment from gambling may even be possible but detachment from woman is not at all possible. Attachment to women generates other vices, viz. apathy to work, unjustified act of passing time, ruin of religion, deviation from possibilities of worldly reputation and development and addiction to wine and other inebriants.]

"Drabyanasat satrubedanam gariyay."

(*Arthashastra* 8/3/18)

"Drabyanasah kosabodhakah
Satru bedanam pranabadhakam iti." (*Arthashastra* 8/3/19)
"Anarthya samyagat duhkha samyogo Gariyan.
Anarthya samyogo muhurta partikari
Dipgha klesakari duhkha namasanga iti
Tasmat kopo gariyan" (*Arthashastra* 8/3/20—22)

(Creation enmity is a greater problem the loss of articles. Loss of articles causes loss of money, but creation of enmity brings in situation for loss of life. The problem arising due to loss of lives is a far greater problem than loss of money and articles. Being in the grip of rage is a problem causing loss of money and being in grief becomes long-lasting and rather a companion throughout life.]

Kautilya has laid much stress on the problem related to rage and lust. Affiliation of rage and lust is enemy not only of the inner life of a man but also of his external life. These vices create trouble in the respective circles of individual. The restraint of these vices is essential for the administration of state also. Inner scarification is news for tracking these problems. That is why Kautilya has spoken of inner scarification of all.

Liberation of State

One would not have bothered about the effect of these vices, if only defense and sovereignty would have been necessary for flourishing of a state. Even being aware of the outer area and extent of the total state and basic importance has not been laid by Kautilya's state system on these. Kautilya's state system has given due importance to the context of defense but at the same time has laid importance toward the inner and outer lives of individuals. Inner and outer lives of individuals take a combined shape in the state. State is just the reflection of the combined lifestyle of individuals. Combined desire and endeavours for people build up a state.

That is why Kautilya has stressed more on external structure than on the inner structure of people of the state. Now here in any political union such attempt for building up of character and purification of the same is met with. Generally, a state becomes eager to pay attention to its needs and on its desires as well. Kautilya has pictured an ideal form of a state. This ideal form comprises building up of external infrastructure, observing duties and waking of inner consciousness.

State consciousness is combined consciousness, the combined form of integrated consciousness of the people. Consciousness of the state wakes up at the glow of consciousness of the people. As also in case of men, incitement of consciousness is required for transparent and sinless character which clears up the flow of the power of consciousness, so also, in the case of a state. To release the power of consciousness of a state, a boundless and open environment is required, where the state becomes a suitable field for austere practice of consciousness. Austere practice of consciousness happens in an individual no doubt, but the state makes the field ready for getting it flourished.

There is liberation of fatuous feelings and consciousness. In the liberation of materialism, materialism includes the necessity of a state for flourishing accomplishment. This involves knowing and understanding the whirlpool of needs, where the state rests and acting accordingly. The consequences thereof is to reach a minimum stage devoid of hunger, poverty and discrimination. This results in fulfilment of inherent desire of men—to fulfill the mind to a higher stage.

Along with the liberation from insensate feelings comes the blooming of consciousness. Liberation from insensate feeling and blooming of consciousness are intimately connected. Such liberation paves the way for spread of consciousness. Blooming of consciousness is possible at the background of liberation from the insensate. Kautilya has wanted a balanced and equilibrated state-system with economic development.

That is why aspirations of a state are not only limited to flourishing defense, sovereignty and power, it wants mental waking and liberation for all the people. Liberation of consciousness can make the waking of the state certain and firm. On the basis of this will an ideal state system be built up.

13

Sovereignty of a State: Kautilya's Instruction

Aspects of sovereignty and security of a state have been vividly discussed in Kautilya's *Arthashastra*. The *Arthashastra* discusses all the subjects under the preview of the state from different points, which includes a proper economic arrangement and infrastructure of a state. Besides, *Arthashastra* has vividly discussed the context of leadership and the contexts preserving the security and sovereignty of a state. To discuss these contexts, the *Arthashastra* has introduced a number of new subjects like foreign policy, facing inner and outer enemies, spying agency rules for punishment and correct judgement and the principle of introduction of a sequential system in the leadership of a country.

In the context of economic security, Kautilya has cast his look upon the people. In order to find economic ability among the people, he has laid much importance on three points. These are agriculture, livestock farming and industry. A stable social bounding is required for agriculture. Agriculture is not possible without the support of a stable social collectivity. Therefore, for agricultural bonding in society, communication and collection of power and wealth in the state's interest are to be thought of. Kautilya has urged the state to be attentive to acquire the support of these endeavours of society. To think of the stability of the state, feelings are to be rooted up to a greater depth.

Agriculture needs long termed thoughtful investment of money and desire or demand of the market in conjunction with productive ability. Unless the agricultural products are accepted in the market, there will be a shortage in agricultural production. Preparation of the field is the first step of the agricultural process. After proper cultivation of the field, seeds are sown. These seeds would grow into crops as long as there is no lack of fertility. If the land's fertility remains intact or is increased, crops grow in conformity with the nature of the seeds. As crops take time to grow, agricultural production is a time-consuming process.

Judgement, in accordance with time, is required for building up a social system fit for agriculture. The measures suitable for agriculture are to be judged by the standard of time. All are to be made prepared for patience, abandonment labour and attachment demanded by produce through agriculture. Agriculture has its own movement, and it proceeds rather slowly. Slow but promise-bound, these are the truths of agriculture. Sometimes, agriculture is thought to be all-enduring, as it has to move enduring everything. The produce generated by agriculture is associated with nature in many ways—it increases by the influence of climate and rainfall sufficient for farming. In an opposite circumstance, agricultural produce can get upset. A society worthy of agriculture must build up cooperation. The usual mode of cultivation is to be maintained even at times of both drought and excessive rainfall. For this reason, a cooperative federation of families is required to build a society worthy of agriculture. A mutually cooperative relationship is also to be built among families. Only then will it be possible to realise the full essence of agriculture.

Thus, mutual agriculture requires a bonding between family and society, much like how livestock farming requires some arrangement framed out of an assemblage, giving rise to mutual cooperation. A compassionate heart is required for livestock farming. But for compassion and sympathy for herds, livestock farming becomes merely a trading endeavour. Kautilya has stressed on building up the character of the people. He has emphasised the study and practice of the people before they enter the economic system. Kautilya's firm effect is that the study and practice of the Vedas will lead to the purification of the guilt of people's character. Spiritual practice kindles nutritious jumps of the hearts. A possessor of noble character would grow up learning from millions of individuals. Such a person will be the storehouse of all good qualities. Kautilya prefers to see such people placed at the helms of the administration of a state of society. He wants honest and good chartered individuals at the front of both agricultural and livestock farming fields. As a result, a suitable background for economic development would be framed.

The excellence of agriculture and livestock farming can be accomplished by cooperative, associating, diligent, enduring, modest and largehearted people. Only he who has a mind filled with responsibility, compassion and love can understand the truth of smile and leans of the heads. Neither agriculture nor livestock farming is the job of a single individual. Different types of people are required for preparing agricultural land, irrigation, sowing seeds, reaping and marketing the harvest. Cooperation and association of many people of different types would harvest the action and endeavour in agriculture. In livestock farming, too, the combined efforts of many people are essential, especially if it is to be promoted to the state of a big industry. This calls for the importance of cooperative and associative people.

Economic Development

Agriculture and livestock farming constitutes the first phase, and industry grows up based on the same. At the time of Kautilya, cottage was the only industry. The main provision of individuals growing up in the present industrial civilisation has come from agriculture. What form the industry would take depends on the condition of the agricultural sector. Industrial development does arise as an extension of agriculture. One of the main conditions for the extension of the college industry lies in the arrangement for marketing the products. Neither stability nor expansion of the cottage industry is possible if a favourable market does not exist. Additionally, one of the conditions for creating such a market is support. There is no question of this support when there is no industry. Support from consumers is needed for the cottage industry to complete machine-made articles.

In modern India, arrangement for support for this government has been introduced for cottage industries. A great example is the provision of subsidies in different phases of production and distribution. As a result, products of cottage industries can occupy the market, even competing with machine-made products. There are, of course, some fields where products of the cottage industry cost less than the machine-made ones, such as machine parts of electronics and computer industries. Able workers, artisans and technologists can manufacture these at low cost and sell them in the market at a low price. Here ostentatious expenses of the top-heavy system of big industries are not to be managed. Consequently, products of cottage industries become much less costly than products of high technology of big industries.

Agriculture, livestock griming and cottage industries gradually contributed to the gain of the society, became associating with these professions. If the buyers at large, producers and people, in general, come forward to support this profession, it is to be ascertained that power is being gained. Similarly, if agriculture, livestock farming and cottage industries gain power, economic development of the society also becomes possible. Economic development provides happiness and fields for happiness.

Practice of Power

Kautilya says power is needed, waking of strength is required:

Saktih siddhih ca Balam saktih Sukham
Siddhih

(*Arthashastra*, 6/2/30-32)

[Both strength and attainment are required. Power signifies strength; happiness signifies attainment.]

Saktih tribidha jnanabalam mantrasaktih,
Kausadandabalam prabhu saktih
Bikramabalam utsahasaktuih

(*Arthashastra*, 6/2/33)

[Strength is of three types: the strength of mantra, originating from people's power, the strength of dominance, originating from economic power and the strength of inspiration, originated from physical power]

Ebam siddhih tribidhaiba mantrasakti
Sadhya mantrasiddhih prabhusakti sadhya
Prabhu siddhih utsahasakti sci dhyah
Utsahasiddhih (*Arthashastra*, 6/2/34)
Tabhih abhyucitau jyahar bhabati
Apacitau-hinah, tulyasaktih samah. (*Arthashastra*, 6/2/35)

Tasmat saktim siddhim ca ghatet atmana
Abesayitum,
Sadharanau ba drabyaprakrti svanu
Antayerna saucabasena ba

(*Arthashastra*, 6/2/36)

Dusyamitrabhyam bat papakrastu yal etah

(*Arthashastra*, 6/2/37)

[Attainment is of three types. Attainment of mantra is the result of practice of strength of mantra, attainment of dominance is the result of the strength of dominance, attainment of inspiration of the result of the strength of inspiration. The more would be the practice of such strength the more would be the procurement of such strength; without any practice, void of strength would result; and if the practice is equal, procurement also would be equal. The practice of strength would take up attainment. The practice of strength should always be inside and outside, and the consequence would be right on all things. Along with the practice of strength, there should be an attempt to create a distance for evil powers.]

Kautilya's *Arthashastra* has stressed on power attainment. From strength and attainment rise up power and happiness. Power and happiness are due solely to wandering and extension of the world. They are required specially for the establishment in this world. Kautilya has laid stress on power, strength, happiness and attainment and said that they are required for all. Not only for a king of leaders but these are required for all. Also, for the people, power, strength, happiness and attainment is required. To create a background for economic awakening, strength and attainment for many people is to be practiced. This practice of collective strength and attainment can get economic liberty to a country.

Kautilya has spoken of three types of power. There is power of knowledge, power of money and physical power. Power of knowledge is essential for a king and the people as well. A king should be knowledgeable. If the king is not enriched with knowledge, danger is inevitable for his country. To be enriched with knowledge is essential for state leadership. Competency of state leadership comes from three types of knowledge. These are knowledge of the past, present and future. Knowledge of the past can find out the right path for state leadership, which can ascertain what is to be done at particular circumstances.

Knowledge of the past, too, is necessary for the people. People can ascertain which incidents yield what results. It is the un text of receiving instruction from the annuals of history. On the annals are within the past incidents and the causer and effect power behind every mentionable one. If the circumstances under which a particular decision has been taken can be realised, a thorough review of the results becomes rather easier. As a result, the enterpriser may be careful in the event of initiating one such attempt, which may even bring in the modification theory. For example, in the case of framing and applying the economic policy, the consequence of promulgation of kinder one on previous occasions in different places may be easily ascertained. As this matter is applicable to country and society, a case of a family judgement in the past may lead the facility towards future paths.

Knowledge of the past is helpful, but so is that of the present and future. Unless there is no delayed knowledge of happiness at different corners at present, it is not possible for an individual to frame the right plans. Detailed knowledge of the happenings of different places at present is essential for maintaining the security and sovereignty of a state. It is essential to know the deployment of arms and ammunition, forces and steps taken by the neighbours. Enough deep knowledge of the happenings on the inside and outside is required for securing territory integrity and sovereignty of a state.

Acquiring knowledge not only of the past and present but also of the future is necessary. How the future days would be shaped is to be known. Similarly, how the future would be framed further depends on clean ideas. Greater opportunities for future success would appear before those who have a better comprehensive understanding of the future. Especially for the economic development of a country, thinking about the future is necessary. One should know what the demand and supply in a future market will be.

No step can be taken in a market unless a clear idea of demand and supply grows. First, a clear idea of the market available for the product of a factory or how these would be sold is required; then and only then the investment in that factory would be effective. For investment in marketing, the possibility of marketing these products is needed. On the way of marketing, there exist knots of many important matters, for example, how much of the goods would be produced, how would the standard of their quality be and what would be the cost. The quantity of produce would be judged by the total demand of the market and the total supply at present. If the product is presently available in the market, then the total production and demand should be judged. Moreover, what would be the measure of the increase in this respect should also be judged. From these, a clear idea of the new factory would materialise.

To have an account of the future, one has to ascertain the nature of the future market. For example, what would the normal nature of the market be, and what would happen if the market is booming or slumped? Here, the reasons for the market to be booming or slumping should have to be carefully asserted. The principle is caked probability. Applying the principle of the probability of the most acceptable number shall have to be brought in this account of production and sale. If it is found that this account of produce and sale brings profit to the working of a factory, only then investment in that factory becomes profitable; otherwise, it does not.

Awakening of People's Power

Just as an individual becomes crippled without the power of knowledge, a state also becomes incapable and static. Next, after the power of knowledge comes economic power. As the proverb runs, money brings money. Without economic power, a state becomes weak and parasitic. In this case, the state loses its very desire to survive. It is not that with monetary power, it would be possible to frame up an economic infrastructure—but it is true that without monetary power, a state becomes dependent on others.

All that comes out in judging the wealth of a state can be measured in terms of monetary value, an example of which is natural wealth. Natural wealth comprises land, water, forest, mineral, human resources and so forth. All of these are to be consider while judging the economic wealth of a state. Moreover, the state shall have to calculate the amount of money made ready to be circulated in the market. The valuation of any resource is considered in the standpoint of its utility, such as mineral resource. What is to be done with wealth confined within mines is to be learnt. Moreover, it is also to be learnt how can that mineral resource be prepared for utilisation. As a result, a notion would be created on its market value. Thus, the value of mineral wealth is ascertained.

To build up economic power, on one side, the power of knowledge is required and physical power on the other. The march begins with the ability to think and take a vow, from which devices comes out gradually.

For the economic development of the state, the ability to think and taking a vow is required. If such abilities are there, one is to think that man likes to do something. The strong force of thinking then supplies the working force and brings in results. It is true for an individual and a state as well. Just as an enterprising individual blooms up, the enterprising state also multiplies its growth. A collection of enterprising people opens the door for the blooming of a state, which cannot grow without any enterprise. If many people, or rather all enterprising people, gain interest in the running of a state, economic advancements will be possible. The state here either unifies the enterprises or extends its hands of zeal, inspiration and cooperation. Just as an individual or a family prospers at the background of an individual enterprise, the state also develops at the background of the enterprise of state leadership.

Economic development assures the sovereignty of the state. If a state cannot provide food to eat, clothes to wear and shelter to rest for the people, it fails in its duty. The state is to be active in founding its fundamental right. Its basic responsibility is to make arrangements for food, clothes and shelter for all. If a state fails to fulfil its basic responsibilities, it loses its fundamental right to exist.

The economic power of a state is not judged by accumulated treasures only. If such satiation arises as there is some money in the treasury, but people have to starve, this economic development of a state cannot be said to have been achieved. Economic power is to be spread. In the proposition of Kautilya, the power of knowledge, money and capability are applicable to all. In the same way, these are essential for the leadership of a state. Kautilya wanted everyone to be economically powerful. As the dominance of strong people in the case of the power of knowledge, money and capability increases, so does the development of the state.

Demand for Sovereignty

This world is a field of strength. Everybody salutes a strong man. If a strong man speaks of peace and amity, all pay heed to it. The say of peace and amity on the part of a weak person is often taken to be a way to save himself.. That is why strength and velour cannot much on this world. Incapable and weak people draw compassion from all, but they can never demand respect from anybody whosoever. Once weakness disperses, a feeling of respect and reverence comes in. As the spread of economic power is helpful for maintaining sovereignty in case of internal administration of a state, being strong is also required for external security. Power of capability would supply the strength of defence. That is why it is urgently necessary to keep one's eye on all the matters concerned with defence of a country.

A state is to gain strength from the power of its people. Strong and valorous people make the state strong. If every man possesses strength and valour, the state thereby benefits greatly. The state becomes a welfare one bestowing happiness. Pleasure and happiness are required for the whole of the state and, at the same time, for its people too.

Yadi ba pasyet amitrau me saktiyuktaqu
Bakdanda parusya arthadusani h prakrti
Rupah nisyati
Suddhiyuktau ba mrgayah dyuta madah
Stribhih
Prasadam gamisyati sah birakta prakrti
Rupaksinah
Pramantau ba sadhyau me bhabisyati.

(*Arthashastra*, 6/2/38)

[If enemy be strong, it becomes necessary to keep a watch on him. There may be attacks with speech, attack from economic front and even physical attack. On the other hand, at the time of happiness, all addictions get augmented. For example, addiction to liquor, addiction to gambling and attachment to woman. As a result, enemy occupies the greater field and takes away happiness.]

As in the case of an individual, so also for a state; unless one becomes a storehouse of strength, one does not reveal the measure of capability. Strength has perturbation. A resource of strength becomes dynamic and creative, and when there is a lack of strength, there may be an attack by others. Just as how with tardiness of the life force, one may face an attack of diseases. First comes the onslaught of diseases in the form of tiny organisms such as viruses, bacteria and so forth. Next, gradually comes bigger bacilli, which are visible to the naked eye. Parasites and worms fall upon corpses and thrive in decay. Similar is the case of a state. The sovereignty of a state is amenable to strengths; even if a weak state speaks highly or utters big words, nobody pays any heed to them. However, mild advice of a strong state counts much more. Kautilya wanted to exercise and inauguration of strength in the house. Exercise of strength is quite unavoidable to the state and its people as well. Strength is indispensable for worldly development, and without development, sovereignty is quite unthought of. For the sovereignty of a state, the development of the people inside is essential. Likewise, a suitable arrangement for the defence of the country is also required.

Kautilya has drawn attention to the two points of the defence system—political and military. Kautilya wants the state to be equipped with friendly powers using political arrangements, which means that a state first locates its friendly and enemy states. Next, it would take steps to crush down the enemies from all directions, utilizing its own power and that of the friendly states. With continuous pressure, the enemy would always remain on their toes. Another side of this aspect has been mentioned, which is its economic strength. By the influence of the state's economic power, enemies may constantly be kept under economic stress.

Another side of the political solution is the extension of diplomacy. Kautilya wanted to increase political friendship and control enmity through the extension of diplomacy. Such pressure can be exerted on an enemy state through diplomacy, which confuses them. Besides, Kautilya has also spoken vividly of the detective agency and its skillfulness. Military power is to be built up of political and diplomatic skillfulness on one side and detective experience on the other. Then and only then, sovereignty would be properly protected.

Kautilya wanted to harness all the powers within the state helpful to it and to increase resources of knowledge, money and capability of all. By the combined influence of these three elements, there would be a mass rising. If people of the lowest level of society, the poor helpless and miserable people, can be filled with their own power and energy in search of happiness in life, the sovereignty of the state would be properly preserved.

14

People's State: Economic System of the Masses

The first speciality of a people's state refers to a state system formed by the people. This state system is directed right to the people, which means that a people's state is by the people and for the people. The main theme of a people's state is to give priority to the interest of the public, and similarly, it finds out the real problem of the public. People's state brings to the public a big promise. Again, the call of the state is towards the joviality of the public—it marches towards their fulfilment. A people's state can rise to be enterprising for the fulfilment of the desire of the minds of the people. A true people's state can bring people's liberation.

Kautilya's *Arthashastra* has not directly dealt with people's state or people's economy. The way in which these proposals have come in the *Arthashastra* apparently shows that people's state and economy are quite far off topic. Even the word 'people' has not been used in Kautilya's *Arthashastra*. But still in the *Arthashastra*, the proposals are such that when designed will frame the concept of people's state and people's economy. The *Arthashastra* looked upon it from different corners.

The case of a king has been discussed in detail. In this context, inheritance, character, quantities, his protection, extension of the sphere of his influence, failure of interest and more have been discussed. In every case, the direction of the kings' activities has been aimed at the people. That is, all the kings will do will be aimed at the people. Kautilya's proposition, while centered on the king, is actually people oriented. The subject of the rise of the people's state has been thought of in two ways—building up of people's organisation at the lowest level after taking decision from the above and building it up after taking collective opinion at the lowest level. A people's state is under the pledge of confirming the responsibilities of total judgement and total power over the people.

Plans of a people's state can be taken from the level of the leadership, or by the spontaneous demand of the people or it may even be proposed from spontaneity. Whatever may be the nature of a people's state, it shall be extended up to the grass root level. If the authority of the state is extended to every corner of society and, if in their own way, every person can apply the authority of the state, it is to be realised that a people's state has been established. A people's state not only delivers offerings of all kinds to the people but also makes people initiate actions for the state. In other words, demands of a people's state include receiving and, at the same time giving too.

A people's state becomes engaged for all and, at the same time, it moves to all with the demands of a complete sacrifice. The state demands capability, that is, a people's state likes to have a background of support, cooperation and sacrifice in accordance with the respective capability for all. Thus, for founding a people's state, such mental preparation is required, where people would have to be prepared to offer extreme cooperation and sacrifice individually.

Basics of People's Economic System

For the foundation of a people's state, there should be clarity on the basics of abandonment and simple and common cooperation. The same condition applies to the basics of people's economic system. People's economic system aims at carrying the benefit of economic richness and economic arrangements for all. Different types of endeavours should be undertaken by the public. There should also be provisions for the livelihood of individuals. But there should be a halt to the minimum provision of livelihood; rather, the continuous march towards established economic status in life is required. As a result, the standard of living has improved. After crossing the minimum level of requirement, gradually, man becomes desirous for an improved standard of living. Consequently, the market of commodities becomes people oriented. Demand for commodities increases, and the market for commodities gets extended. Commodities spread in the market in different forms.

In the people's economic system, the approach of the commodities is to be directed to the masses; that is, for many people, the production and distribution systems are designed. Association, cooperation, and active participation of all are inevitable in the economic system. In people's economic system, the benefits of the system are to be carried to all people. The main object of this system is to establish economic power for all. Thus, necessary buying capacity will come to all people. As a result, the economic ability will be extended everywhere—necessary factors for the act of living of men will come under their control, including the unimpeded right of men to food, clothing, housing, education, health and thinking. There should not be any discrimination of poverty and inequality in a people's economic system. This system will find out poverty, ascertain where the root of poverty lies, and how poverty extends itself, gradually making the preparation for the eradication of poverty effective. A mode so efficient will be extended that poverty is eradicated to the root. Poverty, along will the causes of its origin, will be eradicated completely.

With poverty stay the accompanying problems. Without the provision of adequate funds, the right to education and the right to health does not come. A child of a poor family is to become capable of learning by offering physical labour. He has to first learn things that will get him some earning by dint of his child-like capabilities. Meeting this instant necessity becomes so important for the child that thinking about the future becomes rather irreverent.

The future of a child is eager to sell labour in childhood. Building up a better foundation for life becomes quite beyond the range of his capabilities. Therefore, firstly, the provisions he consumes come from his own daily wage. After that, it is not possible for the earnings to be invested in education from an educational institution. Secondly, even if education is free of cost, it is not possible to study because his income would be affected if he spends the time devoted to education. There is a quest for income, and at the same time, the sphere of work also gets extended. Thus, the child manes far away from education. Since the future foundation of his life has not built up, the ability to struggle in life becomes weak.

As the education of a child inflicted with poverty remains far off, so is his health. In this venture, beginning right from childhood to earning a livelihood by selling his labour, the child becomes quite fatigued. He becomes a victim of malnutrition and other infectious diseases. Besides, these children are occupied by weak sightedness, shortage of hearing, different types of incapability and indisposition. The structure of their mind also remains incomplete for getting the society's care required for a child despite being a child themselves. There is no blooming of the mind, which stays far behind. Why talk about the balanced development of the mind when even the basic mental faculties cannot grow up? Such a child engaged in labour can never be a perfect connoisseur of beauty and flavour of life. Continuously facing rough and rude treatment from society, the attitudes of such children towards the world also become rough and rude. Feelings of compassion, love and sympathy are lost, and many fine sentiments of life are devoured by poverty. Many other social problems also arise out of poverty. Just as children, their health deteriorates by the influence of poverty, creating an unhealthy flow of life for poverty-stricken individuals. It is not possible on their part to select food in consideration of health. Thus, the problem of poverty here becomes a control problem stemming from the lack of education, nutrition, health and many other social diseases.

Modern Endeavours for Eradication of Poverty

Though the matter of eradication of poverty has been taken up by many organisations, governments and individuals, the problem has effectively remained unsolved. The nature of poverty has remained unchanged. Poverty has expressed itself in many forms in many countries. Generally, 'poverty-stricken' is the term which is used if minimum purchasing capacity is judged on the basis of foods habits and common likings of different countries. Almost all countries have their own judgement of poverty level. The background of this judgement of poverty level is roughly the same. Food habits, tastes, minimum requirement of goods in case of individuals are pointed out, the market value of each is ascertained and then the poverty level is marked.

When the poverty level of the background of land and time is ascertained, it is then dependent on cultural judgement and cultural character of the people. Accounts of food, clothing and housing is applied on the daily purchasing capacity. The level when food, clothing and housing come within reach is designated as poverty level.

The World Bank has assessed the international measure of poverty level in two ways. It has set its target to remove poverty in the short and long terms. Short term means instant and long term has an extended sense attached to it. In the short-term measures, judgment has been on the basis of present valuation. On the other hand, long-term evaluation is on the basis of the future value of money. World Bank's through analysis has found that whose daily purchasing capacity is one American dollar generally becomes eager to be relieved of poverty and get permanent rid of poverty.

In the global study continued by the World Bank for some past years, two standards have been fixed for assessing poverty. The first one is the number and percentage of people with a purchasing capacity of one American dollar per day. The second one considers the right to have purchasing capacity of two dollars daily. Poverty is being assessed in two stages. The larger goal is fixed on the complete eradication of poverty. But there are norms, problems and questions on the way of achieving this. The world has accepted a basic principle to consider these problems and questions—proper unison of unity in a state and cultural liberty. As a result, a proper judgement of the different aspects of cultural freedom will be there, as well as the proper solution to the question.

The World Bank gives proper respect to the worldwide movement of going to the roots. In almost all cases, such movements have turned aggressive. In many cases, some admixture has erupted into such movements. Thus, these movements of going to the roots have turned separatist. Such a movement is trying to create small states with a state. Occasionally, there is support from big powers behind such attempts.

There are some common factors in the movement for going with roots. The main factors are:

(1) Speciality of identity of the group.

(2) Protest against financial exploitation and introduction of a particular monetary system.

(3) Cultural liberty and dignity.

(4) Proper recognition of political rights.

Speciality of identity of groups is assessed in terms of their past and present conditions. Groups with generally bright past demand future security and solvency. Different types of grievances grow when there is shortage of security and solvency. These grievances continue until special honour as a practical group is granted. These movements for moving with roots often turn into political and other movements. The direction of these movements often gets changed. The demand of recognition of the speciality of the group takes this form of separation.

Such endeavour for founding liberation of the people gradually takes a separatist and aggressive form. Demand for economic liberation now becomes important to people. Whatever may be the outline of the people's movement or some aggressive movements, economic exploitation, economic injustice and demand for liberation from these become more important. In such cases, even terrorist movements get people's support. Consequently, the terrorist and separatist movements get the claim of the liberation movement.

Behind any movement of economic liberty always remains a demand for cultural freedom. The point of freedom and dignity in people's own culture becomes important. People become united at the question of cultural freedom and culture. As movements for economic and political demands of the people become indicative of external things, they also indicate internal affairs. The demand for cultural liberation is also a demand mainly for acceptance of the speciality of the existence of the people. The movements turn into demands for freedom of cultural activities of the people and for presenting cultural rights.

Different types of grievances prevailing in the people gradually turn into political movements and demands for political freedom. In the ring of the influence created through participation of the people in the struggle for political freedom, economic demands, cultural demands and the demand for dignity remain mingled up. The collective face of expression of these turn into political demands. As a result, political demand not only becomes dominant but behind these also comes power. As a consequence of people's support and cooperation, these political demands become rather intense. Sometimes this political struggle goes on trough, sowing firm faith in democracy and sometimes it becomes aggressive, fighting and armed. Sometimes it becomes democratised and armed at the same time. Collecting documents on these propensities, the World Bank has conclude that cultural freedom is a necessary condition of economic development. Economic cooperation comes along the path of cultural freedom. On greeting united cooperation, economic system gains motion and economic awakening is hastened.

The 2004 human development report has attributed central importance to cultural freedom. In the preface of this report, it has been said that cultural freedom is of utmost importance for human development. Freedom of culture awakens conscience in man. He becomes able to express his identity proudly with respect to religion and language. As a result, the inspiration of social accountability arises in a group of people. The World Bank thinks that because of cultural freedom, feelings of cooperation and sympathy would flash among the people. The economic endeavour would be condensed and spontaneous.

The World Bank has been designing plans depending on and with faith in some factors. The aim of this is to strike against common belief. The common beliefs the World Bank has disregarded are:

(1) A deeply conflicting relation exists between special identity and characteristics of the groups of people with their identity in respect of the state.

(2) There is conflict in the groups of people among themselves on the basis of mutual tradition and values. There exists a relationship of conflict with regard to mutual dignity and long-term endeavour for a place among groups in a country of varied groups. One is to be achieved at the cost of the other.

(3) Cultural freedom is intimately connected with heritage and tradition. In other words, cultural freedom is to be achieved on the basis of heritage and tradition. It is the road to economic freedom.

(4) Economic growth is slow in multicultural countries, or these are economically developed.

(5) There are some cultures which have the ability to march forward more rapidly in respect of economic status in comparison to others.

The World Bank has given opinion against these beliefs, as stated in the foreword of human development report of 2004.

(*Human Development Report 2004*, Oxford University Press, p. 6)

Something more than health education, balanced act of living and political right is required for the advancement of man. Cultural freedom of man fills up this gap. Every state should give dignity to its people's cultural freedom and to accord befitting approval. Men should be given the opportunity of enjoying their cultural freedom irrespective of other things. In short cultural freedom is a human right with which economic development is intimately connected. That is why the responsibility of the state is to make good arrangement for cultural freedom of the people, as a result of which economic advancement gets hastened. Meanwhile, the World Bank has stressed on the standard of education, health and act of living. Recently, they have admitted that amelioration brings change in the act of living. If men get the freedom of their minds and get cultural freedom change in education and health can be affected.

By cultural freedom, the World Bank has specially aimed at men's rights speech express, behaviour, dealings and observance of social rules and norms. When these rights are established self-reliance and feeling of unity grow in men. In such cases, one feels that the attempt to improve one's own economic status is right, as the attempt of economic advancement of the country; that is, a feeling of harmony grows up. This is called cooperation in the economic system.

This context of cooperation in the economic system is an important depiction of the *Arthashastra* of Kautilya. Kautilya, on the basis of economic arrangement, wanted the development of characters of the leadership and people. For both the leadership and people, Kautilya has prescribed the spiritual development of every man on the basis of Vedic learning and practice. The basic idea of the development of character means formation of a godly atmosphere and the development of mind in that godly atmosphere, which flourishes godly qualities in man. The more these qualities flourish, the more the visions that move many. This shift of vision for one-to-many men practice of not 'I' but 'You' is the very attitude of an individual who comes to think of others' welfare and to act for others' welfare. This is loosely the exercise of an individual. In this role, a man will be the possessor of the divine mind and a heart of happy sources will not only remain continued with the development of the standard of his own living, but he would long for the upliftment of the standard of others' living as well. He would desire education, health and cultural freedom for all.

Keeping in view the cultural freedom of the groups of people, the right thinking and decision-making of all worlds has to be looked upon as a step toward economic progress. The most recent review from the World Bank has paid dignity to the cultural freedom of men. But there is no proposal of any fundamental change for man in it.

On the other hand, the proposal put forth by Kautilya has a possibility of a forward march in it. Kautilya has come forward with a proposal for change. He is eager to stop the possibility of any low taste and mean possibility in man. Kautilya's call is for elegant culture. No one else has yet cast a glance at the taste and at the character. What Kautilya has tried to strengthen is the culture of elegant and charactered people. The meaning attributed to cultural freedom in the proposals of Kautilya is the findings of the basic identity of creations, and that basic identity is the recognition of divine entity.

Actually, the godly self is moving along life's path in the form of creations. This culture is marching forward. This creature is gradually being troubled by the heavy burden of culture. Culture can be the carrier and bearer of loving propensities, and so it can also be of higher propensities. Kautilya has preached in favour of Vedic learning and Vedic practice and attainment of the power of character. As a result of this, high propensity would rise in man. Culture will be awakened.

On the other hand, in cultural freedom, the World Bank has just begun to think that there is no scope of judging the qualities of a culture at all. Perhaps this fact will come to their notice after a few decades.

The more intense would be the waking of divine culture through freedom of culture, the steadier would be the cooperation. A new term in economics is cooperation. Thus, the more intense and extended the cooperation, the wider would be the road to the liberation of the people. Provision for food, clothes and housing for all people as well as the opportunity for education, health and more improved balanced living for all, would be created. A very special modification of the economy in history will come off. This modification would surely bring in people's economic system.

15

Kautilya's Principle of Trades

Trade demands mentality, capability and capital. The principle stated by Kautilya contains a suitable arrangement for mentality capability and capital. While discussing trades, Kautilya's *Arthashastra* has composed views of one judgement and another special judgement. The judgement is to find a standard for the aim, target and measure of trade. Similarly, the special judgement is to judge the effectiveness of the mode and principle adopted for a special trade. In special judgement, both the trader and the tradesman is taken into account. In both general and special judgements, Kautilya has laid special stress on the interest of buyers and consumers. Along with the interest of buyers and consumers, Kautilya has brought in the aspect of interest of the state as well. He has looked at the overall interest of the state and especially into the principle of trade and the field of application.

Thus, in *Arthashastra*, the principle of trade has been discussed from a bigger perspective. From the angle of view of the state, different industries and enterprises have become topics of consideration in the field of trade.

In discussing the topic of trade, Kautilya's *Arthashastra* has adopted a particular method. The methods are to look at the decry from an overall outlook of a state. In order to see trade from the view of the state, the trade is to be divided into different factors. As the requirements of the factors of the trade may be ascertained in different ways, there should also be a standard of judgement for each factor. For economic development, Kautilya has divided the economic zone of a country into three fractions. These are agriculture, livestock farming and industry. On one side are the enterprises of agriculture, livestock farming and industry and on the other side are different types of organisations and departments for the state's observation. Kautilya has kept the role of the state under control. In this respect, the basic principles of Kautilya are discussed ahead.

The state would not be involved in any trade, nor will it be associated with any trading enterprise. The state will frame rules and apply the same for controlling all types of trades in the state. Kautilya's *Arthashastra* has given a direction for controlling the role of the state in controlling the trades. The main significance of it is in running trades—the interest of the buyers is to be considered as the main thing. If there is a difference of opinion or different types of propensities, the state would apply its minimum power and be eager to fulfil the greater interest of the state.

The principles a seller has to follow in running trades are:

1. Right cost.
2. Right measure.
3. Right standard of quality. Marketing only of the salable goods.
4. To keep the market clean, there should be no cause of impairment of social wealth.
5. To pay due respect to the tastes, culture and traditions of the country.
6. Not to market any commodity that would cause impairment of people's health.
7. To spell out both the merits and demerits of the commodity to the buyers.
8. Kautilya wanted the state itself to not take the role of tradesman but keep detailed information of the trade and would go on judging in respect of the interest of the buyers and the state itself. Kautilya has divided the field of trade into two divisions, which is trade and interstate trade.

Role of the State

With respect to both economic and lawful controls, Kautilya has tried to bring the state closer to the people. The state would, at the same time, keep watch on the public and national interests. Kautilya wanted the state to take a particular attempt in it on its part. He has liked to set up respective departments for each case and to create different responsible posts in every department. Each department will be under the control of responsible people who will have enough expertise and knowledge of the activities of the respective department. The minimum qualifications of a worker are detailed knowledge of different types of activities of the same department. There are two aspects of the minimum qualification—the first one is the minimum eligibility for different activities the department, and the second is the attitude to accomplishment of work.

Kautilya's *Arthashastra* has actually cast eyes on their two aspects and has been eager to realise with emphasis on a common principle in these two aspects. Each department continues to accomplish definite actors of a department on behalf of the state. Responsibility has been vested in the department to be in control of judging in respect of the state. In being controlled by the interest of the state, a department cannot take any step against the interest of the state. If it does, it will have to face the music, for the overall evaluation of every department is being done continuously. When a department gets engaged in work, Kautilya has proposed a device to keep vigilance on that. Thus, the state would have control in two ways. One, a controlling device should be arranged in a department through the creation of quite a number of tiers in the department. Besides, there are different attempts to keep coordination among different departments and to have overall control.

1. To fix up purpose and target of the company.
2. A philosophical basis necessary for activities of the company.
3. To take proper inference to determine the mode of working.
4. Framing of the plans.
5. Shaping of the plans.

Modern companies distribute these activities in different ways to augment their effectiveness. From such divisions, different streams of activities arise. On the basis of these streams come up with different divisions, departments or centres. Centre of profit and centre of expenditure are two terms used quite commonly nowadays. Different companies divide their streams of activities among different profit centres. Each of these has to make a profit. For this, each has to choose such ways which make the trade profitable. All the workable ways on the part of a trade to become profitable have been encouraged by Kautilya.

Kautilya's financial administration and organisational extension of financial infrastructure have been quite balanced. The extent of activities of a state is all-pervading. Right over the authority of a state lies all forms of activities of a state, but the state itself does not perform all the activities. Activities not undertaken by a state are:

1. A state itself does not get involved in a trade or become a partner of any trade enterprise.
2. Despite being entrusted with education, health or service to the masses, the employee of a state themselves does not perform these works.
3. A state does not become a partner of any profitable financial enterprise.
4. A state does not initiate or administer agriculture or industry.
5. A state does not enter into any trade in mineral and forest-grown resources.
6. A state does not get involved in the trade of gold or precious stones.
7. A state itself does not get involved in livestock farming.
8. A state itself does not get involved in any production or service-based enterprise.
9. Except in a few cases, a state does not straight away appoint people expensively in service or work.

Kautilya's Economic Practices

Kautilya's economic philosophy relies on three pillars. These are:

1. Benevolent role of the state.
2. Cooperative leadership of the state.
3. People-oriented role of the state.

Resting to this belief, Kautilya has pointed out in which direction the indirect role of the state would play. The *Arthashastra* has defined the state as a primary instrument for farming and applying laws and rules. The activities of a state would be to give impetus to all types of financial enterprises and to help them flourish with cooperation and support. On one side, the state would provide the means for cooperation, and on the other side, it would also keep the regulative device. Regulation would be from the point of view of the people and the general principle and justice. This job may be done quite smoothly if the state has a clear idea of the consequences of different deeds, that is, which one is supportive of the state and which one is against its interest. Kautilya's *Arthashastra* has clearly indicated the role of a state that would be helpful for the financial progress of the state, including which financial actors a state would resort to.

The actors that would be specially undertaken by a state are:

1. Set up the treasury and regulate the same.

2. Farming rules regarding all types of trades from the standpoint of people's view and application thereof.
3. Building all types of arrangements by direct enterprise of the state for internal and state-related defence.
4. Fixing up principles relating to production, distribution, evaluation and arranging proper application of the same, with respect to people's interest.
5. Farming rules of the state in respect of mineral of forest-grown resources and applying the same.
6. Arrangements for running markets so that small sellers and common buyers do not feel differently or become prey to injustice.
7. Farming rules on production, distribution, marketing and valuation of gold and other mineral goods and promulgation thereof.
8. Farming clear-cut rules relating to livestock farming, presentation of livestock and slaughter of animals and creating proper laws.
9. Giving impetus to all types of production and service, according to adequate encouragement for creating a proper background of production and service and adopting proper planful means in this respect by the state and its people for this interest.
10. Taking proper steps so that the scope of employment increases and this venture is set in motion. Above all, static duty is to make the provision of employment in accordance with the support to endeavours of extend doing job facilities.
11. Kautilya's *Arthashastra* has paid attention to some procedural means to accomplish these ventures.

The most important of these is to pay attention to the most important aspects and to bring gradually the makers of less importance into consideration through lending lesser importance to there. To create departments of correct assessment for proper thinking, enacting loses and implementing them properly in the interest all such ones. To set up arrangement and acquaintance of works to be done and of in every department and to protect the overall interest of the state and its people through effecting coordination among all the departments in the long run.

Arrangement of the *Arthashastra*

The first one among the application procedures of the *Arthashastra* is worthy of mention. The prescription laid by Kautilya is to judge the most valuable subject with the greatest importance. In the modern administration system, this is called the A-B-C analysis. Resorting to this process is of utmost importance in modern arrangements. The background of this procedure is about 20 percent activity of different financial enterprises of a company get 60 percent of the money; on the other hand, about 60 percent of activities get 20 percent of the money and the rest 20 percent activities get 20 percent of the money. Of these, the first fraction, that is, 20 percent activity related with 60 percent money, is called activity class A. Thus, the fraction with 20 percent activity and 20 percent money is activity of B class and 60 percent activity getting 20 percent money is C class activity.

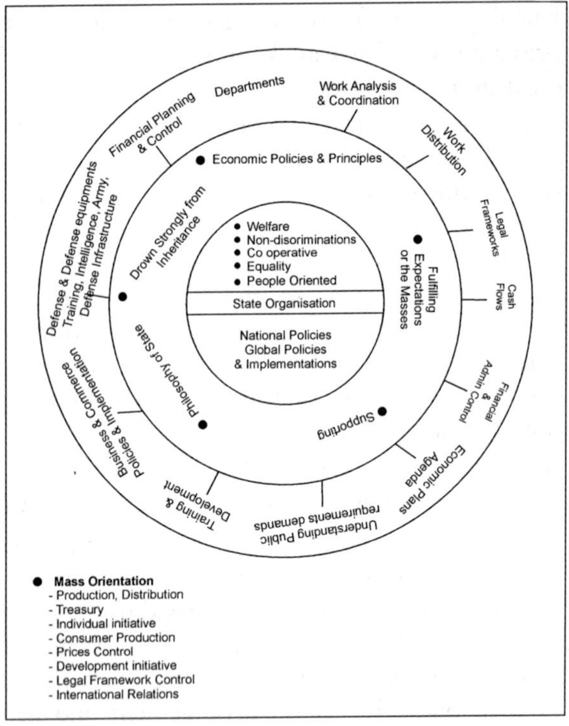

Figure-1: Fulfiling expectations of the masses

Kautilya has laid maximum stress on the activity of A class. Next comes B class and C class activities, which come last with minimum importance. Kautilya wanted their secretariats in the arrangement where the ones that control the maximum number of financial matters should be considered with the greatest importance. Thus, there is a secretarial of minerals looking after the mineral products, farming of rules, thinking of different aspects and financial development. However, there are special arrangements for gold mines as it is more precious. Kautilya spoke of special arrangements to be made for the gold mines. He had designed proper classification of organisational levels for controlling gold mines. Besides, he has proposed the deployment of a proper number of intelligence personnel here. Thus, defects and deviation from fairness of those who are at the helm and hold different responsible positions can be controlled properly. The basic philosophy of the economy there is winged; welfare, cooperating with leadership and a people-oriented state system. To give this system a perfect shape, Kautilya cast special attention to state leadership and buyers' protection. In some cases, the interests of the state and the buyers have coincided. For example, Kautilya recommended strict rules for weights and measures, also for the slaughter of animals. Kautilya wanted to respect weights and measures and said that description here amounts to a loss in treasury. The matters of taxation are dependent on weight and measureless and also for protecting the right of buyers. So severe punishment is prescribed for the tradesmen indulging in such deviation. There is a provision of direct punishment in case of the slaughter of animals. For example, a provision of punishment is there for deviation in the country's tradition. Proper punishment is prescribed for the slaughter of cows.

Kautilya's Classification of Secretariats

Important departments that would run Kautilya's state are:

Secretariat of Classification of Rural Settlement

The duty of this secretarial will be to assure arrangements for the settlement of all in consideration of professional fitness and requirement of the villagers. Under the four views of such consideration are brought settlement for agriculture, the interest of the farmers and the interest of the agricultural workers.

Department of Distribution of Uncultivable Lands

The main task of this secretarial is to demarcate the boundaries of cultivable and uncultivable lands. Uncultivable lands would be allotted to big or small industries and urban habitation under the guidance of this department.

Secretariat of State Defence

The function of this secretariat will be to build different types of forts in all corners of the country. For different people and states, there would be different forts and their varied forms. There would also be proper arrangements for perverting enemy attacks. Construction of wide road inside the cities would also be within its jurisdiction.

Secretariat of Godowns

This secretariat will set up godowns of different sizes for different types of goods and would store the goods in those godowns. Right from construction of roads down to the arrangement by different processer for storing the goods, the deparment would take care of all programmes related to godowns. Some of the godowns would be underground and others would be on the surface. In some cases, the godown would be built of stone and in some cases of salt and heavy wood.

Secretariat of Tariffs

The duty of the department will be to impose proper government tariffs on different trade and other financial organisations. In those cases, proper arrangements are to be made for collection of those tariffs. This is the main source of revenue. Two types of tariffs will be collected—current and long term.

Secretariat of Audit and Accounts

This secretariat rest supervise works for all other secretariat, auditing and controling their accounts.

Secretariat for Prevention and Removal of Corruption at the State Level

This department will be for event entry of corruption among the government workers. For this, there would be different clauses of act and principle.

Secretariat for Assessment of Works of the Executives

The duty of this secretariat would be to supervise the work of the officers and executives of different departments. It would also periodically assess the result of the work of the executives.

Secretariat for Prevention of Special Crimes

This is to prevent social maladies, including drinking of wine or violence on woman.

Secretariat of Language and Scripts

This secretariat will work for the improvement of important languages other than the mother tongue and to extend the utility of these.

Treasury Secretariat

The government treasury will be under the control of this secretariat. One of its duties is to evaluate the costly items collected and to make proper arrangements for their presentation and use.

Secretariat of Mines and Factories

This secretariat makes arrangements for collecting mineral wealth. It would also prepare true accounts of the quantity of mineral wealth at different spots and to preserve the same. It would also set up favourable background for founding factories according to requirements. It would also fix up the quality and quantity of work and to control the same.

Secretariat of Gold Mines and Production of Gold

The duty of this department is mainly to arrange collection, treasure, presentation and proper utilisation of the country's wealth of gold. Production and modes of marketing are also included in the duties of the department.

Secretariat of Information

Collection of information and proper communication of the same are the duties of this secretariat. The information department would collect important information for all parts of the country for production, distribution, evaluation and more of all systems connected with financial possibility and financial set up and communicate the same to proper places. If anybody happens to supply information and earn profit, this secretariat will prevent him for doing so.

Secretariat of Commerce

Farming and shaping of the rules of trade and commerce are vested in this secretarial. While forming the rules, the secretariat would take the opinion of buyers and sellers. Comparing these with the ideal of the state, this department would frame the principle of trade and commerce.

Secretariat of Forest Management

The responsibility of proper record of forest growth, which is the wealth of the country, its preservation proper, its proper utilisation is vested on this department.

Secretariat of Ordinance Production

The activities of the secretariat could be looking for necessary weapons for the defence of the country. It would take the initative for discovering these and make arrangement for the production thereof. The means for preservation of these are different in different cases—the department will be conversant of all the means. It will also apply the knowledge judiciously.

Secretariat of Wealth and Measure

This secretariat will place the weights on proper measure. All types of trade, commerce and transfer would come under the tour view of this secretariat. This secretariat would keep watch on the use of correct weight or the correct measure of different goods in case of transfer. It would prepare correct standard of weight and measure.

Secretariat of Measurement of Land and Time

This secretariat will control the methods of land measurement and the measurement of time. It would set up proper standards and measure of land and time, for example, working day would composed thirty days. Solar month will have thirty and half days, lunar month thirty days. Steller month twenty-seven days; a month for mobilizing armed for would comprise thirty-two days of thirty-five days month for running a tamed elephant forty days. Time will be recorded by the shadow at noon of the twice Asadh (June-July)

Secretariat of Custom Taxes

This department will impose customs and taxes on different commodities, transport, markets and business. The assessment, application, inspection of these customs and taxes would be the responsibilities of this secretariat.

Secretariat of Fixing and Controlling Price

This secretariat, for securing the interest of buyers, will keep vigilance on other departments and their functioning. This department would intervene if the sellers of commodities are not in accordance with the interest of the buyers, keep up the standard of price and would bring the price down to the correct level.

Secretariat of Clothes

This secretariat will always look into the affair of clothes and thread. Proper supply, price and standards of quality of clothes and thread come under the jurisdiction of this department. This secretariat will take proper steps after considering these things.

Secretariat of Agricultural Production

This secretariat will control the affair of agricultural production. It will consider the amount of production of different crops and will assess the price of these. It will classify the product in categories like agricultural food products and consumable agricultural products. Coordination between the two would have to be determined in terms of total requirements of the country.

Secretariat of Excise

This secretariat will judge the merits and demerit of intoxicants and take proof steps for their control. It will also enact and promulgate laws in this matter.

Secretariat of Production of Slaughter of Animals

This secretariat will keep vigilance if careless slaughter is undertaken anywhere. It will control the same. This secretariat will keep vigilance on cow slaughter. It would keep close watch to prevent cow-slaughter in the country. Severe punishment would be afflicted on anyone who would for some reason another kills a calf a mitch-cow or an ox etc.

Secretariat of Amusements

Affairs of cultural amusement belong with secretariat. It will consider and control different types of amusements.

Secretariat of Ship and Transportation of Merchandise

This secretariat will consider transport system for different types of goods and men specially transportation of large quantities of merchandise and would urge the business hours accordingly.

Secretariat of Livestock Farming

This secretariat will be enterprising for rearing of the animals. Different modes of rearing of different types of animals would be considered by this secretariat separate departments would be there for rearing cows and leases. Rearing of elephant will also come under the control of a different secretariat.

Secretariat of Building Army

This secretariat will take initiative for training of the soldiers to make them fit for war.

Secretariat of Forging Tour and Travel

This secretariat will look after foreign tours and travels and give permission and passport for to and for travels to different countries. Function of this secretariat is also to keep account of the foreigners and watch on them.

Secretariat of Intelligence

This secretariat will procure different types of news and information and forward there to relevant authorities. Both military and civil detectives would have to be adequate in number and properly skilled.

Secretariat of Urban Development

This secretariat will keep watch on weather service to people in properly maintained. It will be applied for making civil rights and opportunities proper and adequate.

Kautilya's *Arthashastra* eagerly goes deep into the administration of the financial system to solve problems. The main function of the secretariats discussed in the *Arthashastra* is to maintain and introduce contact. There is a specific clause about what should be the nature of administration of each of the departments, who would perform their duties and who would supervise. Kautilya has also specified the relationship between a secretariat and money. Had those who are presently at the help of the financial administration shown a bit eagerness towards Kautilya, widely siding with their Harvard knowledge, many burning problems might have been solved by them. Kautilya's *Arthashastra* is the possession for future.

16

Vedic Principle of Agriculture and Rural Development

The Vedic principles of economic management have put a very high level of importance on the issues of agriculture and rural development. This concern is common between the practice and thoughts of managing the aspects of agriculture and rural development, as depicted in the policies of Yudhisthira in the *Mahabharata* period and that in the *Arthashastra* of Kautilya. We shall follow the pathways of Kautilya for the study of agriculture and rural development for managing the economy of a nation or the world.

Kautilya's Approaches

Principle of Segmentation in Practice

For the overall economic growth of a country, Kautilya has divided the economic factors in a number of ways. These sections have been designated by him as different secretariats. The basis of the division is the foundation and regulation of the financial system. Each of the sections designed for the convenience in foundation and regulation of financial systems has a special identity and programme. Each section has its own limit of income and expenditure and its own target. Kautilya has exposed the function of each secretariat to the public, but each has its own problems too. So, for supervision of and coordination of activities, all the sections of a state have set up a specific secretariat from its part. A secretariat does not involve itself in the financial production or trades but coordinates among the individuals and groups engaged in those areas. Behind this, there is an attempt to set up an open atmosphere and environment for production and circulation.

Kautilya has adopted some types of principles in the case of rural development and agriculture. For rural development, Kautilya has simultaneously considered many types of things.

Kautilya's thinking started with the consideration of what would be the nature of rural settlements, which types of people would be involved in these settlements and what would be their respective fields of work. He first considered topics like what would be the individual endeavours of activity. He wanted the development of rural wealth, potentials and possibilities. In an attempt to devise effective development of wealth and possibility, he determined the role of a state for creating a complete network of activities and for binding the whole locality in that network to make the same able and active. A rural locality becomes able and active if all the people, including themselves, in the endeavours of the state with their offerings of ability and possibility, lend their support to the state enterprises according to their own ability.

Settlement of Land for Agriculture

The system of settlement of land comes at different stages of history in different forms. The settlement of the historic stage required land or recognition of the right by state as the main inspiration. Kautilya has presented arguments behind the settlement of land.

The *Arthashastra* has discussed with great importance two aspects of land settlement:

(1) how the productive capacity of land can be increased.

(2) the decision of settlement according to the usefulness of land.

With these two objects, Kautilya settled and resettled rural habitation and in proper cases, affected settlement of unproductive lands. Kautilya liked to keep proper watch on both preservative and productive aspects of land through demographic settlement and resettlement. This results in protection of land on one side and on the other, desired crops may be obtained.

> Bhãtapãrbam abhutapãrbam b~ janapadam paradeÑ~pab~hanena
> SvadeÑah abhisyan ada bamanena b~ nibesayet
>
> (*Arthashastra* 2/1/1)

(All places and all people are important. Authority should be made in all places where there was so long habitation or not by involving all people from those places as elsewhere in the economic initiative for the masses).

It means that the requisite population is required for habitation in every village. Villages will be self-sustaining if there is balanced distribution among area, population and resources of the villages. Thus, opportunities of proper distribution of locations and collection of resources for the villages would be created. In this context, Kautilya liked to have a balanced ratio between the area and the population of a village.

> Đudra Karsak aprayam kulasatabara·cha pancha kulasa tapara gramam /
> Krausah dvikrausah Simanam anyai anyaraksam nibesayat.
> (*Arthashastra* 2/1/2)

(The population of a village is to be determined by agricultural workers and farmers. The number of families inhabitants in a village will be within the range of 100-500. The boundary of a village would be extended to one or two couples of miles and would be well-protected by mutual cooperation. Each person should be involved in the work of the ground and for serving others in the realm.)

Kautilya has given an account of the population of a village. A village will be accommodated by one hundred families as the minimum and a maximum of five hundred families. Those who would form the habitation are mainly families belonging to agricultural location and families working in agriculture. The measure of a village would be 4 by 2 miles, which is rectangular in shape. The security of the village would be managed by the people of the village. The security management would grow through cooperation among the villagers, which means that they would guard the resources from being taken away by any outsider. On the other side, there would be proper management for augmenting the wealth of the village itself and to grow up proper preventive measures for the same.

The best security management of the wealth of a village would be affected if the villagers can manage to grow their own wealth properly by themselves. Kautilya liked to have cooperation and combined enterprise of all for this. The greatest security can be achieved by cooperation and combined enterprise. Natural arrangements lie side by side with human endeavours for security management.

Nadih sailah banah bhustidari setubandhah samih
Slmatih krirabrksat antasu simanam sthapayeh (2/1/3)

(Boundary of the village would be occupied by rivers, hills, forests, heaps of stones, bends of water pools, bridges and acacia trees, silk cotton trees, peepul trees and the like. Creating boundaries should also have sequential natural arrangements.)

Kautilya has paid attention to both of the two aspects of security. Preparedness of people's own security measures and the aid of natural elements like different types of trees, mountain ranges or heaps of stones, boulders and so forth, create situations for security and at the same time, help increase the yield of crops in the agricultural region existing within the boundary.

Astasata gramya madhye sthaniyam,
Catuhsata gramya drauna mukham
Dvisata gramyah karbatikam
dasagramau samgrahena;
samgrahenam sthapayet (2/1/4)

(Within eight hundred villages one 'sthaniya' [local], within four hundred villages one 'dronamukh', within two hundred villages one 'karbatika' and within ten villages one 'sangrahakendra' should be set up to involve all in the collective activity for collective growth.)

That it, a regional office would be set up with every eight hundred villages. Every four hundred villages would constitute one defence centre. Every two hundred villages would form a tax-imposing centre. After settling the internal administration of the villages, Kautilya has been engaged in the external administration of the villages. After internal management is made, this mutual coordination has made the villages live in a state coordinate, having a particular sense of concordance. This mutual concordance among the villages strengthens and confirms the supply and exchange of financial resources among themselves. Just as it results in making the financial bonding of the stage strong, it also becomes necessary for the growth and wealth of its own. Owing to the management of the wealth extension of the wealth of the villages, coordination among them becomes very fruitful.

Independence of the Villages

Economic Independence through higher Productivity

Kautilya saw the villages as individual units by fixing up their boundaries. The aspects of government officers and government administration system of the zonal distribution set up thus have also been discussed. Government officers and office bearers would protect this economic zone properly and would build them up with requisite ability; that is, they would grow up mutual coordination among the villages and among the villagers as well. Thus, would grow up village-zones. The zonal economy of villages would also grow up.

Kautilya has also given a picture of vocations and qualities that are to be borne by the people in these zones.

> Ritwik acharyah purohitah ksatriyabhyau
> Brahmadeyat adanda karat anyabhirupat ayadkani prayacchet.
> Adhyaksa sanikhyay akadibhyau
> Gopah Sthanikah anikah-hasti cikitsakah
> Asvadam ekajan adhikarik ebhyasca bikaya dhana barjati
> (2/1/7)

(Land will be distributed among the performers of religious sacrifices, mentors, priests, warriors and so forth. Those who are engaged in observance and exercise of Brahman will not have to pay any tax. Such a person will be exempted from being punished and for paying tax. This right will be extended through generations. Besides chiefs of secretariats, lord accountants, regional chiefs, drivers of elements, physicians, professional caretakers of horses will get such land without right to sell or transfer).

In order to set up an equilibrium in the qualitative arrangement of the population, Kautilya has inspired different types of people to settle down in a village. Kautilya has kept the doors open for those who would cultivate knowledge, who would work for others' welfare, who would be engaged in medical practice and who would be engaged in financial exchange and security on behalf of the state. They would get proper cooperation for residing in the village, and land would be distributed among them for residence and other suitable uses. These properties regarded to be endowed for deities would make the people engaged in special activities accountable to the villages and the villagers.

This accountability has indeed given them the right to serve society, constantly remaining engaged in these professions and vocations. Thus, this accountability has created a bonding of the society with these people engaged in different professions or vocations. They will always be coordinated in concordance with the village.

> Karadebhyah krtaksetra nyeka purusikani prayacchet.
> Akrtani kartrbhyau na deyani.
>
> (2/1/8) (2/1/9)

(Cultivable agricultural land has been allotted to the taxpayers. The uncultivable land rendered cultivable would belong to the rectifier).

This step of augmenting the productivity of land is a salient feature of Kautilya's principle of agriculture. As there would be an endeavour to increase the productivity of land, there should also be an endeavour for rendering infertile land fertile. The rights of the infertile land turned fertile by a farmer will be vested on him. That is how Kautilya has tried to induce zeal for increasing the productivity of land and the total agricultural produce.

> Akrsatamat chhidyat anyebhyah prayacchet.
> Gramabhrtah kabaudehakah ba krsesuh.
> Akrsantauh babahinam daduh. (2/1/10-12)

(Uncultivated land would be taken away from the farmer to be bestowed on the other. Or it will be cultivated by worker or farmer of that village. The owner of the land would have to compensate for uncultivated land.)

Kautilya has laid stress on agriculture. A land must be properly cultivated. This would result in bringing adequacy of agricultural produce. There is a provision for realising compensation from one who would deliberately leave the land fallow.

> Nibesa samakalam yathagataka in ba parihara dadyat.
>
> (2/1/17)

(Tax should be exempted wherever necessary or proper help should be accorded from the royal treasury.)

As the *Arthashastra* has laid stress on agricultural produce and productivity, it has also stressed on being sympathetic towards the problems of the people. Sympathetic judgement regarding men may be possible only through the judgement of the context, which means that one has to be stern where sternness is necessary and when the situation demands slackness, one would have to be slack promulgation of the principle of agriculture is just making the interests of both the farmer and the consumer of the agricultural product well-secured.

Infrastructure for Agriculture

Proper distribution and utilisation of tributary lands have been arranged in view of the interests of both the taxpayers and agricultural yield. At the time of Kautilya, the technology used for agriculture was mainly physical labour and an ancient mode of farming. The main mode of farming then was by using the combination of plough and bullock. Proper attention has also been given to the vocation's concomitant with farming. For example, people would be attracted towards villages by giving their right to land through development in the respective fields of the profession, such as development in industries, development of trade, development of education, development of religion, spirituality and so forth. Thus, a balanced characteristic bloom in rural society. Thus, for the development of the balanced characteristic, people of these categories have been given the right in a village in proportion to their numbers.

Even then Kautilya had spoken of irrigation for farming. The need for irrigation can be met in two ways—irrigation by the endeavour of the state and by individual or non-government enterprise. Whatever might be the arrangement for irrigation, government or non-government, Kautilya has not insisted on the dependence on natural processes or natural resources only. In case of the mode of irrigation solely dependent on nature reveals its dangerous side when nature becomes hostile. If nature becomes hostile, agricultural yield is jeopardised and may also cause havoc in the productive ability of farming. For this reason, Kautilya has recommended lessening dependence on natural processes and insisted on introducing irrigation processes on individual and non-government enterprise.

The irrigation process needs dams, canals and other arrangements for controlling water. For these, Kautilya wants the farmer or someone well-connected with the rural financial system, or any number of people that would come forward with the initiative, or whoever might like the initiative, the financial burden would be vested on all. The responsibility of meeting the financial burden would rest on those regions that would benefit from the irrigation works.

> Sahah udakam ahayaudakam ba setum bandhayet. (2/1/20)
> Anvesam ba bandhatam bhumimargah
> brksah upakaranah anngraham kuryat
> purnya sthanaramanam ca. (2/1/2)

(Irrigation works are to be affected by natural water or water carried from elsewhere. If others accomplish the irrigational work, the state will help them by providing land, trees and other components or with pleasant things).

Some things of common use in the village were under the control of the state. These were pleasant places, common gardens, dams constructed by the state and so forth. On the other hand, when these had been affected through individual enterprise, these did not come under the control of the state. Kautilya has accorded inspiration to individual enterprises. It is not that individual enterprises would be welcomed in setting up trade, but many different activities would be brought into effect through individual enterprises. In Kautilya's financial mode of private enterprises, along with government ones, have been welcomed in all cases, like creation and preservation of infrastructure, their renewal and extension and so on. Just as the state that first gets financial benefit from the infrastructure created by a state enterprise, so in the case of enterprises set up by individual endeavour, the very first benefit goes to the enterpriser. In both cases, the principal monetary provision is created for all men.

Managing Agriculture for Prosperous Society

Kautilya has paid attention to social management with enough importance. His outlook is in favour of setting up such a balanced society. He has paid attention to creating proper management for all types of men in society. On the basis of this social arrangement are these individual families. Thus, Kautilya wanted to get financial obligations within the family solved through balanced distribution.

Apatyadaram mata pitaro bhratrn
Apraptabyabaharan bhaginih
Kanyah bidhaba aksyabhibhratah
Saktimatau dvadasapanau dandah
Anyatra patitephyah anyatramatuh (2/1/28)

(If any capable man does not support his children, parents, minors, widow sisters and the like, twelve sets of adequate punishment have been prescribed for him.)

In this case, the responsibility of social distribution also has been bestowed on the directions of the secretariats created by the state. They would see that there is no deficit of justice in society. In every house, the responsibility of a financially helpless member will be vested in the member capable of earning. He who earns will have to take responsibility for his wife and children. Besides, he will also have to take responsibility for his parents, unmarried sisters, widowed sisters, minor brother and so on. There would be provision for punishment on the part of the state for the individual who would fail to take such responsibility to refrain from taking initiative in such activity. People eager to take such responsibility get help and munificence from the state. As the state has provided encouraging principles for people of some special professions to set up habitation in villages or agricultural fields, it is also eager to take up proper principles to solve social problems also.

If in spite of staying in a village and a being occupant of agricultural land, someone fails to cultivate the land owing to some calamity or misfortune or if in spite of cultivation, the land does not yield crops, help from the state would appear before him. Loan taken from the state will have to be paid in the future with the results of his toil.

> Dhanyah pasuh hiranyani aksetah anugahaniyat. (2/1/13)
> Tani antuh sukhena dadyuh. (2/1/14)
> Anugrahah pariharau ca etebhyah
> Kosabrdhikaraudadyat
> Kausah apadhyatakau barjayet. (2/1/15)

(The representative of a state would favour the needy with crops, livestock, money and so on. On arrival of good days, these are to be repaid to the state treasury. This would enrich the state treasury. State representatives would not make the treasury void through extension of favours.)

Through the review of Kautilya's principles of agriculture and rural affairs, it becomes clear that all sorts of attempts for development in agricultural and rural development were mentioned. Kautilya had not taken any one-sided outlook. As the state extended its charitable hand in the case of agricultural and rural development, it also kept watch on the good and bad of the royal treasury. The treasury is in the best state of existence, in which all remain happy. Thus, the state extends its helping hand during hard times. During good times, the state has to be repaid. It is the obligation of the good times to return the bounty of the state with proper dignity. In Kautilya's state management, this bonding has been so designed that nobody can deny this financial obligation.

17
Role of Vedic Economics

India has laid emphasis on simple but deep living all along. On the contrary, the Western world has emphasised the basic enjoyment of life. Indian sagacity has not only preached in favour of limited enjoyment on the basis of renunciation but also brought renunciation in the exercise of living and has, in the real sense, accepted the sensual pleasure and luxury on the basis of a sort of abandonment. Indian living system has grown up on the basis of a balanced understanding between renunciation and earthly enjoyment. Since the most ancient times, there has been no cut in it. The West is now drawing us to another type of lifestyle. They say, "Squeeze life for its favour and enjoy all pleasure." Enjoyment is the ultimate satisfaction in life, nothing else. As we keep brimming with joy having Western degrees, we also beam upon being habituated with Western fashions. This very attitude has shifted us from India's own customs and norms and brought us close to the practice of a separate system. We have become habituated to an artificial taste and system. Artificiality has gradually started to take the place of originality. Our lifestyle is becoming a follower and pursuant to the West.

What would be the direction of life's movement just depends on the instance of what would be the outlook of living or what the path of movement would be. From this, would be built up such a system as would be cast its consequence on all concerned. The main principle of economics is to be collected from life. What is economics? The answer has come in one form in this new age. The answer of the ancient age was completely different.

In the modern view, economics is the principle of setting a system of balance between need and supply.

The ancient view was quite the contrary. In ancient definitions, economics is the pursuant of lifestyle. Money is the temporary means for fulfilling the final desire of life. Economics is a part of the principle of life. Both the modern and the ancient views are connected with the mode of living. The modern view is to get a thing by hook or by crook and to build up a life on the basis of that attainment. On the contrary, the ancient view is to give, to build up a life on the basis of the bestowal. The modern view is mainly of the West, and the ancient one is of India. Modern economists have provided principles of solution to economics, keeping concordance with the West.

On the other side of the ancient ideals, the measures prescribed for India are of Western style and have settled on the thought and perception of the West. Amartya Sen of India has caught the sight of the West through a Nobel prize. Sen's prescription is also no exception. The main theme of the model on poverty and hunger that he had framed him is to build up an economic system on the basis of social justice.

The position of a country is selected in the Human Development Index, framed to fix the standard of living of different countries and in terms of that position, the ways of development of that country are stated. The main objective is to alter the relative importance of the proper distribution of wealth inside the country and its investment and to give a human shape to it. For example, the benefits of education, health, service and so on are to be carried to the people and to relieve that system distribution from the grip of corruption. Besides, the allotment of many towards the account of defence, for example, is to be reduced, allotment towards social development is to be increased and similar other changes are to be brought about.

The standard of the Human Development Index used by Amartya Sen is basically the contribution of Pakistan's economist, Mehobubul Haque. To the people submerged in the extensive capital and capital business of the modern world, it is not only attractive but also worthy of appreciation. The matter is somewhat like the behaviour of the rich engaged in capital business in listening to the tremor of the voice of poverty and enjoying the same. The picture of India presented in the recent report (January 2020) of the Centre of Economics set up by Mehobubul Haque rather causes uneasiness. In many cases, even Pakistan stands above India, but most of the

Western economists and social scientists are not only looking at the economic awakening of India, but they are also seeing the future of India as one of the best economies of the world. The first phase of which has already started.

Individuality of India is preserved in its mentality, in its practice and in its recollection. In the light of common standard of Economics, India, through detailed calculations, may be made censurable, may be pulled down but still it shall not be understood. Indian aspiration is embedded in its realisation of life, in its eternal and long-borne ideal. Amartya Sen probably did not like to pursue this, possibly due to his affinity to Marxian notions. The solution that has been provided by Haque and Sen for a country like India is rather superficial. Being shorn of national tradition, the intimation of the main flow cannot rest even in the corner of the mind. Thus, without caring for Indian culture and ideas, but only through evaluation of what has been the production and distribution in a few states like Uttar Pradesh, Rajasthan, Kerala and such, or what is there in the Western standard, the structure of Indian economy cannot be framed. Reference of Shree Sen and Md. Haque comes here becomes they have used India as an example in economics more than anyone else.

Any outline whatsoever of economics should be very intimately dependent on the lifestyle and aspirations of the nation as a whole. Viewed from the angle of the vision of economics, the real situation may not be identical to the picture as shown. The true picture can really be ascertained after proper judgement.

Economic Growth: Prevailing Mindset of People

Until now, no economic notion has attached any importance to the national mentality. The economy has grown on the basis of two factors. One, what is the overall wealth in the country, and what is its management for all. Two, in what form and measure which wealth should be supplied to the whole country and to an individual.

All financial management is judged in the light of these two standards. Importance is laid on the gross national income, per capita income, per capita expenditure, per capita purchase of consumable goods, per capita expenditure in educational account, expenditure in health account, per capita overall income and expenditure, stock of foreign exchange, deficit in foreign exchange, deficit in national income and expenditure, surplus or deficit in foreign trade and the like. Above mentioned factors become important in framing the annual budget and plan for different states. The advancement or recession of a state is also judged on this standard. This is also the standard for deciding how the economic problems of the state will be solved. Though such a basis has got enough acceptability, if not based on correct basic grounds, these factors may lead to wrong inference.

The basic grounds need to be pointed out first. For this, it is important to know the mentality of the nation. It cannot be ascertained by the craving and gain of a clan or group. The mentality of a country remains mingled with overall national consciousness and national rise and fall. National Outlook is the sum total of the individual outlooks plus something more. The matter may be understood with an example. Let us take the cases of India and China. India had divided the eastern part of Pakistan to found Bangladesh solely by dint of its own power. India could have retained its authority over the newly created Bangladesh in different ways. There might be some minor hue and cry, but it would not have been so difficult at all.

Indian sagacity has never been allured to seize other countries and mainly for this, India did not try in the least to spread its authority on Bangladesh; nay, it did not try to do so at all. After Bangladesh became Islamic, some things, like spreading malice against India, utterly destroying the Hindu temples, constantly abusing the Hindus by the term 'Kapher' and above all, rendering the Hindus into second-class citizens, are going on there. Every such disgrace of the Hindus did not cause any extensive retaliation here, as nobody demanded Indian intervention only due to the fact that India is tolerant, democratic and non-aggressive.

On the other hand, China is known as apt to seize other countries. The temperament that has worked behind China's war against Vietnam has also worked behind occupying India's portion of Tibet and a great part of India. It is a general perception of many in the world that Chinese authorities are covetous of other countries and others' wealth, proving to be the aggressor by nature. This national attitude of theirs is rather a reflection of their individual character. In spite of being a country of old civilisation, China is still very much keen on its aggressive outlook. China does not have the tolerance and compassion that India has. So, while agreeing to the Panchashila, there was a stabbing at the back in the power of aggression of 1962. Landing India quite unprepared and careful to the friends into the problem and seizing a big portion of its land is in the compatibility of Chinese temperament. This basic outlook and character in an important factor in framing the outline of economics. The complete outlook that is required for building up a future economy is the national mentality.

Amartya Sen is eloquent in praising China, repeatedly drawing others towards China. He says that the Chinese model is essential for India and that we have to learn from China. This advice is far more for the allurement of his personal reputation than in terms of a deep sense of economics. Mr. Sen is quite covered up with his own ignorance. The foundation on which India has built up its economy is far more lasting and dependable than that resorted to by China. It is true that the advancement achieved by China during the last decade has a foundation much more fragile in comparison to India. The Chinese economy is built from the angle of an opportunist outlook. Three tiers of this are as follows:

The first tier has big port cities and here free economy exists. The control of the state or party here is very loose, almost nil. Unrestricted investment and uncontrolled distribution here are big attractions for foreigners. The market is mainly Chinese and foreign. This is open to the upper class and high-middle class of society.

The second tier has locations like big towns, state capital and such. Here, everything has been controlled partly. The mode of working here is with some license, permit and going along with the party leaders. Hence it formed the basis of the extended market and ingredients for the companies of the first tier. The standard of living here is intermediate.

The third tier includes rural regions, suburbs and industrial towns. Here, the standard of living is very low. State and party have full control here.

People of the third-tier travel by their own cycles. Cart and public transport are limited for them. In the second tier, there is a dominance of public transport, but in the first tier, there is an overflow of consumer goods. Profusion of inland and foreign models of foreign cars is there. This controlled three-tier system has provided a temporary advantage to China. But in terms of the future, it may not be trustworthy. In coming years, things may be extensive slide like some other Asian economies in the Chinese economy also.

The foundation the first tier of the Chinese economy rests on is extensive consumption. What can be the nature of unlimited and extensive situations confined in consumption can be exemplified as follows. The report of the Associated Press first appeared first on 14–15 April 1995 in different countries of the world and created much agitation. Different multinational companies producing consumer products read the report and became up and doing to avoid themselves of future 'opportunities'. On the other hand, it seemed to be the beginning of a dreadful intimidation to the good-natured people.

The report of the Associated press was as follows:

Human embryo considered palatable and calorie dish for some people:

In different port cities of a country, the sale of the human embryo has spread much. Human embryos are powdered in an ultra-modern machine and sold in small pouches. Doctors of a state hospital also are preaching in favour of this. It is being said that embryos on male babies born of girls of tender age are the most popular. A single such pouch supplies a full dose of calories for a man for one whole day. It is a very good drug for heart, lungs, kidney, skin . . . (A.P. 15/04/1995).

It is a very sad ridicule of the civilisation of consumerism. We boast about being civilised. We see men be fetishists and also find great support in favour of that. This is a very good piece of news for the vendors of consumer goods. It is so because it is possible for them to call upon men apt to feed on their own species for consuming any commodity whatsoever. The sale of consumer goods begets enormous profit. This profit may be inflated by increasing the extent of consumption.

The more one's attention would be drawn to consumption, the more this consumption may be made the most coveted aspect of life, the more would appear deficit and dependence on conflict in one's life. Too much consumption brings in profuse deficit. Situation of the West, now, is such that three sources of income are required for maintenance of a family of three members. That is to maintain parents and their child, both the parents are employed and one of them is to be doubly employed.

Only then would it be possible to maintain that family solvency. Nobody knows how far the list of requirements would proceed and where it would terminate. A large portion of the Americans are now to consult doctors for their purchasing habit. From one to six percent of Americans are always after buying. They do not know what and why they would buy, but they always feel the urge to buy something. Doctors have called it Compulsive Buying Disorder or the craving for purchase. It is being called a lack of mental balance or a mental disease. Doctors have of course found medicine for this. Such a victim will have to take fluvoxamine for quite a long period. Other medicines also are there. On the whole, the cure for this disease is rather costly. People who suffer this and are always running after buying something have cast extensive influence on society. Some of them are even losing their jobs. Say, coming to the place of employment, someone thinks about buying something, immediately they would rush to buy the thing, placing the kettle on the chair. On coming back, they would find the kettle there with the departing letter and the last cheque. Many people have thus gone out of employment.

This is the consequence of the highly extensive consumerism of the West. Indian mentality is just the opposite. Here too much consumption becomes unbearable. From the times of the Vedas and the Upanishads, India has valued renunciation mos. Life here becomes fruitful not due to external plentiness but by the inner wealth. Man becomes great, becomes noble by the power of his soul, by his spiritual awakening. The 'pouch of human embryo' of China will not be accepted here. Consumerism is there as well; keen competition among the rich exists for purchase, but everything has a limit. There are many such big industrialists who wears nominal dress, takes a nominal good and maintains a very simple standard of living. It has been found that the number of buyers thronged at by an advertisement of a product with one hundred dollars attracts less than one-fifth of the enterprising buyers out there in China. Indian people are contented with just a little.

As soon as a businessman earns some money, he thinks it is far and no further. Repeated use of the same thing is not appreciated here, but there is also not any possibility to change often. One can just beget satisfaction. Here, contentment and satisfaction neither have been judged by houses, cars and amount of money, nor would be judged thus. Of course, there is a demand of all such things in India.

The market in India nearly equals the total market of Western Europe. Any product whatsoever, if launched here rightly, can bring one million sales. In spite of there being such a market of enormous possibilities, the problem is with the culture of the Vedas and the Upanishads. The basic appeal of this is that what lies within the heart of an individual and drags him to the dearest self. An individual gets the perfection of his life by the standard of his quality. Judgement on the basis of external education or literacy would rather find that a vast number of people in India are illiterate, and so they are spending days in utter poverty.

But the fact is that here every individual has his own feeling about life. Every Indian is a philosopher. They like to see the truth in their own way, and they know how to do this. This particular form of the Indian mind has been bloomed by Yudhisthira in the answers stated to the God of justice (Dharma of the *Mahabharata*) when he appeared in the form of a heron. Yudhisthira had said that a man who is free from debt, who does not live abroad and who lives on very nominal food is really happy. This is the basis of the Indian economy.

Such a person, free from debt, is eager to build up a self-dependent financial system. Such was the condition from the very ancient times of India down to the advent of Muslim invasion. A temple of a god is present at the centre of village life. Everything there has happened in the name of God. God is the owner and controller of everything. Quite naturally, man's feeling of religion was under the control of God. There had been a tendency of everyone to do duties for others, and the basis of life was little enjoyment but plentiful abandonment. The Muslims came and gradually broke down the situation, but the maximum disintegration happened during the British regime.

Not being exiled is something like not being in debt. Man had agreed to the abidance of five debts, and so no ambition occupied them. At present, we are being called to build up our lives on the basis of ambition. Its tenure is short, and the consequences are painful.

Renunciation is the main saying of India. The world economy of the future is to be built up on the basis of this saying, drenched in the Vedas and the Upanishads. If the economic set-up of India is different from this, the consequence will be distressing. Sayings that have been preached by Amartya Sen and Mahbub-ul-Huq are not enough for India. Rather, these are similarly distressing; India would have to stand up on the foundation of its own tradition and mentality. Others will be really amazed at the glow and speed of the Indian elephant.

18

The Test Place of Vedic Economics: Vedic Financial System

The main theme of Vedic economics is supremacy. This supremacy stands on the very supreme stage and the land of confidence of Vedic mentality. Lord Shankara is a great example. Lord Mahadeva is known by many names such as Sadasiva (always beneficent), Mahasiva (the Great beneficent), Hara, Sankara and the like. The significance of his names is the same. He is filled with the pleasure of experiencing his own savour. He is always pleasure condensed. Lord Siva of the *Mangalakavya* (the books of verse depicting the glory of different gods and goddesses) has established a family in his abode. The mistress of the house is Annapurna herself. The little family is maintained with alms. The Great Lord (Maheswar) himself collects alms, but in this work, he has got neither mind nor attention. He lives on alms, but he is not a beggar. He is the king of all kings. His activities impart comfort to minds and lives.

Lord Shankara is the background of the Vedic mind and character. The Hindu society stands with a supreme mentality just like him. A simple, easy and common life. The beckoning of desire there is very scanty. The demand for giving has surpassed that of longing. The mentality of giving is depicted in the anecdote of the mongoose referred to in the *Mahabharata*. The anecdote in brief, is as follows:

Yudisthira has become the emperor of his own empire. After the battle of Kurukshetra, he is now on the throne of a sovereign ruler. His sacrificial horse has brought all the states and territories within the boundary of his empire. So, a sacrifice to establish his suzerainty is being performed as a token of such admittance. All are welcome in the sacrifice. Yudhisthira, the emperor, is giving free money to all; all are easing to their habits, content and receiving gratifications. Brahmins, after taking meals and receiving gratifications, are engaged in conversation with the emperor.

Everyone is eloquent in appreciation. Nobody has ever seen or heard of such gifts before. During such discussion appeared a mongoose. The upper part of his body is golden, bright and very nice, but the rest is filthy and dark. The mongoose stopped all and said, "No, you are all wrong. You don't seem to have seen what really is called 'gratification'. I have seen a selfless gift, which is not related to any returns, nor is there any expectation of domination and reputation." The mongoose then narrated his experience.

He lived on the branch of a tree at the remote outskirt of Yudhisthira's kingdom, by the side of the hut of a poor Brahmin. During the war, the financial stringency that cropped up became more complex due to the shortage of rainfall and drought. The members of the family of the Brahmin had to go without food, often for a few times at a stretch. But on that occasion, they had been starving for continuous four to five days, for people had practically stopped giving alms. That day the Brahmin happened to have a small amount of rice. After cooking, they were about to have lunch; everyone had a little bit of food as a share. At that very moment, a beggar came to the door and asked for alms. The Brahmin engaged himself in the service of the stranger deemed to be God. He gave away his share of food to him. The beggar was not satisfied. He was not satisfied with the whole of the little amount of food the Brahmin happened to have after starving for four days. The Brahmin's wife then gave away her share to the beggar. Even so, he was not satisfied. So, by taking turns, the descendants of the Brahmin followed their parents and became indigent. They all remained unbeaten and, within a few days, died of the pain of hunger.

The mongoose noticed the affair. When everyone died, the mongoose began to roll about on the floor. A few grains of food of that eventful day had been lying strewn on the floor. In contact of that holy food, half of its body turned golden. Before coming to Yudhisthira's sacrifice he had thought that as Yudhisthira was so religious a king, nay religion embodied, his charity would also be similarly an act of piety. But coming over here and rolling on the grains of food the rest of its body did not turn golden. Some vanity, some pride or some expectation must have lain dormant in Yudhisthira's charity.

We thus hear of the charity of a poor Brahmin from the mongoose. This is the common custom of the third mind. A Vedic mind values charity above acceptance. An all-renouncing ascetic is appreciated more than a king. To Hindus, renouncing men resembles gods where Europe has bestowed appreciation as the heron on the triumphant. A Hindu appreciates a renouncing and munificent person. Religions like Islam and Sematic appreciate reputation while Hinduism appreciates magnanimity. The West has attributed greater volumes on the brain and its scientific attitude. The driving force of the Hindus is his conscience and wisdom mingled with stoicism. While others have clung to a part, Hindus have worshipped the whole. Asceticism for the whole.

The Source of Power in Vedic Economics

The most mentionable part of the sequence created in the Hindu society is religion. Religion is more superior than even the king. Religion is also superior to money. At the very root of life is religion and at its end stands emancipation.

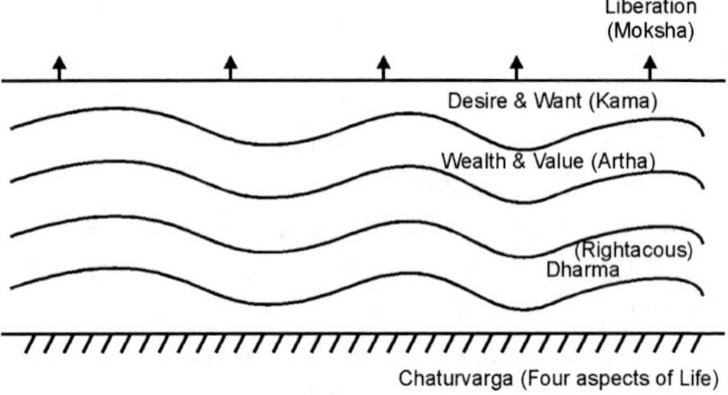

Figure 1: Vedic way of life

Figure-1 shows the Vedic way of life. Religion stands at the basis of life. A Vedic life grows up on the basis of religion and religious belief. Standing on the basis of religion, a Hindu mind moves in the quest for money and lust. Not only collection of money, its conjunction, modification and everything else gets accomplished on the basis of religious belief. Emancipation comes in the long run.

The ultimate goal of life that has been fixed here is its compliance with the good qualities of life to the godliness. Among the valued posts designated here of the Hindu values, the main one is 'renunciation'. Power and dominance are quite lusterless before renunciation. The authority of a king is very weak before the power of righteousness.

In the oldest social system of India, the power of a king has been confined in the enclosure of righteousness. In the *Ramayana*, the saying is:

Aikyamatyam upagamya sastradrstena caksusa
Mantrinau yatra iratastanahu mantram uttamam (6/12)

(Decision taken through unanimity is the most acceptable one. A king will take decision on the basis of counsels of the ministers and ministers in their turn would give counsels in the light of scriptures.)

This notion of the *Ramayana* is applicable in all cases—common and special. But in some especially urgent cases, there may not be any unanimity, in that case, the king would accept the opinion of the majority of the council of ministers. Kautilya's *Arthashastra* also holds the same opinion. In the *Arthashastra,* the king has been advised to abide by the opinion of the majority, even in special or urgent cases, but the king has the right to think otherwise.

Yatra yad bhuyisthah Karyasiddhi karam
ba brauyustata kuryah

(*Arthashastra* 1/6)

(The king in all cases would stress most on the accomplishment of the action and in possible cases, he would abide by the opinion of the council of ministers or of majority).

The main principle of Vedic politics is that a king would, in case of decision and effectiveness, abide by the democratic values. This democratic value also stands on the religion's feelings of good and bad. The king and his personal matters are always to be taken in the light of the feelings of righteousness in totality. Otherwise, the prestige of the king will be at stake and as a consequence, he might even lose his kingdom.

A perfect example of this is available in the *Rigveda*. The king, from the idea of the general principle of justice, in the interest of righteousness and interest of the state, had given capital punishment to his son for committing fault. The verse of the hermit Kaksiban, the son of Dirghatama says:

Ajah abinasatya kara bam mahe yaman purubhuja purandhih

> Srutam taechasuriba badhrimatya Hiranyah astamasvina badattam.
>
> Asno Brikasya Bartikam abhike yubam narana satyamum uktam
>
> Uto kabini purubhuja yubam ha krpaman amakrnutam bicakse. Caritram hi beri bacchedi parnamaja Khelasya paritakmyayam Sadyo janghamaya sim Vispalayaai dhane hite sartabe
>
> pratyadhattam.
>
> Satam mesanVrikyae caksadan amynasvam tampit andham chakara
>
> Tasma aksi Nasatya bicaksam adhattam dasra bhisaja banrban. (*Rigveda*, 1/116/13-16)

(O the two Nasatyas (Asvinikumars)! You are the lord of bestowing desired fruition intelligent Badhri mati had called upon you repeatedly through respectful verses and you heard that call. You gave him a son named Hiranyahasta. O the Asno! You had snatched bartik? away from the grasp of Brka. You had been pleased to show the godhead to a truly respectful wise man. Your kind heartedness had caused the replacement of the tibia of Vispal, the wife of Khela broken in the battle by iron ones. Rjrasva Vriki who had destroyed hundreds of sheep was blinded by his father.)

Rjrasva got rescued from the offence of homicide in the exchange of blindness. This behaviour of Briki is an example of social justice and rule of justice. Rjrasva, of course, got back his vision through later asceticism.

Just like a king, in case of an empire, in case of family, the role of the father was to take steps for initiation of righteousness. The rule of righteousness and religion is preferable to rule of laws. For founding and rearing religion, it is customary to shun personal comfort and interest. A king used to take a vow to religion even before ascending the throne.

A Vedic king had always been identified with his kingdom and mainly with the truth and religion for applying his power and preserving the same. A king would have to respect this vow of truth and religion in every field of his life. Otherwise, the reign of the king would be wiped out. The king would be dethroned. Another king would have the opportunity to reign. There is detailed dissension on this in the *Mahabharata*.

Thus:

Pratnam cabarauasva manasa karmana gira
Palayasy amaham bhaumam frahma ityeba casakrt.
Yascatra dharma ityuktav danda nitibya baksayah.
Tamasamkah karisyami svabasau na kadacana.

(*Mahabharatam* 12/58/115-16)

(The king in administration of his kingdom is under a pledge of controlling through provision of punishment any insult or violation of the religious principles. The king takes the vow that he, with all his heart and soul, would rear all his subjects, especially who are religious and righteous; he would value more the religious activities and arrangements than those of his need and choice.)

Kautilya's *Arthashastra* has specially recorded the norms of the later period. The *Arthashastra* has also advised how the king would spend his days and what would be the time to be devoted to his additional activities. The *Arthashastra* has granted one-fourth of a day, which is six hours, for personal repose of the king. (1/19).

Overall, the source of power has been obedience to religion. If the king is religious and devoted to truth, only then would he wield the sceptre. Otherwise, the power of the king becomes rather temporary obedience and as a consequence, the king may have to bear much trouble.

The social system of the Vedas stood on such sovereignty that the administration of the state or any big organisation whatsoever was the society. The primary source of power was society, the social mind or the social system. All powers were under the control of society. The king is bound by obligation with also such control of society. The king is not controlled only by the counsels of the council of ministers or high officials. He is always obligated to religion. The king's exceptions to such customs have turned autocratic and have invited their own ruin.

Financial System

Kautilya's *Arthashastra* has submitted detailed reports of much of the affairs of the ancient administration. Right from a pay-structure of the ministers and officials, one would set the outlook of administration of the state. Salary used to be paid in accordance with the Sukra principle. The basis of this principle was that for every lakh of coins earned, the ministers and officials collectively would set 300 coins as salary and other allowances. The financial system was in conformity with total production and fiscal collection.

As a result, there had been no chance of any fiscal deficit. The pay structure that Kautilya had presented is as follows.

Table-1: Pay Structure in Ancient Royal Management

Post	Salary (per annum)
Queen, Crown prince	48000 coins
Prime Minister, Army commander	48000 coins
Deputy Commander, Chief official and other ministers	24000 coins
Regional commander, Regional ministers and other officials	12000 coins
Superintending officers	8000 coins
Physicians and professionals	2000 coins

(*Arthashastra*, 4/7/24)

It is to be noted here that the picture depicted in Table 1 is at the initiation of even the Maurya and Gupta eras. Kautilya here has only followed the Sukra principle. Right on the basis of this principle, the system of financial grants has been commissioned from the Vedic period.

The coin used in the table provided by Kautilya is possibly a copper coin. This type of coins was in vogue and acceptable all over the country. The fundamental basis of running a state was self-dependence in every sphere. The revenue department was permitted to expend in accordance with its collection. For expending every coin, the respective department would have to earn a sufficient number of coins. This very system in modern economics is termed administration in a profit-centric form.

In the financial system of Kautilya, the basic picture of the most modern corporate administration of today can be noticed. It is not unnatural to think that the modern corporate system is a reflection of Kautilya.

The picture of the financial system presented by Kautilya is much later than that of the Vedic period.

The basis of the financial system of the Vedic age was basically built across agriculture and agricultural industries. Agriculture was vastly pervasive. Farming used to be accomplished with bullocks, using plough and yoke. Farming techniques still in use had its origin in the Vedic ages. The agricultural produce was dependent on the cooperation of Nature.

The Vedic belief was that natural cooperation was quite likely in religious and honest social system. The irrigation system was known to exist in the Vedic age. Rainwater would get collected and that water would be brought to the land for cultivation through small canals. Among the produce, the predominant produces were paddy, cereals and pulse. Besides them, there were permanent crops and fruits produced in different seasons. Due to abstemious use of the cultivable lands, production capacity was very high.

In the Vedic economy, the role of the cow was very significant. Cows and oxen were adored. They were called 'Aghna', which means not to be slain. Careful nursing of cows and oxen was a part of life in the Vedic social system. Cows and oxen used to be reared in the hermitages and also in households. Hermits used to fulfil many of their necessities of hermitage through the milch cows. Cow milk was considered to be the most palatable food of the residents of the hermitages. These residents used to give greatest importance to the rearing of cows.

There is a number of anecdotes about this in the *Upanisads*. One is the anecdote of Jabala and Satyakam. In the story, Gautama, the hermit, had received his disciple, Satyakam, for his truthfulness. Satyakam, quite unaware of the identity of his father, had boldly disclosed the identity only of his mother to his mentor. Immediately after inducting Satyakam as his disciple, Gautama handed over some diseased and weak cows to him—numbering about three hundred—and said, "Go to the forest. Rear them there in forests and when their number would reach one thousand, come back here." Satyakam left for the forest with those cows. After the number had reached one thousand, he came back, but there was a beaming but pleasant glow of the knowledge about God on his face. The mentor himself was struck with wonder. While rearing the herd of the cows, he had developed a deep friendship with nature. The plants, wind and creepers, all would come and speak their hearty words in his hearing. A limitless, infinite state of equilibrium had occupied him. Thus, while grazing the cows Satyakam had attained the supreme knowledge.

Among many other anecdotes in the *Upanishads,* that of Naciketa is one of the best. Naciketa also was first pained at the action of his father. Naciketa's father was performing a sacrifice of excellence and was offering old, crippled, worn out and diseased cows to the Brahmins present there. The tender mind of Naciketa became inquisitive at this gesture. On questioning the father, the father happened to insist Naciketa on going to the abode of Yama (the lord of Death). Naciketa went there on the order of his father. As a result, the world, as a gift, received the precious mine of supreme knowledge—the *Kathopanisad.* The knowledge of absolute self is depicted in it. At the root of this story as well, there are cows.

Besides, there is the famous anecdote of Surabhi. This cow was the bone of contention between the hermits Vasistha and Viswamitra. A number of references are there regarding the nursing of the cows in the royal circle of Indra. That is why in Vedic civilisation, the careful nursing and worship of cows is a precious custom. In the Vedic civilisation, a cow is regarded as an especially mentionable animal and a medium not only because it gives milk and is used in farming but also for its calm and saintly behaviour.

Trade and Commerce

Trade by barter, which means buying and selling commodities directly by exchange of one for another, was customary in the whole Vedic society. Many hermits of the *Rigveda* have longed for wealth through prayers. For example, Rishi, the sage has said in his prayer to God Agni (Fire):

> Ayam agnih subirya syese mahah saubhagasya
> Raya ise svapatyasye gomata ise brtrah athanam.
> Imam naro marutah sascata brdham yasmimrayah sebr dhasah.
> Abhi ye santi prtanasud udhyo bisvaha satrumadu bhuto.
> Sa tvam no rayah ssihi midhvo agne subiryasye
> Tubidyumna barsisthasya prajabatoana mibasya susminah.
>
> (*Rigveda* V. 3/16/1-3)

(This very Agni is the possessor of the highest capacity; he is the lord of great fortune, lord of wealth, of cows and the like and also of wealth with descendants; he is also the lord of the killers of the britrasie cloud and darkness. O ye the maruts, the best among men—be united with Agni, giver of wealth and promoter of fortune, because in Agni lies wealth that augments happiness. The maruts will defeat the enemies in battle and receive the mercy of Agni. O Agni! In you lie the store of all wealth. Please bestow that wealth on us and make us prosperous.)

This begging for wealth from Agni is taken in an ambiguous sense. The deeper meaning is the spiritual wealth that is man's highest longing—the wealth of spiritual wisdom. That wealth gives man his utmost wisdom. This longing is for fulfilment to be achieved in life.

In another sense, this wealth is earthly wealth. It is evaluated in terms of financial measures. It makes a man rich in the earthly sense. It brings the capability of earning enough profit, enough happiness and prosperity.

The financial aspect of the Vedic people was not limited to their prayer only. There had been trade in agricultural commodities as well as in different handicrafts. The kings were experts in hunting, which had really been in their jurisdiction. Trade and commerce mainly involved the Vaisya community. Of course, there was no such hard and fast communal distribution. The main principle of trade was service. All of the trades were run on the basis of basic principles and religious faith. Thus, the purity of trade had been maintained and through its use and in its light, trading would be established.

Religion is the proper field of application of the call, as summon sounded in the *Rigveda*. The principle of trade has been determined on the basis of religion. However, society has achieved the fullest solvency, the power of controlling the self and complete sovereign management. Modern society will have to observe the Vedic ideal with care for solving all problems, big or small. Only then there would be real development and a permanent solution for financial problems.

19

Vedic Economy: Eradication of Poverty

The pain of not having is poverty. In economic discussions, poverty is measured on the basis of the act of living. Many types of indexes are used in measuring the quality of living—the collective measure of these is used for characterising poverty. Poverty may be of many types. The pain of not having the required factors to maintain the body is called physical poverty. There exists mental poverty even. The pain of not having the proper expansion of wind brings mental poverty.

As poverty is a subject of external measurement, it is also one of the internal realisations. As there are procedures for measuring external poverty from different angles, there are many angles for looking at internal poverty. Most of the opinions discussed so far in the purview of economic exercise have measured external poverty and would like to eradicate the same at a later stage.

Of the opinions that have stressed the problem of poverty during the last two centuries, mentions may be made of Adam Smith, Keynes, Schumacher, Mahbub-ul-Huq and Amartya Sen. Karl Marx mainly focused on the problem of discrimination. While trying to solve the problem of discrimination, he has also brought the problem of poverty into discussion and has set in for its solution. Schumpeter, Ricardo and Merton have also brought the problem of poverty into the discussion for getting balance in the financial system and given solutions as well. Almost all junior economists have somehow or other presented the problem of poverty and have suggested a few points on the solution thereof.

Kautilya's *Arthashastra* has made detailed discussions on the problem of poverty. Actually, Kautilya was the first person to place poverty as the main problem of economics. Recently, Amartya Sen and others have been discussing much about this problem and have contributed as well.

In spite of attempts to throw light on the problem of poverty by different people in different ways, no economist of post the Kautilya period has been able to get to the root of the problem so far. Everyone has exaggerated the outer covering and offered solutions. E.F. Schumacher is, of course, an exception among them. Schumacher paid no attention to the poverty of individuals. He rather aimed at eradicating poverty at the state level. Schumacher tried to introduce a new financial system through the new and old systems, the main aim of which was to extend the purchasing capacity of the people. He wanted to set up a new financial system through the involvement of the poor people, the chief target being to spread the good effects of the financial system. Amartya Sen and Jean Derex have had detailed discussions on the problem of poverty. They have presented many examples, have done many calculations and as a result, have provided solutions based on the social indexes. Amartya's discussion is covered with a sheath of ideology and is rather one-sided. If one goes through the latest works of Sen, based on which he received the Nobel Award, one will find a fundamental trend viz malice against India. Amartya's malice against India can be traced as a basic pillar of his discussion on economics.

A small example may be cited, however, many such examples can be found out. Amartya Sen has discarded, with no proof or document, the financial system of ancient India in Maurya regime, as presented by Megasthenes. Megasthenes reported that in Maurya reign there had been no trace of poverty at all. If this is admitted, the glory of ancient India is established and possible that is the grudge of Amartya Sen.

On the other hand, he said that Kautilya has discussed poverty—so in pre-Kautilya period, there had been severe degree of poverty in India. Possibly, the aim behind this remark is to use Kautilya purposely, according to his opinion. It is so because he seems to be acquainted with the *Arthashastra* of Kautilya. If he is really conversant, he must have known that Kautilya has dealt with the problem of poverty from the pre-poverty status. That is, he has narrated the duties of a State for not allowing poverty to come in.

Amartya's one-sided opinion cannot be discarded, because a good number of people are attracted to this; so, it is to be analysed in detail. E.F. Schumacher is one of several people who up till now have made the most effective discussions with poverty.

The present discussion has been made on the basis of a total view of poverty and not at all letting this to be regarded as one-sided. Consequently, one world gets here the hint of dependable solution to the problem of poverty.

What is poverty and why is it there? The World Bank has defined the poverty level in terms of the purchasing capacity against demand for calories. But the procedure should normally have been as follows:

(1) determination of calories required for the act of living, normal growth of an average man and calculation of the price thereof in the light of the existing market.

(2) determination of minimum requirement of clothing for living and fixing its cost.

(3) measure of money required for common dwelling places.

(4) provision of emergency goods for living, such as money for treatment of diseases, expense for providing means to get rid of natural, social and political calamities (for the people of countries with developed financial system, this is designated as different types of insurance and premium thereof.)

(5) expenses towards education and establishment of self, needed for the heirs and those for the next generations.

The sum total of the present cost of all the above items may designate the poverty level. For convenience of calculation, an example may be cited. Say, Abanita Tafadar wears two pairs of shoes a year which cost 365 rupees, which means that she needs 1 rupee per day towards the account of the shoes. So, she requires three sets of clothes, costing a total of 730 rupees, which is 2 rupees per day. She purchased a house for 365,000 rupees, having an average longevity of 25 years, which is 40 rupees per day. The total cost of food per day is 15 rupees and, on average the daily requirement of medicine is of 5 rupees. On this basis, it can be said that if Abanita Tafadar earns 63 rupees a day, she can manage her requirements.

Consistency needs to be brought in assessing poverty in the world financial system. For this, the World Bank calculates poverty in two modes. The purchasing capacity of one American dollar per head per day and of two American dollar per head per day. In the light of modern market value, the stage of one dollar may be taken to be the Indian poverty level.

p = poverty-level

Lm = lower middle class ('x' number) Um = upper middle class ('y' number) r = rich ('z' number)

sp = scantily poor ('u' number)

mp = moderatey poor ('v' number)

vp = very poor ('w' number)

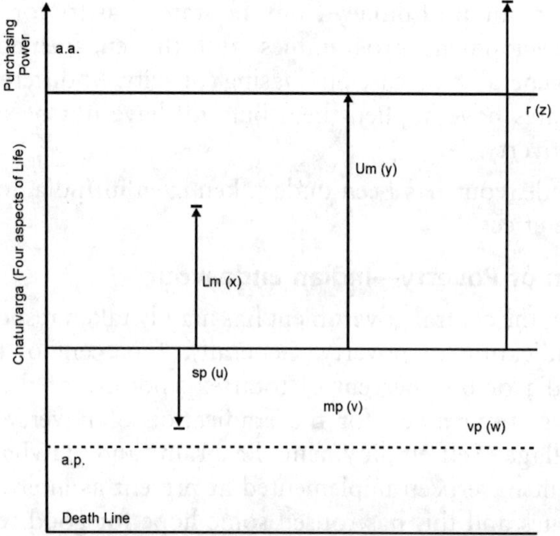

Figure 1: Poverty level—purchasing capacity order

In Figure 1, the order of the relation between the poverty level and the purchasing capacity has been shown.

Poverty may be assessed with a common calculation.

Total purchasing capacity of the poor = (sp)×u+ (mp) × v+(vp) × w

$$\text{average poverty (ap)} = \frac{\text{(Total purchasing capacity of the poor)}}{(u+v+w)}$$

Average poverty is the position of the poor people as per purchasing capacity per head.

Poverty in economics = (p - ap) × (u + v + w) Similarly, affluence can be assessed.

Total purchasing capacity of the affluent = (lm)× x+(um)×y+r×z

$$\text{Average affluence (aa)} = \frac{\text{(Total purchasing capacity of the affluent)}}{(x+y+z)}$$

Measure of total affluence in financial system = (aa - p)× (x + y + z)

From the above discussion, it becomes clear that if there is a lofty show of affluence, poverty naturally disappears. It is very clear theoretically, but practically, it is not so. It is nearly absurd for money to move to poverty from affluence.

Of a number of prevailing modes, there is the role of a state to a considerable extent in two cases. These include the investment of a greater amount of money from the state treasury for expenses towards development programmes and the engagement in an attempt to generally increase purchasing capacity. At different times, different states have applied them but still have not been able to eradicate poverty.

Such endeavour has been undertaken even in India and still is but to little effect.

Eradication of Poverty—Indian Endeavour

In India, the central government has mainly taken responsibility for the eradication of poverty. Generally, 1 percent of the total GDP of India or 6–7 percent of total expenditure of the Central Government is expended for the eradication of poverty. Golden Jubilee Village Self-employment Program and Jawhar Rural Development have been implemented at present as alternatives to the older ones and this has roused some hope for good results. In spite of expending 6–7 percent of government expenditure, nothing more than creating some temporary employment in villages has been possible.

Temporarily some movement of money has been made but owing to extensive corruption, the money has gone into the pockets of the political or the local agencies on whom the responsibility of running the programs had been vested. Though the programs had been designed with the aim of extensive transfer of money, in reality, very little transfer has been affected. However, in rural and semi-urban regions, a class of suddenly turned neo-rich class of people has come up.

In many cases, this neo-rich class has brought up the black market in the financial system, outside the mainstream of the financial system of the country. One example is enough to realise the situation.

Subsidised food materials are given in the custody of the state governments for distribution among the poor through a public distribution system (PDS). Average accounting of the last few years has revealed that a very small portion of the total quality of food materials is reaching the poor. Out of say, 100 kg of food supplied, only 40 kg reaches the doors of the poor people, 20 kg gets damaged in different godowns during storage and rests there as a remnant. No trace of the rest 40% can be found. States provide varied explanations and in connivance with a class of officers at the centre, the matter is quite hushed up. One of the states that act thus is West Bengal.

On the part of the government of India, a new management process has been announced. It is a proposal involving a huge amount of money. The proposal for work involved in the development of road and transport at an expense of 15,000 crore has been floated. The purchasing capacity would be extended with the transportation of money. All opine that, at the influence of this, the effect of poverty would necessarily be reduced.

A little observation of the matter would reveal a basic possibility in the same. The inner sense of Maynard Keynes' proposal of public spending, which is the increase of expense from government fund, is that man, by nature, is enterprising. Enterprise is lacking owing to the want of the fund. If there is a supply of funds, man would be necessarily enterprising. This idea of enterprise is always not uniform in all countries or in the same country. For example, it was much successful in Germany in the initial stage of World War II. It has also been successful in America on several occasions. On the other hand, during the movements of Gandhi in pre-independent India, many such enterprises had appeared behind German and government expense.

In India, there was no monetary help at all, rather there had been much opposition. However, in spite of the unrest, the enterprise expanded rather extensively. At the root of this, there was the national impetus or an inspiration of an ideal. If there is an inspiration of an ideal, enterprise necessarily comes. In the government enterprises of our country, huge amounts of money have been expended towards rural development and upliftment under different headings during the last fifty years, but no permanent result has been achieved. This is because if somebody calls upon me for road construction under the scheme of working for 100 days and giving some daily wages, my basic propensity would be to give satisfaction to the starving members of the family. The first preference would be for good materials, next would be clothing. Similarly, a liking for other luxury goods would gradually follow.

The measure of poverty cannot be changed only through public spending. The miserable consequence of IRDP or Jawahar Earning Program has been specially proved it in the Indian situation. Unless and until an enterprise is created, no change in the measure of poverty may creep in. Eradication of none of the forms of poverty—mental or physical—is possible through the supply of money.

Let us assume that the Marxian method is successful. It is inferred then that poverty is completely eradicated by taking surplus money and wealth from the total affluence. The process that has been used to stop discrimination. However, this will also not eradicate poverty. Only the feeling of satisfaction can bring an end to poverty. To eradicate poverty, we must begin looking for satisfaction.

Recovery from Poverty Through Spreading of Satisfaction

The question is what begets satisfaction. Is there any common measuring standard of satisfaction? Or is it different in different countries or in different people? Basically, satisfaction may be classified into two classes.

Obstruction Before Satisfaction

(a) starvation, want of clothing, want of dwelling house, lack of education, lack of hygiene and so on.

(b) mental stress, uncertainty, worry, unrest, anxiety for the future and above all, the tendency to consume.

Expansion of Satisfaction

(a) praise, cognition and position in family and social fields.

(b) Feeling of renunciation.

(c) Life based on spirituality.

Supply of funds or provision of education and hygiene has been admitted by all as means for removing the obstruction. Structure of character, cultural environment and mental identity become prominent.

Satisfaction comes sharp before a person with a spiritual mentality. A person having a thirst for spirituality always thinks that since everything here is quite well, nothing more is to be expected—

let me now remember God. If we take account of the cravings and earnings of most of the Indian ascetics living at hermitages, we will see that their earning is very nominal and the list of their cravings it also almost nil—yet they feel fully satisfied in being able to call God twice a day and to sing in praise of Him. Coming out on the road they are toiling hard in service of God and their mentor; still, they are highly pleased with such toil in life, considering that as their service to God.

They, having come out in the name of God, like to cross the pleasure of life on the boat of joyfulness. They are satisfied. The supply of funds for them is nothing but superficial. The mentality of renunciation and the basis of spirituality have brought their life the fullest satisfaction. Hunger for things is always minimum. People are satisfied when the basics of life are fulfilled and they are in a position to serve guests and visitors.

The satisfaction of an ascetic is normal and spontaneous. But it may be applicable in the case of any person whosoever. It is essential for a state. It reduces the problem of a state based on religion and spirituality.

Eradication of Poverty: Initial Management

The above discussion reveals the effect of character and mentality. The spiritual environment would reduce poverty, bringing satisfaction with little effort. As soon as the obstruction against satisfaction is removed to some extent, a feeling of satisfaction begins to appear.

Standing on this basis of environment, the state can start taking steps for dispelling poverty of individual through:

(i) self-dependence

(ii) enterprise and

(iii) attempt to set up balance

For self-dependence, the country shall have to be divided into smaller financial regions, and self-dependence is to be brought in these regions. For this small technologies, small investments and a cooperative financial management through the coordination of many people need to be built up.

Enterprise would come through the coordination of the state and its people. It is the responsibility of the state to create an environment of idealism and the responsibility of being enterprising within that environment is vested in individuals. It is the spirituality that would provide mental power for such enterprises.

There should be balance between enterprises of the state and the individuals. A really concerted union of self-dependence, enterprise and balance is able to eradicate poverty in the state and the world. Through the very same management, poverty had been eradicated in the reign of Rama in ancient India, in the reign of Yudhisthira at the time of the *Mahabharata* and later in some other time during the Maurya reign. It is possible to come back anew to that stage, where there would be no starvation, lack of education and pain of lack of hygiene. Satisfied men have established lives in the stage of divine beauty through singing the praise of God. Such days are at the door.

20

Technology in Vedic Economics

Technology determines the form of economics. Right along with the change of technology, new types of production systems bring change in the economic field, a new direction of producer-owner relationships get exposed through this. Technology initiates new types of mentality and social relations.

In the commencement of the twenty-first century, we find that computer-driven technology has entered all the spheres of life. The fashionable name of this is the information technology revolution, in brief, the IT Revolution—computer technology has dispelled the distance between the different ends of the world. All information about one end of the world may reach the other end within a moment.

All sorts of communication and exchanges are being arranged to come to effect within a moment through e-mail just like a flash of lightning. Any happening or discovery at one end of the world moves to the other end within a moment.

Not just information, but starting from trade and commerce, down to the sale and purchase of shares of different companies also have become instantaneous now. As the internet has arranged the exchange of information, it has also made arrangements for the sale of commodities. Through the internet, a buyer at one end of the world can manage selling of services from the other end. At the time of purchase, one can even negotiate prices and judge the merits and demerits of the commodity. IT has brought us in such a situation that a global society has come into existence.

More or less a group of people in all of the countries of this world have been united among themselves and while effecting the exchange of ideas, words, commodities for sale, service and above all, culture has turned into a separate nation. This number is comparatively smaller in developed countries than in the less developed ones. This society is a global society or international society. Their identity would be independent of the identity of their country as a nation.

A rootless society is raising heads inside the global society. This very society has turned into a main party in the control system of the world. Their feelings and demands will reign over those of others. National mentality, national tradition and sequence have gradually been intolerable and mean to them. Whatever will be offered under the cover of nationalism has become mean and be forsaken in their propaganda.

The revolution in the IT industry has brought the arrangement of a new relationship. The lack of any relation with nationalism has already been referred to. Another thing that is very special is the indulgence gradually accorded more and more to mechanisation. The problem faced in the initial stage of the industrial revolution was the change of the names of the workers to numbers. One Arun Chandra Roy, on entering the factory, was identified as worker number 3421. In spite of being designated numbers, the name as an identity prevailed in the age of the industrial revolution. The name and identity of the man behind it had to be identified to inspire him for the work and to get him linked up with the work. In the age of the IT revolution, this has lost importance to a great extent. Arun Chandra Roy, in spite of being an individual, will work here as A, the man. His personal identity here is of no value. It is his intelligence that counts here. A, the man, would be judged in terms of his intelligence and skill.

The extent to which one would rise to get importance would depend on one's knowledge of computers and the power and force of its application. Only having knowledge will not be sufficient, Mr. Arun would have to apply the same promptly. It is useless to evaluate who has accomplished the work. What is only to be judged is whether the work has been accomplished. IT is going to wipe out the consideration of space, time and objects. As a result of this, a new society has arisen in the present world system, which is identified only by its standard of living.

It is not at all to be judged to what extent he thinks. Whether any spiritual longing has developed in him or whether conscience, abandonment has grown in him. What is to be judged is his income and the number and quality of cars he uses; how many residential addresses he has; how many cities of the world he has covered; what is his capability of buying on credit; how far his identity is international. Changes in technique have opened the door to such changes.

Provisions of Technology

Different types of provisions at different stages of technology often become absolutely important. For example, let us use the *charkha* (spinning wheel) for the production of khadi clothes or use the ultramodern computer-driven weaving machine. The efficiency of a machine of the first type in producing khadi is very limited. The machine will have to stand on a small extent of production. If that machine produces to the maximum extent, it would be possible for the machine man to have little surplus; otherwise, the operation will just somehow earn his livelihood.

On the contrary, the efficient driving of surplus, which is able to get the livelihood of funds required to set up a computer-driven technology, is a few lakh times that required for setting up of spinning wheels for *khadi*. The investment required for a computer-driven technology for an employment of the ordinary level may be used for creating about a few thousand employments in the khadi or cottage industry. As a result of this provision, technology has become a very important factor. If the amount of investment demanded by ultramodern technology possibly be invested in the village, cottage or small industries, a revolution may be brought in the employment structure. A small example will clarify this situation. When we were in the jurisdiction of the ninth five-year plan, half of the period of this plan passed in the meantime. In the ninth five-year plan, special importance has been laid on the development of the infrastructure for the Indian industries. Infrastructure is very much essential for flourishing industries.

As for example, if the cable of the optical fibre is spread throughout the country, and the internet connection is affected through that, then the bandwidth available thereby cannot be had from ordinary cables. Thus, the enormous investment in the telecom industry has been noticed. During the next five years, at least five lakh crores of money (in the present rate) will be required for the extensive development in telecom, roads, rail, air transport and communication management.

If the provision for these five lakh crore rupees is affected and if the investment becomes proper, the infrastructure required for the extensive development of industries will be set up. If, along with this, the extension of the measure of infrastructure industries is also developed accordingly, investment in the industries will also be needful in almost the same way. These types of industries, having rapidly flourishing character, will not look back at the older technology.

But this aims at computers or robot-driven machines that would go on producing without caring for human effort. Japan and America are now vying with each other in terms of the usage of robots for developed and quickly producing industries. A very recent report of Morgan Stanley (October 2000) reveals that about forty thousand and twenty thousand robots are engaged in various activities in Japan and America, respectively. They are continually being replaced by newer robots. The first robot that had been undertaking the work of one hundred men was removed to be replaced by another that could accomplish the work of two hundred—a robot that does the work of five hundred men but cannot provide bread to a hundred men. Making this type of technology useful is the consequence of extensive investment in infrastructure.

If, after extensive investment in infrastructure, there is no investment of equal extent in the development of industries, the whole endeavour would be futile. The sum total of these two investments is a rather pervasive affair. Under the present circumstances, such investments on the part of the state are merely a fancy. The amount of five lakh crore rupees required for extensive development of infrastructure or rather a revolution in infrastructure would bring good results only when that same amount of investment would come into the industrial field. Let us assume that it is possible. Even then, the benefit would reach those countrymen who have enough buying and expending capacity.

If there is any deficit of buying and purchasing capacity coming within the purview of this, the benefits would not be possible—of course, there may be some indirect influence on it. The situation of the villagers, the people below the level of buying capacity, is liable to remain unaltered. Here, the problem is twofold. Firstly, providing such a huge amount of money for investment is beyond the capability of the financial power of a state. Secondly, such a great investment, too, will not be able to cause much damage to the basic financial problem of a country. The problems of poverty, famine, deficit of education, hygiene and of lack of social balance would remain unaltered.

On the contrary, if the investment required for infrastructure is made limited and that money is invested in rural industries in modernising agriculture in the cottage and smaller industries, the scope of extensive employment would be possible. There would be a flow in the employment structure and would cause an extensive increase in purchasing capacity. Affluence would come in every house, but it would not be possible to have the right to profuse surplus.

Compensation for Technology

Being tempted by a fascinating name and lustre for better technology, we are running after it. We have had the idea that computers would wipe out all diseases. This notion about computers is not at all correct. Computer-driven technology ushers in a blow of development. Production increases manifolds by this and the quality of production also improves. But it is useless to think that with this, there would be an extensive change in the financial position. Let us take an example. It is a rather recent past incident. Chandrababu Naidu liked to be known as the Chief Executive Officer of Andhra. There is no denying the fact that he has brought speed and transparency to the activities of the state. Naidu was running the activities of the state in a corporate fashion. The basic driving force in the activities of all departments of the state is a computer.

The computer had brought a change in the movement and management of the government activities of Andhra. As a result, it gained extensive publicity. The degree of publicity was so loud that Bill Gates, the legendary figure of Microsoft company, and Bill Clinton, the President of America, rushed there. Both Gates and Clinton praised the flow of development brought about by Chandrababu Naidu. But does the real situation admit the authenticity of these claims and publicity? Most probably not. During the past one year, the GDP of Andhra has fallen below, as compared to that of previous years. The production per head has fallen down.

In all, the financial condition of Andhra is waving instead of increasing. Recently, a new problem has cropped up in the field of agriculture. Due to the rise in the cost of production of agricultural commodities, the sale and selling measure of the surplus crops has also decreased. The actual development in Naidu's state was less than the publicity it had gained. Here, one-sided investment had caused a disturbance in the financial equilibrium and the investment in the agriculture-related industries had not risen enough.

Qualitative change in the act of living gradually changes at different stages of the development of technology. Change in the standard of living takes place from qualitative and quantitative changes in consumption. More developed technology is applied in the blooming of beauty and excess of life to a much greater extent than being used in supplying the basic needs of life. Thousand times more developed technology applied in food, clothing and shelter is bringing about a variety in clothing, fancy foods and decoration of a decent-looking dwelling place. Developing technology is as if it were a black hole. If plunged into it once, there remains no scope of coming back.

A separate order comes out after looking at the industrial picture of India. The Indian mentality and traditional flow have cast greater influence than the financial endeavour planned by many behind the serial order that has brought about by the picture of the Indian industry. The speed of development in the mixed economies so far reared by independent India is very limited. The financial investigation of 1999-2000 shows that in some fields important on the part of industrial production, the speed of development is rather very scanty. The following table gives an idea of this:

Table 2

Year (Assuming 1993-94=100) April-December	Mineral production (10.47 parts)	Manufacturing (79.36 parts)	Electricity (10.17 parts)	Overall percentage (100 parts)
1995–96	10.3	13.7	8.9	12.8
1996–97	-1.2	8.3	3.8	6.9
1997–98	5.5	7.0	6.0	6.8
1998–99	-4.8	3.9	6.8	3.7
1999–2000	0.0	6.7	7.7	6.2

In case of industrial production, the rate of production sometimes (for example, during the first three months of 1995) has been 18 percent and again has gone down to 1 percent (during the last two months of 1999). However, from 1995–96 up to 2000, average advancement has been 7 percent every year. Not only in these years, after 1980, but the average industrial development of India has also increased by 7 percent every year.

In agriculture, during these two decades, the annual change has been at the rate of 3.5 percent a year. From 1980–2000, development of industry in China has been at the rate of 12.5 percent and agriculture has increased there at the rate of 5.1 percent. During the same period, the industry of America has increased at the rate of 2.5 percent and in agriculture, the increase was by 1.2 percent. The rate of annual development of the developed countries is rather low. On the contrary, it is found to be maximum in case of China. In developed countries, it has come to the lowest limit. On the contrary, in China, the financial discrimination has risen to the highest degree. India stands midway. If India continues to maintain its own style, it would not be possible to solve the financial problems. India should take a well-thought-out decision, while deciding the economic policies.

Outline of Vedic Technology

By September 2000, all over the world, a total of 7,50,000 robots were prepared to be engaged in action as they were already in action. In 2003, the number rose up to 9,00,000. There were about 2.7 million industrial robots in use across the globe. Roughly 4,00,000 new robots enter the market every year. The global market value of the industrial robotics industry is 43.8 billion USD in October, 2022. It is quite natural that in India also these will be utilised for action. Now the question is, would we move in all cases for total mechanisation, or would we bind ourselves within limited mechanisation?

As mentioned earlier, the commodities produced in huge amounts by fully automatic technology have no application in the basic needs of living—they have cosmetic utility, only to add fragrance to life. Thus, an individual can well control their use. A Hindu mind, as does not shun enjoyment, also does not forget abandonment. The Hindu mentality is in a state of being extended in maintaining a balance between enjoyment and abandonment.

As a result, a Vedic mind quite naturally feels tired of accepting many useless products to be useful. A Vedic mind, as such, would not drag the cosmetic makeup of mechanised production to a great extent. The use of technologies that have no ultimate use in the development of the country would gradually be limited. The technologies that do come in conflict with the tradition and culture of a country would gradually be waning. In the long run, a unified technology would come into play; at one end of it would remain a limited use of ultramodern technology, and on the other, there would be an extensive use of small technologies that would give a scope of employment to crores of people.

21

Creating Economic Equilibrium Using Vedic Economy

Two main economic problems have appeared before us in this modern world—first is the problem of poverty, and second is that of enjoyment. Poverty on one side and propensity of consumerism on the other have brought forth uncertainty in the world economy. Big companies selling their commodities all over the world are occupying markets one after another and finally are collapsing at the shock of the rise and fall of the market. Fall of a great man has been a very common matter today in many forms in the world economy.

By virtue of globalisation, even small and poor countries have paced towards this path of marketisation. As a result, they are getting the propensity of the same type of living standards as demanded by the kings. The mental affinity of most people is running towards the mainstream market. A much smaller number of people have possibly succeeded in the attempt. But in their mind, they are peeping that type of living that makes one an international or universal buyer.

The medium and flow of publicity of the companies are mainly people-oriented. They constantly say, "Buy this, buy that; use this more; pay more attention to that. Don't buy their products, buy mine. I provide commodities that are more durable and of a better standard than theirs and I supply commodities with proper prices. Something more would be available along with the purchase of my product."

You would be fortunate enough to have such things, and your life would be happier. The market brings change in many things. A new trend of liking and disliking has set in. Man tries to discover the rhythm of life in a newer form.

Commodities used yesterday may not be of use today. Commodities appear anew in the market and the older ones get lost. This is called the higher standard of living. Previously, there was a great demand in society for typists for manual typing. They were needed in every office and company for running activities therein. In the changed circumstances, such people have almost been useless. Manually operated typing machines are now obsolete. Now, computers are active, and this will grow further. Machines of older types and men related to those have lost their demand today. The market has given them a verdict—find your way home, the market has no room for you.

Technology has brought a new wave of changes. All of the rest are being changed with the change of technology. The old downfall at the nook of the straight machine. If we pay keen attention at the stage of change, it would be quite clear that all economic models prevailing in the past are now obsolete. None of capitalism, communism, socialism, radical socialism and even any mutual mixture will do in the slippery path of change. Behind the new world, management to which is directed, our present journey is a beckoning of creation of newer men. The market will glow along the strong currents of globalisation and would bring about such an arrangement where all the activities will be run by people different from the crowd. They look at life with a new vision. They cast a newer vision at everything of this world. By character, they are different. On one side, life experiences a beckoning of infinite consumerism, and on the other side, life experiences endless pain, poverty, lack of education and hygiene—from these a newer man would emerge who would stand up straight above his own bounds of interest.

Poverty And Inequality

In world economics, poverty and inequality have assumed a more turbulent form. Although the number of people with higher purchasing capacity are gradually increasing, the number of people having purchasing capacity about nil is also very high. This is the main problem with the developing and poor countries. Let us review the matter in detail. The recent report of the World Bank (August, 2000) has cast light on this point. The World Bank has classified the layers of the economic principles of the world in terms of GNP or gross national production.

Type of economy	Average national production per head (at the rate as in 1998)
Poor country	760 dollar or less
Lower middle-class country	761–3030 dollar
Higher middle-class country	3031–9360 dollar
Affluent countries	9361 or higher

(World Development Report, 1999/2000)

Japan and Singapore are affluent countries of Asia. Korea and Malaysia are high-middle class. Philippines, Thailand and Sri Lanka are lower middle-class. Finally, India and China are poor. Other instances of affluent countries include America, Canada, Eastern Europe countries and Australia.

If classified in terms of population, it would be found that most of the people in the world are poor, next comes the lower-middle class. Economic management is going through an augmenting discord and inequality, which has been shown through a simile by a renowned economist, Charles Leadbeater. Leadbeater has given (1990) the hint of possible slide in world-economy. He has said:

On the seacoast of Farai in Thailand thousands of crabs fight among themselves in every evening. They first divide themselves into groups and then continue to live among themselves. In the social system of these crabs, there is an attempt to keep up their identity in a dignified way. These propensities, in many cases, are identical to ours. Then, they start to fight among themselves. One pierces the other. If one tries to rise up, others drag it down. They do not offer any cooperation beyond that required for living. Now the question is—is the socio-economic situation of men much different from this? The only difference between them and us lies only in their claws and stings causing wounds.

We are biting one another in the name of competition. The basis of the civilisation set up by us on the foundation of competition is to resort to any means whatever to fulfil own interest and to protect the capital interest. Another famous economist, Herbert A. Heller, also has presented the fact nicely. He has written:

The basic pillars of capital economics are—open market, individual ownership of wealth, investment for personal interest and mutual competition. These are the same in all places of the world. But the situation and environment where the managers of the company's work are different in different regions.

The external environment is not the same throughout the world. But the target of all is same. How can the market be occupied and by what means the competition may be won over? It is an overall war. While explaining this, the renowned Japanese management pioneer Kennedy Ohamaze (1990) has commented that to win a battle is good but it is better to win without war and resorting to tricks.

There is enough substance in the remark. But the question is: could there be no alternative device for those enterprisers who, like the crabs of the Thailand's crab valley, are dying and would die in due course? If keeping the standard of the market and the living standard undisturbed, the circumstance of the market could have continuously been increased, then the crab-war would possibly not be required.

If the market goes on increasing, increase of the circumference of the market nears a situation when people of newer purchasing capacity would come up to buy common customary goods of the market. As a result of this, a new situation of relations and new equilibrium would come in the world economy. The first principle of establishing new equilibrium is to drag the people at the lowermost level of the economic-system upwards—to provide calories to those who are crippled due to the want of needful calories; to provide education to those who have met permanently crippled due to the want of education; to distribute materials of good hygiene and healing from diseases among those who have somehow managed to live on in the beckoning of diseases, decrepitude and death.
Sir James David Wolfensohn in his recent addresses held the marketing system responsible for this discrimination, lack of education and lack of hygiene, warning that unless these are solved, this danger would approach everyone just like a timebomb. The World Bank has forwarded this picture through poverty, lack of education and hygiene prevailing throughout the world.

The picture of poverty in this world at the beginning of 2000 is rather dreadful.

Of 600 crore people, 280 crores have a daily income of less than 2 dollars, which is 90 rupees. Twenty-two years later, even though the population of the world has grown fabulously close to seven hundred and fifty, the economic output, in real terms, has not been properly matching.

The daily income of 120 crore people one dollar, which is less than 45 rupees. Of these men, only 2 percent live in Europe and Central Asia; 0.5 percent live in the Middle East and North America; 6.5 percent in Latin America and Caribbean; 23.2 percent in East Asia and the Pacific region; 24.3 percent in Sahara and Africa and the rest in South Asia. The average national income of the twenty poorest nations is 1/37 of that of the twenty most affluent nations. The problem of lack of education and hygiene lies side by side with the problem of poverty.

In affluent countries, the death rate of children of less than five years is 1 percent while in poor countries it is 20 percent. In affluent countries, 5 percent of below five suffer from malnutrition, while in poor countries, the figure rises to 50 percent of children attaining the age for going to school—9 percent boys and 15 percent girls get nothing to eat. The severity of poverty is getting reduced to some extent. But the rate of inequality is increasing. The future is at stake. Now the question is—where lies the solution?

Why This Poverty And Inequality?

The picture of poverty and discrimination just presented is rather frightful. The question arises—where is the main reason for this hidden? The solution of which of the problems can reduce or eradicate such discrimination and poverty?

On the opposite of poverty and discrimination lies an excessive lure for enjoyment. Within 1–6 percent of the Americans, a terrible attempt always plays to buy something or the other. Such purchase, in no way, emerges from necessity. They even do not know why they like to purchase. They only know that purchase can lift one up. Purchasing is the nature of life; they get to relish their purchases. On the other hand, the essence of a life addicted to consumerism lies in excessive enjoyment and wastage of limited basic wealth of the world.

Excessive propensity to consumerism and a mentality of wastage have appeared as a characteristic of the developed countries. Personal philosophy has been excessive enjoyment and too much wastage for one's own pleasure. The main driving force of society is this mentality of enjoyment.

The more dominant is the role of a person as a purchaser, the more indispensable and attractive he would be to trade and industry. The identity of a man lies in his purchasing capacity. One who can purchase more becomes more precious. One whose purchasing capacity is less, becomes of lower value. The power of dominance lies within purchase and wastage. The basic principle of poverty and discrimination is also hidden in this propensity of purchase and wastage.

Solution Lies In The Vedic Mentality

The net result of excessive consumption and wastage has been the self-aggrandisement of the moving power. Every person is moving fast towards the accomplishment of his own interest in order to fulfil his desired end. At the same time, he is denying his responsibility to others and to society. Almost all of the pioneers' economists right from Adam Smith have taken self-interest to be important in many ways. Almost all of them have the main assertion—the more self-interest would be satisfied, the more developed would be the society or civilisation. If, while satisfying the self-interest, a man does not mind in the least for other, then that would mean accomplishment of his own interest in opposition to the interest of the society and civilisation—the seed of the problem lies in such propensity. This is compelling to augment the discrimination.

A complete balance lies in the Hindu mentality. The Hindu mentality has instituted consumption on the basis of renunciation. The firm faith is that behind everything of this universe, God himself stands with his creatures. This world does not belong to one individual only, it belongs to all.

Pancharin Or Five-Fold Debt System

According to the Vedic faith, there lies the theory of five debts. The essence of the theory is that from our very birth we are indebted in many respects. We are to clear off the godly debt. Godly debt comprises of debts to the sky, wind, light and life. We have not longed for these things but still we are living with these. This debt may be cleared off to some extent at least with prayer and taking refuge. We have incurred the saintly debt ourselves through being great by acquiring knowledge from different sages and seers. The sages who have composed our language, knowledge, science, arts, literature, scriptures have made us equipped with wisdom of the present. Our debt for this is saintly debt. We can try to reduce this debt through daily reading and practice. Bowing down to the wisdom of the hermits that stand behind all the wisdoms, man will have to admit this saintly debt.

All have parental debt to their ancestors. The influence of the parents and forefathers are behind all of the physical and mental factors of life, right from heredity. Through admitting responsibility to the family, we admit parental debt. Through this admittance, sequence and family line flows on. This admittance helps man be family creatures. Such a management makes the intensity of consumption and wastage much reduced.

Manly debt is the admittance of our debt to all people. People engaged in placing food, clothing and shelter in orderly management have made us indebted to them. The clothes we now wear have behind them the untiring effort of many people. The food we take is the outcome of the effort of many. Our daily life is thus the result of different achievements of thousands of men. The healthy situation is to admit these achievements in a submissive mood.

Last of all comes the debt to the creatures. This is our duty to subhuman animals. Trees, beast and birds are constantly serving us. We are indebted to them all. We are in the living state only because they have jointly built up a proper environment for us to live in.

These five debts conjoin us with a vast universal management. The theory of five debts rebukes the idea to fulfil one's own interest without caring in the least for the rest of the world. This theory of debt fixed up our duty—what we are to consume, what would be the form of consumption and what would be the wastage. This gives rise to a complete outlook towards the wealth of the world. I do not belong to myself only. I and we all are meant to exist for the whole world. Thus, we are so eager to solve discrimination and poverty. If one can lift oneself from the sense of '7' to that of 'we', solution will be available—this is the gift of the Hindu mentality to the world.

22

Economy of Renunciation

Beginning from Adam Smith, Marx down to Blake, Morton or Amartya Sen of the modern times—basic and inner conviction of all discussions are embedded in consumerism. However, the stream of age- old economy of India is just its opposite. The tradition of Indian economy is abnegations. Right from the pre-Vedic times to the times of Ashoka, touching the time of Yudhisthira in the *Mahabharata*, this flow of abnegations has remained intact. Even so, this notion has got its fullest manifestation in the time of Yudhisthira. The state system that had been established following the victory chariot of the virtue of the *Mahabharata* is in many ways especially instructive.

In Yudhisthira's state was established social justice, economic balance and national unity. The state was run on the basis of religious faith, humane justice and morality. Though Yudhisthira would administer as a king, the specified duties and works, basically the administration system, was held in a religion of morality and truth. Yudhisthira, the emperor, has laid the highest dignity to the rights of the people in the way admitted by the justice due for the people. The state and economic policy of Yudhisthira were not bound but held by the free system of liberal justice.

In the field of administration, Yudhisthira had employed liberal-minded men in greater numbers. He had inspired them and accepted them spontaneously in the profession and activity.

The emperor wanted blooming and manifestation in many forms and in many ways.

The basic convictions in Yudhisthira's administration were:

1. spontaneous manifestation,
2. blooming of possibilities
3. distribution in terms of due dignity

4. basis of religion

The continuity of these principles was maintained in the state administration of the age of *Mahabharata*, even in post-Yudhisthira systems, specially up to the times of Pariksit and Janamejaya.

Economic Tradition

The evidence of pre-Vedic social systems available to us till date have at the source the discoveries of Harappa and Mohenjodaro. What was thought of initially from the presentation of information and proofs, could easily be marked later to be erroneous. For example, the theory of the arrival of the Aryans. The Britishers, with the help of sufficient proofs of the principal verifiable points of the historical factors, had showed that the Aryans were outsiders. Aryans taught India was a better civilisation after possession through wars. The inner idea of this notion was to prove India inferior. These people like to prove that the cause of India itself is rather inferior, the origin of any noble thing it possesses is at foreign lands. Paying a bit of attention to the references appended to the preaching of the scholars reveals how fickle and motivated their notions are.

The modes of preservation of tradition of different nations are quite different. While the Western attitude is to preserve its own achievements in a rather magnified and more beautiful form, giving these a permanent form for the future through proper care. India's temperament is just opposite. The West likes to frame up its achievement more preciously, while in India's temperament, the very idea of ownership is rather insignificant.

The nature of abnegation has brought a continuity of state in the Indian temperament. People here do not like to praise their own deeds, but rather try to avoid this. To know an Indian and a European, appraisal of this special aspect of tradition is necessary, as it also is necessary to realise this continuity of economic position. The exposition of economic status blooms mainly from the sequential arrangement and temperament. To realise the economy of abnegation, one has to have detailed knowledge about the economic arrangement of a consumeristic society. Thus, two economic systems may be brought to the field of discussion—modern world economic system and the economic system in the reign of Yudhisthira.

Consumerist Vs Abnegationist Economic System

What is the aim of your life? What is the factor that can be the cause of your satisfaction? What is to be done for the augmentation of the satisfaction of that society? Shall I, myself grow up, be satisfied or is thinking for others also necessary? Answers to many questions of this sort would tell what the tendency of a society would be—consumerist or abnegationist. A question may naturally arise—how does consumerism or abnegationism come in the field of the economic system. There is no difference in it. These poor would like to be well-off. The well-offs would like to be rich and the rich will like to be richer. There is no end to craving and no end to satiety either.

There is no regulating stage for the standard of living. It goes on increasing continuously. A lofty show of craving is quite natural, where there is the problem of poverty, starvation and lack of necessary requirements of life. Dissatisfaction and pain of non-fulfilment is there even at the root of this craving. Men of all stages feel the most acute pain of satiety. All types of men have been moved by the pain of being deprived. The pain of non-fulfilment gets transfused in the minds of all. As if there is no scope of having had the proper attainable objects, having been no blooming of possibilities.

All men are being goaded by circumstances and are think that blooming has not been possible due to inclemency of situation. They have had to yield to the pressure of the situation. The situation goaded by circumstances denotes misfortune. The attitude is that having had a congenial situation, they would have done many things. It could not have been so, hence the pain of dissatisfaction, the expression of non-fulfilment.

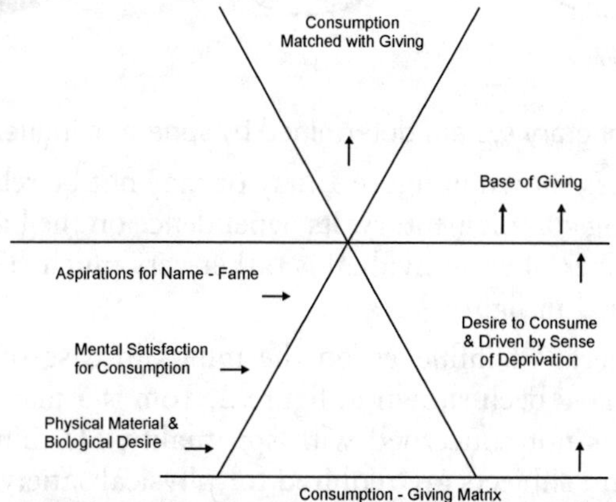

Figure 1: Consumption and Abnegation Matrix

Figure 1 denotes the relationship between consumption and abnegation. In this figure, we find a number of layers. The portion labelled by 'p' denotes the lust for consumption for physical ease. The portion labelled as 'm' denotes the lust for consumption directing to mental satisfaction. The portion designated as 'f' denotes lust for consumption goaded by desire of fame. The portion labelled as 'a' directs abnegation. On the basis of this, abnegation is established. Different distribution of lusts for consumption may be or may not be displayed layer wise, which means that it cannot be so that after satisfaction of the first, the second would arise. The lust for consumption in all the layers emerges from the feeling of want. For example, let us take the layer labelled as 'p'. Here measure of different types of satiety beyond physical needs is affected. As for the example, one may think that as Ramprasad had expressed in his song, the idea of being contented with little gains, so as soon as simple requirements like living ordinary, simple and easy lives, earning daily meals and meeting other, very simple needs, are satisfied pleasure foils monetary objects. The divine pleasure then lies in singing praises of God. In terms of the standard of money, the standard of living here is rather very low, but as far as satisfaction is concerned, it is the greatest.

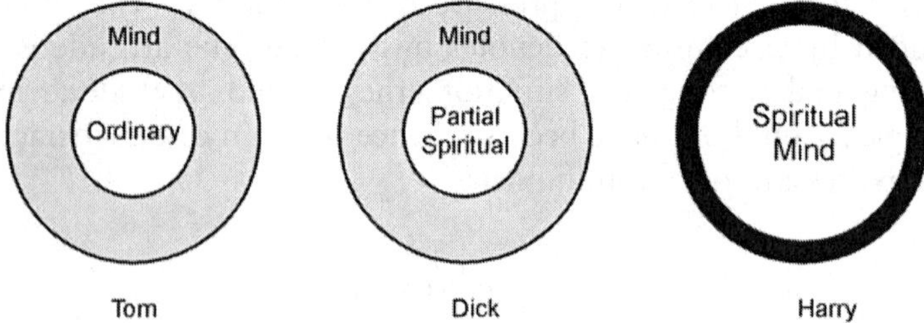

Figure 2: Monetary system determined by sphere of influence of mind.

The layers shown in figure 1 may or may not be related to each other as being complementary. Its dependence on the basic qualities of the character of an individual is rather very much. This has been well explained in figure 2.

The spheres of influence on the minds in case of Tom, Dick and Harry have been shown in figure 2. Tom is a man of ordinary stature. He is not concerned with spirituality. He thinks that lots of objects and subjects are required for physical satiety. Everything whatsoever is included in the list of Tom's demands. He thinks that life is consumption, and in consumption lies the fruition of life; success in life is in being a consumer.

Tom's physical content is never to be fulfilled—the reason is embedded in his mind. Since the intensity of craving for earthly pleasure is high in Tom's mind, his idea is that the desire for something more can bring his satiety to the fullest extent. It is rather hard to fix up the limit of his satiety. The pain of satisfaction always occupies Tom's mind. He always hankers after newer elements of pleasure, although no such element can satisfy him fully.

The case of Dick is somewhat different. He seeks an intermediate stage. After having physical satiety to a certain extent, he becomes mentally satisfied. Next, his attention is diverted to satisfaction of spiritual hunger. Thenceforth, he wants to move continuously on a spiritual path to make his life successful. The more intense Dick will make his move in the spiritual path, the less would be his longing for earthly pleasures.

As a natural consequence of spiritual movements, the extent of his longing would decrease. Contentment would come easily. The fact is that Dick can give some honour to both consumption and abnegation. Dick knows that consumerism cannot get him everything. The consumption of earthly pleasure can bring temporary satisfaction and the knotless form of dissatisfaction. Dick, standing in between satisfaction and dissatisfaction, suffers from constant swinging between greed of earthly pleasure and beckoning of abnegation. His mind can bring some control over craving, but complete control is beyond his capacity. For Dick's satiety, both elements of consumption and influence of mind are necessary.

Harry is in search of spirituality. The fundamental basis on which Harry has placed his life has as its main theme: life is for God only. The basic significance of living is doing everything centering God. Harry's basic confidence is in godliness. In the very longing, the essence of godliness is being drenched. When life is dedicated to God and seeks God, the influence of the factors of enjoyment gradually become contracted and limited. Consumerism loses its sphere of influence. That is why Harry thinks, "that is enough; no more is required." What is the use of running after money, what would one gain in having property, wealth or fame? The success in life does not lie there. Life would be fruitful with the quality of character, not with pervasion of money and fame—this sort of confidence makes Harry a monetary unit of different type. Men like Harry are controlled by their mind, and here the mind is in a state of its fullest purity.

Harry's mind is transparent, simple and pure. He seeks this state for many. The satisfaction of many is the object of Harry's consideration. For satisfaction of many, Tom is quite indifferent to his own enjoyment. He wants all types of monetary systems to be extended for everyone. His life is under the control of his mind and Harry himself is thirsty for spirituality. This thirst for spirituality in him is giving rise to the basis of a special arrangement, the main theme of which is, "Give him, them, not me." Such men initiate newer monetary systems in this earth.

The merits of the monetary system influenced by the dominance of Ram are:

- Creation of financial equilibrium among different financial groups of society.
- Introduction of social justice in financial management.
- To keep the financial systems always moving.
- To bring motion in the financial improvements in the state level, in the people's level or maybe in both. It is very hard to introduce a monetary system based on abnegation at the state level.

However, it may be possible in the level of the society through influencing the prevailing attitudes by spirituality. If the attitude prevailing in society is saturated with spiritual ideas, the introduction of economy of abnegation in people's level becomes rather possible. Both may take place together in probable cases.

In the state system of the *Mahabharata*, 'the economy of abnegation' was first introduced at Yudhisthira's regime through wide management of the state. Prior to this, of course, in the social system of the Vedic age, the economy of abnegation had been embedded in the very distribution of the society.

Economic Consideration and Management Of Yudhishthira

Immediately after the Kurukshetra war, Yudhisthira got the right to administration of the state. Vyasdeva, the great hermit, arrived at the palace for two reasons—consolation to Uttara and proper direction for running administration by Yudhisthira.

Parikshit's life was gradually being transfused in the womb of Uttara. Recalling this aspect of preserving the family line, Vyasdeva consoled Uttara and she desisted from grief. Next, Vyasdeva gave Yudhisthira two directions. The first was to get gold and jewels from gold mines and gold storages of the North-Eastern (Afghan and Persian) region. The second was to distribute surplus wealth at the command of the state widely among the people.

The source of the first was the gold mines and the gold storages build up by men of the dacoit class through long endeavours. Taking the vow of collecting jewels from these sources, Yudhisthira sent the armies and the brothers. There had been not much trouble in collecting this wealth because, after the war of Kurukshetra, nobody had the courage to go against the Pandavas. The armies of Yudhisthira collected enormous quantities of gold and jewels, exceeding the total carrying capacity of all types of transportation of the armies on their way back.

Right after the collection of the jewels came the occasion of the horse sacrifice. At the advice of Vyasdeva, Yudhisthira, after the final offering in the horse sacrifice, distributed money unflinchingly. In the sacrifice, there is a huge assemblage of people from different communities. For the poor people of the country, there were arrangements for offering gold, different types of jewels, milch (or would be milch) cows and other sorts of monetary wealth. Yudhisthira, the emperor arranged mass distribution of wealth procured by the state. The bounty of Yudhisthira was so vast and extensive that it roused awe even among the recipients. Charity after the horse sacrifice is rather customary. But customarily, 'charity' remains confined within 'surplus wealth'. This is highly mentionable in the case of Yudhisthira. Because he was mainly a munificent man, he had founded the economy on the basis of abnegation. Yudhisthira's personal belief had prompted him to initiate this abnegation-based economics. We shall recall here a mentionable incident of the *Mahabharata* through which we can ascertain that in the regime of Yudhisthira, charity was a social propensity. Man was contented with but little. The economic system had been built up through wide extensions of a small amount of consumable goods.

The standard of public living was rather ordinary but solvent enough. Problems arose with the nature-dependent agricultural system. Due to occasional drought and flood, at lapses of years, owing to laws of nature, there had been changes in yields of agriculture, leading to the paucity of food and provisions. But the state, by dint of its mass-oriented role, could solve these problems befalling the country.

Besides the cooperation of the state, the other thing that is worthy of mention is that a mentality of abnegation was transfused extensively within the people. The anecdote of the mongoose of the *Mahabharata* fears many a hint. The anecdote has influenced the main consideration of the horse sacrifice. The anecdote was as follows:

After the offering in the sacrifice, Yudhisthira was bestowing bountifully on the public, with unflinching charity. People of all castes—Brahmins, Kshatriyas (warriors), traders, and slaves—received the fullest charity. All were praising Yudhisthira. Such a charity had never been seen by anybody before, nor was heard or thought of. It was rather incomparable. When the distinguished people were praising Yudhisthira highly, a mongoose entered the court. It could speak in a human voice. The mongoose said, "you are not aware of real charity; hence you can say so. I have witnessed such charity, compared to which, Yudhisthira's charity is not charity at all. It is rather insignificant." Everyone was taken aback at the words of the mongoose. When asked what charity it spoke of, the mongoose said: "Listen then. Once upon a time, I would reside on a big tree just behind the house of a Brahmin. The village is at the remote end of this state.

At the time of war, agriculture in the village faced a severe shock. Food problems were prevalent. The Brahmin family had to starve for days together before procuring some good. Cooking those, all at the closing of the day, sat to take meal, after starving for quite a good number of days. After the ritual of rinsing and washing, they were about to eat their meal, when a hungry Brahmin beggar came at the door and begged for food. The householder became eager to fulfil the beggar's prayer. He gave away his full meal to him. But the beggar was not satisfied. He prayed for more. The house's mother then gave away her share. But as the beggar did not feel satisfied, even the son and the daughter-in-law gave away their full shares. The satisfied beggar departed. In reality, the lord of justice had come to test them in disguise. All the members of the family died after this incident. However, they achieved the celestial abode of Lord Vishnu. I found all to be dead, as I merrily rolled on the floor of their house. Consuming some grains of food lying scattered on the floor, my body came in contact with them and half of it turned golden. Such impoverished and selfless charity glows more than anything that comes in contact, just like gold. I took Yudhisthira's charity to be so selfless, so that I can make the other half of my body golden as well, but this did not happen. Even after rubbing my body with the food here, I found no change in my colour. That is why I call this charity to be mixed. Yudhisthira's charity is noble, but it has some inherent purpose in it. Therefore, its value is insignificant compared to the charity of that family."

The description of the mongoose unveils the characteristic of a truly charitable person. Such charitableness of characters is very rarely met within public, but at the basis of the state system, is built up by Yudhisthira. The emperor attempted to increase in the society the number of people thirsty for spirituality. That is the extension of people like Tom, as a result of which, monetary balance and equilibrium may get established in society. This is the reason why the economic system of Yudhisthira is really one of abnegation.

23

Future of Economy

Many people have researched economic faculty and economic ideas to find that though from the standpoint of application, those two exist the dawn of the history of man, from the standpoint of theory, they are in many respects rather new. Western ideas of economy ranges through few years only. Economic faculty is still a newer concept. As the European renaissance brought about a stir in culture and social ideas, it also led to cultivation of economic ideas and economic faculty. The situation in many other parts of the world is also likewise.

For living, an economic settlement builds up at all places; in many cases, it may be a 'happened-to-grow' stage, which means that behind this, there is no land of confidence or any philosophical basis. Greek philosophy was discussed the necessity of money and wealth as a part of life. A gradual and deep discussion followed. An extensive discussion of monetary affairs and a separate philosophy has been offered by Adam Smith. If judged, it is Adam Smith who gave economics a basis.

India has a distinct separateness in this matter. Just as Indian civilisation set out on a journey with the cultivation on truth, beautiful and God, from the very down of civilisation, India also had a fixed outlook on economic policy. In the Vedic age, there had been a call for combination of all the faculties. Money took an important position in the four principal pursuits, which were virtue, wealth, love and final salvation. The spiritual quest and realisation of India never deserted life. Rather, it always gave an importance to the blooming of the faculties of life. There is ample evidence of this in the eras of the *Ramayana* and the *Mahabharata*. The economic management in the reign of Rama demands special attention. The economic management in the reign of Rama had been more advanced than the economic ideas set up towards the end of the twentieth century and even at the twenty-first. Varied reasonings and arguments may be presented in support of this. Only a few of them are being forwarded to make the subject clear.

(1) **The Rybczynski Theorem:** This is a theory for the consideration of wealth. This theorem states that if the supply of a special type of wealth increases, then the productions and enterprises that utilise that wealth would go on increasing. The extent of their production, on the other side, the production of others would decrease.

(2) **The Stolper-Samuelson Theorem:** This theory aims at fixing up the relative influence of the different elements of determining prices. This theorem states that if the price of elements produced by a labour-based industry or enterprise increases, then the cost of labour will not only increase but will also increase by a greater extent than the cost of the merchandise. The cost of other things outside the labour that goes to determine the cost of the merchandise would increase. This theory is helpful in determining the price of the elements based on provisions.

(3) **Samuelson-Jacobian Matrix:** This observation tries to set up a balance in the market. In this observation, an idea is given how the market, through causing a modification of charity and supply, rectifies any disbalance in commercial transactions. A part of it is the behaviour of buyers. This theory tries to assess how the buyers, through the selection and refusal of commodities, help set a balance in price and rise and fall of the measure of the supply of commodities in the market.

(4) **Scholes-Martin Theory:** This theory tries to create a suitable environment for investment by fixing up the influence and mutual relation among the factors determining the price of the shares of the companies in the share market. The movement of money between the investor and recipient of investment depends on the identification of the environment of investment, the capacity of the market to affect investments and the suitable field of investment. This theory helps assess the background of the market.

There was no share market during the reign of Rama, but the distribution of ownership was present. The share market has two aspects: (a) distribution of ownership and (b) distribution of monetary value. Through distribution of ownership of the same organisation, business may come under the proprietorship of more than one person. Actually, the association of many in responsibility and proprietorship is an ancient custom of India.

The matter of supplying price and money through the market was not directly present in the ancient custom, but it was there rather indirectly. The theoretical discussion on the relationship of price with the role of demand of monetary investment and deficit is there in Indian tradition. During the reign of Rama, the balance of supply and demand was repeatedly highlighted. Light was shed on how natural calamities and artificial deficits take the commodities out of the buying capacity of the common people.

The ideas embedded in the Rybczynski Theorem or the Stolper-Samuelson Theorem are also recorded in the regime of Rama. The king was fully aware of the affairs related to his people. A king's full awareness of the weal and woe of the subjects, which are the people, casts a direct influence on the fixing up of the cost of commodities in the market. A comparatively better method of fixing up costs through chaotic movements of the market is to maintain a steadiness on the cost through adequate supervision and control over the chaotic movements. As a result of this, there is a distribution of buying capacity, the purchase is extended, and consequently, the good result of the monetary system gets engaged in accomplishing the good and welfare of many.

The theoretical discussion between Bhisma and Yudhisthira cast much influence at the root of the monetary system built up in the post-war period of the *Mahabharata*. While speaking of the royal office to Yudhisthira, Bhisma, lying on the bed of arrows, stated the duties of a king and also spoke of setting a balance in the price for bringing happiness and ease to the people. In the later period, Kautilya's *Arthashastra* cast light on the distribution of the mutual relationship between the king and the people, bringing a balance of the price of commodities in the market and so forth.

Financial thought is intimately related to the old tradition of India. This would seldom be met with. The financial thought of the West, though new, is rather glum before the ancient thoughts of India.

Flow of Financial Thoughts

The financial and social arrangements proposed by Adam Smith in his book, *Wealth of Nations*, came to be known in the contemporary quarters as the commercial society. This is the initial basic foundation of a market-based financial system. Money and trade hid in his family tradition. Smith's father was the Comptroller of Customs. Smith had seen in the environment of Edinburgh, where he grew up, many types of harmful effects of money.

The luster of money shows the fickleness in the morality of men. Slackening the closeness of relations among families, societies and people, money has become more valuable. Adam Smith's life had allowed two applications of this instruction.

One, he himself was not confined into the network of any relation—he remained a bachelor. He did not allow himself to be related to any woman. Two, he always kept aflame with the fire of moral valuation along with financial propositions.

Thus, Adam Smith rose to be the sole propounder of economic morality.

David Hume has written on the market-based financial system.

The natural attraction for foreign commodities keeps expanding the external market throughout the world. The countries are constantly strengthening their financial condition to get success in external trade, so they have become much more careful about keeping the price level restricted enough. This trade management is comfortable for the market and buyers as well.

A market-based economy is gradually gaining ground. It has been presented in a number of ways. Propounders of welfare economics and society stipulated that economics also follows this line.

Some indices of economics like GDP or Gross Domestic Product, per capita production, per capita income-expenditure-debt, rate of domestic production and such have come at the root of financial management. Recently some economists have been expressing the future of the internal economics of a country through the discussion on individual industries. For example, Jeffery Sachs, R.L. Vershney and Ashita Bajpai (2000), have in their discussion on economic restructuration of India, shown how computers and the IT Sector are casting an influence on foreign trade in India and, as a consequence invigorating the national economy, companies like Infosys, Wipro, Tata Consultancy Service and Satyam, through expansion of their own trade, have not only brought a change in the financial condition of the country but also created such an environment as the Indian economy as a whole has been benefitted. India's name has spread in the world market, along with old ideas, new ideas have come now so that other aspects also throng with the Information-Technology. A new environment is being created.

The method by which Sachs, Vershney and Bajpai have discussed financial management, as in keeping with the theory, is also predictive for the future. They, of course, during thinking of the future, have been much dependent on the past; still, it is to be admitted that this notion will slow path in the future, at least to some extent. There is no investigation of probability or future in this notion, but there is a hint of support by which the gateway of the future ideas would open. The economic notion and theories have been judged on their merit of explaining power. Reasonability and acceptability of a theory depends on how far it can explain the past. This line is rather a danger to financial management and economy.

New Notion: Spiritual Economics

What is to be intended for having a hint towards the future? At the very beginning, it is to be understood how long-term happiness of all or the majority would be affected.

For these are required more:

(a) to know and understand the present.

(b) to keep correct information of the possibility.

(c) to correctly know the factors rousing the blooming of possibility and the means to break through the obstruction, if any.

(d) to know the essence of past experiences and to always observe the same in the background of application.

(e) To distribute demands in the light of requirement and to try to give shape to the future accordingly. Up till now, financial practices and notions have been dependent on the past. These theories have acted as a bridge between the past and the present. The conditions of the people are unknown. The basis of the financial system of the country would be such an outlook as would at the root search for the system required for all.

For example, in countries where there is death due to starvation and such, the basic demand that is to be filled for all at the very beginning is the demand for food. Before discussions on other things, the first and foremost need is to get food for all. This can be accomplished through the state enterprise or some associate or joint enterprise. The money extended towards this may be taken to be an integral expense of society. If the mechanism to get food are completely run by the state, then its fate would be the same as what happened to the Food-For-Work Programme of India. Close to 10 kg of wheat would be rewarded below a thumb-impression, but supply would be one kg. This would be the scenario. In other words, it would increase corruption. What a joint social enterprise can give rise to is the spread of food and observation, such that any corruption might not creep in.

The very first thing that is to be ascertained in economic management is what possibilities are there and how they are there. Advancement may be in all countries at all ages. For this, the requirements are:

(1) Enlightment of an individual; not only I but we would live.

(2) Life has deep, underlying significance. Life does not mean only being big, living happily or earning fame; it has a far greater adventure.

(3) Life that emerges out of spiritual feelings is the greatest. This gets engaged in giving nourishment to the fundamental wealth of life, which takes life to the peak of nobility.

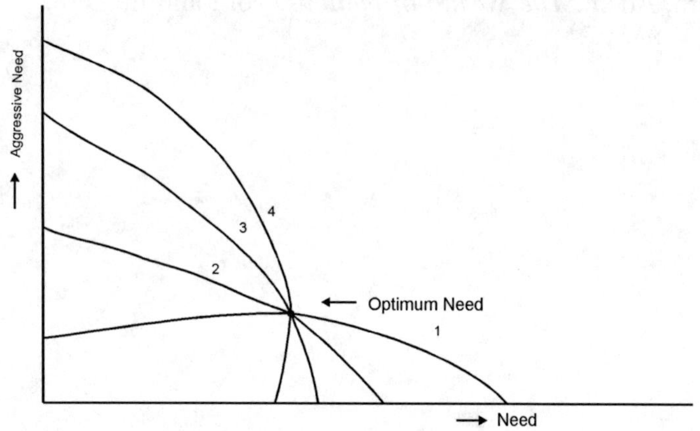

Figure 1: Convergence of Necessity

In financial management, there has been a discussion on utility. Its position is fixed up in the light of the complete utility of the same.

Different positions of necessity-hyper necessity are being shown in the figure. The necessity-hyper necessity that is shown in the figure is determined by different types of outlooks and arrangements that will be known from the displacements of (1) - (4). The point where they meet is the point of convergence. The move of food discussed above would have its rate in the form of necessity-hyper necessity. Future possibilities and blooming would also be measured on the basis of this. True knowledge of necessity-hyper necessity would be able to open the correct path.

What is a necessity? The answer is there in everyone's mind and also in their tongues. There are many necessities—to live well, to stay in happiness, to be big, to have affluence, to be rich so on and so forth. There is no end to it. The remission of enjoyment and lust cannot come with the supply of objects for the same.

What is hyper-necessity? It is unknown. Most people do not know this. It is to be known. If necessary, knowledge of the same is to be awakened. The future pervasion of the continuity of life through which we are moving on is a hyper-necessity. It is something spiritual. Life is to be felt deeply with the faculty of the heart. It is the heart that would direct what is right, what can be done and what cannot be done; this life would long for that. The management would be built on this foundation. This economy is for all, for this world.

Bibliography

Smith, Adam. *The Wealth of Nations*. Vol I and II, 1776.

24
Index of Economy

Whenever statistics are to be consulted during the discussion on economics, different types of indices are used. The indices are classified to realise the true meaning of statistics. Different sides of the economic situation are made clear through different types of statistics. For example, some statistics are used for clarifying the collective situation; other types of statistics clarify comparative situations among different countries. Each of these statistics bears a basic similarity, so the basic differences also exist. Some statistics are expressed by indices, and some are expressed by full values; besides, quite a good number of statistics are there whose basis is continuous, though with respect to other problems or subjects. The more variegated the statistics will be, the more dignified would be the respective economic model. Gradually the economic picture becomes as if eager to pass over from the mutual encirclement of statistics.

If not based on statistics, an economic model loses its credibility. Statistics are necessary. How much the connection of the main problems deemed to be main in deliberations on economics with the past conditions of each of them can be judged from comparative discussions. The use of statistics here is limited.

Statistics-based economic models are gradually becoming dependent on indices and comparison, which is maybe making the situation more complicated. Their role in fulfilling the main target of statistics-based economic policies is gradually becoming feebler. New economic ideas are also in the whirl. Too much introduction of indices and statistical economics has caused the entrapped condition of economics. Total possession of statistics is gradually devouring economics.

Freedom of Economics: Among the indices that have been accepted by are:

- Rate of GDP
- Index of per capita GDP
- Per Capita Productivity
- Advancement Production
- Per capital debt, saving of money advancement of saving
- Per capita efficiency f expenditure
- Per capita and total collection of foreign currency and increase of collection.

Besides these, there is a human development index. Some of the factors what are brought in the discussion of human development index are as follows:

- Different indices for assessing the standard of education.
- Index for assessing the rate of spread of education and measure of education.
- Teacher-taught ratio
- Index for spread of literacy
- Arrangement of total and per capita health service
- Child-death and overall standard of adult-health
- Overall and comparative account of fertility
- Measure of poverty, rate of people below poverty limit and measure of social discrimination.
- Guinea-index.

For mutual coordination and comparison among these indices, sometimes tabular distribution is taken and, in some specific cases, perimeter. As each of these indices has a specific field of use so also there is a limit of application. Sometimes or in some cases, the same index may be differently meaningful, the index for determining poverty level. Some of the elements brought in the purview of consumable goods for determining poverty limit may get changed sometimes. For example, there would be a difference in the measure of calories with changes of foods taken for having inference relating to the intake of calories of food. This will bring change in factors for assessing the poverty limit.

Almost all of the statistics and indices are judged with respect to the foundation year, whether any change has come to the outlook about the change that might have crept in depending more or less on the change taking place in the division concerned. If there is any change in the situation, it is to be inferred that the time has come to think about the matter in a newer light. This brings in newer ideas. Newer ideas sometimes come in a continuous flow and sometimes in a scattered manner. All of the outlooks expressed in the continuity of ideas remain in some way or other, conjoined with one another.

It is rather natural for these ideas not to come through this continuity. There is a tune of unification in the very fundamental basis of every idea. Statistics and indexes stand on this fundamental basis. Now a question may arise—how far this basis is fundamental and how far it is questionable. Confidence is the fundamental basis. The point of confidence in economics determines its consequence. The freedom of this point of confidence signifies freedom of economics. The first symptom of a new economic idea is to have a discrete and clear impression of this point of confidence. The second symptom, the method of the proposition, is independent of past ideas. The third symptom is the application of an overall solution to economic problems and the next symptom is the clue for solution from inland situations.

New Ideas

All of the post-World War II economic theories are dependent on statistical indices. The discerning factors of these are more or less as follows:

Discussion on and analysis of the theories among the old ones that are in vogue are:

- Proposition of future principles on the basis of the consequences of observation of the past by creating new statistics and indexes or with the help of statistics of the measures in fashion.
- Observation of the results in light of the current index and establishment of the result come out.
- Evaluation and foundation of new theories through solutions to past problems after searching them out.

The overall observation shows that the post-World War II notions have been set up on the points of consideration and observation of the past; in the past observations, in many cases, the difference of space and time became valueless. It has been assumed that all the theories will profitably be applied throughout the world. Any endeavour of economics may ultimately be set up on the index of the increase in GDP. As a result of this, on one hand, a worldwide outlook and method of measure have been introduced, and on the other hand, there has been an end of the mutual relationship involving measure in different contexts.

The increase in GDP makes us assume that there is economic progress, and that the economy has yielded good results. However, it is rather wrong.

It is wrong due to the reason that an increase in GDP in comparison to that of the past has not always proved the financial and national capability properly. In spite of being indicative of the present situation of the state, GDP is not the only or the correct indicator of national financial progress. The factors on which total domestic production particularly depends are as follows:

World situation (Financial, political, social etc.)

- Situation inside the country (Financial, political, social etc.)
- Management of production and work-culture.
- Supply for production and distribution and sale of the produce.
- Measure and direction of flow of money.
- Qualitative condition of technology.
- Purchasing capacity and extent of purchase.
- Propensity of consumerism.

Direction of movement of technology

If a country or region does not have the power to control the internal situation of the country, then no control can be brought over production. It is the market which is the regulating power. Marketing on the basis of demand and supply can bring a considerable amount of coordination between production and consumption. Production and movement through the market should be the only condition required for production. Few such cases, as may be taken, are where there is much difference between the total production and marketisation. If a produced commodity is not marketised and is rather stored in warehouses or even after marketisation, it is not consumed or sold to a proper extent, then that commodity hampers the overall financial health. Say a steel factory has produced one thousand tons of steel in a year. Of this one thousand, only five hundred tons are suitable for consumption and the rest five hundred is not fit for use or consumption and so, has remained confined in the warehouses. This steel stored in warehouses is not helpful for monetary movement, bringing about a number of harmful effects. These harmful effects are as follows:

- misuse of the main investment for production.
- expense due to storing of the commodities in warehouses and looking after the same. investment to be used elsewhere.
- damage in the coordination between overall demand and supply in the market.

Even in production, attention is to be given to other aspects. The effective portion of the gross national income can be assessed as follows:

(1) present cost of production.
(2) total sale and use of the produce as per present price.
(3) present price of unused produce.
(4) price in respect of the investment of unused produce elsewhere.
(5) expense in the modes of attracting for production and
(6) total expense or investment of the unearned portions existing in the production, distribution and marketisation system.

Gross national production = (I) – [(2)+(3)+(4)+(5)+(6)]

[Here service has been included in production]

It is different from the current system in fashion. The current system takes account of the present monetary value of production and service.

The method given above is more dependable than the current system of index and statistics. In it, the measure of possibility has not been included. If the measure of possibility is added, the statistics will take another shape. This outlook can be applied in case of two countries—India and China. The scenario will be clear if the application is made during the period 1995–2002. Instead of going into numerical details, the following figure is presented to give a clear idea.

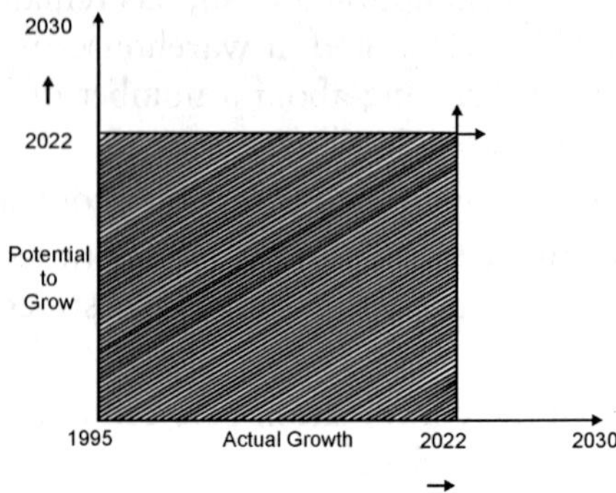

Figure 1: Gross national production: India, China

Figure 1 gives an idea of the gross national production of India and China from a new outlook. Here, in the possibility part, India's condition is superior to China's economy. India has been shown to be susceptible to possibility and that of China as directed towards attained state. A new outlook of gross national production is on its basis.

The new outlook will certainly undertake the observations necessary to be made with respect to the merits and demerits of the economic system. Let us take an example from India—food and agricultural problems therein. Some days back, there had been a discussion with Professor Erich, a renowned scholar of statistical economics, in the courtyard of City Hall of Nobel (Nobel Prizes are awarded at this venue) in Stockholm, Sweden. While teaching at Stockholm University, I occasionally had the privilege to discuss with Professor Erich about this. Two mentionable questions of Erich were:

(1) In spite of the fact that India's annual food production nears that of two years, why do people here still die of starvation?

(2) Whether India is benefitting or suffering by imitating America?

Many others had these questions. In discussing these the subjects that would gain prominence are discussed ahead.

The natural circulation process of marketisation of the produce has not been introduced in India yet. The government acts as the regulator here. The government has a few problems before it—such as providing minimum price to the agricultural producers to get food to the people at a terminal level or below the poverty level at a definite price, to look into the possibility of surplus produce being invested in foreign markets.

Firstly, to maintain a minimum price for agricultural producers and to provide food to the poor at a reduced price, a subsidy is to be introduced, striking the common principle of economics. The time has come to look at the matter in light of current economic ideas. As a solution, there should be a subsidy on one hand, and different announcements for the circulation of money on the other. The supply of money needs to be in the hands of the desiring and deserving people, through creation of government employments in rural and urban areas. To get a great number of labourers involved in the programs of construction, repair of roads, irrigation and similar other development plans through the investment of money and to provide different types of works to them continuously for a pretty long period.

As the primary stage of getting the labour market up to the international standard, a highly spread opportunity has been given to different multinational organisations to employ workers and according to that, equality in prices of labour is going to be established. Two streams of their management have attracted notice:

(1) determination of the price of labour in international standards.

(2) management of a number of activities by outsourcing of labour.

The first case is a step in the unification of the world system. As a consequence of this, intellectual labour gets a proper price right within the country. But as a reaction to that, outsourcing manages to buy or deploy general labour at a very low price.

Men of the first type represent the management of the world class consumerism. They have the right to have financial solvency to be able to enjoy all the good things. Men of the second type lag behind in this respect. They would have to depend on the lower priced purchasable commodities of the market.

American system of living is in the grip of the men of the first type. The theory of economic exploitation cannot be applied here. But men of both types do stand on the intensity or the surplus of agriculture. Both of them indirectly enjoy the surplus of agriculture. If the price of the agricultural products gets low, labourers of the second type are especially benefitted. They also gradually come closer to the American style of living.

American living is mainly a craving for enjoyment. When you are always buying, you will continue buying even after crossing your buying capacity. You do buy a home, car and everything on a loan. Ultimately, taking another loan, even before paying off one. One would go on taking loans. As a consequence of this, the demand for things will increase and with this, movement of money will also increase. In economic terms, it is called a duo boom. One of these, in a later stage, casts an influence on the other. Thus, from both sides, progress shall proceed the economic index.

The problem that has been created in the case of India by American living or could be created to a greater extent is the socio-economic classification. Until now, India had assimilated itself into American management. As a result of these, the enjoyment of consumable commodities is going on, but it has not crossed the limit yet. Individual loans here are also within the allowable limit. This means that the touch of American living is enjoyed by the first group of men but not in the American way.

India has built up a style of its own in the economic management system. Behind this is a cultural influence, which exceeds the role of the government. In Indian mentality, the eternal influence of the *Upanishads* and the *Vedas* is like a subterranean river. Individuals, whatever community or belief they may belong to, have in the inner depth of their self, a Vedic and Upanishadic land of mentality. As a result, an Indian, if he is not very obstinate, will not be able to be too attached to sensual pleasure. At the valuable part or stage of life, his craving for enjoyment will be drenched with restraint and a condition of unification would be built up. Consequently, an individual will be allured by enjoyment but after some time, he will be existing by satisfaction and think, "enough is enough, no more."

Indian observance of living has set up a few streams that proved proper in accordance with economics. Monetary longing of India has begun to wake up in different ways. The problem is that economists like to judge all in the light of other countries, especially China or America. There is nothing unjust in the fondness towards China or America. Different people may have a special affinity for some countries. For example, Amartya Sen is fond of China, while a large portion of economists are fond of America. But unless India is understood, new principles of economics will also remain unrealised.

A few new principles are being brought into discussion and they may be applied everywhere under the Sun. But the method of application of these principles will be different in respective places. These are:

(1) Satisfaction index.

(2) Index for perspective deprivation.

(3) Index of social homogeneity.

(4) Index for fulfilment of ambition.

(5) Pointer to sustainability index.

The five indexes stated above are the first step of the spiritual economy. The spiritual economy specifies basic objects, necessity and provision of the people. Its application in India may be quite natural. To some extent, there has been so—but quite out of the knowledge of men. Propounders and experts in economics have taken men to be rather a lump of desires—as if lust and desires are all that is concerned with men. All of the basic elements, noble qualities and aspects of life have been rather wiped out. Herein lies the main principle of disparity.

Poverty exists because spirituality has moved apart. When spirituality gets out, heartiness disappears. Spirituality helps one realise that every man is an icon of God. The God in man cannot be kept unfed. The realidation of godly wealth within inspires one to be assiduous for work. On the other side, waking of spirituality gradually makes man recede from enjoyment and pursue pleasantness. This is against the living of the Americans.

A sample of factors that one would have to pay attention to for determining the index of satisfaction is given below:

- amount of money generally for goods, clothes and living.
- to ascertain in terms of money—what else is required to move life towards a smooth rise.
- present monetary price of the endeavours meant for deepening the distribution of family and social relations.
- present overall monetary price required for creating balanced management of the future.

An annual or half-yearly satisfaction index may be formed, taking the total figure of the above monetary prizes as 100.

The satisfaction index will be different for different groups of people. Thus, in North India, Central India and South India, its application would be on a regional basis. For every region, the product of total population and satisfaction index is to be found out. At the end, such products are to be summed up and the total will have to be divided by the total population, when the average satisfaction index of the country at that time will be bad. This satisfaction index is very useful to determine the flow of progress and the regional disparity within the country. The capabilities of the satisfaction index is very much greater than any of the indices in vogue. Consequently, other indices would be able to ascertain their position with respect to it.

Like the satisfaction index, other indexes can also be found and used. For this, what is required is a continuous special type of investigation on the people of the country, which would fetch the right answer or account of every factor of the index. These indexes can rightly judge the economics of China and India. As a result, the future economic system of the whole world will be able to take a new turn.

25

E-Economy in Eradication of Poverty

The electronic economy, or e-economy, has given a severe blow to the root of the monetary ideas reared so far. The e-economy has brought to the world a new possibility—the eradication of poverty. Ideas so long in vogue have, in the background of the e-economy, been untenable and gradually become obsolete. Distinctions like capitalist, socialist and Marxist became useless before the e-economy.

E-economy will bring a tidal wave of change, also among social arrangements and social relations. The structure of identity in the first, second and third world will become obsolete, and a new network of identity will bind them. By this time, even the e-economy questioned the division in the world and gradually, it will bring greater changes in the factors of the division of the world. The e-economy is gradually rising beyond the current measure of indexes. The way the economic indexes have so long judged the good or bad—will no longer be possible in the new system. Indexes of new types and new standards would be required to measure and express the new system. Demands are there not only for a change of the indexes but for a new light on economic ideas.

The precondition and prerequisite for having the opportunity of e-economy in one's possession is rather different. Amid the economic arrangements managed so far, opportunities of newer economic management may come to those who, in the meantime, have advanced somewhat in this respect, which means that money begets money. Hence, if you want to make money, come out with a bagful of money. If you are an insolvent person, you have no way out.

There was a time when up to the premodern age, power in this world was in the possession of owners of lands, that is, the landlords or the zamindars had a special advantage. If you own land, you also are a part of the driving force of society, and if you are the owner of all the land, then it is you who has the sole possession of power. You are the target point of any type of social change. Just as the extension or distribution of the state system is affected with landlords or owners of lands, in a venture of bringing any change by giving a push to the state management, their interest is to be judged with the greatest importance. In modern times, the role of land has been but secondary.

Nowadays, there is no consideration in the light of land. In this modern period, the measure of judgement is the ownership of industries, factories and machines. Up to World War II, there had been unopposed dominance of the owners of these people. During the post-World War II period, again a change had begun. Ownership of industries, machines and factories has particularised the centre of monetary and social power. The greatest influence on the policy and administration of the state has been cast by the interest of the owners of industries, machines and factories and the overall interest of the industry. Society and the state have lost the courage and ability to ignore the interest of the industries, especially in the case of temporary interests.

After that, during the sixties of the last century, change of another step has set in. The order of the change set in during the sixties and the later period has at its top, the influence and role of the money marketers. Generally speaking, any trade, especially financial trading, has appeared as the main driving force. The financial systems have deviated from dependence on production. Gradually, transfusion, supply of money and the source of connection have been the main driving force. The trading groups and the groups supplying money have appeared to be most influential in the state management system.

Gradually, the driving forces of society have been captured by the business groups. They have come to the very centre of the main driving force of society and the state. Dependence on the part of industry, machine and factories has increased on the businessmen. Firstly, businessmen have greatest knowledge of the requirements, demands and satisfaction of the buyers. They have started to be fully aware of the points of special requirements of the buyers. What is in the minds of the buyers? What types of commodities, at what times, at what type of locations, at what price and at what intervals of time would they like to have?

The experiences and knowledge are being stored with the organisations engaged in the trading and supply of money. As a result, they are gradually being eager to control production. The result of the investigation collected continuously depends on what type of products would be produced, in what amount and after production, at what price, at what measure and through whom these would be supplied.

It is nearly impossible for the manufacturing organisations to run these types of investigations continuously, so their dependence gradually increases on those who go on supplying full particulars of the buyers. As the businessmen are always in constant contact with the buyers, they can form ideas of instant mentality of the buyers, their choice and the favourite products and service. Not only does it find use for the industrialists or in the production of machines and factories but it also gradually brings the production system under control. These groups have come to the very root of the monetary system.

The next stage started in the decade of the nineties of the last century. At this stage, the setting influence of ownership of lands can no longer control the power. Manufacturers are accountable to businessmen and money suppliers just for the future of their industry.

So, their role is just in the back row. The role of businessmen and money suppliers will also be gradually negligible. Here, intellectual power takes their place. In the new high-tech management the driving force of the world would come under the control of the intellectual power. This intellectual power becomes the main bearer and carrier of the basic and practical force of the state and society. The new management has tarnished all the earlier managements. Land, industry, business—all of these have just become secondary to intellectual, inventive power or have become an object of compassion. The following figure shows the driving force of the financial system at different times.

Controlling the power rests in the hands of different stages of the organisations of social power in different situations. When there has been dominance with ownership of land, the ability and power of farmers have also risen opposite to them. Labour force and power, in many cases, have been united and constantly applying their influence and ability on the industrial environment. Owing to problems and consequences of state management, wide change has often also come over. For example, in communist and other countries, it has cast an influence on their state industries and organised sectors. Change has come.

From the decade of seventies of the last century, the influence of managers and executives has more or less been found to be cast on society. The driving force of the power of the business and industrial world has already come into the hands of managers and executives. They have gradually been controlling and occupying the direction of the financial power of society. Authority over the corporate world, over the organisations for financial supply, transfusion and the basic driving force of financial infrastructure of society have gradually come over in their hands as well.

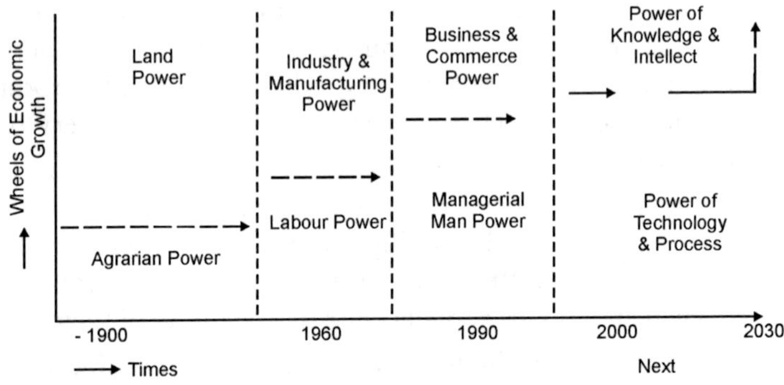

Figure 1: Situation at different of the financial system.

All of these are now going to be history. Now a new march is on—the flow of intellectual power. Direct or indirect authority of intellectual power has been controlling, right from the financial infrastructure down to the transfusion of money, expansion and contraction of activity employment, coordination of demand and supply and so forth. The intensity of authority in both instantaneous and distant application gets exposed thorough technology.

People of all types may come over to the sphere of information technology. The present basis of information technology has helped bloom the latent genius and intellect of man. On one side, information technology has brought in a great store of information and on the other side, it has created an opportunity for unrestricted communication. In the supply of information and unrestricted communication, dormant genius and intellect have bloomed.

The manifestation of intellect and genius would be extended gradually and build up the field of application of financial power and force. As a result, direct or indirect control and the driving force would come to the disposal of those who possess intellect and genius at the point of blooming. Gradually this manifestation of intellect and genius would break down the equilibrium set up so far in the countries of the world and a new equilibrium would be set up. An interchange of financial power between the first and the third worlds would be rather natural. The controlling power of a greater part of the financial management of the first world would come in the grip of the enterprising and hardworking people of the third world.

High-Tech Financial Management

The economy has also changed its movement. The overall form of virtual products, which are commodities shown on computer screens have started to offer continuous challenges to the brick or wood of the house and the burnished products of machines. In the direction of development of technology, information technology (IT) is now going to rapidly augment the gross domestic product. Normally the average measure of the total national production of the world has continuously increased during the last one thousand years. Figure 2 presented a rough picture of the per capital total national income of world during one thousand years.

Per head International Average of Total National Production

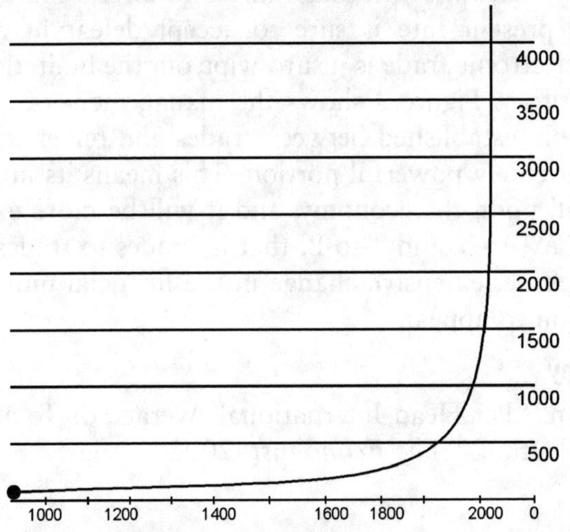

Figure-2: J. P. Morgan (*The Economist*, E-Trend, 2002)

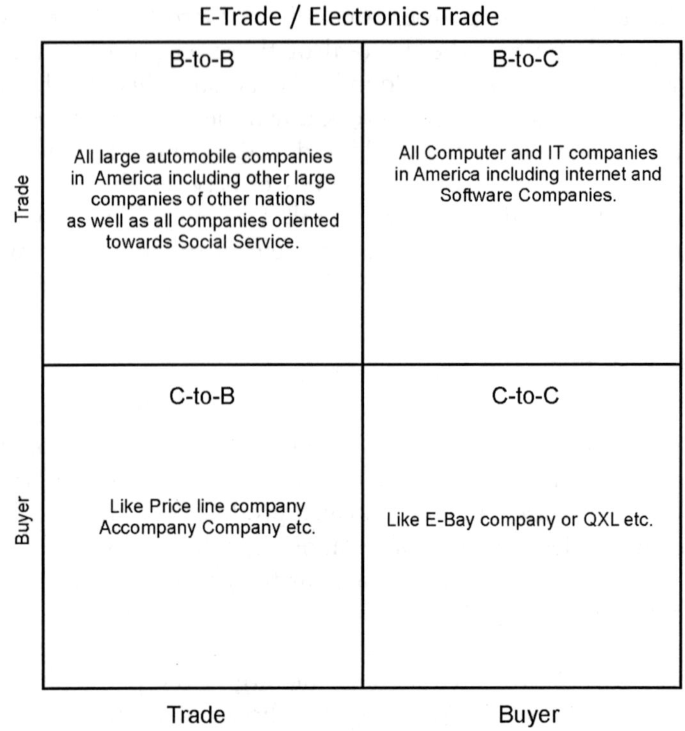

E-Trade / Electronics Trade

	Trade	Buyer
Trade	B-to-B All large automobile companies in America including other large companies of other nations as well as all companies oriented towards Social Service.	B-to-C All Computer and IT companies in America including internet and Software Companies.
Buyer	C-to-B Like Price line company Accompany Company etc.	C-to-C Like E-Bay company or QXL etc.

Figure-3: Understanding the relation between Trade and Buyer in the context of new Financial-System

The rate of advancement has started to increase in the modern phase. The present rate is sure to accept defeat in the future. E-trade or electronic trade is just to wipe out the limitation of local or state territory. Figure-3 shows the management of a new type of relationship established between trades and buyers. T-to-T has been the extremely powerful portion. This means its influence has begun to fall upon the economy, and it will be more extensive in future. In the T-to-T and T-to-B, that is, trades to trades or trades to buyers' phase, extensive change in the financial movement has already begun to appear.

Bibliography

J. P. Morgan. "Per Head International Average of Total National Production." *The Economist*, 2002.

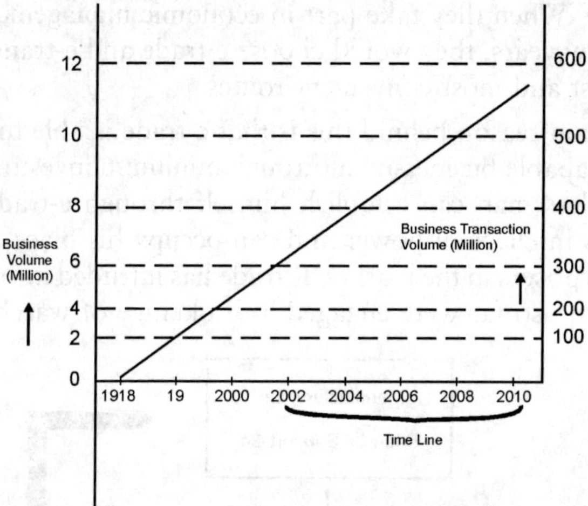

Figure-4: Germany Brokers' Market

Figure-4 gives the idea of transactions in Germany or the brokers' market there. This market is gradually turning fully into e-trade. E-trade is experiencing immense changes between the methodology and basis of the market. Among the European countries, Germany is conservative and at the same time, advanced in technology. For the last two decades, the market for monetary transaction is rather booming. This is supposed to increase in the future. The contribution of Germany in an attempt to get the greater part of Europe within the purview of the euro has been the most acceptable. Gradually, Germany is going to spread its dominance in the financial market of the euro region. Figure-4 clarifies the condition of the brokers in the financial market of Germany and the future outline of the days to come. In 2010, nearly 12 million or 1 crore 12 lakhs traders would carry on a transaction of nearly 60 million or 60 crores of business transactions through e-trade. According to a current calculation, through each transaction of about 0.01 million, 10000 dollars would be the price. For example, a transaction of 6 lakhs crore dollars would be there. Such a great ostentation of other developed countries.

In India, e-trade has not yet been so wisely introduced, and enterprise is not so much in this direction. The Indian economy has reached the door of the enterprise of e-trade at a greater rate or in a greater measure than the cases where endeavour has taken so far. In India, there has been a flood of computer education. At present, most of the college students are well-versed in computer technology. When they take part in economic management within the next few years, they would choose e-trade and e-transaction as the simplest and most convenient routes.

The main reason behind this is that e-trade is able to establish man as a capable businessman through minimum investment. Even a resourceless man can establish himself through e-trade by dint of only his intellectual power and can occupy his place among so many enterprisers in the market. E-trade has intruded into the rights of those who so far were engaged in brokerage of warehousing.

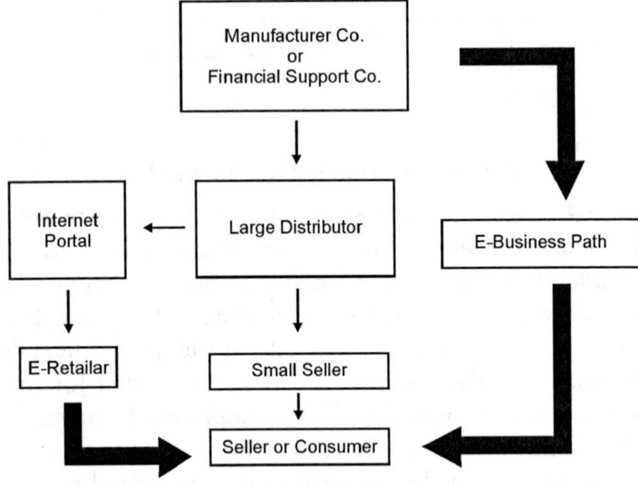

Figure-5: Route of E-Trade

Figure-5 has clarified the route of e-trade. Through the route of e-trade, buyers can directly come in contact with the manufacturing or investing organisations. In e-management, hoarders are going to face the most dismal misery. As a result of this, buyers would get all types of commodities and services at a much lower price. This system is bound to make the advantage available to the buyers, its target because here, competition would be at the top.

There was nothing called e-trade at the very beginning, but that e-trade and e-trade movement has grown up now. Initially, this is spreading within the wealthy section, and in the next stage, the public would be bound to be its buyers.

E-Economy

The measure of the e-economy will not be fixed up in the light of capital. With this, the movement of capital would keep on increasing. Online service is gradually becoming popular in developed countries. Not only in the West but in the East also is gradually gaining confidence in the 'e' or electronic medium. Public participation in the same is also increasing. A business can be started even without any initial investment. The investment that is of utmost importance is intellectual power. Intellectual power can meet the lack of investment in large measure with a rather meagre expense through the internet. To him, who has the proper knowledge in this respect, e-trade is very easily understandable and available too. Some of the main pillars of e-economy are:

- to earn full confidence in the methodology of trade.
- continuous arrangement of measure and review of time.
- complete awareness of merits and demerits.
- to maintain the other portion through cross-subsidy, that is, from the earning of one portion.
- continuous innovation.

Up till now, the standard of the economy has been cognition of merits and demerits through ascertainment of quality, measure and monetary value of the financial management. The protesting voices of financial management are bringing education, health and social indexes into the purview of discussion and trying to judge their merits and demerits. The e-economy is going beyond these and looking at men to be blooming and fixing up their value in the light of their possibility, development and honesty.

The measure of the e-economy demands newer ideas and newer valuations.

Bibliography

J. P. Morgan. "Per Head International Average of Total National Production." *The Economist*, 2002.

26
Kautilya and Solon

During the seventh and sixth centuries, the long-lasting disorderliness was shattering Greece. By that time, India had already brought in a message of a new life. At this time, a stir had come to the life of the Vedic land, drenched in Vedic messages in a venture to find out the meaning of a newer philosophy and life. Indian sages engaged in the quest for truth had even brought in social life the infallible touch of truth. In the basin of social life, the touch of truth has an incomparable aspiration in man. Men in all spheres of their life have been eager to find out the meaning of life in different ways. Thus, a touch of consciousness has come in life.

Man has learnt reverence, and love has grown on the basis of reverence. A fundamental linkage of unity has come in between one and the other. Inside society, there has been a sincere attempt to follow the object and end of life on the basis of this linkage of unity. A vow of attributing mutual dignity is at the root of the relationship designed in the social system of India; it is a novel endeavour to look at one another with the look of mutual dignity.

The financial system has also been developed likewise. With respect to the ultimate longing with all vocations and professions, here is basic coordination among men of different vocations and professions. In the ultimate desire, men of all professions become inseparably unified. Being associated with the daily movements of life ushered by the godly urge at the very centre of life and the godly urge captured by the Indian wisdom, life is moving in that direction—so on the foundation of reverence, society has grown, which sees everyone through the mirror of God; normally realised just as a replica of God.

A different picture emerged at the very initiation of the setting up of European civilisation. Man has sold far too much of his lifelong service to others. Thus, a great number of men have had no opportunity to collect the wealth of life. Life is searching for liberty. Lives are eager to get the taste of liberty from the confinement in which commonplace life has been detained. Widespread groups of people have had the same fate in life, in spite of the differences in vocation and profession. All of them have lived the lives of captives being sold to the wealthy and the aristocrat.

Within the desires of life have been primarily included endeavour and susceptibility to the liberty of the exterior, which is also the accomplishment in their lives. The life and death struggle to attain liberty from the flow of works in captivity has extended its background everywhere. He, who likes to be free from bondage, has to take a life and death vow. Either he would live, gain liberty or would bid a permanent farewell from the scenario of the world.

The longings of Europe and India are quite different. Europe is searching for the initial solution to the problems of daily life, and in a venture for that solution, they have offered direct attention to that. It has searched for the truths deeply rooted in men from his outer arrangements. That is why the extreme truth comes to Europe, nay the West, through the exposition of the outer identity. Nature becomes predominant. But they have had no time to search for the extreme self-staying beyond nature. So, man also has been designated by his outer identity. The external has marked the identity of vocation and profession. The end of this is the line of judgement in the light of success. The line of judgement in the light of achievements makes it evident that the extreme price of the man is through the judgement of the extent of success achieved in life. He, who has become an aristocrat and is wealthy, has a life more precious than the lives of common citizens because he has developed the competency of being aristocratic and wealthy. So, this man is more elevated and great. Others will have to remain submissive to this man and bow down to him.

Appointment of others at the service of this wealthy aristocrat would be easily accepted. It is here that the clue to the mentality of a slave system exists. All men are not equal. Some are big and some are small. Small people will have to be engaged in the service of the big people. He who has had success in life will be big in all respect, from all sides, and so this big man will be allowed to be established in his right and dignity. If, in this process, small men are to be sacrificed, even then, no judgement will be needed at all. The fundamental truth in the Western people would be sought through external propensities, so their ardent desire is to move near that fundamental truth. The infrastructure of society has thus been built up.

From the perspective of the modern age, much change has come into this very attitude of the Western mind. As the Western minds were struck and surrounded by science and technology, they were widely disturbed; thus, change has also been achieved in the external structure. Just for this, for men engaged in the struggle of life, the doors of prospect are lying open. He can build up his future in the light of capability, genius, worthiness and proficiency. He has the liberty of free movement on the horizon that would be unveiled before him in this venture of building up the future. He is free and has the nature of roaming freely. He would be able to set out for adventure in the path of life in an unopposed and non-attributed situation. He can snatch an inexpressible future for himself. The man, who is free today, being directed by the force determining the success of his tradition, has grasped the success in life as a token of his ability to move. If he is not successful, he would be worthless. Man is getting worth in the light of success. An unsuccessful life is, therefore, accepted by the successful; he is rather a follower of the successful. Modern West has made success the hymn of its life. It is similar to its background, ranging back many thousand years in the past.

India has cultivated success, but that has come hand in hand with the practice of the truth and the right. Man has been moving after the truth embedded in his life. He has realised that man is leading and living a symbolic life. Every man is a form or symbol of a Brahman, the Absolute Self. In his heart stands the condensed entity of the Absolute Truth. Being condensed to this, the Supreme Entity staying in the small, limited circle has been the central force of life. He has realised that this is not applicable to him alone; it is rather applicable to everyone in the field of life. Brahman has dwelt from heart to heart; he stays in one's heart and life in the form of an eternal and constant companion. Thus, Brahma, in the form of a seed, has been the only inducing force in the atmosphere of the feelings of life. That environment is the environment of the blooming of life.

Man has realised that just as he himself has emerged from Brahma, so is everyone else. Thus, a mental state searching for the truth has been exposed in his propensity and capability. He has been eager to give a call to the truth in different forms, on different occasions, in different states and identities. Reverence is enlivened in him. He likes to see and understand everyone. Being seated at the altar of reverence, he accepts and embraces all.

He has received men lovingly as the abode of Brahma. That is why he has never dreamt of making man a slave and the system of slavery was never set up in India.

Solon and Kautilya

Solon is an Athenian and Kautilya is an Indian. There is a difference of about two hundred years between them, where Solon is older than Kautilya. Still, in them exists the principle of change. Both of them, in their respective societies and the economic system of their lands, have brought about wide changes. Kautilya's *Arthashastra* and other principles have been applied in the perspective of widespread disorder and back of allegiance in a big portion of India, under the Nanda rule in post Bimbisar, the king and Ajatsatru period.

The rise of Chandragupta was not only the initiation of the re-establishment of the great Indian unity, but its main accomplishable object was to set up a state and its economic system in the form of an edict of justice, judgement and religion. Thus, Kautilya can be called a revolutionary philosopher, a possessor of confirmed wisdom and force applied in the respective fields. When Alexander was victorious in Punjab, his army started facing the power of the great empire of Dhanananda in North India. The Greek army perhaps felt the urge to go back the severity of the military power of Nanda rule. Selucus, the Chief next to Alexander, who came to India for an invasion, found that the picture was just the opposite in a course of only a few years. The boundary of Chandragupta's empire crossed the entire Northern part. No more brandishing of power; now, a clue of the treaty was required. The propensity and plan of this change in the situation were of Kautilya. The *Arthashastra* in Punjab had not only presented a philosophical belief in this case but Kautilya also properly applied the philosophical belief in the field of life.

An unendurable span of time had arrived in the life of Athenians. Society was divided into a number of streams. Oppression in society reached a maximum stage; the situation was so grave that unless the rift was prevented, national havoc would be inevitable. People were quite done with the oppression of the aristocrats and the wealthy were constantly adding fuel to the fire of rebellion. At this point of time, a great man, Solon, came to the rescue of Athenians (630-560 BCE). Some have described him as an important sage of

ancient Greece. What Aristotle says about him is the most remarkable. He has written what was the role of Solon under the circumstances prevailing.

"For a long time, there was a strife between the rich and the poor. For the state was oligarchic in all ways, and the poor, along with their wives and children, were enslaved to the rich. And they were called "clients" a "sixth partners", for it was at this rate that they worked in the fields of the rich. All the land belonged to a few people; and if the poor did not render their dues, they and their children could be sold overseas. And before Solon, all loans were made on the security of the person; but he became the first champion of people."

Frank N. Magill, ed., *The Ancient World* (Chicago: Fitzry Dearborn Publishers, 2000), p. 803.

The phase of the advent Solon was like this:

There was conflict regarding the rights to the island of Salami, between the city of Athens and the city of Megra to its west. Athenians, at this time, had given in and had been quite frenzied with pleasure and happiness of their own. Referring to the dreadful situation in the fifth century BCE, Aristotle had said that one-fourth of the population had then been enslaved. They had no civil rights. When the rich were engaged in buying and selling slaves, the export of slaves had rather been a topic worthy of discussion. How many slaves belonged to one became the identity of one, while another measure was to become rich through the sale of slaves abroad. The slave market became very powerful. The pomp of buying and selling slaves occupied the whole city of Athens—not so much by the commodities as by sheer disrespect.

Economic Principles of Solon

When disorder was at its maximum, quite a good number of respectable people apprehended their difficulty, realising the fire blazing in the winds of the slaves. These would burst out at any opportunity. These aristocrats had been searching for a device so that by this, their condition does not change much and the fire of rebellion remains under control. They designed Solon as their savior.

One day, Solon, in philosophical confidence, extended his call from the Dais at the centre of the city of Athens. Calling upon all, Solon said that change is required in the social management, financial arrangement and political situation. All were pleased noting Solan's endeavour and he was entrusted with composing the principle's deeds worthy of accomplishment.

Solon provided a good number of plans of enterprise and works and their materialisation also began. Aristotle remarked, ". . . Solon established the council of four hundred to prepare measures to be voted on the assembly of all citizens and set up the law courts as the central democratic organ" (Ibid. p.805).

To recast the political system, Solon classified the male citizens into four classes:

1. Top Class: They are called Pentakosio Medimnoi, who are the citizens with the highest financial capacity (500 bushel)
2. Hippeis or Knights: Their financial capacity is next to the top class (300-500 bushel).
3. Zengitai: Youths suitable for posting in infantry.
4. Thetes: They are mere workers.

Distribution of political power was as follows:

Top Class: They would be leaders and only they would have the right to have the high posts. Democracy would be built under the leadership of these people.

Second Class: They would hold the authority of the middle order. Whatever political or financial power they may have, they will always be under the command on the people of the top class.

Third Class: They would be devoted to duties like defence, security And so forth. With such works, they would satisfy the top class.

Fourth Class: They would do all sorts of laborious work. They would have no rights at all. Oswyn Murray, *Early Greece*, 2nd ed. (Harvard University Press, 1993).

Discrimination was right at the root of the democracy set up by Solon. In spite of this discrimination, the slaves responded to this system very strongly because Solon had been able to bring back many slaves to the country from abroad. Besides, he brought changes to the loan management system. He had introduced the system of giving loan on the basis of working days and property, instead of personal security. Slaves amply benefitted from this.

The system introduced by Solon did not last long because both the rich and the poor began to feel amiss. It is not that Solon failed, but his efforts were obstructed. The social and financial distribution that had been set up on the basis of western mentality, had at its root the socio-political distribution of Solon, based on financial management.

At the root of Solon's socio-economic classification was the same propensity to pay higher, from dignity to ability. Immense power would come to those who have at their disposal profuse money and property. As a result, power is the basis. The West had, thus, allowed human fates to be crushed by the weight of the wealthy and made money the basis of financial capability.

The financial reformation done by Solon has been called *Seisachtheia*, which means one that breaks down the wall. Truly, he could break down the walls of bondage. But in the new wall he built after breaking, the dominance of the rich became lawful and permanent. Solon has been recognised as the genius who saved the seed of the central pillar of the socio-economic intellect of the West. Aristotle accepted him thus.

Kautilya not only surpassed Solon but was also much more advanced. Kautilya made the state leadership realise that people do not belong to a separate class—rather, the people must rise to be the main target of every state. The king will not be concerned with his own priority, but that of the people in every sphere. If the people arehappy, the king will be happy.

> "Praja Sukhe Sukham rajnah, prajanam ca hite hitam,
> natmapriyam hitam rajnah, prajanam tu priyam hitam'.

(People's happiness is king's happiness, welfare of the people is the king's welfare. The king would accept only that thing to be favourite which is taken to favourite of the people).

Kautilya has introduced the account of different vocations and professions in the financial distribution of the state. He has given a detailed account of the arrangements to be made for agriculture. He has discussed livestock farming, industry and commerce vividly, giving a detailed prescription for all of them. Administration of the localities, social conditions therein, maintenance of social reforms and customs—he has entered into a detailed discussion of all of these. But everywhere, he has kept the people at the centre. Kautilya has not made any classification on the basis of money or ability.

Kautilya's financial management was drafted through paying proper importance to the people.

Kautilya liked to have the spiritual view to be present in the background of leadership. He had given priority for all to Vedic practice and procurement of knowledge. Kautilya has made Vedic learning compulsory for all. This will rouse a spiritual outlook. The net result of Vedic practice is to proceed in the path of having spiritual knowledge. After having spiritual knowledge, one knows that the Absolute Truth has himself has been this world and its creatures. He has different forms.

'Rupam rupam pratirupah babhubali

(He has spread himself in different forms).

Self would be the identity of all the men that have spiritual knowledge. He himself has manifested himself through all. So, man can never be trampled, what to speak of enslaving. It is quite natural for the classification made by Solon to be rather dangerous. In a later period, this became the fate of Athens that was demolished by the Spartans. The bit of democracy set up by Solon was destroyed completely. On the other hand, Kautilya's prescription has furnished an infrastructure of financial management spread far within the Indian intellect. This very structure has flown even to this modern time.

In spite of the time difference between Solon and Kautilya, there is a similarity with respect to perspective and the propensity of taking enterprise. Thorough and correct judgement would reveal how deep and far-reaching mental achievement Kautilya's *Arthashastra* has furnished, not only in the Indian background but of the world too. Kautilya was not only for Chandragupta's regime but of much later ages—he is of today too.

Bibliography

J. P. Morgan. "Per Head International Average of Total National Production." *The Economist*, 2002.

Magill, Frank N., ed. *The Ancient World*. Chicago: Fitzry Dearborn Publishers, 2000.

Murray, Oswyn. *Early Greece*. 2nd ed. Harvard University Press, 1993.

27

Application of Agriculture in Economic Awakening and Removal of Inequality

More than one economist has won the Nobel prize for propounding theories influencing economic awakening and inequality. There has been coordination between economic awakening and the problem of inequality. Deliberation on this subject has come from different angles of vision. In modern economics, the connecting link between economic advancement and economic inequality has been discussed with much importance.

Here, coordination among different financial professions—industries and financial factors of different measures—smoothen this advancement, which has been taken to be secondary and not primary. In modern economics, the rate of advancement has the greatest weightage and because of this, the role of agriculture in this field has been made limited.

The far-reaching thought on this subject is there in Kautilya's *Arthashastra*. Kautilya wanted the path of economic awakening and removal of inequality to be built on the application of agriculture and mainly on the background of agriculture. Kautilya wanted to bring the far-reaching awakening through the path of agriculture and to establish economic equality through the removal of inequality.

The main theme of Kautilya's economic policy lies in the blooming of manhood in state managements and above all, in the right use of wealth. Kautilya liked to set up such an arrangement as a result of which an ideal of unified lives would exist through the usage of wealth.

There is a motive behind the right use of wealth. If wealth is suitably augmented, it would be easy to carry the same to all concerned. Kautilya liked to realise a fundamental basis of wealth, and the matter of division and distribution would also be much easier from this basis.

The basic foundation is necessary for augmentation of wealth. Kautilya wanted agriculture to be known as this fundamental basis. His proposition of expansion of wealth lies on this basis of expansion and extended distribution of wealth becomes possible. The basis of economic advancement formed through the expansion of wealth would make carrying wealth to all possible.

Kautilya's *Arthashastra* is specially dedicated for economic distribution and advancement. Kautilya has built up the economic distribution in such a way that inequality can be removed completely.

There have been extensive attempts among modern economists to remove inequality completely. Nobel Laureates in economics of 1954 and 1955, W. Arthur Lewis and Simon Kurznet respectively, have deliberated on the relationship between economic awakening and financial inequality. Lewis' theory was economic development with unlimited supplies of labour. Lewis showed in the model of development theory that advancement and accumulation would grow in the modern industrial civilisation through the workers' employment and investment of capital. Possessors of capital would deploy workers in adequate numbers for guarding and augmentating the capital. When the market would grow up, these possessors of capital would, in case deployment of workers, follow the market rate.

Cooperation would be obtained from the workers byengaging them into rendering the financial enterprises of the possessors effective. Capital and labour have their contribution in the profit gained by such application. The possessor of capital would run after greater profit and as a consequence of the profit, would try to inflate the capital. According to Lewis, the rate of agricultural production and development is much lower in comparison to that of industries.

Agricultural labourers, eager for improved living, would leave agriculture and be inclined towards industries. The rate of improvement in industries would surpass that of agriculture. Not only that, but agriculture would also be unable to provide the varieties that would come along with the industries. For that, the worker ignoring the age-old field of agriculture would move in uncontrolled speed towards the more improved living, much more income and prosperity of the industries. This would bring in varieties in income. Low-income group workers would be inclined to high income.

Lewis has stated his invasion of men from low to high income fortheexploration to be his natural expedition. This propensity of march from low income to higher income would increase the discrimination of income by a greater extent. Just as there is a difference of income between the downright cases of agriculture and industry, the start of the propensity to race towards the industry for agriculture further increases this income discrepancy.

In such cases, the total income of the whole economic region goes on increasing and with that, the measure of the average income also increases. A discrepancy of increase remains even between the advancement of total income and average income. One of the reasons behind the increase of average income is the rapid increase of income in the upper stages of the economic region. Average income increases due to rapid increase of income of the people of higher income groups.

Due to such an unequal increase of income on one side and an advent of slowness in income of the majority on the other, the discrepancy in income goes on increasing in spite of an increase in average income. Of course, such a stage does not last long in an economic system. In due course of time, newer attempts to come back to the status quo sets in. In this process of economic development, inequality comes in at the very first stages. Up to a certain stage, this economic development goes on increasing inequality.

When inequality becomes excessive, a flow of spontaneous change comes in the economic system as a reaction to this excessive inequality. These two opposite reactions suddenly stop, to some or much extent, the movement of men between the two economic systems. As a result of this break, a reverse action sets in. Much of the newer increase in the average income in this reverse action comes from the income of the lower level. In this time, labour and capital goes anew for economic success. The possessor of capital becomes eager to march anew for more capital. As a result of this, now the capital looks for a newer field. In this arrangement, variedness comes in the economic system. In the market, there is an attempt to move from one to many.

In the fields of capitals arrives a tendency to multiply. As a result, there are endeavours for marching from one company to many, from one financial enterprise to many. As a result of this, the opportunity of activity gets extended and so, the fields of activity also spread out. Keeping up with the increase of opportunity of activity and number of fields of activity, the market rate of workers rises up.

Workers or enterprisers can now aspire for enhanced market price, right from their position. This expedition of workers and enterprisers directly causes enhancement of their income, which transforms into an economic propensity—that is, the ascension of average income of an economic region.

When such expansion of the economic system happens, average income starts its march towards a permanent and proper consequence right then. This results in a new opportunity—a new opportunity to build a new distribution of the economic system. Inequality of income of the new arrangement begins to decrease. If this position can be achieved, then at the same time, the descending tendency of inequality of income and the ascending tendency of economic development takes place. But the problem is that just the reverse process is taking place in reality. Where this is possible, there is built up an extended economic system and as a consequence this, the extended economic system becomes effective in removing the inequality.

Simon Kuznet, the Nobel laureate in Economics, 1955, of course, holds a different opinion. According to Kuznet, the transmission of labour from one field to another is not essential for economic development. Kuznet argues that the proper use of wealth in a particular field is possible only in that field. In other words, people associated with agriculture will be able to have full reliance on agriculture if they get variety and expansion in agriculture only. The case of agriculture can also be applied to the case of industry and supply.

Reliance on agriculture will bloom in agriculture only, reliance on industry will bloom in industry only and in both cases, the expansion of wealth will take place in their respective cases and the economic development will be extended. The expansion of the respective fields can be affected in this line and at the same time, the tendency of the difference to decrease would start to come into play.

According to Kuznet, the movement of people from one field to another would be required as long as one field lag behind others.

This means that enhancement of inequality is inevitable. Despite facing no change in the status of one field when moved backwards, in other fields, inequality grows again in advancement. Imbalance seeps in the financial distribution. Inequality increases with increase in financial imbalance and ordinarily financial ability also goes on waning.

Lewis has stated his invasion of men from low to high income for the Kuznet Curve. The economic development and inequality of income are inversely connected—this theory, in figure, is like the inverted letter 'U', which means that at a certain stage, economic advancement and inequality of income awfully connected inversely and, in some stages, a balanced condition exists again for some days from this inequality. This equilibrium is the ideal state because from here, the opposite movement starts.

After the equilibrium state, for some days, the opposite movement starts its journey. In this opposite movement, as economic advancement increases, inequality of income decreases. Thus, the whole relation has three stages. In the first stage, economic advancement causes an increase in inequality; in the second stage, in spite of economic advancement, inequality remains fixed at a state and in the third stage, the economic development lowers the inequality. This means that the reason behind the economic advancement in the first stage is the extension of the field. Bands of people move away from agriculture to industrial and other fields and the speed of income of people increases rapidly. In the second case, at the insistence of the market, these people revert to their initial fields and help bring speed in their income.

On the third stage comes the progress of the lower level. The extension of economic advancement would start taking place in accordance with the broad base economy. As a result of this, inequality of income will also decrease with the expansion of income. There had been two classes in the countries from examples of which Kuznet came to an inference. One class consisted of developed countries like England, Germany and America; the other class consisted of India, Sri Lanka and Puerto Rico. Kuznet's curve has been thoroughly discussed for four to five decades in case of the relation between inequality of income and economic advancement.

Hypotheses that have the basis in the features of Kuznet curve are in most cases, not quite proper. Hypotheses on the basis of which Kuznet curve has been designed would have to face questions far reasonableness. Rabi Kanbur, in his book *Handbook of Income Distribution* (2000), has elucidated upon the Kuznet's theory and shown that the aspect of inequality of income has been so connected with the exposition of the economic system that the influence of the exposition of the economic system is a must to fall on the inequality of income. The main theories among all economic theories that have been framed on the basis of mentionable investigations on this subject are: 'Growth is good for the poor' of David Dollar and Krary Aart (2000); 'Simultaneous Equation of Growth and Inequality' of Squire Lyn and Mattius Lundburg (2003); 'Growth, Inequality and Poverty: Looking Beyond Averages' of Martin Ravallion (2001); 'Can we Discuss the effect of Globalization on Income Distribution' of Banko Milanovic (2002) and 'Income inequality in OECD countries: Data and Explanations' of Anthony B Atkinson (2003).

The research of Atkinson has exposed detailed works on how income inequality has been built up in the countries, included in OECD (Organisation for Economic Cooperation and Development) during the second half of the twentieth century. After 1970, inequality began to increase, especially in America and England.

During the second half of the twentieth century, as on one hand, the extensive economic advancement had been achieved, on the other hand, income inequality had been inflated. Different aspects have been brought in observation for discussing the increase and decrease of development and inequality. The factor that has been broadly exposed in Atkinson's research is that the new avenues for economic advancement may, at the same time, be favourable for development and inequality. Economic advancements takes place whenever a large number of small or medium enterprises begin setting up in a place with fewer numbers of big-sized enterprises or organisations; along with this begins the tendency for inequality to get reduced, especially mentionable among those who have undertaken detailed research on e economic awakening and income inequality of China by Martin Ravallion and Chen Sheohua (2004). Their theory, 'China's (uneven) Progress Against Poverty' (World Bank Policy Research working Paper Series 3408), demands a special reference.

Ravellion and Sheohua have proved that in the interior field of almost all enterprises in China and in the overall Chinese economic system income, inequality is increasing rapidly. The income inequality in the 90's of the last century has much surpassed that in the 80's. In between, inequality has increased rapidly but still, the overall rate of economic advancement was not uniform. In case of the rate of overall economic advancement, sometimes there has been a rapid rate and sometimes sluggish one—but in both cases, inequality has increased. As a result of this, the Kuznet curve could not be applied here. In case of investigation on India also, it has been noticed that even when the rate of income inequality is decreasing.

On some occasions, it takes an upward move, though economic advancement in different measures has remained undeterred. Bhaskar Majumder (2005) of Princeton University has shown in his research that in America, economic advancements have been very rapid, as the Black community has had a propensity move apart from their locality and financial flow to join the rest, but as a result of this, income inequality has increased. The research paper of Thomas Hertz (2005) has supported Majumder's view.

In Hertz's research, Majumder's opinion has been expressed owing to the transfer of the Black community's economic advancement has been hastened, no doubt, but at the same time, inequality has inflated. Consistency has been expressed among the research accepted recently by the World Bank. Now, the opinion has grown that economic advancement will not have to be considered separately. The attempt to remove inequality is to be made strong, along with the attempts of advancement.

The first step of removing inequality along with advancement is expansion. The old technique of expanding the wealth of a certain state in its own locality has been replaced by the attempt to expand the possibility of one place to various other places. The public sector came along the path of expanding the wealth of a certain locality.

The public sector took the social responsibility for the expansion. It has utilised the finance of Government Treasury through many channels and engaged in the job of financial expansion. It cannot be said that the public sector has failed in all attempts. There are many such fields where the public sector has been successful and is running successfully, vying with the private sector. In extreme cases, attempts for economic awakening through public sector have failed everywhere under the sun. The main reason behind this is the existence of expansion of wealth in the theory of the public sector. It did not pay any heed to the possibility. The reason of there being no blooming of possibility in proper measure, in spite of expansion of wealth, is that the economic system has been quite dependent on wealth.

Even the private sectors that appeared in places of public sectors had confidence on the expansion of wealth. Changes in this attitude have come through a span of only one decade or so. In line with this change has risen the economic system of the basis of possibility. For example, a balance sheet gives an idea of the assets of a company, but no idea of its conjunction with the market. In place of the real value of a company, what becomes the most important is at what price the company might be sold on the market. To apprehend this, the company would have to judge its present price structure and its future status. The consideration of the future prices lies in the judgement of present and future price status.

The more financial thoughts would be able to overcome the dependence on wealth, the more would economic development expand and people of lower monetary ability would be able to come up gradually to higher levels. The first result is monetary progress and the reduction in other inequalities of the consequences. All men have their own contribution in the field of possibilities. In all, there is a latent ability. Brahman (Absolute Spirit) resides in all human structures, from all can emerge personalities full of possibility.

When coordination of many people appears in the economic system, at that time, all of the possibilities turn every individual into an economic unit. Something is to be taken and in return, something is to be given. Moments of remaining dependent on others flow out. Latent possibilities and capabilities wake up in men. Extensive collection of latent possibilities and capabilities can bring economic revolution in societies and states. Economists have not come up with anything to say regarding this coordination of possibility and capability of the economic system till now; the only exception is Kautilya. It is Kautilya who has laid stress on the blooming of possibility and ability of an individual so far, the judgement of wealth Kautilya has wanted is the expansion of wealth.

That is, he liked to hasten the advancement of a state through expanding the wealth of the country among the multitude and collecting from many people taxes generated from the wealth. Kautilya has wanted simultaneous expansion of wealth and simultaneous blooming of possibility.

The more rapid would be the blooming of wealth and possibility the more would be simultaneous advancement and revelation of wealth. Revelation of wealth comes from its expansion in the possession of many. As a result of this, economic inequality continuously increases. As soon as economic inequality starts to increase, expansion of wealth begins to reduce. For this, Kautilya has wanted proper expansion of wealth in the field that owns that wealth. Expansion of wealth and possibility can take place simultaneously in the path shown by Kautilya. At the root of the expansion of possibility is the inauguration of the dormant factors within one's own existence. Kautilya wanted to open the door and to extend wealth, keeping a balance with possibility in the proper field.

Thus, Kautilya's *Arthashastra* has pointed out that the first stage of financial development is the exposition of the economic possibilities that are dormant in the fields where financial enterprises have been contemplated to be undertaken. Right at this stage, the end of all of the economic inequalities begins to be indicated. Economic inequality starts to get reduced at this stage of exposition.

The more would be the reduction in the economic inequality, the more would be the awakening of the possibilities. The awakening of economic development and the diminution in the load of inequality take place simultaneously. Kautilya wanted the possibilities in the agricultural fields designed to be bloomed right in the interest of agriculture; on the other hand, if economic development begins in other fiends of economic possibilities, then it would be possible for development and equilibrium to attempt to be affected simultaneously. According to Kautilya, development has priority on the basis of possibility.

Kautilya has analysed all the subjects that have been inferred by economic profounders like Lewis, Kuznet, Hertz and others through judging the modern economic system at a different time. Kautilya's inference is far more far reaching and deeper. At the very initiation, Kautilya has made an economic observation on application and blooming of possibilities. In case of these economic observations, Kautilya has solved the problem of inequality right with the problem of advancement.

28

Fields of Application of Spiritual Economy

How to ascertain whether economic advancement has taken place or is ongoing? How would we realise whether we are moving in the path of development? Someone has quoted, "we have had a simple principle by looking at the faces of many people of many countries." This simple principle is related to development.

The simple way to realise whether there has been development is to understand the mental condition of the people. While walking along the road, if a garland of many faces is seen to move on beaming with pleasure, it is to be understood that they are well. To remain well, they have a fixed measure of their own satisfaction. It would naturally be ushered if they realise that they are well in their own measure, if they have this feeling.

The feelings and ideas of this satisfaction would spontaneously spread in their movements and appearance. On the other hand, if in some locality, the appearance of a sorry and burdened mind is spread on the people, it is to be inferred that they are not well. Arrested in anxiety, dissatisfaction and apprehension, they, with gloomy faces, are moving every day from one work to another. Looking from the outside, one has to normally understand how they are.

Now the question is: are dissatisfaction and poverty the same measure? All dissatisfaction is not indicative of poverty. Different measures of dissatisfaction bloom at different times. Even the richest of all people may have plenty of dissatisfaction. If despair, anxiety, apprehension, darkness of mind—all these combines with dissatisfaction, it is to be understood that poverty must have been one of its reasons.

Rows of soiled people stooped forward reveals the intensity of poverty. Change comes in the presence of the overall form of man with economic development. If the change augments the measure of gloominess, it is to be taken that there has been no economic development, or the flow of development would get deterred. The flow of men beaming with bubbling inspiration and filled with life force is the index of economic development.

While walking along the roads of New York, Tokyo, Washington, Paris, Stockholm, Hong Kong and Seoul, one would note the overall unity blooming on the faces of men. It would seem that the difference in physique is the only symptom that would characterise their separateness.

The standard of bearing and living of the people of the big cities has been maintaining nearly the same standard all along. Now, the slogan of a place is 'Money is God'. Everything is weighed in the standard of money. Money can get each and everything in the grip of man. Endless pleasure, plentiness of enjoyment, innumerable ways of physical and mental satisfaction, constantly newer tastes of consumption, arrangements of limitless happiness—money can get all of them. A unification of the throb of life will be felt at every corner of a supercity. The demarcation of countries, societies and nations in this respect is gradually becoming meaningless. In different countries, a national or international society has grown up.

Citizens of the international societies are all of a different blood. In spite of emerging from different cultures, a uniformly unified society has been built up where there is a unity of mentality and uniformity of living. They may speak in various languages, but they have the same style of speaking and same style of living. They were born on the soil of the country but have been a part of the world. They have no roots. They have lopped the roots linked with which they were born on the country's soil and have grown up.

They have shed from the root to become universal. Now, they do not belong to any particular country. While walking along the road of Shanghai, they think of New York. The very topic which they deliberate on sitting at a park of London, becomes the topic of a fluent discussion at the parks of Stockholm or Chicago. Sitting at a comfortable restaurant in Delhi, they bring in their discussion about the affairs of the people of Tokyo, with the mentality of the people of Paris or Washington, but in comparison to that, they have rather very little attention towards the villages of Orissa, West Bengal or Karnataka.

They speak the same language, represent the same mentality, are accustomed to the same living and are moving in an indomitable speed towards the same target. It is not difficult to understand that they are very close to one another. They can very easily recognise a man of their own class. All that is developed so they are different. They are men of an elevated world. So, they are considered to be great.

Great men have big dream. Their wealth is far-extended, and their expansion is great. Big men walk as if they carry royal blood. They have money, so the world is at their command. They bear a different identity. Some are traders, some are industrialists, some are politicians, some again are intellectuals or company executives. They have one and only identity—they are all developed and big men of the world. They are the residents of a global village.

This global village has wiped out their mutual distances. Any day of theirs is as if trapped in a dream, spread in a number of flows. Science is lying in their palms, so are all of the discoveries of technology. They do not care for the assurance of nature. In the tropical countries, so many cooling appliances are after them. There is a cooling arrangement in their houses, cars, offices and everywhere. In cold countries, heating devices run after them.

Everywhere they have a scope of being warmed. Technology has got for them all sorts of services. There is nothing called distance to them. Having breakfast in Frankfurt, they hold an official or business meeting, having a lunch in Stockholm or Copenhagen and come to dine in London. The whole world is lying in their palms. Their food menu, clothing and clearing devices—all are international with Japanese cars, European cosmetics and food.

With an American style and mentality, they embrace some articles of their society or country at all corners of the world. In the event of illness, the means of treatment for them extends all over the world, starting from America. They consume and enjoy. They are eager to enjoy. They believe that enjoyment is life, that enjoyment begets satisfaction. What living is meant for is enjoyment.

This life is not much extended, so enjoy as much as you can. Search out which is the best at which place of the world. Loot and catch hold of that. The more plentiful would be the arrangement for enjoyment, the more advanced would be the standard of living. Living is marked at the instance of enjoyment. That country is called developed where majority of the people fall in this category.

A land where rather a smaller number of men belongs to this category is undeveloped. In the countries of big people, there is a competition to be far bigger; most of the big people are dissatisfied. There is no way in the country for them to be satisfied. In spite staying on the land, they are beyond the land, beyond the time. They think themselves to live in the future; technology, too, is their offering.

On the other side stand the group of small people. Either they are extremely poor, or they somehow manage themselves. They never have all their requirements met. They belong to their country and time. They have to search for all their requirements within the country. The country and society before them are their one and only one. Beyond the country, there are beckonings of many kinds before many of them. Some also set out on adventure. They aim to join the cluster of the big people. They seek the opportunity to move and live with big people.

Perhaps they also aim at being beyond time, they move about in search of a philosopher's stone. When would they reach the state of the big people—this is their desire. Their target and movements are directed towards the world. They like to find suitable articles for themselves and get those components and arrangements that would make them universal. In reality, their condition is very miserable. They hope and long for the lives of big people, but the stroke of reality comes to them in rather a violent form. Their lives are burdened with wants—wants of education, wants of food and nutrition, of proper treatment, of monetary help in case of calamity, of proper accommodation, of the environment of growing up, of proper hygienic arrangement, of supply of objects beyond needs, of capability of fulfilling dreams and of cooperation.

Let us take the case of Mr. Ranjan Bhattacharya of West Bengal. He used to consider himself a low-middle-class man. He was employed in the office of a business. During the last fifteen years of his career, he had the post of cashier. He was a man of old mentality—a father of three daughters and two sons. He somehow managed to build up a home in a mofussil at a distance of a one-hour train journey. The education achieved by the progenies was rather scanty.

Only one daughter was about to be established, one of the sons has managed to get a minor job. The income of both the daughter and son is rather meagre; Mr. Ranjan is retired and ailing. He is only sixty-five. He has been suffering from different diseases for quite some years. The first and the third daughter is not engaged. So, he had somehow managed to get them married rather early. The family runs on the combined income of the second daughter and the second son. They are running into debts and quite embarrassed at the illness of their father. Now, Mr. Ranjan has an ailment of the heart. Hospital kept him for a day and has installed a temporary pacemaker. It is now to be made permanent. Money is needed. The pacemaker has to be bought, money is to be collected for treatment, or otherwise, he would have to leave the hospital within few days.

Under such circumstances, Ranjanbabu's son and daughter are moving from door to door. Everybody advises, "There is no need of installing a pace maker, how long would he live? Take him home, provide oxygen and that will do. Alas Ranjanbabu! This world is pushing you towards death little by little. For your announcements of all the developments of this world is but empty."

Advancement of science and technology, development of medical treatment in different countries and medical technology is all futile in the case of Ranjanbabu; balance of payment of the country, GDP per capita are all baseless to him. To him, this world is a distant abode. It is just not his own residence. Here, he is an alien who came from outside, uncalled for and taken possession of without a right. So, there is no arrangement here for him. His family cannot procure money to save his life. Ranjanbabu will have to move to the land of death little by little, just before the eyes of the members of his family.

Let us now hear the other side of the story of Mr. Punit Jain. He is a businessman of the middle order and a native of Kolkata. Big car, big house—all are in his posession. His business has extended to different cities, and he often flies in between Kolkata, Delhi and Bangalore regarding his business. Punit is very health-conscious and has made a large amount of Mediclaim. He undergoes annual check-ups from big centers. Punit consulted a doctor on account of a sudden pain in the chest and some problem of valve were detected. Punit flew to America, underwent an operation, returned completely cured. He returned to his business.

All amenities of this world are at the grip of big men. Advancement of science and technology, global village, everything involved in development—all are for big men. Liberalisation in different countries and globalisation are primarily for big men.

Newer markets are required for expansion of business of big men. Globalisation is a step for such expansion of market. Liberalisation brings in change in the internal management of a country to expose it before the world market. For forming of the big people, newer and newer markets are necessary.

Because either they are getting forward their own trades and business or the industrial organisation on the routes of the world have become helpful as representatives of the companies in expansion of the market for that company. In both cases they have become synonymous with their companies. The company goes on increasing itself in different countries hoping for more success, gain more franchises and enjoy greater profits. Here, the interests of the company and its executives are running almost towards the same target. It is the executive who is to earn for the company. How would a company earn? Respecting the laws and abiding by the rules, a company would move towards its target. What would be the target? Some would say that it is service, some would say expansion, some again say that it is to get profit. Whatever may be in their announcement, profit is compulsory.

Every company grows depending on the wealth of its own connection and capability. Capability and wealth are created through connections and again connections get capability and wealth. Both managements aim at expansion and greater profit. Big companies aspire to be bigger through their worldwide expansion and profit. As big companies are creating big men, big men also continue joining or creating big companies.

Big companies and big men go hand in hand. They coordinate with each other. They are complementary and the force of inspiration for each other. The combined power of big companies and big men is now moving forward to set up a global village. They, at any time, are able to devour small companies and enterprises. They undertake, they seize and grow rapidly, they can augment the measure of their profit more rapidly through enormous expansion.

To run after profit, they often even deceive others. One who is big gradually becomes eager to earn more wealth and capability for being bigger or to remain big in the teeths of competitions. All of the big American companies that have been caught for fraudulence are all of big dimension—they are included among the companies known to be the best in the world. Most of them are "Fortune five hundred companies", which is in the category of the top five hundred companies in the judgement of Fortune magazine. Such a company is Enron. To influence their investing agencies and people, Enron was exhibiting the financial position of the company in such a way so as to augment its attraction. This profiteering organisation showing increased profit and alluring for a greater profit in the future became eager to influence the shareholders. This action was not only illegal but also bad taste.

Such a big company, in spite of its high reputation, high decoration and so much skillful use of words, has such a low taste. The company is being engrossed in the pursuit of expansion by any means and having greater profit was caught red-handed. As a consequence, the company was closed down. Those who were associated with that big company as executives were also shares of the sin committed. The purpose of this type of behaviour was to import investments in great quantity, deceiving not only the common people but also other investing agencies of the market and the wealthy investors. The company and the executives had the same type of intention. They only looked after their own interest in deceiving the society.

The executives had a great property along with that of the company. Their fates are tied to each other. If the company grows and its profit increases, the executives can also increase in their money. Big companies and their executives stay within the same circle. They jointly want to grow up to a great extent through extending financial and trading influence on the other party. Big men are eager to deceive the small men. Big men like to appropriate the wealth and possibility of small men in their own interest. Big men want to be bigger at any cost.

Society of Big Men, Society of Small Men

Big men are eager to create and maintain communication among themselves. Of these, those who are engaged in industry, commerce and trade have made themselves united and incorporated. All of them have clubs, associations and different types of organisations. The object of these clubs, association and other types of organisations is to maintain the interest of the big men and to extend the same. At the root of these united efforts of big men, these are union and confidence as subtle factors. The union is framed on the basis of interest and possibility of common measure. They join hands for protection, expansion of interest and possibility of common measure and become coordinators of reciprocal enterprise.

Their reciprocal coordination depicts mutual interest. The primary object of certain commercial organisations is to extend common interest of those commercial concerns and common organisations.

Being earnest in such activity, if they find that to increase the depth of the market, some actions are to be taken against the interest of common people, they take a leading role in these cases. They take the role of the initiators in the attempts against the interest small men; that is, the common men, commercial clubs or associations. This is a main part of the social management of the big men and these men use these organisations for extending their own wealth property. Chambers of commerce in different countries perform these duties.

They have twofold ways before them for expanding the extent of the market—one, to allure the people who have at present become their customers to buy in greater measure and to serve newer commodities in greater amounts so that the way of purchasing becomes rather easier for the present buyers; two, to find out newer buyers and to please them with newer commodities. Either these buyers are buying customers or commodities for the first time or have begun to buy the newer ones.

It has been found, after frequent application of the first process, that much time is not required to reach the limit. The limit can be reached rather easily. That is, here competition is much and in comparison, the opportunity for profit at present times or in future is low enough. Comparatively, new markets of new buyers are conducive enough for the supply of commodities. Different commercial associations, therefore, are keeping watch on new markets of new buyers, which bring twofold opportunities before the companies.

One, extension of sales and consequently opportunity for making enough profit and being expanded; and two, the economic possibility of mass production, owing to having opportunity of manifold productions. This means reduction of selling price of each of the factors for mass production and as a result, greater measure of sale. That is why big companies and big men always extend hands towards small men. They continuously try to inspire them so that the commercial organisations become great, industrial production increases, resulting in speed in their monetary movement. It directly casts an influence on the economic status of the country.

That is, such changes begin to appear as the causes consequential economic progress. As a result of these, ample possibilities bloom out before small men.

Gradually, they become charmed by opportunities and possibilities and become attracted to the big men. The society of big men gradually make the society of small men attracted towards them. The society of big men becomes, at the same time, the dreams of small men and oppressor, the big men, continuously apply their concerted endeavours on small men. The society of small men becomes supporters of the societies of big men and at the same time, become troubled and demolished by them.

Like societies of big men, there are societies small men also. But the main difference is that in the societies of big men, there is an inner basic unity, just in the form of an inseparable tie. In the societies of big men, there is competition and mutual struggle. For example, Pepsi and Coca-Cola. Between them, there has always been an inimical relation. But still there is also a far-reaching unity.

This point of unity will be evident if the history of spreading of their business in India is observed. First, they divided the Indian market in between them on the basis of a mutual understanding, created their sphere of influence in particular regions and later both of them spread throughout the country and entered into competition between themselves.

The first intention was to organise oneself in particular regions to give a permanent shape and the second was to purchase small but popular local companies. Thus, their business became monopolistic. They have not only occupied the market of soft drinks in the country but have also given a new measure to the market, so that anyone of them has become the regulating authority of the market at different ends of the country.

Social binding among big men appears through monetary power and ability. On the contrary, societies of small men are formed keeping in mind the problem and requirements. On one side, they are quite embarrassed with the spread of problems; on the other side, their eagerness is extreme for meeting the needs. But all of their attempts often become futile for want of ability.

It is a spiritual economy that only can initiate development. Such a relation has been set up between societies of big people and small people that as it has at its root the separateness between the intensity and outlook of the two groups, without the support and coordination of one part, the counterpart cannot survive.

If the society of small men are able to reject boldly the efforts of the big men, then there would come a slide in majority of their enterprises. It has already been discussed that to get expansion in the enterprises of big men, expansion of market is required. This is the reason why they would have to approach the society of small men.

On the other hand, the urge for development brings primary dependence on money and wealth. Why is development required? More employment, greater amount of wealth, greater measure of provisions and much greater coordination, in case of possibility required for the small men, who is to provide these? The state and social organisations are gradually getting weaker in consideration of the financial standard. The state is unable to support it. Small men are to build up management for the development of themselves in their own way. In many places, this development may be possible by their own methods. But in most cases, they require a coordination system and coordination of property and wealth. Mutual predisposition depicts mutual relationship.

If big men, by the power of their living and power of enjoyment, cast looks of apathy and injustice on the small men, it would be evident that their days are on the wane. On the other hand, if small men bear a mentality of contempt and hatred for the big men, their future will have to be thought to be perfectly overcast with gloom. Awakening of spirituality can change the direction of this mentality.

As this change of mentality is required for mutual survival and in the far spread interest, for keeping mutual interest intact, one is to also understand the other, one is to realise the weal, woe and pleasure of others. Big men have big problems, big miseries and big pains. They have no want of money, wealth and enjoyment, but they are very poor withrespect to mental wealth.

They are quite distressed; their feelings and realisation of satisfaction are so pervading that all the pleasure of consumption to them becomes just the happiness of a dream. They are dissatisfied because their craving is infinite. Their craving goes on increasing. It is true for an individual so also for the collectivity. Their craving goes on increasing by the measure of many multiplies of their having or being. So, the difference between craving and having goes on increasing.

This difference is an index of dissatisfaction. If big men go on moving, it would be merely a dream to them to get relief from inevitable destruction and calamity. Spiritualism would open the door for them. Spiritualism would be able to get into them the realisation that endeavour, profit and expansion are required, no doubt, but all of the requirements are to be met with the basic objects of life in mind. Financial rise is required for life. That rise is not acceptable by life, which breaks human society into fragments of the big and the small. Truly big men are improved in spiritual standard; he knows whom the worldly wealth belongs to, where it originates from and what the consequence it has. This feeling would come down in the societies of the big and the poor and gradually the force of unity within the societies would be stronger.

The main pillar of spiritual economy is coordination. The deeper would be the coordination in economics, the more powerful and smooth would be the financial management that would be able to accept all types of healthy compositions. The basis of this competition would be coordination. The spiritual economy would open up the door of this coordination.

The basis of the competition also would be coordination. The spiritual economy would open up the path to this coordination. Coordination can come through many paths. For example, in a democratic system, coordination of the majority is the best way to set up coordination in a state system. But only a democratic infrastructure would not be able to get this coordination.

Something more is needed for this. The attempts of some such people are needed here who, through leadership, would be able to inspire the people. This means that as coordination is somewhat dependent on the endeavour of some men, it would also depend much on proper leadership. It is possible only as the part of proper leadership to inspire men. This is the initiation of spiritual economic management. At the consequence of this would come a world economic system that has equilibrated gracefulness.

29

Creating Humane Money

A slide may come down on the monetary world. The mighty dominance of money is facing a challenge. This mighty challenge has come from within the world of money. Besides, there is a challenge from the outside as well. Now, the stage of the natural face of money for the dominance of world power starts. Even in the meantime, there has been a shortage of the dominance of money. The main time of capitalism, in the last years, was that money is the last word. The power of money has begun to yield before other powers from the end of the last century and at the beginning of the twenty-first century. There are attempts, no doubt, to claim even now that money is the last word, but in many places, money is not getting the chance to utter the last word. In many cases, the voices have faded.

We have heard that money begets everything. The power of money is all-pervading. World society is occupied by a situation and nation that none has the power to obstruct the flow of money. Anywhere in the world, we may be dominant, and the right of money is seen to be admitted and taken for granted. Man has come to believe that with money, one can buy anything and everything. One by one, through the use of money, house and buildings may be built up and demolished, overload ship can be established on different lands, companies may be purchased one after another. Indirectly, governments and their targets may be brought one after another into the sphere of one's influence. Even man can be bought out right. Under the influence of money, man's mind also gets perturbed. In many cases, the human mind abides by loyalty before money. The dominance of money blooms quite unnoticed. There comes a change in the voice at last and even in longings. There is a touch of change. Entanglements of culture sometime seem to be immature and unwanted before dominant money.

For a long life, a heavenly adobe of money has been built up. Just after the promotion of men, the evolution of living creatures has been upward. Man's cognition has been unveiled and awakened. The attention, which in the kingdom of beasts was directed towards the self, has been radiated coming to men. Man is very much eager to realise his own interest, no doubt, but he has cast his notice through to a small extent. To others, the disparity cognition has created the disparity in difference in human mentality to different extents.

Some men have come out overcoming the earlier beastly cognition and cultural entanglements and been lifted to a great consciousness. This main spite of being men are engaged in beastly fastenings. They are a man in form but a beast in mentality. Such people are many in number and a great of number people in between these two groups. They are partly covered with beastly cognition. They are also possessors of great consciousness. There are rather vacillating flies, sometimes resting on sweets and sometimes on stool.

With respect to money, they are not so trustworthy, but sometimes they seem to be the most deserving. In order to increase the dominance and acceptability of money, a fair role of money is to be presented before society and man. As a result, the trustworthiness of money increases. This trustworthiness creates a market in favour of an increase in the dominance of money. Coordination and support are required to increase the dominance of money. Those who accord coordination are men of the inner sphere of money. With the pervasion of money, they also get improved. Affluence and power would get into them. It is the affluence that would make them quite different from other people in society.

Living within society, they are possessors and mentors of separate societies. In an attempt to offer coordination in the dominance of money, man has practically yielded to money. Money, here, has the last right to speak. Here, words are original in terms of money. It is money that tells how their living would be what type of mentality would be acceptable and what type of consideration they would have.

In many cases, the dominant role of advice and the influence of money gets access to the practical lives of man. If it tells what the practical life of an individual should be; how he would maintain his personal relations; how much time he would devote to his family;

how many specific times he would be selected in the personal life; what would be the field to lay stress on and from where the propensity support and endeavours servitude of money. His dwelling face is the hell of affluence.

Defeat of Money

Money is not lost before management; it loses before conscience. Beckoning of conscience has dimmed in a moment the dominance of money and removed it. Awakened conscience is rich and makes a man rich with the wealth of conscience. Their significance surpasses the case in life. Those who hanker after case in life judge and arrange everything in terms of money. Considering the utility of money in various ways, they place money at the top and sometimes at the topmost. Value Ease is judged with respect to the desires of the individual.

As is the influence of desire, so is the limit of ease. The need for money for uncontrolled longings becomes boundless. Uncontrolled longings like to establish the dominance of money. The very first point of uncontrolled longings becomes the establishment of cravings whereby any means, attainment is needed. Cravings can be pulled at any stage whatsoever and the control over craving can be lost. As a result, the significance of the life of an individual becomes a desperate attempt for boundless money. Not only the dominance of money but the sovereignty of money also becomes desirable in such life.

Full power is required for the establishment of sovereign influence. To those who are eager to establish a sovereign influence of money, the power of money is boundless. This boundless power just becomes the cause behind the dominance of money. The main point of this power is the buying capacity and capacity to spread the influence of money. Thus, the buying capacity is determined with respect to the market.

Just as the value and flowing measure of money determine its buying capacity, similarly, the structure and management of the market determine the spread of its influence and also fix up the route of the movement of money. The process of the movement of money depends on the management of the market. The movement and collection of money simultaneously assures the flourishment and capability of money. For the movement of money to be effective, changing hands become necessary. This changing of hands augments the measure of the application of wealth. As a result of the changing of hands, the tendency of money to be accumulated in a single spot led to gradual dominance. The movement of money from one spot to different or many other spots. Starts. As a result, the tendency of money to be centralised begins to decrease.

The meaning of the dissipation of money to varied places is the expansion of the case. Since the case is very obedient to money, the case also spreads with the spreading of money. Ease of money comes in exchange for the case of one—both of those who endeavour for the case or do not have the right for the case. The spread of the case again augments the flow of money. With the spread of money, the flow of money continues. Just as money increases its capability with spread of the market, with spread of the case, the power of money also spreads. The purchasing capacity of money began to increase. As a result, the form of money aspiring to occupy the first place becomes evident.

Man endeavouring for the case never denies the form of money occupying the first place. Accumulation and centralisation of money are required for the case. The spread of the influence of money is required for newer arrangements of the case. Money becomes inflated in an amount from here. The first consequence of the flow of money is starting a greater extent of centralisation. As a result, instead of the case of a great number of people comes the multiplied case of a lesser number of people.

Money begets money—this common proverb is especially applicable in the world of money. Where there is centralisation of money, there is a greater flow of money. As a result of centralisation, the amount of money with which the journey had started rapidly increased. The natural movement of money is in the direction of the mine of money. Wherever there is a mine of money, there begins the dominance of money. This dominance continues till the influence of another mine falls here. The dominant mine of money enters a conflict with the person of the mine. As a result, there is a rift in the world of money. Through the rift in the world of money caused by this type of conflict, the usual nature of money remains behind this.

Money is by nature restless. It does not like to rest in a place. It wants to move from one pocket to another, from one place to another. As restlessness is natural, the movement of money becomes rather easy. Slept money gradually wanes out. The money that remains asleep in a pocket or a place gradually becomes thin in figure. Sleeping money becomes deprived of the scope of intelligence. As it cannot increase, it gradually beings to dry up. As a result, the glow that had already been established earlier has got its changing stage started. It is the confined state of money that makes its power feeble. Money loses its capability in the confined form. Sleeping money is a slave to its confined state. Sleeping money cannot expand its dominion and cannot even preserve it, as sleeping money is incapable. If it is new money, it is incapable of creating a bigger amount of money. Sleeping money can be used to spread its influence in the world, so in spite of its possibility of being in the transaction stage, its effectiveness becomes lean.

Market Money

The power of application of a big amount of money is naturally to be big. For the movement of a big amount of money to be effective, there should be a very big setup of management and enterprises. Now, the big setup of management and big enterprise does not depend on money only. They depend on money factors such as the big extent of the enterprise, and management depends on the capability of the market. If a big enterprise does not get wide acceptability, then it becomes very hard on its part to maintain its existence. For a big enterprise to be sacksful and money-making, there should be wide support and coordination.

The market is standing on the combination and support of money for people. The movement of money for people just makes a market vigorous. Cooperation and participation of many people occur through small amounts of money. Small amounts of money for many people just set up the wide capability of the market. The source of the wide capability of the market is a collection of a good number of small bags of money. A wide accumulation of small amounts of money can give the market a stable form. A small number of big bags of money can set up a big market, but its periphery is limited. That last reason for this big amount of money would supplicate before the small money. In the long run, the link of small amounts of money nourishes the extension of big money. The existence of big money is dependent on small money.

It is the small amount of money that fixes up the demand of the market, of big people. The more would be the demand, the stabler the enterprise would be. The ultimate target of the enterprises is to augment the measure of demand, to create new and greater demand, just with the increase of demand necessity of enterprises would be created and enterprises would be eager for enterprises.

Big amounts of money would be required in association with big enterprises. Now, the sleeping condition of the big money would be over. The more flourished would be the enterprise, the greater would be its extension and the greater would be the measure of the field of application of big money. The spread of an enterprise is the field of extension of big money. In the long run, the existence of big money is dependent on the units of small money. If there is no movement of small money within the market, if small money does not become market-oriented, hand in hand with the demands, big enterprises would dry up. Big money will have to go to its deathbed. Small money is the life force of big money, its field extension. It is the small money that fixes the future of big money. The inner view of big money is the failure of small money in spreading the life force. This is the utter failure of big money.

Liberation of Money

The captivity of money is at the resort of the big, and its liberation is in the resort of the small; so long as money is confined in the mine, it is a captive, and the free air of liberation is at the outside money just gets its ability of application outside the mine. 80 to 90 percent of the money is the custody of 10 to 15 percent of people in the world. This is the resort of the big 80 to 90 percent of the people who have only 10 to 15 percent of the money. This is the captivity of money. Money does not fall at the case in this captivity. It wants liberation. In the resort of the small money gets the air of liberation, the environment of liberation. Wide circulation of money is effective from the resort of the small.

Money just moves about from one spot to another. It comes over to the market and buys, engaging in purchases. The purchases of exchange of hands, exchange of pockets and of traces go on. It becomes eager to create a capability of the market from one field to another. The greater the boundary of circulation of money, the greater the extension of the possibility. The flourishing of money and its power of generation will increase with the capability of living circulated. Money at this stage is eager and able to generate new money. Wide use of small money brings glow and extension of demand in the market. The gradual influence of demand spreads the field of small money, with increasing demand, the advancement of small money increases. This results in the creation of new money by the influence of the small money in different forms and through this circulation, newer fields of requirements are created. Consequently, it draws new enterprises, which gradually make the innovation of small money speedier. New enterprises grow up from small firms gradually to big firms.

The new enterprise of small firms draws up one of the bigger firms. Consequently, a big amount of money becomes essential for an enterprise of a big firm. A big enterprise creates a field of application for big money. It is time for a big enterprise to be extensive and made. This is because all the support needed for a big enterprise is now ready. The demand in the market has grown through the combination of small enterprises, the small enterprises, now in a concerted way, would make the market able to circulate money. At the stage of the wide circulation of small money, a boom would come in the market.

Consequently, big enterprises will also gain life force. The big enterprise would get the life force with which it can survive and expand from the combined capabilities of small enterprises. The big money that has made the big enterprise lively will also be living. The success of money comes from the success of an enterprise. Thus, the success of big money comes from the success of a big enterprise. Big enterprises are the field of application for big money. So, when big money becomes lively by coordination and influence of small money, it achieves liberation from captivity on the part of big money.

The liberation of money is the liberation of the masses; the liberation of small money means the flavour of the case of affluence is carried to a large number of people. Just as it is useful for those who hanker for the case, it is also useful to those who are indifferent to the word case. Ease-loving men attribute undue importance and excessive coordination toward big money. Ease-loving men thus gradually surrender to big money or become slaves to it. Ease-loving men become obsessed with dreams or the urge to use big money for their own service until it fulfils their interests. Consequently, such a man would help make the foundation of the world of money more stable. Until now, the world of money has become strong by this method. Liberation from this situation lies in the urge to hide, spread and become fully dedicated. The extreme dedication to money has been revealed in the attitude of ease-loving people.

Slide in the Power of Money

This attitude has so long built-up civilisation. Ease-loving people are running after money. The change in the attitude of man towards money is inevitable with the advancement of conscience. This change of conscience signifies the change of character and outlook of men. The effect of this change of character and outlook of man would bring a basic change in man's appeal to money. The upward movement of conscience does not rouse any concept of the lack of interest in money and at the same time, it also does not bring in any attachment to money.

The desire of the modern consciousness moves to the side toward contempt and lack of longing for money on one side and on the other side, it moves against the sovereign influence of money. The flow of consciousness now does not admit the governance of money and at the same time, it also does not disagree with the same. As a result, men interested in money can no longer be traced out. This means that the dominant influence of money would no longer be effective on all. Even a man, who has waked up from beastly instincts and moved halfway in the path of human consciousness, moves by the attraction of money and is obsessed with money, but here, the condition is not as earlier; these have become complete slaves to money. The condition is now in both ways loose and completely devoted.

More upliftment would continue with the awakening of consciousness. This is the stage of divine consciousness. The divine feeling, divine idea and divine state stay within man by the touch of divine consciousness. Newer exposition of new life comes along the flow of divine consciousness. This man is human in an apparently acceptable life. The man, human in form, human in the outer situation, becomes divine in the extreme state. This means that this man takes up divine attire. The life of such a man is just in the whirl of the divine through.

The assimilation of divine ideas makes the life of this man divine. Thus, in contact with divine consciousness, a divine effect becomes evident in his body. As a result, the identity of this man gets lost in the extreme. In this situation, the mind of this person does not get engaged in the service of things. He would never be eager to serve objects. This man becomes quite above the service of objects. Instead of serving objects, he attempts to rise up along the stains of a more improved life. He wants his life to move toward a more improved life. He is no longer an aspirant for the fulfilment of his own interests. His own interest becomes secondary to him. He becomes engaged in benevolence and arranging comfort for money. To this man, money would have a very scanty demand. He does not yield to money; rather, money tends to become his slave just with a written bond.

The wealth of money becomes dim before the glow of consciousness. He, who is aspiring for divine consciousness, is gradually respecting the appeal and influence of money in life. He does not admit submissiveness to money; rather, he gives indulgence to money with mere compassion for the provision of minimum support and ability in life. The influence of money began fading to him.

We have now reached the gateway of divine consciousness, moving along the path of the evaluation of consciousness. There is now such a man as believed in divine existence and living entry of divine consciousness. To such a man, divine consciousness is the main theme. Such a man likes to have only God in his life. In the same way, as once man himself appeared in a tiny form in the world of the beasts, so also there has been the advent of the stage of appearance of a divine species master of more improved consciousness from among the collection of man. Such a man would reject the establishment of the kingdom of money. There would be a slide in the world of money.

30

China, India and Spiritual Economy

China has advanced very fast. On judging the few advancements, it is clearly understood that if the advancement of China is termed as racing, India's is to be called walking or stumbling. India's economic development has been much less in comparison to that of China. Direct foreign investment so far affected India's market has been rather scant in comparison to that of China. Not only in the case of foreign investment but in other cases also, the advancement of China has been much appreciated all over the world. Respectful reception of China to the American architects of the industry is known to all.

Intense eagerness about their placement in the group of Western commerce and industry has been expressed, just as it has been expressed on the part of different places of Asia, especially Japan. Like American organisations, Japanese organisations have also made wide investments in China. As there are organisations which consider investment in China to be risky, there are even more organisations that have invested knowing well that it is highly risky. After completion of their investment, that is, after reaching the time of having the effectiveness of investments, there are some where practically no profit has been there.

The main theme of the investment that has worked well in different cases is to invest money, do some work and then reinvest the profit gained in the investment of money at a time elsewhere. One aspect is strong in the Chinese mentality—the expansion of investment in the national background and, in the end, to lend an extension to the investment and its outcome. As there is no obstruction in going the harvest if the how is within China. In the same way, the manufacturing organisations of China are continuing to produce different commodities inside the country or to meet the demands of outsiders. Manufacturing organisations in China had been dependent on foreign wealth to meet the inner and outer demands. The most mentionable wealth received by China from outside is technological knowledge, methods of applications, elements of basic scientific research, profuse money for investment, extensively outspread banking management for circulation of money and unrestricted and unforeseen market.

On the other side, the Indian situation is otherwise. A major part of the advancement achieved by India in the post-independence period is by virtue of its own endeavour. The important coordination and help India have received from outside are:

1. Coordination and support in the field of defence,
2. Exchange of knowledge in the field of industrial and technical fields,
3. Help in building up infrastructure for heavy industries,
4. Help and cooperation in the basic structure of technical education,
5. Exchange of market and
6. Cultural exchange

There are some similarities between India and China regarding development. Among them mention may the made of is the expedition to the west of meritorious youths and students from the country.

There are different contradictory interest groups and classes in the social systems of both countries. In respect of development, both of the countries are, to a great extent, dependent on others.

On drawing a comparison between the economics of models of India and China, one would find similarities and dissimilarity in more extended fields. As the political liberty of India has given the country a very deep basis, similarly, a different type of power within and outside have taken advantage of the same. Among them are the self-seeking of different nations and paths and, at the same time, industrial and commercial groups of different ideas and identities. The future and ability of the country have been preying to the political liberality of India. In many cases, programmes of improvement have been extremely frustrating merely due to obstruction. Even as a result of this, slackness has crept into government administration and in different enterprises inside the country. Corruption has seized government administration. Forms of social right and wrong have been determined by the dominance and influence of money.

Mafia groups are continuously controlling the power of society. Separation and terrorism are constantly eroding the basic ability of the country. Above all, a large portion of the population of the country is mentally against the country. They have a greater connection with the power antagonistic to the country. They take the country to be hostile and join such activities, which result in the loss of power and disaster in the economic ability of the country.

India is a country of soft temperament and has not been able to make its future plans successful, especially owing to the exercise of non-cooperation in the internal fields. There is apathy in the mainstream India. Outside the mainstream, this apathy is rather extreme. To those who look at the country from the angle of political and cultural points of view, with eyes tinged with foreign shades, search for a group of self-interest have surpassed the people and advancement of the country. For the satisfaction of the group or self-interest, they have thrush the overall interest of the country or nation in the dustbin.

There is no scope for this in China. China is not a soft country. In political cases and even social cases, Chinese principles are not particular; that is, taking self-mentality and hard steps are very common and natural in China. This means that it is very hard to ask to maintain antinational objectives and to translate them into action from within the country. State management of China does not accept it. It is not possible for Chinese society to hold such a natural mentality. It is not that Chinese society strongly discourages such activities, but the state also represses such actions firmly.

Chinese state management has divided a portion of the country into different economic regions and has been restricting free movements within these regions. Chinese workers have to abide by the local rules of labour. Consequently, there have been extended opportunities for different commercial organisations to make the workers work. The flow of work culture created by China has spread great influence on natural income and the measure of production. In comparison to India, China is in a much more comfortable position. In spite of this, India is being filled with individual power, while China is on the verge of having three separate existent, three separate Chinas. This is being created as the land of application of spiritual economy, and China is gradually for its sphere.

The Basic Ground of Spritual Economy

It is the establishment of spirituality that can build up a spiritual economy. The position of a spiritual economy can be definitely understood in the consideration of the financial systems. Common financial systems can be divided into two classes:

1. Financial system created at the capital.
2. Mass-centred financial system.

At the end of the decision, no financial system possibility cannot be classed as simply capital-centred on mass-centred.

But all the systems are very near to these two classes.

Table I: Different financial system

Capital-centred financial systems	Capital and mass-centred	Mass-centred financial systems
America	China	India
Canada		Russia
England		Israel
Japan		Poland
Germany.		Hungary
France		Yugoslavia
Italy		Romania
Sweden		Singapore
Australia etc.		Taiwan
		Middle East countries

The position of China is going to be the most compelling. The result of the introduction of various powers inside China has been that China is eager to fulfil its financial aspiration to keep its political status intact. For this, in spite of there being an inclination to a mass management system derived from communism, China had to compromise with the capitalist power, and in many cases, it has had to yield before the dominance of the power of capital. America is at the top of the list of countries which are faithful to the strength of capitalist power and dependent on the dominance of the power of capitalism. What is pervading in America and other countries of those is now the form of money.

The system of these capital-centred countries, which have yielded completely to the demand of this form, can be designated, thus, the main theme of the capital-centred financial system is:

1. Consideration in terms of money.
2. Dominance of money.
3. To ascertain the demand for money in the interest of increasing the quantity of money and to abide by that.
4. To unite the social powers in accordance with the demand of money and to reorient the society at the demand of money, to determine the movement of everything in the direction of movement of money.

On the other hand, the main theme of mass-centred financial system is:

1. To ascertain the requirements of larger number of people and build up the system accordingly.
2. To assume the supply of social wealth for the people, according to the measure of their taste.
3. Efficiency and capability merit.
4. Orient and reorient the financial system according to the desires of the people.
5. To gradually inspire people towards a path of better living.
6. To give inspiration and assistance to the people for a better living.
7. Breaking barriers in the background based on the desires of the people.

There are both merit and demerits of both capital-centred and mass-centred systems. Circulation of capital is needed for economic development and improvement of the financial superstructure. Lively and moving capital carries it forward. The two adjectives viz 'lively' and 'moving' signify the applicability of capital. That capital is lively and moving, which is gradually getting multiplied. Lively capital grows up its own urge and the moving capital moves from one place to another by its own power. As a result of being lively and moving, capital creates a background or atmosphere, the main theme of which is to increase the valuation of money.

If the money lying with an individual changes hands and later returns to the same person in a larger amount, then that capital would considered as moving. Moving capital does not stop changing hands, but it gradually expands. In terms of its valuation, moving capital creates various components that play an effective role in the development of society.

There is, within society, a scope that fits its necessary craving and consequential gain. Capital-centred financial system has gradually become headless. Human values there become meaningless. Anything and everything here can be done for money and only money. Every judgement is made with respect to money. The value of money evaluates everything. The demand and value of money want business—it has an oriented relation. Assets and liabilities exist in any relation whatsoever. Calculation dominates everywhere. Whether the relation would be able to get any profit, in the long run, is ascertained through tests by estimation. Thus, there would be some business in every exchange process. The nature of business would judge everything.

The mentality would be just like a businessman. This mentality may open or be dormant. Be it open or dormant, in the long run, it is the commercial transaction that takes the stable form. The root of a capital-oriented financial system lies hidden in this mentality. The spread of capital-oriented financial systems is commercial expansion. As a result of this, some new dimensions are added, and some new opportunities are created by this system in every field. The final stage of these new dimensions and opportunities is greater involvement in the capital-oriented system. There is scope for some coordination and advantage in the capital-oriented system.

There are many stages in even these advantages. For example, in the platform of the chamber of commerce, active participation and coordination of big and small companies, instead of being direct, may be indirect even. Besides, there is coordination among the sellers and among the buyers. In each case, this coordination has grown up in the interest of the groups and individuals. Selfish motive is not only very strong in this case, but sometimes it becomes the only thing. Any method may be adopted in this condition to fulfil self-interest. Let us cite some examples.

The company is not running well. Let there be retrenchment. There is no time to see what the workers would do, what would be their fate, whether they would live or die.

The company engaged an expert and fitting technologist with much care and expense. At the cost of much expense, the company sent him abroad. He also returned having training and just after doing so, he joined another company being tempted by higher salary. All the secret facts about the former company were divulged through him.

Capital-centred financial system flourishes through such diverse managements. Fulfilment of interest of one's own self is to be done abiding by the law or everything is to be done ably with evasion.

On the other hand, mass-centered systems become rather soft. In rearing soft attitude, the demands of men become important. There are many examples in favour of this:

For example:

"Sir my son is sick. I would like to leave a bit earlier."

"Well,"

"Why so late again today?"

"There was a jam on the road."

"Why was not the job completed?"

"The union has already framed a rule—daily five cheques are to be entered and five customers are to be honoured. But if you grant over time, I will complete the job."

The ordinance factory new technological workers have joined the duty of preparing compulsory weapons. On the first day, eighty units of work were already completed before lunch. Just getting the information, Kestoda remarked, "You are just a Kalidas, cutting your own branch. If you do so much, how then over time will be realised? Complete at best eighty units of job per week, otherwise I will let the union know about it. We won't tolerate the workers being deprived of their dues."

"What do you want?" The worker of a government store asked the approaching buyer. "Wait, let me have a through look at the newspaper. Sourav Ganguli has had very bad luck. What do you think?" The buyer left disgusted.

Management, mixed with compassion, wears a new type of weapon for exploitation. The masses have introduced this culture on the basis of its organised form and structure. So, the mass-centred financial system has broken down. Those who are creating hindrances find a way to organise themselves and earn unrestricted entry into the upper stage. As a result, those who stand at the middle ground either leave the steer or succumb to the conventional flow.

The matter would be quite clear if we consider the case of public sectors in India. Neither business nor service to society is affected if business is directed from a social viewpoint. A healthy and complete man can grow through either of these two processes. India's democratic tradition and culture originated from the Vedas and the Upanishads have made India a noble-minded country. As a result, even harmful groups and communities are being looked upon here with care and compassion and giving importance.

The attempt to break India into fragments has been a long practice separation. Secessionism has been gaining ground in different portions giving stress to the notion of the 'Son of the soil'. Terrorism is getting direct support and help from a large portion of the population, who are the binding forces of the opposition. Consequently, advancement is generally hampered. In spite of this, India has remained united and will surely remain united in the future, or maybe the old parts will be completely united. On the other hand, China's mentality and the real condition are trisected. China has divided financial management into their tiers. The first tier consists of the port and metro policies, the next of other own and the third tier is of the villages. The financial management of the first tier is of American style; that is, it is capital-centred and the third is commodity-centred. Government control is slack in the first tier. In the third tier, it is executive. In both the first and third tiers, the Chinese mentality is expanded.

The second tier is as if in the middle, as a united form of both. The primitive background of this trisection of Chinese financial management is implied in the history of China. The very first and real form of mass tradition bloomed between 1554 to 1545 BCE, the reign of the Shang dynasty. During that reign, financial power used to be produced by nature. For this able and active worker used to be appointed when the workers had been engaged in job, there would have been an 'Ethic of Service' for them.

It is as if the heart was used to judge the job of individual workers. The regular succession of the Shang dynasty has given a strong foundation to mass culture—people, land and mass—financial system. Next came the Zhou dynasty, which also had an extensive range from 1122 to 221 BCE. They were sometimes of mass outlook and sometimes of self-centred thinking of their own interest. Both streams existed in them. They are occupiers of modern Chinese power. The third portion have their thoughts filled with kindness. During the period of long struggle (403-221 BCE) among China states, the Chinese wall was partly constructed. The Kin dynasty connected the parts to build up a federal wall. This kin mentality had in it a sharp knife or speedily thrown spear. Thus, it is fit to give rise to a heartless commercial attitude. At the same time, it claims to be progressive.

The first tier of the Chinese financial system is drenched with the kin mentality, the second one is drenched with the Zhan mentality and the third emerged from the Shang mentality. Links between history and financial management have definitely separated them into respective identities. These separate identities are the main theme of the Chinese financial system. In the long run, the separate identity comes out to be the one and only factor.

The reason is the target of easily comprehensible living and the aim of life. Such a wide difference between the standard of living and the aim of life is carrying the capitalistic commitment of thinking to gradual erosion. Tien-an-men possibly would not be able to prevent it.

Promotion to Spritual Economy

It is the spiritual economy that can get the desired life for all. It is a life of satisfaction, a life of invention. The Chinese mentality is a barrier to the spiritual economic system. It cannot be established by force, through pressure and under duress. Through this management, the path that is characteristic of an Indian can go for. It is easy and possible for India to be conducive to the liberal and tolerant mental realm required for this. In spite of opposition, action and relation of destructive forces, India would be able to proceed through the integration of the mainstream. It would gradually reveal, in the whole world, as a model in the field of augmenting coordination within the mainstream.

31

Field of Application of Spritual Economy

Significance of Spritual Economy

Economic ideas have reached the final stage of ability and manifestation. Shaping of economic principle, judged only on the basis of attraction to enjoyment, would no longer be worthy. Economic principles have not been able to realise any of the pledges they had wrought. It was thought that with the establishment of the authority of the working class such a change would come that poverty would be eradicated, there would be no discrimination and all the requirements of life would be obtained in due time; it was also expected that life would be filled with perfection and satisfaction. It was a deep rooted belief that the establishment of socialism was the most definite path to human development.

Beside this, many have preached other means for social and economic development. All of them have, in their view, the definite key to that process. Some of them have advised the control of commercial and financial systems through the share market. Some have wanted to change financial arrangements by solving problems of education and health, and some again have stressed on overall economic development of the state through setting proper balance in between investment and disinvestment. Different ideologies have proceeded towards the same target along different paths. All endeavours have been to convince others of their ideology. In that respect all ideologies have a basic similarity. All assume that man is susceptible to enjoyment. So man will remain filled with satisfaction if he feels enjoyment. Thus, to bring a change in economic conditions consumption goods are to be supplied in bigger amounts.

When judgement is done solely on enjoyment, the question that naturally occurs is 'what would be the target for liberation?' Whether the meaning of financial liberation is opportunity for more enjoyment or being able to access consumption goods of higher quality and higher standard after assessing them in terms of their merit and demerits. 'Requirement' and 'enjoyment' have been used in a different sense. If judgement is made in terms of requirement, it would be found that financial liberation would come after all requirements are satisfied. There is no need of any extra arrangement for taking decision on subjects more than what is necessary.

The limits of requirement need to be known. Whether those requirements are being fulfilled needs to be known. Requirement needs to be marked, permanent arrangement is to be made for gradual comprehension, so that new dimension can be properly designated. Requirements of allure have to be shaped in a combined form. It is to be understood that in a world where even one person starves, poverty has not been eradicated. Development of a place where many people are spending their days without any food, being deprived of the light of education and the benefit of minimum health care, is but to be ridiculed. Gandhiji talked about the rule of Rama to make one understand that there should be such administration of a state where the king would share the weal and woe of the people. The king would starve till even a single man remains deprived of food.

The aspiration of king Rama's state philosophy is founded on equality, justice, pleasure and happiness for all. The king has no separate existence as an individual. He is just a representative of the collective. Language of the collective is the language of the king, the consciousness and mind of the collective are those of the king. So in an integral sense the collective is the shaper of ideas of an individual.

These subjects have remained outside the sight of different economic philosophies. Qualified leadership is required to cast a deep sight into the state. What direction a state would move in depends on the situation and qualities of the leadership. Development of any country would be possible if good and befitting leadership is in hand. Flourishing depends on leadership, not on situation of wealth. If honest liking and honest heart are there, a man may easily reach the state of flourishing from the opposite one. Heart and mind form the driving force. Where leadership has heart and mind, the evaluation of financial status gets a new dimension.

Heart and mind of a leader should be great and wide. He should have the ability to accept a large number of people.

Elucidation of the correct definition of 'consumption' and 'necessity', and establishment of a mutual relation between them, is necessary. Endeavour will have to be made to determine the measure of consumption and necessity through judging them sympathetically in order to fulfil the same. A leader would gradually spread his self-culture idea and sympathy within the people. "Consumption" and "necessity" would gradually come in a single row. This is the ideal situation called for. One of the enterprises that becomes essential for an ideal situation is the part of leadership and the others from the original situation. Both leadership and related situation become essential in respect of application and consequence. Now of the current financial models have spoken on leadership through a mix of mind, sympathy and financial power originated from the situation. Spiritual economy begets a basic confidence, the main principle of spiritual economy stands on this fact: restoring life properly into human resources and through proper application and use of the same an economic revolution of a state may be affected. Spiritual economy is largely dependent on human resources in solving financial problems.

Judgement of Wealth of Spiritual Economy

When these matters are judged with respect to consumption, the quantity of consumption and its qualitative measures become the objects of judgement. An example would clarify that the qualitative measure and quantity of consumption in many cases fix up the minutiae of the financial system. It is consumption that shapes the consumable goods. We would understand the matter if we discuss the kinds and quantity of food intake- For example, if physical labour is the only means of income, rice and bread are to be consumed to hearts content. The quantity of rice, pulse, bread does not remain the same all along. With advancement of the standard of living the amount rice-pulse-bread consumed would decrease and other items like fruit, fish, milk, meat would increase. That is, instead of common types of food, costly, high calorie food gradually form a part of life. Quantity of common food gradually decreases and the quality of finer things increases. Let us consider some statistics from the annual reports of National Sample Survey.

From 1970 onwards per capita consumption of cereals in India began gradually decreasing. Beginning from 1970-71 up to

1997-98 annual consumption of cereals has decreased by 0.70% in rural areas and by 0.2% in urban areas . In 1970-71 per capita consumption of cereals in rural areas all over India was 15.35 kilogram. In 1997-98 it came down to 12.50 kilogram. Similarly in the urban region the amount came down from 11.36 kilogram in 1970-71 to 10.11 kilogram in 1997-98.

(National Sample Survey Organisation, 2000)

The main reason for the decrease in use of cereals was the upliftment ofthe standard of living. With upliftment in standard of living a change comes in the quality of foods. Consumption of cereals in West Bengal, Bihar and Orissa increased during this period. It means that beside West Bengal, Bihar and Orissa, standard of living in all other parts of India was uplifted. Man's adventure in search of high calorie foods is a common upward movement of living.

Not only an Indian organisation like National Sample Survey but other international organisation like World Bank and IMF also determine the standard of living in terms of quality and quantity of consumption. If the desire for consumption is satisfied, it is to be assumed that the route for economic liberation is open. Desire for consumption has been assumed to be external. Man has been taken to be an animal longing for consumption. Here desire for consumption is the driving force of economy. It is not necessary, but consumption is the open route. Consumption fixes the direction and speed of economy. If consumption is lost the moving wheel of economic system would stop.

Combination of consumptions appears in financial system as demand. Supply is to be depended upon for satisfaction of demand. The principle of financial management is just to bring demand in line with satisfaction. It is supply which satisfies demand. And the quality and quantity of supply fix the measures, management etc. of supply. As a result of this the power production of economy or financial management goes on increasing. Varieties of demand joins and is saturated with varieties of supply. The journey that began from demand crosses with supply to reach the end in the creation of a flow of activities in the financial system. The demand makes one understand the necessity of machines. Import of newer technology, new inventive knowledge and learning and arrangement of newer ideas etc. are used for desired satisfaction of demands. As a result, the relation between demand and supply becomes the driving force of modern times and a directive for the future.

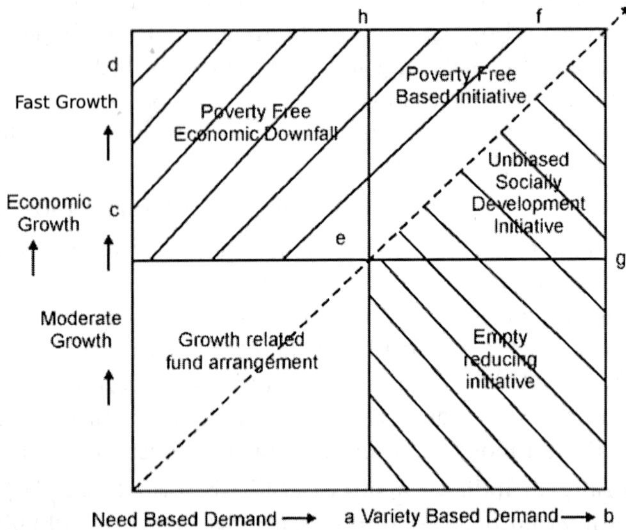

Figure 1: Variety of Demand depends on the scenario of economic process

In financial management for rapid progress such types of demands are required which have mass appeal, i.e those types of demands through satisfaction of which satisfaction of the people is brought about. This means, demand would have to be of the measure of 'necessity and 'compulsion'. Necessity of the wider section of people would be the real demand, satisfaction of which would economically liberate the under section of people. When demand becomes dependent only on necessity of man, the economy rests in a particular stage of flourishment. To allow demands to also be variegated is equally necessary. If variegation is lost from demands the future of the economy becomes at stake.

In the previous discussion it has been said that almost all the endeavors taken so far to remove the curse of poverty, and discrimination have failed. One of the many reasons of their failure is the absence of direct judgment and prejudiced approach.

Demands can be divided into two classes: necessity-oriented demands and variegated demands. Necessity-oriented demand swells up in numbers. That is the greater number of people would come within the purview of these demands for which there is a rough minimum requirement limit for each individual. This limit can be different in different cases but on the whole requirements spread within the limit. The limit of the requirements may alter to some extent but not very widely.

Figure-1 shows the nature of economic advancement as a result of different types of demands. In figure-1 the portion X-A specifies necessity-oriented demands.

(I) Developing economic system.
(II) Beginning of economic policy free from poverty.
(III) Adventure for a society free from poverty.
(IV) Adventure for a society free from discrimination.
(V) Beginning of contraction of the extent of discrimination.

In the upper axis, X-C portion has signified development economic stage, thus the field X-A-E-C signifies developing economic stage. Economic development in this stage is slow, but in many cases stern and far-reaching.

The following stage also has been shown in Figure-1. Along the base in the portion A-B variegated demands have been signified, that is to say, demands of this regard have surpassed necessity. Variegation of demands depends on cost and valuation. On the other hand, variegated demand in most cases go on increasing quite independent of evaluation. In figure-1 C-D along economic development index marks rapid progress, which is possible if there is wide variegation in demands. In figure-1 the portion marked A-B-G-E has been shown as the beginning of the contraction due to the mass use of discrimination. If its significance is to be stated in brief, then it can be said that the more the demands are variegated, the greater is the scope of circulation of money. Each of the commodities or factors one would buy has a value added complement. That is, there remains scope of earning more profit on value added commodities than an ordinary commodity.

Psychological pricing becomes necessary for such commodities. If a certain commodity can be adorned with its own specialties by psychological pricing, then plenty of additional wealth may come through the value-added route. As a result this unconventional productive power has scope to appear in financial systems. The first opportunity from the rise of unconventional productive power may be held by established industrial organisations, but in many cases wide scope comes with new enterprises. This results in the expansion of financial arrangements. The controlling rope of the financial management comes to the collectivity, avoiding possession by the few.

The portion marked as E-G-F-H in figure-1 may be further divided into two divisions: E-G-F portion and E-F-H portion. E-G-F portion signifies a progressive and balanced financial management. On the other hand the portion marked as E-F-H is approaching a society gradually being freed from poverty. According to figure-1 the portion E-G-F-H would fulfil the financial expectation. This is an open route for financial management to flourish completely.

This discussion has helped elucidate a matter which is rooted in the mentality of man regarding consumption and demand. Diversity of consumption and demand opens up different directions of financial progress. At the root of these is the mentality and mental condition of man.

Basic Foundation of Spritual Economy

Human resources are the basic wealth in economics. So far human resources have not been considered in economic judgement. They are included in the receipt section of economic management. Such that they bear the good or bad effect of financial management. Financial management grows on the basis of other resources, for example, natural, mineral, industrial, commercial and foreign. Those aspects are considered as resource which have selling and buying value. Except selling and buying values, other items and factors are to be neglected in financial management.

Each of the convictions and announcements on the basis of which financial management and economic philosophies grow has its own basis. For example, the basis of capitalistic system begins and ends in money. For money this system renders all other subject matters and components into its slave. Similarly, in socialistic system the main object is to remove social discrimination. Just as Marshall's theory of "aggregated surplus" promised to distribute the surplus wealth of society among the unfortunate, later on other philosophies of social welfare also took this to be the last consequence. The basis of calculating Marshall's aggregated consumer surplus was taken to be the extra price over the payable one enjoyed by the consumer. Much of this extra price emerges from a feeling of mentality or satisfaction. If we proceed with satisfaction as one criterion it would be quite clear that different stage of satisfaction signifies the merits demerits of a financial situation.

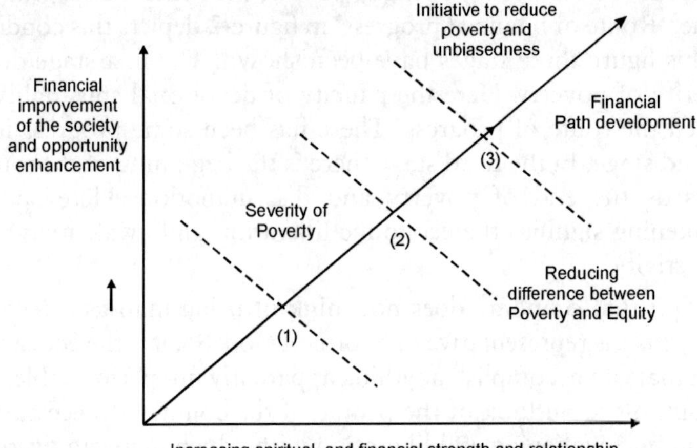

Figure 2

The main point of spiritual economy: Man is the basic resource and possibility. Creation provision and augment action of the standard of evaluation has the role of man at the top. Proper management of this resource would be the most important for carrying the merit of the financial management. It is the human resource that can bring revolution in financial managements.

In case of the fulfilment of the basic demand of man, investment in financial field demands investment of many people. What is meant by investment of lakhs or crores of men? Their savings or properties? These are just insignificant. Investment of man is his human resource. The basic foundation of human resource in his spiritual resource.

Just as an individual is judged on their spiritual resource, so is a society or collectivity judged with respect to the spiritual resources of the society or collectivity.

The route of economic liberation becomes wide if the spiritual power of the collectivity is awakened. With the blooming of the spiritual power of the collectivity come a mentality of coordination and inspiration. The mentality of coordination gradually urges an individual to cross the periphery of 'I and mine' and to come to the feeling of 'You and yours'. Giving up the belief that self-interest is the only target, the individual gets engaged in the interests of the many.

Not only well-wishing, but for the well-being of many the individual's endeavors are engaged. If spiritual ideas are engaged thus, for the well-being of many people, then social evils gradually wane. 'Route of financial progress' in figure-2 depicts this condition. In this figure three stages have been shown. The first stage depicts severity of poverty. Here the paucity of devotional spirituality has closed the route of progress. There has been some progress in the second stage. In the third stage there is the beginning of the journey towards the end of poverty and discrimination. Here spiritual awakening signifies the economic liberation and awakening of the collectivity.

Spiritual economy does not think of using man as a resource. Every man is representative or a form of God. So, it is the endeavor of man that can accomplish anything apparently un- performable. Such an optimistic outlook of the people of the country is necessary for economic awakening and liberation with which man can overcome all hurdles and disappointments. An individual occupied with disappointment and distress cannot flourish as a resource. Within society itself rests the power of awakening and liberation, and the necessary financial ingredients for its realisation. In spite of being at the margin of full possibility society has so far not been able to bloom. Spiritual development would liberate the society and open up the route to economic liberation.

32

Spiritual Economy in the Global Background

Introduction

The main object of spiritual economy is to build up the infrastructure of economics on the basis of spiritual consciousness. Many commentators have provided many solutions for the problems of financial system that have gradually been seizing the world-society, but all of these ended in despair and disappointment and new theories were always sought after. New theories or new application of old ones, in whatever way the problems have been looked into, there remains in every endeavor a deficit that in the long run one has to return to the old problem once again.

It is not that there has been no change in the form and turn. Rather change is a constant phenomenon. But in the new form problems, instead of decreasing, are constantly increasing. There have been many kinds of problems, both independent and dependent.

While analyzing problems those of the latter type are called derived problems. Those of the former type are called basic problems. Solution of a problem, be it derived or basic, must be in both theoretical and practical perspectives. Going to the root of the problem one would realize what its components are and what factors are directly and indirectly influencing it. While basic problems are concerned with the totality of all aspects of economics, derived problems are concerned with individual parts of the financial system.

Of the problems some are just temporary and others far reaching. Both these types may be regional, indigenous or international at the same time. In whatever form the problem may begin, by the influence of different factors it may constantly change form. If there is some change in form and quality, some consequent change must come in the viewpoint and method of solution of the same. In a circumstance where the problem has changed form, but the viewpoint and methods of solution have remained unchanged,

all attempts of solution will fail. Factually this is the tradition of human history. At every stage of history assiduous people have endeavored to address different socio-economic problems and in most cases the difference created between the form and nature of the problem and the form and nature of the solution has cast influence on the system. This is problem that has recurred in different ways.

Real Nature of the Problem

The question is: which are the basic problems and which are the derived ones. The chief among the basic problems which have been persistent throughout time are:

Poverty, inequality, lack of education, lack of health.

Some of the derived problems are: dissatisfaction, unhappiness, lack of desired consequence.

Every one of these problems has its own norms and arrangements. In the discussion of basic problems, it would be realized how far solutions have been made and what type of endeavors are important in the present circumstances. While discussing poverty we would see that it has only changed its form.

James D Wonfenshon, the erstwhile president of World Bank, raised some important facts at the International Conference of Auditors in Washington on 26th June, 2002. He effectively said:

Out of 600 crores of population of the modern world 500 live in the Developing countries. 80% of the total income of the world lies in the hands of 100 crores of people of the developed. About half of the total population of the world, i.e., 300 crores have on average a daily income of one to two dollars (U.S.D) and about 120 crores of people are living with an average daily income of one dollar or even less.

The world background of discrimination and poverty has been revealed from Wolfensohn's remark. World Bank always judges discrimination and poverty with special interest in its eradication and the removal of discrimination. World Bank itself and through different organisation has gone on to arrange for investment for the world to use. Allotment of World Bank is continuously increasing for the development of the 500 crore poor people of the world.

Thus in 2001-2002 World Bank invested thousands of millions of currencies towards development of the poor people. From this year this amount has increased and for next three years it has been 1500 crores of American dollar per year.

Along with the endeavor of world Bank many other organisations also allot money towards development of poor countries. European Union is such an example. The amount of money may seem to be big but actually is rather meagre. This amount of money towards coordination and development is only 0.3% of the total national produce. World Bank likes to raise it to 0.7%. Let us look at the investment in the rich countries contrary to this. Only during the first three months of 2000 in America 5600 crores of American dollar had been invested. Now investment fund has been granted to make up for the deficit of the external trade of different countries. According to World Bank data 100 to 150 crores of American dollar had been necessary to meet the deficit.

In discussion of the problem World Bank has designated two types of poverty. According to World Bank poverty in two types—absolute poverty and relative properly. In absolute poverty, the deficit of comfort may be designated as poverty. What are the signs of poverty?

World Bank has marked poverty with some conditions. These are:

- Existence and extension of hunger
- Want of residence,
- Want of clothes.
- Want of care and treatment even in illness,
- Obstruction of education, improper implementation and lack of institutional opportunity.

Absolute poverty stands for want of food, clothes and residence and lack of appeasement of desires. Right at the root of these in paucity of income. If income is scanty nothing can possibly be acquired. Then an individual is to be a prey to deprivation. An individual becomes deprived of adequate food, proper clothing, suitable residence, proper treatment and service and lives a helpless life perplexed to the extreme. In such condition both blooming and manifestation of the individual gets hampered, Amartya Sen too has opined thus. According to Mr. Sen this deprivation results in the obstruction of "the route of competency and eligibility of the individual selected by himself"

Income poverty: In the study by the World Bank, persons of different countries of the world have explained income poverty in different ways. According to a poor woman of Ethiopia: 'We live through oscillations from hour to hour.'

According to a poor man of Argentina: 'You have employment, it is good. If there is no employment you will have to starve. This is your fate.'

A poor old lady of Bulgaria said: 'To being (in) good condition means the well-being of grand children to find them being established (in) life and to serve and cajole this at every encounter; and never to beg money as help from them.'

An old Russian opined: 'Poverty means not being well to do and of daily paucity of fund in case of requirement'.

The poor of Jamaica: 'Poverty means lack of self-reliance.' According to the poor people of Kenya: 'Look at the holes of my broken house, look at my torn away clothes, look at my want of health and recognize my poverty.'

Right from 1990 World Bank has been keeping account of the poverty of the whole world yearly. There are two forms of such accounting of world bank: people having a daily income of less than a dollar are extremely poor and those with daily income in between one dollar and two are morally poor.

Generally, 'income' and 'consumption' are the two aspects used for the estimation of poverty. The basis of income in different local currency is converted into international currency. Based on this the extent of mutual poverty is judged. Different countries have designated their own poverty line. Just as multiple collectivities make up the whole country, so also multiple poverty lines may be ascertained for different regions of a country. For such ascertainment sample survey are required.

The estimation becomes correct if sample survey is conducted properly. As a result a complete picture of poverty may be had. Taking the information supplied by Mr. Wolfensohn to be authentic, it is clearly understood that 80% of wealth belongs to 20% of world population 80% are living with the remaining 20% of wealth. As a result, possibility of life and flourishing of wealth are gradually decreasing. Problem of poverty is being extended; absolute poverty is decreasing but relative poverty is on the increase.

Unequal distribution of wealth is the main cause of poverty. Where starting is with unequal distribution of wealth, there the measure of poverty is increased by lack of equity in opportunity and lack of balance in possibility of development. The methods used at present for determining poverty have different directions. The main directions are being discussed here briefly:

World Bank has fixed up two indices of poverty. These are:

H.P.I.I (Human Poverty Index One)

H.P.I.II (Human Poverty Index Two)

$$HPI = 1\left[\frac{1}{3}\left(P_1^{\alpha} + P_2^{\alpha} + P_3^{\alpha}\right)\right]^{\frac{1}{\alpha}}$$

$$HPI - 1 = \left[\frac{1}{3}\left(P_1^{\alpha} + P_2^{\alpha} + P_3^{\alpha}\right)\right]^{\frac{1}{\alpha}}$$

Where,

P_1 = 100 times of the probability of a new born baby at the moment of birth living up to 40 years.

P_2 = The measure of lack of education among the adults.

P_3 = Number of people not getting supply of pure water, access to healthcare and number of malnourished children below five years of age. A new measure is added in the estimation of HPI-II. which is P_4.

Deprivation begins with deviation from the target of a long and healthy life. The depth of deprivation is the index of poverty. Just as poverty is not having and not getting, 'not being' is also poverty. Forms of poverty and deprivation discussed so far have all signified not having and not getting as poverty. Not being has not been regarded yet as poverty.

Path of Liberation from the Course of Poverty

The latest stand of World Bank is that cooperation is needed for eradication of poverty. Poverty begins with lack of co-operation. Recent conviction of World Bank is that the democratic system and open environment gets cooperation in economy. Cooperation is the main principle of economic development. Cooperation augments ability, increases possibility, capacity and competency. The more extreme and spontaneous the cooperation would be, the stronger and more direct the resultant economic development. Amartya Sen Perez, Merton, Soaks and other renowned economist have laid stress on cooperation. This is the darkest period of history, to get light cooperation from all corners is needed.

Human development report, 2002 of World Bank while describing the overall situation of the world has remarked that in economic, political and technical judgement the present situation of the world stands on the most liberal yet most extensively unjust basis. (World Bank, *Human Development Report 2002*, p. 1)

The World Bank Team has found the way of recovery from this situation and placed the same on behalf of all. Their inference was: the greater the number of people cooperating in the economic process, the greater would be the rate of economic growth. Economic management would be much more organized. According to the World Bank Team a democratic administration (from the stand point of infrastructure and outlook) controlled by the people for themselves in required for true human development. (Ibid, p.3).

That is a full-fledged cooperation would be there whose basis would be above the cravings and attainments of the people,that is, spontaneous cooperation of the people. Along with cooperation comes the question of explanation. It is through cooperation and mutual dependence that a world-wide economic system may be built, where the main reason behind origin of poverty may be judged with sufficient importance. The farther the cooperation can be extended at the time of taking a decision, h the greater number of people would be helped during the execution of the decision. Best result would be attained if cooperation may be blended with explanation in the economy.

Cooperation gradually asked for compulsion on giving weightage to some factors like, Rightful due of the cooperators, long, healthy, educated, happy lives for them alongside personal progress and development owing to their world-wide roles.

Addressing the discussion of poor people on H.P.I through cooperation of all people in the economic system would ensure a bright and wide future. But the question is, when would this co-operation be possible? - Which mental state can get cooperation, what is to be done to make the cooperation sincere? Full co-operation is not possible without mental preparation. To inspire and fulfil the co-operation, self- realisation is required along with a mental expression that teaches us to make others our own. It is barely discussed that wealth does not belong to someone, rather it belongs to all. Right to use and consume the wealth is vested in all, so also is the right to create and coordinate wealth. It is only the spirituality that may raise such a mentality. It is the knowledge cum cultivation of spirituality that can wake up the dormant Shiva (i.e. well-being) in man.

Spiritulity in Shaping of Economy

Life is on one side while on the other stands spirituality. This is the common custom by which spirituality has been rendered to be against life. Such a thing the adoption of which makes life lean and thin. Since life is not the field for learning and cultivating spirituality, a situation should beyond the common activities of the society is necessary. As a result, the influence of spirituality on common social activities seem to be just outsider intervention. That is why life processes have been quite devoid of spirituality.

Relief can be brought by coordination of economic management when we have reached a situation to realize this. Then it also has to be understood how we this coordination can be steered, and be brought into the scope of the right propensities natural to man. It is not possible through any philosophy whatsoever, -nor can it be made possible through hundreds of quotations and sayings. For this, spiritual awakening is necessary.

Spirituality is not a luxury, it is a necessity. Spirituality is necessary for economic liberation. Awakening of spirituality is necessary to build up a worldwide society free of poverty. The dormant power and possibility in men are to be roused. Man will have to be made alert of his true form. In order to realize the right in life, and deliver the rightful to the world, one has to know their true form. Life and the world are connected in a fundamental unity based on spirituality.

Actually creatures in the form of Shiva (God) processed by different shapes and traits exist as different people. In the state of Shiva lies unitedness. The sense of the state of Shiva makes one understand that all men are different forms of Shiva.

It is good for one to have limited right on what exceeds one's necessity.

The global wealth is not for me; it is meant for all.

Life begins at the inspiration of the state of Shiva. Life consists of the recollection of this state of Shiva where, in the end, it will be enjoined with this state of Shiva.

As a result of this, the propensity for co-ordination grows. So long money and opportunity has been depended on for creating co- ordination. It was taken for granted that all could be inspired with money and opportunity and this would bring about the final results. But the contrary has happened. The inspiration lent by money and opportunity has had just a small and temporary effect. It is only the awakening of the state of Shiva that can give rise to such a wide and broad notion based on the idea of development for all. As a result of this, true revolution would come in the economic system. Just when a flow of change would come in the mentality, a change in the practice of purchase, in the mentality of behavior and in the mentality of consumption would follow. and this will fix up such an invasion which would result in the eradication of poverty.

Bibliography

Anand, Sudhir, and Amartya Sen. "Concepts of Human Development and Poverty: A Multidimensional Perspective." In *Human Development Papers 1997*. United Nations Development Programme, 1997.

Sen, Amartya. "Poor Relativity Speaking." *In Resources, Value and Development*. Basil Blackwell, 1984.

World Bank. *Human Development Report 2001*. Oxford University Press, 2001.

World Bank. *Human Development Report 2002*. Oxford University Press, 2002.

33
Rural Development in Spiritual Economy

Rural Situation in the Indian Context

India is village-dominated. Just as awakening of India depends on the awakening of the villages, so also does the awakening of the villages in all corners. If the village wake up the country will too. If villages do not gain momentum, then in all parts of the world the flow of development would be obstructed. Various arrangements are needed for the awakening of villages. Villages have declined owing to the weight of their isolation. 'To wake them up this allotment is to be stressed on. Urban preventives will not be able to solve rural problems. If Villages are to provide service, are to grow, keeping the separateness intact is necessary. If villages shun this separateness' and try to develop in the urban line then instead of advancement, collapse would be more evident. The clue of advancement of villages is to be found out through searchs within villages. Villages banking on their own separateness would be able to find out the means of solution to their own problems.

We have been noticing long different endeavours in the name of rural development. In India many an endeavour has been taken up in the name of rural development Most of the endeavors taken for so long have been through government enterprises Many have also been taken in extra governmental, non- governmental and foreign fields. In many cases cooperation and help from government have been noticed in case of many extra government endeavorus. In cases where the endeavours that have had help and support from the government, they possess basic confidence and philosophy for liberation of the people.

Religious and social organisations are playing special roles behind these endeavours in many cases. Even individual attempts to affect rural development have been made in many places. In spite of such varied endeavours the examples of effective rural development is rather scanty. In many cases there has been rural development no doubt, but most of the development has been connected with a small group of people inside a village. The development the of wider section of people is still a distant illusion. In the name of development through government endeavours or different plans, the extent to which villages have been developed has been far surpassed by the extant of enlivenment carried to a small group of villagers.

Small islands of development have been set up within villages. Such islands would exist in villages in ancient times as well. Mutual coordination has been observed within such islands. But there was no consideration between the developed and undeveloped segments of the same village. There had been connections between them only on the basis of give and take relations. It is thus that social relation would grow among them and on a personal level. As a result, in spite of there being different types of development, in the society a bridge of human relation would be built up among them. In recent times' system tradition, has had a slit in it. Presently any glow of lamp brings about the least change in the dark and undeveloped rural society. Social duties and responsibilities of the developed section of the village towards the rest has gone to oblivion.

Sense of responsibility has disappeared in both sides. Just as the developed portion feels no responsibility towards the undeveloped fraction, so also the undeveloped fraction feels no sympathy for the developed. As a result, such a condition has crept into the village society as human order has completely vanished. Villages have turned into heartless places where there is no glow of development, nor any love or warranty of heart. Due to disappearance of the warmth of the hearth the villages have turned into undesirable living places. These places are not only undesirable to live in but also rouse a strong desire to be left, with a view to moving to towns. The tendency to leave villages and move towards towns is growing greater. This has cast direct influence on both the villages and the towns. Usually, the people leaving villages to move to the towns are the creams of the rural society; they form the most developed brains.

The most enterprising portion of the village-folk, the portion having the greatest possibility, the portion that can create the noblest wealth and who are the most creative, leave villages and go to the towns. Of course, there is some expiation to this trend. A small number of exceptional persons remain back in villages. Inspite of staying in villages in many cases these people lose their interest and enterprise. As a result, those villages are not at all benefited by their staying there.

Endeavours of the villages themselves for development of their surroundings are thus gradually becoming nil. This is because a portion of the villagers being the life force of endeavours has left the village and a portion has brought themselves down to the level of indifference in the flourishing of the village like a mere onlooker. In the interest of economic development of human and cultural fields cooperation and endeavour of all of the able villagers are necessary. Development of the villages by their own power has become insignificant due firstly to the life force on the villages leaving its own place and secondly to the villagers living in the villages being indifferent about the village's affairs. Any discussion on the development of villages would lay stress on the case of the self-development. For the life-force of a village, one should feel no need of depending on any power outside the village.

When external power search for the life forces of a village, they are found to depend on those forces inside the village which are apparently visible. The factors not visible from outside do not come into consideration. Only the factors apparently visible come under the purview of the consideration of the external powers. In order to get the clue for the latent possibility of the villages they should have to be completely mingled with the living and environment of the villages.

It is not possible for the external visitors and organizers to get the real account of the self-reliance of the villages unless they become part and parcel of the village life. The task of changing the condition of a village cannot even be started until the real account of the human resource and possibility of the village are not available. An account of the material resources of the village need be taken and at the same time the financial resource of the village must also be taken into account. It is possible for the external power and different organizers to take a full account of financial and material resources of a village. But it would not be possible for them to have an account of the human resources of the village.

That is why cooperation of the people of different financial and social identity in the village is of utmost importance in case of rural development programs. Not only in regard to the villagers because the participation of all the people of all sections would be necessary. People of all classes of the village would need to come forward for the development of the village.

Clues Towards the Solution of Problems

There is a novel similarity among the rural problems of different corners of the world. It is possible to classify the problems in the following classes:

1. Lack of special eagerness for development
2. Want of acquaintance with previous human, material and financial requirements for development
3. Want of necessary and proper outlook or philosophy of development.
4. Overall distress of a village.

In most cases it is observed that want of eagerness about development continues to frustrate rural development in different corners of the world. Glow of eagerness is about to disappear from all the rural fields. The main problem behind this-lack of collective work is the want of real leadership. What is now required for rousing collective desire for work is leadership engaged within the rural environment. For emergence of rural leadership from the very core of the village the first thing that is required is to create such an environment under the influence of which persons with enough possibility would come forward to initiate enterprise for solving the recurrent problems. To create such an environment inside a village self-manifestation of atleast some person would be required.

Manifestation of the talent or genius in man is possible only through the awakening of humanity's spiritual wealth. Just as merely a tonic of philosophies stone turns anything in, so also through awakening of spiritual power the divine genius and capability lying dormant in man located in his self-acquaintance is freed. First comes self-acquaintance, next comes spiritual relation. The step to self-acquaintance is to be engaged in knowing 'who I am' . From this extreme enquiry comes the sense of man's incompleteness and the incapability of 'I', the individual person. The inquiry gradually unfolds the petals of ignorance one by one. As a result of unfolding of the petals of ignorance the boundary of smallness, incompleteness and incapability in a person gradually begins to break down and they begin to get a hint of a new horizon.

It comes within the purview of an individual that there exists not only an individual identity but also another identity beyond this. An individual would realize that there is a horizon of a bigger and wider identity where the individual himself would gradually be lost within the greater identity. The closer an individual crossing the boundary of the smaller identity comes to the greater circle of identity, the more he would learn to realize that the big and great external truth which is always existing, which holds, rears and augments the whole creation, is latent in the practical existence of the entity. This is the moment when the individual now likes to wake up. The more eager this big and this great would be for being wakened within an individual the firmer change would come about in the individual's own propriety. The change is like returning to the house, knowing all the objects of the house. It is not like coming back to the realm of the unknown. It is returning to the nest in one's own entity with one's total desire. It is the realisation that it is not transient; expedition of an individual does not belong to the past, it is the expedition of the external and the perpetual to the future.

The divine brilliance dormant in an individual will now be revealed with a glowing manifestation in all sides and in the distant horizon. It is not that tiny and mortal individual of old fashion confined in a small, incomplete self bounded by verity; it is that external, perpetual magnanimous individual within whom there is endless possibility, within whom there is the trick of being great and of being grown up. He is rich with the matter of the Absolute.

Exposition to the glow of this identity increases the confidence of an individual and gradually makes the extent of one's consciousness wider. The individual realizes that in the expedition of consciousness towards the Absolute consciousness has an embodied self which is vast, wide, great and external. The flow of this power of consciousness wipes out the darkness and fitness of ignorance inside and thus gradually converges towards the endless existence of the individual.

An individual is to rise gradually to be desirous of this endless identity. An individual would not look at incompleteness or verity, rather seeking a great and vast existence, without casting a sight on being on his own, would be blooming for extremity and endeavouring towards immense possibility. Blooming and manifestation are not now in the possession of the individual, but by dint of notional and spontaneous propensity the blooming becomes the unrestrained exposition of the endless entity of the individual. The individual will now be motivated, not through private endeavours and individual desires, but through the possibility of his gradually developing endless identity, established in the consciousness, pervading the world. Thus eagerness is the first step of development. The eagerness within the individual will gradually be clear in the background of the pervading spiritual consciousness.

Fitting Identity of Resources

After creation of eagerness regarding rural development the individual has to be acquainted with different types of resources. Resources maybe of different kinds, like-human material and monetary. In case of rural development human resource is the most important. Pioneers in different fields of economics have, through the last decade, made many deliberations on "the index of human development". Human development has been considered on the basis of same factors such as, the human aspect of financial infrastructure, opportunity of education, presentation of health, measures of living and the qualitative value of living. The fundamental basis of human development is participation in development process and eagerness in development. After having an idea of human resource, the human power of the village may be classified in some groups. The methods of classification also may be different.

The first basis of classification would be age.

After that would come classification on mental ability, followed by knowledge and education.

Next would come the judgement of possibility. Brief accounts of the groups are given below:

Table-1: Analysis of Population Power of Village 'X'

	Teenagers	Youths	Adults	Aged
Male Female	(number) "	(number) "	(number) "	(number) "

Table-2: Particulars of Mental Ability of the Youths of Village 'X'

	Of Firm Mentality	Of General Mentality	Of Weak Mentality
Male Female	(number) "	(number) "	(number) "

Table-3(A): Youths of Firm Mentality

	Literate	Entional Education	Technical Education	Others
Male Female	(number) "	(number) "	(number) "	(number) "

Table-3(B): Particulars of Knowledge of Persons of Firm Mentality in the Village

	General Knowledge	Theoretical Knowledge	Practical Knowledge	Overall Knowledge
Male Female	(number) "	(number) "	(number) "	(number) "

Table-4: Judgement of Human Possibility of the Village 'X'

	Firm Mentality Knowledge (number)			General Mentality	
	Theoretical Knowledge	Practical Knowledge	Overall Knowledge	Theoretical Knowledge	Practical Knowledge
Male Female	(number) "	(number) "	(number) "	(number) "	(number) "

Some factors are to be specially taken into account in order to prepare the above tables. For example, to understand mental ability, a psychological analysis of the villagers is necessary. Some simple procedures may be adopted for psychological analysis so that the job may be accomplished with small expense and little effort. For classifying the store of knowledge of the village folk study of the rural field of population is specially needed. Particulars of different classes of people, of different educational standards in case of rural population study and proper calculation among them is necessary. Essential data and information gathered in the mass investigation at the government level.

Classification and arrangement on the basis of efficiency of the people of different standards of education through educational identity and taking proper steps and endeavours for their blooming would be required. After having an idea of education full idea of the power of knowledge would be necessary. Blooming of knowledge in rural people occurs in different ways and different phases. Some people are there whose knowledge is held in regular succession.

There is a 'continuity in the process of their procurement of knowledge and blooming of the same. Knowledge held through different successions gets specific characteristics to different persons. A characteristic line of his own develops. For example, inspite of being a poet one has features of a scientist and vice-versa. Deep knowledge is very strong in case of some people. Others might be lacking in deep knowledge, instead having subjective knowledge. Some again possess philosophical or spiritual knowledge.

There is subjective knowledge in many people, but unless there is subjective knowledge in proper measure on special features, the right path for manifestation of an individual cannot be discovered. So, for correct information an individual is to move towards the path of proper blooming of his own knowledge power. If proper knowledge power of a man with firm mental power blooms, the gate of possibility will be wide open. Scope will be there for proper blooming of all types of possibilities existing in the village.

Blooming of scopes will fetch the village opportunities of proper use of its own resources which would result in the development of the village.

34
A World Free From Poverty

Dream of Freedom From Poverty

A dream indeed! A world free from hunger and disease is but a dream. It cannot be imagined that everyone would have a house to live in, would have supply of medicine and diet for disease. One cannot even think of a situation where all of the bright children would go to school to have unrestricted knowledge. When all would have potable water; all would have access to the necessary measurement of daily calories; there would be adequate arrangement for prevention and treatment of diseases for all. A situation when screams of despair would not burst out of the breast of the mothers.

When fathers thrown out of employment would not commit suicide under pressing hunger. When one would not have to shoulder the responsibility of others' obligation right from childhood and to be in routine service with a smile on the face and agony within. Let there be a situation when human mind would leap up with joy and in the newer and constant expedition of joy would be eager to quest of its inner and mental world.

Would such a day ever come? It seems just like a dream of fetching the moon of the sky by hand. It is as if an absurd event in the quest of which many a person has spent a lot of time. They have framed a good number of theories, opinions and groups. But in the long run they have all failed and become reactionary. The dream has remained simply a dream. Poverty, hunger and the agony and misery of human fate has gradually assumed a newer measure and form. Maybe one of the wants has been removed, but newer wants have appeared. Fulfilment of one demand has brought in heaps of newer demands.

Heads of 180 states have signed in the regulations of bringing this dream into reality. This charter signed in 2000 under the supervision of the World Bank is the declaration of the millennium. In this declaration 2015 had been marked as the target year and it had been resolved that by that time poverty of the world would be removed by a large measure. The target was to not allow poverty to come anew and to bring an end to the poverty that reared up so long ago. The steps these states have taken have been looked upon as the indicator of advancement in the new millennium.

So long eradication of poverty has been demanded of by philosophers and social reformers. Now modern states and international management have become collaborators of this dream. One of the routes to get rid of the dangers of poverty undertaken by international organisation and forums is expansion. Expansion and extension relieve the state of depression. The first action taken by this expansion and extension is the augmentation of the real buying capacity of the market. A small number of people would buy many things: this may be an acceptable situation, but at the same time it has some limitations also. There is a limit for a small group of people buying many items. They change choice and rapidly shift from one to another. As a result, there is an explosive situation. The situation can handle a much greater number of people than it could before.

Organized endeavors have so long been considered to be the only way for eradication of poverty. There are conflicts and struggles in such organized efforts. Struggle is there between one group or class with another or there is an effort of establishing one's own right. The notion that the open market can play any role in the endeavour of eradicating poverty has not so far caught the sight of philosophers or social reformers. Command over the open market does not remain in the hand of any particular group, community or class. Even the government guardianship on open market becomes rather limited.

It is mainly an enterprise of man for man. All of those who join an open market have the target to draw maximum profit. But the methods and processes of the market do not allow to have high profit at one's disposal. In this process gain of one may turn to be the cause of loss or danger for the other, but in the long run spread of opportunity is bound to come. Open market does not stand on the income of an individual. It stands on the power of the market.

There are many forms of exposition of the power of the market such as, power of the buyers, power of technology and power of money. There is coordination between power of buyers and technology. The process of innovating technology for creating convenience of the buyers goes on. Thus, the main function of technology becomes the service of the buyers.

Constant innovation of technology results in much convenience of buyers. That is consumable goods and services constantly come up in new forms. This acquirement of merchandise and services continues in a competitive environment. In other words, technology has no single door, it rather comes up through many gateways. It is the market which competes with itself to use new technology.

The power of buyers may abandon commodity and service resulting from a certain technology and may prefer those of new technology. This process makes the market multi-dimensional. A veritable explosion of the market occurs. Just as there are many suppliers for the same commodity or service, so also many types of management come out. As a result, open market comes within the reach of common people.

Just as new commodity and service grow by this process, so also grows those of low cost and inferior quality. Commodity and services gradually come within the reach of consumers. This forms the initial phase of causing expansion of the market.

In the same way there is a tension within the power of buyers. Monetary power gradually develops under the influence of the power of buyers. As in case of the suppliers so also in case of common buyer, a monetary explosion occurs. In case of buyers it goes on increasing as the organizers keep supplying money. Gradually the trend of supplying money shifts from wholesale to retail. The less is the scope of supply of huge amount of money, the greater becomes the dominance of small amounts. By way of supplying wholesale money, the investing agencies begin to have their profit lessened, on the other hand, their profit increases, if they can supply retail money. So, the natural target of the monetary power becomes the people, the buyers, the public in general.

Expansion is the natural trend of movement of a market. Market initially remains limited within a small area, a small group of people of a particular identity. Gradually the market comes up from this situation, in many directions, and through the attraction of large number of people the market achieves success.

Success comes to the market through association of money. As a result of this the phase of gradual expansion of total resources begins. Though the main resources initially remain under the control of few people, gradually that expands to reach many. This brings in a new financial stratification in the society. A new wave and new tide of attention reach even the poor. Economic rise finds a scope to flourish.

35

Trend of Freedom From Poverty

Market Dominance

Rise of the open market has fixed up the target of economic advancement at changing the standard of living. If standard of living is upgraded, it is to be granted that economic development is there. Upgradation of living standards means qualitative change of life. Modern economic thoughts are directed to this direction.

Poverty has many directions. The main one is economic poverty. According to modern definition a person who is poor cannot afford to spend one dollar (American) daily. This type of worldwide measure is required to build up a balanced picture. Beside financial poverty there are problems relating to lack of education, concern with health, social discrimination and other situations.

In order to get rid of poverty, capability of earning one dollar per day is to be attained and so also liberation from the curse of lack of education is also to be earned. Sound health is to be acquired, as well as liberation from gender discrimination and similar other social users.

Thus, a balanced natural environment is to be had.

Different aspects of the market declared by the one eighty heads of states in the proclamation of the millennium are:

1. End of excessive poverty and hunger: Number of excessively poor and starving people is to be halved in every ten years and in the long run, effect complete eradication.
2. Introduction of primary education everywhere and for all: The target fixed here is to make arrangement for primary education equally among the males and females and see that everybody can complete the phase successfully.

3. Removal of discrimination between males and females and enhancement of woman empowerment: Overall endeavour for eradication of discrimination between males and females in the field of education and empowerment and to ensure priority for women in proper places.
4. End of child death: To reduce the death rate of children by at least two-thirds and to bring an end to it in the long run.
5. Improvement of health of the mothers: All round attempt for good health of mothers so that deaths of owing to bad health is reduced by three fourths of the present number.
6. Rescue from severe diseases: Eradication of virulent diseases like HIV-AIDS, cholera and the like.
7. To set up environments congenial for stability: To build such an environment by bringing back the balance in environment so that the green talent gets a longer life
8. International cooperation and sympathy for development: To consider development as a global problem through expansion of interdependent markets in the world and spread of the target of development and to make others consider thus.

This charter with eight items came from the joint declaration of the heads of one hundred and eighty states. International organisations are chief partners of this charter. Many states have made declaration in favour of development and eradication of poverty many times. But in most cases, they have been rather meaningless, only empty slogans.

In most cases very little effect has been there. When there is a declaration, fulfilment is not necessarily a surety. Rather under the cover of declaration there is an abundant display of interests of particular groups or individuals. International experts have written many books and papers on the experiment of México. Some Nobel Laureates have forwarded the main theorems and principles with Mexico. With the Mexican model they have tried to show the ways for development and eradication of poverty. Both in spite of lots of advices, cooperation of the world Bank, International Monetary Fund and other developing countries the condition of Mexico has remained nearly unchanged.

China and India form another set of examples. China's is a special case, China promised economic liberty for all in the path shown by Marx and Mao. But coming down to the seventies experience showed that this path would not be able to retain power because although the sayings from the philosophies of Marx and Mao may bring people to agitation, and all sorts of favors and facilities may be enjoyed through achievement of statepower. Self-enjoyment and enjoyment of near and dear ones may be arrived at, but these cannot lead to development of state and liberation from poverty. So, they have resorted to the real path.

Due to the absolute control China has, the very primary scope of breaking the economic situation according to the social will have split the economic system in three layers. The first layer consists of the big cities and port-towns like Beijing, Shanghai and Shenzhen. The second layer is formed of other state capitals and big suburban cities. The third consists of the rest country and the rural areas. In the first layer they have arranged free economic systems as in America, to do whatever you like.

Thus, a liberal economic system has grown. This has even caused large amounts of American, Japanese and European investments. The advantage China has achieved during eighties and nineties of the last century is the capital of money in the world market.

Money has accumulated in the custody of investing financial organisations, but scope of investment is lacking. Under these circumstances FDI or Foreign Direct Investment has been showered towards China. This is money-running after temporary opportunities.

At the time of investment all took it for granted that the whole of Chinese market would come within the sphere of this money. But the result was not so. Now after about two decades it is found that industry and enterprising activity started under the influence of that money have come to a half, reaching a fixed border. Number of maximum buyers that were apprehended has been reached -it is not increasing any more.

This is because rural people have practically no buying power. Common workers are neglected and exploited. Noneof the labor laws expected to be there in a good industrial system exists there. In agriculture the process of storing food in granaries has already begun. Some big concerns have somehow had the control over big cultivable landand dominating over the produce there from. Whoever is able to earn something from these are leaders of big or small parties.

The rest of the people living in rural area are somehow managing to earn the livelihood. But the overall control invested in the government through international agencies has remained unexamined. No internal agency, no personal or non- government enterprise are able to bring out any statistic without government control. There are of course few exceptions. These exceptional statistical data point at the impending danger before the investigating agencies. They are now seeing that the lifestyle of rural and semi urban regions has remained rather old fashioned. Income is meagre. There people are living through giving labor in exchange of food. It is very hard for them to come up, and unless they come up the market would not grow in size.

That is only the goods produced in the market within China would find ways to be sold, no more advancement would be there. The second layer [prevailing in the middle]are people ofthe lower middle class. Their individual taste and buying ability are very little but through cooperation system they get multiplied to get the mistress of purchase in the market. That is, they purchase in the form of groups, not individuals. Their transaction is with different, stores from organized sale countries. The extent of such truncated consumption is very limited. Its increase is rather very slow.

The announcement made publicly in favour of development of China by some individual agencies is based only on the financial demand in the first layer. People in this layer were so long enjoying the benefit of the development without any disturbance. The Nobel wining economists have pointed at them and continued showering advice upon India. But irony of fate is this- they have now leaned towards India to know India has flourished within the periphery of liberal management-by . It is now the turn for the world to cast eyes on India lifting the same from China.

36

India Would Liberate the World from Poverty

'India freed means humanity saved'. An atmosphere of liberty has appeared in this world just after freedom of India from British rule. One after another different countries have been liberated from foreign rule. The power of consciousness emerged from the soul of India has been controlling the world. When India wakes, the world wakes. It is India who has supplied the world its spiritual power, a power of the soul.Anything that is positive, that is beneficial in the world, that has been conforming to the stability of the world has got India as the source. It is India that has told the world the gospel of deathlessness. Again, it has informed us about the other of life.

Britain's greatness lay in the fact that it had occupied India; that is why Britain had become the greatest power of the world. It would occupy India due to a unique opportunity;India's open andcareless attitude rather paved the way of the occupation. Had India been aggressive then, Britain could not have occupied her. A tiny state of India- that of Porus had halted the world-wide invasion of Alexander. Again, the whole of the Eastern and Northern hemisphere of the globe have grown up through the spiritual power of India. More than half of the Chinese civilization has grown under the sphere of influence of India. China has grown up just in the form of a Buddhist ideas and rural socio-economic system of India.

Time has not yet come to realise separately the influence of India. Some people or organisations who possess free and far-reaching thoughts have of course been realising slowly. The big world organisation have now realised that the root of success so far achieved in the eradication of poverty is in the hands of India and China. For a considerable period of time, they used to mention only China, but reaching a certain point, for last few years they have been referring to 'China and India'. 'Now the order has changed to 'India and China'.

The World Bank has written in its World Development Report 2004.... 'The world as a whole is in track to achieve this first goal- reducing by half the proportion of people living on less than 1 dollar a day-thanks mainly to the rapid economic growth in India and China' (p. 2). In this report the World Bank has admitted with due importance that the world has advanced towards reaching the pre-assigned target of eradication of poverty due to advancement of India and China.

Warburg Pincus, a famous private equity company of wall street, America has said that it is not China, but India that is the target at present. India has just become the center of gravity of world economics. J. P. Morgan, in its latest, report has remarked the question is not centered around whether there would be extensive rise of economic development in India, but it is what would be the extent of the rise. Michael T. Clark, the executive director of the Indo-American Trade council has said 'I can see a hurricane approaching'. The next five to seven years belong to India. In the opinion of Clark, economic rise in India is coming with the speed of a hurricane,

We are standing face to face with the economic rise of India. Some have explained the same to be the key to a golden store house. But what are the points of importance of India? One point was thought to be the computer and software industry. But presently it has been observed that the main power of India lies in the cases so long moved ahead of in the government enterprises. But success has remained beyond reach. It is found that internal power of India has revealed in the field of basic industries, manufacturing service and outsourcing. This would result extension and expansion of Indian enterprises within and outside India.

The main causes of economic rise of India is the inflation in currency for three to four years and hide extension of service. The market of construction of building is increasing by 30% a year. It has cast influence on steel, cement industries and the like. Stress has been laid on infrastructure and good result is evident in the extensive efforts of binding all regions of India, from Kashmir to Comorin and Assam in a common link of highways have yielded results. Cable lines about 80,000 km conjoined with about 30,000 km of roadways have excited both ability and possibility.

The interim account of just the last month shows that there is again an emerging explosion in income. The share market of India is blooming. In the last few months foreign investment in our share market has increased at the rate of about 20%. This indicates that Foreign institutional investors (FII) are being rapidly attracted towards India.

The problem of India lies within itself. As a country it is advancing, but the condition of the states is just the opposite. West Bengal is gradually backing out and irony is that this backout is proudly being announced a success. Such an instance is seldom found history. Great harm has been caused by Bengal in driving out computers. Even China has been suppressed in the world market. The technological world powers are dependent on English. China had not realised the value of English- so it has just rushed at the learning of English. Starting from Beijing, Shanghai etc. in all big and small towns of China there is a great rush for learning and teaching English. Setting apart computers West Bengal has retreated abou two decades, as computer-based activity and education system is now reigning supreme.

We now have engaged our life and thinking to source a place just at the back. The last nail has been driven into the coffin of West Bengal through the dictatorial mentality of getting everything under the control of the party. They like to bring control over everything and as such this state is not exposed to the market at all. And consequently, no explosion of buyer's power has been affected here. And without an explosion of the power of buyers there would be no blooming of technical and economic power. And as a result, poverty would be just at the same state as it had been before.

For economic development and eradication of poverty what is needed is not class struggle nor conflict nor malice but the state of a completely free market. The more a state keeps itself engaged in framing and applying laws and preserving internal peace the better. The right of a state is not trade. It has to be protector of the market. The rise of man would come by holding hands of open market, but on the basis of spiritual consciousness of India.

Bibliography

World Bank. *Word Development Report 2004*, 2004.

37
State Authority in Economic Development

State and Financial Management

The role of the state has been observed in different ways in the financial management of a country. As in philosophy so also in action, different roles of the state have been recorded in the history. Some times state has been the controller and director of financial management and sometimes again the role of state is linked in a slender joint. The role of state has changed in different stages of history. Sometimes state has been somewhat indifferent and sometimes it has been quite involved. The state authority always has concern with financial management of the state-it is quite natural; consideration of financial matters is important because money is required for running a state. Whatever maybe the process of running a state, to run the administration state has to be careful for procuring money. In the presentation of financial matters Kautilya's *Arthashastra* has considered the matter of running a state with importance. Kautilya's Arthasdastra is not only a charter of philosophy but it also contains a detailed programme of implementation.

The state system contained in the *Arthashastra* has total authority, but its responsibility is also universal. Kautilya has created a balanced system between authority and responsibility. The king would enjoy authority as the state leader. Authority of the king is universal. The king has the right to know anything and the right to play his role. Intervention of the king is always granted. The will of the king may be the ultimate word in all cases. The whole of the state is in the sphere of king's influence. The king may add up his choice in every aspect of the state. Law can be framed in accordance with the king's will. Application of laws may be affected according to king's will. King may be the first word; he may even be the last word. But that is not possible in any way.

Kautilya's *Arthashastra* has given the king authority and responsibility parallelly. The burden of responsibility would come upon the king engaged in enjoying. Besides *Arthashastra* has so defined the character and qualities of a king that it is rather easy for a king to observe the authority. But he could never apply his authority abruptly. Inherent personality of the king would prevent him from doing so.

The king would never be eager to apply his authority unjustifiably right because of the qualities prescribed for him by the *Arthashastra* and the knowledge possessed by him therefrom, nor he would allow any body else to be engaged in doing so. If a king assures authority, he would first have to admit the responsibility of the public and above all he would have to work for the public. Only after completing the welfare activities of thepublic, the king may look after his own interest. Until and unless the king is fully successful in bringing welfare to the public it would not be possible for him to be engaged in accomplishing his own interests.

According to the instructions of the *Arthashastra* the king as such plays a benevolent role in financial cases of the state. At the very beginning Kautilya has attributed importance on the personal ability of the king. He wanted the topmost official of the leadership and all others to be proficient in Vedic learning. He had introduced learning and practicing Vedic education for leadership. This is because the kings all have to be free from longing and desire. Unless the king is free from longing and desire, it would not be possible for him to bear the responsibility of his country's rule, responsibility.

Foulness infiltrates in the king if he himself remains occupied by longing and desires. Instead of protecting the interest of his people, the king would become an exploiter and a tyrant. Kautilya as such advised a king to not only start his life through learning and practice of Vedic education, but also to make the practice of Vedic learning his beckoning every day.

If Vedic learning influences the living of every day and every moment, a touch of spiritual knowledge comes to the life of the king. If the king becomes able to lead his life through practice of this Vedic learning, spiritual knowledge begins to bloom in him. The king becomes spiritually knowledgeable.

A Vedic King is Free from Desire

Kautilya has placed a proposal for the king to be free from longing and desire, because he has seen in the Puranas and in history highly disastrous effects. Endlesss wealth is required for blooming of endless longing and desire. If endless wealth is utilised for service of the king then that wealth is procured from the subjects or the public. Public is to bear the responsibility of the enjoyment of the king. Kings' money comes from the wealth of the people. It is the people who are to pay for keeping the king immersed in enjoyment and pleasure. Kautilya has learned instructions in this respect from the *Mahabharata*.

The history and description of Yayati the king has been depicted vividly in the *Mahabharata*. Nahus, the father of Yayati was called a royal ascetic.Everybody respected him as an ascetic. Yayati also has this sort of reputation. The royal influence of Yayati was wide spread. His administration policy was also beneficial to the subjects. The attraction of Yayati's personality was tremendous.People were also attracted to him for his beauty. Yayati had been married to Devyani, the daughter of Sukracharya, the mentor of the demons. But it happened so that he got involved in a relationship with Sarmistha, another daughter of that mentor. As a consequence, a curse of Sukracharya came down upon Yayati.-experiencing the infirmities of old age for the duration of a thousand years.

Yayati of course got such a power as to transfer his infirmity on some other person and to enjoy his health. Endless desire descended in Yayati's mind.And to satisfy that desire he presented the proposal to his son-to accept his infirmity and to give him, in exchange, his youth. Only the youngest son, Porus agreed to this proposal, Porus reached the stage of infirmity of Yayati and Yayati got back the youth and with that the proper power to enjoy With the juvenility of a thousand years, Yayati enjoyed life to avery large extant.

Getting exemption from infirm life for thousand years, Yayati enjoyed juvenility and then returned the same to Porus. Yayati did not become happy through enjoyment of juvenility by transferring infirmity to his son. Instead, hefelt severe remorse for transferring his infirmity into his dearest son during the golden period of the latter's life. Gradually Yayati became firm in the opinion that enjoyment of desired objects does not make one's life better.

The more is the supply of the desired objects the more becomes the incitement of the desire for enjoyment. Satisfaction of one desire for enjoyment generates another such desire. The lust for enjoyment gradually extends in life. There is no liberation from the same.

Yayati then returned his son his youth. He said to Porus

Na jatu kamah kamanam upabhogeno
Samyati
Habisa krsnabartmeba eba dhuyah
Etabhi bardhate

(*Mahabharatam*, 1/37/12)

[Enjoyment of the desired object never inhibits lust, rather just like as fire gets more blazing in contact with ghee, so also lust increases through enjoyment of desired objects]

Yat pathibyah brihiyabam hiranyam
Pasabah striyal
Ekasya ap na paryaptam tasmat trisanam
Tyajatah sukham.

(*Mahabharatam*, 1/37/13)

[Even all of the monetary wealth, wealth of food, wealth of hands and wealth of woman collectivly cannot satisfy the desire of enjoyment of an individual; so, it is better to give up the desire.)

Yah duh tyaja durmati abhih yah
Na jtryati jirtyah
Yah asau pranatika rogah tam
Trisnam tyajatah sukham

(*Mahabharatam*, 1/37/14)

[An individual captured by vile thought cannot easily forsake desire; desire does not wane even if body wanes; and he who can shun the thirst which is like a total disease, is happy.)

Purna barsa sahasramme bisayah
A saktah chetas
Tatha api anudinam trs nava
Mamaitesva abhijayate.

(*Mahabharatam*, 13/37/15)

[Being addicted to desire for long thousand years. I was completely merged into worldly possessions but still newer desires have constantly hindered me.)

Yayati was the lord of a big empire. He possessed all of the qualities of a king and he had acquired Vedic knowledge. Still the desire of flesh infiltrated his character. Just a single gush of lust got Yayati conjoined into a longer heap of lusts. Anything that had come in the purview of his lustful nature, got fulfilled. Satisfaction of one lust at one level generated lusts of a newer period. After endless enjoyment Yayati came to the realisation that enjoyment cannot stop aggression of lusts, but only increases it through newer forms.

Kautilya has set the basis of the *Arthashastra* from the view point of an attempt to found a state-leadership free from the influence of longings and desires. According to Kautilya's philosophy a king would have a character free from infatuation- denying pleasure and good charactered.

Rajnau hi bratam utthanam Tajnah
Karyah anusasanam.
Daksinabrttih samyam tu diksa
Tasya abhisecanam.

(*Arthashastra*, 1/19/33)

[The king becomes big and great through his observance of vow; the basis of his royal injunction would be renunciation. And the aim of the influence of money in the royal treasury would be setting up of equity. King will be impartial to all.)

Tasmat tat utthitau rajah kuryat artha anusasanam
Arthasaya mulam uthanam aharthasya Biparyah.

(*Arthashastra*,1/19/35)

[A king always engaged in work would run the administration of the kingdom in such a way as to attempt truly for the economic rise of all. Devotion to activity lies at the root of economic rise. The king would render the economic system free from any adversity only through devotion to activity.)

Combining all the main principles of Kautilya's economic philosophy one would get a balanced principle of economic development. A great possibility in the philosophy of Kautilya. It was not possible for Kautilya to present his economic prospects in the form and language of modern economics. Influence of time is there on all earthly matters and objects no doubt. Just similarly it also acts in cases of theories and philosophy. Economic philosophy of Kautilya contains some such matters which were connected specifically with contemporary societies and requirements of the country. But there are some more things which surpass contemporary needs, casting far reaching influences.

Much of the items the productive capacity of which has been stressed upon in the economic philosophy of Kautilya are rather periodic. Examples are agriculture, protection of cows, of livestockand proposals on trade and commerce. Kautilya has selected the periphery of a village as the criterion for distributing villages. Not only that he has mapped a coordinated system among different professions and communities of people in a village. Within a village there should be multple people of proper mentality and profession to provide labour for agriculture.

Next would come the context of men of associated professions. In order to build up things like agricultural production, controlling agricultural systems and the like, menof associated professions are necessary. Beside these, what more is required is the fusion of knowledge and spread of education. In order to make the village people join the cultivation and learning which would extend the light of awareness among them, people of those professions are required who desire only the practice and cultivation of knowledge. Kautuilya's economic system has chartered a balanced distributior among many.

Economic and overall principles have been included clearly in Kautilya's proposal. While Marx's principle of equilibrium is one sided and partial, that of Kautilya is balanced and holistic. Karl Marx wanted dictatorship of the proletariat and to mobilise all of the productive powers of the society under the control of the proletariat. As aresult, building up of different types of divisions within the society was inevitable. One division in between the haves and have-nots, Another between the old and the new; Marx is impatient towards the old tradition. He has said in the third page of the German edition(1867) of *Das Capital*;

'Alongside of modern evils, a whole service of inherited evils oppresses us, arising from passive survival of antiquated modes of production, which with their inevitable train of social and political anacronism. We suffer not only from the living, but from the dead'. 'Le mort sadist le vie'. For Marx the good side of tradition has escaped his notice. To Marx tradition has seemed to be oppressive.

So, the traditional civilization failed to appeal to Marx, rather he has searched for all sorts of defects and dishonest points in them. That is why Marxian economics is not only partial but also an incomplete and detrimental theory. In comparison Kautilya's economic theory is far more developed and favourable and complete. If the basic principles of economic theories of Kautilya and Marx are compared, it would be found that the basis of Kautilya's philosophy is much more sound and its future possibility is more powerful than that of the other.

Kautilya's *Arthashastra* has emphasized on setting up of a balanced equilibrium. It is a holistic work. This outlook is there in the character of the leadership. The king or the leader of a state should have to be initiated into renunciation. The chief target of the king or the leader should be to stake his life for the economic upliftment of all. No importance in the least would be placed on the interest of the class, group or individual. The target before this leadership would be the balanced advancement of the people. The ultimate target of the king or leadership is to set up balanced equilibrium.

Balanced Equilibrium

The theory of balanced equilibrium is subject to the nature of the individual. That is an individual has been called on for getting himself lifted beyond his base interests. As a result of this an individual would enter into the greater idea. The greater idea is that all men depending on their individual capability and efficiency, are to be brought forward into a greater field. Economic awakening is to be achieved through one's own endeavour. Personal endeavour would gradually unfold an individual. This would open the gates of creation. The state would create newer values by dint of new ideas, new activities, new methods. Not to remain parasitic on surplus values, newer values are to be created which would cast its influence on allacross the state.

Kautilya has demanded co-operation in economic flourishing. With cooperation, new productive idea and activities would come into the financial management. Since a perspective of new creation appears, the influence of shortage of production and the aspect of surplus value would disappear to make way for the creation of the state of newer value. New values increase the resource of the state and reaches everybody- balanced economic advancement come to everyone.

Certain Features of the Vedic Economic Philosophy

It is based on the good qualities of tradition and civilization. Constant endeavour is there to procure basic propensities from tradition and civilization to build up newer economic theories.

Spiritual awakening of an individual is essential. It helps an individual expand himself.

The advancement of the state should be channelized along a balanced stream. All sort of possibilities of complete flourishing are required for a balanced society. For example, for agriculture proper distribution is required within a village.

Kautilya wanted the men in the leadership of a state to be eager to earn divine knowledge. Thus character of the leadership free of personal interest is very much essential for the public, for if the leadership seeks his own interest, he would utilise all the resources of the country for his own benefit, or for that of his own group. The leader of a state would have to be self-denying, sacrificing his own life for others and would be the shield of mankind. He would not cast any sight of difference on the public.

Kautilya's proposal is that state would intervene in others' business. The state itself would not be directly involved in case of produces of the state, but it would have its opinion in case of all aspects of a state, including what it produces, distributes and arranges. Based on its own views, a state would frame laws and apply them for full protection of the interests of the public. This is because happiness of the leadership is in the happiness of the public. The leadership would give up interest of its own, or of its class or group. Only then it would be fit for running the administration of the state.

Cooperation is the very first thing in economics. Thesecond is balanced equilibrium. Economic arrangement gets expanded by cooperation and if cooperation of all is achieved, then the economic arrangement would get a new momentum by the inventive faculty of all. Again, balanced equilibrium comes from cooperation of the state. The monetary good effects achieved by balanced equilibrium will reach everybody in terms ofcapability, necessity and quality.

Principles of the Economic Philosophy of Marx

It is against tradition and civilization. Natural instincts have been derived from tradition and civilization.

Spiritual awakening is to be forsaken just like poison. It is detrimental to society and civilization.

There is no mention of balanced equilibrium either. What exists is an industry controlled by the participants in the interest of the proletariat. All the aspects of the industrial management will not be included here. As too much importance has been laid on the leadership of the working class of productive management, there is no mention of balanced equilibrium. Problems and possibilities of agriculture are considered the same as those of industry.

Marx's concern about traits of character of leadership expands only upto a certain mention of class distinction. An individual becomes an expert in consideration of the interests of a special class only when he is well informed about the nature of the class. The meaning of the establishment of the leadership of the working class is the fulfilment of the desired interest of that class. Here an individual also blooms up in concern with this interest. The matter of being eager to look after his own interest naturally becomes quite reasonable on the part of a man who is ardent about the interest of the class.The administration of such leadership may be rather poisonous with the greater public.

Marxian state will behave in the authority of all productive and distributive agencies. Only the state would produce. Industry and commerce would grow under the direct control of the state and as a result state will have the right of profit and loss of the industry and commerce. The surplus value coming from the management of production under the control of the state would go as the right of the working class. Since the life of the state would run under the control of this working class, direct control on the surplus value would come with leadership. Those who will remain outside the productive management will not be able to come inside the directive sphere of the surplus value.

The first thing in economics is class-distribution and class-animosity, while the second thing is inter-equilibrium of classes. Unity would be established right through class-animosity and consequently they would fight unitedly and earn their deserving rights. The produce in this struggle would be in the control of the state. The result of the control of the state would bring inter-equilibrium among the working classes.

Bibliography

Marx, Karl. *Das Kapital*. Verlag von Otto Meisner, 1867.

38

Kautilya's Labour Policy

Identity of workers: Interest of the labourers has been dealt within Kautilya's *Arthashastra* with special importance. Whoever tries to earn by offering his labour is a labourer. If through giving labour they earn they are a labourer, if they do not earn, then also they are a labourer. The only criterion of being a labourer is the ability, efficiency and opportunity of giving labour. He who has had ability, efficiency and opportunity of investing labour is admitted as a labourer.

The identity as a labourer means arrival of opportunity to give labour. Kautilya wanted the assurance of opportunity of giving labour with respect to ability and efficiency. The meaning of appearance of an opportunity to give labour is to arrange jobs for labourers. Different types of enterprises of the state would arrange jobs for labourers. State, here, is the manager, controller and arbiter of proper justice.

While considering the efficiency of a labourer, his racial identity, the identity of his locality and that of his worthiness becomes prominent. Racial identity is the stream of activity practiced along his family line. In this identity becomes evident the type of activities his ancestors were involved in and in which their efficiency was manifested.

By the racial identity an individual becomes able to express his own qualities. With help of racial identity, it becomes easier for others to recognise a man efficient in the performance of a particular line of work.

Many of the aspects on the basis of which efficiency and utility of a labourer are characterised are embedded in the racial identity. Kautilya has laid importance on these aspects in case of welfare of the labourer. As a result of this a labourer would not have to move from door to door for justification of his worthiness. He would have the key to his own settlement in his own hand.

This type of management is very much essential in the perspective of the modern open market. Sometimes it becomes necessary for an individual to be associated with his own publicity. This is evident from the experience of modern society. Perhaps Kautilya had approached such possibility and judged the racial identity with importance. Consideration of racial identity may also go against a labourer, but commonly it's beneficial role is more mentionable.

Kautilya has considered the interest of a labourer from a holistic angle of humanity. He has not considered a labourer only as a labourer. The first identity of a labourer is that he is a man, so a labourer is to be understood from the standpoint of human consideration, and not only as a common labourer offering his labour. Within the limit of identity of a labourer as one offering labour much of the qualities of the character of a labourer and much of the traits of possibility likely get lost.

Inferiority complex grows in the labourers. If a labourer knows that his role is limited only within the limit of his labour, his utility begins to diminish. Desire of waking up in the labourer gets lost. He becomes complacent with his limited existence. The desire to do something big, to do something great in life disappears.

Lust breeds perpetuity of greed in such a fashion that it kills the positive identity of that person in different organisations. The racial identity of the labourer is one such medium. With the help of racial identity, the minimum standard of efficiency and gradually cumulative efficiency of work gets restored. A labourer can make the wealth of these efficiencies to be elements of the route of development of his life.

In order to be a dealer of labour, a labourer is to be conversant of his efficiencies and qualities. What are these efficiencies and qualities? How are these to be matched with accompanied changes? So on and so forth. This means that a labourer will not be and will not remain to be a dealer of labour. He would rise to be a creator of labour, a controller of labour. That is, he would create and control labour, mainly keeping an eye on the interest and possibility of production. Kautilya cast his view on this subject. While speaking of the interest of labourers Kautilya's greatest emphasis was on production. A labourer's responsibility is the production of high standard goods. The interest of an organisation or state grows taking resort to the production of high standard goods. An organisation or state becomes very careful about this and expects that labour offered by the labourers would be similarly accepted and appreciated. So, the *Arthashastra* of Kautilya brought the principle of labour under the purview of judiciary. According to Kautilya, proper judgement should be there in farming and applying the laws of labour. At the time of judgement he primarily stressed on one thing, the principle of justice. Kautilya emphasized the actual depiction of the principle of justice. The real depiction would be such as it truly reflects the principle of justice. For this Kautilya fixed up the standard in two levels. The first one is bilateral and multilateral agreement and the second is arrangements determined and decided by the market. Kautilya appealed in favour of the most appropriate, best and acceptable of all the arrangements. It is very much present with respect to the personal interest of the labourers. Though there is no scope of direct contract with labourers, possibilities are there for continuing with the works keeping them in a pleasing mood. As a result of this boundary and ability of work gets expanded.

Division of Labour

Kautilya's *Arthashastra* has thought of protecting the interest of the organisation and the state together with keeping the identity of the labourer firm. The subjects that become essential for this are aspects like labourers' views and the elements of economic awakening of the country. The awakening is essential in the light of both the labourers' interest and the country's.

The basis of division of classifications of labours is demand for work. In other words, at the requirement of work by the organisation or state, labour may be divided in many ways. Every division would move separately with its work. There are different laws of this division of labour. For example, the matter of offering labour for agriculture is quite different from that of live stock farming or any other rural enterprise. In case of industrial enterprise also this division of labour is very important and useful.

The division of labour is based right on the basis of qualitative standard and utility of the labour on offer. For example division of different labourers of some standard of quality would be on the basis of usefulness of individual labours. The theory of division of labour presented by Kautilya is useful in modern economic management. The process of division of labour in the *Arthashastra* is holistic.

Along with the division of labour, assessment of many other things have come forward.

> Karmakarasya karma sambandham
> Asana viduh (*Arthashastra*, 3/13/26)

In modern management regulation of work is done on the basis of the respective period of time, but the merit of the work is not always judged on the basis of circumstantial elements. In modern management. there are many methods for assessment of works.

Among these a few worthy of mention are: to determine the standard of quality; to determine the level of income and expenditure through budgets; to determine the level of control over human resources. Along side this there is the procurance of the essence of experience gathered from the running of other organisations, to introduce administration in that tune. Examples are procured from comparable organisation in the national and international level to setup or improve administration systems.

Kautilya liked the administration system catering directly around the work of an individual instead of being limited to manner and custom. As a result, direct influence comes on the quality of work assessed together. The quality of work is not made independent of individuality but dependent on it. Work independent of individuality is impartial and does not have any impact of the impositions of the person on it. In this system very little inspiration remains for an individual. In case of assessment of works independent of individuality, the good and bad of the organisation and its relation with work are the only aspects brought into consideration.

Aspects of good and bad of the individual or other workers are not brought into consideration here. But for the permanent stability of the organisation the aspects of an individual must be considered. Assessment of work cannot be made separate from that of a worker. In modern management different organisations have designed different means of psychological corrections and reformation for assessing particularly the condition of the workers. Aim is to make the worker more zealous for work and to create conditions to to generate newer values through that work.

> Yathasambhastiam betanam labheta.
> Karmakalah anurapam sambha sitam
> Chetanah. (3/13/27)

[In case of determining salary for a worker, the primary contract is to be considered. Salary will be fixed according to the primary contract. Of course, without any primary contract the pay structure would be determined in accordance with the current rate of the present market.]

For determining salary for workers Kautilya has accepted the process of division of labour and the procedure for selection of the definite standard of the market. With the help of division of labour. particular work is to be brought in the purview of a particular class in accordance to its individuality and contract with the labourer is to be made in order to hasten the same and to complete it in a balanced manner.

More than two thousand years before introducing modern laws of industrial control Kautilya honoured the aspects of the labourers. Kautilya valued a labourer just as a human being. A labourer's duty is not only to offer labour. As he is engaged in offering labour, so also, he has some human activities. As a result, labourers can demand to be a partner in the process of taking decisions in offering labour. Kautilya has given that right to a labourer. Kautilya wanted the labourer tobe associated with greater roles. When one is intimately associated with the good and bad of the work being undertaken, theeagerness to do it grows only then. The concerned organisation is also benefitted by contracts with the labourer. Perhaps the organisation would get that much from a labourer as it could expect from him.

Kautilya has seen a man as a unit and that is why he has been eager to enter into salary contract with a labourer. He has not thought of coming into contract with trade-union or the organisation looking after the demands and rights of the labourers. This is because the organisation itself has thought apriori of the demands of labourers.

In case of giving salaries to labourers a part of the produce is to be given to them, if part of the unorganised sector.

Kjarsakah sasyanam, gopalakh
Sampisam vaidehakah
Panyanam atmana byabahatanam
Dasabhagam sambhasitam betanau labhet.

(*Arthashastra* 3/13/28)

[Farmers, cow herds and labourers engaged in industry would get one tenth respectively of produced crops, milk products and total trade, provided there is no bilateral agreement.]

Agreement of salary maybe there with those who are connected with different works for rural economy. If there is no agreement, one tenth of the produce effected by them would come to those labourers as salary. It is to be taught to those who are constantly beating drums on modern land-reforms and reforms of rural economy. To have the right on one tenth of the produce is profitable and connectable to any worker.

The labourer has not to invest any money to get that much. In such a case, one-tenth is an exemplary division of wealth. The division will in one way increase the work-culture and in another way the augmented appeal to work would get qualitative change in the work.

Through work Kautilya has increased the pervasiveness of the authority of the organisation in many ways. The pervasive presence would create attachment in the workers, and newer ideas would grow in their minds. Propensity and suggestiveness like this sows in a great number of workers the impetus to be helpful for the economic development of villages. Such idea of expansion of wealth is very essential for awakening of agriculture and allied industries, Appeal of an organisation in the community of workers would increase if such endeavours are taken to the heights possible.

Sambhasikh betanah tuyatha sambhasitam.

(*Arthashastra*, 3/13/29)

[If of course, there be any agreement, salary will be fixed up in terms of the same.]

Kautilya's principle is very easy and simple. He has wanted the interests of workers to be protected as labourers themselves are also eager for the development of the organisation concerned. If there is any dispute or difference in opinion, it would be settled in accordance with advice of the experts. Advice of the knowledgeable in the line would have to be abided by the workers and the authority equally.

Karusilpah kusilabah cikitsakah bak
Jibanah partcarakah
Rasa-karikah bangel tu yatha anyal
Tadbidhah

Karyat yatha ba kusalah kalpayetuh
Talha betanam labhel
(*Arthashastra*, 3/13/20)

[Technologists, experts in fine arts, physicians, orators, professionals, story-tellers and the like would get salaries in the same way as received by others in the market. Of course, if such standard in the market is not available their salaries would be fixed by the experts]

The *Arthashastra* has laid such importance and such well thought out opinion on salaries that difficultly would hardly arise at all. Kautilya has taken steps so that writers, physician, artist, experts in fine arts and people engaged in kindred professions are also not deprived. The topics *Arthashastra* has commented on are all based on a basic principle. Kautilya's principle is to give dignity to labourers as then and at the same time to pay dignity to labour. If labour is equally dignified the concerned organisation will by benefited and gain profit and at the same time the economic condition of the country would experience a change.

Kautilya has not indulged in the idea that labours and proprietors are two opponent groups. In the *Arthashastra* the relationship between labourers and the proprietors is depicted be complementary. The management recommended by Kautilya depicts labourers as not only working for themselves but for the organisation and the country as well. Labourers would not initially think for themselves, but their initial thinking is to be for the organisation and the country. Kautilya's labour-policy would move the economic status of the country firm and would bloom the labourers in a greater role.

39

Kautilya's Economic Diplomacy

Preface

Diplomacy on the basis of politics and economics is quite common nowadays. Diplomacy has occupied an important place within the havoc of political invasion. Diplomacy brings a coating of peace in battle and an unfailing truth of coherence in conflict. As in political management of a state, so also in economic distributions, many a situation of conflict of different types occurs. Application of diplomacy helps control such situation. Application of diplomacy keeps such situation under control, free from conflicts and urges one to be ardent in solving the problem in a new way.

Diplomacy is the messenger of peace; peace is to be bought with a price. This price is determined along the way of diplomacy. Diplomacy becomes the hailer of peace and appears on politics and economics. Diplomacy is quite customary for a state in politics. Kautilya has extended the application of diplomacy in economic management also. Use of diplomacy in economic system is rather novel. Kautilya has not emphasized this but has taken it to a considerable depth. The method of using diplomacy in economic management shown by Kautilya may be very attractive in modern economic management policy.

Economic Tricks

In modern times economic management of almost every country has a number of divisions. When judged in the background of global standpoint this division will show to have a sort of uniformity. These divisions have been very tightly linked in a uniform fashion and are going on to accomplish definite activities.

The primary division of economic management are:

1. Capital market or markets for buying and selling different kinds of shares.
2. Money market or the market prevailing for buying and selling of currency
3. Banks and financial organisations.
4. Different types of financial enterprises big or small under the auspices of the state.
5. Government treasury and related controlling system.

Some common principles accompany this financial system. Works are accomplished in every case through the rules and principles of the country and in accordance with the ideals of development of the country. Thus, there are institutions for controlling the capital market their duty is only to frame up proper rules and laws to control these activities and applying the rules accordingly. There are many security-devices in the capital markets. The value of these securities is ascertained with respect to their demand and supply in common markets. Besides demand and supply there are many other important factors for fixing up values of these securities.

Thus, conducts of buyers and investors are to be specially considered. Conducts of buyers and investors depend on their mentality. For example some prefer temporary investment, some like long term investments and some again invest to become rich overnight. Thus, different investors have different types of intelligence. It is not that an investor is guided by his intelligence only, this propensity of investment depends on many others factors, like, relation between income and expenditure, financial forecast, structure and governance of the markets, etc.

Movement of money of the country happens through purchase and sell of equity shares or bands in the capital market. The main object of buying and selling of money is business and to keep the movement of money in different activities intact. In phase of movement the role of banks and financial organisations would act as the principal mediums. The role of financial organisations in movement of money is worthy of mention. Their duty is not only collection and investment, they also help increase the extent of investment. That is banks and other financial organisations are the supporting pillars of investment in many enterprises.

Programme and target decided by the government are applicable to the organisation under government enterprises. Among the programmes taken by the government enterprises mention may be made of those which are catered around social responsibilities. The programs of the organisation specified by the government are framed around the social responsibilities of the government in different cases. For this it is not always possible for these organisations to come out properly profitable in the market. In the long run a question mark is posed on the worthiness of such organisations.

They lag behind in the competition with other non government organisation and enterprises and ultimately become liabilities of the government. These are of course exception to this , for example there are some organisations even in government fields which have been much more efficient with respect to ability and proficiency of them the comparable non governments counterparts. The rise of this organisation has been due to technological and administrative efficiency. They have occupied special position even in the market. Government treasury has to bear the responsibility to maintain the government enterprises that have lagged behind in competition or been proved to be inefficient in the market.

Treasury procures finance from government activities; it moves the monetary value produced by the government and in many cases even controls the investing media.

Treasury procures money from government wealth for proper management of the vast family of the state and at the same time a big portion of this wealth is needed for supervision of the same. Treasury not only thinks of increasing financial development, its function is also to set up the balance of this increase within the state. That is the state itself would be flourished with riches and wealth. Treasury is intent on extending this ability further. So treasury has got the right of control over creation of wealth and printing of monetary notice and at the same time it has an overall control of the system of movement of money.

Economic Intelligence

How does treasury control the movement of money? Answers to this question are different for different writers. The reason is: there is no hard and fast structure of the management for control; there are many a structures. Each of the systems has some characteristic which are the essence of that controlling system. That is, if those are attended to control is right and proper. An aspect of financial control prevails everywhere in this world, in all the countries and that is economic intelligence,that is, a secret system for financial system. This financial secret service remains directly related with the treasury and the financial department. Some other departments are connected with it as well.

Revenue intelligence and banking ombudsmen or control over banking administration are some such departments. India has the Securities and Exchange Board of India; America has Securities and Exchange Commission. Function of these is control of capital market. Under their command is business intelligence or secret service for share management. Control of money market is vested in Reserve Bank of India and the control banks of respective countries.

Financial secret service keeps an eye on a number of matters. For example, for the government treasury this function is to fix up income tax, sales tax, wealth tax and other types of taxes and realisation of these. Treasury is filled through realisation of taxes. The more is the quota of taxes realised from different sources, the smother and more perfect becomes the management of state administration.

But the problems are, financial service system or financial supervision in whatever name we call these, these have not brought any flourish of efficiency in respect of financial irregularity in methods of tax-collection and tax management. The standard of efficiency is a continuity of the past. Efficiency flourishes in line with the continuity of the past. A bit of greater income, a bit more realisation of tax, a bit of improvement in management investment is taken to be the token of efficiency. The argumentative routes of carrying augmentation of efficiency or pushing it to a dignity limit are considered in respect of the past and one is contented with the same. If any state befalls a disaster for this, a long time is required to pass over the situation. On the part of the state or an organisation the period of passing over becomes rather too long.

Just as there was the object of development, so also there is the question of administrations with honesty and righteousness. Few recent examples catch glimpse of this. Collapse of big companies like Enron or WorldCom or financial and commercial disaster of different states clearly depict that present day financial and controlling system are not enough. On the financial disaster of the state, Peso-disaster of Mexico and Rouble-disaster of Russia in the the last centuries are subjects of thorough study. One very important point had been neglected right from the process of salary review of these disaster. This is the invisible standard of control.

All types of control have been in terms of visible standards. But the time is now ripe for everyone to look for the invisible control system. In case of American and Japanese financial, management this invisible control system has been rather parallel to the visible control system. Not only that, in the system of parallelism this visible and invisible system are working hard in the review of the financial institution and movement of money in the financial systems.

In spite of this there is maximum uncertainty in every case. What would be the price of Yen in respect to the dollar, or how the sale and purchase relation between them would rise and fall in the interim, an approval market Secret service might be active behind these. In every capital market there is a special group called market maker. Just as their market making keeps themselves busy in preventing anything abnormal in the market, but the more important activity is to procure advanced information of different directions and objects of the markets. This activity of procuring advanced information is a special duty of these market makers.

Methods applied here comprise of taking financial statistics to review the nature of the norms of purchase and practice of purchase of the buyer and to make proper assessment and decisions by surmising the future mode of the action of the government. Slides often befalls different capital markets. The market makers have not been able to stop that trend. What the market makers have succeeded in is to know the power and ability of the market through reviewing the steps one after another and to take action accordingly. But they have not been able to control those powers of different or opposing natures.

Kautilya's Proposal (as derived from the *Mahabharata*)

In *Arthashastra*, Kautilya demands special respect for-the management of economics for the state as a whole. If this management is applied in case of capital market banking and financial organisations, money market, cases of government enterprises and government treasury, unbelievably good result can be had there from.

Kautilya's economic diplomacy, as derived from the *Mahabharata*, can be divided in four phases. Every phase has got a theory behind it along with the principle of their application. The theories can be brought into shape through application. The divisions in Kautilya's theories may be as follows:

Kautilyan theory of economic diplomacy:

1. Conflict peace-conflict-victory theory.
2. Peace withdrawal-conflict-victory theory.
3. Application-withdrawal-application-rescue theory
4. Judgement of field and right theory.

Kautilya's *Arthashastra* has placed these theories in respect of backgrounds. For different backgrounds the forms of theories would be different for example, when the state has its own capability, the first phase for its financial expansion would be one of conflict. Conflict would be put up somehow. It would be made clear through conflict that solution is possible only by application of force. But the route of solution may be introduced only by application of force in the form of principle instead of application of full force. The same method may be applied in case of the companies. As for example strong measure is to be taken to realise unrealised taxes. In order to be efficient in realising extra taxes imposed on local and foreign companies the route of command is to be decided from the very beginning.

But the ultimate goal cannot be reached only through attack or conflict. The ultimate goal is to realise adequate amount of money. For this peace is to be purchased. Diplomacy would have its way. So just after monetary injunction dealing out of peace comes into the field. Peace is distributed through diplomacy. This situation is one of confidence. As a result of this instead of stretching hands for force, right money can be realised through compromise. Kautilya's proposal here is to recognize the weak point of the organisation or individual and to give a severe stroke on that weak point and this make the victory of a permanent measure, not just monetary.

The second theory for those who are enfeeble. Peace is to be bought at the very beginning through extension of diplomacy. It may be so that high price is to be paid for this, but still, it is essential. The reason being that the attempt for peace is for a victory in the future. It is applicable for comparatively weak government or weak organisation. Resort to diplomacy is required for attainment of peace in weak condition. That much money is to be procured through this path as is possible to be earned. Next is required apparent recession from the field that is, withdrawal. Withdrawal is the accumulation of power. Under such circumstances power is accumulated behind the eyes. In the long run conflict is required to achieve victory. Before world War-II the rise of Germany was primarily as eco-military power.

The background of rise of Hitler on state power had been created from financial disaster. At the severe shock of worldwide depression of 1929, the price of one American dollar jumped to one lakh eighty thousand. About half of the German labour power was unemployed, which equalled about sixty lakh people. At the initiation Hitler resorted to his own usual path of peace. Completely vegetarian as he was, he did never take any salary-he donated his salary to the labourer welfare fund. He even donated about 20 lakh dollars, the royalty of his renowned book "Mein Kampf or My struggle". He had bought the massages of peace at the very beginning in the financial administration. As a result of this extended co-operation generated from within the country in course of a short spell of time. Unemployment reduced rather drastically, -within three years the number reduced to 10 lakh and just before the War there was shortage of labourer, that is a market without unemployment. There was the seed of war in the very background of peace. Proper provision of victory in War come in his possession with this financial peace. Few American Banks like, Morgan Stanley also applied this principle. Initially there is a touch of peace for expansion of business and later wide phase of undertaking. In India also sometime back Hindus spent their lives under the direction of Mr. S.H. Dutta, and had taken up the same principle for a period of time, and become successful.

That is why in case of application of the theories of Kautilya consideration of the perspective is very important. If there is a blunder in judgement of the perspective, this theory can bring disaster, but if it is correct amazingly novel development may be brought in.

40

War Economy

Fund for War

History of war is very old. War was there at the beginning of human history; it was there in the middle and will also be ther at the end. Continuously there is war. It is very hard to find a time without war. War is there in between two countries, war is there even without the country. There are beckoning of reasons behind the trumpet call of war, constantly something all over the different types of war. Different countries may be engaged in the same war, at the same time in the same country war can bring different types of troubles; similarly multidimensional problems may arise under the influence of war or avenues of newer possibilities may open up.

War brings death and horror. Under the influence of war, a great number of people will lose their lives, at the same time in post war situations, epidemic, long term obstruction and devastation and confused condition may befall them. Beginning and end of war brings great agitation inside the society. Heat generated in the beginning of war casts influence on many fields.

Spread of the destructive effects of war casts widespread consequences. Inimitableness of war brings in many possibilities even within widespread destruction and slaughter. Thus, as a result of war the infertile financial phase begins to be freed from traps. War carries with it ideas of newer technologies and applications thereof. Even during a war newer researches and ideas of development get created. Newer researches and technology lend a newer dimension to war.

The Effect of War

As war carries danger with it, so also it brings a number of new possibilities. It is due to war that many field of financial development move towards newer possibilities. War begets revolution of technology. At a stroke, avenue for forward movement opens up due to war.

The dreadful sight in modern war far surpasses the horrible slaughters of the war in older times. In spite of that the extent of great actions going on in the name of war is undeniable. Kautilya's *Arthashastra* has discussed war economy in many ways and from different angles. The first methods adopted by the *Arthashastra* in this respect is to classify the activities of war according to their nature. Next step is to review the topic in different ways in each class.

Kautilya has laid stress on war for multiple reasons: One, war is inevitable, so it is better to face it than to avoid the same. Second if the preparedness for victory in war can be accepted correctly, financial distribution of many other things would be formed. If preparation for war starts as advancement takes place towards protection of the state so also its benefit would come from other sources as well. While discussing preparation of war Kautilya has introduced two topics specifically.

These are human powers appropriate for war and equipments and ordinance for war. According to Kautilya ordinance is important no doubt, but still more important is the act of arming oneself and deployment of persons for administration and application.

Kautilya has vividly discussed standard of quality, mentality, character and loyalty of a solider. This discussion has occupied a large portion of the *Arthashastra*. Kautilya has paid special attention to the facts of how a soldier should be, what should be the traits of the characters of a solider to make him useful for the state, how the standard of soldiers can be improved and the like. Collection of different of information becomes essential to assess the real situation at the time of preparation for war and the time of war. Preparation for war not only essential for going into war; accumulation of power and to be fitting through application of power are required for preventing the invader and to avoid the inimitableness of war.

The *Arthashastra* has considered different aspects of war and this has imparted different types of advices for it. After proper judgement Kautilya has found that a state should always judge the real situation to come to the conclusion who is loyal to the state and who is against it. Those who are loyal are to be prepared properly for war. The management of defence of the state is to be made sound by decrying the loyal persons in different posts. Kautilya has liked to associate war economy with the political economy of a state so the state can be benefited. War has many far-reaching aspects for example the associated production and distribution systems. The most mentionable are the following points which have been specially emphasised by Kautilya in his vivid discussion on war economy.

- Appointment in army and allied forces. Training of army and the others
- Production of war-equipments and testing of their quality
- Distribution to avoid shortage of these war-equipment in different regions.
- Introduction of war news system and administration. Accumulation of proper provisions for war and preparation periods
- Transport system for war and its management
- Prescription for mental satisfaction of army and the allies.

Appointment and Training

Kautilya has securitized the context of appointment and training with utmost caution. At the very beginning he has judged the fitness of a soldier. That person would be describing for the defense of the state only when his attitude is proper in respect to the state. For one who is loyal to some other country or to the enemy of the state it is not at all possible to become an ideal soldier and would not be appointed as a soldier if one has minimum connection with the opponents of the state or has any connection in the list with the opposition of the state.

In case of training, Kautilya has laid stress on two factors. The first one is technique and the other is loyalty. Of course, the *Arthashastra* has discussed loyalty with the greatest importance. Army and concerned people remain like a very important power of the state till their loyalty are beyond any question. If loyalty be in question it is detrimental to the state as enemy power. That is why Kautilya wanted loyalty beyond any question. If such soldiers who have loyalty or healthy build are contacted and are appointed or trained, it not only poses a problem to the defence of a state but also casts a harmful effect on the economic system of the same. The mailer is very important, so much so that building up and making effective of a secret service with great expense becomes needful.

Another responsibility of the state is production of ordinance and to keep up a control over its standard. In comparison with the vividness of discussion in the Arhashastra on the principle of commending a war that on production of ordinance and keeping up of its standard in rather less. But Kautilya is very careful about the control on the standard and. The *Arthashastra* has looked upon the subject from the stand point of sovereignty and financial profit and loss. Kautilya has paid attention to the distribution of war equipments and storage of the same in different regions.

Many types of possibilities of war have cropped up in his discussion. For example, if there is in any part of the state, activities against the state, then war might be inevitable there. Prior preparedness is required for victory in a war. So in case of making plans deep in sight as to where war might happen is to be thought of. Preparation should be in accordance with that plan. Preparation for war outside the state would be required to combat the probable neighbouring economics. For this Kautilya has uttered special precautions.

Gaining power of a neighbour, friend or foe is always dangerous. That is why Kautilya has insisted on collection of detailed information of the war-power of the neighbours irrespective of the fact whether they are friends or foes. Kautilya has vividly discussed where, as a result, war-equipments are to be stored and in what amount and what would be the financial liability for this. Keeping in mind the necessity of different resources the standard of war equipment for that region, quantity thereof and the duration of storage are to be ascertained. For this Kautilya has openly brought in the context of expenditure for materialising the management. Discussion is also there on the consequence of each arrangement if not accompanied through the controlling principle.

Collection of information is very important in any type of war. The methods of collection of information may often be very dangerous. Specially in case of collection of information from the enemy camp danger of the collector may go to any extent. Sometimes the expense in relation to danger is reasonable and sometimes it is abnormal. Whatever may be the expense the work of collection of information should be kept up uninterrupted. Kautilya has enumerated different ways for collection of information. The *Arthashastra* has discussed different aspects of the subject. The *Arthashastra* has brought into discussion some aspects of the subject with importance, such as proper attention is to be paid on different aspects of activities and movements of provable enemies; how they have prepared themselves.

What are the numbers of weapons and soldiers and what is the distribution thereof: this information is to be collected, how they are moving on in different fields is very important? Information at a certain instant would not do, it is necessary to have constant flow of information. Kautilya has designated that the basis of any information is to be correct. That what is had as information should have dependability. Otherwise, all of the action taken on the basis of such information would be futile.

For getting true information truthful loyalty of the server of information is required. Kautilya has asserted that and taking action on the basis of information served by such person's appointment in such posts without taking tests of loyalty may invite disaster. The enemy camp may be assured to be always prompt in this respect. So, first step of success in collection of information is selection of collectors of information. In this subject Kautilya has said of the necessity of collectors of more than one tier. If there be any defect or wicked motive in collection of news in easy term, it would be mended in the mind. Thus, if there is arrangement of collecting information with another, side by side, then the authenticity of the information can easily be ascertained through comparison. Sinister motive, if any, of a collection of information would also get detected.

For war are important equipments like ordinance, similarly important are the provisions necessary for war. Arrangement of all types of provisions for army and its allies is a must for states. In this arrangement on one side the state in landed into a state of huge expenses, so also at the same time it casts influence on the productive power of which in its turn causes augmentation of production. Under such circumstances there is direct influence on the economy of the country. Creation of provisions for war and its supply constitutes an extensive network of actions. Its expansion helps much in moving through financial crisis.

There may be many reasons behind financial crisis of a country like decrease in agricultural and industrial production. Crisis in world markets, political unrest and natural calamity. In case of financial crisis, different measures may be taken for the remedy. Preparations for war and supply and procurement of provisions among its allies at war times are able to give speed to the economy of the country. Extension of this provision increases movement of money, and consequently buying capacity increases. Kautilya has insisted on being prepared in all respects for all eventualities. The king who is able to gather power and thus integrate the same would be respected by others. Even if there are many enemies, no one would attack him so easily. Initiatives like procurement and storing of provisions casts and enormous influence on the different aspects of the people. The system for his control is connected with many factors, like the management systems of movement and the mentality regarding commodities among the common people and also of those under the control of the government for movement and distribution. As a result of this the state can understand correctly the matters that influence it and its ideas directly, and this administration and control of the state may be beneficial to the people. Kautilya has insisted on being very scrupulous in regarding the subject. As a consequence, its influence on the financial system would be beneficial.

Transport activities of war are an extensive enterprise. Just like provisions, its role is also far-extended. Proper management for supervision on the personals connected with the system by the state is required. The *Arthashastra* has considered with much importance this system of supervision as a result of which amenities for war can be transported in time in proper spots. The *Arthashastra* likes to have efficient planning and communication in this matter. To set up correct communication is very important. Kautilya has all along considered with utmost importance the mutual coordination in financial systems. If this system is correctly managed, its direct influence is sure to come there in the financial condition of the country. Through discussion of their subject the *Arthashastra* has judged the capability of getting the financial benefit of every activity and to congregate them to spread the benefit. As a result of this the financial benefit will spread clearly, far and wide.

At the role of the financial benefit are the considerations of the mental state of a person. Involved in all the fields, Considering the mental state one can ascertain to what extent the country would be benefitted by the work of a particular person. The context of the mental state is very important. If the mental state is stable, two people engaged in the same work will be able to help the state grow identically. If the mentality is against the state, then the influence of their work would be detrimental to the state instead. Of the different training matters the *Arthashastra* has dealt with, the matter of causing mental satisfaction of the person engaged in working for the country is important. Besides army and its allies, the *Arthashastra* has said of making also the lay person engaged in conducting war, manufacture of equipments necessary for war, etc. to be helpful for the state to try to build them up in the form of a power conducive to the state. Considering the nature of emphasis, One would easily comprehend that to Kautilya more importance has been received by the matter whichever makes the state stronger, increases the ability of a standard cause that results in the overall good of the state. Kautilya has made a note of the all the characteristics of a state and its ruler than help in conditions of war.

Bijigisuh atmanah parasya ca balah
Abalam
Saktih desa kalayatra akalah badah
Samuhan akalah.
Pancat kopa aksaya abyaya labhapadam
Jnatvah
Bisista balau, anyetha tat asit.

(*Arthashastra*, 9/1/1)

[One is to judge through experimentation who is strong and who is weak, where and when the opponent is definitely stronger and when the superiority of the capability is permanently stable- with such ideas further steps are to be taken]

Utsahah prabhabat utsahaha sreyan. (*Arthashastra*, 9/1/2)

[Of the power of inspiration and power of war the former is definitely superior.]

Svayam hi raja surau balaban orogah
Krta sa strauh dandah dvitiya api saktah
Prabhababantantam rajan jetum.

(*Arthashastra*, 9/1/3)

[If a king is inspired, bold and at the same time ready to face any disease, he cannot be defeated by some other king who is more powerful but not that much inspired.]

Alpha api ca anye dandah
Tejasya krtakaram bhabati

(*Arthashastra*, 9/1/4)

[A vigorous king, though deficient in ability and power, gets victory by dint of his vigours.]

Nirytsahah tu prabhababan rajah
Bikrama abhipannau nasyati, iti acargah

(Arhthasastra, 9/1/5)

[Even if a king, lacking in incitation, is powerful, he gets defeated by some other king who is weaker but flourished with inspiration.]

No iti Kautilyah.
Prabhababan atisamdhantam ta
Visistamanyah
Rajaham abahya bhrtva kritva
Prabinapurusan.

(*Arthashastra*, 9/1/6-7)

[As Kautilya says, a powerful king by virtue of the force of his power can hire or deploy deserving warriors full of energy from elsewhere and can defeat weaker kings.]

Ebam gtsahah prabhabah mantrasaktinam
Uttarit uttaradhikau iti samdhante. (*Arthashastra*, 9/1/16)

[A king who is thus filled with inspirational power, moral power or power of mantra can defeat other kings.]

Desah prthibi
Tasyam himabat samudrah antaram
Udicinam
Yojanam sahasrah parimanam
Tiryaka cakravartikseterm.

(*Arthashastra*, 9/1/17-18)

[The whole world is to be made one's country. There would lie a plain ranging from the Himalayas down to the sea; there are also transverse lands and desert like one. Resources are to be created here and this is the success of war in case of a mighty emperor]

In case of war-economy Kautilya has emphasized on the occupying of proper fields for creating resources. His advice is to specially to make use of wide lands and to set up such measures there as to have proper number of provisions.

Kautilya has noticed certain useful things for war. Firstly, one must have capability. A state has to accumulate power. In the leadership of a powerful state there should be inspiration full of vigour and that must be accompanied by a power of mantra i.e spirituality which would move the state ahead. Combination of these three would turn a state into a great power and only such a power can be victorious. Why should a state be eager to be victorious? A state would be victorious for creating resources. Success would appear crossing over the financial burden caused by war. Kautilya has called for war for firm establishment of the spiritual power. He wanted a state to be engaged in war for spiritual power. And as a result of that the economic process for flourishing of life would be hastened as well. War is not for the sake of war, it is for life.

41
War Trade

Rationale Of War

War carries with it destruction, so also roots of creation. The seed of new creation remains dormant in destruction. Much money is required for war. A war leads to extensive loss of money. Such is our attitude towards war. War causes great human devastation on all sides. It takes away lives, it destructs the environment, it causes extinction of wealth or causes war of resources. The horrible and dreadful idea of war is generally over spread. Extinction of money, wealth and lives that is the account of the effects of war. But, war has the capacity to engage the roots of a newer rise.

Kautilya has furnished vivid extension of war. The reason behind this explanation in the *Arthashastra* is to warn the state of the equipments and methods needed for war and to make the state properly equipped for this side by side with the presentation of a detailed explanation of war. The *Arthashastra* has well raised the economic side of the matter. Alongside these, one may consider the plays and endeavour of war as presented in the *Arthashastra* in the perspective of war-trade.

The main theme of war-trade is to gain profit through war. Profits gained through war are manifold. In the hints provided by Kautilya about war economics he has also given special importance on the financial side of the subjects along with the means of making the object of war successful. Kautilya has given clear opinion on the important subjects in respect to the financial side of war. The *Arthashastra* has tried to make clear that war can open a new horizon to a state. Kautilya is against war-trade. But he has insisted on perfect preparedness of war within the scope of indomitableness of war.

In providing an attitude of war-economy, Kautilya has given the stress on the process of war for victory. He has asserted that victory is not attainable without a strong will. Without will winning victory is hardly possible. Kautilya has explained that war can be waged in two ways: one was that has been forced up a state; two, the war that has been contemplated. Financial benefit for a war that has been forced upon is possible only when there is enough prearrangement. And the success of a war that despite being well planned and well-contemplated, depends on the rightness of planning and the capability for war.

War for Victory

Kautilya has prescribed many a preparation for making victory inevitable and creation. The *Arthashastra* has specially insisted on lacking too many endeavours for being victorious in war. According to the *Arthashastra* the resource behind war must be made clear to all. Why the war would be waged; why war could not be avoided; why proper leadership must be there with them in a strong grip; all these are parts of the war preparation. Step to be victorious is to turn up as warriors. Kautilya has placed much importance on soldiers throughout all the phases of war. The greatest importance associated with the tactics and qualities of warriors are their mentality of endeavour and earnestness. If a warrior is not properly earnest, then in spite of preparedness the affair would not be fulfilled. Kautilya has advised the head of the state to inspire the soldiers properly through detailed discussion and clarification. Gaining inspiration in warfare begets victory in the war.

Kautilya's assertion in the *Arthashastra* is to tail war and to get its result and direction under the control of the state. As a result of this when a state would innovate for war it will be able to earn wealth properly in exchange of war. If the result of war culminates in continuous victory, a thought of valour would be raised in the soldiers. Kautilya has asserted that this air of valour is not only required for victory in the war it is also very much useful in increasing power of reconstruction of the state. If the state becomes powerful and everything required for war victory is present therein , other states would not take decisions against this state. Different factors become dominant in case of a powerful state e.g. military power, financial power. Intellectual power and power of leadership. For a state to become powerful it has to earn power in every aspect.

Kautilya has done a detailed discussion on war with some specific targets. The first one is overall preparation for war. If a state remains indifferent of war, these is full possibility of it to be burnt in the flame of war from within. War as it were, has been captured in the invisibleness of the life of the state. Kautilya has wanted to ensure that victory through combination of overall preparation for war and strong desire to win. This result in a craze in the state for procuring and storing power.

Power is to be procured and stored from the resources prevailing in the state. Though initially procuring of power from the resources within the state is possible but gradually its probability decreases Kautilya has advised to use the periphery of the state to procure resources from. As the territories conquered through war come within the command of the state so also do the residents therein. Kautilya has advised the state to be sympathetic and powerful as well. Who is powerful may be sympathetic. Kautilya has advised the state to have all hurdles on the way of being powerful to be removed. In the respective of war, a state exhibits power and at the same time generally procures and stores evenly.

Man brings opportunity of experimentation to the arena of war. The atmosphere of war brings inspiration and enthusiasm. If the direction and effectiveness of war becomes correct, sort of enthusiasm comes to the mind of the people. An example may be cited as war or struggle for freedom. War for freedom has a good number of significances. Being involved in struggle for freedom a person not only strengthens the power of the state but also causes the flourishing of individuals. At the time of struggle this flourish of power casts influence on all wings of life. This influence falls on literature, arts, science, technology, religion, philosophy etc. -all fields of life.

Background of Liberty

War for liberty brings about a flow of flourish. The possibilities that are lying dormant in men gradually wake up. Anything latent tries to be exposed. An artist builds up newer art with his genius, new techniques also grow. A literature presents new literature, the invocation of a newer life, a dye-breaking wave of newer thoughts; he brings in eager inauguration of new type of consciousness. Thoughts and research of a scientist now get merged in a whirl within his illuminating flow of eager genius and goes on beckoning, with renewed zeal, new creations. New sayings of manifesto wake up in the domain of thoughts of the scientists. And these sayings of manifestation means for war the flow of manifestation of thoughts. So, to the scientist it appears as a unique sensation. He gets engaged in deliverance of the news of unique discoveries which move the human civilization ahead towards a new domain, hails the instinct of awakening of the new.

The wakeful conscience of a scientist is the basis of new discovery. The force of inspiration in him lays out in the form of provisions of new discoveries. A scientist getting on the chariot of his discovery moves ahead the great vehicle of civilization. The inspiration for liberty gets bloomed in a scientist in the scientific domain in the form of scientific terminology.

The environment of freedom movement comes a fall in life. Transformation appears in the economic background of the state. Prevalent financial favours that had so long been enjoyed by some people of groups may get lost. In the country a new financial bondage grows up. Many rises and falls may occur in the scope of new financial distribution. In the backdrop of war economy, construction and destruction become natural. Extensive changes may come within the people of the society.

Extensive investment for high expenditure in war and its allied fields increases the possibility of employment. War makes this employment process either short-term or long-term. War-time recruitment in army directly increases the employment process. Besides there is scope of employment in supply of commodities, supply of weapons, building up of infrastructure required for war. At war-time many an imposition is laid on movement and demand or necessity of commodities in common market. So, in this very backdrop of war extensive change crops in prices of commodities of the market. Somewhere price get raised due to extensive deficit; somewhere price soars up without deficit but by the influence of common indices of the market. Just as wealth of the rich slips out of the grip during a war, so also at war times new groups of rich people may appear.

Financial System Influenced by War

War brings a great stir in the financial system. That is why post-war reconstruction becomes important in case of different states. Post-war reconstruction is to be accomplished with the inspiration and enthusiasm of the war. If this work is accomplished through the inspiration of war time, injury of war is not only removed but in the state economy also new thoughts come in and new awakening starts. At this time coordination is more important than contentment. If coordination begins to come up from all the spheres of the society economic upraise becomes very smooth, easy and facile. Awakening becomes easy where labourers, directors, owners, social-workers, educationists, state-workers, artists, litterateurs, scientists, technologists and intellectuals, all get engaged to work in a concerted manner. Relatives of the victims of war become distressed and they may be offended with the state or may be filled with pride of labour. If offence is replaced by pride, then and then only state would be able expect much coordination from such people.

Coordination is required for upliftment, coordination of many people. While composing principles of war Kautilya has laid stress on coordinating attitude of people. Through war a state may be profited in different ways, if it gets a taste of victory. And extensive change may come in the post-war financial distribution if during that period full and active coordination comes from the people.

Reformation of financial distribution is not possible only by the ability of state. Power and ability of a state are quite important in this case no doubt but it is not within the range of sole capability and power of the state. What is required here is thinking for the state in a big multitude of people on human thoughts within a greater periphery the seed of coordination lies in the national thoughts. People may be cooperative in all works of the state if they become pleased with state enterprises and activities and if they can hold the same opinion with the state. And cooperation of a big multitude of people is the sole principle of the rise of a state.

That is why Kautilya has mentioned war with utmost care. Whether there is likeness of opinion and coordination is to be the judge of the outcome. That is, Kautilya has tried to estimate the measures of support for the contemplated war from the army, suppliers, producer of weapons and common people. In the period of preparation for a war Kautilya has laid the greatest importance on the attitude of the people connected directly or indirectly with war affairs. If the attitude is coordinating, success in the war affairs becomes more likely.

Thorough and Comprehensive Victory

The victory in a war which has with it coordination of all, and behind which there is a definite principle, brings wide change in the economy of the state. As a result of war comes a thrilling sense of work, production gets into motion. It is not so that production gets a temporary boost, the new line remains unperturbed if the eagerness of the state remains. Through the virulence of war newer change come to the financial capability of a state. The capability on the part of a state to enterprise in financial matters becomes multiplied. The experience of war begets the call of newer enterprises in the public. This is to advance to a great extent within a short span of time that is, war brings the possibility of many kinds of enterprises with a small capital and in a short span of time. Kautilya has wanted the right application of the same in financial upliftment in the background of invisibleness of war.

History also teaches this. History has shown the preparation for world war had brought extensive external changes in human civilization in later period. Change came in the outlook of living and moving forward. Since World War II waves of changes have struck human societies. The first change has come in the outlook of living. The primary call for life has been victorious. Commerce has come forward to strengthen the needs of life. Commerce is the underlying truth in everything. Moves for all activities are taken after thorough calculation. If calculation goes against something then that work is not undertaken. Life of idealism and values has moved at the back.

Commerce has gained so much prominence that specific instruction are inspired in research work only on the basis of the possible results obtained. Investment in a scientific discovery, however inspiring it may seem to be, would be hampered if there is no sale value in the market. Profit and loss of the traders are to be there in the artwork of artists also. If profit does not come through artistry, it will not be indulged in. If procuring learning is only for an acquiring knowledge, society of family will not have any support for the same. The aim of procuring learning would only be to have money. If there is no return of money, learning would be decreased. Mutual accounting of profit and loss is very important even in the distribution of human relations. The basis of human relations would be said if it is apprehended that it would get profit in the long run.

Kautilya has not liked war for war's sake or for the sake of commercial interest. He had lived a life of deep wisdom which is full of profound dependence on God, but possessed proper outlook absent in the outer world. War is inevitable so it is necessary to be prepared properly for war. As a result, instead of a dreadful consequence of defeat an unadulterated pleasure of victory would come. The whole world is to be conquered. All the hurdles on the way of life are to be conquered, war is outside of a man and also within. Kautilya has insisted on the application of inculcation of Vedic knowledge and application of the same for the war within an individual. For external war he has prescribed weapons, soldiers and competition of other arrangements. One has to be victories in both the war within and war of the state outside. To be victories one should be powerful. Through internal war power of honour, power of life would infiltrate an individual and national war would add on them intellectual and physical power. Financial management for maintenance of the triumphant warrior has a long-term position and its movement is directed everywhere. It carries with it the message of newer life.

42

Economy of Disaster: Disaster of Economic System

Hints of Disaster

Economic disaster sometimes comes suddenly or sometimes appears with a proper notice. When one disaster comes the very form of it, its nature and movement and the possible state of the final consequence can be approach end to end.

Disaster brings havoc. Country, society, the basis of economy, everything gets ruined. Everything becomes topsy-turvy at the shock of disaster. Even if disaster comes prior notice, it becomes unbearable in many cases. The common nature of disaster spells continuity, one after another. When a disaster brings a stream of destruction, a newer wealth of experience grows out of the blazing fire of the devastation. This experience becomes very important in post-war reconstruction. The power of combatting a disaster comes from the disaster itself. One disaster gets the power to combat impending disasters.

As disaster brings ruin, it also brings possibility and opportunity. The shock of disaster makes one understand the beating influence of the same.

There is even a distinctive meaning of disaster. Structures fall down in storms, planned forests get exhausted, old and big trees get uprooted. In its midst emerge newer creations. New trees get lives. The old, fallen, bored get possibilities of awakening and inauguration of the new structures ruined at the strike of tempest again reaches the gate of new possibility. All older resources come forward in the form of a new appearance, the old become expressive of the new.

In disaster all the resources get new life to bloom. The old comes forward and gets engaged with the new in creation and extension. This is an overall endeavour of the old to be new.

Just as disaster brings in nature the possibility of the new, so also it gets a transformation in the financial management. With a possible disaster in view, it remains a transformable position of inspiration. The detailed preparation required for transformation of financial management is quite readily available through preparations against disaster. And a financial management devoid of preparation is reviled as ruinous.

The financial management planned with the possibility of disaster in view have embedded in them the power to change or to be changed. Kautilya has presented this fact. He opines that disaster may befall at any moment. So, it is very important to judge the different aspects of the disaster. It is to be clearly understood how disaster comes and what is to be done when it comes and also which one is to be controlled in what way and so on.

A new power emerges through disaster. Many organisations of people lie in wait to take advantage. As soon as disaster appears they all jump out. They aim at gaining something from the disaster. The advantages they aim at are all transient, instant and temporary.

There are even cases where plans to incur disaster is there and in majority of those terms the target fixed is to earn profit from the disaster. In other words, there are not only direct and indirect attempts to create disaster for others but also investment made for the explicit purpose. But investment here cannot be direct, so the investor has to remain controlled with indirect investment.

Indirect investment may be made in a number of ways, like, War, obstruction, natural hindrances, causing interruption in production through striking are some processes for it. Terrorism causing loss of wealth and lives may also be included. Besides there are topsy-turvy situations caused by natural calamities. Many people wait to benefit even through natural disaster.

Rise from Disaster

Power of life and awakening remains dormant in destruction. Planned disaster of course does not have such power. For these planned disasters lack balance. In such disaster there remains no ability to rise up, on the contrary citizens become upset at the sudden stroke of such disasters. But still different kinds of provision grow up from this type of disaster. While discussing possibilities of disaster Kautilya's *Arthashastra* has kept in mind the inimitableness of this type of disaster.

The economic principle and arrangement described in the *Arthashastra* is a total phenomenon. There almost all fields of life and financial management have been brought under discussion. Economics is not just confined in the produces of factories, agriculture or movement of money. Kayutilya has spread economic management in all of the active principles of life.

Whatever is essential for life, whatever instinctive tour and connected with other natural activities are related with economic and economic system. Kautilya has brought in many such subjects in the purview of economic management which apparently do not belong to the domain of economy. So for the true foundation of economic system, its example and its evaluation all of the cases of a natural life are useful.

Thus, in the economic philosophy of Kautiulya war, disaster and the like have been part of economic discussion. Commonly accounts of incidents subsequent to war or disaster are made. Taking the disaster of war to be inevitable Kautilya has attempted to coordinate the good effect of the same with the economic management. As a result of this Kautilya's *Arthashastra* is continually attentive to bringing all activities of life distributed in accordance with a certain principle. All types of plans should be indispensable to the economy that cares for the possibility of disaster. Ruinous effects may befall a planned economic system due to many reasons.

Disaster in economy is caused by many things, for example, that distorted effect of the movement of money can upset this system. That is if pervading strikes come in the movement of money, its far- reaching effect would be indispensable, disasters striking on the system of production would hasten economic disaster,, disturbing sabotage within the economy, terrorist attack of striking on the production and distribution system under the influence of foreign or opposition power, etc. may bring in financial disaster.

For the countries which remain dependent on foreign trades or trades outside the country or a foreign capital, may be rather dangerous on the part of the financial situation. Sudden changes in the international currency system may bring change on the environment and management of investment and management of many of the countries concerned. It levels a strike on the economy of dependent countries. If dependence of the country on another be high, the strike becomes rather ruinous. During last few decades this type of great international ruinous effect has befallen the fate of many countries.

Another new aspect has been dominant in modern age- it aims at getting money or other resource at the centre of all plans, activities and connecting links of life. That is, the mentality of trading is at the root of all activities. The target of this mentality is to earn profit from all events of life catering at the trading mentality through integrated efforts and endeavours. Attempt for earning profit entered at disaster are designed keeping in mind the human side of disaster. When such a period of disaster continues in a country the persons desirous of earning profit from disaster come from other countries, get entangled in facing disaster and human activities related with disaster or post-disaster organisational opportunities to satisfy their own interests. In such cases traitors within the country become their intimate associates.

Judgement of the *Arthashastra*

Kautilya has laid too much importance on this subject. He has advised utmost and well thought out decisions to be taken against these traitors. Kautilya has liked to judge the cases where the disaster mongers might be active and the types of disaster they are likely to commit. Kautilya has judge among different professions and vocations to find which class of the people are honestly affected. Judging thus he has discussed and shown that the effect of the disaster-managers may be ruinous to the people of some professions. In such disaster Kautilya has classified into providential and human disasters to make the same simple.

Daivapididanam- agnihudakambyadhih
Durbhiksammadakahiti. (*Arthashastra*, 8/4/4)

[Conflagration, flood, morbidity famine, epidemic-this fall under the class of providential rage.]

Kautilya could not agree with the earlier mentors in respect of providential torment on rage of conflagration and flood. The earlier mentors had thought the former to be more important. According to them consequence of conflagration is irrevocable. Articles reduced to ashes by fire can never be got back. On the contrary Kautilya opines that when judged in respect of the havoc created, flood is far more damaging.

So utmost care is to be taken against flood.

Agnihgramamardhagramambadhati
Udakabegastugramahsataprabahoti

(*Arthashastra*, 8/4/4/)

[Conflagration can blaze one village or half of one. On the contrary virulence of flood may affects hundreds of villages]

Comparing between morbidity and famine the earlier mentors have given more importance to morbidity. But Kautilya has attributed more importance on famine

Ekadesapidanaaubyadhihsakyapratikarah ca
Sarbadesapidanamdurbhiksampraninamah Jivanayanti

(*Arthashastra*, 8/4/8)

[Morbidity can cast its virulence on a portion of a land but that of famine can extended far and may causethe end of the lives of many.]

Kautilya could not agree with his predecessors in respect to epidemic either. Earlier leadership considered epidemic to not be as harmful as common people because those in the leadership can provide relief work. Kautilya has opined otherwise, however. According to him if epidemic touches the leadership, the consequence may prove dreadful to the country. Common people are many in number but persons in the leadership are few. So, if a void comes in the leadership, it would be dreadful on the part of safeties of the whole country so carefulness in this line is very important.

Sakyahksudrakaksayahpratisamdhatum
Bahulyatksudrakaram
Sahasresu hi mukhyaubhakatiekaunabai
Satvaprjnahadhikyat tat asrayatbai
Ksudrakarnamiti

(*Arthashastra* 8/4/11-12)

[Post epidemic consequence in case of common people may be brought under control because they are many in number. But the number of chief officers is rather low, even less than one per thousand. So common people remain dependent on these officers with an intention to be guided by their instinctive knowledge and wisdom.]

Kautilya has judged consciously the dangers of uprising within the country of one's own and foreign invasion. His advice is to be on one's guard first against foreign powers. If there is any association of the any foreign power within the country, it is to be uprooted. If there is any possibility of anti-national uprising within the country, it also is to be destroyed from the roots. For these the person wielding the sceptre would have to be self-denying, conversant of the state, compassionate to the people, in short virtue would be a friend of the people in leadership, as indulging in amusement and recreation is very much detrimental to the interest of the state. The state is to be careful about this. Excessive amusement and recreation of the leadership is dangerous for the state.

Kautilya has liked the leadership to refrain from these, otherwise disasters would engulf the state.

Desabiharahkarmahsramahabadhartham
Ampambhaksayati
Bhaksaitva ca bhuyahkarmasuyogam
Gacchati
Rajabiharahtusvayamballavesca
Svayamgraha
Pranayahpanyagarakaryaupagraheh Pidayatiiti

(*Arthashastra*, 8/4/23)

If state leadership indulges in amusement, his charge would be captured and this would cause much trouble to the public. On the other hand if common people get absorbed in amusement, eagerness and enthusiasm in their respective activities would increase. As a result, there would be improvement in qualities of activities.]

People are to be quite bouyant in pleasure. It would be possible if their immediate and future requirements are satisfied and they can spend their lives easily being free of any burden of the minds, Kautilya wants such people to be citizens of a state. All would be merged in pleasure and drenched in amusement, but would contently engage as workers of the state. But leadership of a country would have to be watchful.

Their duty would be to keep careful watch on all matters and to assure fully the security of the state. People establishment in leadership would forget their own happiness, comfort, amusement and recreation and be absorbed in the interest of the state. State authority would have to pay fullest attention to the matter of security of the state and happiness of the people and overall advancement in economic and social affairs.

State is, therefore, to look specifically after certain affairs: firstly. manage the job of the boundary-guards; secondly, to keep watch on the trader community so that they cannot do any detestable job, so that traders in greed of excessive profit do not raise abnormally the prices necessary commodities.

> Artahpalapanyasampatanugrahenabartayati
> Vaidehakahtusambhuyapanyanam
> Utkarsa-apakersa Kurbanah pane panasatam
> Kumbhekumbhasatamitiajibanti.
>
> (*Arthashastra*, 8/4/36)

[Boundary-guards may help illegal movement of commodities with special favour from outside or even abroad. Worse disaster many befall owing to sale of commodities at price increased some hundred folds by dishonest traders.]

Economy of Justice

Kautilya has advised to move with utmost precaution with price of commodities inside the country. Inflation takes place in the country owing to price index upset by dishonest traders. Poor and insolvent people are worst affected in this situation. Kautilya has taken this situation to be utterly upsetting and has advised to avoid this. That is why Kautilya has suggested having control over dishonest traders and advise the state in this tune. He has undertaken judgement of this from the standpoint of state treasury and financial solvency of the people.

> Abhyantarahmukhyastambhaubahyah
> Amitratbaistambhah
>
> (*Arthashastra*, 8/4/48)

[Disaster is as likely to come from any chief or authoritative person inside the state or firm, as from someone from outside the state economy.]

Kautilya has always advised a state to be alert for the office-bearers. Connection of the office-bearers with man-made disasters is very likely. Man-made disaster cannot be brought into effect without undesirable collaboration of the office-bearers. Dishonourable traders often causes abnormal hikes in the price of commodities-here also there is unholy connection with the office-bearers.

Pidananamanutpattahbyutpattanam
Ca barane
Yaetatdesabrtarthamnasau ca
Stambhasangayauh

(*Arthashastra*, 8/4/50)

[State leadership has to, very carefully, combat the disaster or face the same. Man-made disaster is to be removed to the very root so that these are uprooted completely.]

Kautilya has judged disaster in two ways. One, natural or providential disaster and two man-made disasters. Kautilya opines: -if the state authority goes on working honesty, devotedly and selflessly for the state and its people, then there would be no chance to effect natural disaster or providential rage. Dishonest, characterless, self-seeking leaders of a state continuously accumulate vices for themselves and the state. Their collected vice summons natural providential disasters. Kautilya has therefore, all along advised running the administration of a state on the basis of truth and justice. The chance for a state run by truth and justice to face providential disaster is rather reduced.

On the other hand, Kautilya has advised the state to be stern in respect of man-made disaster. This stern attitude should be there from the very beginning. Anybody in the state trying to commit treason against the state is to be pointed out and destroyed at the root.

Both natural and man-made disaster strikes at government treasury or wealth of the state. If there is prior indication of impending disaster the state would promptly have to take preparation so that the blow does not fall on the economic situation of the country. The capability to face the disaster grows from within the state. As a result, it would be natural for governments and transformations to appear in the economic situation. If movement occupies the economic situation transformation is evitable. That is instead of a stand-still there would be advancement of few steps. For this state leadership should be proficient in spiritual learning. By the leadership grown through self-denial, truth, justice and devotion, it is possible for the state to reach such a condition. A state under the control of such leadership would able to overcome bad effects of natural and man-made disaster, at the same time the foundation of the state would be very steady.

43

Financial Responsibility for Security of State

Advent of Security

Thinking of the security of state is increasing through ages. With the very advent of state its security has been thought of through short-term and long-term projects. Fixation of principles of state, application of the same and future plans is embedded in both of these long-term and short- term projects. Collection of proper information and news for fixation of principle, lies within the jurisdiction of state administration. At every period of these activities and enterprise there is financial change and responsibility.

Financial responsibility of the state for all activities related to security is undeniable. It is the state's duty to build up properly all person and organisations connected with security of state and to give proper suitability in consideration of the state administration. How would a state meet the financial responsibility of security? This question is very reasonable, and Kautilya states that the state would manage the security arrangements of its own and at the same time would try to get rid of the financial responsibility as far as practicable. That is state enterprise would be instituted in different fields for security keeping the expense of wealth at minimum.

Kautilya has considered the subject of security with special promptness. In his observation on security just as very common and simple things have come up, so also have very deep and distant aspects. Kautilya has discussed different aspects of security. He has stressed upon being on guard against evil people. Evil persons are more harmful than economics.

Dusyebhyahsatrubhyahcadvibihasudra

(*Arthashastra*, 9/6/1)

[Two types of dangersare to be apprehended: evil person and enemies.)

Dandabarjanupauresujanapadesuba

Dandabarjanupayanprayujjita

(*Arthashastra*, 9/6/2)

[Tactics are to be applied to restrain evil people. There is no need of wasting ability for this.)

Dandah hi mahajanekseptumasakyah. (*Arthashastra*, 9/6/3)

[It is not wise to enrage the whole public by inflicting punishment.]

Kisptauba tam ca arthamnakuryat

Anyam ca anarthamutpadayet. (*Arthashastra*,9/6/4)

[Instead of having desired result hazard may befall if force is applied against greater public.]

Mukhyesutuesamdandakamihakabacam

Ca cestet. (*Arthashastra*,9/6/5)

[Even if the chief of a clan is punished for becoming voluble the state remains secured.]

Kautilya's line of judgement is clear. He has wanted control over the situation and a settlement out of it. For this money is required. Kautilya's solution contains hitting the mark and saving at the same time. Expenditure of money of any sort for attempts in security of state is detrimental with interest of the state, and publicly answered security measures are to be taken in such a way as the far-reaching consequences do not fall on the financial system. For this Kautilya has wanted the matter to be distinctly clear to the authority so that taken decisions are correct.

The authority eager to keep the security of the state intact should recognize the nature of every citizen. Enemies of the country are of two types. One type is well-marked. They can be recognised and understood. Kautilya has demarcated them as enemies. Enemies may be within the country and also outside. If condition, location and identity of enemies be well ascertained, their prevention and eradication becomes easy.

The more clearly and intimately the enemy is recognized the better. Now enemies may be recognised in many ways. Just as an enemy is recognised through enmity so also this can be achieved through amity. The amity has can many types such as, real family, pretence of family, or a mixed one. Kautilya has wanted tricky amity. In modern terminology this is called strategic alliance or strategic partnership. Behind this amity remains dormant the true reason. Attempting to make the path of amity smooth should be untiring.

War and Diplomacy

Kautilya opines that it is the best to prevent war through diplomacy. The enemies can be more intimately recognized and understood through diplomacy. If diplomacy can be successful, then better function will be ascertained than successes or position achieved through victory in a war. Kautilya wanted to weaken enemies thus if enemies drift from their position, then it does not become very difficult to subdue them.

In such cases enemies are subdued without much expense of money. To do the job of subduing enemies profusely, they are to be removed at their roots. If enemies can be made to deviate from its position through diplomacy there they can be destroyed by application of force.

Evil people are more dangerous than marked enemies. They are not marked; they wear different types of masks. State authority often fails to recognize them. They remain mixed up in the public in different ways. They create such an atmosphere so as to make it seem that the whole of the public is committing treason or holding opinion against the state, such a situation is very troublesome for the stability and future of a state. Generally public gets influence by bad motives of evil persons. Such influence is sometimes transient, sometimes temporary and sometimes long-lasting.

Such persons find places in different groups by some plea or other. It is very difficult to isolate them. Evil people get mixed up in groups and create unrest within it. As a result, it seems that this group is engaged in an intrigue against the state. In some special cases the description of the situation is incurred. But in majority of cases such generalisation creates an opposite disposition. Kautilya has warned against this. If the state does not become ready to solve the matter carefully then it may so happen that the state would have to declare or practically engage in war against that whole group of public.

Application of force against a big group of people does not yield good results on the country, as it may rouse reaction. Kautilya has wanted to avoid application of force against big group of publics.

Avoiding application of force, attempts are to be made to gradually estrange the evil persons from them. If the whole public is punished, they would be enraged.

This sort of action would be good enough for the state in the long run. It would be most wise to recognise the patronising evil persons in those groups. There evil persons lead the public astray. If evil persons are punished, it would not be possible for the public to understand the reality. On the contrary, the state has to take up the heartless responsibility to punish fewer evil persons. That is why Kautilya has wanted to isolate the evil persons, punish them and thus to place the jobs of maintaining security of the state on strong foundation.

Application of Penal System

Kautilya has advised to introduce system of judgement also in case of backing known enemies. The *Arthashastra* has given special instruction to make difference between enemies and consider the primary and secondary enemies separately. If true identity of enemies can be apprehended through proper judgement it would be rather mentionable in the eye of the state. State would look at different enemies differently and would act likewise. If enemies are not classified, there would be no other way than to apply the same principles in case of all. The result of assuming a common attempt would be effective in some of the enemies cases, while in some cases it would be quite useless.

That is the attempt of demolishing them would be hindered or futile.

Satrusuddhayamyatahsatruh
Pradhanahkaryauba
Tatahsamadibhihsiddhimlipseta.

(*Arthashastra*, 9/6/6)

[Without subduing primary and secondary enemies together, temporary success may be achieved in some cases through proper understanding with them.]

Svaminyayantapradhanasiddhih
Mantrinahbayantahanyatahsiddhih
Ubhayantapradhanayantasiddhih.

(*Arthashastra*, 9/6/7)

[The leader of the state himself needs be engaged in subduing the main enemy. The charge of subduing secondary enemies may be placed in the hands of ministers. To subdue both types of enemies together the joint endeavour of both leadership and the council of ministers is required.)

Dustahadustanamamisritatvat

Amisrah. (*Arthashastra*,9/6/8)

[Persons of evil nature get mixed with common people and bring about mixture of evil nature.]

Amisrayamduisyatahsiddhih

(*Arthashastra*, 9/6/9)

[Common danger is to be considered wisely and proper arrangement of security should be made.]

Alambanahabhabehialambitana

Vidyante (*Arthashastra*, 9/6/10)

[In want of the pillar meant for basic support it is not possible to hold objects on the pillar.]

Different mechanisms for security will be created in consequences of different categories. Security earned through tricks causes minimum expense of money. Between enemies and evil persons relatively unknown evil persons are comparatively more harmful than known enemies. These evil people are to be removed at the roots. If evil persons get mixed with the public and create anti- state agitation those evil persons are to be controlled so as to subdue them properly. Otherwise result would not be achieved even with undue expenses of money.

Kautilya has insisted on planned invasion. By drawing comparison between enemies and evil people it is to be judged which one has an instant necessity. Instant necessity cannot be ignored. But being confined within instant necessity it would not be possible to be truly engaged in future activities. One has to be eager for both instant and future needs. One is to be desirous for accomplishing both temporary and future requirements. Wherever that evil people would be suspected to be engaged in spreading anti-state malice, proper endeavour is to be taken by the proper and adequately skillful spreading of the news of existence of evil persons and their intention.

All the people should be conversant about the main intention of the state. People should have transparent outlook about the process of running the administration of the state by the leadership, their specialties and intentions. If state leadership maintains fullest honesty in their actions and enterprises, if public gets examples of this subject in different ways and becomes able to follow them through experiences, then only respect, sympathy and emotion would arise for the leadership.

Due to respect, sympathy and emotion no inconvenience grows in people for accepting mentality and dealings of the state with eagerness. The state itself should have to be enterprising and eager, desires of the state gets inevitably expressed in the way of activities and the route of growing up of a state. For example, some states are eager to occupy other states and like to grow through occupying land and wealth of other states. Again, there are states who do not indulge in such intention.

They never venture to occupy foreign states. But they are never reluctant to prevent foreign aggression. This type of states grow as self-dependent. Beside there are a third type of state which are all along weak, depending on others and living and grow with the favours of others.

Economic Fluorishing

Selection and adoption of processes for economic advancement also indicates mentality of the people about the state. It is rather easy for a state which advances along the way of sovereignty and total development in economic field to acquire confidence easily. Such type of states always remain especially eager for extensive economic advancement of the people. The state becomes welfare state due to being thus directed with people. The state generally gets support and cooperation of the people. Welfare state becomes flourishing with cooperation of the people. In such cases anti-state voice and endeavours are deprived of public support. All anti state endeavours and propensities gradually get severed from the people.

In economic management some states for direct and rapid economic advancement create pressures in different ways on the people to keep control. In such cases a distance is created between the state and big public groups. As a result, any intrigue of evil persons may get public support. Or intrigues of evil persons easily get a public basic. If public interest is properly maintained in economic managements and the public is not deprived of expressing their problems properly, cooperation spontaneously comes for the state enterprises.

The more extensive and firmer becomes cooperation to the state enterprises, the greater number of varied groups of people will come forward in respect of state affairs and would easily sever anti state groups from public life. Anti-state envisions of evil people in such cases do not get fulfilled. That is a special aspect of security of a state to be build upon an economic foundation. A state sympathetic to the public problem related with financial matters and the like generally gets control support from the people, who might become earnest in subduing the evil persons.

According to Kautilya if a state along with moving forward along the route of advancement becomes able to extend its economic foundation the burden of security gets minimised to a great extent. The more advanced would become the mass foundation of economic management, the more sound would be the basic foundation of security of the state.

If awakened public emerge in the form of a force in support of the state, evil persons intending to do harm to the state would not be able to raise their heads. They would even refrain from striking the administration system of the state. The marked enemies of the state also retreat. That is why Kautilya strongly believes that management of economic status strengthens security.

Kautilya has wanted public distribution of economic management. This means that the financial liability of the country would be admitted for all. The most important point of administrating the financial situation: how attention and love for all have been extended in the minds of those responsible for controlling the financial situation. If love rises in mind there would be no trouble at all to run the financial administration. That is state leadership with a compassionate attitude admits the financial responsibility of the public and takes it as the burden of the state itself. Such a state is termed welfare state.

A welfare state gradually builds up a natural sphere of security within itself. This security sphere is made of human elements. That is the common people become partners in the security sphere. The state will only be a coordinating agent. So, the people are also cooperators. The state, with attention and consciousness, looks after the problems of the public and so the people also apply their attention and consciousness for the endeavours of the state. For these reasons support and coordination comes from the people for the activities of the state.

While paying deep attention toward the aspects of security, Kautilya has drawn a connection between the security of the state and the flourishing and building up of the economic foundation of the state. The sounder and people- oriented would be the economic foundation of the state, the more would be the availabilities of coordination and future security of the state. Only defence and alliance activities are not sufficient for security of a state.

Defence is necessary no doubt. Carefulness about the different aspects of defence is also necessary, proper steps about the activities of the neighbouring state and the marked enemies are also to be taken. Productions of ordnance, mastering the latest techniques of war, preparedness for able movement of war-equipments etc- all are necessary. Equally important are to keep information about the movement of war-techniques across the whole world and to be likewise prepared.

Army skillful in war and associated works are to be created in large numbers. Preparation is to be taken for research in different aspects of warfare-new success and advancement come if researches become successful. But all these may be turned into failure if active support and cooperation is not had for the people, the true pillar of the country.

That is why Kautilya wants the people are to be looked at first. Leadership drenched with Vedic knowledge can create a stream of total development in the lives of the people. In a life quite surrendered to God has no backing of self-interest, no association with any unscrupulous work. The economic management that can create such a leadership has behind it an extended and far-reaching divine inspiration.

As a result of this the pillar of the sense of responsibility of the state for all wakes up. Awakened public always has inseparable unity with the desire of the state. The desire of the state creates such an atmosphere as every citizen becomes able to sacrifice himself for the country. Such condition may be the most successful and long-lasting as if it is a building made of granite. When every citizen lives for the country, any attempt of evil people to create mass-resentment is nipped at the bud. Besides the aspects of external defence system also becomes firm. None dares to disturb such a state, the state of real power.

44

Labour Economy

Preface

Man was never enslaved in the history of Indian civilization. But in Europe man had to be so. The line of slave trade found in Greek civilization had been in vogue in different forms in different p of the world. In some portion of western civilization, it has been evident in detailed form. Types of living, cruelty, unkindness, heedlessness in human qualities and the line of judging men in terms of material cost have been noticed in European experience but in India any trace of this can be hardly come across. The west has run after success while India has searched truths. The west has wanted the reception tray to touch all the wings of life.

And there is no harm if the process is instantaneous. India has always been looking too far. That plan has suited the character of index which may last long. That is why in all ages India has looked for that solution of the problem as is natural and realistic. The west judged society in the light of individuals, while India has judged an individual on the background of society. So, the west has been concerned with rights of individuals; India has been alert to the duties of individuals. The line of judgement of works prevalent in ancient Indian tradition has been confidential and secret aspects of modern corporate organisation.

The judgement of actions had first been taken up from the viewpoint of experts. This has been termed judgement of the intelligentsia. In this system in one would have to be specialised in the subject in which he has gained expertise. During the phase of being specialised one can go through different stages, but when it is completed, that individual would have to carry with lines that identity.

Not only that, one would have to go on increasing the depth of that identity to make the justification on one's placement in that class firm and sound. This is called sharpening. The constant endeavour to make one's position firm is the attempt of addition of knowledge to increase one's qualities.

Greater portion of repeated foreign invasion of India has been possible due to liberal attitude and the enduring and accepting mentality of India. Evil invaders have taken advantage of this nobility. Powerful but evil persons have been engaged in bringing down the flow of change as a result of which the chief bonding in society and the basic outlook behind these, existing for so long, have received a shock. Still India has remained glowing in its own greatness. India has kept intact its civilization, prevailing through thousands of years by dint of its own greatness.

The loftiest summit where at the stage of Indian life had been established has remained unperturbed capability in the rooms of the society. In the western tradition there are few lives swelled up by the satisfaction in life through contentment at oppression of the people. Indian tradition is,

'Samgachadhvam, Sambadadhvam, SambomananaSijanatam'

(We would walk together with the truth in mind). Here society has grown up through mingling of people of different professions. The first and foremost view of society is to build up life through the basis of long cherished love, foundation of godliness, faith, and cooperation.

So, in the tradition of India in spite of there being difference between the high and the low, interest of financial ability, man had never been through utmost indifference and oppression; there had been no enslavement. In course of having comparison of Indian society in respect of the Greek society Megasthenes had noticed the elevated characteristics of India.

'People here are possessors of free professions and longings. India lives have all along been spent being spread in excellence of respective profession with a view to a better reform of the mind. Megasthenes has written. The Lakedaemonians, however hold the Helots as slaves and these Helots do servile labour but the Indians do not even use aliens as slaves much less a country man of their own.'

(J.W. McCrindle, *Ancient India as Described by Megasthenes and Arrian*, 2018, p. 211–13.)

Then in Indian society dignity of labourers has been universally instilled. Not only the greatness of Indian society but its external influence would be quite obvious in course of applications in depth of the principles of selling of labour' and 'offering of labour.' The west has inspired labourers to sell labour. While India has insisted on offering of labour. Kautilya has clarified the rights of labourers. Considering from the end of the institution Kautilya has made the matter of rights of the labourers clearer.

While the world had been prepared to attribute human values to labourers through judgement of the capability of workers to sell labour, India had judged the human qualities of labourers. It is not sale of labour but the eagerness of offering labour that has been made the labourer's central power. Looking at the industrial management of the west, it is exhausted in carrying the tradition of the system of enslavement Karl Marx had shown the operation, exploitation and torture of the labourers. This is absent from India's own tradition. Imposition for less civilized power from outside has come upon India's tradition. This imposition has created troubles here. Western influence has infiltrated in this management through lending from outside or through impositions.

India has given the labourers organisational right. When the other part of the world is eager to fix up the price to purchase labourers India has given them the right to form unions. Labourers got rights of their own and that of forming organisation. The right of persons offering labour had been established even before Kautilya. He only made the right lawful.

The rights mentioned by Kautilya is applicable in both the interest of the state and the labourers as well. Kautilya has been inspired to look after the interest of the labourers in conjugation with that of the state. As a result, the right attributed to the labourers by Kautilya has satisfied both the state and the labourers.

Alongside labourers have got responsibility. Labourers would earn and enjoy their own right no doubt, but at the same time they would have to observe some duties also. A labourer would come to terms with his own right and at the same time he should have to be careful about his own responsibilities.

The rights Kautilya has given to the labourers are:

Right to be organized.

Right to have lawful wages for work.

Right to have wages intended for the work

Side by side with their rights the responsibilities vested on the labourers by the *Arthashastra* are:

Responsibility to complete the work promised to be done. Application of intention of work definitely.

Responsibility of finishing the work completely and decently.

The *Arthashastra* works at the labourers as a unit. That every worker is engaged independently in his domain of work. In case of work everybody would be considered as an individual with respect to the job. But in respect of maintaining or establishing the right this individual would be considered along with the totality. Here Kautilya has laid greatest importance on the job. Completion of a job is the primary responsibility of workers. The responsibility for the job promised to be completed would be vested on the worker.

Responsibility goes to the workers whenever the intention for the job becomes evident and whenever a plan has been chalked out for a certain job. The job will have to done by him. If he backs out without performing the job or when the job would be left out incomplete the organisation involved or the state will have to face a loss. So, it is not acceptable by the state. On the other hand, if a worker has appeared with an intention for performance but the circumstance is not congenial or materials are lacking so as to complete the work the responsibility would not be vested on the workers. If a worker be present at the initiation of the work, he would be eligible for the whole of his wages.

The aspect of the freedom of the workers had been sounder before Kautilya. At that time the custom was such as whenever a worker arrives at the working field on invitation, whole of wages would be due for him.

Upasthitamkarayatahkrtameba
Bidyat-itiacharyah. (*Arthashastra*, 3/14/6)

[Predecessors are of the opinion that attendance on being called would become the work to have been done.]

'Na iti Kautilya' (*Arthashastra*, 3/14/8)
[Kautilya says, 'No'.]
'Krtasyabetannamnaakrtasyaasti'
(*Arthashastra*,3/14/9)

'Sahcetalpamapikarayitvanakarayet
Kartamebaasyabidyat'
(*Arthashastra*, 3/14/9)

[A creation job will not be deemed to have been done if that is not attended to. If on being called a portion of the job is completed, then only the job will be assumed to be complete in case the authority fails to supply favourable conditions for the same.]

Desakalahatipatanenakarmana

Anyathakarane

Nasakamahkrtamanumanyena'.

(Arthashasta, 3/14/10)

[If a worker commits mistake in some place, time or ascertainment or he fails to perform the allotted work then in spite of his desire the work may not be demand to have been completed.]

Sambhasitatadhikakriyayamprayasam

Na maudhamkuryat.

(*Arthashastra*, 3/14/11)

[If someone performs more than the stipulated work it would not go in vain.]

Tenasamghabhrtahbyakhyatah

(*Arthashastra*, 3/14/12)

[By this the existence of organisation is honoured']

Tasamadhihsaptarathamasti.

(*Arthashastra*; 3/14/13)

[A worker will not work for seven days at a stretch, organisation would engage some replacements.]

In the *Arthashastra* Kautilya has kept provisions for creating union by the workers. This association would be kept proper control over the line and field of work of the workers. There are two sides of such control over work. One is related to the timing of work. How long would a worker work for, how many days would the work continue for, all of this would be correctly quantified by worker's union. Union will keep watch on all the workers and be aware of their works. As a result, no work would be like a torture on the part of workers, but the work would be quite acceptable.

Workers would come to the field of work by the allurement of the work and the attainment there from. He would not work only by the consideration of remuneration. Thus, taking part eagerly in a work and completing the same signify offering of labour from the part of a worker. A worker becomes contented by offering labour.

So, offer of labour and pleasure of completing a job and earning of adequate and respectful living bring this contentment. So, one who has once completed the work would come back to the field again and again. In modern terminology this is could delighting work.

The main significance of the line of work introduced by the *Arthashastra* is to define right and power of labourers ranging for the creation of a nation of the work down to completion of the same. Workers union would not only be limited within timing and wages of the workers, but would spread itself even to the qualities of the works. The *Arthashastra* has given the workers the scope of having the right as units and at the same time it wants to create attractive propensity in the work and thereby attract the workers.

Some have opined that Indian labourers have achieved freedom in some cases, but in others they have still remained subdued and exploited as social groups. Foreign observers have considered this aspect in India with much importance. There remain many groups of people having different ideas and notions in the way of a nation building. Some have very clear views while views of others are always covered by baseless principles.

To their idea, that anything Indian is condemnable, such a balanced and well managed status of labourers in Indian tradition does not become evident at all. So, through right to labour, right of labourers, arrangement of building up of workers union prevailed in Indian tradition long before Karl Marx, the same did not transpire in the researches of the desks of the imperial library. It was not possible to surpass the idea that everything in this world belongs to the same pattern.

E.F. Schumacher has recorded the tears of the poor people in the narration of the invasion of one bound for one's home. He has expressed the status of the labourers and the poor as:

'– We are poor, not demigods.'

'– We have plenty to be sorrowful about and are not emerging into a golden age.'

'–we must concern ourselves with justice and see right prevail.'

'–And all just, only this, can enable as to become peace peacemakers.'

(E. F. Schumacher, *Small Is Beautiful*, 1975, p. 131.)

It is a reply with "Parable of demigods" in the Christian gospel. Schumacher has announced the condition of the poor in their own voice. Condition of a labourer is like that of this poor man who has many a source to make him unhappy and there is hardly any possibility of appearance of a golden age of happiness before him.

The picture of the severe suffering of penury presented by Schumcher is one very much familiar in the traditional life of labourers in the west. Selucus, the Greek chief succeeding Alexander made friends with Chandragupta Maurya through offering of his daughter in marriage and in many other ways. The territory of the vast Maurya empire then had spread up to that of Persia. Megasthenes, the state representative sent by Seleucus lived at Patliputra for a considerable period of time and noticed Indian managements closely.

He built up a report on the internal affairs of social condition of India on the basis of his own personal experiences. That is why when he says that in India there was never any custom of keeping slaves that is quite trustworthy. Among what Meagasthenes had observed on poverty mention may be made of the statements of different income of people of different professions, of different social endeavours and of setting up of a splendid balance among these.

Thus, it can be said that the picture of poverty Schumacher has drawn in a partial description of Indian arrangements in the modern phase. Possibility and wealth of the principal group of Indian people have become extinct under Mughal, Pathan and British occupancy. The plunderers looted the wealth, India's store of wealth got crushed one by one by foreign invasions. Foreign invaders come to India being allured by its affluence and wealth. They looted, taking advantage of internal conflict, but still, they could not break down the structure of Indian social system.

Megasthenes has written:

"The inhabitants, in like manner, having abundant means of subsistence, exceed in consequence the ordinary stature, and are distinguished by their proud bearing. They are also found to be well-skilled in the arts as might be expected of men who inhale a pure air and drink the very first water. And while the soil bears on its surface all kinds of fruits which are known to cultivation, it has also underground numerous veins of all sports of metals, for it contains much gold and silver and copper and iron in no small quantity and even tin and other metals, which are employed in making articles of uses and ornaments as well as implements and accoutrements of war"

(McCrindle, *Ancient India as Described by Megasthenes and Arrian.*)

Social picture of India during this period is beyond poverty, Affluence was the natural picture. Not only that, affluence spread among the people and they were very efficient in arts and work-culture. They had plenty of pure air to inhale and potable water. Innumerable fruit trees pervaded lands and there was plenty of mineral wealth underground. These mines were very rich in gold, silver and copper. Different types of articles were being made of iron and other materials. Besides ornaments made of gold and silver application of iron and allied metals in manufacture of war materials and ordinance were easily fulfilled-such was the management.

Indian labourers, therefore, stood with their heads held high. They had dignified position from the very beginning. A labourer established in his own dignity was not bound to sell labour. Rather offering labour was natural and instinctive to them. Labourers and unions have grown up at different quarters. If is clearly understood that union's respective location kept watch on the affairs regarding labour., As a result it is expected that such union used to help labourers select suitable jobs.

It is also knowable that union has helped determine wages correctly. Through assessment of timing of work in a day, week or a month union have built up a basic structure of labour-economy. This helped the authority to ascertain the expenses toward labour charge in the manufacture concerned, and the productivity of labourers. Unions have tried to assure that in spite of attendance of the workers in the field of work, the work remained suspended owing to want of necessary articles, raw-materials. In such cases workers would get proper wages. Such rights of workers are found to be widely unavailable in the modern world.

At the time of Kautilya also such freedom, dignity and respect were not available anywhere in the world except India. Even on the part of modern workers, unions and proper acquaintance with correct role to be played by the labourer is a rare experience. Labour-economy was established in Kautilyas *Arthashastra* on the basis of the dignity of labour and labourer,

While discussing different aspects of labour economy Kautilya cast his eyes on financial structure, financial distribution, economic system, etc. Labourers were collectively looked upon as a special pillar of economic system. What Kautilya has demanded is that labourers would be careful of rights and duties at the same time. Workers would accept work gladly and run to the field being attracted by the same. Workers would try to establishe their rights everywhere and just similarly they would bear the responsibility in their respective fields and observe this duty as workers. The *Arthashastra* has looked upon an important factor of economic system.

Bibliography

McCrindle, J.W. *Ancient India as Described by Megasthenes and Arrian*, 2018.

Schumacher, E. F. *Small Is Beautiful*, 1975.

45

Uprooting of Inequality and Poverty: Vedic and Modern Economic Ideas

Basics of Inequality

Unequal set up of wealth is the index of inequality. Wealth is in much excess in someone's possession and while lacking for someone else-. Such circumstances augment inequality. If wealth is judged before proceeding towards the future, crossing the present situation one would understand the direction towards which the spread of wealth would help the economic situation within the society. In the path of use of wealth there is a possibility of loss of wealth and at the same time there is also a possibility of influence of wealth. In the background of a society, creation of any wealth whatsoever becomes acceptable.

Wealth is judged on the status of the factors of money and money-value under consideration at a certain time. The word 'wealth' has come from weal'. This means the condition of keeping well. In common usage it means this has come to mean anything which has got monetary values and which comes under the purview of possession. Wealth and its possession are linked separately.

Aiming at measuring the difference existing in the British Society of the 20th century' Jack Revelle, the economist has defined wealth as: (1965, p. 368)

"The wealth of a country consists of two elements-the value of tangible assets located in the country and the net total of claims on overseas residents. The wealth of an economic unit within a country, such as an individual or a household can also be seen as consisting of two elements the value of tangible assets owned by the individual household and the total of the individual household's claim on tangible assets, the second element comprising financial assets net of liabilities......"

Methods followed by the commission formed by the 'Royal Commission' engaged by the British Government to judge the balance and consequence of income and expenditure of wealth of the people in considering the judgement of wealth getting the particulars of inequality have directly influenced nearly all of the chief international organisations concerned with financial and social matters. Stewart has published its conclusion: "Marketable wealth which includes all assets for which a value can immediately be realized, net of liabilities.... plus, value of occupation and state pension right.... (But also) the net worth of the company sector, collective wealth of the public sector, the value of human wealth contingent rights to forms of income other than occupational and pension rights.... and the value of restricted access to certain assets like subsidised tenancies."

Measure of Inequality

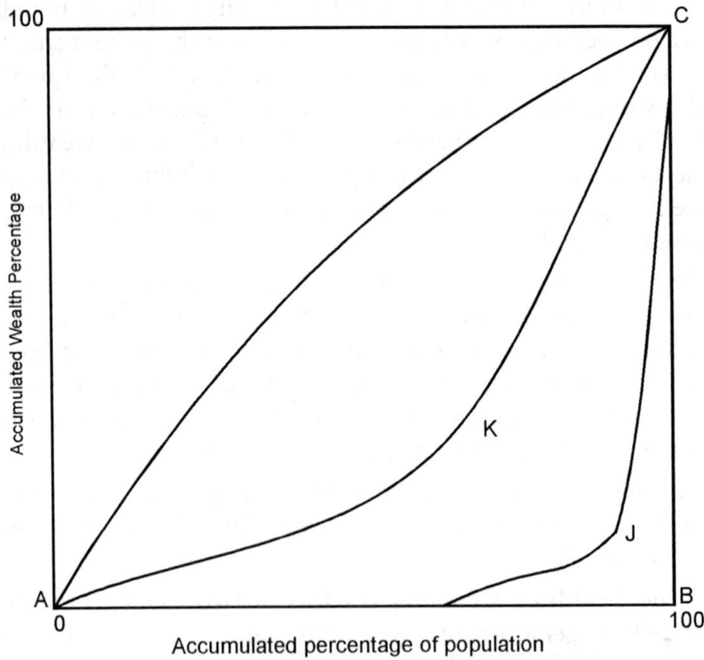

Figure 1

Gini Co-efficient and Lorentz Curve are discussed with utmost importance in case of measuring inequality. Corrado Gini showed (1914) in Lorentz Curve that the triangle within the hypotenuse determines the whole equilibrium system. Gini Co-efficient for measuring inequality extends from zero (0) to one (1). If the co-efficient is 0, then the condition is in complete equilibrium, and when it is 1, it signifies complete inequilibrium. In figure 1 the lines K and J signifies two types of inequilibrium. The ratio AKC: ABC is less than the ratio AJC:ABC. This shows that in the Lorentz curve designated by K-line there is less extent of in-equilibrium condition, and there is greater extent in equilibrium in the J condition designated as mentioned.

In Lorentz curve the right to wealth and influence of change in case of high-income group of people is rather higher than the influence of wealth in case of middle and low -income group people. There may be coordination between Gini Co-efficient and Lorentz diagrams of two countries or two times of the same country. If the financial management in the financial groups of people be at nearly equilibrium state, its measure with Gini Co-efficient becomes easier, otherwise in case of financial distribution of complex types this co-efficient does not signify the correct picture. Lorentz Curve of course, helps to outline an overall idea. Atkinson and Harrison have given hare a comprehensive opinion (Atkinson & Harrison, 1978):

There measures give different weight to different parts of the distribution and man in effect that one has to examine the underlying Lorentz curves in order to understand what is going on (p.124).

There is but little discord in the notion that in case of having a correct picture of the financial management, statistic often leads us astray. But real judgement is impossible without the help of statistics. So measure of wealth is to be considered keeping in mind the limit and ability to mislead of statistics.

Frank A Lowel has presented (1977) an acceptable opinion in this subject.

'There are basically two ways of collecting .... information: 1. You can ask for it. 2. You can make them give it to you. Neither method is wholly satisfactory since in the first case, some people may choose not to give the information, or may give it incorrectly, and in the second case, the legal requirement for information may not correspond exactly to the date requirements of the social analyst (p. 106-7)

Not only in respect of use of wealth but also to inflate the wealth one has to be careful about the inequality in judgment of wealth. Inequality of wealth is a natural part of society. Inequality sometimes hastens the movement of wealth and sometimes hinders the same strongly. Inequality has two forms -one relating to poverty and the other with respect to strength. When there is impairment in social strength, the process of creation of wealth becomes rather one-sided. The social wealth accumulates with the affluent. It has a good effect also for example If attempt is there to create social wealth on the basis of affluence, rapid growth of wealth and situation of the route of wealth become easier. The march that begins with affluence often has a strong basis of advancement and as such progress also becomes definite and coordinating. As a result of this the whole society gets inflated.

Economic Development

On the other hand the invasion for economic development that begins on the basis of affluence alone often fails. The reason behind this is that the coordination of a large portion of society is lacking. As a result, social distribution comes on the vergee of a devastating situation. Co-existence of poverty and affluence is not at all healthy in any way. Leaving aside the possibility of poverty striking against affluence, it may be asserted that the first hurdle before affluence to co-exist with poverty is mutual acceptability and attitude. Poverty and affluence can coexist up to a creation limit only.

If due to this co-existence the depth and rate of poverty begins to decrease, then this co-existence is beneficial for both. Otherwise, the main link of coexistence would get severed and distrust would develop, its consequence may be disastrous and even destructive.

The recent thought developed in course of observation and measure of inequality and poverty stands as quite different. The inequality may often be augmented in a venture to remove poverty. The reason behind this is that in open situation holders of affluence in market and open trade may get tradition of work very similar to poverty. Such freedom on the part of affluence may attempt to inflate wealth. On the other hand, building up of freedom on the part of poverty like this is not possible. That is, identical circumstances of advantage turnout to be of two different forms to the groups. The quality of advancement from affluence surpasses the liberation from poverty and its rate of increase, and becomes many times of the same. When a poor man advances by one step affluent person by that time would advance ten steps. As a result, in spite of some remission of poverty inequality increases.

This movement of inequality (increase or decrease) becomes different in every society, economic situation or state. The extent of inequality brought about by a certain society or economic situation may not be applicable to others. If the means for eradication of poverty are controlled by the state, result may be otherwise. By the control of the state the possibility of inflation of affluence in the phase of eradication of poverty may be brought under control. In such cases the state itself would have to be endeavouring.

If the state itself becomes engaged in different enterprises in different economic processes, then it may become possible. In this case the state should take the responsibility of expansion of job possibilities and of wealth. Through such expansion processes the state would gradually be able to bring people in the purview of regular income. If expansion of wealth be conjoined with the endeavour of expansion of work culture creation of works for the entrepreneurs would be possible. It is quite natural for the entrepreneurs to be associated with new types and forms of works and to create new spheres of work. Expansion of the fields of public sector and state enterprise is the path to follow.

Some instances in the post-World War II economy show growth public sectors, while at the same time their devastating end have also become inevitably true in other instances. Public sector has faced such consequence in almost all countries. Economic situation under the state control has been ruined. Economic situation based on private proprietorship emerged from within that and got established everywhere.

The direct consequence of this is complete surrender of the economic situation before the power of the worker. On the way of surrendering before the power of the worker many problems arise without means to get rid of them. In this situation there is no scope, favour or reproval is there. Only competition is there. Both poverty and affluence get compulsorily engaged in competition in these respective fields. In the market-based management poverty is deprived of any favour, so also affluence is deprived of opportunity and favour. There both have to be established in their own merit and capability. Both can move on in their respective paths. With the power of social inspiration. Since commonly affluence has greater support it may advance with greater speed.

Neo-Economic Management and Kautilya

In modern economic management this situation has also changed. In spite of starting from the same position different consequences may appear in case of different types of enterprises. As economic management has come within the control of information technology and intellect many forms of advancement with multiple qualities may appear here. Both poverty and affluence can be improved by information technology and intellect. Use of intellect and possibility thereof can bring rapid elevation from the state of poverty.

This is also possible in open market management. In open market management incitation of intellect and unveiling of information technology are able to bring rapid change. It is possible in both organized and non-organized sectors. Due to incitation of intellect, the enterprising attempt of an individual gets unveiled in terms of price of intellect. As a result, setting up of a new economic basis becomes easier. Two matters are important in case of incitation of intellect. These are, one, intellectual possibility of an individual and his agility to shape up that possibility and two congenial environments for sharing up of the possibility of intellect.

The second point means that in congenial environment incitation of possibility of intellect gets hastened; but the store of that possibility is the individual himself. This possibility of intellect coming out of the store of the individual has the capability of changing its own economic identity completely. Until this possibility of intellect is not incited, this possibility remains dormant. Even if the individual connected with the possibility of intellect is devoid of wealth, it would be possible for him to turn into a glowing luminary in his economic stride. 'Intellect is the basis of wealth' – This is the new perspective of modern market economics. Kautilya's *Arthashastra* had realized the importance of human intellect and engaged himself in regeneration of intellect.

Kautilya has said:

Dhanahitahna ca hinah ca
Dhanikasasunisca yah
Vidyaratnenahinah yah
Sahhinahsarbabastnsu.

(Kautilya, Principle -268)

(A poor man should never be looked down upon. A learned man is superior to a rich man. A man devoid of the jewel of learning is practically devoid of all things.)

Na astividyasamamcaksuh
Na astisatyasamamtopah
Na astiragasamamduhkham
Na astityagasamamsukham

(Kautilya, Principle-287)

[There is nothing which uncovers vision, there is no asceticism like truth, there is no sorrow like anger and no happiness in anything like renunciation.]

Kamadhenugurahvidyaakalephaladayni
Prabasematrsadrs'tvidyaguptamdhanam
Smrtam. (Kautilya principle -96)

[Just as the wishing cow gives milk at all times, so also learning yields truth even in bad times. Learning is like mother when one is in foreign land. So learning is disguised as hidden treasure.]

Kautilya is very clear in regard to the role of learning. He has called learning a hidden treasure. A poor man may become rich with learning. A learned person is honoured in the world. So, wealth comes in the custody of learning. Intellect is expressed in learning. This intellect is the hidden treasure within an individual. The phase of participation of an individual in economic management gets expanded through incitation of intellect. Through this participation an individual becomes able to cast influence in the economic management process, the right of the individual gets established in this situation incitation of intellect becomes carrier of procuring wealth. Intellect becomes the carrier of wealth. First intellect begins to be established with the support of wealth. Gradually the right of wealth gets expanded and spreads in all corners of the field of intellect. As a result, the unification process between intellect and wealth becomes sound.

The modern economic management has been established with the help of the invasion of technology and the judgement of the excellence of consumers. As a result of this stronger attention for articles and services to these materials spread much farther. Thus consumers are the main strength of the market.

New Evolution and Kautilya

Consumer God

Modern economic management system is aiming at imparting satisfaction to the consumers of articles and services and at giving them pleasure. In this process of imparting satisfaction and pleasure, consumers have been set up at the topmost position. When consumers appeared as the power in the market in the form of buyers' right, then the market itself had to bow down before them. That is why consumers have been called God of the market. Keen competition has been set up among the organisation of different countries engaged in production, supply and offering service to society the consumers in the form of God. This competition is rather extreme. Success or failure -come what may, organisers would have to move on along the path of competition. Consumers wait very eagerly to enjoy the good effect of this competition.

There is a continuous evolution in the demand and expectation of the consumers. They do not feel satisfied with older articles. They want newer and newer goods. To accomplish this the demand for continuously more improved goods and services becomes strong. Consumers become eager to realise value for money. They are not fully satisfied until and unless they get service and goods befitting the value paid for. Problem lies in the felt that the outlook of the consumers is constantly changing. Besides there is newer distribution of information. Consumers are gradually becoming aware of the process and mechanism of offering consumable goods and service at different corners of the world. Gradually factors infiltrate before him in comparison. Attraction becomes stronger for other service providers setting wide other produces and suppliers. As a result, craving becomes more severe for new goods and services in place of older ones.

This attraction created among the consumers brings in new goods and services. Demand has been created and so there has been earnestness in innovating new goods and service. Intellect with innovative possibility gets engaged in research for improvement and has brought a competitive ability among the companies. Companies engaged in competition are continuously looking for avenues to find out goods and services more pleasing for consumers.

In this work research and development play important paths. If pleasing and pleasant goods and services are to be carried to the consumers at low prices, the process may be of two types: one, to arrange for supply of low-price goods and services through better technology and mechanism and two, through arrangement for distributing wider and much multiplied production and distribution systems on the basis of demand. What is required here is wider and far-spread demand. Unless the demand is much multiplied such wide scale of production and supply is not possible. So, the first duty of the market is to bring regular flow of newer goods and service. The second is open explosion of demand.

Regular flow of new goods and service is possible only by dint of the blooming intellect. Blooming intellect originally brings to the bosom of the society newer goods and service. Constantly these is a transformation of economic management system. This transformation of economic management system is possible only by the influence of blooming intellect. Blooming intellect has been the backbone of modern economic management system. By virtue of its bounty a certain company is in a better position that the other. It can move fast.

Kautilya has clarified with the importance of knowledge and intellect that the value of knowledge and intellect is more than that of wealth. In comparison between a rich and a learned person Kautilya has given the former a lower rank. The superiority of a learned person has been said not only in respect to the background of the society. But according to Kautilya the wealth of a learned person counts most.

A learned person, with of his blooming intellect is constantly engaged in inventing newer goods and service. So, there is not only an explosion of demand, but also there comes change in the qualitative standard of demand and directive in direction. After the blooming of intellect, poverty and affluence both are of same value. Not only that, poverty and affluence come down from the same background during the phase of blooming of intellect, but they would have to move along the same path. As a result, in the newer background the so long existing difference in the comparative forward movement of these gets lost. Active people by dint of blooming of intellect become able to transform rapidly, their financial identity.

Whatever path may be followed to eradicate poverty, it would cast influence on the poverty. The path of blooming of learning and intellect is very direct. In these paths due to blooming and application of learning and intellect the way of transformation of poverty into affluence may get exposed and becomes wider.

The basis of intellectual economy rest within the man; with the blooming intellect. Exposition of the blooming intellect possessed by a man is of value to him. This value forms the external value of an individual. With the help of this an individual is capable of the neo-economic management system is eradicating poverty and inequality at the same time.

Bibliography

Assen, Robert. *Visions of Poverty: Welfare Policy and Political Imagination*. Michigan State University Press, 2002.

Atkinson, A.B, and A.J Harrison. *Distribution of Personal Wealth in Britain*. Cambridge University Press, 1978.

Brickley, James, A. Clifford, W. Smith Jr., and Jerold I. Zimmermann. *Managerial Economics and Organizational Architecture*, 1996.

Cowell, Frank A. *Measuring Inequality*. Oxford, 1977.

Demsetz, Harold. *Enterprise Control, Wealth and Economic Development. Economics of the Poisiness Firm, Seven Critical Commentaries*. Cambridge University Press, 1995.

Pandey, Tusarkanti. *Chanakya Sloka*. Granthana, 1988.

Revels, Jack. Change in the *Social Distribution of the Property*. Britain during the Twentieth Century, Conference Internationald'Histoire. Economique, 1965.

Schneider, Michel. *The Distribution of Wealth*. UK & USA: EdwardElger, 2004.

Stewart, I. "Estimates of the distribution of personal wealth II: marketable wealth and pension rights of individuals 1976 to 1989." *Economic Trends* 457 (1991): 99-110.

Town, Richard D. *Managerial Economics*, n.d.

46
Economic Revolution through Spiritual Realisation

Elements of Economic History

So far, the history of human civilization has reflected the evolution of consciousness. Man has found the wealth and provision for living, growing, and moving ahead. As wealth and provision have come, as man has found them out, so he has set up the management, and through this, the economic basis and financial groundwork have been built. Financial management has also grown on the basis of this groundwork. Man has built up this management so as to suit himself; on this financial management, therefore, the kingdom is dependent, otherwise dependent on the creation of nature, while sometimes again has come dependence on agricultural enterprise created on the bosom of nature by his own attempts.

Man has advanced by his own attempts resorting to his genius, creativity and ability to work. So, in agriculture this one attempt of evolution at different steps. Agriculture had to depend long on nature, but gradually, it became free. Agriculture face from the dependence on the right of nature has exposed the gateway of wealth to men. Crossing the dependence on agriculture, man is moving towards a phase of exposition of industry and technology. Not only that the economic management system has been experiencing quantitative change, but also, a qualitative change has also grown spontaneously.

In economic management, man is the basic resource. There was a time when wealth used to be measured in tenses of how many orchards a gentleman had, how much land he possessed, and how much gold and government securities he held. The more one had, the wealthier he used to be considered. The dominance of land, and dominance of money reigned supreme.

One the way of man's living dominance of a new wealth has appeased now-the wealth of merit, wealth of genius, wealth of knowledge has surpassed all and moved ahead. Intellect, genius, and knowledge have come as the dominating factors of man. Moreover, organisational rights and influence have gradually become weak and useless. Wealth of intellect, genius, and knowledge would bloom on the basis of the extreme capability of an individual wealth of intellect, genius and knowledge would be considered and discussed in terms of monetary values. This wealth in the possession of an individual would gradually be strong in terms of monetary value and be inflated in terms of the same. In the stream of evolution of history, this is an index of measurement. The social management system of the future will be judged in terms of intellect, genius, and knowledge.

Different types of transformations have come in the qualities that prevailed and predominated in man in the initiating phase of civilization. The excellence of civilization was expressed in its overcoming the wild society and upliftment into agricultural one. The situation set up in the agricultural society is certainly different from the wild one. In the latter, there had been sheer slavery to propensity, lack of endurance.

Severity muscle power, lack of feeling for others and one-way nature of longing and desires and hunger. In the sphere of wild society comes dominance of the external ability of an individual, a merely temporary outlook. Wild society has been organized from the measure of immediate necessity. Mutual endurance and alliance were evident in wild society. Where laws had been established, the main principles were the source of individual power and its dominance or sphere of influence. Within this sphere of influence was created a certain social management. Inspiration and enterprise of agricultural society have emerged from this very wild society.

Emergenge of Wild Society

It is the agricultural society that has carried the seed of civilization. To achieve fruits, one has to wait after sowing seeds is the most important principle of agriculture. This also has a long- drawn periods of preparation. Land is to be bought into true form with long toil. Even the fertile land is to be made cultivable through ploughing. Infertile lands to be brought into form through patience and perseverance. Infertile land is to be watered, exposed to proper sunshine and air is to be circulated within through ploughing. Besides, many types of monitoring are necessary. A land is made fertile by adding manure and then field becomes suitable for sowing crops.

An experienced farmer waits for a number of seasons for proper situation of ploughing and for suitable environment. He never sets in cultivation work until the land is formed. For proper preparedness of a land patience, endurance and technique are required. There may grow and flourish in the individual self. Blooming of such patience, endurance and technique in an individual is not enough. Besides these individual qualities a collective exposition should be there. For again a collective enterprise of many hands is required. The basis of agriculture grows on the foundation of collective enterprise of many people. For agricultural work therefore, a bonding of mutual linking becomes necessary. From the necessity of this bonding have grown the external enterprises of family, society and collectively.

Bonding of unison, feeling of stability internet of relations of affection-love-respect and mutual dependence have lent a strong foundation to the family. Success in agriculture may get an endeavour an dependence while has a far spreading result. Such a unique situation of endeavour and dependence creates a separate civilization. Agricultural society and agricultural civilization have grown for agriculture.

Personal entity and collective presence of an individual have been factored of external excellence of both agricultural society and civilization. The more has been the exposition his personal entity the more he has learnt how to mix up, how to befriends, how to established friendship and in the long run he has learnt how to be identified in the form of collectively instead of a unit- At the basis of agricultural work these is an attempt for a united enterprise of the multitude. He who among many moves ahead to give leadership hold the role of the senior in agricultural production for this reason in agricultural society and civilization there grows a basis of idealism right on and spirituality idealism religion and spirituality are needed for proper control of the society and for it to reach a befitting end.

Basis of Agricultural Civilization

The line of connection between man and nature has been important in agricultural society and civilization. This alone has built up the agricultural civilization. What is wanted hare in union of human lives and the means of mutual coordination. Union of lives in the medium of manifestation oflife-force. The act of blooming of the life force is the main phase in agricultural management.

With the blooming of life force of an individual go not the phase of endeavour of the collectively, coordination of the collectively and attempts enriched with support the bonding in union with nature the chariot movement of agricultural management has moved on. As a result, in the agricultural management have come up influence of enterprise, influence of coordination and influence of nature. By the support of nature, the influence of enterprise and coordination become very much effective.

The bonding of union of enterprise and coordination becomes effective even in unfavourable situation. At the basis of enterprise and co-ordinationare mutual endurance, affection and dependence, muchmore favourable situation in with men than that created on the part of nature on the basis of coordination between new or nature. In course of discussion on the relation between nature and man in Brahman in the first part of the last century, Fielding Hall has hinted at duties towards animals.

Fielding has written

'To heir men are men, and animals are animals, and men are for the higher. But he does not deduce from this that man's superiority gives him permission to ill-treat or kill animals. It is just reverse. It is because man is much higher than the animal that he can and must observe towards animals the very greatest care, feel for them the very greatest compassion, be good to them in every way he can' (Fielding, 1920)

Fielding's opinion cast influence in social left of England and right before World War II being accelerated by the impact of such opinion the movement of love for nature and animals advanced somewhat which has been much more forceful in recent years. Such a feeling had been specially embedded in agricultural societies, especially in the lifestyle of hermits in ancient Indian civilization. That is why big trees, creepers, shrubs, etc. have earned the dignity of gods. Introduction of the custom of worship of big trees signifies deep love and devotion to nature. In the civilization related with hermits all the factors of nature have been identified as forms of the Brahma identity.

That is why act of tilling of the cultivable lands begin with worship of cultivable land. Reaping of harvest is also a festivity.

Through worship this reaping is made successful and effective. Reaping of harvest is concerned not only with crops, but is a part of worship of the great. The manifestation of Brahma in the universe has been called through different techniques like worship, embrace and the like in the perspective of life.

Cultivation is, therefore, not merely a financial profession; it has turned to be offering of love and adoration of men eager for achieving unadulterated treasure. So, nature and all of its factors have turned to be idols in Indian view drenched with Vedic realisation. Thus, towards them the basic view of life has been of reverence and love. They cannot be harmed; they cannot be envied; ruin cannot be called upon them. Effect of this thought and view has fallen even in Europe and other place of the world.

Modern Management

In European views, natural wealth has been evaluated chiefly in the interest of living. Western society has been eager to use property the natural wealth (derived mainly from forests, animals, mines, water etc.) in the interest of living. Europe, in this case, has taken the leading role. Towards the end of seventies of the seventies last century British government submitted a charter at the Stockholm conference, Sweden, on the conservation of natural resources.

The report runs this:

'The most important off all resources are obviously the initiative imagination, and brainpower of man himself. We all know this and are ready to devote very substantial funds to what we call education. So, if problem is survival, one might fairly expect to find some discussion relating to the preservation and if possible, the development of the most ferocious of all natural resources: human brains. However such expectations are not fulfilled. Sinews for survival deals with all the material factors mineral, energy water etc. but not all with such immaterial resources as initiative, imagination and brain power.(Schumacher, 1979)

Attempt for conservation of resources has been taken not only in Europe but also everywhere to small and large extents. The main development attempts for procuring wealth have, in many cases, been spoiled. In many cases, in the interest of conserving and procuring wealth, man has been eliminated as the basic resource, and confidence has been placed on external and other resources. A consequence of such confidence and extreme resources has been rendering the power of possibility in man weak or deeming to be reduced.

This power of possibility has generated attempts for work. In the invasion of man, work and attempts for work have undergone many transformations. Schumacher, through his study, has shared that the attempts for work may have their special reasons building, for example, "First to provide necessary and useful goods and services. Second, to enable every one of us to use and thereby perfect our gifts like good stewards. Third, to do so in service and in cooperation with others, so as to liberate other selves from our inborn egocentricity." (Good work, 3-4).

In the condition of work referred to above, the basic principle is to point out that conviction by which a clear feeling of an idea goods about the object that is worth giving on the part of an individual. At the basis of such notions is the act of knowing as the basic source of man and his invent power. As a result of these endeavours, genius and intellect that were doormats in the form of financial get bloomed.

One after another, the tranches of possibility go on blooming. It is not merely exposition in the light of judgement of utility of the possibility. It is rather manifestation inflation and blooming. As a result of this, conjunction grows between man and society in the light of extreme truth and capability. Here, choice becomes one unidirectional. When an individual marches forward along the path of completeness, the companion of interest does not gain prominence, it rather becomes only secondary.

Instead of satisfying self-interest, attention falls on the others. Attention to others becomes the feeling in case of choice. If one bread is procured for two, there would be no attempt of snatching; one would rather pay greater attention to the other. He would like that the whole or the lion's share of that single bread to be enjoyed by the other. As a result of this, a balanced distribution would grow in the society or civilization. A change would come in the basic outlook of economic matters.

Beyond Selfish Motive

This principle is not effective in through of modern economic shape, principle, and applications. Professor Amartya Sen has quoted with importance from Ragnar Frisch's memorial lecture in the context of choice. The problem raised by him in respect of choice is whose requirement is to be met first.

Professor Sen quoted from a writing of Ragnar Frisch (1977):

"Assume that my wife and I have dinner alone as we usually do. For dessert two cakes have been purchased. They are very different, but both are very fine cakes and expensive- according to our standard by life hands me the tray and suggest that I help myself. What shall I do? By looking up my own total utility function I find that, I very much would like to devour in particular one of the two cakes. I will propound that this introspective observation is completely irrelevant out for the choice problem I face. The really relevant problem is which one of the two cakes does my wife prefer? If I knew that the case would be easy. I would say, "Yes please" and take the other cake, the one that is her second priority" (Sen, 2002, p,177)

This question of choice is important in the consideration and distribution of resources. The feeling of requirement and meeting the requirement exists in all of society or state. For this, everybody has his own choice and judgment in light of that. The movement of new commodities in the market for greater satisfaction of those who are able and affluent becomes a problem. At one side, there exists the necessity of providing minimum requirements for the greater population.

The necessity of a small residence, food needful for living, clothes, shelter, education, and health becomes more fundamental. When the provision is small question of priority arises. The mode of distribution of provision and certain newer provisions would grow on the consideration of giving priority to a particular aspect.

If attention is paid to the greater public, the economic foundation becomes firm, but the appearance of a lack of speed would be quite natural. Long waiting would be required to infuse motion right from a sound economic system. On the other hand, in the case of an affluence economic situation, it would be easier for the investment and enterprises launched to grow. That is, speed is infused in the economic cycle by greater enterprise and investment in the economic cycle. But the basis for blooming and investment remains unstable if importance is laid only on this. It is not possible to settle on a strong foundation without the rise of a big public.

When both get involved in strife between them regarding matters related to their interests, then the minds blinded by the cause of their own interests shut up the scope of the infinite possibility of a new line of economic flow. If the stream of infinite possibility gets exposed, the fly of economic blooming would go on uninterruptedly, the principle of. It is proper to consider the principle of consideration between man and nature in this light.

Cooperation and Conflict Between Agriculture and Industry

The basic relation marked between man and nature in agricultural society and civilization has undergone in the society of industrial technology. Search of science and technology has started to cross the boundary, right, and obstruction of nature and fly along the path of victory. Man has conquered nature, and the world has conquered more- this is the chief of the desire. Service and technology for being free from the right of nature has been hostile to the basic culture of agriculture civilization.

In this respect, Schumacher's line of thinking is noteworthy. He (Schumacher, 1973/1990) has remarked:

"There can be no doubts that the fundamental principles of agriculture and of industry, far from being compatible with each other are in opposition. Real life consists of the tensions product by the incompatibility of opposites, each of which is needed, and just as life would be meaningless without death, agriculture would be meaningless without industry. It remains true, however, that agriculture is primary, whereas industry is secondary, which means that human life can continue without industry whereas it cannot continue with agriculture" (91)

Spiritual-Revolution driving Global Economy

Through the deliberation between agriculture and industry is not the last word, the fundamental principle has been apply said in it. The background of may grow up on the basis of the coordination between agriculture and industry lines of history exhibit such occurrence to some extent, both coordination and conflict have been partial and temporary. The reason behind this is that there has been a basic implication of a material basis the method of judgment by which man has arrived at this situation. Rene Descartes has discussed his view of the world classifying everything into two classes.

There are 'res cogitans' or right of mind and 'res extensa' right of the insensate. He has placed the right of the in sensate. The mind mentioned by Descartes on the basis of conflict -coordination but men right of mind and right of the insensate is also an insensate mind, The relation between the two entities of insensate measure is only the tendency to manage one's own provision; the phase bestowal is absent from hare. Existence of the phases of acceptance barring those of bestowal makes all relations to converse at conflict; coordination remains absent. This insensate conflict is in the right of the insensate. Liberation from this lies in spirituality.

Waking up of consciousness is embedded in the basis of spiritual realisation. Awakened consciousness makes divine inspiration and desire in forceful. As a result of this the phase of marching towards an infinite desire crossing one's own entity starts. The feelings shunning interest and offering oneself without being restrained within the enclosure of one's own interest wakes up in mind choice here becomes very easy.

Others aspects gains prominence in the choice of an individual-the feeling 'Not me, but thou' becomes strong. This 'Thou and thin' feeling and realisation may create a new revolution in the economic field. This confidence lies at the root of Kautilya's attribution of importance on the spiritual expansion opens the gate of intellect, genius and knowledge of an individual; builds up coordination; becomes helpful in expansion wealth and; its application for the benefit of many. In the true sense spirituality creates an economic background for mass development.

Bibliography

Fielding, Hall. *The Soul of a People*. London: Macmillan, 1920.

Frisch, Ragnar. *Cooperation between Politicians and Econometricians on the Formalization of Political Preferences*. Federation of Swedish Industries, 1971.

Schumacher, E. F. *Good Work*. HarperCollins, 1980.

Schumacher, E. F. *Small Is Beautiful*. Blond & Briggs, 1975.

Sen, Amartya. *Rationality and Freedom*. New Delhi: Oxford University Press, 2002.

47
Mahabharatiyan Trade Principle

Preamble

Mainly two classes are found in the statement depicted in the *Mahabharata*. One is based on improvidence in lack of principle. Too foreseeing and based on the foundation of religion. The second type of state-management was introduced by Yudhisthira, the emperor after the war of Kuruksetra. And the main example of the first type is the state-management of Dhrtarastra or Duryadhana. Priorto Kuruksetra there were many a settlement whose state-administration used to be run on the basis of religion. There social distribution and public life were especially in accordance with religion. There are many exampleson the leaves of the *Mahabharata* which depict the principle lying at the base of administration of the states. There are examples of different state- administration where financial administration principle, trade principle is compatible with religion. Trade principle lies at the post of economic principle of a state.

But for a proper trade principle a sovereign economic principle cannot be built up. On the trade principle stand on the movements of commodities within thestate, marketing of the commodities, valuation of the commodities, production of commodities and exchange of things; trade principle of a country has these at its bare.

Just at emergence of trade principle has been the judgmental basis of state management and remained at theroot of the decision taken by a state; so also, if it is inclined to have a stable position public life in the state, that is also reflected from the state of public life. How are the common people? How are their life processes? In the front word meaning of the estimation of the form and measure of the element required for carrying on day today-to-day lifethere should be right decision and confidence about the true form of life.

What form of life one requires? Common healthy life at the root of which there is an idea of minimum requirements or one of aggressive greed at the root of which there are strong desire and gradual dissatisfactionof the same. Necessity of realisation and blooming of the confidence that stand at the base of life determines the measure of life. Now question is: what is the feeling of realisation? What is its basis? Yudhisthira has given his opinion in this context:

AnyoDharmahsamasthasyabisama
Sthasyacaparah
ApadastuKathamSakyahParipathena
Beditum.
(*Mahabharata*, Santiparva, 255/4)

[Religion of ascetics is one, that of a householder is different and at the time of danger it is still more different. Solow can their religions be known through reading of the Vedas?]

In different managements and at different ages religion of an individual, of a state and of livelihood become different at different times. Yudhisthira is finally convinced in this the remarks:

Anyekrtaynge dharmastretayamdvapare pare
Anyekaliyugedharmoyathasaktikrataiba
(*Mahabharata*, Santiparra, 255/8)

[Religion is different in different ages. In Satya era religion is of another type, in Tretaera it is of another type, in Dvapara era it isof a third type and in Kali era it is skill of a separate type. Thus, it seems that the sages have introduced religion in accordance with the power of the people,]

It is not that the norms of observing the rites of a religion differs with difference in nature of man. The principle of observing religions rites is embedded in the reforms, nature and traits of one's character reforms, nature and character grossly determines how an individual would behave in public or in family; what his modes of living and behavior in public and family would be; what his mode of living and philosophy of life would be. An individual would turn decisively to be addicted to enjoyment, to be helpful, Snatcher of others goods of parasitic mainly in the perspective of such characteristics. In other words,how a man would behave as a social animal depends in many respects on the personal specialties of his.

Reforms, nature and character are specified by these specialties. What would be the form of purchase of commodities in the market, how and to what extent would these be, and where would be the inclination of the process are determined by the individual characteristic of the man.

The trade principle of the state depends on the outlook of the people about trade. Where the number and influence of persons addicted to extreme enjoyment is, there trade would depend on the theory of gross profit. Compliance of trade would be this gross profit. Behind gross profit there would be the direct support and coordination of those who are addicted to enjoyment.

'Profit' or 'Auspicious Profit'

The question that arises is gross profit or something else. Unless profitable an organisation producer or marketing firm cannot survive. Of course, it is quite natural to be somewhat exceptional in case of government enterprises. E.g., in development of infrastructure, basic industrialization or urgently essential cases subsidy from government treasury becomes necessary for running those. This is needful in developing the fundamental economic base of a country. Organisation that would be run standing on this fundamental base are to depend on profit. Depending of current Year's profit movement will be assured in the next year. If profit of the current year is nil or less provision for the management in the next year would be in available. So, profit ability is not only desirable but also very essential.

But presently the aspect which has disappeared from the traders in an attempt to earn profit is a feeling of religiousness. As earning of profit is desirable. So necessary is think of the question of profit; how these profit would be earned? If there is net profit why one would take an endeavor of trade an enterprise? Profit is the only attraction that money and labour are being invested. If this is no profit, no one would be interest in investment. So profit is not only desirable but also urgent.

Satisfactory answer to the question why is this profit lies with traders. But there are two other questions: what is the quantum of profit and how would be earned? Proper answer to these question does not lie will all. Practically majority cannot answer. Profit or unlimited profit is temporary good for an organisation but in many cases it is improvident. Government enterprises with subsidy in case of infrastructure have been referred to earlier.

Reaching a certain stage, the necessity of this subsidy just ends. E.g., In America and the developing countries development of infrastructure is also profitable enough. In these cases,also therefore lack of endeavour is not noticed. Similar situation has also appeared in India also. One such endeavor must be cited in this context. RelianceInfocom Company had undertaken the programme of Asia. This company had started the programme of laying a cable network of a length of about 80000 KM in India with optic fiber. It took three years to complete the work. It is to be noted that the diameter of the earth is forty thousand Km. with the cable of this than the earth can be wrung truce. The cost of the programme was thirty thousand crores of rupees.

It was proposed that Reliance in the first phase would invest five thousand corer of compound rupees ten thousand corer would be taken on loan by which work would continue for one and half years. In the meantime,programme would begin to fetch money. In the first phase this income would be ten percent greater than the total of investmentand expense. In the next phase this would rise to be in between twenty-five to thirty percent. This enterprise would continueto give profit to Reliance Infocom company for next fifteen to twenty years. This optic fiber cable line programme would get in the country a financial transaction of about ten lack corer of rupees. As a result of these much employment would be created such propensity of profit that gets much profit for the company and at the sometime meets social and financial demands may be called good in one sense.

Good because the propensity of profit of the company and all other related things are seem in the perspective of movement of money. Justification of enterprise of oneself is embedded on these two facts. Excessive profit does not become beauty. So also, is the profit for a limited period. Profit is essential for the very survival of the company, but the methods of earning profit is also to be considered. This combination may be affected by the religions feeling of trade.

There is such example in the pre-Kuruksetra war of the *Mahabharata*. One such splendid example can be had from the account of Tuladhar, the merchant of Jajoli. The mater would be clear for the story and their conversation.

Account of Tuladhar and Jajali

The Santi parva of the *Mahabharata* has depictedthe conversation between Bhisma and Yudhisthira. In course of discussion on the religions of a king, a merchant a worker and a scholar Bhisma has said that religion of any one of them may not be similar to that of the other. Actually, it is often found that religion becomes different on the basis of the form of character of the person concerned and the essential factor of this different comes from within the man. Protection of the difference comes from support of the state.

> Yenaibanyahprabhabatisoparanapi
> Badhyate,
> Acaranamaraikagryamsarbesamupa
> Laksayaet. (255/19)

[Meaning: The religion by which one person gets flourished becomes the cause of oppression on others. So, it is to be noted that religion is not identical everywhere.]

Just as religions of person of different nature are different so also that of different professions.

Jajali and Tuladhar has cast sufficient light on this.

Jajali is a scholar a Brahmin and Tuladhar a merchant. Jajalibelieved that he had acquired the superior knowledge (Knowledge of Brahman) He used to be engaged in severe asceticism. He lived in a hermitage, had been to the sea coast and become expert in continuous fasting, restrained meal and disciplined life. Mattedhair, a small price loin-cloth and deer skin were all he had. Jajali remained long smeared with gluey mud and refuses and at stained from speech under a vow.

Owing to this meditation and asceticism a dazzling glow bloomed in Jajali and he became a state of divinity and power. Factually he could assume astral body and could move as speedily as wind. He could move under the water of the sea and could even roam in the sky. On one occasion Jajali determine to see the universe. After roaming through forest and jungles he saw the heavenly path. All of these had been accomplished with the victory of the mind. After being able in all such practices jajali through that he had a glaring strength and power within himself. No one else in these three worlds has such power, he through, God has bestowed this power only on him hearing this even the demonical animals having under the see got started, one of them said, "O Lord, please go to Kasi. There you will find a merchant named Tuladhar.

Jajali set out meeting Tuladhar, the merchant when they met, Jajali found Tuladharselling his merchandise. Tuladhar welcomed Jajati and told him something in context of his past which made jajati taken a back and he found that Jajali through engaged in business is vastly wise. He asked, 'O merchant, how have you got this superior knowledge? Jajali had taken the man to be slaying in the midst of all types of true significances of worship. But for one who sells accumulated goods and fruits of trees and the like have acquired superior knowledge was really a wonder. In very Tuladhar said, "I am aware of the Vedas.

I have known Vedic Knowledge.

> Adrohenaibabhutanamalpadrohenabapunah
> Yabrttihsaparodharmastenajibamijajjlet (256/6)

[Meaning: O jajati the living the causes no or little harm to animal is the greatest virtue. I earn living through that religion virtue]

> Parochinnihkasthatrnairmayedam
> SaranamKrtam
> Alaktampadmakamtungamgandham
> Sceccabacamstatha.
> Rasamscatamstanbiprarsel
> Madyabarjyanbahunaham
> Kritvabaipratibikrineparahastamayaya. (256/7-8)

[Meaning : I have built this house with cleangrass and wood and purchasing lac, padma and tunga woods, Different types of essences, many types of liquids barring wine I sale these without found.]

Besides the principle of my sale is:

> Tula me sarbabhitesusamatisthati
> Jajate I (256/16)

[My balance is same for all]

From this conversation of Jajali and Tuladhar is it clear that Tuladhar's profession did not stand as a barrier before attaining the greatest treasure of life, the knowledge of the absolute for him. Both hard and difficult asceticism of Jajaliand the spiritual principle of Tuladhar have brought identical results. Tuladhar's principle of selling is "fraud less' and equal measure (balance) for all. Virtue is the main word of Indian trade principle Virtue and devotion to principle has been mere forceful than the propensity for profit before the merchants. As a result profit has turned into auspicious profit. Tuladhar has been owner of wealth, and at the same time he had been the possessor of a blissful complete life.

Trade Principle

Tuladhar's trade principle echoes the trade-principle of the eternal India. The main thing in it is the basis of successful balance in life. Behind the propensity for extreme profit is a strong desire to be wealthy and resort to any path whatsoever to fulfil that desire. A question arises in Yudhirsthira's mind-low the thirst for wealth can be removed. He asked Bhisma this question. Bhisma narrated to him the conversation between Janaka, the king and Mandabya, the great hermit.

Mandabye had told Janaka:

Arthahkhalusamraddhahibadham
Duh khambijanatam
A samrddhastvapisadamohayartyabicaksanam (269/5)

Meaning: Plenty of wealth cansus worst unhappiness to the conscientious again little wealth always causes infatuation of the tools. Mandabya clarified the subject with example he had said:

Yathaibasrngamgoh kale
Bardhamanasyabardhale
Tathaibatrana bitten bardhamanenabardhate (269/7)

Meaning :

Just as with gradual graving up of a cow itshorns also grow bigger; so also, as wealth increases thirst for the same also increases. Janaka, the emperor is called royal ascetic. This means one who in spite of being a king is an ascetic. Administration of a kingdom by a royal ascetic differs from that of a king. In case of kings rule personal desire and its fulfilment, profit and loss, satisfaction of interest become prominent. In case of a royal ascetic there is no scope of such things.

The rules in the interest of pleasing the subjects his rule is only in the interest of the subjects. His leadership is fully dependent and God and directed to God. A royal ascetic controls his kingdom as a respective of God. To him all persons deserve some dignity and due. A royal ascetic knows that is God's management of the world everyone has fundamental and universal rights and at the same time there are fundamental duties for him to be carried out. Family of the royal ascetic is vastly spread he knows that case and this result of economic flourish one to be carried to all. For this is required production is enough measure within the country and movement and marketing of the produce.

The Royal ascetic here observes the duty of a real king. A king in the reason development if the subjects and as the same time he may also be the reason believed this run.

Rajaibakartabhutanamrajaiba ca binasakah
Dharmatma yah sakartasyadaharmatmabinasakah. (189/9)

Meaning: It is the king who is responsible for prosperity of the subjects, again it is he who destroys them. A religions king is the reason behind prosperity and a irreligious king behind the destruction.

Not only ruling over the subjects, but to give inspiration and well protection to the merchants in their trade also is the duty of a king.

Yada sasaranikan raja putrabatparibaksan.
Bhinatti ca no maryadamsarajno dharma neyata. (189/36)

Meaning:

King's duty is to protect the merchants like his own sons and make such arrangement as to see that none loses his glory. Kings' duty is not only to make arrangement of the trade of the merchants but also to give well protection and befitting glory to then. The king will arrange him state. Management in such way as to make all arrangements for economic development in the kingdom will be compulsory. But all should be done on the basis of virtue. Virtue will be the fundamentals basic of trade also. Trade will not stand an injustice. In the interest of the trade the king would not only give protection to the merchants but he would also control and subdue the basic of injustice and dishonest merchants strongly. If necessary, merchants may be brought under the control of the king and undertake their rectification. The duty of the king would be to remove all obstacles from the path of flourish of the merchants. The fundamental duty of the king would to give the merchants opportunities of earning money. But the king will keep vigilance so that this earning of money by the merchants be in honest way.

Arthasiddhahpranamdharmammanyeteyomahipatih
Brddhyancakurutebuddhimsadharmenabirajate. (190/7)

Meaning: A king who takes virtue superior to money and gives attention to him and to the kingdom, becomes a learning by dint of his virtue.

King would pay importance to virtue. That is money would be controlled through virtue. Under the control of aroyal ascetic this virtue becomes universal. If trade becomes conjoined with the social views and state principle the king if would become complete and beneficial to all. The merchant who conducts his trade unjustly the expectation of extra profit would cross the injunction of the royal office and necessity would be punished. In the context proficiency of Tuladhar in virtue in the story of Jajati-Tuladhar is worthy of mention.

It is not that Tuladhar has done a noble deed through using correct weight, but his principle is to have justified profit, his principle is lawful profit. As a result, earning of wealth and surplus money has not been a problem to Tuladhar, at the same time he had no problem to walk in the path of virtue.

In spite of being a merchant he has become a great hermit with full knowledge of the Absolute self. The separateness and superiority of Tuladhar's trade-principle should be realized if it is discussed and observed in the light of modern trade. In the light of moderntrade-principle the matter may be discussed in two stages. First, on the basis of principle of process i.e. what would be main note of the trade-principle and what would be the process of its shaping. Second, on the basis of experience i.ewhat has been the result of the trade what are the from and consequence of the merit and demerits caused by the trade. The present discussion will briefly through light on both.

Custom of World Trade and Trade Principle of the *Mahabharata*

The context of Tuladhar is recurring because he directed such a trade as developed him spiritually. We are coming to the discussion why Tuladhar's instruction is useful is bringing change in the trade principle of modern world'

World trade Organisation abbreviated as W.T.O is now the controller of trade in the world. There was a time when portion of world economy was limited within a country and in many cases controlled by the government of the native land. Presently this situation is being changed. Europe, North America and Australia are unopposed lands of open market economy. That is in their region greater path of trade in under the control of the power of the market. The main object of market is the power of demand and supply many other regions then those mentioned are now coming under the control of the power of the market. Many Asian countries are examples, China and India have recently entered into the circle.

The main object of world trade organisation is to roses the power of demand and supply throughout the world and to set up a single market in the world. That is to build up the same trade system everywherestarting from America, Mexico down China India, Nepal, that is introduction of the same principle irrespective nature. Tests, behaviour target and significant of life. The consequence may be both good and bad. The true from of the subject come out on going deep into it. Influence and reaction of different agreements of World Trade Organisation would be different on different countries. Let us now discuss the effect of different agreements as India and the trade principle emerge dent of the same.

India has come under the provision thirteen contracts is all. Of these the special ones are:

First: Gatt Agreement (1986-94)

The main object of this agreement is to bring force in movement of commodities within the country and in the world market, is lift up domestic control from foreign commodities. As a result of this Government of India has withdrawn tax and control of number in majority cases. A disaster has come on the inland industry. Two mention able points of this subject is reaction of the producer and reaction of the consumer. Producers have not always been able to apply would quality technology and for that they often have had to face disaster. A small example will clarify the matter.

Heavy engine of Tata, we all along had known that Tata products are of high standard. Truck engine of Tata had the reputation of being of high standard. No doubt ever arose with standard in production of engines is the function of Telco in Jamsedpur and Pune. No question did arise till there had been any chance of seeing other engine to draw comparison. Tatas instantly apprehended the danger. They took joint venture with Cumins Company of America for constructing new engines. This new engine is of would standard Consequently Telco closed down the engine section of Jamsedpur and attached the engine product at the joint enterprise named Tata,Cummins with the Telco, trucks. Ready wit of Tatas saved their business. But in many other cases companies had to face fall and closure due to free trade of the post-Gatt period.

Tenth Agreement: Agreement of Agriculture

By this agreement there would be no subsidy in agriculture. Application of fertiliser pesticides and hormones would have to be increased. As a result,agricultural productswould come to India from abroad. Foreign rice and pulses would gain prominence in Indian market. Reason is that the government would not be able to retain the measures taken by bit in different spheres nor would be able to retain the price in future. Some countries are being able to produce extensively rice, wheat etc unexpectedly low price (rice costing 215 may be purchased with rupees one or two)

As a result, Indian buyers would be inclined to that side, i.e there is disproportionateness in the interest of agricultural produces and agricultural consumers.

Objects shown in different agreements of the world trade organisation are much different from the real picture. Rights of living and affluence will not be met with this. Because if during liberalization of trade real situation is not paid attention to development of different measures will only increases the economic also on other side, if there is control of trade on the marketor on the balance between demand and supply; its serviceability to common buyers increases because price rises and falls, newer innovative measures of we are added.

Conclusion

The main object of the trade-principle of the *Mahabharata* is to carry the effect of trade to all and to accomplish trade as the basis of principle and virtue modern world-trade is far off from this. The good effect of the agreements and principles of world trade organisation would go to the rich countries. Poor and backward countries would be just market and buyers of the manufacturing and supplying organisation of the rich countries. The principle of Tuladhar is needful in the case of world trade.

If the principle is applied, the clauses of agreement would be determined in the light of the financial, infra-structural and social conditions of the concerned status in case of every agreement and endeavours of world trade organisation. On the part of world trade organisation, the trade process of Tuladhar can be a very important custom. The outcome of this process is trade on the basis of virtue. Trade for the benefit of all future world make Tuladhar its ideal.

48
Trade Principle of Asoka

The Hindu economy began to develop during the pre-Rigvedic period. The same stream has flowed in the Indian economy through Vedic, Puranic ages and the age of Indian Valley Civilization. There has been some deviation in post-Christ ages, viz., during the rules of the Muslims and the British. The primary economic thought and flow have remained unaltered. The mixed economy of the post-independence period and the liberal international economy of the current time have not changed the flow of that basic economy.

The strength of the basic propensity and effectiveness of the Hindu economy lies in the Hindu mentality, which has swelled up in Indian civilisation at every stage. The pressure of the nation or dominance of external influence has not been able to make the flow of the Indian economy weak, rather it has strengthened it. Of all the endeavours of setting up national integrity around the spirit of India, the most mentionable is that of Asoka, the great. Just as Asoka's deeds are an integral part of history, Asoka's economic principles are also one of the best instructions left in economic history. The principles laid down in Kautilya's *Arthashastra* are partly applicable here, and so is the economic belief in the reign of Rama.

Greatness of Asoka

Information obtained about the early life of Asoka is quite different from the latter parts of his time. Before accepting Buddhism, Asoka seems cruel, dexterous and selfish. Sri Lankan (Ceylonese) sources provide ample information about this period. Buddhist report 'Divyabadan' states that Asoka occupied and ruthlessly preserved the throne after his father's death. He slew all his ninety-nine brothers except Tisya, the younger one. Buddhist scripts have tried to show much difference between the two parts of Asoka's life. These aim at proving that Asoka, before accepting Buddhism, is quite different from the man after taking the Buddhist vow and that it is Buddhism that made Asoka great.

But the course of events is quite different. Asoka's ascent to the throne and holding of power had the scope of cruelty, no doubt, but it is not true that he had killed all his brothers. Stone inscriptions depict that he had engaged many of his brothers in the kingdom's administration. Some of them were killed in Patliputra and used to take an active part in administrating the stone inscriptions. Asoka has been described as 'Devanamapiya' and 'Piyadarsan', meaning appreciated by God and amiable looking, respectively. Asoka's place is at the top in world history. H.G. Wells in his globally known title *The Outline of History*, has termed Asoka as the qualities king Asoka has given the adjective not based on the extension of his empire.

Asoka's empire was vast and extended through greater India, barring up to some of the portions of the border of the Persian empire. H.G. Wells has termed Asoka as the greatest king because of his character, personality, ideal life, and principles of administration. Asoka administration trio called to be the three most significant rulers of the world—Alexander, Caesar and Napoleon.

As man and ruler, none of them is at par with Asoka; Asoka ruled his kingdom based on virtue and religion. He looked at his subjects as his own and treats likewise. Asoka's ideal and philosophy of life and preachings of peace, fraternity and faith. He mentioned coordinating the economic system for salvation from mortal life and residing man's virtue and virtuous feelings and showed them the path to a more improved life. As a king, Asoka flourished on this path through the activities and endeavours of the state.

Power and prescript of unity of the state is quite interactive for Asoka. As a prince, he had overseen Ujjain and Taxila; he successfully subdued revolt and succession in the kingdom. In the eight years of his rule, Asoka's conquest of Kautilya was a vast, bloody war. Almost a lac of soldiers and co-warriors died in this war. Besides, 1.5 lakh were prisoners of war. This wide bloody war made Asoka think of the consequences of war, and he took the vow of Buddhism from Upagupta, the Buddhist monk. Henceforth, all of Asoka's thoughts and life were dedicated to the welfare of humankind.

Economy in the Service of People

Of the stone inscriptions obtained on the life and administration of Asoka, fourteen are the inscription on stoneslabs and seven are inscriptions on stone pillars. Stone inscriptions were found in different places of Odisha, Delhi, Junagar and caves in other sites' hills. From deciphering the inscription, Asoka made his path of life stand on the inherent ethics of the Buddhist. The factor of Buddhist philosophy that is beneficial for people worldwide turned out to be the principle of Asoka's liking.

The main principle of Asoka's administration of the state economy was religion. Tolerance, non-violence, self-restraint, equal treatment and gentility-social conditions in Asoka's time had been built up based on their qualities.

Asoka described his socio-economic situation in his sixth inscription. He said, "All subjects are my children. My prescription is to give pleasure and happiness to my children; my desire is their equilibrated state and spiritual upliftment; in the same sense, my duty is to prescribe happiness and welfare to all people. Through my works, their moral life be full of joy and interest, and later course, they would have the boon for heaven." Since Asoka's view extended towards the moral and spiritual lives of the subjects as he was eager to meet the requirements of natural life, he also engaged himself in satisfying this spiritual hunger.

He extended full support to Buddhist monastic guilds, divided into different branches because of the influence of various quarters, and spread everywhere within the society, the state and even outside. The state had patronised the monastic hermit ages carrying sayings of improved culture and life through support and favours.

Asoka had dispelled the limit of his personal life before the requirements of administration. It is known from one of the inscriptions that he had said, "My primary duty is the welfare of man and the world. I am always ready to do beneficial work for men at any time. Whenever I stay in whatever condition I may be in -on hunting, in forests in the inner portion of the place - my doors are open welfare of the people. I am ready to render service to man and the world. Asoka did not stop only. He expressed his hope thus: My sons, grandson, the great-grandson would observe constant endeavour to maintain the structure and economy of the welfare state and will attribute the most outstanding care for the welfare of the people."

Welfare State

Quite a good amount of description about state administration is available from the stone inscription of Brahmagiri, Sahasram and

Rupnath. Asoka drew everybody to the path of religious lines. Firstly, authority was directed at the officers. He timed fervently to bring change in their lives. In some cases, he had to resort to the punishment process. After the high officials and bureaucrats, he drew ordinary workers to religious lives. Next came the people.

Asoka gave the rule of law and the basis of the rule of justice for all. The target of economic justice was the provision for the living of all and protection for the future. He punished even prominent officials for community injustice to the public. An incident from the inscriptions of Dhouli and Jaugada threw special light on the aspect. Complaint of that locality to the effect that he had punished some persons for no-fault and shut them to jail quite unjustifiably; he had also committed some monetary malpractices. Asoka had genius had severe punishment and thus warned all ministers and officers against the consequence of the harmful practice.

Asoka had passed orders for workers and officers for rectification of character. He wanted men of calm and handsome appearance, of principle and firm nature. Asoka told them, "Your basic struggle is to acquire the strength of your character and honesty against the dacoits on the roads. He wanted liberation from malice, greed, hardness, worry, unrest, laziness etc."

Asoka made the government and social workers realise that to be engaged in the service of humans through works of their own is the noblest duty. He was always eager to make them learn through a call for idealism and creating himself as an example. But still, a part of the ministers and workers disobeyed.

Asoka's principle: To prevent such propensity, he introduced. '*Mahabharata*'. *Mahabharata* was used to audit the works of the chief officers and directors in charge of all religions every five years for vigilance against obstruction. The decision was taken in terms of the reports of *Mahabharata*'s inscription. The most important and urgent task was to give the emperor's principles a concrete shape. From what Asoka had said in the description of the fifth stone inscription, it becomes clear that the duty of *Mahabharata* was not only to cite mistakes but also rectification. They are basically like monks. These mahamantras were eager to give assurance and advice for proper management so that the lives of the workers and enterprises may go on under the control of religious injunction. Their duty was to be initiated into welfare in mortal life and, at the same time, to associate spirituality with life beyond.

Financial Administration

The mahamantras initially only investigated the application of government policies. They used to look after the correct installation of an aberrance from the right principles and ideals of the state and, at the same time, used to take steps for rectification. Later mahamantras were transformed into dharma mahamantras.

These two primary duties were: financial administration and religion injection. The central theme of financial administration was public welfare. The first step of general interest was: taking responsibility for the lonely old helpless ailing and poor people. The state has borne the whole of the financial burden of such people. When dharma mahamantras could find such people, they would make proper arrangements in their zones.

The second step of public welfare is the prevention of injustice. The state would have two-fold management for this. First, punishment of those who acted unjustly and second, social and financial relation of the victims. The most mentionable aspect of this arrangement is a sequence of endeavours. Who would take the first initiative state or the one who takes welfare? Obeying the *Arthashastra* of Kautilya, Asoka has vested the responsibility on the form. That is, it is the state's duty to search if anyone suffers from starvation.

Even if the starving citizen fails to apprise the state of problems, it would be the duty of the state's representatives, ministers and workers to find out the starving man and to arrange for his living. Of course, in respect of this living, the state would act per its custom and nation just in the same way crippled, old, attacked with old age, a desire, affected by fortune can expect welfare by the endeavour of the state.

In the third step of public welfare, every citizen is instructed on more improved living. Asoka expected from every citizen resident worker minister such a life borne by firmness and higher character qualities. As a result of this, on one side, the administration would be responsible, restrained and sensitive. At the same time, on the other side, people would be careful about their duties and would not be involved in any anti-state activity.

Thus, the state would be more dynamic, righteous and able to run the administration based on justice. Asok was very much restless in this regard. Frequently he did take the influence of all the zones of the country. A stone inscription depicts. I can never be satisfied in respect of work. To bring welfare to the world is my vow. The basis of fulfilling the vow is completing the job speedily and honestly. Asoka has laid the most significant value on the people. In his administration, all types of work related to the public's welfare have been given priority.

Source of Income of the State

Works related to the public's welfare were a medium of expense of money from the state treasury. From the infrastructure of state communication, development and reformation down to the maintenance of the old, infirm, crippled, poor and helpless and service-besides provision for money for widespread citizens. The state was determined to incur such expenditure by opening its bear shop. Another feature of Asoka's rule was that the people living in the mountains and forests were satisfied with the state administration. All the wealth apt to be distributed reached all classes of people.

Now, the question is: how and from where would money be supplied to the state treasury? What was the source of the income of the state?

In Asoka Kingdom, revenue was earned in two ways: one from taxes on produce and income and two through other types of taxes. Asoka's state itself was not directly connected with trade or works of agriculture. State only fixed up principles and investigated the application of the same; officers and workers of different stages of the state related to the realisation of taxes city-magistrates used to work on the application of law and at the same time, they were to look after the completion of taxes. No enterprise was related to the grip of taxes, but there was a difference in the rate of taxes. Stone inscriptions of Sarnath, Udaygiri, Khandagiri and Delhi depict the rates of taxes were:

One-fourth of the total income
One-sixth of the total income
Or,
One eight of total income
Depending upon the situation and cases.

In the case of surplus production in agriculture, which works up to expectation, generally one-sixth of the tax was levied. The state used to take produce as tax, e.g., agricultural produce was used to meet taxes. The state would collect and distribute the same on a zonal basis.

One-sixth of the tax rate in Asoka's reign reminds one of the rules of remark. There also, the rate of tax was one-sixth of the produce. In case of any inconvenience met by the state, rate was increased to one-fourth. Again, issues of reduction of taxes are also observed in the activities of the state. e.g., there had been a notable reduction in taxes for Lumbini, the birthplace of Lord Buddha and habitants of Lumbini had to pay taxes at the rate of one region of the produced.

A detailed description of the distribution system can be seen from any inscription. However, based on the sources available, in Asoka's rule, the distributor's approach had not been limited zonally. It instead spread through the neighbourhood and even to distant places. As a result, any zonal discrimination in this state had been eliminated.

Zonal representatives of the state used to fix up taxes, and at the same time, city magistrates had been entrusted with judging the justness of the same. If any case, it would sweat that the tax had been increased out of grudge or reduced to show favour, the concerned officer won't get warned of punishment. City-magistrates were to arrange for this punishment.

Special Types of Taxes

In Asoka's rule, there was a provision for taxes on produce. At the same time, there were some other types of taxes. In social cases, wrong doers had to face two kinds of punishment. One for social crime-this comprised imprisonment, exile etc. And delicate along with. The power of imposing fines had been vested in the city magistrates. They were to fix up the amount and term.

Besides, there were special taxes on religious celebrations. On many occasions, there had been exemptions in this, e.g., for Lumbini, the birthplace of Lord Buddha. But in the case of the erection of Buddhist temples in some places, the tax would have been imposed. Given this line, it is seen that religious nobleness Asoka is rather scanty or may instead, he is said to be absent. Different inscription depicts the realisation of religious tax in the erection of Buddhist temple. Still, any sign of endeavour to erect a Hindu temple or renovate the like is absent.

Economic Mentality of Asoka

Just as Asoka, in state administration, had laid the most significant importance on public welfare and economic management, he has stressed a unique mentality. He opined those men are indebted to one another in many ways. Men are accountable to the solar system, to rational persons, to the ancestors and commonly to humans. So, Asoka has repeatedly reminded the people of this duty to pay off these debts. According to him, fixing up tasks is the most significant step to paying off debts, "I am the king; my duty is to live and let live and with good with of my own to cast kind notice on others. State management and the social system will be perfectly well if everyone becomes aware of one's duty." This debt principle of Asoka has been taken from the Upanishads. The theory of the five debts of the Upanishad itself has been reflected in this. But in Asoka's assertion, there is no acknowledgement of the same. In this sense, Asoka is the borrower of money.

His activities showed that Asoka had been careful about transfusing this same debt to the royal workers. After the conquest of Kautilya, there was vast devastation and losses, and waste, especially the condition of the woman folk, was the most pathetic; forsaking violence widows of the families of one lac dead and 1.5 lac captives began to feel helpless. Asoka showed sympathy to them. Besides, people needed financial help. Asoka supplied the same. Secondly, at the same time tax imposed on the people of Kalinga was at the rate of one-eighth. Thus, Asoka had expiated or became eager to pay off debt.

Religious Travels of Asoka

Through acknowledgement of debts and side by side through the inspiration of people towards religious conscientiousness, Asoka was able to get some reflection on the reign of Rama in his empire. Religions stepped in to engage people in work and duty in the mortal and make them productive. Asoka repeatedly cursed laziness. His order was that a man, whenever he might be or in what condition he might be played in, would be immediately contacted and active in the state's need. Thus, he set examples and brought a workflow among two government workers and ministers. On the other hand, this religious inspiration and conscientiousness have helped people follow the ideals of just principles and, simultaneously, have made them cooperative with the state and society.

Due to the invigoration of religious conscientiousness, man gradually has reduced his craving and, on the other side, has augmented his propensity of giving and satisfaction. The tendency to enjoy has decreased; man has been handy and cooperative instead of being an obligation to the state. From a small inscription, Asoka is known to have said. As a result of bringing a man on the path of spirituality, his sense of responsibility has been attributed to others, and man has attained godly character. After death, the sacred soul of such men would go to heaven.

In the stone inscription, Subarnagirihe had expressed his hope adding to be of virtuous character, the capacity of doing work of the people, workers, and ministers would increase and half times at least. The king's responsibility here is to judge the problem-able people with sympathy, compassion and affection. On the other hand, if the king committed a mistake, the public would keep his patience and, to a specific limit, forgive his omissions and commissions.

This endurance would no doubt reform both sides, not only, but would increase the effectiveness of both sides. Accordingly, Asoka, for the king's endeavour to set up a welfare state, would require the active cooperation of the people. The association of the people would naturally be with the king if the administration and infrastructure of the state were made to stand based on virtue. The Asoka's victory through integrity (dhamma Vijaya) was a more developed step in changing the state's economic infrastructure.

Conclusion

In the state of Asoka, the emperor was a benefactor and welfare. In the name of seeking the interest of all states, had never shown looseness in realising it due. Suppose anybody unjustly evaded dues of the state or deprived the state. Asoka penal code stood as the countermeasure. Asoka's penal code followed Kautilya' s views. Asoka has explained the corrective-code as provided by Kautilya. This is when the hand strikes heart bleeds. Even in the case of commandment and punishment, a tender and sympathetic heart would weep for the wrong doer. This means that presently is a date deviation, not a far penalty. The motive behind correction. So, heartiness side by side with finally would not increase the distance between the punished and the one who inflicts punishment. The space would instead decrease. One who is punished would be able to realise that the man in him is not being punished; instead, the mischief done is.

In Asoka's rule, economic management is an overall balanced one. Information on poverty and epidemic needs to be included. But inequality and mismanagement have often thrived. In this respect, Asoka's rule is weaker than that of Rama Factually, in the flow of the Hindu economy, that of Asoka is a slighted step.

49

Economic Wisdom: Kautilya and Keynes

Kautilya's *Arthashastra* glows with the wisdom he procured in his lifetime. If the perspective of the economic principles printed by Kautilya is seen in a different view than search and research, he might need to be more understood. Factually, Kautilya needs to be more understood. Many questions have been placed to debate whether the theories specified in the *Arthashastra* are related to economics. Kautilya has created so comprehensive background to present his economic views that these are often lost in the environment, social management policy, social reforms and principles, defence, foreign policy, etc., had combined, as presented by Kautilya, cattle farming policy, treasury management policy, income and expenditure policy, saving policy and above all, the policy for shaping the economic character.

Kautilya is the first economist to be called to be glowing with economic wisdom. He has churned the past and judged the how in the perspective of the past and, at the same time, has presented to society and stated a new economic principle in the light of his wisdom. As such, Kautilya can be accepted as a possessor of a combined knowledge in economics.

The excellence of many subjects in which Kautilya' s discussion and theories are moving had gotten lost at that time. What is the role of statecraft in the debate on economic awakening and economic flourish? How much is the financial part of diplomacy, war principles, foreign policy, politics, the principle of social administration, etc.? How does the good or bad of the king affect the country?

Where does state economy converge on the war principle? Where does the training in spiritual learning, Vedic learning, and good character influence economic management? Kautilya has given the last of the state for activities divided into many classes. During the discussion on the excellence of agricultural lands, Kautilya went deep into the explanation of the size of the land and how different articles would surround it. Kautilya' s view glowing with wisdom has so widened the periphery of economics that much later and even today, it is essential in discussion and deliberation on the theories of economics. Great economists of the twentieth century have earned depth and spread in respective topics, but the pervasion of Kautilya still needs to be discovered.

Without comparing with the pervasion of Kautilya, it may be impressive that Keynes' economy is also extensive. But compared to Kautilya Keynes, 'extensiveness' is only a part. John Maynard Keynes (1883-1946) is the brightest luminaries in Western economies. Keynes' influence has spread in every sphere of society and state. The economic recession that appeared in Europe and almost the whole Western world from 1929 created a stir in Keynes' mind; Keynes not only apprehended that Europe would be prey to great war but warned all concerned against this eventuality.

Keynes accompanied David Lloyd George, the British Prime Minister, as his coordinator at the Versailles peace conference held to perform Versailles agreements after the havoc of World War II in Europe. Keynes was perturbed at the burden placed on Germany at this conference. He realised that this Versailles agreement, instead of bringing peace would cause more war and the devastation in Europe.

Keynes vehemently criticised Woodrow Wilson, the American president, and the British leaders at the conference. He wrote an easily killed economic consequence of peace (1919) to express his own opinion against the resolution taken at the meeting.

In his opinion, Keynes fell prey to the wealth of the government. In 1921, he returned to Cambridge as a teacher in economics. His father, John Neville Keynes, had been a professor of moral philosophy at Cambridge. His mother was the first lady graduate of Cambridge and had become mayor of Cambridge. As a student in Cambridge, Keynes had Alfred Marshall as his teacher. After graduating from Cambridge (1905), he joined the British Civil Service.

The first appointment was at the Indian office in London. While working here, he collected different economic materials about India. His first book, *Indian Currency and Finance*, was published in 1913. At that time, he had returned to Cambridge with a teaching assignment. At the break of World War I, he was called back to the government centre. He came back to the service. At the time, his primary duty was to advise the British government about the measure of currency, the movement of foreign currency, and the financial relations within the allied power and to frame principles for the government.

After returning from Cambridge with a teaching assignment as an after-effect of versatile agreement, Keynes felt pain for world mode unemployment, poverty and economic depreciation. Going through the classical line of financial management, he presented a new theory to develop new management of financial movement. In 1936, Keynes's most outstanding achievement, the book on originally fundamental theory titled General Theory of Employment, Interest and Money was published.

As a means of a solution to financial problems, Keynes has laid stress on the removal of unemployment, the movement of money and the proper use of resources. In the following year of publication of the general theory, he had a massive heart attack. In establishing international institutions that began to organise and control the financial management of the post-World War II world, the role of Keynes is worthy of mention. In the New Hampshire Breton Woods Conference, 1994 for post-World War II reconstruction and enterprise pro-establishment system infrastructures and enterprises were through. In the later period, those pro-establishment enterprises have grown to be vast enough to control the financial management of the world. The fame of Keynes spread far and wide in the post-World War II period. In his general theory, Keynes presented a separate faith and confidence in the pervasion of the wealth of nations of Adam Smith regarding economic thought.

In his general theory, Keynes has looked at unemployment in two ways: voluntary and involuntary. Involuntary unemployment paves the way for financial and social for true in society. Keynes asserts that men are Involuntary unemployed if, in the event of a slight rise in the price of wage goods relative to the money wage, both the aggregate supply of labour willing to work for the current money wage and the aggregate demand for it at that wage would be greater than the existing volume of employment. (Keynes General Theory, C42., Sec 2).

Involuntary unemployment brings a change in financial management in two ways. Firstly, applying economic awakening factors gets furnished; secondly, a downward trend may be infused in financial management. The new realisation of consuming may get a fresh impression in financial management.

For this, Keynes judged the taste and reasonable factors of consumerism. An accurate estimation of unemployment in a country can be ascertained by industrial and financial classification. The point those graphs of aggregate supply and aggregate demand meet is the measure of aggregate wage deployment. Thus, with the charts of the collection of labour, the estimation of unemployment becomes easier. Keynes wanted to boost the demand for money by increasing the supply in the market. With the bloom of demand, one would be the spread of supply; the aggregate graphs of demand and supply then meet at a higher point. This means an increase in labour supply and a diminution of unemployment.

Keynes's theory depicted that some comparative considerations are essential for the aggregate increase in demand. One must consider whether expense increases with an increase in income or whether the propensity to purchase consumable goods increases or decreases with the rise and fall of income. Comparative growth is essential when there is an increase in income. The tendency of expense becomes comparatively greater than the rate of revenue increase.

The possibility of supply of labour becomes bright. Keynes has advised to reject older theories and apply newer ones, especially in the case of financial distribution and expansion. When an individual's propensity for income decreases, the extent of expense decreases. Again, if the market price rises, but income remains the same, an individual becomes alert of expense. In the case of economic depression, aggregate expenditures do not decrease. As a result, the initial repression becomes fiercer and speedy falls.

Keynes was very much vocal and enterprising in this matter. He believed that it is impossible to get rid of the depression of the market through the balance of power of the market in the future or by activities of the same invisible hand of different powers in the market. Keynes had written an open letter in the New York Times to intimate Roosevelt, the president, that government expenditure was to be increased to combat the falling demand in the market due to revision and, at the same time, proper alteration needed to be brought in the tax structure of the government.

In the language of Keynes, In the long run, we are all dead›, so correction in the effect and process of the market is to be brought right today; economic balance may be set up, keeping unemployment intact. The government is to come forward to create balance in the economy. Different types of mass enterprises are to be taken by the government whereby government funds dissipate throughout the country, and other goods and services would come back into the market as demand for purchase. As a result, there would be an awakening and an explosion of demand.

Keynes established his theory with respect to 'marginal propensity to consume, marginal propensity to save and average propensity to consume and rescue, etc. The method of determination of marginal propensity to consume is to consider the extent of expense for consumption against the additional income. Also, the marginal propensity to save is determined by the portion of income that is saved. That is, the propensity to consume saving and propensity to save are advised to be determined regarding income.

Keynes, of course, did not judge only in respect of income. Factors other than income are also to be taken into account of such factors other than income may be made of indirect income or factors favouring income. It cannot be accurately inferred that a sudden increase in revenue would result in a proportionate rise in expense. There is an opportunity for the expense to increase with an increase in income. Still, if there is a balanced relation between income and expenditure, it is possible to be conversant with the marginal propensity to ensure and the marginal propensity to save.

Sometimes, the propensity to consume is not directly dependent on income. In such cases, individuals or organisations, without caring for payment, move forward for expense works, dissaving the propensity to keep waiting. Dissaving propensity is when the tendency to save exceeds the income value. In such cases, such a person either runs into debt or begins to expend continuously from his earlier savings. As a result of this, no saving takes place. Instead, such moments come to him as he completely exhorts his resources earned through saving through his propensity to consume. If such activity is on the part of a business organisation or another such institution, it sometimes becomes injurious for resources or adds to the existing resources. If that institution with that expenditure collects some capital goods, it will be detrimental to the help.

Increased the value of capital goods or elements will be used up for the creation of resources or the addition of finance. This increase of resources or addition of finance would be helpful for the instant financial development of the institution and, at the same time, for the creation of resources in the future. It has been found by different types of experiments that the balance between income and consumption in the financial picture of other developed and developing countries, especially in the decades of the seventies, eighties, and nineties of the last century, can be detected. Consumption and propensity to consume increase with the increase in income.

Consumption and propensity to consume moved parallel to income, sometimes at the same speed and sometimes at a different rate. If income propensity to consume through expenditure increases, the financial distribution improves. If money is spread in many hands market also begins to spread from different stages and directions. The retail, wholesale, and swelled-up markets of different types of goods help aggregate the economy's speed.

But even above this, proper distribution of the tax system is needed to correct all sorts of market propensities. This distribution is designed as a balance between an increase in income and expenditure. Tax may be imposed in different forms to balance income and spending. In such cases, two targets are there for the imposition of taxation, e.g., to provide additional revenue for the state or to be ardent for imposing a restraint of expenditure in case of surplus income through the imposition of tax. As a result, with an increase in revenue, the propensity for an increase in spending will flow along the desired channel, and the flow in the undesired channel would be hindered, too.

Expenditure in all fields or of all types cannot bring the same effect on the market. As some types of expenditure influence the market, others cannot do so. For example, with an increase in the sale of goods, production that brings variations or casts a direct effect expands the financial circle. On the other hand, such commodities production only maintains statuesque instead of getting diversity in the market. In the first case, buyers' contribution not only improves the market but also causes its expansion. In the second case, the effect of the buyers' market maintaining statuesque sometimes causes improvement, too.

The forecasting effect on Keynes looked at the government enterprises, especially the widespread ones. Due to government enterprises, different development programmes would continuously hasten the development process. At the same time, those would be rapid movement of money. A new set of buyers would be created through this movement of funds. These new buyers come with the expansion and swelling of the market. The purchase and use of new buyers are often quite different from those of old buyers. So, new buyers are always attractive to the market.

Keynes thought of expansion and the wide rise of the market under the influence of government expenses and enterprise and developed his theory accordingly. Financial endeavour is to cause an explosion of demand in the market through mass expansion of money because of government and public enterprise and to reduce this direct and indirect unemployment, because of this financial status quo would be maintained Keynes has through this Kautilya has observed the basic situation of financial status quo. He has wanted to create a status quo in the financial system through mass initiation and has tried to.

He, at the very initiation, has tried to expand government enterprises within the masses. For this, he has constituted different departments. Initially, he thought of taking various programmes and endeavours for other departments. Kautilya has judged the source, effect and consequence of the main propensities in economic systems. The solution should be started from the leading economic principle befitting the time.

Public spending makes the enterprises active, moving and profitable from the point of financial consideration. Keynes's public expenditure was pledged to relieve the economic system from the grip of direct and indirect unemployment by causing an explosion of demand.

But it was never possible. Kautilya had been far ahead in this respect. Kautilya's plan started with division into departments and bringing every critical activity under the jurisdiction of the respective department. Distribution of departments had a specific aim to be achieved. Each department had its account of activities and plan to move ahead. Each department would act in its circle, yet there would be mutual correspondence between them.

A department would be serving the purpose of much expansion by acting in accordance with a definite programme. The essence of

Kautilya' s theory would be evident in the example of a department only.

In the *Arthashastra*, the department of Jananadines (placement in settlement) has been given first place.

Bhutapurbamabhutapurbambajanapadavahananena.
Svadesahabhisandabamanek a banibesayet.

(*Arthashastra*, 2/1/1)

[For mass distribution of those who have meanwhile got rehabilitation on those who have not, it may even be necessary to bring people from the country or abroad.]

For mass distribution, the first step is to assemble people from different places in one region or zone and give the same balanced form. A balanced distribution of habitation means that it becomes flat with respect to the profession due to the assemblage of people of different occupations there. As a result of this, the locality becomes affluent and self-sustained. The affluence of people of other faculties and professions of a locality brings in a self-sustained economic characteristic.

A balanced distribution of faculties and occupations is set up among the faculties and professions. Additional faculty and professions in a locality disturb the economic balance of the place. Keynes has considered and deliberated on direct and indirect unemployment in different ways. Suppose continuous mass distribution among other localities is affected for balanced distribution within faculties and professions. In that case, the imbalance between faculty and profession can be removed through the propensity of faculty and profession of some other locality.

Every faculty or profession has two sides. One is the supply of men of faculties and occupations and the necessity for those faculties and occupations. The wider the faculties and professions, the more the economic expansion. For financial stability, the development of faculties and professions is required, and at the same time, it involves the blooming of each of the faculties and occupations. The isolated assemblage of faculties and professions does not cause economic awakening; instead, it happens with proper measures and conditions. Manifestation of faculties and professions builds up the favourable way to financial management. Establishing economic stability in a locality is the direct consequence of setting up the balance between faculty and professionals. Proper distribution and growth of faculties and professions hasten financial stability.

Aggregately and side by side removes the imbalance in economic management to a great expert. Kautilya has wanted a basic solution. Economic balance may be temporarily set up by increasing public spending, but both permanent stabilities cannot be achieved. Kautilya has instated on continuous redistribution of population pattern become this many men will be established in newer faculties and professions, and at the same time, there would be newer manifestations of faculties and occupations.

Simply, it means that this will cause the inception of the propensity of invention manifestation and new inspiration. As a result of the distribution of population, there would be the distribution of land, and a newer distribution of industry, agriculture, etc., also would take place. Each distribution and redistribution of economic management would bring detailed and vast changes. As a result, the government's role would be to market afresh.

The change in economic management would guarantee the economic awakening of an individual and the state.

Economists of almost all views and groups feel disturbed by the modern form of a problem that Kautilya had solved with a fundamental outlook. Essential solutions are possible only when it is realised with their basic definition. Kautilya has spoken of affecting economic distribution through the distribution of population.

Distribution of the population is the way to a basic solution. As a result, a region or a country would be agreeably stabilised on an economic basis. The sequential process of population distribution within the periphery of a part or a country crossing the limit of the area, or the government would spread beyond and even abroad.

As a result, the process of sequential population distribution becomes the primary step of economic rise. Modern technology would management and living have no conflict with the direction given by Kautilya of the way of the primary solution. Kautilya' s opinion provides the all-pervading solution from the fundamental viewpoint, while Keynes is a temporary solution.

50

Consumption and Saving: Views of Kautilya and Veblen

Consumption and Financial Liability

Modern economic management has been built up in respect of consumption. In modern financial management, the outline has been built up through different types of change conjunction in the consumption, quality, and standard measures. The more the extent and diversity of consumption, the higher the possibility of economic development. Consumption in or cases the apparent satisfaction of man, so at the same time, it also widens the limit and pervasion of his need. In consuming, man realises that more consumption and satisfaction are necessary. More consumption and satisfaction presage the direction and activity of life.

Consumption brings apparent satisfaction in living; at the same time, it signifies the possibility of moving forward in life. Man feels the necessity of adjoining wealth due to the urge to move or in the path of life. Satisfaction does not continue uniformly with consumption. The satisfaction that appears at the first stage of enjoyment as it gradually fades away and is coming for newer satisfaction appears. As a result, the satisfaction of the desired desire for consumption only appears if the desired desire is transformed into some other source of enjoyment. Satisfaction of consumption takes place through consumption allurements does not come to an end. For filling of the allurements are required change in goods of consumption, and of its quality, measure, from any situation. As a result, consumption becomes a pleading stream with the unsatisfied and untested stage of desired desire as its source. On the other side, a concrete stream of newer allurement appears.

Symptoms of the explosion of allurements result from dissatisfaction with enjoyment. Due to this explosion, seeds of allurements spread on all sides, i.e., allurements enjoyed a significant rise. Consumption that blooms in the background of life cannot be still without glorifying it. So, life cannot be celebrated with consumption; the economic situation may be.

Capability of consumption is supplied from the life end. Consumption crossing a life may be spread to many. So, for consumption success, one side requires proper resources and collection, and on the other side, the capability of life. Preparation for enjoyment is only possible with resources and supply, so if this is not the capacity of life, such practice becomes futile. Enjoyment becomes preps with a capacity of life and joint procurement of resources and collection proper enjoyment; proper fun gets apparent beauty to life; give pleasure.

Proper enjoyment can have enough effect on economic management. Economic management imposes speed, and the focus of financial management begins to be forceful. The capacity for enjoyment and resources, of course, begins to wane through consumption. It weakens the ability for enjoyment, and attractive power gradually becomes weak by being expended in the flow of life. Just as the warning of the capacity of life is signified through loss during usage and passing of life, so also grows its value and the scope of the change in the economic base.

The state of consumable goods is just like the reinvigorating of a tired traveller with rest and service. The capacity of enjoyment face of fatigue runs towards newer consumable goods to be engaged in recent attempts for enjoyment. Apparent satisfaction of consumption carries an extreme increase in consumption. Mention in Monu Samhita in this context helps realise the proper form of pleasure.

Na jatukamahkamanamupabhogenasamyati
Habisakrsnabartmaebaabhiyahebabhibardhate.

(*Manu Samhita*, 2/94)

[Desire never gets pacified through the enjoyment of the desired object, just as fire is not extinguished with ghee; instead, it flares up more.]

The notion and situation about consumption expressed in the Manu Samhita is practically inveterate. It is not so that it is confined to a particular case, a particular animal, or a particular subject.

Virulence of consumption is universal. As fire is all-devouring, so also the fire consumption devours up everything. The fire of consumption gradually exhausts all that is honest, noble, and moving and leaves quite empty. Whatever may be the reason for one to be plunged into the grip of consumption, once he is merged, he would come to the verge of problems. For such a man, it becomes quite difficult to proceed along the path to God, to the absolute self, to yoga.

Vedastyagascayajnascaniyamascatapamsica
Na bipradustabhabasyasiddhimgacchantikahircit

(*Manu Samhita*, 2/97)

[For those who have been addicted to earthly attraction and so especially of wicked nature, it is never possible to succeed in the study of the Vedas, charity, sacrificial performance, devotion to rules, asceticism, and the like]

As a result of the exposition of the picture of the consequence and effect of consumerism in different phases of the Manu Samhita, the aspects of consumerism directed toward life are just opposite to the sphere of the divine flow. So, it is said where there is lust, there is no Rama; Good keeps himself aloof from the spot where life is engaged in sowing the seeds of passion and desire.

The Market of Desire

But the life's hornet of modern civilisation is enjoyment. Any parallel to consumerism is quite unbearable to contemporary society. Lifestyle in traders' outlook has glorified consumerism. This outlook not only stops at saying that consumerism is good; its central theme is that consumerism is necessary; the more enjoyment, the better, and the most violent consumerism is the best. This attitude likes to get diversity in consumerism. So, different companies and different industries have entered multi-furious consumerism.

Through advertisements, publicity, and different types of notifications and papers, they have highlighted the utility of various forms, tastes, and colours of consumerism for the necessity of excellence, enjoyment and prosperity. The existence of industrial technology has continued from the propensity of consumption. If the tendency of consumption decreases, its effect will fall aggregately on society and the market; its influence will be distracted by the community and the market. If the overall demand for service is not swelled up, there may be a deficit in the supply measure.

If demands decrease continuously, the market forces will be relieved of attraction for these factors and science. As a result of this, due to a continuous decrease in demand, there would be a downward effect on the measure of production. Ardour for an increase in production appears with an increase in demand; of these impairments in demand would be the creation of demands, the most role-worthy is the propensity of consumption. The central part of modern civilisation's fundamental force is this consumption propensity. Propensity of consumption and modern society go hand in hand. While discussing his famous theory of the leisure class and its economic influence and methods, Thorstein Veblen has observed different aspects of consumption. None has regarded the influence of the measure of consumption on the financial situation and its consequence so extensively as Veblen. So, Veblen's theory has appeared in a crucial role in this context.

According to Veblen:

"During the earlier stages of economic development, consumption of goods without stint, especially consumption of the better grades of goods, ideally all consumption in excess of the substance minimum usually pertains to the leisure class." (Torstein Veblen, p.31)

If the super derogatory goods can be carried to the gentleman who is a regular in the path consumption, then not only does his satisfaction increase, but the attention for consumption also remains intact, and all other objects of life gradually come under the control of consumerism. The social status of the consumer is indicated based on qualities and measures of the goods and services that come under the purview of consumption. This factor must be taken to be young. Even now, the element is more applicable.

According to Veblen:

"The quasi-peaceable gentleman of leisure then not only consumes of the stage of life beyond the minimum required subsistence and physical efficiency, but his consumption also undergoes a specialisation as regards the quality of the goods consumed" (Ibid, p. 31)

Veblen's view is very much relevant in the background of the modern socio-economic situation and the market. The domain consumption is at the gateway of the kingdom of sin. Temptation of consumption beckons the path of evil. In the domain of consumption, there is instant satisfaction, and at the same time, there is pervasive disappointment, dissatisfaction, and pain. A man earnestly searching for long-term satisfaction for temporary satisfaction becomes eager for newer factors in the background of consumption. These goods of consumption of newer production systems bring a sense of satisfaction in a new form. The wider the satisfaction, the greatest the economic flow. Crossing the moment's airiness of the satisfaction lying behind the temporary consumption, the more it advances to stability, the greater the financial flow.

Production of consumable goods- their movement, flow, and distribution -all are to be discharged in the economic situation. At every step, there is the expense of money and investment. Right through the cost of funds and investment, the forces in the market are not only nourished but also, they get swelled up. The more consumption and inclination consumption increases, the brighter would-be possibility of the market expansion can be swelled up by two types of uses creation of permanent buyers and the influence of temporary or periodical buyers.

Consumers-Society

The market gets stability through stable buyers. Such buyers may be tempted by the production in the market by this trend that remains known to the definite sellers, companies, and producers. Acquaintance of manifestation and any identity related to this means expansion. This trend may exist inside or at some portion of the market, but it influences it. Like the stable buyers are interested in long-known goods, they also feel attracted to newer interests.

Instead of being interested in repeated purchases of the same thing, it is natural that a stable buyer would search for diversity. Running after diverse, stable buyers helps the companies grow. Such coordination of stable buyers stands as a primary strength of the market. The companies want the increase the extent and stability of the permanent buyers. The forces of the market come forward in support of the permanent buyers, and in that case, the market enjoys expansion. The way of growth of the market is paved in the background of the coordination of the permanent buyers. The endless strength gets the chance to extend itself. As a result, the permanent buyers' influence in the market begins to increase. The sphere of influence of temporary buyers is created right in the sphere of influence of permanent buyers.

Swell up the resources and power of the market. The more sales increase, the more production, supply, and distribution. As a result, the economic situation rises. The cycle of economic development acts on the purchase and behaviours of the buyers. Both permanent and temporary buyers offer coordination to increase production power and make economic development firmer in the long run.

The nature of the market is to inspire the buyer to buy. If the market buyers are successful in listening to the process, it makes the buyer's activities primarily established and causes the expansion of the market to be more stable. There is no amazement in buying commodities in case of necessity. But there is amazement in crossing the regularly renewed list of goods and including temporary goods in the list of conditions. As a result of this market gets speed. At the same time, the list of necessities of men gets longer. Thus, the market receives new types of inspiration and capability. The inspiration that helps the market move forward has a propensity for consumption at the base. But at this time, in the background of consumption, rapid expansion begins to set in the business interest of the trading organisations.

Owing to the scariness of consumption, a decrepitude infiltrates the prevention and measurement of the markets; modern civilisation is now mainly being identified as market civilisation. The central pillar of it is the demand for the commodities in the market. If demand increases, production increases, distribution increases, and sale increases. With sales increases, the market's glory rises, and the limit of the market spreads out people in more significant numbers than before into the market domain. As they get involved in different processes in the market, the market will grow stronger. Inclination to consumption becomes the primary source of power in the market. Inclination to consumption is the life force of the market. Inclination to consumption has not bloomed, moving based on minimum requirements. The minimum requirement is irrespective of the desire for consumption. However, a new dimension is being added to the minimum requirement so that it could take the consumption path.

Living according to minimum requirements is impossible for one who has so many ways to follow. A life minimum requirement also can make the forces of the market more active. But it is not so that all the forces of the market.

Get liberated from this. In the background of the minimum, the market becomes slack. The significance of slack demand is that the forces of the market increase very slowly. Consequently, the development process becomes inhibited. Distribution of the goods of a minimum requirement is made at a minimum cost. As a result of this, management of low cost.

Limited qualities and casting for the small period would grow strong. The boundary of requirement needs he expected in the interest of the business. The more the swelling up to the limit of requirements comes in thinking, the more the personal feelings of men. Awakened expansion of desire tightens the propensity of consumption at the basis of life. Life spreads further, crossing the boundary of minimum requirements. Creation of support for the inclination to consumption becomes helpful for infusion of the capability of the fore of market, sometimes directly and sometimes in different ways. Giving allowance to the objects to be influenced by desire on the path of movement in life an individual makes the face of the market more capable and active.

Life Free from Consumption and Saving

The minimum requirement in the moving perspective brings stability to an individual. This is half of a spot or a path to cross through stumbling. Halt age at a site may make the provision of life one way and unidirectional. As the requirement begins to increase, so also increases the right of market culture. Market culture moves to expansion in different ways. Growth of consumption increases in man the propensity of the market. Being inspired by consumption and suitable to consumption in many ways, man carries contrariety in culture.

In the context of savings of resources, Veblen has said:

"The end of acquisition and accumulation is congenitally held to be the consumption of the goods accumulated, whether it is consumption directly by the owner or by the household attached to him and, for this purpose, identified with him in theory." (Ibid, p. 11)

Veblen has looked at the elements of consumption rather widely, and since the subjects and articles strewn in consumption are engaged in effecting consumption are regarded as consumable goods. According to Veblen, whatever is taken for activity in life is consumption. Take for living, designate the elements of consumption. There has been conflict and battles among new Claus, among countries for the very initiation of history.

The possibilities of the conflict lie in attempts for procurement, presentation, and expansion of personal resources. These possibilities sometimes come openly and sometimes secretly. When it comes openly, the conflict gets formed. As a result of this conflict, different sorts of propensities regarding consumption at different levels within men, classes, societies, and countries get expressed. Using something sometimes gets into the consumption class and becomes a coordinating agent for life. When the meditating entity of an ascetic takes fruits, it becomes a measure of his living.

Acceptance of fruits or their consumption is generally a form of consumption. There is desire, longing, and lust in this. But ascetics' acceptance of fruits is not driven by desire, longing, or passion. This process is a part of regular movements of life. There is no urge of desire, longing, or last to have these. The flow of living of ascetics within a divine flow, the path of flew of life naturally becomes evident. The lives of ascetics are intimately connected with the eternal flow. So, there is no place for desire, longing, or lust in this case. There is the inspiration of two forces in moving along life's path- a manifestation of the divine will and becoming drenched in surrender to the flow of holy will.

Right for blooming the divine will in life, the life of an ascetic is the manifested form of the eternal flow of energy. So, in an ascetic, there is the awakening and manifestation of divine will. There is renunciation in the life of an ascetic glowing with holy will. The ascetic knows the absolute, eternal, conscious, and joyful self (Sacchidananda) has been formed. He has adopted a manifested form and appeared as everything in this visible world. Everything in this visual world that was in the past or would be in the future manifests this. This world, this life, this flow of energy, all are this. He has been the aquatic, earth, or aerial life and its elements. So, before an ascetic's view, this is the fullest satisfaction and pleasure. He has nothing to get; he has nothing to long for. He is full of a feeling of the complete form. Acceptance is the life of an ascetic, but there is no scope for desire-longing lust. How does consumption enter the energy that goes on at the will of God? God mile blooms constantly in the life of an ascetic, so life comes to him hand in hand with yoga when necessary.

The ascetic realises that there is nothing called necessity. What is there is to give away the self-little by little to the living flow of the will be God. That is why device longing lust has no place in the life of an ascetic. The basic flow of an ascetic life is offering renunciation, exhausting the sell, and employing it at the bathing feel of Lord Vishnu. An ascetic takes his meal as the grace of God, not as an enjoyment. All the activities in an ascetic life are a cascade for the warship of the absolute self-there. There is no scope for any pleasure. Life around an ascetic is that of renunciation.

The gateway of wisdom is always open for renunciation. The glow of high that woke up once in the ascetic life as the down of his life has gradually been dazzling with the midday glow in the ascetic life. This increased flow may be taken as the stream of the wisdom of the ascetic. In his life, there is no acceptance; abandonment and renunciation have made the possibility of attaining truth firm in ascetics. In life, the ascetic established on renunciation comes with the flow of truth. Always, knowledge of the absolute self (Brahman) gets transfused to be captured in uttering the ascetic. Life is due with eternal is expensed in the views of ascetics. The external himself assumes form procures truth and moves along the undeterred path.

The glowing becomes the procurement of truth in the wisdom of the ascetic the more is his transformation into the embodiment of the full. In the knowledge of the ascetics, his advancement along the path of life, his procurement of truth, and making that truth glowing in the light of wisdom. A bit of acceptance is at the summit of the mountain. Consumption funds have no place in such a life. Kautilya wanted procurement of truth at the base of the ascetic's life. So, consumption is just a background of renunciation.

Economic Situation with Dominant Consumption

But in society, going to parties for consumption. In different phases, at other times, life is floating on different types of consumption streams. According to Veblen, Thorsten Veblen has looked upon life as a field of consumption involved in conflict. Wherever the institution of private property is found, even in a slightly developed form, the economic process bears the character of a struggle between men for the possession of goods. It has been customary in economic theory, and especially among these economists who adhere with least faltering to the body of modernised classical doctrines, to construe this struggle for wealth as being substantially a struggle for subsistence (Ibid, p. 10)

Minimum procurement or earning, pointed out by Veblen, is not acceptance at the base of ascetic's wisdom; it is consumption and acceptance of the consumable goods. It is not merely the minimum component of living imitative are beckoning and determination of the most distance flow of consumption struggle. The reason behind the different stages of economic history is not the pain of not having the minimum. This is the unparalleled attempt to live contentedly with having the minimum. This is a remarkable attempt to earn the right of consumption of life, and in that attempt, the activities of one are generated from greedy desires and lustful looks at others. Consumption is the beauty of life. Consumption is the satisfaction of life at the very base of the economic flow created by the chastisement of such feelings. This is at the base of the background of a bloody path for tasting the pleasure of consumption and procuring goods for consumption.

The life stream of the development of consumption is moving along the path through which consumption is continuously heaped up, and the excess possibility of consumption over the capability of enjoyment is initiated. Veblen has realised that the inertia of laziness infiltrates the life of one who moves along the consumption path and brings in the flow of inactivity.

A qualitative transformation of inclinations to consumption and activity would take place. The sense of laziness and craze bloom in the balanced, serene feeling of life, life flows downwards. Life's direction runs away to the consumption stream for that of action. The propensity of being content with consumption within the justification of self-proprietorship gradually, a social stream of flowing consumption is found. This flow of society, combined with consumption and laziness, changes the very form of life. Veblen has made us comprehend that consumption of inactivity severs the flow and inspiration of work and alterations its overall direction. Life deviates from the productive flow of work and gets engaged in nonproductive work; absorbing sleep takes the place of awakening. Veblen comments:

"As seen from an economic point of view, leisure, considered as employment, is closely allied in kind with the life of the exploit and the achievements which characteristic of a life of leisure and which remain as its decorous criteria, have much in common with the tithes of exploit. The decay which the (ceremonies) code has suffered at the hands of busy people testifies all depreciation apart to the fact that decorum is a product and an exponent of leisure class life and thrives in full measure only under a require of status" (Ibid, p. 20)

Leisure is a particular chapter of consumption and enjoyment. The leisure process leads to procuring pleasure and happiness in exchange for others' labour under the dominance of money and power. In this view of Veblen, leisure of any type rouges a separate economic pledge. Leisure occupies a special place in financial management and steps up a parasitic class fond of cases.

Consumption should have been considered in Kautilya' s economic proposals. He did not place a beckon for a life of consumption; instead, his beckon was for one of renunciation. He has lived a life which will be directed at the attempt to know the eternal, the pure, and the beautiful.

Kautilya has made two divisions in his discussion on movement in pleasure and happiness; the first is the royal movement, and the second is for commoners. Of these two, the one for commoners becomes comparatively more detrimental than the royal one.

Desarajabiharayohdesabiharahtraikalyena
Karmaphalahupaghatamkaroti Raja bihahahtu
Karusilphihkasilababakjibanrupah
Ajibahvaideheka; upakaranamkarotitacaryah
Na it KautilyahDesabiharahjikarmasramanaabadharlham, alpam
Bhaksyati
Bhaksayitva ca bhuyahkarmasu
Yogamgacchati.
Rajabiharah hi svayemballabhath
Ca svayamgraha
Pranayapanyagarahkayam
Upagrahaihbidayatiiti (*Arthashastra*, 8/4/6)

Kautilya has despised those who are living in pleasure. According to him, a life of pleasure is detrimental to the route of the economy. Kautilya has a life of action. The life of action would be built only based on intention and pure propensity. This would bring inspiration and zeal in the life of action, because of which works would accomplish beautifully.

The main problem of the life of pleasure is becoming the cause of torture of the big. No doubt, a big group of society is regulated by this life of pleasure, but society falsely prays for devastation. Kautilya has described the royal pleasure to be more harmful. This means if the state leadership, despite being the holder of power, pleasure and its effect would ruin him. For people, this influence of pleasure may be a source of enjoyment. But the central propensity of economic management would have to be free of pleasure. Kautilya' s management would build up not based on pleasure but based on necessity.

Bibliography

Torstein Veblen (1899-1973), the theory of leisure-class: An Economic Study of the institution in Great Books of the Western world, by Mortimer J Adler (series editor-in-chief). (Macmillan, Encyclopaedia Britannica, Inc. Chicago 1990 Edu) p.31

51

Equality and Progress: Kautilya versus Marx

Introduction

This world is full of inequality. Wherever our eyes are cast, these are evidence of inequality. Dissimilarity exists in every field of life. Dissimilarity among countries is wide. Within a country, too, the wall of dissimilarity is firm. Dissimilarity is everywhere. Somewhere it is narrow, somewhere wide. There is dissimilarity in capability, dissimilarity in education, dissimilarity in identity and acceptability, and dissimilarity between high and low. The difference between the rich and the poor is eternal. There is dissimilarity in other measures too. Somewhere dissimilarity in very intensive, and somewhere it is rather mild. Dissimilarity in education, health and capability is universal. Somewhere, the wall of dissimilarity is hereditary, while somewhere, it has been set up anew in modern trams.

The dissimilarity between high and low exists in every field. It is unsurpassable. Ten students of a class have ten types of stages as conditions. This difference has originated from the capability of intellect and, aggregately, all other differences for learning and teaching. There is dissimilarity in keenness of influence. There is dissimilarity from man to man. There is dissimilarity in the capability of judgement and again in the stages of being grown up. Dissimilarity exists in the constitution and prevention of nature. Dissimilarity exists in each and every field of human history. Dissimilarity is the universal law of the natural world. However, all dissimilarities originate from one and the same original source of eternal truth and supreme consciousness.

The five fingers of a hand are of different sizes. The capability, strength and efficiency of the two hands are different from those of the two legs. In the majority of cases, there is an incongruity between two persons. The propensity of people from two different countries is different. With apartment similarities between two persons, the wall of difference is rather firm. Despite being of equal financial ability, other matters between two persons are full of incongruity. A lot of inequality might exist between two persons otherwise equal in education and eligibility. Much inequality exists in appearance as well. The rainy, autumn, spring and winter seasons differ greatly from summer. Differences and inequality exist between East and West, between North and South. Similar to the inequality between the two sexes, high and low, rich and poor, inequality exists between white and black, educated and uneducated and so on. Besides, there is inequality in religious identities, caste identities and national identities. Despite so many inequalities, a measure of equality exists.

Reminding the inequality between good and bad, Friedrich Nietzsche said:

There which divides two people most profoundly is a differing sense of degree of cleanliness. Of what good is all uprightness and mutual usefulness, of what good is mutual good with the fact still remains- 'they cannot bear each other's odour! The highest instinct of cleanliness places him who is effected within it in the strongest and perilous isolation, as a saint for precisely this is saintliness- the highest spiritualization of the said instruct. To know indescribable pleasure in bathing to fail in order and thirst which constantly drives the soul out of right into morning. And out of gloom and gloominess into brightness into the glittering, profound perished- such as inclination is distinguishing -it is a noble inclinator but it also separates -The saint's pity is pity for the dirt of human, all two humans. And there are degree and heights at which he fell pity itself as different, as dirt.

Friedrich Wilhelm Nietzsche, *Beyond Good and Evil* (Macmillan, 1907), p. 539–48.

Even the Charter of the National Liberation of 1789 began with: 'Declaration of the Right of Man and Citizen of 1789.'

This declaration stated:

The representatives of the French people, organized in National Assembly recognize and proclaim in the pleasure and under the auspices of the supreme being, the following right of man and citizen.

Men are born equal and remain free and equal in rights.... The aim of every political association is the preservation of the natural and inalienable right of man, these right are liberty,property, security and resistance of operation...

Liberty consist of the passer to do whatever is not injurious to others, these the enjoyment of national right of every man has for its limit only those that assure other members of society the enjoyment of those same right.

(Adler 1789, 437)

In Nietzsche's theory of difference there is the source of spiritual awakening in the theory of proclamation in the French revolution of coming to and enjoyment of the world as equals. There it is undaunted surrender to and faith in the Absolute Self. Faith in the Absolute Self was so deep-rooted that in the very charter prepared for being announced in the National Assembly, it was said that the Absolute Self had himself given consent to the procurement, and the presentation of the charter had been effected under the guidance of him.. The Charter of French Liberation was based on faith. This faith sees all equality. The sense of equality of both is waking, and all are to move forward in the path of life with the sense of equality.

Nietzsche's consideration of the difference is extreme, with the natural principle of productive outlook. On the other hand, the consideration of the French representatives of the people depends on faith. Both national and extreme consideration that depends on faith are acting on the boson of the earth in their respective fields and path. In the application of both has come deviation and aberration. In the long run, French people could not maintain the low banking on which they welcomed democracy in the path of equality, liberty and fraternity. So, the law has stopped being fulfilled partly. French society was not able to ascend the fulfilment of application. So, the slogan of liberation could not cross the form of the slogan and did not bloom successfully in the application in life. The spirituality that came in the theory of difference did not take afros.

The spiritual theory is just like a power to move along the natural path of living. So, instead of the essence of real spiritualism, importance has been laid on the natural form of ethical consciousness of man. Man's desire for the world gets built up on the price of consciousness. What is wanted in this world, how can that be acquired, and how would be life—answers to these questions emerge from living entry to catted at the depth of consciousness. So, cascades of different influences fall on the centre of life. External influences are bloomed from the phenomena of how this world moves and how men like to move.

The internal influence is that man has built up the deep core of their heart and the clean inner from their own existence. The inner form of existence is the Absolute entity existing in their real existence. Faithful life sometimes works in tee light of this entity. Sometimes, their faith is completely ruined again when it no longer exists. This becomes the mundane desire in real natural life. The look of difference becomes keen in the light of this mundane desire of real life. The culture of identity also gets built on the foundation of difference.

After seventy-eight years of the French Charter, Karl Marx brought to Europe the economic theory 'Capital' to find an identity. The thought behind identity here is engaged in the struggle with difference Marx has distributed in his 'Capital'—the thought of identity in the perspective of difference. Marx presented the outline of his theory in the prefaces of his first German edition of 'Capital' published in London on 25 July 1867. He has designated the production system based on capital as the evil power of the modern world.

The production system dependent on capital is an enemy of society. It makes the blooming of society unidirectional, dries up the ability to offer labour and brings an end to it. It brings to life the air of helpless intolerable unhappiness. Marx has written:

> ... The country that is more developed industrially only shows to the legs developed, the image of its future.
>
> But apart from this, where capitalist production is fully naturalised a mans the Germens the condition of things is much worse than in life, England, because the counter poise of the Factory Acts in wanting. In all other spheres we like the rest of continental western Europe suffer not only from the development of capitalist production, but also from incompleteness of that development. Alongside of modern evils, a whole series of inherited evils oppress us, arising from the passive survival of antiquated modes of production with these inevitable train of social and political anachronisms. We suggest not only from the living but from the dead, Le most saisit le vif.
>
> (Nietzsche, *Beyond Good and Evil.*, 19–21)

Marx has primarily designated tradition and sequence as enemies in this economic theory. Tradition has not only been giving pains, but in the economic situation embedded in the sequence, lies the ability to present continuously. The more this capital-based production system would come to fulfilment, the more it would increase the ability and propensity of operation of the offers of labour. In this context, Karl Marx has explained strongly the subject of social difference and mentioned the total show of the dividing power acting in the society of England.

Marx opines:

...In England the progress of social disintegration palpable. When it has reached a certain point it must reach on the continue. There it will take a form more brutal or more humane according to the degree if development of the working class itself. Apart from higher motives, therefore, their own most important interest dictate to the class that are for the nonce the rutting ones, the removal of all legally removable hindrances to the free development of the working class.

(Nietzsche, *Beyond Good and Evil*, 20)

In the battle of moving forward towards the target of the labour-class for this own liberation from the perspective, character and capability are especially required. They will have to stand aggressively against that very arrangement for liberation. In this case, too, what is maintainable is how the basic difference of character would direct the power of the society. All the capabilities and resources of the society have lent zealous support to the labourers, sometimes directly and sometimes indirectly, and as such, move forward with the capability of the society as capital. Having instruction from the division of the English society, the law of the division of the society may be more important elsewhere. Karl Marx wanted liberation despite division.

Giving a look at and considering the arrangement of production in Germany, Marx has concluded that so long as the unified consciousness does not come within the labour class. So long as they are not unified and engaged in proper struggle, the miserable state of the workers would continue, and up to this period, a scientific attitude would be evident in the economic situation dependent on capital.

The meaning of this scientific attitude in the economic situation is the proper environment and set-up for awakening proper consciousness within every man. The set-up would be forward through a change of situation, and the new set-up would be created through scientific production, distribution and investment. To thoroughly review the subject, Marx closely analysed the German production system from 1948 to the subsequent three decades.

He remarked:

Since 1848 Capitalist production has developed rapidly in Germany and at the present time it is in full bloom of speculation swindling. But fate is still unapportioning to our professional economist.... And as soon these conditions did come into existence, they did so under circumstances that no longer of allowed of these really andimpartiallyinvestigated within the bounds of the burgeons horizon. In so far as Political Economy remains in this that horizon in so far, i.e. as the capitalist regime is looked upon as the absolutely final of social production instead of as a passing historical phase of is Evolution. Political economy can remain a science only so long as the class struggle is talent a manifest itself only in isolated and sporadic phenomena.

(Nietzsche, *Beyond Good and Evil*, 24)

Here, Karl Marx is gradually giving form to the very theory of class struggle. The theory of class struggle is based on the principle of division. The deeper the division, the more eyes would be cast on the division, and the feeling would be deepened accordingly. Then, there would be no other alternative than to be entangled with war on the basis of division. At the very beginning of the class struggle, there was the theory of division. Division gradually turns into enmity. Turning into enmity gets earnestness for a struggle during this time as the workers get engaged in struggle.

So, the bourgeons authority of the bourgeoisie takes a side in this struggle. The bourgeons authority of the bourgeoisie facilitates the flow of money to these weapons. And the workers make the process of production itself these weapons. The perspective of struggle is to be strengthened by obstructing the propensities of different properties within the productive capability and making them flow along a definite channel. As a consequence, the grievance of the workers gets strong; the working class get entangled in a direct struggle in the form of opponents of the bourgeoisie.

According to Karl Marx, the surplus value that comes through formatting the productive capability of the workers paves the way for forming the capital of the owners or the bourgeoisie. The bourgeoisie goes on increasing capital on the basis of surplus value. They get value for a part of the labour offered by the labourers, and the rest is added up to the amount of capital as surplus increases the capital. In this context, Karl Marx said:

...The original conversion of money into capital is achieved in most exact accordance with the economic laws of commodity production and with the right of property derived from them. Never the less, its result is.

1) That the product belongs to the Capitalist and not to the worker.
2) That the value of the product includes, besides the value of the capital advanced, a surplus value which costs the worker labour but capitalist nothing, none the less becomes the legitimacies property of the capitalist.
3) That the workers has restrained his labour power and can sell it a new confined a buyer.

(Nietzsche, *Beyond Good and Evil*, 549)

There is a basic truth in this faith of Karl Marx: Workers do not get a proper exchange value. Instead, they are oppressed. As a result, workers go against capital and gradually get enplaned in the struggle. Karl Marx has given a call for charging hands in respect of production systems in the struggle between the workers and the owners of capital. Due to the advent of united and responsible workers, the control system of capital would change hands and come to the workers union from the owners of capital. This is the beginning of the equilibrium system. With the right of ownership, the labour powers would be introduced among themselves in the system of equilibrium. This new authority would supply the necessary commodities for all and give all positions the same dignity.

Executive failure has not been applied to the theories of class struggle and surplus value of Karl Marx. The subject against which the worker class has been advice to be united and fight, workers themselves ultimately turn into that demon. Besides, to think of surplus value from offering labour by the workers in the field of production to be the main path of increasing capital is quite impractical in the modern situation. The role of the workers is to lose their influence and see their helpless from before the situations dependent on intellect. The acquirable goods now need to be acquired not with the power of muscle or hand but with the brain. So, a unified struggle against capital no longer promises to bring basic change, which is rather partial and can provide only a temporary solution to a problem.

Now avenues of possibilities have been exposed as a result of the role of the market. These possibilities depend on merit and wisdom.

Man has set out to conquer new empires with the help of merit and wisdom. The competition is keen, but there is no enemy. There are many warps and loops in the competition, but that is not a mutual fight. Rather, sprouts of new possibilities get bloomed through competition. All those possibilities that were at the very beginning or had no scope to bloom get flourished by the flow and management of the market. So, there is practically no scope for real class struggle. A class has its identities of the respective fields in a combined form.

A common principle in these is the class measure, which might give the identity of the class, but it is not at all possible to organise. There is a mutual interest in making them fight. So, the theory of class struggle is a failure and completely obsolete in respect of modern society. On the other side, it is known that in the capital-based production system, surplus value sheds the blood of the workers to make the right of the capital firmer. In the open market, there is no scope for it at all. New avenues of action are rather available in the continuity of the open market. So, the organisations eager to exploit no workers lost skilled workers on the very thinking of exploiting them. Still, surplus value, if any, gets added to the profit of the organisation. Lots of organisations and workers are tied with some thread. So, sometimes, there is a proposal of provision for surplus value.

Bibliography

Nietzsche, Friedrich Wilhelm. *Beyond Good and Evil.* Macmillan, 1907.

52
Removal of Poverty: Marx Versus Kautilya

Form of Poverty

Screams of hunger come out from the bosom of the earth at every moment. In the history of the world, poverty has proved itself to be an inevitable truth. Poverty has many sources and varied manifestations. Poverty beings unrestrained screams. At the same time, it brings a store of experience. Poverty makes one full of life experiences. Poverty saturates the sequence along the valley of life. So, we can see that poverty is not limited by a single question but flows through gestations—sometimes it increases, and sometimes it subsides. Men engaged in removing the load of poverty can evade poverty. Again, in many cases, all their attempts prove futile. In case of such futile cases, poverty builds up a severe disbalance. On one side, the darkness of poverty gradually becomes dense, and on the other side, resources of society begin to accumulate within the reach of some in advantageous positions.

The form of poverty has been explained in many ways. Revell World Bank began adventure exploration with poverty and inequality. The action of removal of poverty in Africa has been considered a priority. Poverty has been defined to be the pain of not having and not getting. On the other side, equality is a deprivation of opportunity, position and consequence. If inequality and poverty are brought into discussion, it would be realised that there is a balanced relationship between them. Where inequality and poverty coexist, people spend merely unbearable. To such people, the abominable and ugly form of the world becomes evident. They do not feel any attraction to innocent life.

Life there moves forward in an ever-advancing mood. No separate attraction of living is found there. Life proceeds in search of a little way of hope in the minds of severe pains. There has been a revolution in the name of Karl Marx for crossing the load of poverty; politics and state-enterprise for the same are well-known. But if we look at Kautilya's path, it will be realised that the key to the permanent removal of poverty lies there. Where Marx has turned into a ruinous failure, Kautilya can successfully remove poverty and inequality. If a discussion is made between Kautilya and Marx with respect to the position of the modern world, it would be evident that in the case of the removal of poverty, Marx is to be rejected, and Kautilya is to be appreciated.

The discussion begins with the Asian outlook: Poverty is expressed in different conceptual terms in Singapore, Indonesia and Malaysia. In Singapore, an index of poverty indicates a strong connection between slum living conditions and a high incidence of gastroenteritis. Another index measures poverty in terms of certain minimum standards of nutrition, clothing, household expenditure, transport expenditure and rent. A third measure of poverty is the disposable income ratio, which determines the extent to which disposable income is sufficient to provide for a minimum standard of living, excluding the cost of supporting outside dependents, medical expenses and luxuries such as entertainment and cigarettes. 'Living in poverty' then refers to households whose disposable income ratio is less than 100 and whose income is less than that required to support a strictly defined minimum standard of living (Kuo 1976).

Modern Modes

The notion presented by Eddie Kuo on the mode of poverty in Singapore signifies the different indifferent modes to measure poverty in Asia. Keeping the assertion of Kuo in mind, it is possible to draw a comparison between Kautilya and Marx. There is a common feeling about Marx that he is indeed the sole pioneer in the removal of poverty of some people. It is only a myth. Though Marx had perceived the forms of poverty through his experiences, his intention while speaking of the means of removing poverty has moved in such a direction as some people using poverty as a weapon can be eager to enjoy the combined advantage. In 1848, Marx published Communist Manifesto and came into the sight of all—explaining society through the theory of class struggle. He tried to state that in society, there are two types—proletariat and bourgeoisie. Labourers are the one being controlled and exploited by the bourgeois owners and management. He wrote in the manifesto:

> The history of all halter to existing society in the history of class struggles, freeman and slave, Patrician and Plebeian, lord and serf, guild-master and journeyman, in a word oppressor and oppressed, stood in crust out opposition to one another, carried on an interrupted now hidden, now open fight, a fight thateach time ended either in aa revolutionary re-constitution of society at large, or in the common ruin of the contending classes.
>
> (Marx 1848)

In his manifesto, Karl Marx presented the outline of his whole theory and forwarded the preface of causality. On the basis of the theory of class struggle, he showed a fight between the proletariat and the bourgeoisie classes.

> The bourgeoisie cannot exist without constantly revolutionising the instruments of production and thereby the relations of production and with the whole relations of the society, conservation of the old modes of production and unuttered from was on the country, the first condition of existence for all earlier industrial classes. Constant revolutionising of production uninterrupted disturbance of all social conditions, everlasting uncertainly and agitation distinguish his bourgeois epoch from all earlier ones. All fixed, first frozen relation with their train of ancient and venerable prejudices and opinions are swept away all new formed ones become antiquated before they can ossify. All that is solid meets into air, all that is holly is profaned and man is at last compelled to act with sober senses his real condition of lifeand his relation with his kind.
>
> (Marx 1848, 473–479)

Workers and bourgeoisies are revealed in the view of Karl Marx as the oppressed and the oppressor, respectively. Bourgeoisies knit nets of relation at every step of life, including technology and production system nets. The bourgeoistic power breaks down the equilibrium and brings in speed. There is so much amazement in the speed that when viewed for a distant time, the process of transformation of socket relation and the transformed situation will be clear. Marx has marked the bourgeoisie by their own definition and modes. This definition of Marx, especially with respect to the character and activities of the bourgeoisie, is not only obsolete in modern views but also ridiculous. Behind this type of explanation of Karl Marx, the bourgeoisie and workers are an attempt to create a background for class struggle and give a call for class struggle. Karl Marx has taken this class struggle as a weapon for establishing equilibrium and removing poverty. This weapon is obsolete in the modern economic system. On the contrary, the path of cooperation has bloomed on the backdrop of the world. Major portion of economic struggle has been finding ways through economic solutions. People from undeveloped countries are raising their hands. Many undeveloped countries have been lifted up to become developing and even developed countries.

Enterprise Worldwide

World Bank and different international organisations are acting as agents for change in the economic situation of the world. Different attempts to get economic confirmation have been noticed among these international organisations. In the background of the world trade organisation, a foundation of a new trading technological and economic situation. In this situation stands the enterprise of a newer world. In this attempt for a newer world, there exists for the countries of the world the possibility to set oup a fine state. It is not that only the internal resources of a country would supply the elements for solving economic problems within. It is the much-multiplied state of intimal resources of a country that is fit for solving its domestic problems. This shortage of management in the modern world is behind the economic rise of some Asian countries.

Solution of the problem of poverty and inequality can be solved through the creation of newer and more improved resources. A flow of total change can be brought against the backdrop of poverty through the creation of resources. This attempt to create resources has been successful through many devices, such as management of labour at low cost, mass power worthy of using newer technology, innovation and active economic system and a wide market. The newer world situation has brought in the opportunity for open trade and markets. In the open trade market, there is an opportunity for liberal competition under the background of liberal competition, and incidents of rise and fall of economic situation may occur. Not only the transfer of resources but the exposition of the attempt to create resources takes place by the continuous transformation of economic situation within different countries. This continuous transformation does not remain limited in this country as a domestic matter only. Crossing the periphery of the country, it creates the background of procuring resources for the world market. Quite a good number of Asian countries has been benefitted from this process.

Some countries have, in large measure, met up the insufficiency of these resources by procuring resources from the world market in accordance with the law of competition. As a result, the problems of poverty and inequality within the country have been weak. Poverty has almost disappeared, and inequality exists but on the basis of competition and affluence. Inequality, though it exists, has not been painful to society. The Asian countries in such a condition are small in area and population, such as Japan and Singapore. The good effect of this process has also begun in the case of big countries like India and China. Recently, World Bank has announced rather emphatically that the severity of poverty in the world has decreased by a considerable extent. The announcement is correct. But, at the root is the process of removal of poverty in India and China. These two big countries have brought a change in the perspective of poverty through quantitative and quantitative transformations. The process that brought this success has had some effect or reference Karl Marx on it.

World Bank has been studying the principle of poverty and inequality in determining the form of poverty. After standing poverty and inequality in the same sphere, it has been found that the more inequality increases in backward societies, the more severe poverty becomes. Inequality does not pose a social problem in developed societies to the same expert as that affects a backward society. Hato, in his 'Republic' of Plato, and Aristotle, in his politics, described the equilibration of equality in the perspective of society; the same has been indicated in different social systems. Rig Veda first uttered the note of equality in the history of human civilisation. The background of the Vedas is a situation of very subtle equality. The Vedic sages had been observed in meditation for the Absolute self (Brahman). The path of life was determined on the basis of the knowledge of the Absolute self. So, they have not seen any difference in men. They have rather noticed an extreme unity. All men are moving in life in the form of a symbol of the Absolute self. In view of sages, all are mundane manifestations of the Absolute self. So, sages do not find any difference in the base of human identity. They do not differentiate in the meditation of the sages.

The civilisation soaked in meditation and set in by the Vedic society is the best in the path of human civilisation. Here, monetary inequality had not brought the intimidation of poverty because the main craving was not endless; of course, there was nothing to long for. The aim of life is to get the Absolute self. So, life, instead of being established on consumption, is based on renunciation. So, the demand for life has been rather scanty. A man who has gotten rid of desire and longing despite being a pamper can be the constantly in the sight of pleasures. It is not the pleasure of property but the Godly pleasure that makes a man merge in this problem. So, the sight is not kept on the property.

Newer in The Background of Vedic Civilisation

This unequalled aspect of the Vedic civilisation, that is, equality in equilibrium and the situation of pleasure, has changed subsequently. Due to the advancement of civilisation, extraneous movement has been in a quarter number than introspective ones. Man has gradually become dependent on external objects, so their demand has increased substantially, and they are much grieved for the dissatisfaction. Non-fulfilment of desire for wealth is the poverty of mind. Mere poverty is the problem of starvation, food, clothing, shelter, education, health and blooming of dignity. Recently expansion of the market has been accomplished through the explosion of demands, and within the expansion of the market, opportunities for the extension of activities and income of men have expanded. If the market is expanded, resources would extend and spread up from one part of society to another, from one end to the other. In the last decade, Machiko Nissanke, in the context of the melioration of Africa adjacent to the Sahara and East Asia, has struggled with the necessity of the market. He said:

> Statis regulation, ill-defined property right and other constraints restrict rather than stimulate economic activity. These condition result in rent seeking and redistribution, not rising productivity.
>
> (Nissanke n.d., 36)

In the context of control over the market, Nissanke said:

> The market sustaining role (of government) aims to uphold the working of the market by providing proper incentive system for innovations and R&D.
>
> The market guiding role (of government) aims to help the economy to move in a certain direction by providing incentive and coordinating private activities.
>
> (Nissanke n.d., 42)

Control and infirm outlook deter the motion of the market and economic situation because, as a result, a real outlook about the right to resources is not built up. These arrangements do not increase the ability of production but draw attention to enjoy interest sitting idly.

Due to the role the government plays in the satisfaction of the market, the market swells up and becomes speedy because required inspiration and research for the rise in production management and economy have built up the perspective for development.

The coordinating role of the government market becomes the power to determine the right speed in the economic system, because it makes the arrangement for personal enterprise, and coordination is taking the right speed and direction. It is evident from recent research by Nissanke and others on the direction of improvement of the development of Africa and Asia that economic development has been built up for a mixed form of the enterprise of market and society. As the root of the progress of economic management, there is enterprising coordination and active participation of the people in the concerned economic region. Economic rise is resigned. As Japan, Singapore, Taiwan, Malayasia and others have come as the good result from this process, the development process of the most populated countries, like India and China, have also come hand in hand with this process. In the cases of both India and China, coordination of the state with open markets and arrangements has brought success. The poverty of India and China swelled up gradually the problems of poverty in the world. Along with the betterment of the poverty situation of these two countries, the form of poverty situation of the world has also been changing. Actual accompaniment is what is possible as a result of coordination between extreme market and social authority. All of these lines of advancement of the socio-economic condition of the modern world have organised from the union of coordination of state with open market and liberal economy.

World Bank has designated three types of disparities to measure economic inequality. These are as follows: (1) The inequality with disparities and economic measures between two countries, for which prevailing measures would be in the form of economic measures (2) Multinational inequality, which is measured by the problem related to economic management and living and social situation within the same countries; and (3) Inequality of the world.

For its measurement, the whole population of the world is judged at a time and the conclusion drawn thereof. As a result, familiarities in the world population might exist on the basis of the economic and social distribution of all the people of the world. The disparity of income and inequality of the standard of living in world management are being thought of. World Bank has been endeavouring to become a worldwide institute for measuring inequality. Such management primarily includes income, the capacity of expenditure, power of investment, the propensity of savings, earning education-wealth right for living and attempt to be established. World Bank, in its World Development Report of 2006, has stepped in to measure the world situation of poverty and inequality. In the meantime, there has been some accompaniment of the task. Considering the matter from different sides, it is observed that through the world is stricken with the vice of poverty and inequality, the variance of these is gradually on the wave. A day might come when we will be completely free of these vices.

Liberation in The Path of Kautilya

The theory of class struggle propounded by Karl Marx has failed. The world situation is moving perfectly opposite to the nation of Karl Marx. Financial enterprises controlled by the state are becoming obsolete. Again, control of the sovereign land market is also untenable. Viceless management has bloomed, which would bring us a certain condition of the human race. Going beyond the identity with respect to a state of nation, it would be possible to bring about a change in the measure of the worldwide human race and a better stage transformation of this condition. Modern explosive vices in human history would disappear. It would be easier for us to eliminate the vices that have grappled us like an octopus. The Marxian sun has set at the lowest bottom of the modern sense of living. From this perspective, there has been a looking back, an attempt to look anew in China, Russia and elsewhere. It is time now for the Kautilyan sun to rise. The world situation is now directed at the economic system of Kautilya.

Kautilya has turned the authority and common people into the king and his subjects. This king is, of course, not an oppressing king. The authority that is closer to the subjects in an attempt to be in unison with the subjects is the king.

'Prajahsukhesukhamrajnah, prajanamhitehitam,...'

The king is one who does not feel happy with their own happiness; rather, the happiness of their subjects brings happiness to them. All that a king wants is the happiness and welfare of the subjects. Kautilya has said that the first trait desirable for leadership is wisdom.

The leader would be the possessor of wisdom; they would see everything as a manifestation of the Absolute self (Brahman).

'Yatahbai Imani bhutanijayante, yatjatajibanti...'

Wherever has been lively, whatever has been living, whatever may come to the valley of life, wherever may get manifested, all are Bahaman.

Brahman is the manifestation of life. Man is the embodied form of Brahman. So, Brahman is to be known, is to be realised. Kautilya wanted that leadership at all stages should first be earnest in the realisation of Brahman and should learn about Brahman to accept life. An outlook of great equality would rise in the leadership. He who is the possessor of this wisdom, or Prajnah, would know that you men are manifestations of Brahman, so they are equal at the extreme end. This is the first strong flourish for the establishment of extreme equality in the world. All are equal in the view of extreme equality. So, injustice cannot be done to anybody. None can be deceived. None can be exploited. No one can be injured in the interest of anyone being engaged in one's own interest. Men with such an outlook would come out of every sphere of society. They would be a special resource for building up the economic foundation.

Human resources would come much forward with such a special outlook and primordial conjugation. The deeper and wider this conjugation, the greater the changes to the outlook of living. The change of state necessary for a living would follow the resources of the world, which would be the rightful resources of all. A balanced and equilibrated society would grow there not with a look of consumption but with a look of renunciation.

It is Kautilya, not Marx, who is the best propounder of the future.

Bibliography

Nisbet, Robert A. *The Sociological Tradition*. Rawat Publications, New Delhi, 2004.

Oyen Else, S. M. Miller, and Syed AbdusSamad, eds. *Poverty: A Global Review*, Rawat Publications, New Delhi, 2003.

The United Nations Educational, Scientific and Cultural Organization and the Scandinavian University Press, 1996.

Kuo, Edie C. Y. *Families under Economic Stress: The Singapore Experience*, Institute of Southeast Asian Studies, Singapore, 1976.

Charles Lerert. *Social Theory*, Rawat Publication, New Delhi, 2004.

Asen Robert. *Visions of Poverty*, Rawat Publications, New Delhi, 2004.

Harrington Michael. *The Other America: Poverty in the United States*, Collier Books, New York, 1993.

World Development Report (2006), Equity and Development. The International Book of Reconstruction and Development/ The World Bank, Washington.

Nissanke Machiko and Earnest Aryeety, eds. *Comparative Development Experiences of Sub-Saharan Africa and East Asia*. Ashgate. England USA, 2003.

53
Wealth and Division of Labour: Kautilya and Adam Smith

In production, the role of labour has got importance as per Adam Smith; For Kautilya, the most important are the officers of labour. Primary valuation of economic management is formed with labour—such is the nation of Adams Smith. Kautilya knew that for the system of production built up based on labour, there is no way open for the incitation of the possibility of blooming of a man. Kautilya has judged the subjects related to incitation in man. The context of incitation is not involved in the determination of significance by Adam Smith; so, for him, the subject of preserving the value of action by judging right and wrong is important. Smith believed that efficiency and skill only render a man an economic unit.

The more extended the periphery of skill and efficiency would be, the more possible it would be for a man to increase the measure and excellence of a chart having recourse to such cognition. Adam Smith has laid stress on the theory of division of labour. Through division of labour, the right of labourers were assured. Labour gets the scope of being multiplied many times. That is why Adam Smith differentiates between labour and labourer and has shown that by transfusing its own speed, labour might bring the flow of finance. In this flow, the labourer, at one time, lags behind much-multiplied machines, etc., offering labour moves on. Management dependent on labour might be transformed into management supported by (consequently dependent on) machines. Offers of labour are floating on the financial flow regenerated by labour and reaching the extreme, and lack of identification is looking for the support of their own identity.

Differences in the outlook on production and producers have come along with the onward march of history. There should be no doubt about the fact that the present age is, in many ways, indebted to Adam Smith for lending the perspective of modern socio-economic judgement. Through exposition on the phase of production by the institution of industry and use of machines, labour involvement brought special requirement ever and ever again to the economic unit. Judgement of labour is necessary in the case of production because qualitative and quantitative changes of labour become essential at the time of transition from one enterprise to another. One way of bringing wide transformation in agriculture is to make it multipurpose.

The meaning of multipurpose agriculture is to engage in different types of production from the same field and to lend to each production work a basis dependent on variegation. Keeping the basic foundation and methods of measuring agricultural production unattired, the expansion and variation of produce help swell up its monetary valuation. Initialization of multipurpose agriculture demands many types of agricultural labour. The significance of many types of agricultural labours is embedded in various efficiency, mechanism, ability and wisdom. Determination of the correct form of labour in case of offering labour, in the same way, would likewise be marking the continuous distributions, a measure of production and qualities. Production would depend on many factors. In this, quality standards and measures, of course, are important in the case of inclining modern economic cognition. Adams Smith becomes eager to explain this through judgement and division of labour.

Kautilya's process of judgement is different. In judgements and the division process of labour, Smith has considered different aspects of the labour unit and has tried to arrive at a conclusion. But Kautilya's process is quite different from this Kautilya has laid importance on judgement and division of labour in the interest of the offers of labour and the aggregate of the people of an economic region. Agricultural production and quality and quantity of our turn depend on many factors. Kautilya, after analysis, has shown that along with the bounty of nature, condition of the natural resources, quantitative and quantitative basis and other allied factors, the findings on the offers of labour and utility of the people as a whole are to be considered. As a result, the role of the offers and users' labour would be more useful than the consideration of labour. What types of division and consideration are to be made would have to be understood from the viewpoint of the offers and users of labour. In the case of agriculture, a man apt to cultivate paddy naturally would have knowledge about the cultivation and production of wheat, jute, cereals, etc.

With expertise and special techniques in the cultivation of paddy, that person might possibly be engaged, so meeting the production and cultivation of other things as well or not at all. This depends on the technic and efficiency of that person. The same person might be connected with a number of jobs and come out successful and might also get into trouble. Due to moving about again and again in the same profession, the labour for that profession becomes of rotational character, that is, it rotates constantly. Constant rotation makes the labour capable of being accompanied easily. At the same time, efficiency comes in. Constantly rotating jobs become filled with efficiency. On one side, there is the possibility of efficiency, and on the other side, there is a gradual lack of earnestness in the offer of labour. Attraction and fascination with the constantly rotating flow of works would necessarily wane. The consequence of this waning attraction and fascination for the flow of works is the ruination of quality and standard. And even prior to this there was a situation in which due to lack of attraction and zeal, the future of a financial enterprise was endangered. Division of labour is at the root of this disorder.

As the division of labour has been essential for modern management, which is the accepted management in every case, it has also brought along its disastrous factors. Adam Smith engaged himself in exposing the modern aspect of the division of labour but summoned along with its disastrous effect and the possibility of its pervasion. This venomous outlook at the dawn of modern economic management and the heritage of the foundation of the same has developed on almost all economic doctrines and parties. Kautilya exposed the process of the overall economic blooming of the world much before Smith. Smith has presented golden poisonous, and Kautilya, from the distant past, opened the golden door of past modern economic management.

Consideration and Use of Wealth

According to Smith, consideration labourers may be of two types. One type of labourer increases the wealth of the organisation and lifts up the standard. The other type of labourer does not alter the wealth and standard for the workers associated with the production. It is possible to be cooperative in case augmentation of wealth, and the standard of the organisation can be earned. Such propitious workers gain appreciation by the organisation. On the other hand, the organisation need not consider the cases of those workers who do not contribute to the augmentation of its wealth or standard. Wealth grows in many ways. The influence of labour is very effective in this case. Those workers are happy to be accepted by the organisation are effective. The rest are considered either worthless or useless. After completion of work, if there is no speciality to be remembered then it is of no importance at all.

Works that retain any real significance gradually become beneficial to both labour and the organisation. Organisations flourish only by the quality of their work. At the same time, the work quality differs with the experience of the labour. Work is the only point of consideration here. The qualitative standard of work develops on the qualitative standard of the workers. Similar to how the qualitative standard of the workers makes the work graceful, works of qualitative excellence also contribute to the flourishing of the organisation. A primary nation is forward in the domain of economic science to the effect that the production capacity of organisations increases under the influence of work. This is also the primary law of the swelling of wealth. Wealth gets swelled up because, at this condition of the production management of the organisation, flows start coming in. Owing to this flow, new measures are continuously added to the wealth with which the organisation started its merch.

The main wealth of the organisation gets swelled up due to the combination of extra wealth with the project earned by the organisation, and gradually, the augmented wealth gets a proper environment to grow up. As a result, the stage of exposition of possibility on the part of the organisation becomes easier, and now, the march begins with the augmented wealth. While considering the wealth of the nation, Adam Smith has deliberated on how wealth is procured and how it grows up and maintains two types of roles of the offers of labour. He said: 'There is one sort of labour which adds to the value of the subject upon which it is bestowed: there is another which has no such effed. The former as it produces a value may be called productive; the later unproductive labour.' (Wealth of Vatron Bank One n.d., 161)

Two types of offers of labour are scanty in comparison to the whole population of a country. The demand of the market for the produced commodities is the combined demand of all generated from necessities. As a result, the produce required to meet the need of all may come from any place outside the country. Whatever may be the same when the necessity arises, the venture of the markets meeting the necessity inspires newer fields to come in through economic management.

Consequently, the wealth with the limit of which the organisation started this research gets multiplied many times.

Adam Smith says:

Through the whole annual produce of the land and labour of every country is no doubt, ultimately detained for supplying the consumption of its inhabitants and for procuring a renown of them, yet when it first comes either from the ground or from the hands of the productive labourers, it naturally divides itself into two parts. One of them, and frequently the fetched is in the first place destined for replacing capital, or for ownership the provision multiplies and finished work, which had been with dream for a capital the other, for constituting a revenue either to the owner of the capital, as the profit of his stock, or to some other person, as the rent of his hand. (Wealth of Nations n.d., 161).

Both the land and the workers need to be taken care of. Adam Smith is influenced by another thought. Taking examples from the animal world, he showed that the greater the procuring power, the greater the number of animals. Smith suggested that greater provisions bring in a greater number of the kingdom of that animal. He looks for enough income to be the source of enough increase in the number of animals. According to Adam Smith: 'The liberal reward of labour, therefore as it is the effect of increasing wealth so it is the cause of increasing population. To complain of it is to lament over the necessary effect and cause of the greatest public prosperity.' (Wealth of Nations n.d., 39)

> That is, the income of a labourer increases their power of production, so it instigates them to be intemperate towards sensual institutes. So, at the stage of encountering an economic problem, a social procure crops up. But enough income is necessary for the labourers.

With this enough income, a labourer maintains their health, etc. In the long run, it enhances the overall production of society.

According to Adam Smith:

A plentiful subsistence increases the bodily strength of the labourer and the comfortable hope at bettering his condition and of ending his days perhaps in case and plenty, animates him to exert that strength to the utmost.

(Wealth of Nations n.d., 40)

Affluence and Solvency

As affluence and solvency are required for the labourer for happiness and security in their life, these are required to enhance economic production. A labourer, therefore, calls for affluence and solvency in their life. No doubt, they would also carry this affluence in life and would attempt to swell up their life. That is, money would gather in the hand of labourers, and at the same time, the standard of living would rise, and the capability and power of production of the labourers would grow. In this context, Adam Smith could not frame a proper notion about the fate of the money accumulated in the custody of the labourers. Smith is not clear whether the excess income would be moved towards expenses or would create capital. But his definite opinion is that if this money is used gradually to create capital, the standard of living for the labourers will increase, increasing study idleness and fondness of case. According to Smith:

Whenever capital predominates, industry prevails: whenever revenue, idleness. Every increase of doses of capital, therefore, naturally trends to increase or dimension the real quantity of industry, the number of productive hands and consequently the exchangeable value of annual produce of the land and labour of the country, the real wealth and revenue of all its inhabitants.

(Wealth of Nations n.d., 104).

The greatest importance of the effect of capital amount has been revealed by Adam Smith. With the dominance of capital amount, not only the overall amount of industrial production is signified but a change in the qualitative measure is also designated.

A direct association of the increase in capital amount with the process, production and capability of production has been evidenced. Here, the role of labourers is rather insignificant.

A labourer spends the earned money to buy different types of consumable goods to impose the standard of living. As a result, savings grown to their control is very scanty. This meagre saving cannot be invested as capital because a small amount of saving is too meagre in the case of capital investment. The labourer becomes eager to expand this money to buy consumable goods and other objects of daily use and as investments in long-term schemes. Being a partner in long-term schemes on the part of labourers is not sufficient to make the scheme flourish, but still, the effect of taking part in the scheme by the labourer becomes helpful for the expansion of the scheme. So, the expansion of the scheme is possible for every common process.

As the main basis of the division of wealth and labour, Smith has pointed out the expansion and qualitative standard of production. So, in the interest of sequential development of expansion and qualitative standards, the leadership of economic management would have to be eager to increase the quality and effect of these by considering the division of wealth and labour. This too occupied Adam Smith (1723–1790 ADE), Professor at Glasgow from the phase of lectures of Francis Hatcheson on moral philosophy. A special doctrine of Hutcheson is that the target of economic management should be earning a great amount of happiness and affluence for many people. The twelve years Smith spent in Glasgow as a professor of moral philosophy was the happiest phase of his life. He tried to combine other wings of life with economic management. He conjoined politics, moral philosophy, etc. 'Wealth of Nations' is his creation in the last phase of seven years of his life with broken health and in the service of his aged mother. His mother was very fond of Smith and served Smith with her extreme ability. Moving through a life filled with pains and sufferings, Smith earned experience that manifested in his writings. The intensity of restlessness and sufferings in his own life has influenced his outlook. The call for bringing stability in the environment of intensive selfishness owing to the independent intervention of an invisible hand has emerged for his whole life.

Adroitness and Manifestation

While speaking of the labourers' own adroitness, Smith has indulged in the beckoning of the external things. So, instead of one type of work, many types of works have been points of attraction to them. Special proficiency of a labourer would come not in the attempt for the mental awakening of the labourer but with becoming efficient in production with the help of machines. Machines would selflessly increase the capability of labourers in the entire sense. Smith thought that labourers needed to be more alert for their interests; they would even be self-aggrandised. By this, the phase of the monument of capital money partnership of the labourers would be enhanced. Labourers would, to a greater extent, take part in the planning with the capital money. Through consideration of labour, a labourer would get access to different professions and, at the same time, would flourish the economy through the development of the professions. On one side, the division of labour would be helpful for blooming. On the other side, the division of wealth would hasten up the speed of economic flourish.

Kautilya's Path

On the basis of the division of wealth proposed by Adam Smith, economic management has been brought up many times. In the extreme sense, Smith's evaluation and realisation have not been heeded. Compared with the combined form of these, Kautilya's outlook is rather revolutionary—a different significance of the monetary profession has been mainly expressed in the basic view of Kautilya. Probably, Kautilya is the first to propound socioeconomics in world history, dividing the financial infrastructure of the structure of different professions. Kautilya divided economic management into professions. He classified each of the professions in light of the nature of the works—which profession certain factors of labour would belong to would depend on the propensity and from the labour by the offer.

Dividing economic management in accordance with profession, Kautilya has spoken of directive management. For each profession, in all of the divisions of the profession made by him, there is management for complete monetary control. For each profession, supervisors and workers with special technics have been maintained in Kautilya's *Arthashastra*. If supervisors and workers are directed from the consideration of technic and specialty, these professions may be raised to superiority. Kautilya wanted great and qualified persons to accomplish this job. So, the best result would be obtained if persons in consideration of succession engaged and occupied properly in the job be appointed in that very job. Kautilya has made the economic profession directed at the aim and production.

The king, by royal right, would have to be properly earnest for the welfare of the subjects and the country. At the same time, they would have to be earnest for the enhancement of the wealth of the kingdom. Kautilya has considered this enhancement of wealth with importance; the enhancement is, in the aggregate, a part of his endeavour, and so the aim of each department and each division of work is also directed at the enhancement of wealth. Kautilya wanted every department, profession or man engaged in all sorts of endeavours to move with timeless effort in purpose and desired route.

A king would procure and extend their wealth in the path prescribed by Kautilya and, at the same time, would properly observe all their responsibilities. To a king, the people of the state are what members of a family are to the house father. So, they who are seated in the leadership of a state would be established on renunciation, charity and offering. They would not feel contented with their own happiness; the happiness of the people would be certainly by their pleasure.

The king, crossing the bounds of their own interest, would always remain engaged in doing good to many people. The king would always think of statements of endless happiness of the country and countrymen. The practical form of this thought lies in all the phrases, one after another. The king will translate this into action in two ways. The first is the formation of the state and building the structure of the state endeavour of the king within the propensity and sphere of power of the state. The second is to gain the way of the state by spreading the endeavour of the state and the enterprises of the society.

The state would love and appreciate the worthy of all. But the state would certainly discriminate in this attempt. Thus, it would give a higher price to qualified, efficient and delightful persons than others. As a result, the action within a state would be sound. If the state picks up for every division and circulation of work the most qualified, efficient and enterprising man, it would be possible for the state to move fast, to rise to be benevolent for all and, in the long run, to be able to enhance the wealth of all. In other words, under such circumstances, the state does not support the sense of interest of any person or group but inspires all to move forward on the basis of quality, technic and efficiency. Thus, on the part of the state, the perspective of overall flourishing would be created. In the call for a total blooming within the professions classified by Kautilya is the central theory.

Kautilya has to overcome the obstructions in the way of overall blooming and to be enterprising so that similar other obstacles may not form a wall. That is why Kautilya's *Arthashastra* has different authorities for supervision, giving inspiration, etc., that have been agreed for guarding the state and adding to its wealth. On one side, state officials are entrusted with these responsibilities, and on the other side, there are different sources to keep watch on these officials. These are arrangements for setting up of arrangements like detective, law and social structure agencies. As a result, supervision of and growth of the endeavours, of the leadership, of these good endeavours and the workers therein would be preserved, and at the same time, these would be proper encouragement to this arrangement. For the coordination essential at the phase of division of economic division, Kautilya's view is especially meaningful.

Kautilya has wanted the initiation of a special line of economic development, not in the darkness of interest on the path of a glowing high of selflessness. As a result, this would be a blooming of qualities, economic manifestation and flourishing of living. That is why Kautilya's theory of total blooming has surpassed all throughout Adam Smith and been far-reaching. Smith was of the past, while Kautilya has paved the way for the economic development of the future world.

References

Smith, Adam. *An Inquiry into the Nature and Causes of the Wealth of Nations*. Chicago, 1776.

54

Background and Field of Application of Economic Ideas

Introduction

The history of economic ideas is as old as that of mankind. Different sensations and inspirations for economic ideas sprang since the pulsation of life began in the form of a human form. When it was a phase of living only by collecting resources from the forest, it was a mental urge to move about for that living. In the hunting phase, an urge to move forward came from the urge to live and of power. The phase after is one of receiving the prey property and consuming the same. There, a propensity comes in the minds of the hunters of limited expansion, distribution and skill in the use of it. So, a man engaged in hunting did not leave off after having prey. They have been engaged in endeavouring to understand what was to be done with the same, for knowing it and for accepting it properly.

Hunters of the forest have also tried to think of the proper use of the mild resource that human hunters procured through hunting. Hunters did not develop the propensity or tendency to save. What had been present in them was to bring speed to hunting, to have a detailed idea about hunting, to chase a theory with deep attention and to succeed in hunting.

Succeeds in hunting become helpful for real awakening and exposition of that hunter. Through such exposition more skilful exhibition of lack of eagerness towards the prey and the process of the prey becomes evident along a definite line. Following this line, the lives established a form of a hunting society, gradually making the same strong and stout. Hunting society abides by a mutual understanding centred on hunting. Boynes's action on the hunting society brings mutual understanding, becomes stronger, and at the same time, a primordial form of mutual exchange is set in. The hunting society, with time, has strengthened this mutual understanding. This system has gradually got a definite form in the agricultural society.

Economic Principle of State

Historians have been zealous to set concordance between economic history and state and society in many ways. The culture of the history of society and state would obviously be reflected through discussion and consideration of economic judgement and economic management. While judging the economy, the economic historians have related the context of law and justice with economic matters. This idea has spread right through the earliest economists, the attempt of economists for betterment and the attempt made by Carl Marx.

Such ideas or steps on the part of the state are always helpful for men to hold or move on in society. The difference between economic and political ideas has gradually been waning. At the initial change, this differentiation was almost impossible. The economic idea of the state was concorded with political thoughts. The overall idea comprised the life of individuals, their craving and finding, their choices, their past and future—all in a shell. The basis of economic ideas in agricultural society was of this type. Economic ideas of the agricultural society forward centring on the basic driving force of life and on the basis of aims and objectives of life.

The idea of the whole life, society and state were concentrated in this. For an individual, there is the initiation of a separate idea of economic subjects. Even in the background of society and the state, such a separate idea is possible. The idea of the agricultural society had a depth in these. All belonging to the agricultural society wanted to see life in totality, in full-fledged form. The culture formed by the attempt to march on accepting this possibility has given a trace to the agricultural society and the power to bloom up the separateness. A number of important points of separateness come into the thoughts of the agricultural society. For example, in an agricultural society, this special point comprises practices in life, feelings of life, the field of manifestation, the ability to express and, above all, a background for exposition. In life, on the basis of these, an individual has surprised the aggregate. Thus, in the thoughts that emerged from agriculture, the root of economic ideas is within the components of society, culture and civilisation. No relation has been created where there has been no coordination among the components of society—culture is civilisation. As a result, the overall idea has sometimes made society strong and fast and sometimes weak. Like society, the fate of a state has also sometimes been measured by this. The coordinating concordance established between the power of the society and the state is in the form of culture acting in the society and has created a basic perspective for culture. Against this background is the principle of the rise of a state or the awakening of society. In agricultural ideas, an individual has always thought of themselves as a part of the whole. Consequently, self-oriented thoughts and actors also have been working for the development and upliftment of society and the state. The upliftment of an individual has gone up and created wealth, and their domain has been extended. All earnest ideas of an individual have spread among many. In all endeavours of an individual has somehow appeared another endeavour of the objection of the society or the aggregate. One has set up concordance with another, not merely with object or endeavour but also with theory and consequence. As a result, in the life of an individual has come a significant situation of distribution and extension. This can be applied to those who have been able to create wealth and procure and accept the same. At the same time, it can be applied in the case of those who have pride and a void of wealth. Just as an individual has been able to accept the whole, the whole has accepted the individual and enabled them to move on in the path of life as a whole.

Culture Emerged from Agriculture

At the centre of the culture emerged from agriculture an object of faith—worthy of being worshipped. Agriculture demands thoughts for the future, for these are required to combine endeavour and enterprise. Just as the agricultural crops are to be gradually built up from small to big, agricultural works are hastened up by a combination of little enterprises and the assiduous. For all allied activities of agriculture, a combined effort is required. That is why, in the economic thoughts primarily emerging from agriculture, sets a unique culture of social and organizational attempts to bring many people to a common meeting place. The outline of the culture so formed as a field of faith grows there. The spot of faith and dependence is the leadership of the agriculture society. Hence comes the propensity and zeal for all the attempts. For this propensity and zeal, the perspective of culture and deep faith of the society is considered. All of the combined attempts for work and the works meant for the welfare of many in agricultural society have a far-extended existence within a multitude. For far-extension, union and coordination are required among many. The centre of the union of the members is the centre of that faith. Rise and development of the spot whose faith is concentrated are urges of all. For this, within the agricultural thoughts, stress has been laid on the participation of all and the enterprise of the aggregate. Another salient feature of agricultural thoughts is that the results of enterprise and activities are fixed in different measures for all. Anyone would have the scope to realise their specific share in accordance with their primary wealth and ability.

In the culture that emerged from agriculture, the influence of the aggregate is total. Total feelings for the multitude are at the root of agricultural culture. Agricultural culture gives the inspiration for incorporation. All attempts are taken to place the object of faith at the centre. Depending on the difference in inequality at the centre of faith, all the economic attempts would are fulfilled. In all economic attempts, combined and organised action should remain embedded. The vehicle of economic development can move on only by combined attempts. On the path of every country, there should be attempts to keep. This vehicle of economic development on the whole. In this attempt lies the bringing of the possibilities in the stage of perfect bloom. The more certain the balance between possibility and blooming, the better the perspective of economic development. Cooperation and active participation of the groups would be required for economic development. Owing to different concordance and connecting links among different groups, balance can be established among those groups. Considering the comparative positions of different groups, the difference is there in the situations of economic development in them. World Bank Report (2006) on poverty has exposed, in detail, the dependence of development and progress equilibrium between the groups and the aggregate on the basis of opportunity and development. According to World Bank:

In most countries the between group share is noticeably higher for decompositions based on the alternatives, 'possible' calculation. Based on the approach, observed between groups differences are indeed substantial in many countries- for the group definitions here. To the extent that these circumstances are judged 'morally irrelevant' the findings suggest that in economic life, just as in health and education, a substantial portion of observed inequality in many developing countries can be linked to inequalities of opportunity.

(World Development Report 2006, p. 42)

Different Groups, Different Economic Ideas

The variations brought about in the opportunities and arrangements of different groups by considering the difference in those groups can be measured by influence and distortion caused. Topics of the combined decision of the group have come in the agricultural societies, and here lies the speciality of the aggregate, and engagement is considered on the basis of these. The speciality of the aggregate is especially applicable for this very reason for initiation and measurement of economic blooming. The role of the aggregate in both the cases of induction and measurement of economic blooming can be smooth and firm if an identical perspective and arrangement are set for the blooming of all men conjoined in the economic work restoring to the same situation. The financial works here may seem to be burdensome for an individual and the incitement that may be possible for this may also be brought about.

The perspective of economic development may be very much dependent on the situation and the person. In agricultural ideas, an attempt is made to balance this situation and the person. Both the situation and person become earnest for hastening the economic development of the individual, and it is the consequence of the development of the individual that can definitely initiate the economic development of the aggregate. The exposition of the individual and the aggregate may here match on hand in hand. The concordance between the exposition of an individual and of the aggregate depends on external wealth, propensity of procuring wealth, merits and demerits of wealth and the amount of procured wealth. As a result, the blooming of the individual and the aggregate starts together. The consequence itself would judge, in this case, an individual and aggregate. Progress of the aggregate is not the only measure of the process of an individual. An individual carries the aggregate forward, creating an improved form of the aggregate and exposing the same.

Features of The Arthashastra

The methods introduced by Kautilya have all along been followed later. Economic thoughts are advancing from apparent consideration to a compelling one. The *Arthashastra*, as it were, was the first to initial the essence of all economic thoughts. Such thoughts have been included in the *Arthashastra* for which there are objections even up to this day. The main theme of the *Arthashastra* is that economic management is the same for all activities and all kinds of thoughts in life. All thoughts and all sorts of endeavours and this consequence and result have been incorporated into the economic principle of the *Arthashastra*. The real form of the economic situation depends on all sorts of activities in life and the flow of the consequence. This can easily be explained with the modern capital market as an example. The price of the share of a company primarily depends on its financial status. An increase in profit of the company or propensity of such increase and swelling up to wealth, the price of the share will rise.

The price of the share will fall if the situation of the company deteriorates. Of course, there are some such cases where the price of a share does not follow general changes in the nature of the condition of the company—good or bad. It depends on law and order, social and political stability and even the health condition of the same personalities. The rise or fall of the price of a share does not depend on the financial status of the company. It depends on many factors. All of the factors collectively and individually influence the price of shares. What would be the future price of equity shares of the share market, and how would it go on, therefore, depends on many factors. These factors are true in the case of a company. At the same time, it is true for the economic situation of a country too. Kautilya not only realised the matter but considered it not the most important.

After going through and being engaged in deliberation on it, some have felt that it is less of an economic matter. Here, economic matter is being combined with another beyond its range. An example is the mention of different movements and different activities of economic management in the defence management of a country. In the *Arthashastra*, legal management; secrets management; management of leadership; distribution of different departments; principles of taxation, agriculture, amendment, production, distribution; etc., are considered important. Kautilya even thought that Vedic knowledge is the very first requirement for the onward march to economic blooming. A man expert in Vedic knowledge and its practice would naturally become honest and moralist. The scope of corruption would decrease in personal cases and also in the background of the state. Scope of corruption would go down in the countries or organisations where Vedic knowledge has taken resort. To be free of corruption is a definite advancement on the part of the economy of a state. Kautilya wanted to make economic management emerge from a complete thought through the conjunction of the principle of judgement with the judiciary. There are many wings of such complete thought that are apparently unimportant. But in the long run, they prove themselves important.

Besides this sense of completeness, another future of the *Arthashastra* is its active economic thought. That is, the economic thought stated in the *Arthashastra* is engaged in awakening into action. The theory of how best it can be applied through which mode of its setting and through what sorts of attempts is also under the jurisdiction of the *Arthashastra*. Kautilya has thought of the security of the state and the welfare of the leader of the state and has put front laws on these and composed special fields of its application. Till now, modern economists have not been engaged in economic deliberation to that much pervasion as Kautilya attained in his presentation.

Health education, drainage, potable water, conservation of forests, etc., have been incorporated into modern economic thoughts. Without such incorporation, the presentation would not be accepted. Kautilya had laid importance on these at the very primary stage. He also considered the implementation of the law, administrative capability, application of mass-oriented rule and justices, personality, spiritual knowledge, nurture of leadership, trade principles, preservation of influence, etc. Besides these, Kautilya laid stress on a balanced situation, an attempt for habitation and upliftment. Economic development accompanying these would comprise all of the factors of living of the individual and the state alike. At the centre of an attempt to integrate progress of public life and the state would be a perceptive man. Kautilya's *Arthashastra* has called all endeavouring men and those at the leadership in the periphery of this realisation. As a result, only men with realisation would control and direct everything. They would not have only selfish feelings in themselves, and so the attempt and enterprise of an individual would be directed for many or the totality. The *Arthashastra* has placed the financial basis on a bigger perspective and has placed the same feeling before the future society urging to take the result of the same with a view to the attempt for economic development.

55
Liberty of Individual and Society

Significance of Liberty

Liberty in the economic background means liberty from poverty and paucity. A direct consequence of economic liberty is affluence in life. The necessity of economic liberty for affluence and blooming in life has also been accepted in the religious order. Spiritual advice to persons afflicted with hunger and poverty is ridiculous. Religious feeling and faith help one ascertain what would be the expectation with which an individual a society would move on, what would be the opener of the veil of an individual and a society and which of the economic management would be the most important and which would be unimportant. The context of liberty is combined with the individual life and the life of society. The matter of liberty is considered in the background of the life of the individual and society. This is the most acceptable method.

The matter of liberty is to be thought of in the background of individuals and society. The theory of liberty is especially compulsory for individuals or society. This theory may be discussed in two divisions:

- Complete liberty of an individual
- Relative liberty of an individual

The complete liberty of an individual is judged from the viewpoint of the individual themselves and from their own standpoint. And the matter of complete liberty of the individual is addressed by their extreme position in respect of the others in the society or of others in the society with respect to them. The relative position of an individual is, in all respects, a matter of contrast. Comparison between two persons may be made under the same or different backgrounds. So, in the case of drawing a comparison, sometimes, a partitioner stage or standard may be thought of and may be thought how, in respect of the difference, other factors may be combined under a single survey. The perspective of comparison of an individual may be in any field of society. For the economic liberty of an individual, their position needs to be realised through comparison. So far, consideration of the economic longing of an individual is judged as an individual, so it is also necessary to judge them from the perspective of the aggregate.

In the economic consideration of the personal judgement of the individual, there may be different procedures. For example, the first is to accept the minimum requirement of living, the component without which living is not possible. At the root of this, there will also be personal feelings about the life of the individual. The minimum removal of poverty through far living also has different stages. Before the removal of poverty, the feelings of the individual regarding poverty need to be clarified. For example, many a one has taken for granted the notion that having two meals a day and allied things like having common clothing and common shelters are able to remove poverty and for those who have no provision for food have just enough food is to be considered to be a great attainment in life. If such a man can manage to earn two meals a day, they would feel satisfied because, before this, they did not even have this. They had been without food. Now, they had at least something. This is attainment. So, it brings happiness and course upliftment. Similarly, a person who has had the provision of food and shelter and some clothing also thinks that, now, their minimum requirement would be satisfied if they get a tolerable place of residence. They who have the provision of all these three have before them the wealth of this world exposed. So, there would now be an initiation of intentness for life in them for lack of the same.

Economic Liberty

According to an economic study, the perspective of consideration of the economic situation of an individual depends on their own feelings toward life—How they look upon their life, how they like to live, what they like to be, how their life would be defined, how they would move on in their life's walk, where they would go, what type of life would be the most attractive for them, etc. An individual likes to see themselves in their desired form. In this world, food, clothing and shelter are not all that they want. They like to see what type of education they have availed, what type of health system they have full access to, how much purified potable water they have, how clean their shelter is, how pollution-free their environment is and how much free movement of nature is before them. The outline of poverty is different to different people. Attempt for the removal of poverty would, as such, be varied. To one who is engaged in begging, a meagre provision would just suffice. A little bit of food or help would give them great attainment. They become contented with the filling of their stomach with foodstuffs.

A meagre income to them being free from the curse of living opens many wide avenues for them. They feel contented with the provision of food. The provision of food just changes their attitude towards the feeling of poverty. Now both satisfaction and dissatisfaction grow simultaneously. Satisfaction lies in being free from begging. They no longer have to be engaged in begging. So, their living is now more improved than before. They have come to a more improved stage, being free from the stage of begging, where poverty was acute. This improved life is judged from the standpoint of their begging profession. They realise the improved life in the right of their present establishment. But even this life of theirs was stricken with poverty. They have had provision of food, but the provision of clothing and shelter is yet to be had under such circumstances. Dissatisfaction with the effect of lack of clothing and shelter has grown. The other side of satisfaction grows in them for having food.

With one satisfaction, life moves forward to attain a number of such dissatisfactions. Satisfaction and dissatisfaction are back to back. If there is a provision of food, clothing and shelter, one finds one's own dissatisfaction from some other corner of life. The factors responsible for satisfaction no doubt bring contentment, but at the same time, they bring dissatisfaction. Both satisfaction and dissatisfaction come simultaneously along with this flow. When one's condition is very miserable, one finds no scope to back the other side. After being a bit elevated from the miserable condition, one finds the opportunity to look at the other side. From this condition, an individual looking at different sides comes to realise the condition of others. Or their condition in comparison to others. They like to realise how they would improve themselves in a contrasting situation. Satisfaction, therefore, would not come simply from the solution of the problems of food, clothing and shelter. There are many other factors in the minimum requirement for satisfaction in life.

The standard of living a leading life is a very important factor. To determine the standard of living, a leading life is required to prepare essential matters for a commodity healthy and natural life. The standard of living depends on many factors, such as amount of income and expenditure, food and quality of food, education, health drainage system environment, communication for mass use, and the like. Even after having food, clothing, shelter, education, health, drainage, potable water, pure environment and after placing the mass-management in an ordinary manner would come dissatisfaction. Life would move on in the swing of satisfaction and dissatisfaction. Provision of these begets satisfaction and want dissatisfaction. The flow of dissatisfaction may come even after the satisfaction of these. The standard of living is the cause of dissatisfaction. The standard of the flow of life that lay before living gets blurred in the new flow of life. Here, the contrast plays a very important role. Two lives move through two flows of life, and the contrast, therefore, becomes very important.

The influence of contrast of economic management acts in all stages. It is by contrast that the relative poverty of oneself gets exposed. Contrast comes from understanding what own's position with respect to others is and how the position of one group or state is with respect to others. They who are judged inferior by contrast meet a wretched condition. The individual group or country that proved to be inferior accepts the inferiority and makes on. The environment and manifestation of an individual is an endeavour of upliftment for the inferior state. The inferior state becomes heart-rending for an individual. Relative poverty comes to be felt. The heart of an individual feels the pain of poverty in comparison to others. The feeling of relative position rises in them for life and the world. The movement starts from one type of dissatisfaction to another. The feeling of dissatisfaction and non-attainment get spread in every field of life. Life continues to move along in this phase of dissatisfaction. The feeling of poverty now starts to grow from this feeling of dissatisfaction. An unsatisfied mind is pained with poverty. Hence, its comparative position gets the identity of life. In such a case, dissatisfaction might arise even in the presence of food, clothing, shelter, health, education, pure potable water, drainage, a healthy environment and the overall controlling system. The feeling of poverty grows from dissatisfaction. Natural poverty rises from heaped-up dissatisfaction. All stages of poverty are not the same. Despite there being differences in nature, all types of poverty have a conjunction among them. As is dissatisfaction, so is poverty. A keen sense of dissatisfaction is a symptom of poverty. Though keen dissatisfaction is severe in poverty, it has definite nature. This very dissatisfaction binds life in many ways in different stages of poverty.

Position of the World Bank

The World Bank has framed a basic definition of poverty and has called upon different states to remove that basic poverty. The World Bank, from its study, has realised that a great enterprise comes out of pure potable water and drainage system, as a result of which removal of poverty becomes rather easier. In the case of the removal of poverty, the World Bank has decided on eight different targets, which are as follows:

Target-1: Liberty from basic poverty and satisfaction

Target-2: Active programme for primary education

Target-3: Equal rights among males and females and enhanced rights of the woman folk

Target-4: Decrees the rate of child death

Target-5: Improvement of the mental and physical health of the mothers

Target-6: Extrication from HIV/AIDS, malaria and other diseases

Target-7: Creation of balance in nature

Target-8: Cooperation of all for progress

All these targets of the World Bank are collectively called the targets of the millennium.

The purpose of the targets is to place the problem of the world before all and, at the same time, to march forward together to the target. The targets aim to try to get rid of the problem with cooperation and coordination of all and to get liberty from newer problems. Getting beyond the problem and liberty from newer problems signify engagement in solving the problems with the cooperation of all or many. The World Bank characterised the problems and, at the same time, initiated solving those problems in its detailed report on human development (2006) of the World Bank. The same problem of poverty has been looked upon from eight different angles. The World Bank inferred that the solution to any single problem would make provision for solving the other ones. For example, if there is poverty, supply of potable water would be reduced. The World Bank has looked at poverty from different measures. These measures are important state enterprises, so also are individual attempts and personal coordination of an individual in the endeavours of the state.

The World Bank is earnest in making the coordination and participation more intension. In the context of the first target, that is, liberty from basic poverty starvation, the World Bank stated that if pure potable water and proper drainage system are managed, the world would be able to get rid of one's share of the problem of maturation. In assessing the problem of poverty and malnutrition, the need for pure potable water has taken to be a reason. In developed countries, for every one in five persons, there is not at all any provision for pure potable water. In this world, crores of men are deprived of pure potable water. Those deprived of pure potable water are all poor and somehow stricken with starvation.

Except the developed countries, one in two persons has the advantage of a pure and potable drainage system; others are quite deprived of this facility. The number of such persons in this world is 260 crores. In total, two percent of the natural production is lost in different countries due to diseases caused by the lack of truly potable water and a proper drainage system. While eighty-five percent of the population of rich countries gets a better supply of pure potable water, in poor countries, it is only twenty-five percent. As such, water is expensive in poor countries. Sometimes, it is ten times more expensive. Those whose daily income is below one dollar are stricken with the water problem. Besides, problems have cropped up in the supply and use of water due to the use of water marked for agriculture in industries. In rural areas, water is collected from remote sources for domestic work and drinking. Children cannot join the school because they are to be engaged in this work. As such, the water problem has created a problem of education.

It is the womenfolk who try to get rid of this problem. Due to the time women devote for water, they are deprived of effective work and endeavours. Endeavours get flaccid for the use of water. Women lag behind much more. The World Bank has termed the time women have to spend for meeting the water problem as poverty emerged over time. Poverty emerging over time signifies the time it takes to prevent people from being associated with any work of financial matter. That is, due to time poverty, women lag behind men.

Kautilya's Solution

The problems talked about by the World Bank are really true. At the root of these problems are basic poverty and different related factors. Basic poverty is the problem of food, clothing and shelter. Factors related to these are problems of education, health, water, drainage and so on. Basic poverty includes the problem the carrying adequate food for all. The World Bank consider the problem but has stressed an easy and direct solution. The problem of water is grave and deep. If potable water is not obtained, many other symptoms will be evident at the same time. These would be different social problems. But basic poverty did not start from water. It cannot be said that basic poverty would return if potable water is supplied. The total storage of food in the world at this moment is sufficient for all the people of the whole world to have full meals for one and a half years.

A large portion of food and crops stored in the world get damaged by getting wet by water and treated by sun owing to exposure. Food damaged has to be thrown away. But most of the managers that are there for the distribution of food are corrupt. As a result, proper mass distribution does not take place; rather, in the name of mass distribution, this is only malpractice. There is food, but really, it is a hunt. There is food in the store, but the common hungry people have no right to that. This is so because if hunger prevails, many other managements remain. Most of the targets of the millennium presented by the World Bank have avoided the main problem and been applied at the extension of the problem. It is natural to apply the problem from the extended perspective; the problem itself has been avoided, and newer problems have been brought to light.

The World Bank likes to talk about the problem of basic poverty and change the very character of the problem. Problems of water and HIV/AIDS should be given priority, but these are not at the root of all the problems. Thousands of other problems are generated from poverty. All other problems become strong if there is no provision of food, clothing and shelter. If there is provision of food, clothing and shelter, most of the problems of the world disappear, but newer problems arise. If basic poverty disappears, relative poverty appears. If basic poverty disappears, relative poverty stays on. Poverty only changes its form, but it does not disappear. Poverty would stay on the path along which the World Bank is moving on with a target, thousands of attempts would be taken to remove poverty, and consequently, new types of poverty would emerge.

Kautilya moved along two paths for the removal of poverty: The removal of basic poverty and the removal of relative poverty. Kautilya brought the removal of basic poverty under the authority of the state. If people live in ease and affluence, comfort comes to the state and leader of the state. If people do not feel at ease, the situation becomes unworthy of being related to happiness.

The welfare of the subjects or the people is the welfare of the king, the leader of the state. The article on an item considered beneficial by the people is beneficial for the king of the state. The viewpoint with what Kautilya had considered the leader of the people has a temporary significance and, at the same time, is far-reaching. Temporary significance means that the people should earnestly realise their own welfare, and the king should also do likewise. People would be engaged to bring welfare to the king, who is benevolent to the people. As a result, the welfare of the king is accomplished by the welfare of the people.

The personal welfare of the king is not to be judged here. Kautilya has brought the matter of basic welfare to the people within the consideration of the state. The fact that the welfare of the people rests in the hands of the state means that the problem of removal of poverty rests on the state to be solved. The state must be engaged in the duty of eradicating poverty. So long as a single man spends their day without food and in starvation, the king also has no right to take a full meal and be healthy. The king will move in accordance with their people. Kautilya has presented a solution liberty of mind is required in the light of relative judgement. While considering the condition of one's own self in comparison with others, care should be taken to see that the feelings of temptation, ego and conflict do not get dominant. As a result of the poverty becomes minimum, relatives' poverty would always accompany them who would move on with feelings of temptation, malice and conflict. Relative poverty would be universally strong. If the removal of relative poverty is possible, the problem of basic poverty also becomes subdued. By the overall consideration and arrangement of Kautilya and by the intervention of the state come economic liberty of an individual and state liberty for the burden of basic and relative poverty.

56

Distribution of Land in the Removal of Poverty

Right on Land

The land is a great resource for the poor. Despite poverty, the right to land exposes economic capability in man. If the economic capability is exposed, it moves on with definite speed. It is possible to get into another profession through financial processors. The right to land brings in a substitutional process. The right to land brings in a production-oriented work system centred on the provision of work and land in the periphery of the financial profession. The right to land brings many rights, like the right to bread and the right to live, and at the same time, it brings a flow of different opportunities and advantages. The right to land brings opportunities for loans. Many procedures by loan open the flow of endeavours for that enterpriser. Thus, the right to land brings to them such a path whence there is a scope for liberation from provision in danger and, at the same time, would appear possible and blooming. By virtue of the right to land, poor people will be free from the grip of poverty, and at the same time, it can rouse new provisions and possibilities for many others. As the land yields crops, it makes it a source of crops. That is, the right to land brings in an individual primary resource. And the use of these resources opens up the path to the possibility of great provision of wealth in enterprises. From the right to land, different types of bonding and spheres of common dance rise. The enclosure of family, enclosure of society and enclosure of state—at the root of all these is the primary right of land and the extension of this right with respect to different organisations. Direct types of influence grow from the right to land at the base of rise influence are root and prevention. Land gives root, and again, it helps in prevention. As the right to land brings the right to wealth, it also brings the scope of pervasion.

As the wealth of land can be helpful for the expansion of wealth, it can also bring about the expansion of many kinds of financial spreads. If the distribution of the land is balanced, there is a scope for a balanced spread of wealth and possibilities. On the other hand, the distribution of land, despite the spread and steadiness, might bring in very bad consequences. The way of earning the right to land might be many-fold in a natural consequence. The deprivation of the right also brings a consequence just the opposite to it. A balanced distribution of land naturally calls for a consequence, which is an opportunity for financial expansion and hastens balancing, and as a result, powers of comparatively lower speed and capacity gradually become active. For example, real coordinating influence may be on the steadiness of the female and child societies. As a result, self-dependence and becoming an able power in society on the path of the women folk may be easier.

Among minors and children too, the effect of balanced distribution becomes of normal measures. That is, demand and flow to become pure enough for the sake of the society among them become stronger. Balanced distribution has thought of these factors in a historical background. At the same time, the social and family powers that have logged behind become quite evident, Laws that transmit finances become the strongest by this. Long-term foundation groups in the financial flow of society and the merit of this financial management may be transmitted among the backward people. Where balanced distribution strongly results in the possibility of awakening, this determination strengthens. And when it is wanting, the determination quite disappears in unbalanced situation. The wealth of life, success and pervasion faces incapable spread due to fatigue in action from lack of determination.

Opinion of the World Bank

The right to land was granted in the 2006 world development report. It was said in the report that in the attempt to remove poverty, granting the right to land is a big step. It is not that the World Bank has wanted a small extent of the right to land. It laid stress on the balanced distribution of land. According to the World Bank, through balanced distribution, not only in the rural society but also in the entire region and within every country, proper investment of wealth is compulsory. As a result, as the regional distribution of wealth is affected, the wealth would also be properly used. The report of the World Bank has stated:

> Land is the key assets for poor people. Owning it provides a means of livelihood to many facilities access to credit markets., has an insurance value determines influence in local politics, permits participation in social networks and influence intra household dynamics. That is why inequality in the ownership of land has such far-reaching consequences for the distribution of well-being and the organization of society for generation to come. Yet landownership in many countries is highly unequal, substantially more so than income or consumption.
>
> (World Development Report 2006, 162)

The World Bank has estimated the inequality in the distribution of land among different countries and, keeping this inequality in view, has tried to find out a connection between different factors of living and a balanced distribution of land. This research by the World Bank has revealed that in countries where inequality is high, there is a great difference in health education and standard of living are especially applicable. In those cases, inequality has taken a dreadful situation. This statistic of the World Bank shows that the balanced distribution of land is for all men. It is especially necessary for particularising the standard of living of poor people. The result of the research of the World Bank has shown that balanced distribution of social wealth. Investments in different fields can be controlled through the balanced distribution of land. Control over investment or the ability of investment determined by the power of the market becomes helpful for the distribution of social wealth. Distribution of investment of the countries that have taken attempts in this matter are able to be balanced in many respects, and, as a consequence, a good effect has permanently been introduced in financial management.

Research of the World Bank reveals:

> There are strong efficiency resources to address inequalities in land distribution. Pervasive imperfections in land and financial markets in developing countries reduce investment in land and keep countries from efficient land allocation. These effects together with lower human capital investment, reduced social cohesion, and distorted political power are consistent with a positive association between more unequal land distribution and lower GP growths.
>
> (Ibid., 163)

Right to Land

If doubt arises in the right to land, productive investment in land begins to decrease. This becomes panic that grows in the mind of the landowner lest that land may sometimes be out of hand or the right to that land may be questioned. The World Bank has found through judgement that despite there being possibilities in some countries, the effect of land distribution has brought on them such burden of problems that economic development there has come to a sudden stop. Wide economic development through the balanced distribution of land has taken place in Taiwan. And Venezuela is the worst suffered. Besides Venezuela, the countries where the unbalanced situation has been seen are Argentina, Nicaragua, Australia, Paraguye, Kenya, Zimbabwe, etc. Kenya and Zimbabwe took many steps for redistribution of land, but as those are rather temporary, the financial condition in these became very bad. Among the successful countries, Taiwan was greatly advanced, and at the root of it are balanced distribution and orientation of the land. Success has befallen the countries that have been endeavouring, like Taiwan, South Korea, China, Japan, etc. Among the countries where the distribution management of the right to land has not been supported enough are mainly South Africa, India, Egypt, etc. In these countries, a distribution system was initiated through the fixation of upper citing of land and government supervision, but the venture was not successful. It was learnt from the research of the World Bank that the problem with these countries mainly was the attribution of greater value on the protection of political interest over the economic advancement of the country or awakening of the poor. According to the World Bank:

> Why the rather disappointing results from attempts at land reforms? First given that motivation for land reforms is often to address political grievances efficiency and poverty reduction tend to be secondary. Guided by short term political objectives bureaucrats often targeted high productivity areas rather than high potential areas, resulting in costing land acquisition and limited scope for sustained productivity impacts.
>
> (Ibid., 163)

To correctly assess the financial effect of the balanced distribution of land, the World Bank used different measures for financial assessment. The Gini index has also been used for the assessment of the extent of inequality. The inference drawn by the World Bank is that the right to land should be conferred on the present. The more balance and equilibrium would come in the distribution of land, the more would be the scope for the land to give a return. In this condition, land would initiate the investment process and would extend its hand to increase the measure of the same. In other words, there would be a direct exposition of the rights to land and balanced distribution.

Kautilya's Philosophy

Kautilya has presented a highly well-thought-out and effectual principle in respect of the distribution of land. In order to render the use of land effective and efficient enough, Kautilya initiated a relation between the matter of distribution of land with presents and others.

Astasatagramyamadhyesthaniyam
Catuhsatagramyamadhyedronamukham
Dvisatagramyakarbatikali
Dasagramasamgrahenasaniqrahanam
Sthapayet

(*Arthashastra* 2/1/4)

It means: One person in eight hundred villages is a local (sthariya); one in four hundred villages is dronamukh and one in two hundred villages is karbatik. Every ten villages would bring under a collection centre.

Karadethaykrtaksetraniekahpurnmsa
Ekaniproyaechet

(*Arthashastra*, 2/1/8)

It means: For taxpayers, the arrangement of cultivable land would be made as per the requirement.

Akrtanikartrbhyonedeyani

(*Arthashastra* 2/1/9)

It means: Uncultivable land is to be used only for making them cultivable.

Kautilya states that cultivable land should go under the procession of the presents. Land that is not cultivable but is being tried to be made cultivable should also come under the procession of those enterprises. As a result, efficiency would come in the use of land. The more the use of land is efficient, the more self-sustained is the economic situation. That is, Kautilya's conviction is that economic development is possible through the distribution of land. Kautilya has not only thought about equilibrium and distribution. He has wanted to make the distribution system perfect, that is, support should be extended towards cultivating the lands that are being treated for cultivation or to be made cultivable; these must not be used for any other purpose.

Kautilya's discovery has far surpassed the inference arrived at by the World Bank in its recommendation regarding the orientation and distribution of land. The inference drawn from the research work by the World Bank has proved well the far-reaching future outlook and opinion. Even today, it is hardly possible for the World Bank to accept the wholeness of the definition of economic development enunciated by Kautilya. But it is pleasing to the background of the inference arrived at today by the World Bank through a worldwide study that was enunciated by Kautilya at his time.

Economic thoughts and the idea of the present time have all, in that sense, been defeated by Kautilya. If the perspective of that wholeness presented by Kautilya for economic studies is conjoined today with the economic thoughts, the economic interest of the future mankind would be presented and transformed. The final form assumed by the economic health that would be achieved will be ideal and the world would be free of burden.

57

Social Basis of Equality and Progress

Support of Society

Economic quality cannot be established without social support, nor is any progress possible. As the prevailing thoughts and perceptions in this respect are to be maintained, the social values, norms and reforms and culture are also important. The basis of the economic management of society moves on depending on the feelings the society is established on. In some societies, there is an inherent motion to build up great inequality. And again, some have a proper condition for equity. Naturally, some societies have moved on towards equality. Forward movement becomes possible on the part of the social power–taking in to account the feelings of high and low if it exists in the society at all. The role of inspiration comes out of this combined message of society. Some inspirations are for an individual, and some are for the aggregate. The inspiration meant for an individual is helpful in making the individual big, and the one meant for the awakening of the whole would be the driving force for the expansion of the aggregate. In countries where the awakening of individuals is possible, individual heroism has become the chief factor. The individual has gained prominence.

This individual hero has surpassed many. In the case of the aggregate, the message of awakening the aggregate comes out in a zealous and inspiring form. In individual heroism and inseparability of the whole, whatever may be the means for the society to move forward, there would be a unison between the social power and the power and ability of an individual. The individual desires to be big, to be special and to be full of possibility. Blooming hastens up.

In the case of individual heroism, this flow of blooming gradually spreads within a few or a single person, and in the case of whole spreading within many, it not only causes pervasion but also carries the possibilities forward.

A society considers its problems from the perspective of the basis of this confidence and outlook and becomes eager to solve the problem. In the society of the silvern people too, the forest-oriented line of thinking becomes dominant. The lives of the people relate centring the forest. Forest itself is a line of living. There is a serene veil here. These plants collectively lend infrastructure to the forest. They stand with heads held high, calling all to offer themselves to the forest. The extent of life grows right within the covering and infrastructure of the planets and trees of the forest. Lives and movements of wild animals grow up accepting this very infrastructure. There is conflict among wild animals again. There is co-existence too. The custom here is natural selection. It would serve those who have the ability to live among many living beings. The animal that can survive resisting attacks from others has the right to survive.

Living full of severe collisions behind a severe background signifies the separation of wildlife. In this living, the flow of life and signs of ideas lie hidden. Every society has got such type of signs. At the base of every society, there is a horn of judgement, directions of moving on the way and expression of separateness. Society itself gets engaged in solving its own way the problems that appear before it. Thus, a society with a wild line of thinking has got the solution to its every problem in a wild way. Wild solution to problems of a wild line of thinking is not only natural but also a healthy and permanent solution to the problems of a society that comes out of the depth of the society itself. All the possibilities within a society lie hidden within society itself. Wild environment quite naturally brings in the combined and applied form of possibilities. Maybe in all cases, or at all times, there is no trace available. Maybe society has trouble with the problem out of distraction in faith to find out the solution to those problems. But the link to solution lies where the problem originates.

The history of societies moving through evolution states that when society deviates from its inherent line of thinking, it has the power to face problems. Society deviated from its line of thinking as if it preferred to evade the problems. Being deviated from its own line of thinking, society loses its power and ability and becomes dependent on outlines of thinking. This is the time to be drowned in the poisonous pleasure in society. The meaning of being drowned in poisonous pleasure is the enjoyment of pleasure pierced by pain. This simultaneous enjoyment of pleasure and pain carries a temporary solution to society, and newer attempts to solve it continue. History, through the ages, has endeavoured in holidays pleasure and pain together along the path of evolution of the powers of society. There is a difference in the importance of the problems marked by society. For example, there are some problems that are temporary and local, while others cross time, place, etc.

When society ignores its own reforms and custom and moves on–their local and timely problems become glaring in society and obstructs the path of movement. Society must, therefore, realise the importance of problems, their basic nature and the movement of problems. The propensity of the solution would grow if this knowledge is earned. The solution that comes under the influence of the problem is the best solution. And the solution that comes without any problem is all improper for the solution of the problem. The problem and these solutions, as if a background, move together in the same enclosure. Solutions are sought from elsewhere since solutions are not taken to have risen from where problems have grown. The solution to problems inherent in societies that are followers of individual heroism is to be sought in the path of that individual heroism, and the solution in the societies that believe in the unison of the aggregate would come from the background of the aggregate. The attribution of unison of aggregate on societies proper for individual heroism does not yield results. The converse is equally true.

Instruction of History

The history of Europe throws enough light on the change of the line of thinking in societies with the evolution of social powers. Up to about 1500 AD, European societies were held in the feudal system and distributed in different stages. Much progress has been brought in the European societies under the feudal system, distributed in different stages, no doubt. But at the same time, some social discrepancies have also crept in. Social discrepancies prevailed in European societies, but till then, the extent of the same was within the limit of endurance. In these premeds, powerful monody was at the centre of all problems and solutions thereof. In line hands lay the ability to create problems and give solutions. The regions that had become the most prosperous were Venice, Gemoa and Florance, deviating from the feudal system to pay attention to the open system suitable for their needs. These developed cities, in due course of time, brought forward a system and attempted to establish democracy. Of course, the political infrastructure of the city-states became permanent links at the root of trade interests. The Netherlands of Hapsburg state structure also gradually followed the path of the city-state of Italy.

Here, the development comes intensively, but economic equality within the state was at a low ebb. The transformation in social systems from the feudal system to a democratic one affected society differently. That is, societies realise one's own identity and move with other enterprises based on those identities. Retention of the line of basic inequality is the driving force of societies. Just like in the Netherlands, where the rule of law has stabilised society, in Britain, the rule of law has given a type of social stability. Up to 1932, democracy in Britain was rather nominal in character. The Reform Act of 1932 brought the environment of modern politics. During this period, Britain had become rich by invading other countries. Occupancy of India gave unabashed scope of plunder to the traders, producers and merchants of Britain. In this background came the democratic infrastructure of the people of 1867 in Britain. The democracy existing for so long had not pervaded beyond ten percent. After 1867, there was ample scope for the spread of education. But behind all this was an unuttered but real truth, which was indiscriminate looting in India.

Being a partner of this indiscriminate looting in India, British society became wide and swelled. Social power gained proper ability. They advanced. Society got the result of the blooming of industrial civilisation. But the line of economic inequality has remained the same. Due to the industrial revolution, labourers were more costly in the British Market. The power of deterring values came into their grips, and in the same way, they turned themselves into an organised political power. The labour party of Britain has become the spokesman for this new power. After 1906, Herbert Asquith, with his liberation government, gradually built up Britain as a welfare state.

Simon Szreter, Professor of Rochester University, America, in the main essay of the book, edited by himself and titled *Health and*

Wealth Studies in Policy and History (Szreter 2005), wrote: 'Far from being a consequence of successful economic growth recent historical research on seven teen and eighteenth-century British was found that widespread but unique instruction of social security were is existence for several countries before the industrial revolution. Indeed, scholars increasingly argue that a previously under estimated influence on Britain's revolution infect lies in its prior agricultural revolution.'

Britain's industrial revolution was in the background of earlier agricultural revolution. The field of the industrial revolution was set on the infrastructure of the later agricultural revolution. As a result, the line of thinking and outlook of society have transformed.. In the background of the industry, little change has come in the character with which society has advanced in the path of agriculture, but its line of thinking is the same. According to Simon Szreter and other researchers, most of the evolution of the societies of England had been procured from outside, and these were followed. In this respect, England followed the Dutches, but surprisingly, the Dutches had established their own management. Simon Szreter stated:

'The principal comparator here is with the immensely advanced Dutch rural and trading economy of the sixteenth and seventeenth centuries. Many of the most important technical innovation in British agriculture during these period such as land drainage engineering new crop types and rotation were directly borrowed from the Dutch. Yet it was the British agricultural and service economy that was increasingly outfacing the Dutch as the seventeenth and eighteenth centuries progressed.'

Simon Szreter and other researchers could not apprehend that behind Britain, there was ample scope for the exploitation of India, which brought all the wealth it.

Finland and Sweden may be cited as examples of the countries of twentieth-century Europe that have been able to keep their economic progress intact by keeping their own social equilibrium in force for a long time. Both Finland and Sweden are known to be rich countries. Both of these have extensive provisions for social security. Both of them are small stabs, the population is low and there exists a social bonding between the low-income and high-income groups. Throughout the Middle Ages, finance was actually governed by Sweden. In the war of 1808–09 with Russia, Sweden lost its dominance over Finland. In an extensive epidemic and famine in 1867 in Russia, many Finnish and Swedish people were wiped out completely. Through the Russian Revolution of 1917, Finland got the opportunity to become free. Swedish and Finnish societies that emerged through the struggle got the opportunity to paint afresh. The progress of Finland and Sweden gained motion from the time of World War II.

Urho Kekkoken put the question and appeal to his countrymen: Do we have the patience to prosper? Patience is essential for progress. Ken was able, by his power, to form a concerted opinion in the Finish society for the combination of the corporate section market and the state, and thus, the state was able to earn financial progress and success.

In the case of Sweden, such endeavour brought a new height in the character of the society. History gave Sweden an advantage. It was in Sweden that the State Bank system was introduced in 1968. Besides, it was in Sweden that the right to property was acknowledged as a fundamental right. Right from the beginning, peasants and agricultural labourers got connected with the agricultural management of Sweden. As a result, based on their cooperation and influence, a broad market and productive power grew. A balanced combination of all these factors is at the root of the advancement of Sweden. The novelty of the Finnish and Swedish models lay in their growth and building up the whole system in the background of themselves. Though small in size, Finland and Sweden were able to transform into truly significant economic powers by rising up in the route of the character of the cleat.

The route of rise and ascension of every society has been packed in accordance with its character. The character that befits the particular society and is essential for leadership was chosen. Venture for forward movement omitting the choice of character has not been able to reduce the problem but has rather made the same more complicated through its transformation. For the state, choosing the character is important, and at the same time, it is important to realise the nature of the problem.

This helps find the course of the problem. When the cause of the origin of the problem is found, the link for its solution is objected. It is not that the union of the problem and solution is always possible, but its possibility increases by union with the problem. When the rise of Finland and Sweden is compared side by side with the rise of the city-states of Italy and England, it is apprehended that a base of character should be at the root of financial progress and distribution. Urho Kekkonen put for progress a question depicting a call before all. The preparation for progress here has been initiated by inciting a national character. This feeling could spread to the Finnish public because of the start of conflict and devastation. The same route was initiated in the case of Japan and Germany, ultimately embarrassed in World War II. National leadership has attempted to ascertain the character and incite the union of the aggregate. As a result, the union of the aggregate has been established in the nation's life, and it has been possible for the leadership to attempt combining a united solution to the national basic problem. Solution of problems in financial progress and financial management has been organised by ascertainment of character.

Kautilya's Path

Kautilya's *Arthashastra* holds a definite opinion in this case. The basic faith on which the *Arthashastra* is based is the ground of faith of an individual. If this ground of faith of an individual is incited, it becomes possible on the part of an individual to dive deep into the problem quite indifferently. And thus, through deep dive into the problem, the intimation of the solution to the problem would be incited right within the individual. If the national aspiration of the state is combined with the incitement of the individual, a permanent solution to the national problem would be possible. That is why Kautilya compels an individual to move to the realisation of spiritual power and awakening of spiritual consciousness within himself prior to the natural aspiration. The more an individual moves these, the more would be the extension of their incitement. When the incitement of an individual here crosses the limit of their own object, the limit of their own interest will spread in many subjects, among many souls; a unit under this condition becomes a unification of many means ringing of the same note of pain and pleasure from many people. A ring for many tunes is created, which stands for the unification of many. Kautilya has recommended learning the Vedas for the king for royal miners, for state officials and the welfare management of the public.

The *Arthashastra* being engaged in accompanied unification, many have, with this call, also attended the blooming of the power of the unit. As a result, the problem may be looked upon in the light of the experience of many and looked at on the part of many. So, the power of unit intellect may also incite itself and can bring transformation in many. The crop of these actions and reactions is an individual or combined effort by which the whole system can be engaged in a significant solution to inequality and poverty in the state. The *Arthashastra* has opened a significant route for the standpoint of preparation. So, it has also been zealous for the incitement of consciousness within an individual in aggregate for the standpoint of the spread of work and its distribution. Solution to the problem of poverty and inequality is possible only in such a balanced background.

To be significantly successful in the incitement of an individual, the following the model of Kautilya is very certain.

58

Right to Market: Rule of the Market

The rule of the market started three decades ago or more. It is the market health that is now the controlling authority of all. The power of the market sometimes is engaged in mutual conflicts and sometimes in friendship. As a result, the market sometimes becomes dual and sometimes lively and powerful. The market has now unrestrained movement everywhere.

The periphery of the market is widespread and may be called all-pervading. The market has entered into the interior of the house of individuals market has been unrestrained in the extension of one's own self and of one's near and dear ones. In the case of controlling society and the relation within a family, the market has a very strong flow. With the dominance of the market, many beautiful and balanced dreams will be topsy-turvier. Again, this market is getting the beckoning of many impossible bloomings.

The market has brought diversity. The market has entered into different or all wings of life and given stroke on the place and stability of the market, but in return, it has presented many possibilities and effectiveness to life. Consequently, life has got motion. One life is able to miss the mingle with many. The flows of life at different ends of the world have built up mutual coordination, sometimes through mutual conflicts and sometimes through mutual understanding in a placement atmosphere. With understanding and coordination, hence come different types of countries even with tensions and conflicts. Such conditions and conflicts in life have made the periphery of life swell up. Life has become much more alert about the world and its accessories. Unparalleled attempt to use all compounds and beauties in the world in service of life has strengthened by different methods. The flow of life is the speed of life. The influence of life on one side has hastened the rise of life, and on the other side, by the influence of market life, it has been inefficient and is related to the state of fallen leaves. Leaves unable to stand the keen competition introduced by the have break-down under the influence of the power of the market, and the market has been screaming to become exceptional. The power of parallel markets has grown up in societies. The power of societies has affected the fontal war with the market in its resistant role. Again, in many cases, society has been coordinating with the market.

The societies that have been is increasing. These powers and abilities in the circle of influence of the market have been supportive of and helping the power of the market in the country. Societies that have lost before the power of the market and become completely baffled have entered naturally into a struggle with the power of the market. In this struggle, society's own ability has become evident, and at the same time, a different propensity has also been found. The measure of government coordination has also been of different types. Societies are lent on bringing control over the markets with help from the government. The government help also has different measures. Thus, government's intervention in the interest of society has sometimes been transparent, sometimes limited and sometimes again strong. Government's intervention in society is normally measured in the form of a lawful sense. That is, the propensity of government intervention in the market of small measures through farming and implementing laws is turned into a scanty measure. The main purpose of government intervention to measure and keep the route of activity of the market open and to bring control over the antisocial activities or the activities differential to society.

Government intervention invites situations of conflict. In this case, the market is activated under the domination of the state. As a result, the market opens the possibility of open extension and expansion. In order to make the market free from deep influence on it, a new dimension of the market is desirable. In many cases, the market becomes active within the influence of the state. The rise of the market from governmental influence becomes possible only by the patronage of society. The power of the market might grow. Here, the share of governmental influences on the power of the market may be built up. When the market becomes a propitious power society, then and only then the market regions its footing.

Market and State

If the merit and demerit of government intervention in the market are considered, it would be found that the state has come in opposition to the human powers that, so far, have been engaged in the rise of government intervention. But the declared purpose never plays for the rise of the whole. Wherever a state comes forward to impose control on the power of the market, a problem is created right there. The state acts in the interest of society. The state thinks of imposing control over the market only to pave the way for society to fulfil its demands. Consequently, a situation of dependence has been set up. Going to arrange to measures of social powers, state has factually made itself short-lived and dependent on others. As a result, the process of social power to rise has been different.

The rise of social powers is also restricted within government security and control. For example, productive management, medium of production, ability of production, continuity of production and consonant production of excellence become corporatised in a controlled market. The desire for competition or little competition is bound to damage the working ability of different industrial and trade organisations. As a result, government intervention begins to increase in every place of the market. There, the dynamic role of the market gets impaired. The market becomes limited. A limited market cannot be favourable to the interest of the buyers. The basic influence of an open market is in the competition. Following the path of competition, the market can bring different types of favour and advantages to the buyers. It is possible for buyers in an open market to come to a conclusion after judging many factors. Judging many factors makes it possible to hail on to protect the interest of the buyers.

Through comparison between the controls of the market and the state, it can be realised that the power of the market can surpass that of the state. For example, the cooperation discussion believes that through the quality and price of any commodity, one can ascertain the standard and quality and the excellence of price under the quality market and state. Price is determined by the control of the market, control of duty and responsibility state. The ability, duty and responsibility of the state, through its control over the market, can restrict the management of the price of the market. When the state starts supplying commodities at a controlled price, the question of subsidy on the part of the state arises. The state must give subsidies for the supply and movement of every commodity. The more confirmed the system of subsidies, the more the normal movement of commodities and management of trade would break. Government intervention gets engaged in establishing a balance between normal demand and supply of the market. But a limited supply of subsidies cannot establish this balance. If there is the scope for unrestricted subsidy, the establishment of a balance between demand and supply may be possible for at least some time.

The sovereign right to the market opens unrestricted direction of movement of the market opposite. With this, the powers of the market go against the power of society. The powers of the market cross the limit of the market and begin to enter into the lives of society and industry. The market wants to occupy life and get its severing foundation rooted. This rotten condition is attained to make the market the controlling authority or driving force of everything. Then, the situation of conflict with society is reached. Market and society begin to move along opposite propensity. At the end of the conflict, the background of coordination may come in. In the background of coordination, market accepts the rule of business in a great measure and vice versa. This is a combined stage where the form of market is directed to the emerging principles of business.

The more open the market, the more extended would be the background of competition. The real control of the market is affected by the background of competition. When the state becomes eager to control the market through subsidy, the source of this endeavour depends on the capability of the state to give subsidy and the power of the state to maintain economic balance in the situation through subsidies. Only if the state is able to maintain an economic balance can it, on the part of society, keep control over the market. But it is not possible for the state to keep up all through the capability of maintaining subsidies. The state cannot keep up the capability of maintaining subsidies. At the same time, the state, through the creation of the propensity of subsidy, disturbs the balance and incites problems.

Kautilya's Theory

Kautilya *Arthashastra* has spoken of a certain balanced relation between the market and the state. In *Arthashastra*, there is a mention of the intervention or application of force and the part of the state on the market. These are applications to those who have deviated from the general property of nature market Kautilya wanted. That itself would not appear as a productive power, but it would be helpful and coordinating all the powers of production. As a result, an environment of unison is created between the state and the market.

Panyadhayaksahslhalajalajanamnanabidhanam
Saraphalagbardhantarampriyapriyatam ca vidyat
Tathabiksepasamksepakrayabikrayaprayogokakn.

(*Arthashastra*, 2/16/1)

It means: The chief of the trade would be aware of the high and low prices of different commodities, they would procure commodities moved by water or by land, costly or low-price commodities of high or low demand etc.. Proper time and proper amounts of the sells proceeds would be distributed according to requirement.

Ya ca panyampracurasyanta
Dekikrtyedharmaropayeta.

(*Arthashastra*, 2/16/2)

It means: Chief of trade would be eager to procure the agricultural commodities produced amply and fix up price standards on behalf of the producers.

Praptaurdhaibaardhantaramkarayet

(*Arthashastra*, 2/16/3)

It means: When the price becomes higher than the fixed one, it should be refixed.

Svabhumijanamrajapanayanamekamukhan
Byabaharam
Sthapayet Parabhumijanamanekamukham

(*Arthashastra*, 2/16/4)

It means: Commodities produced in the homeland would be stored in a particular sport for being used by the state, and foreign commodities would be stored in different places.

Vbhayam ca prajanamanugrahen a
Bikrapayet

(*Arthashastra* 2/16/5)

It means: In both cases, native and foreign sale prices and the arrangement for sale are to be made in the public interest.

Sthulamapi ca tevamprayanamaupadhatikam
Ca barayet

(*Arthashastra* 2/16/6)

It means: When there is a situation of a great profit then considering the interest of the public that profit has to be reduced.

Ajasrapanyanamkalparodhamsamkula
Dosambanotpadayet.

(*Arthashastra*. 2/16/7)

It means: Trade officials would not intervene in the transaction of goods unless it is detrimental to the interest of the public.

Bahumukhambarajapanyambaidehakah
Krtardhambikrininam

(*Arthashastra* 2/16/8)

It means: Government goods may be sold at different places in the public interest.

Chedanurpam ca baidharanamdadyukh.

(*Arthashastra*, 2/16/9)

It means: If there is any loss due to depreciation in price, it would be compensated.

Sorasbhagau mana byajibimsatirhaga
Stulamanak
Ganyapanayamekadasabhagau.

(*Arthashastra* 2/16/10)

It means: In consideration of the measure, one-sixteenth of the produce would be fixed as tax; in respect of the highest, one-twentieth and in respect of lowest, one-eleventh would be fixed as tax.

According to the *Arthashastra*, the government can intervene directly or indirectly, but in all cases, the object should be the well-wishing of the public. In every case, the government would associate itself with or disassociate itself from different powers of the market, considering only the context of the public. The foremost duty of the government is to have enough information on the commodities in the market for trade officials. According to Kautilya, government should know how much of what commodities are available in the market—what is the future possibility of availability of the respective commodities.

Trade officials would frame government policy on commodities with satisficing from the market. Statistic stand has logistics of the movement of commodities. After the correct direction and logistic has been fixed, trade officials would get the right idea of the movements of different commodities. At the same time, the role of the state would also be determined.

In Kautilya's proposal, the role of a state is both mind and heart. In this case, there would be no bond of inactivity or opinion. This is because at the root of all endeavours of a state is its well-wishing role. The state likes to protect the interest of the public, so the interest of the market has not gained prominence. Kautilya's economics is, therefore, not market-oriented, nor are they apathetic to the market. In case of necessity, Kautilya's economic management has urged to be aporetic to the market, and when the situation demands, it is to be included in the market. Kautilya has not judged the matter from the viewpoint of the market, but his judgement is from the standpoint of the interest of the public. If the price index is the same, the supply of commodities is undisturbed and the transport system is intact, Kautilya's aim is to get the market and its power to flourish. On the other hand, if the price is abnormally high, there is a shortage in the supply of commodities, and no balance in the state of transport controlling power of the state would be operative in the market.

Kautilya's Solution

If the price of commodities is not just, Kautilya's prescription is an intervention of the trade officials. They would take steps for the collection and distribution of extra commodities; if necessary, they would import too. They would manage the storage of the homeland commodities and would take steps for the transportation of imported commodities through the country. They would bring the price of proper collection and transportation within the buying capacity of the public. As a result, the public would be eager to collect shell goods and market use of the same. If, due to special circumstances, there is excess agricultural produce, the government authority would buy the excess and store the same. As a result, the producer peasant would not be helplessly exposed to the power of the market. As the process of storage of excess produce starts, so also the propensity of price index would be a steady reward to the producer. Having created a price affordable to the people and that can continue to produce those commodities help the consumers. At the same time, buyers would get supply of goods with right price and be placed closed to the market. According to Kautilya, the government would be active in this movement activity of the market only in proper cases; otherwise, the government would not be active or would not intervene in such cases.

The activity of the state has been limited in the case of deviation. If any businessman takes the role of evil intentions, the government would come forward to control with the help of law and engage in doing welfare to the public. If there is any attempt to sell a commodity with excess profit, the intervention of the government would be inevitable there. The matter of excess profit would come in the jurisdiction of the state, and the price index would be fixed and corrected.

Not only for determining price index or fixing up price-index befitting the public, but government intervention has been thought of in Kautilya's theory also for conservation of market and the business power of the market. Kautilya has not only admitted the power of the market but also thought of the expansion of the market by balancing the power of the market. He wanted the coexistence of state and market. His aim was to provide maximum opportunity and benefit to people through such coexistence. As a result, a balanced relationship is set up between the state and the market, and people get benefitted from this situation.

Kautilya had also thought of the deployment of the transportation of commodities for the market. They have thought with due importance of the dependence of the power of the market on the logistics or the transport of commodities. The problem of logistics is an important wing of modern marketing systems. No other economist except Kautilya has discussed this matter with importance. Considering the different aspects of the transport of commodities, Kautilya spoke of a combined situation. In such combined systems, strong management for the transport of commodities is built up through the lack of balance but weak demand and supply in different parts of the country are removed. As a result, the power of the market becomes large in terms of covering the buyers and sellers to create wealth. The market begins on its own motion to appropriate the situation of supply of commodities at right price and right qualities and standard of commodities are assured to reach out in the right manner through the transports and passenger services. As a result, the attraction of the market not only increases but also becomes a helpful power from economic management through financial becoming.

Kautilya accepted the market and, at the same time, also presented a management system for its control. Taxes due to the state were fixed in different ways through the sale and purchase of commodities. For livelihoods or commodities, the taxes of which are measured in terms of volume, the government tax is one-sixteenth, that is, 6.25%. For commodities sold in terms of weight, government tax is one-twelfth or five percent and for those sold by counting is one-eleventh or 9.1%. Besides these, there are other sorts of taxes in the case of commodities. For example, the judge on sale price. Kautilya's system is more scientific and modern than the present system, wherein taxes of the state are judged and occupied on the judgement of VAT and government taxes. Kautilya' judgement of taxes is very useful for the future.

Besides this, Kautilya's *Arthashastra* is largely in favour of open trade. If there is any deficit of commodities or there is any difficulty with the transport of the price index of any commodity, it can be improved from abroad. Actually, Kautilya is ready to call any source of power in the country and abroad to ensure the supply of commodities, fix up the price index and, above all, protect the interest of the people through the import of commodities. The aim of the liberal and board out work Kautilya has taken is to protect the interest of the people and to take their opportunity and convenience ahead. If the market has sovereign rights, it can do anything at its will, but if a beneficial touch of the state is conjoined alongside the lofty rights of the market, good effects emerge from the influence of the market, and at the same time, the interest of the people and the state is protected with gradually. The *Arthashastra* has accomplished different adjustments.

59

Natural Wealth of Economic Life: Initial Identity of Wealth

Wealth becomes helpful for the blooming of life in different ways. The effect of the blooming of life is universally accepted. The wealth that has come upon the flow of life has an inevitable economic power and possibility. Such wealth has its root memory and expansion of life. Again, in other types of wealth, these may be attempts of putting obstruction or hurdle against the below of life. It is wealth that can create wealth. It is true, no doubt. But at the same time, wealth can stand in the way of the blooming of wealth. There should be a conjunction in the direction of blooming and coordination at that stage. If the direction of blooming is identified with that of the flourishing of wealth, there comes a chance to be strong with the strongest possibility of wealth. The possibility of blooming wealth is like acceptance of life and living by wealth. Every big of wealth has particles of consciousness in it, which try to carry it to the end. The span of life of wealth is assessed from the merits and demerits of the wealth and in respect of usefulness and significance. Every wealth gets its dignity in terms of its identity. Identity again grows on the basis of the significance of the use and peaceful demand. Economic variety is always prefaced in respect of practical significance and demand.

Inherent material and surrounding articles and subjects try to build up the identity of wealth. Wealth is to move through there. Self-support can be manifested thoroughly in wealth if that weather be allowed to be known by its own identity. Wealth itself can call upon its exposition. The summon of this wealth can be hastened by the eagerness of the user about wealth and the inherent ability of it. The identity of certain wealth is built up on the basis of the usual growth of natural wealth. Demand for and utility of natural wealth makes wealth usable and attractive. If the identity of wealth is ascertained, its movement and measure grow on the basis of that. Based on natural wealth, the endeavour for creating wealth grows. As natural wealth might be engaged in everything newer, its utility may also be extended for the power helpful in the extension and spread of wealth. That is why the extension and expansion of natural wealth may be quite beneficial for any country. Propensity for the wear up of the natural wealth might creep in through the manufacture of other usable goods for natural resources. For example, objects prepared by felling trees carry wealth to their worthiness. Here, the tree of the forest is useful from the standpoint of human necessity and related to its character beneficial to mankind. Similarly, there are other endless elements of nature too.

The utility of wealth lies at a deeper stage. Water is indispensable because the major portion of Earth is water. The demand for water exists everywhere on the earth. River water, water at different layers, under the crust and rainwater are engaged in the service of mankind in different ways. The usefulness of water would be realised in the historical background. The purity and availability of water can be found in human history since its very beginning. Water has many uses. Water is required at every moment for the living of human beings. Life does not move without water. Like human beings, water is important for all animals and all lives, aquatic, wild and aerial. Water is indispensable for plants. Water has different identities in different places.

Water has different utilities, for example, for men as drinking water, for irrigation, for nature as underground water, rainwater and the like. Despite the intensity and abundance of water, an adequate amount of potable water is not always available. Millions of children have to meet death every year due to lack of proper water. Lots of cultivable lands are lying fallow due to lack of water. Water is there but without a drainage system. Under such circumstances, due to poor drainage, real utility of water is lost.

The lower the water level goes, the more the scarcity in natural life. All plants, starting from trees to creepers and shrubs, depend on water. The significance of living depending on water lies hidden in the life-saving ability of water. Thus, the role of water for the living of man or any natural element is universal. The ability of soil to grow crops disappears with a lack of water. Soil becomes rain asunder. Soil loses its fertility and becomes barren. The capability of the soil to yield crops increases with an adequate supply of water and, with that, proper food for increasing retentive capacity. So, water is required to maintain natural equilibrium.

The use of water is continuously increasing in modern life. At the time of supplying water to meet necessity, the extent of misuse should also be taken into account. In modern lives, plenty of water is used for accomplishing and extending cleanliness while moving from and along the path of affluence. A great possibility for misuse of water has grown, and as a result, good and filled water is gradually decreasing. Only in a few countries is there an arrangement of ample amount of water required per capita. In most of the developed countries, the whole volume of water thus consumed needs to be recycled and made available. Developed countries have excess water required to meet daily needs, and others have less. Men befall attacks from many diseases for want due to a lack of clean water. Not only humans but other animals also encounter many incurable diseases due to a lack of pure, filtered water. It is applicable to equality for plants, animals and all types of lives. Crops from which life moves out, the possibility of stability and extension comes in the lives of animals, become naturally dependent on water. That is why in the modern agricultural system, emphasis has been laid on the arrangement of water through irrigation to increase producing capacity of the soil. There have been continuous efforts to have better crops by collecting water from the layers under nature or bringing water for suitable rivers through channels to the land and using it for irrigation. Wherever there is an arrangement for irrigation, the production of crops increases.

Crops yielded by the land with no facility for irrigation continuously undergo transformation qualitatively and quantitively. After obtaining the irrigation facility, lands yielding a single crop now get transformed to yield multiple crops. Quantity of water is not always correct quantity of water.For example, the cultivation of fish may be quite possible with the salty water of the sea, but it is detrimental to the cultivation of paddy. The requirement of water, therefore, is in correct quality and proper quantity.

United Nations has issued different characters at different times with water. The Economic and Social Council of the United Nations, in its Geneva Convention (twenty-ninth convention of the council) 2002, undertook a good number of decisions regarding financial, social and cultural rights of men. Among the decisions, one was related to the human rights to water. It was an epoch, making decision United Nation sent call to all the states to thoroughly convince the rights to water for each and every man. From the report of the World Health Organization, it is known that AOE states could not properly manage adequate supply of water for all. The minimum demand for water is met if a total of twenty litres of water (for drinking, bathing, cleansing, etc.) becomes available to a single person. In this twenty litres of water, there should be five litres of purified water. With water less than this, living would be unhealthy. Eighty percent of 201 crores of people who do not get water live in rural regions. These 201 crores of people do not get adequate water. They live depending on unhealthy, dirty water and among them are spreading different types of incurable diseases.

About 203 crores of people are regularly suffering from water-borne diseases and diseases caused by lack of water. About 240 crores of people have fallen into the group of incurable diseases due to the lack of an adequate drainage system. In the character number 2 of the character of 2002 AOE, the right to water has been particularised. In the announcement of the right towards (Article II and 2 of the international covenants on economic, social and cultural rights) has stated that water is the bounty of nature; water is life. So, the use of water in sufficient quantity and food standards fall under the rights of the people. This announcement of United Nations has stated, 'Water is limited natural resource and public food fundamental for life and health. The human right to water is indispensable for leading a life in human dignity. It is a prerequisite for the realisation of other human rights. The committee has been confronted continually with the widespread denial of the right to water is developing as well as developed countries.

The human right to water entitles everyone to sufficient, safe, acceptable, physically accessible and affordable water for personal and domestic use.' Through the issuance of the charter, United Nations tried to explain the utility of water. United Nations has unified the utility of water with the personal rights of individuals through this promise for the supply of water for every life. These decisions about reaching suitable quality and standard of water for every life have been inevitable for every life. The call later sent by the United Nations to each member country also stated the following:

'An adequate amount of safe water is necessary to prevent death from dehydration, reduce the risk of water related disease and to provide for consumption, cooking personal and domestic hygienic requirements.'

The right to water clearly falls within the category of guarantees essential for securing an adequate standard of living, particularly since it is one of the most fundamental conditions for survival.

The character of the United Nations has also explained the matter of the right to water. Here, it is clearly indicated that the right to healthy, natural and free life is to be honoured by all the states. This right to water has been shown in different ways, such as water for personal use, water for domestic use, water for cooking, water for other purposes, water for irrigation of crops, water for the conservation of the environment, etc. Growing up with healthy, civilised life and normal advancement depends on the supply of purified water. Roughness, dryness and hardness that grow from lack of water are detrimental to civilisation in the natural background. Water brings novelty to life. If polluted water is used daily, then it directly acts as the reason for the impairment of health.

People with access to an improved water source (millions)

Average annual number of people

Region	1990	2004	2015	Target Gaining access 1990–2004	Needing access 2004–2015
Sub-Sahara Africa	226.6	383.8	627.1	10.5	23.1
Arab State	180.1	231.8	335.8	4.7	6.5
East Asia and the Pacific	1,154.4	1,528.2	1,741.2	22.9	24.3
South Asia	840.6	1296.4	1538.1	32.5	22.1
Latin America and the Caribbean	334.3	499.0	527.8	9.0	6.1
World	2767.7	4266.4	5,0295	79.5	82.4

Human Development Report, 2006, UNDP

The target fixed up for 2015 was not adequate. This is because even if this target was fulfilled, a large number of people would definitely earn the rights to water. That is, there was not enough supply of purified water of proper standard for them.

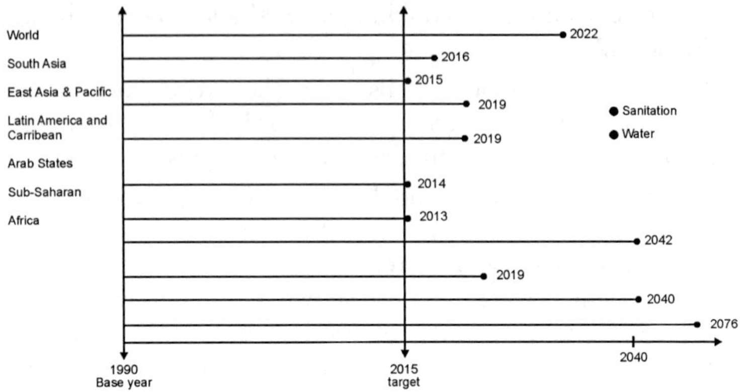

Water & Sanitation Goals for 2015, UNICEF (2006)

Among different regions of the world, the worst situation is found in the region adjacent to the Sahara. People here would have to wait till 2080 to have the minimum amount of purified water. Another four decades would be taken to have a minimum drainage system in these regions. People there would have to wait till 2076. Of the developed regions, the best condition is in South Asia. The situation in this region is gradually moving towards the world average. Countries of South Asia would be able to complete the arrangement of the minimum amount of purified water and adequate drainage system for all in 2016 and 2022, respectively. The condition of eighty crores of people in fifty-five countries is dreadful. They get neither drinking water nor any type of healthy cleansing arrangement. They are constantly living through a struggle against death. The relation between purified water and drainage system is very intimate. If on the basis of this intimate relation, any programme is built up, then advancement in purified water would also be possible.

Special care should be taken while using nature's wealth. To meet the requirement of water, it is constantly being lifted up from underground. Domestic uses in towns, commercial uses, use for the aggregate, water for irrigation for crops taking all these together and in order to get rid of the problems in collective water newer sources of water needs to be created. The underground layer of water is gradually becoming thin and drying up. Besides, with the diminishing forests and plants, natural equilibrium is being disturbed. Formulas presented by the World Health Organization aim at the conservation of the environment. In doing so, the more severe the disappearance of plants, the greater the problems with the transference of temperature and quantity of rainfall. In this respect, the world organisation has opined that to combat the situation, let there be created forests in place of natural fresh or let the afforestation programme be undertaken under the auspices of the United Nations Afforestation Programme in Asia and Africa. Proposal and endeavour of plantation on two sides of roads, on all sides of lands and on all places, including water lands or dry lands, have been undertaken through afforestation.

To make the programme acceptable, seeds and saplings have been distributed free of cost in developing countries. A characteristic of such trees is that they grow fast. For this growth of the trees, some minerals and plenty of water are necessary. They have one tap root and, around them, a small quantity of root hairs. The power of the tap root to move deep into the soil is worthy of mention. Going deep into the soil, they constantly suck water from the lower layers. The amount of water sucked by a huge banyan tree in the course of thirty days is sucked by a young plant of the created forest within one to three days. The shade cast by the banyan tree may accommodate thirty to fifty plants in the created forest. Each of these can suck twenty times more water. So, on average, forty trees, on average, can collectively suck 800 times more water from under the earth. Thus, the underground water layer would rapidly come to an end. If more trees, during afforestation, are planted on the sides of cultivated lands, they would diminish the natural humidity of the soil, and the land would move to dryness. Consequently, regular demand for irrigation would increase for farming, and the problem of water would become graver.

The inherent significance of the target of the world organisation lies in the capacity to increase water supply. The water problem of this world would not be solved through the use of groundwater. This is the current environment equilibrium, which is on the verge of disruption. All of the measures taken so far for improved agriculture are excessively water-consuming. Plants used in a forest action process are all water-consuming. The underground layer of water is sinking. The only way is to use seawater after purification and, at the same time, raid water. But both of these are highly expensive. So, it is clear that full implementation of the 'slogan of clear water for all', as raised by the world organisation, is hardly possible.

Industrial management and unplanned urbanisation by hook or by crook have aggravated the water problem. The position of nature in industry and urbanisation is at the far backside. None can hear the screams of trees and, as such, does not bother our lives. The equilibrium is being disrupted by the mutilation of the wings of nature. Industrial and agricultural management, on the one side, has almost emptied the store of water, and on the other side, open areas of water have been poisoned. This is the consequence of modern economic management. Modern economic management depends on technology and capital, as it has created a propensity to suck dry and destroy water resources. Kautilya's path is quite different. Kautilya said what is just opposite to the management system that has brought faith in these problems of water.

The *Arthashastra* has concluded at a combined situation of agriculture and industry. Agriculture clings to the lap of nature. That is, factors conducive to the nature equilibrium favour agriculture. So, being used for agriculture is agreeable to health. Water used by agriculture comes back by the reverse process. This process cannot be speedy. It is less speedy but contains in it a possibility and imitation of a full motion. So, agriculture moves on while keeping pace with nature in a balanced way. If there is no overuse of water for agriculture, it will eliminate the problems with the water level. Besides, there would be no problem with any afforestation process. This is because, here, there is enough natural forest. So, afforestation is not necessary at all. This is an automatic conservation of water. Undoubtedly, in places where there may be provision for deep tube wells, water from ordinary wells is as good as purified. Even though open, purity is guaranteed as that water has come from lower levels and has minerals mixed with it. So, standards and quality are fully intact.

In economic management, following the *Arthashastra*, the water problem is automatically solved. There is a component in Kautilya's management that can solve problems. So, no problem is there to solve the same. Water has been provided for all. The character and call of the United Nations have urged to admit the right to water. It may not be complied with fully, but in Kautilya's management, right to water is inevitable for all.

60
Principle of Economic Protection and its Necessity

The principle and process of protection in economic management become important in the financial management of states. The suitableness of a process is judged by the consequences of the application and reflection of any principle or ideal in the economic management process. So, in every system is the matter of the application of that principle, ideal and preparation. The time and stability of the principle of a state and, in some cases, its intelligence becomes the point of judgement. Judgement of protection sometimes deals with the stability of the limit, and sometimes it crosses the limit and merchant to a newer limit. Keeping up the stability of the limit or the march crossing the limit in both cases, the main point of judgement is the wealth and possibilities within the state. In the wealth and possibilities of a country definitely lie those points and subjects to be considered but for which it is not possible for any state to live truly. So, the protection of wealth and possibilities is the best thing for a state. The same principle is to be applied in the protection of economic management.

At the root of the principle of protection of economic management are the extension of financial position, financial orientation distribution of financial wealth, and, in the end, the good result of economic management. The urge to protect economic management is bestowed and brings that good results. Yielding and retaining good results depends on the character of economic management. The character of the economic management bears that good result and may be engaged to spread the same for the benefit of many. The most important among the basic endeavours of economic management is to gradually spread that part of the identity, which is meant for the welfare and progress of the people. This identity is created by economic management. For these reasons, intense enterprise and far-reaching arrangements are necessary for economic management. So, the protection context of all classes, groups and coordinators is very basic for economic management. It is important for any economic management to protect all aims, targets, objects and thoughts of the result of the management system and transfuse use and apply the wealth of the country.

All of the components on the way of forward march to the tactful of economic management are to be known thoroughly, and with that knowledge, proper management for movement and connection for all of the sensible elements on the way of march is to be established. At every stage and in every case of these movements, confidence is necessary. Accepting the economic aspiration for every action and in every phase of the financial movement march in the direction of the aspiration is desirable. That is why many types of solutions to any problem whatsoever in economic management may be thought of. Many solutions may exist for a single problem.

Every solution depends on how the problem would be treated and how the solution would be affected by that treatment. Every problem is to be looked upon in light of the theoretical discussion of the solution. According to the theoretical treatment of solution, the problem type may change. An accepted problem has a definite solution when the financial process starts along the path of that solution. Then, what is mentionable is to attempt to solve the problem by looking at its own basis of the theory of the time of relation theoretically established between pollution and its solution. It may be incidentally said that the theoretical conjunction of problem and solution gives a firmer basis for the character of the problem. If the solution is accomplished in the path found by the theory, then it is taken for granted that the perspectives of the problem that had been created, the viewpoint by which the problem had been looked upon, provides the consideration that would inevitably lead to a solution. The phase solution of the problem has not been initiated or accomplished for want of economic protection.

Proposal for Economic Protection

In the context of economic management, therefore both theory and practice of financial judgement so with respect to field of application and field of influence are natural to be thought about. This means as the phase of judgement would be initiated for the base of theory, the base of theory of that phase would also be constantly expanding. The theory would not be limited to a particular spot keeping compatibility with the real situation theory through evolution would be constantly moving on. The field of theory and practice would be expanding and would be engaged in conjunction with each other. There should be unison between theory and practice. A dynamic relation theory and practice would be changing constantly one after another. The matter related to economic protection will always be strong in the field of application of the theory, especially when the practical application would be an inevitable outcome of the theory, and then only the matter of protection would be specially celebrated. Economic protection here would be synonymous with the protection and application of the theory. In the protection and practical application of theory, both the base of theory and the base of application would be judged. This judgement is important in the case of individuals and for the aggregate. In social and government fields, the judgement is as if for regular pursuit at application. Theory becomes quite sharp by regular pursuit; similarly, the application makes the theory so. The sharp form of theory and application hastens economic progress.

Progress is required in economic theory, which through judgement, initials the solution of the problems. Besides, due to the application of the theory itself, the term 'management' comes out. For progress, there should be an assurance of application. If the application is assured, a theory gets its full form. Through the form of theory obtained by the assurance of application, it raises to the state of fullest convection. To protect the theory, the judgement of the problem and application should be made suitable for space-time and groups of people. Through this suitableness, the atheneite of the points of application and exit is determined, and an opportunity appears for the theory to reach perfection.

There are two aspects of a theory. First is confirmed in every theory in trending to be an inspiration in the limit or periphery of the theory. The other is to cross the definite enclose and move on to the annunciation of newer theories through the judgement of the existing theories. At that time, evolution starts within the theory. From the perspective of the surrounding that has been evident inevitably in the field of application of the theory can emerge newer theories or newer applications. There is innumerable consideration of the way of a new theoretician or on the path of a new application. There are many considerations. By such considerations, the rise of economic management may be more intension. The path of the rise of economic management is initiated on the basis of how economic protection is initiated and how new fields of application may be set through the evaluation of economic management. New fields of application often appear in the form of a new theory. For example, the previous field of theory had been seated on a creation background. With the newer arrangement, the theoretical discussion will be held in a new background, moving aside from the previous one. In this case, theory would be protected by application. The correct protection of economic theory lies in the proper application. Whatever may be the form of the theory, it will bring good results through proper application and will bring about economic advancement.

Satruhprakrtibibadahprakrtimukhaupagrahena
Kalahasthanaapanayanebababarayitum Bibadamahastu
prakrbayahparaspara
Raja bibadastupidanacchedanaya
Prakrtinahdvigunabyayama
Sadhya iti

(*Arthashastra*, 8/4/18-20)

It means: Two paths may be resolved to remove quadrat and enmity among the people-one, subduing the quarrelsome men second to remove the cause of quarrel. Through quarrelling among themselves, people lift up both parties to deservingness. If the quarrel occurs in a royal family, then the consequence of that quarrel may be twofold injurious.

Kautilya wanted any problem to be discussed in more than one way and to reach a solution. In the way of such consideration, Kautilya pointed out two main fields: Solutions centring on those about whom the problem is there in solving financial problems and solutions having reason to the link of solution in the burning problem itself. The solution centring the followers or objects involved may even be disastrous or explosive. That is, state power unable to solve the problem of poverty may conceive complete extension of the poor people by taking devastating behaviour to the poor people. On the other side, without looking at the way, the solution may be scratched by judging from the point of view from which the problem itself has been justified. To eradicate the problem, the true form of the problem should be searched. In order to realise the problem of poverty, one must judge the origin spread and different significance of poverty.

With this, poverty is to be realised unknown through querying why poverty has come, how it has come, how it has swelled up, how much is the swelling, which situation is responsible for this, which group has made it swells augment. The true nature of poverty is to be ascertained. As a result of these, a principle of solution appropriate to get rid of the problems would combine new and additional thoughts. According to Kautiulya, the way of solution to the problem of poverty is not to wipe out the poor. The solution lies in considering definite theory and applying the same with deep faith. The consideration of a theory becomes firmer and more proper. Not only this, if the application of a theory in its true form is assured, the problem will disperse. Kautilya's *Arthashastra* advised to reach gradually to a definite conclusion about this. The definite conclusion is the withering of poverty. That is, one has to move forward accepting purpose elements and process for the true solution to the problem so that the problem can be solved. Not only this, one is to see that these problems are gradually sacrificed to reach a permanent solution. What is required for such a solution is an arrangement of the method of constant observation to find out a method for removal. The problem cannot be brought back along the path of this arrangement of a method.

If the arrangement of a method is not props, the path and phases become distorted through being rich in experience or in some other ways. As a result, despite being engaged in the solution of the problem, the solution does not become possible. It would come back again. It would come back in a newer form and shape. Hand in hand with the economic theories of Kautilya's *Arthashastra* have come anneal protection, social protection, social distribution and protection of leadership of the society and overall protection of the people. Kautilya wanted all the problems to be solved. This problem of protection is grave in the case of the state, and inevitably, this context is centred on the state government itself. By this, the state leadership and state are associated with a judgement and are being judged. As a state moves forward, a traditional sequence changes, so an individual established in leadership has a perspective and sequence. When these two come to judgement, they become significantly bracketed.

Leadership and state become included in the same group for protection. That is why Kautilya's solution for reaching the line of permanent solution lies within the solution process by coordination between the state and leadership. With a line of permanent solutions, a prop team may be overcome and, at the same time, determination of the basic nature of the problem is bound to be permanent. Here, the problems are looked at not only with a contemporary outlook but with a universal outlook too. Modern economic principles and theories aim at the assessment of problems only and to be engaged in solving the same in one's own way. Modern economists and experts have almost all cases marked the cases by their own feelings and theoretical consideration. But this has become unitary. That is a one-way solution have come in their cases. States engaged in solutions have tried to solve their own outlook. The judgement of states and leadership flows in different streams.

The line of the solution obtained has the inevitable consequence of the appearance of difference in the form of separation and illusion between the state leadership and people attacked by the problem. Kautilya wanted this difference between separation and illusion to be removed at the very first opportunity. And if this difference is removed, the consequence of the financial situation of economic management would set a line of harmony. By setting this line of harmony, there would be an attempt to look at every problem of economic management from the same point of view. Kautilya liked this attempt to be set in the mind of the individuals. Through the setting of harmony between the state and its leadership, a permanent abolition of the problem would be possible. For a complete solution to the problem of poverty from the viewpoint of persons affiliated with poverty. As a result, constant coordination would be set up between the leadership and persons afflicted with poverty. Through this constant coordination, the form of poverty and the regime flow would be evident.

In any society or state, the attempt at a permanent solution to all main problems amounts to permanent desisting from the effect of the problem. This permanent desisting of the effect of the problem is the protection of economic management. States capable of the fastest and most permanent solutions to economic problems would be able to move forward to the constant exposition of constant awakening by way of organising the economic wealth of possibilities. In this case, Kautilya's proposal is permanently effectual.

61
Modes of Administration

Introduction

Just like the administration of a state, in the administration of an organisation, the role of the mode of administration is important. The future of an organisation would depend on the mode of its administration. With the mode, subjects and consequences of administration have been linked up. An organisation would run as it is directed. The advancement of the organisation and the direction of administration would depend on the mode of action would depend on the mode of taking a decision and the nature of the decision both in government and business organisations. The consequence of an action determines the merits and demerits of the endeavour for the action. In both state management and the trade industry of modern times, some methods are found for liking a decision, and the decision is taken according to those methods. In each case, the decision may be of two types: For permanent management and for timely aspects.

The initial steps for this decision are to make proper arrangements for the aspects especially desired in timely cases. In case of such consideration very distant subject as for future does not come to mind; on the opposite side, there is a study of merely timely affairs and take stapes accordingly. At the time of taking decisions on contemporary and future affairs, the internal aspects of the organisation form are thought of. At the same time, circumstantial situations are also heeded. For example, in the case of thinking up any present, future subject attention must be paid to financial status, political situation of the state, cultural situation, situation of the market, demand and supply, etc. In the case of taking decisions, different types of alternation of the same subject are considered. Thinking of the alternative decision is quite similar to the first one, or those at a little distance are considered.

In choosing a decision from those very close to the first one, other points related to that trade and industry and those related to the organisation that have entered into completion with the organisation under question are also death with. In the modern process of taking decisions, few consequences are naturally thought of. The first one is what would be the consequence of taking the norms of decision in the present case, and the second is what kind of transformation would possibly be brought about in the market or financial fields by the consequence or apprehension of the consequence signifying the judgement existing in the economic field. There is scope for taking decisions in financial judgement, so there is also the perspective of decision. The perspective against which the decision is taken is particularly acceptable. Consequences of a decision may be judged on the basis of the perspective if, of course, the process of taking a decision has been known. If there is any defect in the process of taking decisions, then upset in the case of a decision is quite natural. The upset in the decision might emerge from the steps taken for taking the decision, or it may come out of the internal matters of the decision.

New Theory

There may be different types of relationships among the alternatives that are thought of in deciding modern management. For example, if there is a similarity among the decision, the judgement of the decision may be accomplished on the basis of that similarity. Merits and demerits of a decision depend, in many cases, on the similarity consideration laid to the idea of taking a decision. Among the plans thought of, two opposite ideas are reported at a time. This means that when a decision is taken on the basis of consideration of the circumstances and on the basis of ideas on the progress of a state or an organisation, one must consider what decision can be taken in just the opposite situation. In the theory presented in an article published in a journal related to management from Harvard University, four steps are said to be there in taking a decision.

Roger Martin made a detailed decision from the perspective of integrative decision. He wrote:

...SO what does the process of integrative thinking look like. How do integrative thinking consider their options in a way that leads the new possibilities thinking consider their options in a way that leads the new possibilities and not merely back to the same inadequate alternatives? They work through four related but distinct stages. The steps themselves are not particular to integrative thinking everyone goes through them while thinking through a decision... the first steps in figuring out which factors to take into account. In the second step of decision making,you analyse how the numerous salient factors relate to one another, integrative thinkers do not breakdown a problem into independent pieces and work on them separately or in a ascertain order. They see the entire architecture of the problem how the various parts of it fit together how one decision will effect another. Just as important they hold also of those pieces suspended in this minds at once. They don't parcel out the elements for others to work on piecemeal or let one element temporarily drop out of sight only to be taken up again of consideration after everything else has been decided

.... All these stages lead to an outcome. A leader who embraces holistic rather their segmented thinking can certainly resolve tension that launched the decision-making process.'

(Martin 2007, 64–66)

Roger Martin spoke of four steps of taking an integrative decision; he discovered this as a result of long observation and research. He has been able to come to this influence, considering the methods of taking decisions by fifty among the organisations of the world over a long span of time. The basic thing is that every decision is to be holistic. Different populations have different problems, subjects to be judged and perspectives. A decision is to be taken in consideration of those subjects and perspectives. In the case of making a decision mutual and apparently conflicting subjects may be topics of observation. Those who have taken the path of taking decisions after procuring components for taking decisions from this apparently conflicting aspect have gained success. Another stage of success of the integrative decision is to reach a point balancing struggle and peace among all the opposite opinions and theories. The mutual struggle among the opposite theories and opinions determines the ability and power of these opinions; after that, an attempt to bring peace among those theories and opinions makes possible not only a co-existence but also setting a balance among them. If there is a balance, then the decision that is taken with this may be the basis on which it would be possible for one to move on. This theory by Roger Martin has crossed all the prevalent theories and has hinted at the modes of administration in the coming days.

Applied Attempts

Very recently, there has been a propensity to take decisions in the integrative outlook. This propensity of taking a decision from holistic basis has been more common in these places in the backdrop of the commerce and industry of the world to have a better position for the people. That is, part of the action is changed with spirituality. In this part of action, individuals get burned and change comes in the in animal and animal lives of the aggregate. This propensity is evident not only in the case of theory and principle but has also been glowing in reality. These real propensities will be followed by some recent examples. Jhon R Behner, one of the former chief executives of Nabisco, a famous American company, has said that regarding the modes of administration of companies, they had the idea how buyers may be saturated with service of proper quality. Behner has said that the activity was to whom and some more of his type, just like feeling God.

'Serving everyone in extremely important to me. The idea of serving and to see God is everyone is may cup of tea ...we were having fun of work. What we were doing was a positive thing, making healthy products for the public. We had a wonderful relationship with our clients, and I had good relationship with my employees. The economic outcomewas the result of philosophy of serving; the employees prospered the company prospered, and everyone was happy in what they were doing .'

(Behner n.d., 147)

Nabisco company was not only very efficient, but its position also was among a few of the best companies in the world. Behner was at the El Savador wing of the company. In 1981, Nabisco engaged with the big American Company Standard Boards. Later in 1985. the company named RJ Reymonds bought Nabisco. Then, it was renamed RJR Nabisco. In 1987, Philip Morr's companies bought RJR Nabisco. Still later, Nabisco merged with Kraft Food. Such transformation was due to its worldwide reputation and extension. Every undertaking brought about more expansion of Nabisco.

When John R Behner was the country head of EI Salvador, it was then a flourishing financial region. It was called Japan of the Americas. Account of the mode of administration revealed in Behner's description is especially mentionable and demands elucidation. The fifth is that spirituality may play a role in the spread of modern commerce, and industry has almost disappeared. The integrative outlook mentioned in Martin's theory exists in the field of activity of Behner. Behner wanted to reach everybody through service, and he succeeded. And in the very route, a vast company met overall progress and, at the same time, all persons associated with that company and other companies specially experienced progress.

Kautilya's Solution

It is Kautilya who, from all sides, spread the theory of economic management. Whenever righteous rule has been established, there has been an attempt to apply the practice of spirituality. Modern commerce and industry have left no scope for the application of spiritual practice or thoughts on this subject. Here, extremely mentionable are progress and advancement. That principle would be attractive and favourite to the company taking resort to which the company would experience progress and advancement, but there are some people even in this system who retain spirituality in their personal faith. Kautilya's suggestion is more intricate and deep. He wanted decisions on temporary matters to be taken on the basis of integrative decisions. Decisions are always taken from the integrative perspective who those in integrative feeling theory. As a result, there may be exposition and spread of integrative outlook. As a result of the exposition and spread of integrative outlook, a balanced effect comes on the background of commerce and industry.

A basis of balance may be built up when commerce and industry are built up on the basis of balance that becomes the hour of a balanced consequence on its part. By these, there would be an end to the extremely distressing form that has been spread in different ways, as sometimes, new types of change would come in the economic field. As Roger Martin's theory has risen from the field of application, it is clear from the description of Behner's own experience that economic endeavours may be possible on the basis of spiritual realisation. It is not only possible but the success achieved by these crosses all other cases of success. The success achieved by an attempt for a spiritual basis occupies the top of all success. This is realised from Behner's experience with Nabisco. Behner's experience about Nabisco has revealed that as the company has experienced growing prosperity, so all the people would prosper at a time who are employees of the company, who are associated with the company, who are connected with the company by way of business, the buyers all are pleased and happy. The happy environment created is very congenial for financial expansion. Later identity of Nabisco Kraft Food is now a great trading success with which is embedded or connected the companies' recognition of obligation and line of action.

Kautilya *Arthashastra* has brought spiritual learning to the base of economic ideas. Due to the existence of spiritual theory at the base of economic ideas, it has bloomed the field of integrative faith. Activities and endeavours spread from this field of faith. Activity and endeavour can spread instead of other activities and endeavours. At the same time, new types of the land of concord may grow up, which would make the flow of change forceful and spreading opportunity of rising comes from the land of new theory and faith. The opportunity of awakening would spread and pervade itself. At the opportunity and hour of awakening comes the call of pervasion. The practice that has been accepted in a few cases, the direct consequence of that, has also crossed the expectations of the modern age. The provision of that practice becomes blissful for society, state and human civilisation. The theory accepted by Harvard University and practised by the American Companies has been attractive, no doubt, but entry or groups has not been extensive become at that theory and application thereof has come local influence. It is as if for special cases, for particular individuals and for a definite time. Kautilya has brought liberation from such a situation of delusion. He has spoken of all types of endeavours to place everything on the basis of spirituality.

To be proved in Vedic knowledge is the spiritual victory of an individual. Through this background, balanced and equilibrated feelings are exposed within the individuals. In spite of doing work for one's own company, one can be lifted up in one's own field and can bear a feeling of service, and that would be sprouted in case of taking a decision. Service and mentality of service can primarily build up a background for change. The social responsibility of commerce and industry is particularly pointed out by this mentality. Words, speeches or publicity about the social responsibility of commerce and industry is useless; what is useful is a mentality of service and faith in spirituality. Kautilya wanted to rouse this mentality of service and faith in spirituality in individuals. The principle that is tenable in the case of assets can be accepted in case taking decisions about and administration of a company. As for the leader of the state, for the administration of a company, too, new attempts or enterprises would weaken these by the change of the feelings and both of the leadership. The new types of attempts or enterprises would signify economic thoughts and success.

62
Kautilya's Diplomacy

Introduction

Kautilya's diplomacy is the best of the lot. It falls under most discussed and opt-quoted remarks. From the very beginning, Kautilya moved on with an integrative outlook. The main thing behind this integrative outlook is that the attempts required for the existence, progress and advancement of a state are those behind which are blooming of individuals and the state as well. The field of the blooming of individuals would have to be built up with special care and efforts, and that, in the case of a state, would be a form assumed by a combination of the aggregate. At the base of economic management, Kautilya liked to establish making a proper man. He wanted to fulfil the target of the state with the help of those good and suitable men. Good and suitable men will grow if it is possible to build up this character. If character grows good and suitable, men will grow automatically. Kautilya wanted every man to be fit through building up of character and to be engaged in the welfare of the state.

If the character is built up, the welfare of the state, the welfare of the people and integrative welfare for all would be exposed before our sight. Kautilya wanted men engaged in doing good to be taking multipurpose responsibility and responsibility of many. That is, crossing the personal limit, they would think of the welfare of the aggregate. The individual would work on behalf of that aggregate and would always look after the aggregate. As a result, as a background is built up for the incitation of the individual, a background of incitation of many persons is also being built up. The host of incitation of the individual and the aggregate is an auspicious hour on the part of a state. The situation when the urge of an individual coincides with that of the state is worthy of close attention. Kautilya wanted to build up such a background as special. The effectiveness and background of an individual would always be open for the aggregate. If the full allegiance is for the state and the mode of its administration, then it becomes an auspicious hour both for the individual and the state. So, Kautilya has pointed out a path of judging an individual through some tests. He spoke of understanding through different tests. What is the position of the individual within the state, what is his real mentality, how they intend, which matters are embedded in their mind—there are to be known.

Kautilya's Proposal

Significance of the proposal of diplomacy proposed by Kautilya has far-reaching significance. The purpose of diplomacy is to learn properly about the state and to point out the mentalities for and against the state. What is at the end of the state, which direction it is expected to move on, who are thinking of what and what is in anyone's mind—these are to be understood clearly. Kautilya particularised a method to understand these. The method is to understand who is friendly and who is antagonistic through contradiction. This method has long prevailed in the history of signifying a friend or foe. If the root of friendship and enmity, a fair idea can be framed about its consequence. It is essential for the state and for the market. In modern history, Mao Zedong followed this method to locate his opponents. On the basis of the spreading of and belief in the theory 'Let hundred flowers blossom, let hundred thoughts content', opponents' opinions and thoughts begin to bloom gradually, and the measure goes on increasing. Mao Zedong marked the opponents whose opinions and thoughts were sharp and harmful elements, mixed with them gradually to find out the most harmful man or group and tried to see them in isolation. As a result, when, at a later stage, the time came for wiping them out, it was rather easy. One crore men of opponent view fell dead overnight. Kautilya, of course, did not like such cruelty. Kautilya wanted to discreetly locate the person who had bad intentions, who had different identities in and out and who would wear a mask not to be disclosed. These men would speak of prospering the country but were stealthily associated with activities detrimental to the interest of the state. Kautilya wanted to recognise them stealthily and treat them likewise. First, they would be avoided, and later, they would be set up elsewhere. The vacant place would then be filled up by fitting men of proper attitude. The latter would be of a class whose activities are against animosity to the state or even against any such future possibility. As a result, some people would be aware of the state and its responsibility. Kautilya has wanted to perform some more tests of different types to hasten this action of inducing awareness.

These tests are not meant for common people but for those who are in higher posts, who possess the ability to do harm to the state or who are likely to do so. They may be located at different places, such as within the dignitaries holding high posts in the army and defence, within the high officials engaged in citizen-service management of the state, among those whose words can influence others, including different officials of the finance and tax departments, officers in the foreign department and others who have influential tone in their words. Kautilya has opined that if these high-ranking officials and influential citizens are not definitely known, the line of upheaval might grow out of them.

TESTS:

Test 1: Righteousness and unrighteousness

Test 2: Thirst for money

Test 3: Whether goaded by lust

Test 4: Whether beaten by fear

> Mantripurohitamsakhahsamahye ca
> Adhikaranesu.
> Sthapayttvaamatyaanupasyabhihsodhayate
> Purohitamyajyayajanahadhipateniyukhtam
> Puhyamanamrajabasripet.

(*Arthashastra*, 1/10/1-2)

It means: Special arrangements are for ministers, officials and other dignitaries. Tests required for different officials are to know the mental information of those officials and to know their mentality about the king and his management. To know these, there would also be tests of righteousness and unrighteousness.

The details of the first test are as follows: Trusted men of the king would set out and mix up with selected people. They would mix up in small multitudes and crowds and tell against the authority of the state; they would use different statements and adjectives about the authority. Their attitude would make the audience feel that they are speaking the truth. The test by the secret agent would be performed on the reactions of these on people. The agent would come back from different places and, with such mass relations and information, report to the authority. Such reports are very much essential for a state. Kautilya wanted that authorities would be alert after having the reports and take proper steps. This test has been termed the 'test of righteousness and unrighteousness'. This is because people who have in their mind an idea of a practice of unrighteousness by the state and leadership always, within their minds or in public, discuss that state is engaged in the practice of unrighteousness. So, they were disgusted with the state. This disgust may, over time, lead to displeasure and, finally, even to revolt. To prevent these, the state should take steps; the main one among these steps is to search out the main cause of this disgust or displeasure and to attempt to remove it. As a result, the state would be free from future problems.

The second test is for the thirst for money. Some dignitaries are greedy and thirsty for money. This test is meant for them. Some persons are engaged in conducting the test—these men are engaged in the protection of the state and internal protection. The duty of these persons is to judge how much the persons engaged openly or secretly in different responsible posts are thirsty for money. This is the arrangement to have that information. Through this test, it is possible to judge the practice of taking bribes among the leadership in the authority of the state and to judge matters related to money when the report reaches the highest leadership. The leadership can easily understand what steps are to be taken against the persons eager to take bribes. The next step is to transfer these persons to unimportant posts. If, in these posts too, they are found to have the propensity of taking bribes, they would have to be sacked.

The third test is one of judging whether one is goaded by lust. In this test, a proposal for the queen and other women used to be sent to the ministers through men who had free access everywhere to observe what had been their mentality in this respect. A minister who would express interest would be a suspect; one who would reject such a offer would be judged to be genuine.

Parbrajkahlabdhabisvesahahtahpure
Krtasatkaramahapatramekam
Upajapeta -'Rajamahisimtvam
Kamayatekrtasamagamaupaya

Mahanarthascatebhabisyartiiti
PratyakhyanesuchiitiKamaupadha

(*Arthashastra*, 1/10/8)

It means: If a person having free access to the royal harem and royal court, on whom is deep faith of the ministers and officials, approaches the ministers as high officials and reports, 'Her Highness is charmed with you', consider his words with importance. If a minister rejects this strongly, then it would be judged that he is genuine. This test can be termed the 'lust-inciting test'.

These diplomatic tests are essential for a state to keep the authority of the state unimpaired. The state needs to conduct these tests secretly and stealthily. As the state authority and the chief advisers thereof remain protected by these tests, the matter of allegiance to the state also gets clear. The measure of diplomacy here is covered in a packet and is not evident from the outside. As per Kautilya's proposal, the secret agents, as wings of diplomacy, remain engaged in the integrative interest of the state.

Katva ca antamnibartenasthitla Saturday
Batamghrtau.

(*Arthashastra*, 1/10/19)

It means: The mind that has been blemished by different means, his understanding has also been blemished. If such a mind is inspired like a glowing flame, a lamp character befitting a state is built up.

Kautilya noticed that the officials, powerful ministers, office bearers and other important persons and groups do not always vent their opinions and intentions. Some even keep them concealed in their resentment. They wait to be expressed and burst out at an opportune moment. When a perspective for the outburst is created, the whole situation crosses the limit of control and right of the state. Such a thing is done only with the intention of snatching out the right and stability of the state. As a result, there may be a disorder in the state. So Kautilya has beforehand tried to warn the state authority. The state shall have to apprehend what will come off in future and move on towards sounding and silent active habits. As a result, the problem that might arise in the future may be apprehended much before, and proper steps for its prevention or cessation may be taken.

Security of Leadership and State

Pratyaksahparoksahanumeyah hi rajabrtti
Paroksam
KarmasuKrtensakrtabeksnam
Anumeyam.

(*Arthashastra*, 1/19/4-7)

It means: Among the actions of the king, there are direct, indirect and conjecturable ones. Direct is the one supervised by the king himself. The information intended for others is called indirect. And of which there is no correct knowledge and is determined through guessing is called conjecturable.

When a certain matter comes to the direct experience of the leader of that state, the problem is then quite serious. The problem, having been serious, means it has to be overcome through the application of power and ability of the state. By these, the resources and possibilities that might be used by the state for its progress and development get lost or wasted. That is why the state needs to procure information indirectly and prepare other things for timely remedy. Where there is no scoop for having information even indirectly, or it is time-consuming, a king makes different decisions on the basis of conjecture. Actions that may be taken on the basis of direct, indirect and conjecturable processes are apt for proper control or resistance. Kautilya wanted this authority would be prepared for all possible situations and would not hesitate in the least to take strong decisions if necessary. The opposition force hides in the royal sphere. A king or state would mark the opposition hidden in the royal sphere and, when necessary, take steps against them; otherwise, they would take proper steps to change their mentality. The degree of the problem is to be ascertained carefully. Then, proper steps must be taken too.

63
Proper Use of Land

Price of Land

What is the price of this land? 'The master said, listen Upen, I would purchase this land'. The attraction for land is not of Zeminder alone—it is eternal. This attraction is innate. Who has had the touch of land at the very initiation of life is not to understand the value of the land. How costly is the land? He can assess from the background of the experience gathered by him in life. What sort of land is it? -e.g. 'human land' -Might have yield gold on farming. O my mind; you know not ow to cultivate -so you have left such a fertile land follow. This human land is the field for yielding crops. Here, one has to cultivate, water and thus carry on with the vow of life. In whatever form, one would be able to move on with cultivating the land. So, the activated paths of his life and different elements for cooperation and victory would grow up. One has to rear up the resources arrived on the paths of life. So, in addition to new elements for advancement, human land has a basic unity and similarity. A life glowing with possibility. All lives have descended on the earth with full resources of possibility. All of these lives are held in completeness in the field of completeness. All lives have a perspective of clean fullness. So, this field of possibilities may be given a bright ending by exposing the dormant possibilities of life. The possibility of lying dormant has its perspective of manifestation in life, but that is not possible without proper cultivation and watering. So, the perspective required to advance the productivity of the land, as a result, may be created through practice, observance and proper exposure to the possibilities. This phase of exposition of possibilities under the perspective of life is at the primary group of the owner of human land. When possibilities of life get exposed to personal endeavour, the value of life itself changes. The value which is significantly the life of dormant possibility changes in the phase of blooming life now becomes valuable. The land left out only for future development has a much-reduced value. Again, the land vested in able hands meets an attempt to have a new value. Attraction, too, is created for this new value. Just as ploughing and watering increase the value of land, just as fertility of land forms the perspective of productivity of the land, proper rearing of land augments yield and price too. So to access the price of land, its price primary background is required. Also required is the measure of endeavours taken on the necessity and a clear idea of what has been done for the measure and which steps have been properly taken for the purpose. The fertility of land may be a natural phenomenon, or it can be increased by some methods. Whatever may be the process, fertile land is very precious. A fertile land is not only precious but also has a great scope of movement of price. Fallow land costs less, while fertile land costs more. So far, fertile land should be craving for a high price. The price of land may be assessed from its fertility as also from other appeals. Appeal for land may be created from its position. With this, other sorts of conveniences may be combined. Due to positional reasons with other conveniences combined with it, different types of appealing power are created in the case of land.

Land and Civilisation

Just like human life, in the case of land, too, there is some special support or dependence on any substance. Dependence in the case of land grows from some components lying within. Among the components lying within a land, there are many types of minerals and other natural ingredients. So, often, land develops such attractions that are apparently revealed through reactions. This situation of reaction brings the land an incomparable attraction. This incomparable attraction is formed in the perspective of its expansion. When the land may expand in terms of storage of resources and its identity. This storage and identity help in a newer assessment of the price of the land. In the land are active many types of big and small lives. These are constantly piercing through the land and are giving an endless supply of oxygen, nitrogen, etc. And in this movement are embedded the life factors of all crops and plants growing on the land. So, on the movement and ascending and descending of different types of sub human lives become active within the land and in it lies the chronicle of the land itself. The essence of the possibilities of the land lies in the possibilities of different types of changes happening constantly in it. Tom Dale and Vernon Gill of Oklahoma University, America, wrote in the book *Topsoil and Civilization* (1955):

'Civilised man was nearly always able to become matter of his environment temporarily. His chief trouble came from his delusion that he is temporary mastership was permanents. He thought of himself as 'master of the world', while failing to understand fully the laws of nature.

Man weather civilized or savage, is a child of nature he is not the master of nature. He must conform his actions to certain natural laws if he is to maintain his dominance over his environment. When he tries to circumvent the laws of nature, he usually destroys the natural environment that sustains him. And when the environment deteriorates rapidly, his civilization declines.'

This advancement of man along the road of civilisation is gradually becoming oppositely active on nature. Trees, soil, creepers, grass, flowers, crops, etc., all have been born in the bosom of nature. These elements of nature allow man to move forward on the road of life. For civilisations, man has been rival to nature. Trying to accept and occupy nature in his own field, man has regularly exploited nature and has almost emptied nature. Human civilisation has turned out to be the enemy of man and soil. Man has forgotten the price of soil with respect to soil. Growing prosperity alone is determining the price of soil. As the town is growing, the price of soil is also rising. As the price of soil is rising, its relationship with its own inherent elements is becoming weaker. Determining the price of soil, with respect to its practical utility instead of productivity, is to ignore the true significance of soil and to be associated with other significances. In civilisation, a man wanted to be the monarch of nature instead of like to be confined within their own identity. In order to be the king of nature, man has developed in themselves a strong desire for invasion. This desire for invasion is constantly carrying man towards an enclosure created by themselves and away from the natural surroundings. Within this enclosure created by man's own civilisation, the price of soil has been merely to be a conservator of the base land, surroundings and roads. As a result, man is strolling on the soil only to add the constant disgrace of his strolling. The vehicle of civilisation is moving forward, trembling upon the road for strolling, and along with that, the role of soil is being transformed regularly. The soil that is the 'mother' who got her regular productivity, who is capable of transfusing variegation and who has regular yielding capacity, has been made to deviate from productive ability and to be the basic stand for providing the foundation of buildings. It is now the time for the soil that has been constantly keeping the earth green with crops at the cost of its inner provision to be aware of the identity and the price of that soil yielding green crops. This assessment of the value of soil is aimed at protecting the yielding power of the soil and making it suitable for diversified outputs.

Use of Soil

Eugene Rabinowitch, the Chief-Editor of the *Bulletin of Atomic Scientist*, has discussed a special direction of human civilisation. The only animal whose disappearance may threaten the biological viability of man on earth is the bacteria normally inhabiting our bodies. For the rest, time is no convincing proof that mankind could not survive even as the only animal species on earth! If economical ways could be developed for synthesising food from inorganic raw materials, which is likely to happen sooner or later, man may even be independent of plants, on which he now depends as sources of his food.

Natural resources are priced on the basis of dependence of the man. A certain thing is priced to a stage that coincides with the dependence of man on it. The qualitative and quantitative basis determines the price. Where man greatly depends on natural elements for his food and other things, these natural resources and their sources become precious for them. This price depends on the productive ability and qualitative measures of productivity. But where land has been used for other purposes, it is not necessary to study the productive ability or measure. The price of land meant for urbanisation will depend on how urbanisation would be effective on that land and how that land can be used in the form of a strong foundation for creating big or essential structures or infrastructure on it. The price depends on its use, not on productive quality, power or measure. The responsibility of the land exists as a silent witness in the lifeless building in the form of the bustle of new life and glowing affluence of the township. In the course of describing the relation of man with land, E F Schumacher has commented in his famous book, *Small Is Beautiful*: 'In our time, the main danger to the soil, and there with not only to agriculture but to civilization as a whole, stems from the towns man's determination to apply to agriculture the principles of industry.'

Schumacher has held this propensity to change the character of the land as the worst danger of our time. When crops grow on land, the land expresses its motherhood through this yield. The flow of life moves along the route of the land. Anything that is creative in life that can give stability, customs and principles to society originate from the motherhood of land. The land is the mother. In proper application and use of land is detachment from that motherhood. Land and its productive power are at the root of civilisation. All sides of civilisation have grown centring the land. Primary structure and basis have been created with land at the centre. Innocent gratitude to nature should be there in human minds for growing crops on the land. The proper supply of provisions for the flow of life in human civilisation comes from the bounty of nature. So, favour of nature makes the continuous onward flow of the life of the crops alive. The first thing required for growing crops is to accept the motherhood of the land. The land is the mother herself, so no reckless conduct towards it is permitted. It cannot be destroyed by any means; returning the qualities of the land, one should learn how to bear the land. Besides, patience, endurance and cooperation are required. Patience, endurance and cooperation are intimately related to the productive ability of land. That is why the natural evaluation of land is essential. Accepting land as a mother's endurance, dependence and exchange on the basis of mutual understanding grows within the society. If the character of the land is built up, the character of the society is automatically built; permanent human civilisation grows up centring the land. The significance of Schumacher's statement is that qualitative resources are created in agricultural civilisation. The more the use of land for setting up townships and industry, changing the character of the land, the more rapid would be the ruination of the agriculture-centred civilisation. The fall of land is the fall of civilisation. The civilisation of town and industry destroys the field of endurance, natural bonding of human relations and coordination. Instead, the effects of township and industry, such as restlessness, speed, individualistic flourish and the propensity of applying integrative interest to satisfy individualistic interest, increase. The special observation presented by Schumacher on this is important to realise the flourishing and wealth of civilisation:

On a wider view, however, the land is sun as a priceless asset which it is man's task and happiness 'to dress and keep'.We can say that man's management of the land must be primarily oriented towards three goals-health, beauty and permanence. The fourth goal - the only one accepted by the expert's - productivity will then be attained almost as by-product. The crude materialist view sees agriculture as 'essentially directed towards food-production'. A wider view sees agriculture as having to fulfil at least three tasks:

- to keep man in touch will living nature of which he is and remains a highly vulnerable part.
- ohumanise and ennoble man's wider habitat; and
- to bring forth the food stuffs and other materials which are needed for a becoming life.

I do not believe that a civilization which recognizes only the third of these tasks, and which pursues it with such ruthlessness and violence that the other two tasks are not merely neglected but systematically counteracted has any chance of long term survival.

(Rupa 1990, 93)

Soil is the Mother

The very conclusion arrived at by Schumacher in the perspective of human civilisation of modern time is of relation with the mind, relation centred at mind. In the tradition of our country, the basic confidence and massage of civilisation have been voiced again and again. This soil is the mother. Fixing up the relationship with this mother, the network of mutual relations is set up. If soil is used as soil, only its motherhood is accepted with dignity. Soil cannot be used recklessly for industrialisation and urbanisation. Soil, which is productive, and that, as a mother, has made the men of the society cheerful and strong, beautiful and handsome—judge her with a proper value and give her dignity. Soil is maintaining us, and we should also reciprocate. Let soil bloom before us in the flawless figure of a mother. Indian geniuses have more than once voiced this mystic world of civilisation in human society. They have accepted that the flow of life is victorious over time and have carried it forward along the route of flourishing time. Kautilya has accepted this base of confidence and emphasised proper use and care of the soil. Soil is not only to be protected. Kautilya presented ways for the same. Kautilya's proposal favours the constant rebuilding of the civilisation centring on the surrounding soil, the basis of soil and proper improvement of soil. There is a redistribution of our relation with soil—an extreme relation would grow by which we won't realise that soil is our base. Soil is a provision for our growth and formation. Soil is the field of our orientation. Soil is our ending. Soil is the mother. Kautilya presented an unequalled picture of social orientation. The structure of the villages would be as follows. At the centre would remain land and farmers and men for attending lands. To meet the different requirements of this great number of people at the centre, people of different professions would be differently accommodated. In small villages, one hundred to five hundred such farmers and attendants would stay side by side. With them, there would be people of other professions in the right proportion. Through coordination, agriculture and other professions, the whole region would be self-sufficient. The region would be separated from the rest by canals, rivers, surroundings of plants and the like. As a result, a completeness would come in the village. Kautilya laid stress on this proportionality. At the base of this, there is a proportional existence of deeply related people with the land. The industry would offer coordination with the people related to land in respect of nature. By such attempts, the industry would not alter the character of the land. This identity would be established centring the motherly identity of the land, and land-oriented civilisation would be reared on the basis of that.

Consideration of land merely as a field for production is of modern minds—those who intend to pervade industrialisation. For health, beauty and stability in life, a composed, steady and considerate field and a hint of steady and complete relationship with this life would group up with holism and grace. The land, which, as a mother, can offer consideration in the process of social bonding, is priceless. That land is the mother of civilisation.

64

Public Security and Maintenance of Public Facility

Civil Rights

Human rights have now been a close and sure topic everywhere. Civil rights are now highly emphasised through open calls. Maintenance of happiness and facilities is regarded as a fundamental duty of the state. Kautilya's *Arthashastra* opines definitely in favour of public rights. Maintenance of public facilities is a duty of the state. The state should be prompt in this matter. Farming of outlines of how rights can be established depends on desires, wills, problems and the power of applications thereof. In order to realise this power of application, Kautilya advised the state to try to collect information from society and to pursue the mentality of the people. The expectation of the people from the state is to be ascertained by a secret process or by the patronages of the king. These are to be known in the interest of both the state and the people. The requirement of the state may be temporary and also long-term. The state takes decision sometime temporarily and sometimes on a long-term basis. The decision taken by the state contains in them both types of preparation. To be aware of the opinions and intentions of the people for taking decisions on the immediate requirements of the state is a fundamental duty of the state. The state's responsibility is to change everything or to set everything in order with the intention of the people. Information from different places reacts to the state through the departments created by it. Arrangement for direct procurement of information is included in the duties of the departments of the state. As the direct information comes through different departments, it becomes somewhat tinged. When the information is tinged in different ways, reaches the point of taking decision, a situation suitable for taking decision there of gets created. The decision taken on the part of the state instead of becoming favourable to people is to go against them. For these reasons, Kautilya imposed great importance on the procurement of information. Kautilya has liked to set the principle of state administration and economic management on the basic faith and foundation. Among these seven different theories are important.

Consideration of Kautuilya's Theory

Theory-1: The state and its leader should be farsighted; arrangements for a probable solution to problems right before their appearances should be there.

Theory-2: The state and its leader would run the administration with due consideration of the consequence and would be enterprising enough in this respect.

Theory-3: There should be a clear idea of priority in the works to be done, and in the light of this idea, the turns of works to be done are to be assured.

Theory-4: There should be greater inspiration behind every work. The earnestness of work is to be built up not in the urge of personal interest but in the aspiration of greater achievement. By this, it would not be necessary to look at the result of the work. The consciousness would be directed towards the work itself.

Theory-5: The fare-involved truth lying deep into every subject should be clearly understood; the esoteric theory and idea intricate therein should be learnt. On the basis of this knowledge, work must be accomplished.

Theory-6: Remaining in touch with every work, the influence thereof should have to be realised, and the consequence of work must be ascertained, and endeavour should be directed in that line.

Theory-7: Probable problem of danger behind each work must be apprehended correctly, and prior preparation to face the same would have to be taken.

MundauJatiilobabrttikamahtapah
Byarjanah

(*Arthashastra* 1/11/13)

Sahnagarabhyasauprabhutamunda
Jatilaantebasi
Sakamyabamusthimbamasahdvimasantarah
Prakasamantriyangrhamihamaharami

(*Arthashastra*, 1/11/14)

It means that these men clad in robes of ascetics, with heads shaven, would take shelter near the localities observing proper rites and reforms. They would establish their asceticism in society by taking vegetarian food and a non-vegetarian diet once in one or two months.

Secret agents would enter into the society, and their entry would always be above doubt. As a result, their unrestricted familiarity with men would be possible. Their identity would be not as informers but as really well-wishing to the society and good fellows. When they would roam in society, their position within the society would not only be well accepted, but society would also accept them with the dignity of ascetics. That is why Kautilya wanted a person acceptable to all spheres of society to get the smooth running of the administration of the state. Society shall show unique treatment and dependence to persons who are acceptable and trustworthy in all spheres. On the basis of this treatment and reliability, people of all spheres of society would narrate tales of their pains and sufferings to them. Through such narrations of pains and sufferings, they would get the essence of all activities of the state. This is very appreciated information to a state. That is, through this process, the state would attempt to accomplish works favourable to that society. Kautilya urged to be earnest in solving problems before the problems are created. It is possible when the seat of the problems just in the form of a seed comes to the sight of the state. If this problem as a seed comes to the sight of the state, it must be conceived that proper care might be taken to get it solved. As a result, the establishment of proper leadership and proper management becomes possible. Under these circumstances, two different paths and two lines of information have come before the leader of the state. One of these consists of exposing before all. The other is the process by which worthy informers, in the guise of shaven-headed ascetics, collect the correct mentalities of people in different cases and collect advice from the people.

The news media of the state has the main duty to extend open possibilities and problems and to approach the people properly to collect their opinions. These opinions, in most cases, become to the liking of the government or the head of the state. In the case of giving opinions openly, people only give those that are only to the liking of the informers or the authority. So, there is every chance for erotic distraction to creep in. This distraction is just the same as having no opinion. This is because people do not express opinions that are liable to not be appreciated. The result—the problems prevailing in society lie unknown. And without any correct knowledge, the solution to the problems remains far off. Thus, the king deviates from his duty, and the duty of the state remains unattended. As a result, the trouble is finally met with by the people. Shaven-headed ascetics, to collect information for the state, work here as the most hardworking friends of the state, and the good result of every action devolves on the leader of that state. By this action, the state and people of the state might really get judged and be benefitted.

Thoughts for the Final Consequence

Baidehakantahebaasirah
Arccanah
Samiddhayaugearcaresuh

(*Arthashastra*, 1/11/15)

Sisyah Srantavedayesuh
Asansiddhsh Samahadhikaiti

(*Arthashastra*, 1/11/16)

It means: Men engaged in work or men successful in business would come to these men in the guise of ascetics and accept pupilage through accruing knowledge on observance yoga and ascetic practice and gradually announce their asceticism to others. As a result of this, persons careful about the final consequence become alert and would run to those ascetics for rescue.

In our ascetic practice, high-souled noble ascetics have spoken of the advent of renunciation in mind through thinking of the final consequence. In the routes of asceticism of Pranabanandaji, the master, one main route is the 'thought of death'. The continuous thought of death brings an attempt at asceticism to mind. By this, all would be engaged in asceticism and advance in the route of asceticism. Along the path of this thought on death inclination of the people to religion or fear from the same move forward towards a point of attraction. Even to collect information, one can extend this line of asceticism to others. It would then help advance along the real path of asceticism. Besieged persons now attracted by renunciation and spirituality come forward to express their mentalities open-heartedly. Another side of this thought on the end is the final consequence of consideration of the possible ending. By consideration of ending attention comes to possible solutions. As a result, in the mantel perspective of an individual, frank thoughts begin to flow. Similarly, in the case of state management, a unique endeavour for work grows up. This thought of ending is especially useful for the leader of a state because he has to move forward considering the consequence of work. Due to this propensity of moving on after considering the consequence, in every endeavour of the leader of a state would come a dependence on reasonability and the process of reasoning. As a result of dependence on reasonability and the process of reasoning, all the endeavours of the state would be established on a scientific basis.

Endeavour—One After Another

Kautilya wants that the leader of the state would create conjunction and sequence among the individual works or the works to be done in the distribution of the departments. If this conjunction and sequence among works to be done are created, it will not be difficult to understand which works are the most important. As a result, the leader of the state, despite being engaged in quite a big job in a small span of time, would be able to extend the consequence of work for all. Endeavours of the state, as a result, would extend before all and would be favourable for creating a proper perspective for all. Importance in the case of a certain work might even be less than the extent of eagerness and importance demanded in the performance of a more important work. As a result, the works may move on in accordance with this measure, quality and standard. Kautilya wanted smooth accomplishment of all works. It becomes possible if a proper sequence is marked for all the works. The *Arthashastra* gave an example of a sequence. For example, in the case of a war, the first work to be done is to fix up the target of the war and blaze the fire of war in the minds of all the soldiers. If a soldier feels the heat of war in his mind, then and only then would he jump into war with proper valour.

Kautilya liked a greater inspiration behind a work. Work is not meant to satisfy one's own individual interest; everything would have to be viewed as rising above personal interest. The interest of the nation and of man is also to be looked into. Kautilya liked the happiness of the people to be that of the king. The benefit of the people is the benefit of the king. The leader of the state would not lay stress on his own happiness to satisfy his own interest. He could consider himself happy if that wealth of happiness reaches all his people. For this, the leader would have to be the processor of a great mind. A leader, the processor of a great mind, would be a noble, self-denying, benevolent yogi. The leader would be eager to practice and accomplish these within himself in the best possible way.

Sattva prajnabakyahsaktimsamparnam
Mya rajabhagyamanubyaharetun
Mantrisansyagetubrugat

(*Arthashastra* 1/11/19)

It means: The basket of future possibilities would expose itself to men who are possessors of the highest quality and virtue. So the behaviour and character of ascetics would grow in the hearts of these people. This constant honest attempt would be an upliftment in man—this would be the say of ascetics.

Kautilya wanted to rouse the propensity to be the processor of the greatest virtue among all the persons associated with the department of state administration being quite interested or disinterested. So, this path is one of being 'a man of the highest power'. Kautilya is a traveller on this path of being a man of the highest power. Kautilya liked the munificent men and those who are possessors of a noble mind to present at different corners of society and would be desirous to awaken all good things in the society. The endeavours of the works of these men would bring down a flow of transformation on the path of life. This flow of transformation would touch the activities of each department and cause it to flow. This is because the correct information coming through this honest person would surely bring about the offering of solutions.

Orientation in Depth

Not only a processor of a great mind, a leader of a state should be an accepter of deep feelings. He would enter deep into any subject and acquire knowledge about the same. Special knowledge would make an acquaintance with the root of the problems. If the root of the problem is known, one might feel the urge to get it solved. So, one must understand where truly the root of the problem lies and how deep the root is. Without knowing the root of the problem, its solution is not possible.

Karsakobrttiksinaahprajnasaucayuk
to Grhapatiekahbajanh

(*Arthashastra* 1/19/9)

Sahkrsi karma pratisthayambhumau
Itisamanampurbam

(*Arthashastra* 1/19/10)

It means: As the true entity of real farming of built up by the knowledge lying within the secret truth within the profession of cultivation of the farmers, a man with profound knowledge about the household becomes the head of a family. In the establishment of cultivation, a farmer searches deep into the land for the hidden truth about land and by this, his efficiency of work increases as before.

If one can enter into the deep, it will be knowledge, and if entry into the depth fails, the procurement of knowledge fails. To earn that knowledge, a farmer must enquire about the nature of soil very eagerly when procurement of sound knowledge regarding which soil has what components, which soil is suitable or not for which crop is possible only their suitable cultivation and suitable cropping may be possible. Kautilya wanted all the endeavour of work to be done on the basis of this profound knowledge. The effect of work being done in this way becomes definite. This effect spreads to many people. Kautilya liked this effect spread among many to spread through the state. The good result would then move to the people.

Many problems may be behind all works and endeavours, in the flow and in the consequence. Kautilya wanted to understand the problem and possible troubles quite beforehand and to take proper steps to prevent the same. The attempt to know the problem and trouble in between action and endeavour is really accomplished by different informers. Kautilya specially designed this theory in the case of defiance of the king and the state. A second set of information is necessary for the verification of the information procured by the secret agency. The phase of procuring information is tenable of the special norms. The disguise of the informers remains effective. One example cited by Kautilya is as follows: If the impending threat is apprehended from any neighbouring country at the border, it is, in such a case, prescribed an outright attack. Where there is a dread of stroke, an advanced stroke is advisable. That is, prevention is advisable before the incident practically happens. Such arrangements would have been made even before the happening of an incident as the plan for a solution is hatched beforehand. An attack even before being attacked not only stops the impending attack, but the direction of dread also gets turned. The dread might have been so devastating as to bring a dark night on the state itself and its people. But now, there would be just the opposite result. It will not be advantageous for the state. This is a unique path for the rise of the state and its people by applying Kautilya's theories.

65

Mechanical Control of Economic Progress: Kautilya's Law

Towards Technology: In Past and Present

The excellence of science in the ancient civilisation of India is still a wonder to the world. Many wonders and many wonderful subjects first appeared in India. India was all along inclined to the interior. India has always laid stress on 'Software' than on 'Hardware'. The mathematical theories of Aryabhatta, the master in the fifth century AD, are still objects of wonder. Aryabhatta brought a revolution in mathematics. This mathematics includes the laws of scientific awareness. The decimal theory discovered by Aryabhatta built up the fundamental infrastructure of the current numerical system. This infrastructure of numerical system has found whole numbers as a sum of parts. Ito's Lema, composed of the most modern mathematics, has this viewpoint at the base. This may be regarded as the final consequence of that theory. The use of this final consequence is far-spreading. For example, behind the ups and downs in the price of the share due to the sale and purchase of the shares. Share markets are active in the attitude of the investors, their practical methods and factors acting sporadically on the market. Besides, which of the shares would be invested in the market, how long this investment would continue and how these shares would be protected against loss are also looked into. Arrangements to control the price of the shares to get profit from them are made with the help of Ito's Lema. As a result, the possibility of losing in investment is either eradicated or becomes minimum. To effect this minimum loss derivative, the sale and purchase of shares are going on in the derivatives market.

The idea of the principle of fraction acts behind this arrangement. A main principle of this was contributed by Aryabhatta in the fifth century. In the seventh century came the discovery of zero by Brahamgupta, another master. In the later period, the combined use of zero and fraction brought the mathematical application to a greater perspective. In mathematical language, he carried the theory of numbers to ten decimal places. The perspective of the onward march of the creation that emerged from ever-new discoveries continues with this principle of the awakening of India. In the background of the newly started march of machine and technology, there are always an eagerness and sentiment for doing something new. Indian technologists are continuously making newer and newer discoveries in the fields of application. *Economist*, a famous journal in London, has narrated the possibility of this Indian technology as the result of a special discovery.

> ...India's technological confidences has grown immeasurably thanks to the success of its software and IT firms. The heirs of Aryabhatta and Brahmagupta, India's digital ambassadors have own acclaim for their mastery of one's as well as zeros... As of now, India matters more to technology than technology does to India.
>
> (Special Report on Technology 2007, 4)

In the field of technology, the progress and economic expansion of the world require the expansion of research from the perspective of India's ancient mathematical tradition. The expansion of technology and attempt at research are moving hand in hand in the Indian perspective. Primary research activities are trotting rapidly in many laboratories. The companies have changed the earlier conditions of the medicinal factories, and as the activities of production are continuing in full swing, research is going on at the same time. A small example would clarify the situation. Piramal Industries Limited is now occupying the fourth position at this moment among the drug industries of India. Research activities are happening in their Mumbai laboratories in an arch of nearly two lakh square feet. Robots of very high quality are helping in research in these laboratories. New inspiration has flowed now in research works as a result of the new clauses brought and change effected in the Patent Law of India (2005). This fundamental research has moved far, even in the field of atomic research. Scientific research of India has entered into depth in all cases, including space studies, drugs, atomic and fundamental research. Measures starting from 1/1016 meter to big ones of similar magnitude are in the purview of scientific and technological research in India. This span of expansion in research has been in atomic energy, drugs, space science, nature study, physiology and other fields. An extensive advance has been made in the case of China too. In China, there has been an assemblage of technologies in different countries. There are two reasons behind this: Cheap labour and the rule and authority of a party devoid of democracy. As a result, companies throng in Chinese markets and can sell these commodities. The market is big, so companies become happy if they can manufacture commodities here as well as sell them here. Ordinarily, there is no inconvenience for them if their amount and/or share of the profit remains unhampered. Cheap labour and government patronage make the progress of the companies feasible. The main provision for this progress of China has come from outside.

China and India

China's high-tech firms are cheap; they are also not very Chinese. None on the top, by 2005 revenues, was native born. Foreign firms owned by one fifth of the assets in ICT(Information and Communication Technology) sector in 2004, accounted for his lion's share of the experts, provided sixteen percent of the employment and claimed twenty percent of the earnings. The wages they pay stay in China; as do whatever profits they reinvest.Buttheir know how stems from overseas… But the transitions of the economy from net importer of technology-intensive goods to net exports is likely to take many decades.

(Special Report on Technology 2007, 6)

The line of technology between China and India is different. The technological progress of India has come through its own power and ability, but for China, that has been possible through the idea and processes imported from outside. Behind Indian ideas and the application of technology, its tradition was active. Elements of extensive and pervasive technology exist right in the tradition of India. These technological elements are lying scattered in different sources at different times. At the times of the Ramayana and the *Mahabharata*, at the time of Harappa and Mohenjo-Daro and also at later historical times, technology has advanced sometimes in theory, sometimes in application and sometimes in both ways.

The lofty ideas and thoughts of space science and their application existing in Indian tradition are not rare; the art and science of the arrangements therein is not accessible even to modern technology. Modern technology will have to cross even a longer distance to create something parallel to the wonderful technology of that time. Progress during the periods after the wars of the *Mahabharata* and the Ramayana are wonderful contributions of technology. The plane used by Ravana was completely controlled. It not only crossed a small distance and through a small height, but it has crossed the sea to go on the other side. Sea has been crossed by plane many times; war has been conducted from the plane. On his way back after the elopement of Sita, Ravana was obstructed by Jatayu. There was a battle, and it was in the air. A powerful weapon for destruction as Brahmastra, the divine missile, has not yet been prepared. The atomic bomb is devastating, but the devastating capacity of Bramastra is not only many times an atomic bomb, but it has got some peculiarity of its own. Bramastra may be devastating for a particular object, field and time. Just as Bramastra can be applied in special cases, the ingredients of some weapons also deserve special significance. Weapons used by Arjuna have such novelty and excellence as kindred, which is hardly possible. Such is the case not only in the science of warfare but also in medical science. Revival of Laksmana after being attacked by the deadly missile of Meghnada (Saktisela) had been by the grace of the mountain picked up by Sri Hunumana in which was hidden Visalyakarani, the magic drug to give back life.

Influence of Customers

Living and the viewpoint of living of the consumers or buyers are connected with the advancement of technology. 'Amar Bhide, an economist at Columbia University, goes so far as to say that an economy's technological standing rests as much on its consumers as its producers. 'Venturesome and resourceful' customers provide a great spur to innovators, he says offering them quick feedback of their ideas, and a full deck of behaviors, habits and trends to learn from.'

(The Economist 2007, 16)

This has been especially applicable to India. All forms of possibilities are hidden in the open and democratic environment of India. The more exposed this possibility, the more shining will be the opening stage of economic management. So, new innovations in technology depend on commerce. To bring an object or subject to customers that is not to his liking is useless. So, directions of research are being determined on the basis of taste and choice of customers. What is liked by customers and which job is convenient to them come out as subjects of technology. Let us take an example. Female members of modern small families also are now connected with fields of work. So, they depend on others for domestic work. Their works have been easier by the grace of newer and newer technology. The firms have had new avenues of income. For example, easy dusting with vacuum cleaners instead of using common brooms, washing clothes in washing machines instead of using hands, using microvans to avoid cooking strains on standing long before ovens, etc. New varieties of these are coming out regularly. Each variety is bringer more convenience to men. As the firms are causing more and more convenience to men through different technological varieties, soaring their sales, expansion and profits.

Effect and Expansion of Technology

There are two aims of research after the newer revelation of technology: To find out such a newer element that would attract customers rapidly and to raise the quality of products existing for so long. Both of these are constantly infusing new ideas in the case of mobile telephony in India. The main function of mobile phones is the facility to communicate in any condition whatsoever, even while roaming. But now the customers of mobile phones are looking at what more facilities are available with the sets. For example, in the first state, the aim was to have pictures and the next was to have snaps and videos and register them. There was a requirement to record those pictures from mobile to laptops or computers, and at the demand of the customers, this was effected. Men are now having service of internet in their mobiles and are likely to have the advantage of computers on these mobiles. Arrangements are impending at the demands of the customers. Different companies are appearing with newer advantages and arrangements. As a result, as there are combined facilities to the customers and consumers also the companies enjoy advantages. Different unique arrangements appear for increasing the profit of the companies, and hand in hand with these, arrangements are moving in the stages of exposure and invasion of technology.

According to Professor Robert Jensen of Harvard University: 'The tighter match between demand and simply rained their (Producers) profits by 133 percent a day and reduce the price by 4%.'

(The Economist, Jensen, 2007, 19)

According to Leonard Waver of London Business School: 'Mobile phones can have a disceribile effect on national output. If India were typical of the developing countries, the spread of mobile in the year to March might add about half a percentage point to India's rate of growth.'

(The Economist, Waver, 2007, 20)

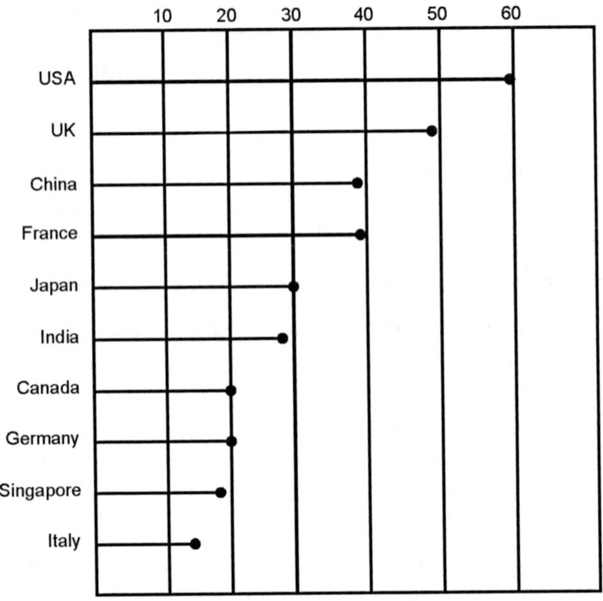

Source: UNCTAD Survey of Big R & D Spenders)

Technological research is advancing speedily in India. Until now, its effect on national income has been rather scanty. In respect of possibility, it occupies the sixth position in the world. Different industrial and manufacturing organisations in India have been engaged in research attempts. So long as it was in the hands of the government, now research has increased to a great extent in non-government circles too. There has especially been a trend of research in information technology and the telecom industry. Two main effects may be noticed in the line of research that has grown in India: Research for all and research for a portion. The theories of mathematics formulated at the time of the great masters Aryabhatta and Brahmagupta have taken shape in later stages. Now time is coming to achieve the ultimate shape of that attempt.

Kautilya's Opinion

If the distribution of subjects in Kautilya's *Arthashastra* is noticed, it will be found that he has supplied provisions of thoughts for technology—contemporary and new. Firstly, Kautilya's proposal for the application of weapon technics has a special type of endeavour in them. The endeavour is always to have new equipments and processes of war. So, new equipments are also required in modes, subjects and sequences of administration of a state. In the financial production system, Kautilya, on one side, wanted improved agriculture, and on the other side, wanted, besides agriculture, industry allied with agriculture. In Kautilya's time, despite technological attempts being multipurpose, the blooming of technology had remained limited within industries connected with that agriculture. In the case of natural calamity and war and other man-made calamities for confrontation, Kautilya laid stress on new ideas and new methods of facing those confrontations. In the case of cattle farming, which Kautilya had mentioned, besides recommending building up of suitable background for cattle farming, he also liked to have more developed technics for cattle farming. Kautilya wanted newer incitation of the skill of application in almost all of the industries and possibilities of industries that existed at that time and of technologies applied therein. The main proposition of Kautilya's economic theory is an attempt of coordination between agricultural produce and non-agricultural commodities. Kautilya thought of other types of works, such as small cottage industries, production of articles of daily use, production of articles that may be used for war and purpose in lands where cropping is not good or where there is no cropping at all. Taking steps mainly for more improved agricultural technic and endeavouring for a greater amount of produce have been recommended for lands where copping is good. Emphasis has been made on methods of application and methods of production as well for enhancing the excellence of cottage industries. If the excellence in methods of application and production is accomplished, then production would increase, sales would enhance and the customers would be inspired to a greater extent. Besides agriculture, cattle farming and cottage industry, there are forest-oriented industries. Kautilya created interest regarding the production in these forest-oriented industries. How such industries may be made more prosperous and how people may be more benefited by the application of such methods was Kautilya's subject of consideration.

The practice of whole and fractions was made in mathematics in later periods. The background of the practice of this whole and fraction is also the background of Kautilya's *Arthashastra*. All would enter into the sphere of activities with Vedic learning and knowledge of the Absolute self. Agriculture, industry, trade and royal duties—all would be accomplished in the background of Vedic learning and knowledge of the Absolute self. The same line, that is, the practice of whole and fraction, is very useful behind the rise of technologies of modern India.

66

Removal of Corruption

Virulance of Corruption

There is violent commotion throughout the world with corruption. Economic progress is frustrated due to corruption—much proof is not necessary to believe this. It is corruption that has made the creation, rearing and distribution of all wealth rather miserable. Virulence of corruption is noticed in the arrangements that are required for the creation, rearing and distribution of wealth among the public. Where is a shortage of supply compared to necessity, there is corruption. There are many methods to judge the sources of corruption. All these processes have admitted the generation and position of corruption centred on men. These are various areas of corruption. Corruption may spread through money, wealth, power connection and the like. Though the effect of corruption falls integratively on all management, it casts a special effect on spreading influence. The effects of corruption are different in these cases. The effectors of corruption on the subjects of mass satisfaction and mass consumption cause a disaster in both ways. It is disastrous in cases of state, society and individuals too. Corruption is one type of disaster-generating disease, which is infectious. If corruption is generated in one place, it quickly spreads to other places. The effect of this disease is so dangerous that it can be compared with cancer. Just like cancer, corruption also quickly swallows all provisions, wealth and possibilities of life and gradually devours up the whole life. It approaches and devours anything and everything. It brings an end to the possibilities one by one and leaves life utterly ruined. The virulence of corruption also brings all possibilities of life to the verge of ruination. Corruption has spread everywhere, such as in society, organisation, individual life, state, religion, practice and application of knowledge, administration, serving, production, distribution, purchase, sale, mutual exchange, etc. The root of corruption sometimes is in one's heart and sometimes of many. The network of corruption spreads from the heart of an individual and gradually pervades in many or aggregate. The state and society—all become corrupted.

Definition of Corruption

In order to realise corruption correctly, its definition is required. The primary definition of corruption is the use of the ability of the aggregate or of power obtained from the aggregate for the facility and profit of an individual. Some international organisations of the present have got themselves busy with corruption. They have provided a definition of corruption. Transparency International (or TI) has taken the leading role here. Year after year, TI has studied the situations of all countries and has been preparing a periodic table for almost all countries. From this periodic table, one can have an account of which country how much corrupted. TI has classified corruption into two groups: Constitutional corruption and unconstitutional corruption. Constitutional corruption is a type of bribe that ends in a lawfully good action. Unconstitutional corruption comprises such actions that include taking bribes for actions that have no lawful significance. Constitutional corruption is very harmful and far-reaching. At the same time, unconstitutional corruption is equally harmful. The first one is disastrous for the integrative life, while the second one is for an individual. Let's discuss an amazing example of constitutional corruption. Vice chancellors of different universities take with them different types of gifts to the institutions for granting funds so that such grants are available for respective universities. These presents are intended to obtain bigger grants or a bigger portion of receivable funds for one's own institution quite lawfully. Besides, international experts have specified the propensity of providing this or that in other ways to fulfil the objects. They have mentioned that these things happen in the case of public sector institutions too. Higher-ranking officials of the public sector are equally eager for the high-ranking officer of the controlling authority to gain government patronage in better ways. The object is to purchase patronage with bribes. TI has mentioned all fields in police service and other organisations, including different government, semi-government or non-government organisations. TI has noticed the propensity of taking and giving bribes in India for personal promotion, different posts and different types of opportunities and advantages. They said that the virulence of corruption is greater where subsidy is concerned. Corruption influences all working programmes and government schemes through rural development, slum development, development of living standards, health programmes, social reformation programmes, etc.. TI has presented different measures of corruption in government management. There are many shameful factors in it. For example, if ten rupees are sanctioned from the government fund for rural development, the net expense is only four rupees. That is, six rupees are manipulated midway. Besides government establishment, there are many serious allegations against other mentionable institutions for taking bribes. Among them are the judiciary, people's representatives (of village, state and country level) and even persons occupying topmost positions. Even previously convicted persons have been included in the ministry. There are many allegations of corruption against the topmost helmspersons of the state. Virulence of corruption is everywhere. These gradually spread from a stage and become pervasive. TI everywhere is propounded of open principles. The basic proposition here is to take a decision and make that decision effective to expose all of the factors within the decision without any prejudice. The object is to make all these factors perspective to all. As a result of this exposure, the action that has been possible is that the factors of the decision have been known to all. And all these decisions and methods of applications thereof would come to the notice of all. Thus, the propensity of men to be associated with the decision and action thereof increases. That is why TI has aimed to classify the eagerness for the removal of corruption into different classes: Administrative, commercial, social, political, economic, cultural, religious, integrative and the like. The principle taken in each is what provision and wealth are required behind the management and how they are provided and used. It would also be decided what would be the basis of the provision and use of these. That is, the steps TI has taken and the advice it has given to remove corruption through the application of some rules and means after studying the policy, object and aims of the organisation have been the last word for the whole world. All are thinking of abiding by these. The endeavours taken from 1993 to the present comprise, on principle, making chief organisation of industry, commerce, society and state earnest for rising against corruption. There should be a depiction of rules for removing corruption and a foundation of sequence and management for action. The meaning of establishment of sequence and management of action means there should remain programmes of proper procurement, conservation and distribution of the wealth, possibility and capability stored in those cases. TI has realised that unless the effect of corruption cannot be lessened, the advancement of organisation, society and state is not possible. The principle taken by TI for organisation, society and the state has been called in their language. Fighting it (corruption) is a step-by-step project-by-project process. Experience is to be gathered from different levels of society, and on the basis of that, vigilance is to be kept on all the new programmes and endeavours of work. As a result of this and as a consequence of this experience, a light would be thrown on new management, and the attempt would be to reform the same. Without going into detailed discussion and deep enquiry about the source of corruption, they have judged the place among different countries and organisations on the basis of virulence of corruption, intensity of corruption and influence of corruption, that is, in short, on the basis of corruption itself. TI has informed that there are four types of virulence of corruption. Its effect primarily falls on individuals and integratively on society, state and civilisation or society, state and civilisation. As a result of corruption, determinant comes down upon political, economic, social and environmental fields. If politics falls into the group of corruption, devastation comes down upon the whole state management. If a political person and leadership be confined in corruption, its effect falls upon nearly all of the fields of a state. Political decisions influence nearly all parts of a state. Such influence extends to kitchens, restaurants, reading tables, schools, colleges, universities, markets, industries, economic management and even individuals themselves. That is why purity is the most important attribute while making and implementing a political decision. A great danger will befall a state if corruption intrudes in making and implementing political decisions. TI has found through judgements that if corruption prevails in making and implementing political decisions, its effect would be reflected in all principles and processes of the state. That is why politics should be free from corruption. If politics become free from corruption, its effect first falls on the administration and management of states. Influence on administration and state management, in turn, always becomes influential for economic management. Factors of administration and state management that have become important have all of the ingredients of purity. Economists have appealed to infrastructural change of state and mentalities of individuals for the ingredients of purity. A state, through infrastructural changes, will attempt to bring about changes in state management in different ways and, through this, make every man free from corruption and make the system, as a whole, free from corruption. Methods taken by TI include the creation of accountability. The more this accountability is created in political decisions and processes, the more different enterprises would be relieved of the influence of corruption. Ways resorted to by different economists include gradual reforming of political processes to be relieved of the structural problems existing in them. It would amount to removing the elements of problems and corruption from the structure through a gradual reformation of the same.

Kautilya's Way

Kautilya has studied the subject from its basic position. He found that without basic change, corruption-free economic management cannot be built up only by structural change. The difference brought about by structural changes is rather external. A man who is dishonest by heart would turn out to be dishonest in any structure whatsoever. A dishonest man quickly turns an honest structure into a dishonest one. A dishonest man very quickly extends the disease of his dishonesty. That is, they become the creator of many dishonest men. A dishonest man can move along a creative path by which they can control a good situation and induce rotting in it. Management can be irrespective of man. Rather these always depend on men. An honest man can attract many by their honesty, and a dishonest man can attract many men into dishonest activities. So, Kautilya wanted a basic change. Change is required in the minds, hearts and character of men. Getting the link from such a change, a propensity comes into men for building up a pure structure. At the root of an honest and pure structure, there is always an honest and pure mind and character. An honest and pure mind and character can gradually build up an honest and pure structure. At the same time, these can transpose honest and pure sensations in many persons. As a result, honesty always stays in state, society, trade and commerce, education, industry, culture, life of an individual, life of the aggregate and so on. Upanisadic hermit uttered: 'Ishall speak what is true, I shall speak the truth.' A man seated in truth and spiritual truth actually resides within hearts, resides in a goodly atmosphere. Knowledge has bloomed in them. He observes a vow.

His spiritual practice is not for fulfilling his desire for anything. Here, there is only submission, no desire for acceptance.

Kautilya has, first of all, said of assiduous study of the Vedic learning, and the significance of this is that truth is seated in honesty. A large-hearted man is seated in truth. Within a man seated in truth and spiritual truth would constantly bloom truth and purity. He is such a man who, at every instant, would think of truth and, as a result, would be fully absorbed in truth. Such persons are required to have an open mind and open conscience within themselves. They would not work for their own interest. Also, they would not be indifferent to their own interest. They would work properly, that is, as per requirements. They would not apply power, ability and opportunity to fulfil their own interest. Their life and ability would be dedicated to all or many. The theory of satisfying the interest of one's own self has created problems and dangers. The root of corruption is within the propensity grown at the centre of civilisation for satisfying self-interest. Men who fail to satisfy self-interest on a straight path like to satisfy that interest through a crooked path. That is why they move towards corruption. These men of impure character like to realise their own facilities from others or are paying attention to fulfilling individual interests through individual management. Had Kautilya's path been followed, this danger would have been nipped in the bud. Men firm in religion and spirituality are above corruption.

67

Kautilya's Solution to the Impending Economic Disaster of China

Position of China

Good results of the economic management of China are now on every lip. Probability in China is now resounded everywhere. But China is now on the verge of a dreadful economic explosion. Almost all of the published information continues to describe the economic rise of China in detail. All raises are judged in the light of that of China. This judgement is in terms of how success in economic management is expressed statistically. Success in economic management may be expressed in different ways. For example, in the prescription of the World Bank, there are accounts of integrative progress and special progress. In order to apprehend the integrative progress, one has to know the total production in the country, the increase in the rate of total production, the production in different cases and the rate thereof and the different types of influences on economic management, especially price-hike, rate of interest and the influence of government, principle and international management—all of these influence the account of integrative progress. There is another measure to understand progress, and that is the people. What type of living is accepted by the people, and how have the sensation and flavor of financial flow reached the people—these influence the account of progress the most. There is a human development index to understand the standard of living of the people. If this index also increases gradually, the progress of individuals is going on with integrative progress. Documents on many subjects that are of utmost necessity for a higher standard of living are supplied in the human development index. These are primary health, pure potable water, proper drainage system, balance between the life and death rates, effects of pure air, etc. Different types of information related to the economy of China are with almost all of the world's organisations. Nearly all of the information support the economic blooming of China. Rate of such progress in industrial production, overall national production, progress in almost all cases of financial fields have suppressed all. As the population of China is the largest, it has surpassed all in financial fields because profuse money flows to China from almost all developed countries of the world. Every country is eager to invest in China. Everyone expects that the best result would be obtained from investment in China. Direct foreign investment is the highest in China, so much so that it has exceeded all other such cases with other countries. China is now not only an economic power of the first row but now is also eager to compare itself with the greatest in the world. The economic measure of China is now second in the world—next to only America. Many big manufacturing concerns of America have now extended their production in China. Factually, nearly all developed countries, including Japan, Germany, England, France and Canada, have come to the Chinese market hand in hand with America. The situation is so favourable towards China that if China extends its hand to any production, distribution and service system, it becomes an object of envy, anxiety and keen competition to all. There was a time when these centres of power were admitted into the world. In the eighties and nineties, America, Europe and Japan were recognised by all as the trio of power- centres. Now, replacing Japan, China has appeared at one corner of the power-triangle. All the top economists of the world opine that now there are three special economic powers in the world: America, the European Union and China. All these are equal in financial power, dominance and domain. China has realised well that this dominance in the economic field is needed in other directions and in other ways as well. The advancement of China is especially recognised in science and technology.

Two Chinas

But only sometime back, the disaster of distant thunder was voiced by the Chinese President. In an open address at the Party Congress of the Communist Party of China, President Hu Jintao and Premier Wen Jiabao brought forth lists of development, progress and success and, at the same time, expressed the possibilities of disasters. Mr

Hu said that China would soon rise to the top of prosperity. China sent human beings to space four years ago, and they are all prepared to leave for the moon. In military power, China had acquired the power to make all amazed. But, the danger had been approaching from inside.

Hu cited two burning problems:

- Abnormal increase of inequality between the rich and the poor in town areas and
- Lack of exposition of an open mind and open voice due to internal democracy.

The condition of the farmers and rural agricultural workers in China when Deng Xiaoping started his cultural revolution about thirty years ago from the rural areas of China was now extremely precious. Instead of the right to land, the right to crops has practically turned the farmers into land labourers. In 1989, millions of students and youths thronged Tiananmen Square in Beijing with demands of assurance of democracy and more improved living. Rural farmers and land labourers also joined this agitation with demands for a minimum standard of living. Chinese government demolished a few thousand men with military tanks. The moving tanks just jumped upon the unarmed public from all sides of Tiananmen Square and crushed them. Communist Party and the Government of China understood from this incident that if urban agitation were managed, there would be relief. The ability and leadership required to organise the rural farmers and land labourers would never be available because such likelihood would be crushed at the very beginning. That is why the greatest importance is attributed to educated urban youths in all the decisions and management. Importance and coordination have been given to these educated youths of urban areas. For the last one and a half decades, they have quite prospered. From them have come many enterprising and endeavouring youths who have set up big companies or organisations. They are importing different products from abroad. A large portion of them are engaged in different activities. As a result, the availability of the world market for Chinese products is gradually expanding. Middle-class people and youths of China, having had internet and mobile in their hands, are themselves trying to understand the real taste of democracy and liberty. On the other hand, the rural farmers and scantily educated persons are being hurt from all sides. They have been quite accustomed to corruption. Health service to them is of a very low standard. The majority of people have been getting minimum education—in name only. However, they have no coordination among themselves. There is but very little opportunity for being organised.

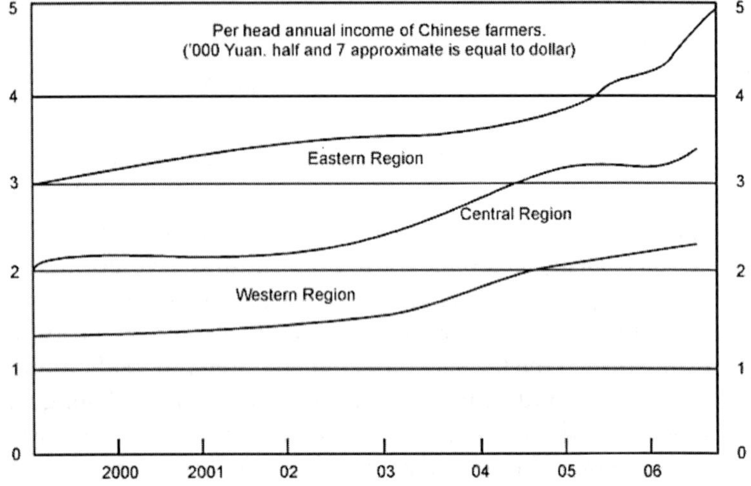

Figure 1: Differences in the incomes of Chinese farmers from different regions.

Social Classification of China

About sixty percent of the population of China still lives in villages. The agricultural measure is now only twelve percent of natural production. But even in 1990 and immediately after that, it was somewhat greater than twenty-five percent. In 1990, the Chinese government used eight to eleven of national investment in the case of agriculture. But now, it has reduced to only seven to four percent. Mr. Hu tried to pay attention to some factors critical in the health insurance for the farmers. But the minimum premium for health insurance is fifteen Yuan. The minimum daily income of a land labourer is seven and a half Yuan, that is, nearly one dollar. In Indian currency, its value is less than forty rupees. It is not so that one would earn that amount by only having the ability to work daily. The job is available only on eighty percent of the days, that is, even less than ten months a year. During the rest of the period, the probability of a job is uncertain, mostly unavailable. There is an arrangement to supply books to the boys and girls of schools free of cost. But still, in innumerable rural schools, there are students, buildings and classes, but chairs are lacking. Some students take their tests on benches, and some are on the floor. *The Economist* of London entered into some rural schools of some western states of China and, after a long investigation, has brought to light startling news and photos. The 13 October 2007 edition of *The Economic* has published a vivid description of the same. The peculiarity of the health Insurance planned by Mr. Hu is that its good effect is beyond the range of anyone's capability. An example may be cited. If a person working in Luochuan whose residence is in the village nearly 300 km away falls into an accident, they themselves would have to bear the cost of the treatment. This is so because the insurance is applicable in the case of a village only. Fifteen Yuan, that is, their two day's income that they have paid as a premium, is a huge expense on their part. Despite that, the majority of workers have no opportunity to realise that amount. Recently, Shenzhen University has conducted a study on the rural education system with a sample of some regions and published the reports thereof. This report showed that the education systems followed by President Hu have but mixed effects. For example, eighty percent of students getting books free of cost as some pocket money instead of being engaged in a job of a daily wage of 10 Yuan per day will remain contented. But school education has recently been wiped out. There are classes, teachers and students, but the standard of education has come to a low ebb.

Li Rui, former secretary of Mao Zedong, voiced a note of warning in the latest issue of Yanhuang Chunaquic, a reputed monthly magazine of Beijing, and wrote, 'Looming Chaos imminent in China unless it embrace democracy'. China is now divided into two parts. The first part may be named 'China of US Variety' and the second 'China of its own variety'. We know and can hear the first part. It centres in big cities and port cities, like Shanghai, Shen Zhen, Beijing, etc. This is going on to swell up the financial fate of forty percent of the population of China. And 'China of its own variety' has got the charge of sixty percent of the population. They are villagers, farmers, peasants and agricultural labourers. The first variety of China resembles America to a great extent. It is even more Americanised than America. The people there ride big cars, move about foreign and abroad, avail higher education, first-class health schemes and large incomes. And the second variety of China spends days in a measured way. They are destined to walk on foot or travel by cycle. They send their wards to schools, sign on papers to the effect that they have got everything and yield to everything, that is, being deprived of two-thirds of the amenities. They have been enduring for six decades. Now, among them too, mobile phones and the internet have spread. The information does not remain stagnant. It has spread far. Now the western region is feeling that they are lagging extremely behind. Besides, they have come to understand the baselessness of the statistic used to elucidate their progress. For quite sometime, agitations are being observed in rural areas. In all the states of western and central regions, men are becoming organised day by day. Citing the Himalayan inequality between urban and rural areas of China, *The Economist* of London wrote an editorial (13 October 2007) titled 'China, Beware! The Country's Rulers care too much for their own welfare and too little about the rural peasants'. The construction of the editorial is: 'The leaders meet, the cities grow, the peasants are left behind.' The article has described, in detail, the villages and rural peasants of China.

Tears in the Eyes of the Poor

The direction towards which the situation of China is moving might be described as a widely devastating ending. The reason behind this devastating ending is the extensive division in basic living. The situation in many places has been of great concern. In a party congress held recently, not only the president and the premier but others were also in favour of discussing the matters of democracy and economic equality. The matter of democracy and reducing economic inequality is now a matter of discussion for all in the party. Present steersmen are trying to draw the attention of all to a thing that is the economic competition with America and victory therein. The main factor is continuously increasing inequality and the right to free citizenship. The political situation of China is controlled by the communist party. If any external voice rings, the punishment of fate is rained down. An eminent Chinese scholar has written: 'In recent years China's Communist Party has been to pay attention to a deep malaise in the countryside: The prohibitive cost of health care and education for the rural poor mounting debtsat the lowest levels of government, bloated bureaucracy and a growing wealth gap between rural and urban areas. Riots have become common, fueled by the attempts of avaricious governments to raise money by selling farmers land (a big edition of Singur and Nandigram). Incomes may have been rising, butso has dissatisfaction. In some parts, of China, move than sixty percent of those in dire poverty have been driven there by medical expenses. And for many rural residents the higher level of schooling are becoming unaffordable...'

(The Economist 2007, 27)

Solution by Kautilya

The root of the problem in China rests on the theory of the dictatorship of the communist party. However extensive the progress in urban areas, villages would like to have their share. Snatching agricultural land for industry is a very common practice in China. Any company would get land of their choice, whatever region it may be in. It is possible in consideration of the development and financial progress of the urban region. In economic management, it is not possible for farmers there to jump into movements, like Singur or Nandigram, because the dagger is always down to stop the contending voice.

The long-term benefits of China would be possible if the leaders of the Chinese Communist Party were a bit conversant of Kautilya's *Arthashastra*. First of all, a change in outlook is necessary. The main point of the outlook Kautilya has put forth is: 'people's pleasure in the pleasure of the leader or the state'. Kautilya wanted that they would have to learn the opinion held by the people, the idea people put stress on. For this, the king's duty was to set out in disguise within the people in regular intervals. As a result, the king would learn what contexts are going on in markets, on roads and so on, and from this, the duty of the king would come out. The king would get information from the Management Information System (MIS), so they would know the state of affairs from their personal sample test. Through these influences, the disaster may be resisted. As a result, upward movement and sidewise extension of financial progress might be possible. Kautilya liked the king's character to be clean and pure. They would, first of all, want to look after the man who is the most problem-stricken. As a result, the flow of inequality is bound to be slow. If the flow of inequality initially begins to be reduced in the end, it might get a balance in the surrounding. This would be sure to bring about progress in the world. There would then be no inequality between one part of the country and another, one field of an organisation and another or one department and another. To resist Chinese devastation, the leadership might take resort to Kautilya.

68

Nature of Economic Slump and its Solution

Why Slump?

The reason behind the economic slump may be many folds, sometimes along an abnormal way and sometimes normal. If there is a continuous downfall of economic condition for a considerable period, if production reduces, sale decreases, work reduces, money becomes devalued, unemployment increases, price becomes high and the standard of living becomes lowered, the integrity of all the indices of economic management become unfavourable—that is the beginning of this situation. If this condition prevails for long, for a few months, it is called an economic slump.

'A Significant decline in economic activity spread across the economy lasting more than a few month, normally visible in real GDP, real income, employment, industrial production and wholesale-retail sales.' US National Bureau of Economic Research (NBER) has furnished this definition of an economic slump. As an economic slump has been found in America. Economists have said a lot about the slump. America's condition at present is as follows: The unemployment rate increased to 5.1% in April 2008. In March 2008, 98,000 men in non-government fields lost their jobs. The chairman of the Federal Reserve of America said to the American Congress Committee on April 2008, 'Output was unlikely to grow much, if at all, over the first half of 2008 and could even contract slightly'. That is, in this case, it is not only that the rate of production has decreased, but it seems to be decreasing for a long time. Thus, a question arises: How long would this reduction of production, increases in unemployment and reverse flow of all economic indices continue? During the period of economic downturn in America because of housing finance crisis, more than 80,000 men have been thrown out of employment. When the keenness of the slump increases, the number might even reach 1,50,000–2,00,000. On 9 April 2008, I.M.F.R. informed the World Economic Fund that the GDP of America would begin to decrease and might reach as low as 0.7%. But it is IMF who informed three months ago that this would continuously increase at the rate of 0.9% at least. The picture presented by IMF showed an analysis that the economic situation of America would remain dull even in 2009. Such a situation befell America in 1990–91 and then in 2001. The consequence of that did not appear as a breakdown in the economic situation. On these two occasions, the economic slump partly prevailed for eight to nine months in the American economic system. Four months passed in the meantime. The economic slump still continued. Warren Buffett, eminent moneyed man exponent of economics and chief executive officer of Berkshire, did not think the economic situation to be trouble or impending trouble at all. At the beginning of April 2008, he said in a meeting of a group of MBA students of Wharton Business School of Pennsylvania University that there are many possibilities in this declining situation of America. The possibility of crossing over this situation is very bright. Factually, this situation would bring great changes in a good number of things.

Which Slump?

Warren Buffett remarked: 'I mean, you don't want a capital market that function perfectly if you've in my business. People continue to do foolish things no matter what the regulation is, and they always will. ...I read all day, we put $500 million in Petro China – all I did was read the annual report – last year Break shine sold the Petro China shares, which has acquired five years earlier $4 billion.'

(Buffet 2008, 26)

Warren Buffett and kindred fellows who can invest through proper judgement and research are getting enormous profits. One of the main reasons for the situation that has now approached America resembles a slump is that it is mortgaged. A semi-government organisation named the Office of Federal Housing Enterprise Oversight (OFHEO) is now looking after about seventy percent of mortgage funds. All had made a big and extensive endeavour to give credit at a higher rate to those who were not entitled to get credit through the subprime rate. Now it is found that many of them have no enterprise to pay off the loan. The condition of those who had situations in favour of paying off debts is now on the decline. As a result, a very big amount of debt has remained unrealised, the amount of home loans is continuously increasing and there is a shortage of new debt too. Many people in America are leaving big residences to shift to smaller ones.

> It is very very hard to regulate when you get into very complex instruments where you've got hundreds of counter parts. The counterparty behavior and risk was a big part of why the Treasury and the Fedfelt that they had to remove in over a weekend at Bear Stearns. And I think that they were right to do it, incidentally.
>
> (Ibid., 27)

Variables in the Market

There are many factors that influence the things in a market. A market is formed on the basis of the total supply of the market, the total sale and their value and standard. The total price of houses, buildings and different types of infrastructures made of bricks, wood and concrete in America is now about twenty trillion dollars. Of these, the amount of eleven trillion dollars is under a mortgage. There is a scheme of investment of a big amount of money in this mortgage fund. Such a situation arose in 2006 too. At that time, 330 billion dollars had been invested in that fund. In the present occasion, too, Federel is going to take the procedure, but the amount in the present occasion is 150 billion dollars. All that occurred in economic fields interactively are not reflected in the share market. What happened in the past is fully known here, but what would happen in the future cannot be known. It is to be apprehended. Besides, in a share market, one invests in a certain way, the other in another way and the rest invest in still different ways. Everyone proceeds depending on individual tests, desire, longing and aim.

At the root of the housing and real estate problems in America was the bluster of housing loans. In this bluster, those who are not eligible to get a loan have been burdened with a loan. The propensity of taking a loan had gone so far that almost forty percent of the mortgage came under this scheme. Now, the problem has come out. Those who took houses are now quite incapable of retaining the same. There now has been a rush to give up the houses. Of course, very recently, this propensity has somewhat ceased. The American government has arranged a special package of up to 200 billion dollars through which those mortgages have had a supply of a big amount of money so that they would be enlivened again. Other problems got associated with this issue, like big prices, hikes in gas and petrol, ncreases in the cost of labour in non-government enterprises and decline in the field of employment. Instead of resisting the gradual devaluation of the dollar, the American government has taken the same as a weapon for compensation in different ways from the perspective of loss in other fields. By this, a big slide occurred on one side in a straight way, increasing the equation of the value of dollars. One thing must be mentioned here. Due to the devaluation of the dollar, the sale of foreign goods in the American market has begun to decline, and the path of sale of American goods in the world market is being opened. During the last three decades, American companies went to China owing to cheap workers and other cheap elements. However, the propensity of carrying some technology there manufacturing goods and buying the same at home and abroad is now facing a hard challenge. Under the effects of political claims on the occasion of the election of the president on one side and on the other economic claims for removing financial problems, the dollar is now proceeding very slowly to spread the disaster of its own country to some other countries, including China. India does not come into this sphere because the sphere has been farmed with the internal economic factors of those countries dependent upon America. Some again had put a question mark on the economic sovereignty of America. Housing crises in America have taught the economic experts of the other countries to think afresh.

American Methods

A study in *The Economist* (12 April 2008) stated: 'Fannie Mac and Fredric Mac, America's Government backed mortgage behemoths will fill part of that whole the Brush administration recently announced changes to these where institution's capital rules, to let them by up to an extra 200 Bellion of mortgages. Political momentum is also building up to an extra 200 billion of mortgages. Political momentum is also building up to prevent a surge of fore closures ...

Despite these hopefulsigns, house-prices will continue to fall this year. Worse house-price deflation is only the first elements of quadrupole whammy that is thumping American consumers. The other three elements are,tougher credit conditions; a deteriorating labour market and high commodity prices pushing up the cost of fuel and food.'

(The Economist 2008, 80)

'... After five years of breakneck growth, a more sedate global expansion will be no bad thing; it would damper inflationary pressures in the emerging world, and weak domestic demand should shrink America's gaping external deficit – Already down from above 6% of GDP to below 5% of GDP...'

(Ibid., 13)

The Past of the Slump

American economic reforms have run fast for five decades. If slackness runs for five months, what would be the harm? The fact is, they have spread the effect of this economic slump in other countries. In the meantime, inflation is rapidly increasing in China, has touched Europe and is spreading in India. Of course, in the meantime, America has decreased its deficit in the outer world to a great extent. The countries dependent on America but engaged in a trade war would have the fate of being struck with the partial slump of America.

If we go to the root of this problem and judge, it would be found that this consequence is the outcome of the homeward attitude of the Americans—home sweet home. This attitude has gained ground in America. The families have pushed luxury to such an extent that if their income is hundred rupees, then they would spend five rupees towards eating, fifteen rupees on insurance premiums, thirty to forty rupees on house-EMI and the rest would go for paying taxes and other expenditures. Everybody takes a house on a mortgage. The same pattern of houses is for all. The house that belongs to someone today may not be to them tomorrow; the mortgage company might evict them if the premium remains unpaid, and then a small apartment would be their residence. They look down upon apartments as the house has been costly enough to make one pauper. The solution to the slump lies in the base of frugality as recommended in the economic prescription of Kautilya. If it is in agreement only with income, then it would be permanent. For this, a sense of temperance is essential. Temperance in consumption is a big obstruction against a slump.

69

The Act of Economic Adjustment is Worthy of Market

Economic Adjustment

The market has its own urge and obligation for survival. If there is no government, but all parts and persons of the market can act properly, then it is quite possible to bring economic balance within a long period of time. Creation of economic balance through government patronage is quite impossible, except, of course, for some special cases. In order to set up economic balance presence of such factors is necessary for economic management that can manage the opposing situations and get them in favour. The act of maintaining the economic balance within the bounds of a certain country is to be done within the factors existing in the country itself. If there is pressure from an international situation, then the association of a reflexive force would be necessary. In creating and maintaining the economic balance, proper engrossment of that reflexive force should have to be timely. When the engrossment of the reflexive force would be in proper measure, then and only then would come the hour of balance. In modern times, there are a few basic problems in the creation of economic balance. The most worthy of mention among those are: Want of state leadership fitting for the establishment of integrative interest crossing the individual interest, the problem of liberating the national economic principles from international influence, gradual exposition and possible explosion of long accumulated pains in the economic management of the world.

It is not that the problems apply to a single country. These have had a wide circulation. Firstly, the attraction of power in the state leadership easily defeats the influence of conscience. Most of the methods applied for sticking to or ascending power or which forces are to be augmented through active support act opposite to the interest of society. As a result, there is a great influence of the state power on the economic interest of society. The stage of exposition of the power of the state gradually makes the state powerless and makes the split within the society more permanent. Society gets bifurcated and gradually moves forward, accepting the separation, and the wall of separation becomes more firm. Such step of the state leadership often creates a perspective of long-lived problems.

Local Arrangements

Apart from these, there is a foreign influence on national economic management. The foreign link in national economic management is mutual trade or exchange. Different companies from other powerful countries come to cast influence on the market and internal forces of the country. As a result, in those forces lies hidden the power of casting extreme influences. It is rather hard to be free from such influence. The main way to be free from these influences is to place the national economic management or civilisation, culture, mentality, tradition and wealth and move on. It makes it possible to accomplish overall blooming, keeping confidence in national wealth and possibilities. Tendency and mentality of consumption turn out to be the most essential among these. In order to be free from the tendency and mentality of consumption, the revival of the feeling of attachment to the country is required to be seated firmly on the culture and civilisation of the country. By this, the revived lives would be associated with the economic flow of the country in terms of nationalism. Inspiration and propensity to be associated with the field where there is inland affluence or speciality would be roused in men. A change in mentality is required to create a balance between demand and supply. The fields of change in mentality are: How the living would be; what the structure of the society would be; consciousness about which factors are more appropriate for life and which are less; and correct conceptions about one's own self and others, the conception of society, the conception of personal role in economic management. All these would grow from the link-line of personal belief, national tradition and sequence. The mortgage disaster about to break down on America and the way by which the regulative agencies can manage to overcome this and actually overcome it are to be specially highlighted. Very recently, the two biggest mortgage investment companies in America have come under strict surveillance from the American Congress, judiciary and security and exchange commission. These are Federal National Mortgage Association, briefly called Fannie Mac, and the Federal Home Mortgage Corporation, or Freddie Mac. The first one was established by the New Deal of Delano Roosevelt to resist the disaster of 1938, and the second one was established in 1968. Both of them are government-sponsored enterprises (GSE).

American Examples

The frightfulness of the disaster of 1938 went rather deep. Fannie Mac was formed for the wide disaster in the market of taking loans for building homes and for paying off the loan. It's function was to keep the supply of money for the mentionable organisations in the market of loan for houses of personal owner ship by the local or other banks. To keep the supply of money undeterred, Fannie Mac began to flow money from the American Treasury. Initially, its function was to arrange for loans at a low interest. As a result, the purchasers of houses would get money at low interest. In such arrangements of mortgage, a new marketing management was established. Through this management, the path of buying and selling houses opened in a specialised form. For these reasons, any man of any income may have a residence to stay in. Fannie Mac has brought greater speed in the rates of interest. But a fixed rate of interest is of many advantages for the buyers of houses. For thirty years since its inception, Finnie Mac incredibly rose to be an associate of the market. However, a disaster followed the Vietnam War. Lyndon B. Johnson, in 1968, denationalised Finnie Mac. As a result, the deficit in the national budget might be shown to be rather less. From that time, Fannie Mac moved forward along the path of gaining profit and enjoyed government favours, such as in the form of a discount on taxes, which proved to be beneficial to it. Again at the same time, this organisation remained lively in favour of the government under such circumstances to get rid of the probable monopolistic situation. American government set up the organisation named Freddie Mac. Freddie Mac came into action in 1970. At present, these two organisations jointly occupy ninety percent of the mortgage market in America. They are now occupying a mentionable position within Fortune 500. They rose to a stage of possessing wealth which was much higher than an average large size American Bank. Recently, a disparity of about 4.5 dollars has been noticed in the annual reports of these organisations. For this, the finance committee of the house might take stern measures.

In the meantime, a question has arisen—why would Finnie and Freddie not be nationalised? Of course, Hank Paulson, Treasury Secretary of the American government, firmly advanced in this respect. The crisis has almost come under control. To bring back the balance in the economic management of the country, Fannie and Freddie need to be brought under appropriate control. They have kept the profit earned by them limited in the service of the shareholders and themselves, and on the other side, the dangers of the load of these problems are being transported tactfully to China and other countries. As a result, the load of problems spreads out and appears in different forms—America has come out of its own danger to remain an unopposed power to itself by spreading the danger elsewhere. A study of the American Senate about this is worth mentioning:

Freddie and Fannie have changed the equation only slightly their importance lies in what their rescue says about the financial system. At Fannie and Freddie and shockingly at the investment banks- the profit were privatized but the risks were socialized.One Republican Senator complained that he thought he had woken up in Finance; Mr. Paulson was still right to intervene; the collapse of Fannie and Freddie would have been a catastrophe. But by not formally nationalizing them, he has let down taxpayers and would do the same deeply uncapitalist mistake the British Government initially made with Northern Rock, a failed mortgage bank it tried to prop up.

(Ibid., 11)

Ascension

In the course of discussion on the economic management of the modern world, Baney Cimbel wrote on the famous annual 500 companies of Fortune magazine and the economic management prevalent in perspective of them:

'Welcome to the new, preciously Bipularworld, while gross domestic product growth is cooling a bit in the emerging, markets, the results be still tremendous compared with the U.S. and much or Western Europe.The 54 developing markets surveyed by Global inside will post a 6.7% jump in real GDP this year down from 7.5% last year. 31 developed countries will grow an estimated 1.6%. The difference in growth rates represents largest spread between developed and developing markets....American consumers is still hungry, but the world consumer in varacious...'

(The Fortune 2008, 58)

An example of one side in economic management is cited. Its influence is everywhere. All attempts to reduce expenditure, this new management in new discovery would, by means of many walls, actually keep intact the economic development, pushing aside the advice of the European representatives.

Kautilya's *Arthashastra* has already given a sure solution in this regard. Self-dependent arrangements are to be constituted in different regions of the country within small financial limits. Dependence on the markets of other countries would get reduced. As a result, a balanced economic region would grow up.

70

Let the Nature of the State be set on Godly Nature

Theocratic State

Paths and attempts of administration in the world have been created for the welfare of mankind. One has to build up oneself to build up the needs of earthly requirements of social life. A child gets continuous support from their family, parents and elders right from childhood till they become fully grown through rearing and tending. The wealth of society and family is to hold the hands of a child firmly. Helping a child grow up is the responsibility of society and family. Similarly, the property of the state is to extend its coordinating and supporting hands among all people of the state. The duty of the state is to stand with greater effect by those who are socio-economically helpless or weakened. Besides, a greater necessity is to wind up the methods of working in life in order to bestow coordination in moving on in the way of life. The power of the truth of life is thus to be carried forward. Six different modes are to be accepted to augment this power of the truth of society, including alliance, idol, posture, transport, resort and duplicity. These modes are like those told by Vaisampayen, the hermit in the *Mahabharata* for associating endeavours with propensities of life. Kautilya has asserted in his *Arthashastra* that these six protective methods can constitute an index. Vasampayam, the hermit, got this way from the revelation of the protective management theory of the state, as stated in the *Mahabharata*. Kautilya has applied all these collectively in every case, right from foreign policy down to the cases of protection of the state. These primary qualities prevail everywhere in the world. But a special combination of these may build up a proposal for offering a consistent protective measure for life. The arrangements defined for the protection of life may become of primary confidence and help accept life for the liberation of living, now-living and consciousness.

Alliance

One has to move on the path of life through the diversities constituted by different types of external forces on the path of daily moves that influence life. This universe and nature have been created in the light of an expectation to exist in the form of a consistent idea. The most successful path for moving on the life is to be coordinated. Around us are thousands of ingredients, including those of nature. Dispute with natural ingredients has been accepted as a propensity of modernism. The propensity to conquer nature is now existing in modern lives. Space-expedition is just an attempt to bring out a special acquaintance to a spontaneous move properly within space. In this stage, this expedition is not against nature; it is an attempt to dive deep into nature and maintain coordination with it. The venture to bring particular fields of space under the control of man in a spontaneous co-existence and alliance. Alliance has been natural in every stage of life. This path of 'becoming' in life is of coordination. The path other than coordination is conflict. Conflict is the acceptance of life only on the basis of the demands of life. Conflicts lack coordination between two opposite propensities. This lack of coordination gradually carries a consequence, and the consequence naturally becomes sized in a fury. Families of life and marching of life have in them a union of life with nature. This union has naturally opened a liberal expansion of life. This union often becomes permanent. Union is taking place in the practice of all forms of life. Expedition on the bosom of nature, afresh or in collaboration with nature, becomes disastrous. Disaster always becomes an impediment to the way of expansion of life. A distant future of growing of life and onward march is built up, and there is an eagerness to take the vow of an alliance of life.

The Lamp of Divine Will

Tatsabita be amrtatvamasubat. Agohyam. Yatarabantaetan.
Tatcit camas am asurasyabhaksanamekamsantam
Akrnutacaturbavm.

(Rigveda 1/110/3)

In that divine glow full of the nector of the Supreme Mother
We've always got the glow of the bounty of God.

That glowing entity with their glow has made thee glowing.
All sensations that come to life have been free.
Now the hour of thy offering has been ready.
For the teste in the constant flow of feelings.
Thou hast spread all around the grace of bounty of those feelings.
Thou hast made the lamp of your will glowing worded.

In the Gradual Blooming of the Divine Glow of Knowledge

Bisadvisamitaranitvenabadhati
Martasahsantauamrtatvamanasuh
Sodhanvanarbhabahsuracaksasah
Sam batsarasamaprcyantaritibhih

(Rigveda 1/110/4)

Thou hast given the power for transfusing supreme science in the World.
Hast given the lamp of life to be glowing always in the hands of time.
Profound wisdom of Thine has been transfused in the stage of divine science.
Divine wisdom of god has been filled with human knowledge.
Has experienced ascension in this life at the blooming glow.
Now time has come for spreading the divine wisdom of the supreme soul in the world.
Let the glow of wisdom spread in the practising route of expedition.
I've concealed that divine wisdom only to expose gradually.

Be Thou Pervaded in Life

Ksetramiba bi manuhtejanena.
Ekampatramrbhabaujehamaram
Upastutaupamamnadhamano
Amartesusrabaiccha mana

(Rigveda 1/110/5)

Gods, processors of divine wisdom, have woken up.
It is the time for human consciousness to be drenched.
Whenever there has been an exchange of receiver in transfusion of wisdom.

A flow of wisdom has set out with endless urges.
Human mind has liked divine wisdom to be on the earth.
And wisdom seers ring again constantly in wakefulness.
Human body will now hold divine wisdom in heart and soul.
Life now blossoms in the divine flow of feelings in every particle of existence.

By the Touch of Wisdom

AmanisamAntariksasysnrbhyah
SracebaDhrtamjuhabapambidmana Taranitva ye
pituhasyasasriran Rbhabobajamaruhandibo rajah
(Rigveda 1/110/6)

Grace of wisdom has appeared on this earth.
In this stage of practice, Thou hast bloomed.
Let the touch of this wisdom of Thine spread bar and wide.
Let it spread in that divine land, sky and space.
Let the glow of wisdom of Thine spread continuously in life.
In the stages of the search for it by the seers and blooming of the same.
Let newer wisdom come against all the offering paid.
Exposition of the stage has occurred in this stage of appearance of goods.

Knowledge of Idol

All of the big and small elements of this space are staying through alliance. The solar system that has been framed with the Sun at the centre has got its tie of basic relation set up. The law of gravitation has been devised to enunciate the very intimate relation and describe the distribution of the relation. The main message in this law of relation is alliance. One has to be engaged with the other in relation. One is to stay with the other through alliance. Not only human society but the propensities of life are also coordination and alliance. There is a significance of alliance between human society, animal society and plants. Coordination is required for co-existence. To move on along this line of coordination is civilisation.

To build up coordination, confidence and faith in each other and receptivity of a noble mind are required. The awakening of life is affected by this. The feeling of the Absolute self lies hidden in the heart, and so there is a vast eternal possibility in the noble feelings within man. Possibility rests and grows in moving along the sequences of life. This path of onward march may bloom naturally to strengthen the mutual coordination among all. For this, we need a sense of strife. This sense of strife tells how the presence of one gets engaged in intimate relations with the presence of the other.

In the Sphere of Succession

To be engaged in succession, a sense of idol form is required. The sense of form is to be framed in worldly views. Framing should be such that every form becomes one idol to be preserved in separateness. The sense of idol reveals external separateness among all. The main theme of external separateness is that every animal is separate from others. Animals are seized in the semblance their individual identities. These semblances individually are units. The deep significance of this is to be ascertained with the help of this form of succession. The deep significance of the interior is that every animal is separate from another. The relation that exists is the external identity is only a view of the moment and for the realisation of a moment. Realisation of a moment makes one understand, and that is the extremity there is a revelation of another type. Earthly relation wants to merge into the interests of one's own self or near and dear ones rather than all other things. Owing to selfishness under such circumstances, humans like to place their near and dear ones on one side and the whole world on the opposite side. As a result, a propensity of one type of narrow-mindedness blooms in the mind. If the outlook of the king is such narrow-minded, then the king would not be acceptable to the society or country.

On the other hand, the succession may be framed in such a way as the relation, free of all meanness, becomes spiritual. This relationship will grow if the small idol grows up correctly. Every idol of life is actually one of a god. This identity of the idol of god is to be judged correctly. To apply judgement afresh means to understand. The idol is in its actual identity, and this identity is that of a god.

When the idol of life would be an abode of god in the consciousness by the feelings of faith, life would be built up in an eternal form. This consciousness of an eternal feeling would make one understand that all semblance can resort to god. Every semblance can be a pure field. And this pure field can rise to be an abode of god. If god rests here for a short time, it would be a temporary abode of god. This temporary abode of god, in due course, can turn out to be a permanent abode of god. A permanent abode of god would be built up through acceptance of god. From this abode of god, gradual forward march contains in it a sensation for god. If this sensation is indicated within a human mind, then this would be an abode of god. This abode of god naturally becomes drenched in consciousness. Human consciousness here becomes inspired by the touch of divine consciousness. By the contact of divine consciousness, human consciousness gets bloomed. External form signifies the human semblance. But within the heart blooms such a transfusion of feelings that a divine feeling automatically weakens up. It is non-living, but not truly non-living, which, in external look, a human form now becomes a divine idol. This call of God in human form becomes a carrier of the feelings of divine consciousness. Divine consciousness exists in human idols. So, this man naturally feels the divine consciousness with all human semblances.

By the Grace of Awakening

RbhurnahIndrahsabasanariyan
Rbhuhbhajebhihbasubhihbasuhdadi
Yusmakamdebaabasa ahempriye
Abhihtistemprtsutihasunvatam

(Rigveda 1/110/7)

In this attractive disfavour of sacrifice has come
All the vibration of life, all the manifestation of feelings of life
Now have become filled with eternal grace.
As long as there is an initiation of the glow of endless wisdom
The lamp that has now become lightened in this world
Givest the eternal grace of constant awakening of that lamp.
I've been drenched with pleasure by being offered
String of mind has become enlivened always to hail Thee.

With the Strength of Feelings of Youth

Niscarmanarbhabogamanimsata
Sat batsenaasrjatamatarampunah

Saudhanvanasahsvapasyeyanaro
Jibriyubanapitaraakrnotena

(Rigveda 1/110/8)

That glow of the light of Thine has always given a feeling of youth
The more I can in that light be bathed in certainty
Thou last taken aside all beauty of manifestation in the succession of life lively in life
Being lively by Thy inspiration, the glow in life
May it rise too long for Thee everywhere.
Plenty of exposition throughout this world has gathered now filled with feelings.
The exposition of youth now has been embodied in full bloom
Let its manifestation in constant bloom hail Thee.

In Daily Prayer to God

Bajebhih no. Baja satauabiiti
RbhumanIndra. A drasiradhah
Tat no mitrahmamahantam
AditihSindhuhprthibiutadyauh

(Rigveda 1/110/9)

Givest Thou the touch of your bounty in my life
Thy endless divine wealth is stored in the divine abode
Now unveil that wealth for the benefit of the world.
That divine wealth is filled with the eternal seed of consciousness
Let the divine consciousness be seated now in this life
Let it spread swiftly for constant pervasion
Let it be spread in Mitra-Baruha-Aditi-Bhumi-Water-Ether
Let it be awakened constantly in blooming in every mind.

In the Observation of Thy Maternal Identity in Celestial Vehicle

Taksanahrathamsubrtam. Bidyamanaya
TakasanhariIndrabahabrsanbasu
Takasanpitrbyamrbaboyubatbayah
Taksambatmayomataramsachabhubam

(Rigveda 1/111/1)

Constant offering has been there in earthly activities in celestial vehicles
Earthly flow has been eternal through constant initiation
Now I have made Thee my own in my life's festival.
Just as a child gets zeal before its mother
Just as life has experienced festivity having Thee as mother
Let this constant flow of life be a divine inauguration
Let Thy motherly identity spread throughout the world
Just as Thou hast spread your deepest sense in the universe.

In the Royal Circle

So long as the mind remains restless, it does not rest on the seat of god. The mind is to be tranquilised. The way to make the mind tranquillised is to move aside all the filths in the mind—all filths are to be dusted out. The mind is to be built up closely with the consciousness of purity. Honest thinking is to be reared in mind.

Honest desire is to be built up. Honest desire builds up the mind in a permanently moving stage. This stage causes pervasion of life. The deep constitution of the mind might cause permanent invocation of the flow and touch of divine consciousness in the mind. By this, the divine sensation of ideas enters into the lives of living beings. A living being in whatever form it may be confined in—common or royal—feels the hour of transformation in themselves. In this hour of transformation, variegation might grow within a king. Necessary principles for the victory of society, state or an international group comprising many states have primarily been recorded in the *Mahabharata*, and its reflection has occurred in Kauilya's *Arthashastra*. If the royal circle is properly constituted, it points out the road to victory. If the royal circle is properly constituted, this proper leadership, the revelation of theory and religious faith are required for its application. Depending on the chief characteristic of the king included in the royal circle, there may be many divisions. Kautilya, in his *Arthashastra*, named twelve such divisions of the royal circle.

These are:

Bijisu (Desirous of victory): The king or the individual who is ready for victory in the world

Ari (Foe): An individual or a king whose character, behaviour and objective are enmity.

Mitra (Friend): An individual or a king whose nature, behaviour and objective is to establish friendship

Arimitra (Friend of a foe): The individual or king who has established a friendship with the enemy

Mitra-amitra (Friend cum foe): The individual or king who is established in the relationship of a friend

Arimitra-mitra (Friend of a friend of a foe): The individual or king who is among the friends of a foe

Parsvanigraha (Para-adversary): The class of other special groups of foes in the circle of an individual or a king longing for victory

Akranda (Protector): Power and associate of the friendship of an individual or king longing for victory

Parsvanigrahosar (Associate of para-adversary): Associated of foe of the individual or king longing for victory

Akrandsar (Associate of Proctor): Allied power of the associate of an individual or king longing for victory

Madhyame (Medial): The power standing in between the individual or king and enemy -power

Udasin (Indifferent): Indifferent, uninterested and unaspiring about the power or influence of an individual or king

In the real thinking of life, the variegation comes within the king or common beings as a common line of thinking. This line of thinking builds up the external or real life in the form of eternal beauty. This beautiful life alone can build up a new life circle, a new flow of thoughts. A royal circle community grows up centring interest. The integrative interest of the state or many a subject relating to the state is to be woven together, and all the subjects are to be combined for the overall welfare of the world. The basic object of the royal circle would have to be the welfare of the mass. There are many aspects of this welfare of the mass. The duty of the royal circle is to provide commodities for the living of man. The royal circle is always accounted for above the mass. That is, the royal circle is always supposed to be endeavouring for the mass.

For the activity of the royal circle, what is always necessary is the alertness of duty and setting up of the right of the king on all the affairs. Just as acquaintance with the identity of friend and foe for the administration of the kingdom of the world, so is needed to direct the personal life properly and to move towards God for which it is essential to recognise friend and foe. Spiritual science is, therefore, endeavouring to point out the six inherent vices. The endeavour to accept god comes only if one can banish these vices and remove them fully from life. Victory over life god is accomplished only when one can move forward after resisting the attack of the non-living. Establishments in the divine route become possible for one who can march forward, being quite indifferent to life. Twelve expeditions of the royal circle actually make the establishment and expansion of the reign of the king in real background possible. Victory over the foes in external life occupies the royal circle. So, the victory of foes at the end of life is different from one in the divine route.

In the Wisdom of Sacrifice

A no yajnayarbhumatbayah
Ai tavidaksayasuprajabatimibam
Yathaksyasesarbabiraya bias
Tat nah saradhayadhamathasuindriyam

(Rigveda 1/111/2)

To call upon the deities in this life
I've initiated an inflow of sacrifice in the path of works.
Life's work has been the landform of that sacrifice.
Just as Thou art always embodied in the initiation of life's work
Let that glow of wisdom of Thin spread now in life
Let right now be the real exposition of eternal Truth in this world.
Touch of wisdom has come into life along the flow of divine pleasure
Let divine power pervade in this flow of life.

Awakening by the Divine Endeavour

A taksatsatimarbatenarah.
Satim no jaitrimsammahetavisvaha.
Jamimajamimprtanasusaksanim.

(Rigveda 1/111/3)

Thou hast become God of gods in revelation of truth.
Thou has pervaded in hearts though invisibly.
Many a life has been lighted with truth in the practicing pervasion of life.

As Thou hast given the divine vehicle for life to move on
Let that divine vehicle be on move in divine awakening.
Let it be in motion hailing in the heart the sensation of Brahman.
Let right now be Thy beautiful blooming within the life
In wakefulness has come your call in a divine embrace.

I Call in that form of Brahman

Rbhunbajan marital somapitaya.
Ubhamitrabarunanunamasvine.
To no hinvantusatayedhiyejise.

(Rigveda 1/111/4)

I call upon all in the exposition of all forms
Givest Thou your formless flow of thoughts on the route of feelings.
Thou hast revealed Thy self in many, many forms.
Let those forms glow and spread in this life.
In this stage of moving on in life provision of your bounty
Has formed a divine air at the touch of Thine.
I've called the worldly passion of all the divine forms
Comest Thou here in life as the eternal guide.

Fillest thou with Light

Rbhuhbhrayasamsistusatim.
Samayahajitabajauasmanabistu.
Tat no mitrahbarunahmamahantam.
Aditihsindhuuprthibiutadyauh.

(Rigveda 1/111/5)

Thou hast call light in the lonely offering of life.
By the noble bestowal of god, that light has
Sometimes bloomed in the inner world.
And sometimes that lamp has been glowing in the whole world.
Thy easy blooming has lent the power to life to bloom.
Let the divine power be exposed in pervaded longing
Let this life pervade throughout heaven-ocean-earth.

The Divine Property

A life established in divine spirit gets a divine character. A divine character is one that has conquered inherent vices. Life has to be free from each of the six inherent vices. The practising routes aim at organising the mind with a view to making it unidirectional. God is to set in this unidirectional mind. Mind is non-composed, even if a bit of a single vice lingers therein. For this, there are so many preparations in the path of asceticism. To build up the intentness of mind, different stages of purification should be there. Purification of mind and intrinsic attitudes becomes essential. The most important is the purification of the mind. Proper selection is required to move on in the path of purification. Arrangements are necessary for the life that is eager to march forward in life, hailing god therein.

Divine property established in faith, love and reverence, restrained on the mind; control over the mind by yogic methods; etc., are followed in asceticism. If God is our aim in life, then the practice should be direct. Who directly want God is required to feel God and move on the path of life, and to move on the path of life, faith is required. One has to hail this faith in life and march forward on the path of life. To love God, one needs to cross the resorts of love between the living and the non-living. Love mixed with respect and reverence is devoid of attachment. This is required on the divine path.

Belief in a more powerful God who intervenes miraculously in people's lives by dispensing cures for various forms of aliments and brings about other spectacular acts;

Prosperity theology - The emphasis on the materials wellbeing of believes;

Emphasis on the power of the devil and evil spirits to herm human beings;

Exorcism as a remedy to evil attacks;

Public confession and being born again as a prerequisite for receiving God's blessings;

(James 2015, 66)

The traveller on the divine path would be full of faith. Divine faith is mixed with good intervention in worldly affairs. Life generally gets protection from God in respect of affairs of the world. Sometimes, that life becomes full of gods bestowal. Again, it might also be such that life would have to bear the charge of the consequence of its own actions on the path of life. The consequences of action might be of different types. There is some action that directly calls for consequence. Again, there are actions whose consequences are observed after a long time. The consequence of a third type of action goes on being accumulated. The type of actions are permanent results. The consequences of actions cross the limit of this life and enter into later life. The consequence is a type of permanent consequence of actions that come up as reforms. Reforms enter into the conscience of life layer after layer. Reforms enter into the wings of life. Reforms enter into sequences of life. Reforms bloom in characters and behaviours. Reforms form the outlook of life and build up feelings of life. Reforms make one understand one's basic character and qualities. Many influences of basic character are lying scattered in different corners of the world that would enter deep into lives.

Faith in the abundance in man leads one to confide in God in all conditions. A great flow of life is created from all sorts of demands on life. This flow of life is the pioneer of moving along the path of life with all that may be involved with it and all the responsibilities of the flow of life vested in lives. The follow of life marches on along the path of this movement of life, and reforms are important in establishing life on an eternal and universal route. Good reforms become carriers of life and the source of the flow. Good reforms rise to be bestowing well protection to lives. Good reforms impact extension to life.

Prevention of Pleasant Sensation

Ile dyabaprltibipurbacittaye.
Agnimdharmamsurucamyamanistaye.
Yabhihbharekaramamsayejinvathah.
Tabhiusuutibhihasvintunagatam.

(Rigveda 1/112/1)

I've known the nature of this flow of life in this world.
Whatever was my gain on the path of life as an experience
Has come as a flow of wisdom naturally in the lamp of life.
Now has wildly pervaded a constant glow in life
Has been transfused as a practice of fire in a newer identity of life.
I have offered Thee this fire set in the sacrifice.
O god! This unmixed gift of yours has pleased us.
Thou hast spread the sensation of pleasure everywhere in the world.

Divine Action, Divine Touch in Divine Life

Yubauhdanayasubharaasasrati.
Rathamictasthu. Dacasam ne mantabe.
Yabhihdhiyoabathahkarmanistaye.
Tabhiyuutibhihrasminagatam.

(Rigveda 1/112/2)

The wave of pleasure has come by the touch of your feelings.
To life has always come your constant call of Thine
Now at this hour of constant flow of pleasure.
I've got the feeling of flawless pleasure at this hour
Hailing Thee with fullest felicitation.
Let the fullest manifestation of this pleasure of Thine be in this world.
Let the flow and through of action of the world be bloomed.
Heap of divine feelings of eternal pleasure in this life divine.

In the Unimpeded Exposition of Deathlessness

Yubamtasamdibasye
Prasasanebaisamksayathoamrtasyemaksana
Yabhihdhainumasvampinvathonara
Tabhihusuutibhihasvinagetam

(Rigveda 1/112/3)

Thou hast been the monarch of life in the abundance of all powers. Customs of this divine land of yours are respect-reverence-commemoration- offering.
Hour has come to give away the peerless offering to the Supreme Soul.
In the divine feeling all the worldly feelings have of lost way.
Time has come to have the taste of Thy nectar of feelings.
I'm merged in your nectar like cogitation being drenched in your feelings.
Let Thy lamp of feedings come down free from all impediments.
Let divine nectar be exposed uninterruptedly like open cow-milk.

Right in your Integrative Wisdom

Dvikmatatusutarahihbibhusati
Yabhihtrimantuhabhabadbicaksanah
Tabhihrusuuthbhihasvinagetam.

(Rigveda 1/112/4)

You are moving on, always being absorbed in the path of judgement
Now it's Thou who has got the link of diversity.
Thou hast come in my life at this hour of self-offering.
Thought Thou I've learnt the phenomenal reality of life.
Through Thou has come in life the feelings of divine phase.
I've been exposed to measures of realisation through varied manifestations of Thine.
Comest connect Thou being merged in life now.
I've practised Thee constantly in meditation cogitation in different forms.

Divine Reforms

If the reforms become strong, they will be strong seekers of truth. Owing to be an honest path becomes a processor of thoughts and conscious feelings for pure works. Reforms crystalise in character. Inherent desires of man become evident on the path of natural reforms. Generally, divine matters remain absent from there. If earnestness for God gets in there, if the mind gets attached to God, then the footfalls of the forward march in life grow there. Whatever may be the reform, it is to be changed gradually and led to the divide path. Reforms settle character, pacing, basic aims of life and values about life. Reforms run in the line of sequence. It as if carries some inherent factors in life. That is why, there are such ways of leaving where darkness is always merged. Outlook, good and bad of life—all remains covered with darkness. Again, there are such lives where the whole is full of light. These lives full of light sees everything bright. These lives filled with trances of truth always remain filled with the supreme (sattva) quality.

Intending is widely considered a practical attitude. It is so conceived because it has an essential connection to action. One basic of this conception is an intrinsic element in intentions: By their very nature, they are, in content, in some way directed to action. A second basic of the conception is relational intentions conceived as bearing a special relation to actions that realise them. It is, however, quite difficult to see just how to understand these aspects of intention. The second aspect has received far more attention from the philosophers than the first without understanding the nature of intentions and their contents. We cannot fully account for imperatives, commands, promises, or discussions. These include Kants' categorical imperative, the famous biblical love commandments, promises to love, and discussions to be less didactic.

(Hear 2017, 2)

The action of our life is determined by the line of thinking of ideas. These are some lines of thinking that naturally become inspirations for works and make one march forward on the path of action. Again, there are some lines of thinking that give inspiration for works, no doubt, but rather prolonged and delayed ways. With these prolonged and delayed ideas of actions, the vanity of the being gets associated. The path along which a being moves their life along the path of action is disagreeing with God. A mind loaded with vanity always makes a mind proceed with its own tastes, liking, disliking and requirements, and so brings ruination of all the possibilities.

Mat cittahsarbadurgani at prasadattarisyasi
Atha cat tvamahan karat nasrosyasibinanksyasi

(Srimadbhagabadgita 18/58)

A man who really surrenders their mind and life to me becomes able to easily cross thousands of obstacles and dangers in life's struggle. By my grace, crossing all abstracts, they would naturally climb up step by step in the invasions of life. On the other hand, one who, owing to their own vain sentiment, would like to disobey me or disregard the path directed by me would have their life stumbled into the cavity of the ruination of progress along the path of resistance and lack of success.

An individual might bloom the possibilities with the help of the strength of competency; naturally, the strength of competency in the life of an individual is of utmost importance. With the strength of this competency, an individual may march on along life's path to gain victory. It is also possible for an individual indifferent to god to move on, on the basis of their own competency. But this victory is held within a limit. Life is an announcement about belief in God or apparent acceptance of this belief in life that has apparently been evident through mental practice. Speech revelation of belief comes within the circle of the bounty of God. Width, pervasion, speed, strength and glow of gods bounty are limitless. On the contrary, the limit of the known circle of man on the limit of human intelligence is very small. Man's decision loaded with vanity obstructs God's will and the strength of His bounty. The unrestrained glow of God's bounty stops there. On the contrary, they who are real travellers along the divine path call freely through a real offering of faith, reverence and love God's bounty in their unhesitating surrender and offering.

Thou Hast Liberated from the Veil of Ignorance

Yabhirebhamnibrtamsitam a dbhya
Utbandanamairayetamsvadrse
Yabhihkanvamprasisasantamabatain
Tabhihrusuvtibhihasvinagaten

(Rigveda 1/112/5)

Thou hast liberated them who have wanted Thee.
Whatever idea and consequence of action had there been
Thou hast removed all siding with effect and ending.
The light Thou hast created in this life
The light that has been the exposer of life's wisdom.
Thou hast exposed that light from the obstruction of the veil.
Thou hast unlocked that flow of light at the desire of the seer.
Let the wisdom of life be exposed amid the pleasure of the arrival of god.

Spontaneously Thou Hast Rescued

Yabhihantakamjanamanamarane
Bhrjyamyabhihabyatibhihjijinvathuh
Yabhihkarkandhimbayyamjinvathah
Tabhihrusuutibhiasvinagatam

(Rigveda 1/112/6)

In spontaneity, Thou art deeply seated
All have been blended in ideas of constant offering in personal whirls.
Thou art in mind in royal circle in constant passion.
That royal circle has been built up to hail Thee in earnest offering. Thou hast always removed the filth of that circle.

A newer measure of motion has been initiated by the touch
of Thy bounty
Now givest the whirl of Thy protection in life
Givest a promise for liberation in all circles.

State Seated in Divine Property

If it becomes possible for a living being to cross inanimate reforms and bonding of the lowest quality and the quality of spiritedness and to be lifted to the quality of virtuousness if they shake off all sort of insensateness and takes resort to God being field with fullest faith on Him with reverence and fearlessness. Vanity of self is the worst enemy of a living being. It is the vanity that confines a living being in their inanimate domain. In their own small circle, a living being naturally thinks their smallness is big. Just as the colour-smell-taste of the small circle linked to be one, so is the initiating phase of possibilities of spontaneous growth of a confined being. In due course, a counterblow comes from that phase, and life goes on being burnt in the fire of desires in mind. So long as the mind loaded with vanity does not shun vanity in their own fields and take resort to God, a living being would have to stay in the inanimate abode being dependent on the inanimate. Liberation of the living being from This small circle is possible through unhesitating surrender to god. They who can resort to God themselves move on fully, catching hold of the hand of life along the divine route spontaneously.

Ahankaarambalamdarpamkamamkrodhamparigraham
Samaritah
Mama atma para dehesupradisantaabhyasuyakah
(Gita 16/18)

He who, despite really knowing God's words, disregards them and becomes eager to move along the path of their own life circle, they who, disregarding God's words, become eager to move along a separate or an opposite path depending on their vanity or their own ability-money-wealth-ego, they who like to move on leaving aside the path specified by God lose their happiness, attainment of divine grace and possibility of having the grace of god. (Na sasiddhimaprotithasukhamnaparamgatim)

Quite unknowingly, support from one's own self, one's circle, family, relatives, wishes, ideas, desires and inanimate powers, one's own self or inanimate strength becomes important. In this way, one has removed oneself from the noble exposition of a great possibility and has confined one's life in a long-drawn imprisonment. The desire for liberty finds a way to move on towards the route of liberty. Real exposition of the desire for liberty can lead one to the divine route.

If not by words or announcement but by faith, reverence, respect and love for God is possible, then an unrestrained exposition of the force of the bounty of God becomes evident in life. If attention is truly turned to God, He will come to remove all hurdles. It would be He who would hail life with the fullest complacency. If God Himself hails a life, then that life becomes extramundane right on the bosom of the earth. All desires are wiped out from there. The man concerned does not have charge of their life. God Himself becomes the resort. God takes charge of a life offered to God quite knowingly or unknowingly. If state surrenders itself at the feet of God, then that state can also integratively make all lives quite full of true happiness. This is the state established in divine property and in mass equality.

Appendix
Spirit of the Vedas

Throughout the pre-historic and historical periods, the human journey has been undertaken as the journey towards cherishing the desires of human intent in any form. Its flavour in life has the usual destiny of self-consumption. In a way, the journey of human beings in the pathways of the movement of life has been the journey towards personal fulfilment in terms of living standards, having more than adequate resources to take sources of and possessions of command in life, fulfilling biological hunger of all kinds, satisfying mental desires and greed, creating unique position for personal identity with respect to other, and finally getting along with the demands of individual ego so that the person's position on earth is charted in a unique way. A person gets satisfaction from the intents of the cosmic command or the cosmic principles as applied to the spirit and development of human progress on Earth. The footprints have been depicted by all categories of mental frame. However, sustained with honour and regard are those who have charted their ways of life in such a way that the imprints of their stepping across the flows of eternal time have not been filthy in any way; rather, these few are those having nurtured and engineered the thoughts of the well being of all and worked for the broader perspective of cosmic life. The human journey has always been a journey through all kinds of explorations and finding out or creating structures, systems and processes in such a way that provides illuminations in the lives of those who want and maintain the ways of having access to the spirit of righteousness in all walks of life. However, a handful of individuals have always surfaced on earth in a way that extends their enormous amount of mental strength to accommodate things that are usually untouched by most on earth. In the ancient period, just after the Vedic period was over, the spirit of goodness was subdued, crushed to the limits of horizons that not only the integrity but even personal respect of men and women not only got affected but was spoiled to dust by the authorities and power of those who used to assert their personal control to achieve selfish satisfactions and gains in the context of the human journey coordinated by a system that was attempted to be authored and monarched by them.

Though the journey of human beings has been orchestrated as the depiction of the victory and superiority of the evil spirit and forces at times, these are also the forces that got crushed through the passage of time. At every phase of the human journey, it was the final triumph of the good spirit in the ultimate game, and the same good spirit had to spread two classes of principles and focuses—the one that is eternal and the other empirical. Eternal spirit looks into real and long-term well-being, whereas the empirical one thinks that satisfaction now is an end in itself, irrespective of the concerns that are truly cured with the surfacing of the scope of things on earth. The seekers of eternal well-being adhere to those values in life that truly support the cause of eternal blissful existence. These are primarily those eternal values that are fundamental to cosmic creations. The values that would aim at or attempt the impact and drenching lives with transcendental truth are the ones that would always and all the time stand by the principle of truth on the hand and see or explore that this principle of truth connects with the spirit of eternity. The eternal principle of existence and creation works across the fundamental force of divinity and nobility. Whatever is noble in its content, structure and form is divine in its essence. Divinity begets the structuring of lives in such a way that the basis of life gets merged in the spirit of divinity and brings forth the field and realm of actions in such a way that all actions of life make proper synthesis with that spirit and get into the wholesome connections of the spirit through the human form to undertake the promise and practice of total truth in the life on earth.

Human progress on Earth has been two-fold. The one that has received the highest importance so far in the history of human civilisation is the material and functional progress in terms of arranging things contributing to the happiness of life. Happiness is construed as enjoyment in the forms and contents of human presence on earth. Science has given birth to superior and constantly engineered forms-structures of technologies to make the functional prospects of life easier and smoother. This progress is properly visible. It is tangible and effective. It has transformed the ways and means of human living, making it more dynamic, smooth and worthy of making a longer or a higher degree of journey on earth. This, in a way, has made the global system merge into the spirit of science and be driven on the wheels of technology. From that perspective, the other elements in the progress of the human journey have been the perspectives in life to make things happen in such a way that this aspect of progress becomes more logically understood by all. The positions of understanding each other and rising above the crude personal domain to a situation where the considerations of a single life turn, in effect, an approach towards redeeming the aspects of human potentials in such a way that the force of understanding others developed by one individual gets spread into the forces of cohesion, become open in mind in terms of understanding others and make a position in the world that would actually foster forward the urge to be a part of an element of the cosmic truth, belonging to the cosmic world but serving as a part of the intent of the creator at the point of creation. This creation has to take along the spirit of it and see that the resources and opportunities are shared among all those who expect to remain a part of the cosmic journey, continuously making qualitative advancements into it and for the benefit of all those who seek to happen in life for themselves and for others.

Material progress through the cultivation of science and technology has been the visible arm of human progress and achievements. It remains a fact always to mention and accept that the progress of the spirit of urbanisation, on the one hand, and that of industrialisation, on the other, has actually captured the attention of creative minds. Some minds have always tried to look into the prospects looming through the facets of existing functional programs, conditions and aspects of time. In a way, the rise of technology has endeavoured to replace the human intellect with an artificial framework creating artificial intelligence for the growth and reengineering of the spirit of human progress. The attempt of technology towards this aspect makes it prominent in a way such that it stimulates thoughts and ideas from green minds to act as engines of movement forward in the way and fashion that makes the journey of life effectively devoted and dedicated to the cause of human growth and sustainability. This process, thus, enhanced the spread of the spirit in such a way that the human actions of making life better ones in terms of consumption, absorption, possessions and drawing perpetual satisfaction for making life a better place for human growth. The other realm of the mental frame has actually created two forces. They are not only concurrent but are sometimes directly or indirectly conflicting. The way of good spirit takes courses of assimilation with the ways of spreading the message of goodness to all. However, in effect, this mental wealth of human beings has led to the strengthening of the forces of fragmentation. On the other hand, attempts are made to have the individual identity prominent enough to capture emotions, perception and understanding of the strength of individuality. In a way, at one point, the essential spirit of individuality was loneliness in life.

Fragmentation and physical distancing at one end of human resettlement has given shape to the previously orchestrated mutual connections and bonding. However, on the other end, a new process of coordination and connections has emerged through the virtues of emerging technologies and their applications that, in terms of the available set of things, is a kind of new identity fixing through which an individual goes beyond the boundary of thoughts that exists and creates something that proves more attractive, more rewarding and more satisfactory. The journey has been fostered by the renewed application of the factors of life in such a way that the involvement of a human person goes beyond the existing boundary of identity. This is gradually becoming more and more prominent as the factors of the basic identity of life are getting gradually rediscovered to give place to a new set of things and catalyse a new kind of order for a fresh identity. Institutions that used to have a higher degree of relevance before, like the spirit of national identity, are likely to take a deep in the face of a technology-driven borderless process scaling up the factors and forces of multi-nationality to replace, to a large extent, the hold and impacts of nationality. Similarly, there are many other areas of the real outpour of personal identity where a person could be drawn into the core of broader dynamics than a unitary one. This aspect of transformation is likely to prove more important than now for making things happen in the context of a pattern of change or un-patterned and chaotic situations of change. The factual position of this change is going to trigger a new set of thoughts and, thereby, actions arising out of that which combines the thoughts in such a manner that creates forces of change or even forces of transformations in the face of the new dynamics having captured the central attention of human communities across different geographical distributions at human settlement. It is very pertinent to understand whether this is a phenomenon of a large or a small number in terms of the emergence of a new spirit centrally driven by knowledge.

Societies have emerged out of this process, with knowledge being the core identity, and newer patterns are emerging among human grouping across the globe where the barriers of previously honoured doctrines of life are considered good to have been diluted. On another scale, the new grouping, termed the knowledge society, has emerged across attributes like individual tastes, individual choices and individual preferences, and at the same time, to talk about the chances of grouping across factors with the likelihood of similarity on a short- or long-term scale. It is thus a kind of regrouping that may or may not last longer than its current estimated or perceived span of significant existence. In this game of changeover from one set of things to another, it is actually a catalysing change—sometimes towards the positive end and sometimes towards the other side of it. Any remarkable contribution of knowledge, thus, is poised to restructure the human settlement in ways that would possibly throw open either new opportunities in life or new kinds of processes be initiated to explore opportunities in a new way. It thus has the potential to foster change on the one hand and see that the process of change continues, rather than getting a position of resting across change and creating identities over and above the dynamics of change to reach a situation of steady-state or tranquillity.

Human regrouping through the process of the dynamics has more or less direct impacts on relations of interpersonal context in entities and institutions. This has, thus, the objective and power to make, remake or break bonds of any kind in the world where the known is likely to become obscure and the unknown to get knitted across the related entities. This process of regrouping is thus the process of the new world likely to emerge in the current century through new types of knowledge-driven regrouping in societies across the globe.

Attributes that are actually emerging out of the process of the new kind of process engineered by the human intellect in place are actually the ones that centre around selfish considerations. 'Me first, others next' becomes the dominant and driving attribute in this new game of change and regrouping. It is thus a situation where a new type of emergence acquires a commanding role. The primacy of 'my satisfaction' emerges as one of the most important points of concern in this game. With individual selfishness being one of the most dominant factors in life, the factors of growth and dispersal are destined to take the forms of chaos-based fragmentation. Chaos being the state of affair and fragmentation being the identity of the dynamism, the ultimate objective of creating a human society with different focus in life would be distanced further in this process. It is the spirit of indirect or direct assimilation of factors, understanding of things and appreciating the facts and factors of the lives of others. One can directly understand and realise that God's design of this creation had a different set of things for human life and grouping to take the shape of. It is, of course, a very strong position enjoyed by human society that unless the limits of actual departures of the factual positions of human beings cross the limits endowed with to have a free play of individual volition, the divine intervention in this game is marginal or absent. Human independence is an endowed factor from the creation, and thus, unless the limits of endowment are broken in any way, intervention from the point of view of the creation is thus absent in the game of humane transformation. It is thus, an important point to note that the true spirit of human unity, true perspective in the human expectations in life and true focus of human action should be understood and adopted with the central focus of the unity of purpose and perspective. Vedic ideas and thoughts appear here, at this point of human understanding, as the basis and the way of new kinds of lives on earth. The process, if undertaken by people, would be enough to fix a new kind of or a new set of attributes to set in and follow on the horizon of new life.

Vedic life is basically the life lived on earth while maintaining the attributes of divinity. It is, thus, a new premise of living with a collective identity through individual emergence in life. In the aspect of collective identity, it is to be realised the similarity and sameness of the spirit of things that are not only engrossed in the facts and process of life but also a kind of understanding that would allow things to happen in a way that individual's position is safeguarded with respect to the remaining all and fulfilment of individuals is construed through the fulfilment of others. The underlying concept is similarity or sameness. It was uttered eloquently by the sages in the Vedic period as follows:

> 'Sam gachchadham sam vadadham
> sam bo manamshi janatam....
> samani vo akutih samanah inanah....susahasati.'

It talks in terms of creating harmony, unity and oneness. Harmony in the context of the prevailing conflicts, contrasts, differences, chaos and general disharmony with harmony as the target objective of life, the further quest and understanding go along to a state where the internal understanding of one and the other gets transformed in a way that pulls things from across with view to have in place or develop a true view of life that understands the conceptual underpinnings and correlates with the agenda for actions in life. With the thoughts conversed to the points of understanding and making things happen in a way that connects the minds in series to respond actively for having the same in the light of identical expectations and actions in life.

The question that was dealt with was the basis of equality and identity. The Vedic sages have always gone into depth and spread the forces of creation and the intrinsic facts of human identity. They visualised the fact that the supreme truth, being the identified entity as the Brahman, is omnipresent and omniscient on the one hand and without any specific form in the realm of existence on the other. He is beyond the limits of time, the span of space and the spectre of any kind of form. Yet, He has an intrinsic identity. This intrinsic identity is the Paramatman or the Supreme in the form of cosmic Atman. He can not be seen in the usual sense of the term and cannot be measured, as He is beyond the span and content of what we try to understand through the term 'infinite'. He is not just vast, but all is Him, and being is all. As the sages have identified the reality of supreme truth this way, they earned realisations of the Supreme Truth as all and sundry and that of an infinitesimally small form, again with the same identity but residing in all living organisms. His special presence is there in the core of the human heart. As He resides within the inner cave of the human heart, He possesses and maintains the same identity of form, being a formless spirit and having the graceful orientation to human existence for their being amid human life. Sage Vaishampayan visualised the presence of the Atman in human personality and expressed the connection of His presence with the organic structure of human beings. Vaishampayan had structured Krishna Yajur Veda with a dialogue between the lord of death, named Yama, and an early young boy named Nachiketa. The intent and urge expressed by Nachiketa were to earn the knowledge of the Supreme Self in the form of a stream of spiritual knowledge called Atma Tatwa, or the theory of the soul. This theory, as it was revealed by the lord of death,

Yama, describes, in detail, the relationship the soul maintains with this empirical human existence. One of the descriptions highlights as follows:

Atmana Rathinam Viddhi Shariram Ratha Eva Tu
Buddhi Tu Sarathi Viddhi Manah Pragraham Eva Cha

In means: Consider this body a chariot having access to movement in the world; the soul, in the name of Atman, resides within the chariot, maintaining a direct connection with it. The human mind works as the connecting cord between the chariot and the soul, whereas the human intellect functions as the driving force of life.

With the human intellect involved in the guidance of life, it steps forward in a way that makes the pathways of life turned to the empirical identity, having full coverage, and demands on the usual aspects of human desires and usual spells of human urge taken possessions of. It is in this context the Vedic sages started exploring further, deeper within the depths of truth, having realised such and gradually getting the unfoldment of truth expanding into the identity of the vast and having touched and present in the various forms of the life's elemental vitals or mentals. This was the gradual opening up of the truth of the Supreme in individual life in one way and getting across the factors of living throughout. It was thus a unique realisation of truth wherein the aspirant realises the connection of this living with the cosmic existence of the Supreme Soul. This discovery by the Vedic Sages was fully endorsed by the incarnate of God, in the form of Lord Krishna, in the context of the *Mahabharata*.

Lord Krishna spelt out the theory and truth about the soul to his most dear disciple-devotee, Arjuna, in the context of the war of Kurukshetra as elaborated in the world's greatest epic, from India, the *Mahabharata*. He has described an intrinsic fact about Atman:

Na enam chhiddanti shastrani na enam dahati pavakam
Na cha cledayanti apah na shoshoyati marutah.

It means that Atman can never be cut apart by any kind of weapon. Nor can it be burnt to destruction or partial damage by any amount of fire. Thus, Atman cannot be washed off in any way, as it has been the case of washing to cleanse things from the clings of dirt across or around. Atman is also so stable that it cannot be blown off by the thunderous pressures of air at all.

Atman is nondestructive and always maintains its autonomous integrity. Though it resides in the life of a person, it does not form any organ or a part of it. Instead, Atman remains within the cave of the human heart as a witness self and remains unattached to the facts, actions and thoughts of life. However, the situation changes with the changes in the mind and attitude of a person. It was the universal call for which the Supreme Soul decided in His volition to be along with life, however unattached. But if a person chooses the form of God as their dear one, cultivates love for God and actually develops within their heart a dedicated love for God, then the soul in the form of Atman fails to remain just witness in life and gets slowly involved in their affairs, thoughts and actions. It is in a similar perspective that Lord Krishna chose Arjuna as His own person, as a friend, and got involved deeply in the destined set of actions by Arjuna. His being with the core activities of Arjuna has a separate set of causes. As God has clarified to Arjuna and mentioned in the Bhagavad Gita:

Yada yadah hi dharmasya glanih bhabatih Bharatah
Abhyuhthanah hi dharmasya tada atmanah srijami aham.

It means: Lord Krishna, as the God incarnate, reiterates saying whenever there is any kind of problem that inflicts upon the principles of righteously, the lord appears on earth with His presence as an incarnate to offer His grace and power to protect the spirit of goodness and to offer a sequence of interventions for rescuing the good souls from the inflicts of those who attempt to crush the truth on earth.

It is thus a point of assurance from Lord Krishna that the power of divinity has been omnipresent with the noble and honest souls to rescue them from any destructive attacks from the evils. It surfaces the fact that God maintains the intent of making the human society a society of goodness and, in this way, transforming individuals from the habit and nature of the world unto the world of good spirit and making goodness the prevailing doctrine of human civilisation and growth. In this context, the realisation of Atman within not only puts the person on a path of a good spirit but helps transform human civilisation into one where God is adored at the centre, and lives are lived across throughout.

Whereas the Vedic sages have gone to the extent of not only discovering the truth of the cosmic creation but undertaking ways to make things happen in a way that has put across the functional ways to live up to the spirit and, at the same time, spreading the cause of the spirit in and among lives on earth. Vedic sages urged upon and constantly prayed to God to remain vibrant and arouse the person from any kind of remote realm of the spirits detached from the facts and principles of life. It is, thus, a situation where God becomes and remains a normal company in life. Sages lived in families and had spouses in the appropriate senses. Sage had their own children, and in most cases, they had a large pool of disciples. The children had to be a part of this team of learners. The disciples and children had to observe the monastic discipline as regular meditation and practice the divine principles in their lives. Different ways of spiritual living, paths of yoga, tantra, sat-chakra, path of love for and devotion to God all were the functional and practice areas. The disciples had to call upon the Supreme Spirit to realise Brahma Gyanah—the wisdom of Brahman. This way of practice and attainment is contained within the domain of the Rig Vedic invocation. The central theme of this Rig Vedic invocation proves to be uttered and conceptualised as 'Prajnanam Brahman'—the wisdom of the Supreme is the revelation of the wisdom principle. This wisdom principle makes their revelation more depiction of Brahman as the realm of Him. It is thus the spirit of the formless, eternal identity that is the fundamental causative element for the treasured living the divine way.

Rig Vedic tradition itself gave the ways of earning divine life. Whenever a person lives normally and constantly maintains regular and usual meditation and consecration, they maintain the spiritual ways of living. Similarly, the sages of the Saam Vedic tradition are based on a differential footing of cultivating the enemies beyond the purview. Sage Jaimini, along with a large number of sages, started with the discovery that God may, at his own choice, prefer to be along the devotee in such a way that a small input factor might turn into their own choice and preferences. Therefore, the identity comes from God as a non-separate entity. Sage had visualised this great realisation as: 'Tvat Tvam Aushi'—I am that. You are this entity, in essence. Therefore, your presence makes life heavenly, enabling the mutual transferability of identity. This existence, being drenched in the love of yours, thereby knows, loves you and you only. 'Tvat' and 'Tvam' refer to the understanding of the duo. This may be construed as dualistic. However, this is not dualistic. Rather, the person having the spirit of God merges in the nectar of it. However, dedicated love requires a form to bestow upon. Devotion is cultivated in the context of having God, and His devotee, remain present in the context of the world but thoroughly maintaining the spirit of devotion and oneness through the cultivation of dedicated love for God.

Devotion leads to ultimate realisation in a condition of non-differentiation. You and I make the sense of separation and intend to maintain the same throughout. But with the cultivation of love very intensely over a significant stretch of living makes the senses of you and I non-differentiated. The loved for becomes an entity of the heart within. Intense love is such that the devotee tends to forget about their own concerns but looks at God for what stands as their concern. Devotee now tends to understand the choice, taste and preference of chosen form of God on earth and thus gets involved in senses such that their life gets drenched in the showers of love from God in such a way that the vision, the audibility, the tastes, touches and perceptions all get somewhat merged together to form a conscious entity that would take the devotee to the world of the consciousness of God. The devotee's mind, vitality and heart now shed tears together in a rhythm that proves to be the Chhanda of God. All the moments carry inward the conscious throws of the elements of love for God. Devotees' mind-vitality-heart get not only engrossed in but totally dedicated to the cause of God. Devotee now thinks of ways and means of how the realm of God could be the realm they form a part of. Now comes the issue of 'Seva'—service to God. Devotee's mind rhythms to offer services to God. It turns into a moment of service to be offered to God. Service that makes the approach physical is good; service that satisfies the wish of God, being mental, is a better service; service that brings in Ananda, that is, bliss in God, is the best service. Arjuna could impart this Ananda in God. Arjuna had devotion and deep love for God. But the transcendent dimension of Arjuna was the destined work of God. When he devoted himself to the work desired by and prescribed by God, he was very happy. His being happy was revealed through the realisation that an Arjuna-like devotee is there, who not only possesses and adheres to the love for God but is one soul dedicated himself to the cause of God with a view to make it perfect in approach and to beget success.

Karma or action is endowed to carry a large flow of the blessings of God. But when the karma becomes the destined karma of God or which the devotee dedicates life to and cultivates the ways so that God's objective gets fulfilled on the one hand and that of the chosen destiny of time on the other, service to fulfil the divine design and God's objective, in particular, stands as the best service to God. Devotee's love for God takes the culminating height with the service to God having identified and offered. However, in the entire process, the devotee's personal intent of any kind should remain absent. Whether it is a personal intent to offer service in their own chosen way or the service that begets lots of factors other than or in association with that destined to God, it erodes the fervour and the potential of the offered service. Devotion, in true form, thus endows the person with the facets of divine intent and makes the devotee rightfully offer that making at the best way of God's fulfilment.

Non-differentiated love for God has the underlying condition of consecration. Consecration is dedication in absolute terms. It makes the devotee oriented to the one and only spirit of God for the fulfilment of all aspects of the divine's presence on earth. Sometimes, God's physical presence in the world may appear alien to the devotee. Alien in the sense that it is not known or understood by them in the true perspective of that. It is thus the object of considering in the spirit of divinity based on the concerns, patterns of thought and actions and, finally, the intrinsics so far kept away or remained away from the already charted path by the devotee. It is in this context and condition of the devotee's growth and journey in the spiritual path. Its identity of the journey in the spiritual path is based on faith in God. Devotee requires the faith to be nurtured intensely so that even a small fragment of doubt fails to creep into the mind of the devotee. This mind becomes devoid of any element of faithlessness or doubt. Devotee's strength of faith helps keep ahead the spirit engrossed in factors of the world to give birth to a new order in the cosmic system, and that emerges into the pool of faith and consecration. It is the victory of faith that puts forward the spirit of divinity in the arms of the passage of time. The devotee's victory through the winning of their love for God makes the devotee further dedicated to the world of the spirit. The spirit of the divine has the power to assert over the stream of things going ahead with the forward movement of time. Devotion wins over all divine forms of worship, meditation, yoga and all other ways to reach God.

Yajur Veda has completed the journey of devotion to consider even through the ways of consecration. The view and vision for that remain unique in the pathways of spirituality. The charted destiny as destined by the flow of time makes one understand that there comes a point of culmination when you find that God and you have turned into God in you, which is this condition 'Aham Brahmashmi'—I am the entity of Brahman merged in. In this situation, the devotee is now endowed with the spirit of being one with the devotee with the entities having merged in. Once this is understood, no chance of impossibility or less possibility remains away.

Vedic sages have consciously attempted to house every fact or truth in the personality of at least one variety where the spiritual oneness can be practised in the self entity through the wisdom of 'Ayam Atma Brahma'. It means: My soul represents the Brahman. It is the embodied and personified position of the soul that collectively, in a way, endorse the functions of this life. This has been put across by Sage Sumantah about the flow of time in the empirical world. This identity is the true revelation of Atman and its presence in the life of a spiritual aspirant in the world. The victory of devotion in the world begets the victory of the self. This indicates continued new revelation by God for those who aspire to that for.